Engineers in Business

The Principles of Management and Product Design

MIKE LANIGAN

University of Kent

ADDISON-WESLEY

*Harlow, England · Reading, Massachusetts · Menlo Park,
California · New York · Don Mills, Ontario · Amsterdam
Bonn · Sydney · Singapore · Tokyo · Madrid · San Juan
Milan · Mexico City · Seoul · Taipei*

To Madge

© 1992 Addison-Wesley Publishers Ltd.
© 1992 Addison-Wesley Publishing Company Inc.

Addison Wesley Longman Limited
Edinburgh Gate
Harlow
Essex, CM20 2JE

Sponsoring editor: Tim Pitts
Developmental editor: Jane Hogg
Production editor: Sheila Chatten
Production controller: Jim Allman
Sales specialist: Davie McGirr
Text designer: Valerie O'Donnell
Illustrators: Chartwell Illustrators
Typesetter: Columns of Reading
Cover designer: Hybert Design and Type, Maidenhead
Cover printer: The Ethedo Press, High Wycombe
Printed in Great Britain by Cambridge University Press, Cambridge

First printed 1992. Reprinted 1994, and 1996

British Library Cataloguing in Publication Data
A catalogue record for this book is available from the British Library

Library of Congress Cataloging in Publication Data
Lanigan, Mike.
    Engineers in business : the principles of management and product
design / Mike Lanigan.
      p.   cm.
    Includes index.
    ISBN 0–201–41695–6
    1. Production management.   I. Title.
TS155.L254   1992
658.5—dc20   92–11533
                                                       CIP

Preface – Why?

A good workman is known by his tools.

Proverb

The basic message

Engineers are engineers because they enjoy applying scientific principles to the solution of demanding technical problems. They are fascinated by the science-based technologies. This is as it should be, because people do best what they enjoy doing. But *engineers in business* need a number of other skills, as well as proficiency in a family of technologies. This is emphasized by the definition of **engineering** used in this book, which places it firmly into a **business** context. Engineering is:

> *the application of technology to wealth creation by providing cost-effective solutions to human needs and problems.*

So the other skills needed by a complete engineer relate to creating wealth, to achieving value for money, and to translating human needs and problems into technological solutions. These are the skills of **technical management** (also termed **technology management** or **engineering management**) in **manufacturing businesses**. The skills include expertise in **product design**.

Technical management is as fascinating as the technologies to which it relates. And it is equally important because, unless it is done properly, the technologies cannot develop or deliver their full potential. Sadly, this basic message is not appreciated by insular engineers until it is forcibly brought to their attention by some looming disaster. This book is *not* about the technologies. It *is* about technical management in manufacturing businesses.

Principal aim

Traditionally, the early education of engineers has concentrated on the technologies, with the management aspects of the subject deferred to training and experience in industry. It is now widely recognized that this unreal separation of the technologies from their business context damages the formation of complete engineers. But

v

incorporating the requisite material into degree courses presents a variety of problems. The principal aim of this book is to provide an acceptable solution to those problems.

Target readership

This is primarily engineering students in universities and polytechnics. The first career destination of most such students is industry. The majority of these start their industrial careers in the **technical function**, working on some facet of **techno-logical innovation**. The book is most relevant to that majority. It covers the *'why'*, *'what'* and *'how'* of the business and management environment in which they must work and develop their careers. The material is also directed at young engineering graduates with management ambitions. So the longer chapters are developed beyond the requirements of most engineering degree courses for that reason. Finally, there is evidence that some non-engineering industrial managers seeking an insight into the activities of the technical function will also find the book of interest.

Contents and presentation

A broad interpretation of the term **product design** is used to determine the topics. These are presented from an engineering management perspective in chapters constructed as relatively free-standing modules. These matters, and other features of the book, are explained in the Introduction. All readers (teachers and students) are particularly asked to study it. It sets the scene for the whole book.

Acknowledgements

Many private communications and/or discussions with colleagues past and present have contributed to this book. Particularly acknowledged are: Fred Myers (1990) of GEC–Plessey Research (Caswell) Ltd for *An Applied Research Project* used in Section 6.3.1; Harry Cather (1991) of Brighton Polytechnic for *Some 'Mechanical' Examples* used in Sections 6.3.1 and 6.4.3; Ayre Freedman (1981) of Plessey Radar Ltd and Hugh Wassell (1979) of GEC–Marconi Ltd for ideas incorporated into Chapter 8; and Peter Greenwell (1989) of Wiebmuller Klippon Electrics Ltd for *Marketing Industrial Products* used in Section 9.4.2.

Mike Lanigan
Canterbury, January 1992

Introduction – What and How?

Oh! rather give me commentators plain,
Who with no deep researches vex the brain.

George Crabbe (1754–1832)

Product design sets the topics

Ideally, engineering students are taught about relevant business topics in an engineering fashion by engineers. This is the best way for motivation to be transmitted, and for it to be received and retained. The book aims to encourage and develop that approach. It does so by equating 'relevant' business topics with those which particularly relate to **competitive product design**. Product design is the natural link between the technology studies which comprise most of an engineering course and the business studies within it. This perspective also provides a welcome constraint on the scope of the book: business topics are in such plentiful supply that a rational selection criteria must be applied.

Product design may be defined as:

> *the process of seeking a match between a set of customer-derived product requirements and a way of meeting those requirements, or of finding an acceptable compromise.*

This comprehensive definition places the process firmly between the **market-place** for the products offered by a business and the **manufacturing operation** that makes them. It is how the term is *most generally* used in this book. 'Competitive' product design means doing the process in such a way that it results in a product which at least matches, and is preferably better (in some way), than similar products offered by competitors. Note that the comprehensive definition includes **technical product design** within its orbit. That activity is the process of shaping the requisite **technological configuration** of a product to meet defined cost and quality targets.

Product design is system design

Note, too, that all **products** are **systems**. But not all systems are products. Products are creations of the human mind and human labour, whereas some systems occur naturally (the weather is one example). So 'product' is a better word than 'system' in the design context.

Skills of a professional engineer

A distinguishing feature of a professional engineer is, or should be, the ability to design competitive products. This demands skills beyond those in the relevant product technologies, critical though these are. An engineer designs a product inside a business, which competes with other businesses to earn its living from the same product market. If the design is competitive then the business may survive and prosper. So competitive product design is part of the wealth creating process. It requires that the product designer:

(1) Has expertise in the relevant product technologies.
(2) Understands the overall operation of businesses, and especially about **marketing**, technological innovation and **production**.
(3) Appreciates the critical nature of time and money in the business environment.
(4) Is financially literate, because the language of money is the language of business.
(5) Is a **manager**, with specialist expertise in the use of tools and techniques which relate to technical management and to the broader issues of product design.

Items 2 to 5 in this list provide a broad specification of 'relevant' business topics as the term is used here. The book aims to present these topics from an engineering perspective in the context of a **structured product design** methodology. The emphasis is on enduring principles.

Theme: Engineers for management

At some stage, many engineers must decide whether to progress along a mostly technical track or to move into management. But when a promising engineer is promoted into management, the net effect is often the loss of a good engineer and the gain of a poor manager. One reason for this is that dealing with technology is dealing with facts, and most technical problems have right answers. The laws of physics have an appealing consistency. They do not change overnight. Management problems are not like this. Hard facts are normally rare and frequently well hidden. Often there are no right answers, and solving *time* must take precedence over solution *quality*. Management is normally about choosing which problem to have, since solving one creates another. Engineers who are stimulated by such real challenges can, and should, exploit their basic training in management roles.

This book aims to persuade embryonic engineers that management is a respectable, demanding and intellectual pursuit which is worthy of their attention. It is not, as many suppose, a dubious distraction from 'real' engineering which is best left to those seeking a more dramatic life style. So a theme of the book is 'engineers for management'.

Management is product design

Management and product design are closely related subjects. Both are about problem identification, analysis and solving. Management problems and design problems share many features. Both are susceptible to the problem solving methodology offered in the book under the guise of 'structured product design'.

Overview: Presentation and scope

'Business studies' is treated as a subsidiary subject in most engineering courses. This factor has conditioned both the presentation and scope of the text. Ideally, student appreciation of the business context of engineering should be built up, in parallel with the technology studies, during each year of the course. There is ample material here to support that strategy applied to full or part-time courses. Each chapter introduces a distinct topic and, generally, the intellectual level of the material increases as the chapter progresses. This allows for flexibility between the options of topic concentration or topic diversity in course planning. However, Chapter 1 covers business basics and it is the recommended prerequisite for the rest of the book. There is then a natural flow, in chapter order, from topic to topic with an extensive Glossary and Index at the end of the book.

Modularity and repetition

Not all course directors will wish to use, or be able to accommodate, more than a fraction of the total offering. So each chapter is deliberately structured as a relatively free-standing module. This inevitably leads to some repetition between chapters. 'Flags' and cross-references are provided where this occurs. An interesting consequence is that the total illumination of linking material is greatly improved. It is this teacher's experience that students are rarely damaged by viewing important subjects from a number of different positions.

Advanced material

A number of chapters include concepts which are more challenging than the norm and/or are more easily appreciated by readers with some industrial experience. This material is termed 'advanced' (for want of a better descriptor) and flagged as such in the text. It may be omitted, when first encountered, by readers new to business ideas without gravely compromising their progress. But serious students (undergraduate and graduate) should return to these matters, because they provide valuable insight into some enduring and fascinating problems.

Businesses and people

The material is presented from an engineering management point of view in an integrated, analytical, 'systems' approach. The style may suggest to undergraduate readers that business activities are always rational, logical and tidy. This illusion, if allowed to persist, will not survive their first few weeks in industry. Businesses are systems containing people as the dominant elements. So business behaviour often reflects human behaviour. People do not obey the laws of physics. Their behaviour is not always rational, logical and tidy. This glimpse of the obvious does not undermine an engineering approach to business management. It does suggest, however, that the approach should be tempered with an appreciation of the critical elements involved.

So Chapter 4 outlines the relevant facets of **behavioural science**. Additionally, some comments and observations on these matters (distilled from real life) are woven into the text. Their purpose is to tell the story as it actually is, by leavening the logic with some of the realities.

Technology independence

In principle, the material is technology independent. However, most of the examples within the text relate to electronics, communications or computers. This bias merely reflects the technical background and obsessions of the author, and it should not be allowed to compromise the generality of the underlying messages.

Bibliography

Each chapter includes a small bibliography comprising 'References' (cited in the text) and 'Suggested further reading' (not cited in the text). References to journal articles mostly reflect the historical development of the chapter topic, whereas references to books identify those found most useful in developing the text. The books listed under 'Suggested further reading' contain material which extends that presented in a chapter text, and they are commonly relevant to more than one chapter. The Chapter 1 bibliography lists books covering broad areas of management and business. Note that *this* book is largely experience-based and the author has not traced all of its messages and idiosyncrasies to an earlier source.

Questions and (some) answers

A number of questions are included at the end of each chapter, with some answers at the end of the book. The questions are designed as vehicles for further learning and understanding, not as model examination questions. So some are long, searching and suited to small-group teaching situations. The nature of the subject requires that many questions seek essay or (better) 'structured note' type answers. Questions of this sort are not popular with engineering students. But they cannot be avoided. And students will find that rephrasing seemingly obscure concepts into their own words is a short cut to understanding. Answers to such questions are to be found within the text, but some also achieve a commentary in the 'Answers' chapter. Numeric answers are provided for the mathematically soluble questions.

Contents and structure

The book contents match the broad specification of relevant management topics listed earlier, and its structure reflects the overview of a manufacturing business within its environment shown in Figure 0.1.

This simplified illustration (adapted from Figure 8.2) identifies only the salient features of a more complex system. In particular, the environment of the business shown here contains only the **customers, competitors** and **constraints** which make up its markets. Similarly, the business itself is reduced to just five **functions**. It seeks to generate wealth by selling solutions to customer needs and problems at prices which exceed the costs of creating them. The solutions are the products of the

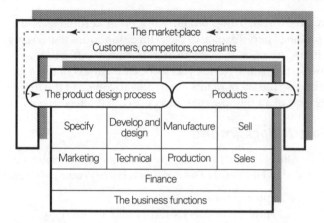

Figure 0.1 **An overview of a manufacturing business within its environment.**

business. If the product price–cost differential is adequate the business will survive. If it is more than adequate the business will prosper. The business functions cooperate in the wealth generating process in a sequential fashion. These functions are:

(1) **Marketing**, which seeks to influence customers to favour the products of the business and to understand their product requirements. The marketeers formulate **outline specifications** for new and enhanced products which are the precursors of product development and design projects.

(2) **Technical**, where *engineers* charged with **product development and design** seek to transform the outline specifications into proven **manufacturing specifications**. These define how to make the products *and* meet acceptable quality and cost targets. The product development and design activity is supported by a longer-term, more speculative, **research** activity (which is not shown in the figure).

(3) **Production**, which seeks to transform manufacturing specifications into a stream of products meeting pre-determined quality and cost boundaries. Rates of production depend on the nature of the market, marketing policy, production capacity, product competitiveness and customer order rates.

(4) **Sales**, which seeks to achieve an acceptable level of **product orders** from customers and to deliver those orders in accordance with the agreed terms of supply.

(5) **Finance**, which aids the business managers to **plan, organize, monitor** and **control** the performance of the business in terms of **profit, profitability** and **cash-flow**.

Note that the (broadly defined) product design process, while centred on the technical function, actually spans the marketing, technical and production functions. It is an **investment** type activity, because its costs come before its rewards. The costs can be substantial, the time-scales long, and the rewards uncertain. For these reasons it is also a focus of financial attention.

Note that technical function activity on product development and design is the interface between the marketing and production functions. Without wishing to get involved in debating which wing of an aeroplane is the most important, it is the combined performance of these three functions that largely determines the success or otherwise of a manufacturing business. All the other business functions play supporting roles. Actual and forecast business performance is measured in financial terms, so the accountants are deeply involved in the three crucial business functions. In view of all this, the main text is divided into three parts. These are now outlined.

Part 1: Background

This material underpins that which follows by considering facets of the whole picture revealed in Figure 0.1. The approach here favours 'why' and 'what' rather than 'how'.

Chapter 1: Business Basics
Chapter 2: Business Strategy and Technology
Chapter 3: The Role of the Technical Function
Chapter 4: About People at Work

Part 2: Technical management

This comprises four major topics in the broader field of technical (or technology) management. Here, 'why' and 'what' are covered as before but substantial attention is also devoted to 'how'. Chapter 8 is a discourse on structured product design. It is the *focus of the whole book*, because everything before it and after it can be regarded as supporting material. The methodology is relatively informal and non-prescriptive. But it establishes a way of thinking about the problems of product design which is equally applicable to other management problems.

Chapter 5: Technical Organizations and People
Chapter 6: Technical Project Planning and Control
Chapter 7: About Costs and Costing
Chapter 8: Structured Product Design

Part 3: Interface topics

The effectiveness of the technical function largely depends on the ability of its inhabitants to communicate properly across the functional boundaries shown in Figure 0.1. Such communication is most efficient when the parties share the same mission, understand each others' part in it, and speak the same language. With this in mind, the purpose of the first two chapters in this part of the text is to illuminate the nature of the marketing and production functions. The next chapter recognizes that a healthy business has always got more ideas for technical projects than the resources to implement them. The material covers business-level mechanisms for the proper evaluation and choice of such projects. The book then concludes with an introduction to **financial accounting**. This is a common thread which links the individual business functions into the total business, and its terminology is the language of business.

Chapter 9: The Marketing and Sales Functions
Chapter 10: The Production Function
Chapter 11: Technical Project Evaluation and Choice
Chapter 12: Basic Financial Accounting

Contents

Preface   v

Introduction   vii

Part 1   BACKGROUND   1

Chapter 1
Business Basics   3

   1.1   Introduction   4
   1.2   Different sorts of business   8
   1.3   Functions and organization   12
   1.4   Business objectives   22
   1.5   About management   25
   1.6   A financial model of a business   27
   1.7   A manufacturing business model   30
   1.8   An example exercising the model   34
   1.9   Concluding summary   40

Chapter 2
Business Strategy and Technology   44

   2.1   The strategic role of technology   45
   2.2   About planning in general   48
   2.3   Business planning   52
   2.4   Technology and strategic position   68
   2.5   Building a technological strategy   73
   2.6   Concluding summary   81

Chapter 3
The Role of the Technical Function   84

   3.1   Introducing innovation   85
   3.2   The primary tasks   89

3.3   Innovation is investment   102
3.4   Secondary tasks   106
3.5   Software innovation   112
3.6   Concluding summary   114

Chapter 4
About People at Work   **117**

4.1   Organization: Why and what   118
4.2   What about the workers?   119
4.3   Organization design: Overview   131
4.4   Organization design: Company level   135
4.5   Speculations on the future   142
4.6   Concluding summary   149

Part 2   TECHNICAL MANAGEMENT   **153**

Chapter 5
Technical Organizations and People   **155**

5.1   Introduction   156
5.2   Technical function: Role summary   157
5.3   Profiles and objectives   161
5.4   Design constraints   166
5.5   Design implementations   177
5.6   Concluding summary   191

Chapter 6
Technical Project Planning and Control   **195**

6.1   The context   196
6.2   Bar charts and resource tables   201
6.3   Flow diagrams   208
6.4   The PERT network technique   219
6.5   Task time versus task effort   248
6.6   Project control   259
6.7   Concluding summary   264

Chapter 7
About Costs and Costing   **270**

7.1   Introduction   272
7.2   Why is cost important?   272
7.3   Cost and costing problems   277
7.4   Budgets: An overview   281
7.5   Cost categories   287
7.6   Cost behaviours   296

7.7   Project costs and costing   301
7.8   Product costs and costing   310
7.9   The profit equation revisited   318
7.10   Concluding summary   331

Chapter 8
Structured Product Design   337

8.1   Motivation and content   338
8.2   Explanation of terms   339
8.3   The product purchasing decision   343
8.4   More about design and designers   346
8.5   Requirements definition: Design   352
8.6   More about functional architecture   362
8.7   More about design constraints   366
8.8   Product design: The whole process   370
8.9   Concluding summary   376

Part 3   INTERFACE TOPICS   381

Chapter 9
The Marketing and Sales Functions   383

9.1   Introduction   384
9.2   Marketing, sales and the business   385
9.3   Marketing: The four Ps   394
9.4   Marketing: Mixing the four Ps   400
9.5   More on price and promotion   406
9.6   More on sales   412
9.7   Concluding summary   414

Chapter 10
The Production Function   417

10.1   Introduction   418
10.2   The manufacturing operation   421
10.3   Manufacturing support services   435
10.4   An arena of conflict   457
10.5   Current production technologies   460
10.6   Concluding summary   464

Chapter 11
Technical Project Evaluation and Choice   469

11.1   Motivation and content   471
11.2   A review of project types   474
11.3   Project evaluation: Background   481

11.4	Evaluation of BR and AR projects	485
11.5	Evaluation of PD&D projects	489
11.6	Product creation projects	490
11.7	Project Evaluation Tool 1 (PET1)	493
11.8	The cash-flow model	497
11.9	Cash-flow shape techniques	501
11.10	The cost of negative cash-flow	506
11.11	A compounding technique	510
11.12	Discounting techniques 1: NPV	513
11.13	Discounting techniques 2: IRR	520
11.14	Project choice: NPV and IRR	524
11.15	Cash-flow models and inflation	533
11.16	Project Evaluation Tool 2 (PET2)	539
11.17	Concluding summary	543

Chapter 12
Basic Financial Accounting   **550**

12.1	Introduction	552
12.2	Basic accounting principles	555
12.3	The birth of Adastra	571
12.4	Adastra: The end of Year 1	585
12.5	Adastra: Year 1 accounts analysis	596
12.6	Concluding summary	613

Appendix A: A Requirements Definition Example		620
Appendix B: Tables of Discount Factors		643
Answers to Selected Questions		646
Glossary		670
Index		692

PART 1

Background

Chapter 1   Business Basics

This chapter provides the context for the rest of the text. It describes, in broad terms, *why* businesses exist, *what* they have to do to continue to exist and *how* they do it. The emphasis is on technology-based businesses. The aim is to enable those readers who claim no prior knowledge of the business world to cope with the rest of the book. It is also commended to those readers who do not start from that position, since its perspective flavours the whole offering.

Chapter 2   Business Strategy and Technology

Modern businesses operate in increasingly complex competitive environments. Technology is a potent weapon in the competition. It offers **opportunities** to those businesses which use it properly and **threats** to those businesses which do not. This chapter examines the role of technology in **strategies** aimed at ensuring business survival and prosperity. Although it is properly placed within the background material, this chapter builds quite rapidly from basic principles into relatively complex considerations. It may be omitted at first reading or, alternatively, early attention can be restricted to the first two sections.

Chapter 3   The Role of the Technical Function

The **primary task** of the technical function is technological innovation (which is commonly, and confusingly, termed **research and development** or **R&D**). A number of **secondary tasks** are also assigned to this function. This chapter examines technological innovation in some depth. A relatively **distinctive view** of this key subject is introduced, which permeates the rest of the book.

1

Chapter 4   About People at Work

This chapter is concerned with the organization of people in industry. The topic is treated at company level and from an organizational *design perspective*. The structure of an industrial organization is necessarily a compromise aimed at meeting the conflicting **constraints** imposed on its design by its business purpose and by the people that it contains. The design emphasis allows this compromise to be examined. The chapter links into Chapter 5, for which it is recommended background reading.

Business Basics

*If there were any difficulty in commerce those
who now conduct it would not be able to do so.*

Dr Samuel Johnson 1709–1784

1.1	Introduction	4
1.2	Different sorts of business	8
1.3	Functions and organization	12
1.4	Business objectives	22
1.5	About management	25
1.6	A financial model of a business	27
1.7	A manufacturing business model	30
1.8	An example exercising the model	34
1.9	Concluding summary	39

 Advanced material Sections 1.6, 1.7 and 1.8 comprise a more searching examination of how a business works than is contained in Section 1.1. Readers with no prior knowledge of business notions might find the material somewhat demanding. It may be omitted at first reading. But it provides a first insight into business accounting which, contrary to engineering mythology, is a thing of beauty and a joy for ever.

The overall objective of this chapter is to equip readers who have no prior knowledge of businesses with the ability to cope with the rest of the book. The material is also commended to more experienced readers, since its perspective flavours the whole offering. Objectives by section follow:

1.1 To outline the nature, purpose and operation of businesses.

1.2 To illustrate three different ways of classifying businesses.

1.3 To describe the major activities which cooperate in a business, and to explain some basic forms of business organization.

1.4 To examine eight critical performance areas where business managers should set and strive towards demanding targets.

1.5 To review the nature of the management job, and to identify the desirable qualities of managers.

1.6 To introduce the basic financial model of a business.

1.7 To present a model of a manufacturing business which combines two earlier models.

1.8 To explore the financial consequences of trading operations in a manufacturing business by means of an extended example.

1.9 To identify its salient points and summarize its major messages.

1.1   Introduction

It is not sensible to discuss the role of *engineers in business* unless there is some shared understanding of businesses. This chapter paints that background for the chapters that follow. It is an engineering view of businesses which examines:

- why they exist
- what they have to do to continue to exist
- how they do it.

To accomplish this daunting ambition in one chapter requires that most of the subtleties are glossed over and a vast amount of detail omitted. But enough is left to equip readers who can claim no prior knowledge of the business world to cope with the rest of the book. The chapter is also commended to readers not in that position, since its perspective flavours the whole offering.

Sections 1.6, 1.7 and 1.8 explore a financial model of a manufacturing business. They are a little more demanding than the earlier material, and may be omitted at first reading.

1.1.1   What is a business?

A first (engineering) answer to this question is *a business is a black box for creating wealth*. This is a good place for engineers to start learning about businesses because they already know about black boxes, which turn inputs into outputs with the aid of transfer functions. So, in this book:

- A **business** is defined as an entity which aims to transform inputs to outputs in a way which increases their *value*.

A business incurs cost in acquiring inputs but receives an income, called **sales revenue** or **turnover**, from selling outputs. So the **added value** created by the transformation process is the difference between the sales revenue arising from selling the outputs and the cost of the inputs which are transformed into those outputs. This added value is **wealth** created in the business by the transformation process. Creating wealth is what businesses are about.

Note the definition used here deliberately excludes 'businesses' which are not concerned with creating wealth. Some charities, for example, are concerned only with redistributing wealth.

A basic business model

A representation of a business is shown in Figure 1.1. It is based on the black box concept and views the business as a number of cooperating activities. These distinct activities are called **business functions**.

In this basic model, the **production function** is supported by a number of other functions which appear simply as a list of names. The production function includes the process which transforms inputs to outputs of higher value. The way in which the other functions support and sustain this critical process is described later, in Section 1.3. The nature of the inputs depends on the nature of the business. For example, the inputs to a business which makes and sells bicycles are bicycle components ranging, say, from alloy tubes to tyres. On the other hand, a business which makes and sells financial products, such as insurance policies and home purchase loans, processes money inputs to create its outputs. The outputs that a business offers for sale are commonly termed its **products**.

A set of **resources** is assigned to each function. Resources are the people and things (such as buildings, machinery, tools, furniture and computers) which enable the functions to perform their duties. All resources incur cost, both to acquire and to employ or use. The resource cost of the production function is labelled 'process cost' in Figure 1.1. Those relating to the other functions are lumped together as 'operating cost'.

In principle, the operation of the business model of Figure 1.1 is quite simple:

- Inputs are processed, in the production function, into products of higher value.
- The products are sold to yield sales revenue.
- The sales revenue is used to buy more inputs and to pay the **process cost**, leaving a surplus called the **gross profit**.
- The gross profit is used to pay the **operating cost**, leaving a surplus called the **operating profit**.

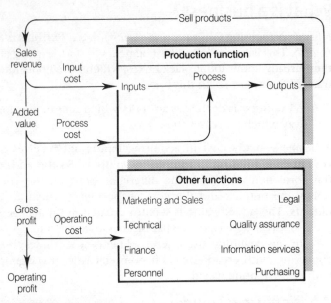

Figure 1.1 **A basic business model.**
In this simple picture of a manufacturing business, the production function is shown as a process which transforms purchased inputs to product outputs. This function is supported by a number of other functions (marketing and sales, technical, finance and so on) whose roles are discussed later in the chapter. Products are sold to give an income called sales revenue. This is used to pay for inputs to the manufacturing process, for doing the processing and for the work of the supporting functions. Hopefully, there is something left over after paying all these costs. This surplus is the operating profit. Equations 1.1 to 1.5 in the main text describe the left-hand side of the figure in mathematical terms.

Note that the operating profit must be sufficiently positive if the business is to stay in business. What is meant by 'sufficiently' in this context is explored later in the chapter (under the 'Profitability' heading in Section 1.4.1).

Some fundamental equations

The model depicted in Figure 1.1 establishes a number of fundamental business equations:

$$\text{Gross Profit} \quad = \text{Sales Revenue} - \text{Cost of Sales} \tag{1.1}$$

where

$$\text{Cost of Sales} \quad = \text{Input Cost} + \text{Process Cost} \tag{1.2}$$
$$\text{Operating Profit} = \text{Gross Profit} - \text{Operating Cost} \tag{1.3}$$
$$\text{Added Value} \quad = \text{Sales Revenue} - \text{Input Cost} \tag{1.4}$$

or

$$\text{Added Value} \quad = \text{Process Cost} + \text{Gross Profit} \tag{1.5}$$

There is an inherent delay in the **trading** (buying and selling) loop of Figure 1.1 due to the processing. It is likely, also, that there are additional delays due to buying and selling on credit. But the equations only make sense if all the quantities involved are measured over the same period and relate to the products sold during that period. The problem is resolved by measuring revenue and cost in a way which is not solely based on cash. The technique is known as **accrual accounting**. It is examined in Chapter 12, which is devoted to business accounting. The measurement period is never longer than one year and shorter periods are often used.

Equations 1.1 and 1.3 have a central role in all business matters because of the critical importance of profit. Equation 1.5 is an illuminating variation of Equation 1.4. It illustrates that added value measures the effort of the business in transforming inputs to outputs together with the reward for that effort.

The basic business model of Figure 1.1 is developed further, in Sections 1.6, 1.7 and 1.8, at the end of the chapter. The approach adopted there introduces the pivotal concepts of business accounting. (Note that accountants usually approach the profit concept by first introducing **balance sheets**. This approach *is* used in the later discussions, in particular in Section 1.6.3, under the 'Non-compensating changes: profit and loss' heading. The treatment used in the preceding introductory discussion is less formal, but it gives the right answers more quickly.)

Product value, price and cost

Product value is not a well-defined concept but it is clear that it is regarded differently by sellers and buyers:

- Product value is perceived as less than **product price** by a seller, because the seller would rather have the money than the product.

- Product value is perceived as greater than product price by a purchaser, because the purchaser would rather have the product than the money.

However, from the perspective of the supplying business, **product cost** is quite different from product price and product value. Product cost is the cost of those inputs which are consumed in the process which makes the product *plus* the cost of doing that processing. There is *no direct connection between product cost and product price* in the sense that determining one automatically determines the other. They are independent variables.

1.1.2   Section summary

This section has introduced a number of fundamental notions about businesses. In summary, these are:

- A business is a system which is designed to buy inputs, work on them in some way, and sell the resulting products for more than the cost of the inputs plus the *whole* cost of working on them. If this happens, the business earns a net income, termed operating profit. If this is large enough the business will survive and, perhaps, prosper.

- Some fundamental business parameters are gross profit, sales revenue, cost of sales, input cost, process cost, operating profit and added value. The relationships between them are summarized in Equations 1.1 to 1.5.

- Product price is what a purchaser pays for the product.

- To the business supplying a product, product value is less than product price. But the purchaser who buys the product perceives its value as greater than its price.

- Product cost is the cost of the inputs consumed in the process which makes the product plus the cost of doing that processing.

- Product cost and product price are not mathematically connected. They are independent variables.

1.2 Different sorts of business

There are many ways in which businesses can be classified and only a few of these are considered here. These are by the nature of the product, by size, and by type of ownership.

1.2.1 Classification by product

In broad terms, there are only two types of product. These are the tangible, physical sort and the intangible, non-physical sort. Motor cars, computers, bridges, food and software packages are examples of tangible products. Examples of non-tangible products are transport, consultancy, education and banking. This product classification allows two types of business to be distinguished.

Manufacturing businesses

Businesses which create tangible products are termed **manufacturing businesses**, indicating (nowadays) that their products are made with the aid of machines. The products may be called **manufactured products**. Most of the inputs which are processed into the tangible products are tangible inputs. Typically, the ratio of product price to input cost is about two or three to one (added values in the range one to two times input cost). Manufactured products range from high value, high complexity items produced in relatively small numbers to low value, low complexity items produced in relatively large numbers. Ships and air-traffic control systems are examples at the high end of this range, whereas such products as cassette tapes and wood-screws are at its low end. The spectrum is covered by three broad classes of process, which may be termed **project manufacturing**, **batch manufacturing** and **mass manufacturing**. Thus, manufacturing businesses can be further classified by the nature of the process which dominates their manufacturing operation. These topics are examined in Chapter 10.

Service businesses

Businesses which create non-tangible products are termed **service businesses**. They usually depend on specialist skills and facilities, or on a particular location, or on a combination of these features. The inputs that they process into their service products are more diverse than in the manufacturing case. The taxi, hairdressing and education businesses, for example, add value to people. Consultancy businesses take in customers' problems and create higher value solutions. Banks, insurance companies and building societies have money inputs which they use to create money products such as loans, policies and mortgages. Retailers offer local availability and support to the end users of some tangible products.

Manufacturing and services businesses compared

The feature which distinguishes service products from tangible products is that *service products cannot be stored* in anticipation of future demand. Most Christmas crackers, for instance, are sold to end users in December but they can be made and stored all the year round. Skills, however, cannot be stored in this way. The same is true of specialist facilities such as transport capacity and telecommunications capacity. So service businesses may have the problems of excess processing capacity in times of low demand, and not enough in times of high demand. But, wholesalers and retailers excepted, they never have the problem of a redundant stock of tangible products that no one wants to buy.

Many real businesses offer both sorts of product and are classified in a way which reflects the dominant activity. For example, a manufacturer of air-traffic control systems can also sell training courses in operating and maintaining the main products.

1.2.2 Classification by size

The size of a business can be described in a number of ways. The measures most commonly used are the number of people employed, the annual value of product sales, balance sheet parameters (discussed in Section 1.6) and **market share**. This last factor indicates what fraction of the *total* sales in a particular market over a period have been captured by the business. It is one indicator of the relative competitive status of the business.

An interpretation of tiny, small, medium and large

An interesting non-numeric 'measure' of size relates to the *structure* of the business. Most large businesses have grown from very small beginnings. A number of writers, Channon (1973) for example, have suggested that there are distinct structural stages in developments of this sort. The consensus appears to favour four such stages, described as follows:

(1) *Tiny*   A single business managed by one individual (who probably owns the business) and trading in a single limited range of related products in a restricted local area.

(2) *Small*   A single business managed by a team and selling a single broad range of related products in substantial quantities, probably over a wider geographical area.

(3) *Medium*   A central organization managing several small businesses as described in (2) above. In this structure, the small businesses are usually distinguished either by the nature of their product range or by their geographical area of operation, or by both of these factors.

(4) *Large*   A central organization managing several medium businesses as described in (3) above. The medium businesses are likely to be substantial operations in their own right with their own semi-autonomous management

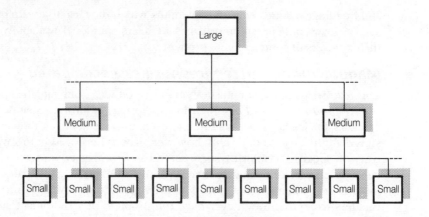

Figure 1.2   **A large business as a hierarchy of businesses.**

One non-numeric way of measuring the size of a business describes its relative position in a business hierarchy. The small businesses in the figure are team-managed operations trading in a single broad range of similar products. They are usually distinguished by product type and/or location. The medium businesses comprise several such small businesses which, typically, serve different sectors of the same market (such as security, communications or domestic appliances). The large business is a central organization controlling a number of medium-sized businesses. Thus, the large business is an ordered structure of small businesses. This type of organization offers the only reasonable way of managing a large business. It is examined in more detail in Figures 1.3 to 1.6.

teams. Taken together, the whole organization offers a broad range of diverse products over an extensive geographical area.

Figure 1.2 illustrates a fully developed business which has grown into a large–medium–small hierarchy. It is essentially an ordered structure of small businesses, each trading in a specific product market.

There are two basic reasons which favour this type of growth pattern:

- There is a limit to the number of subordinates which any one superior can manage effectively. So, as the volume of activity within a business increases, further layers of management are introduced.

- Managers are best motivated, measured and controlled by being given a total business responsibility. So, when it becomes necessary to subdivide a business, there is every reason to split it into a number of smaller self-contained businesses.

1.2.3   Classification by ownership

A business always belongs to an owner or owners who hope to benefit from its activities. Owners can be individuals, other businesses or institutions, or governments. When businesses are classified by type of ownership there are three major categories to consider:

(1) **sole-traders**

(2) **partnerships**
(3) **limited liability companies** (known as 'corporations' in the USA).

(A small proportion of all companies are *not* limited liability companies. These forms are not discussed here.)

Sole-trader businesses

In this case the business is owned by *one* individual, a sole-trader, who may also manage the business. Many businesses start (and end) their life in this way. There is no legal distinction between the business and its owner, who is personally responsible for any debts that the business might incur. Typically, sole-traders run small retail and service businesses.

Partnership businesses

A partnership business is exactly like a sole-trader except that it is owned by *two or more* individuals, who are the partners. They are jointly responsible for any debts that the business might incur, and can share the business profits (or losses) in any way they choose. Again, many small retail and service businesses are structured in this way, as are some very substantial businesses such as large legal, accountancy and estate agency firms.

Limited liability company businesses

Companies are quite different from sole-traders and partnerships in that they are constituted, in conformity with the laws of the country in which they 'reside', as *legal entities* in their own right. A company, therefore, is legally distinct from its owner or owners. Ownership of a company is split into **shares**, so a company belongs to its **shareholders**. They are entitled to benefits of ownership in proportion to the fraction of the issued shares that they hold. However, they are only liable for the amount that they have invested in purchasing shares in the company. This **limited liability** protection means that the owners cannot lose more than their stake in a company, whatever sort of difficulty it gets into. This is in sharp contrast to the situation with sole-trader and partnership businesses, where the owners have unlimited liability for the debts of the business without regard to the size of their investment in it.

Companies whose shares are *not* publicly traded are termed **private companies**. Most companies are in this category. In Britain, this status is indicated by the word 'limited' (or the abbreviation Ltd) as a terminator to the company name. Generally, these companies have a relatively small number of shareholders, who are also its managers. They tend to be the smaller companies.

Companies whose shares *are* publicly traded are termed **public companies**. In Britain, this status is indicated by the phrase 'public limited company' (or the abbreviation PLC) as a terminator to the company name. These companies normally have a large number of shareholders, which means that ownership and management are usually separate. They tend to be the larger companies.

Because of the fund-raising possibilities implicit in access to a large number of owners (actual and potential), and the limited liability provision, companies have become the dominant form of business organization.

1.3   Functions and organization

The primary aim of this section is to describe the various business functions which comprise the business represented in Figure 1.1. This leads into a brief discussion of some organizational issues, which links back to the business hierarchy concept illustrated in Figure 1.2.

Figure 1.1 shows that the production function is a system which transforms product-related inputs to product outputs of higher value. Conceptually, it is useful to regard the other business functions as systems which transform *information inputs to higher value information outputs*. For example, the technical function transforms product specifications into 'how to make it' instructions for the manufacturing operation. As it is used in this book, the term 'function' usually implies that the inhabitants of that function share a common *business purpose* rather than a particular *professional skill* (though they may do this as well). For example, the technical function is dedicated to technological innovation and employs technically qualified people. But it also employs accountants and personnel managers who share its ambitions without claiming technological expertise. This is now the common usage of 'function' in businesses and business literature. But sometimes the word *is* used, here and elsewhere, to denote a group of people with a common professional skill. In these exceptional cases the meaning is made clear in the text. The role of each of the major business functions is now discussed.

1.3.1   Marketing and sales

The **marketing** and **sales functions** are most usually part of the same organization within a business. This is because both interface the business to its market-place, and both are concerned with products, customers, prices and costs. Only rarely is this organization called the 'Marketing and Sales Department'. The titles 'Marketing Department' or 'Sales Department' are more common, although variations on the 'Commercial Department' theme also occur. The term 'division' might be used instead of 'department'.

Marketing can be defined as the task of capturing and keeping customers by ensuring that the right product is available at the right price with the right promotion in the right place at the right time. This potted definition allows the following sub-tasks to be identified:

(1) **Market research**, which is aimed at locating, defining and evaluating customer requirements.
(2) **Specifying** new products and enhancements to current products. Marketing will probably also lead business-wide projects aimed at turning those specifications into profitable reality.
(3) Defining and implementing product **pricing** strategies.
(4) Defining and implementing adequate and economic **promotional** strategies. These are plans aimed at persuading actual and potential customers to favour the products of the business over similar products offered by its competitors. Promotion applies to current, enhanced and new products.
(5) Defining and implementing adequate and economic product distribution arrangements. These relate to the **time** and **place** factors.

(6) Defining and implementing adequate and economic arrangements for after-sales **customer support**, such as product warranties, good documentation, servicing and repair facilities, good spares availability, and so on.

Thus marketing emerges as an essentially strategic activity concerned both with developing the current trading activity, and identifying and exploiting new profit opportunities.

The primary objective of the sales function is to achieve, economically, the planned level of firm orders for products, which is the ultimate 'pay-off' purpose of the whole marketing activity. It often involves selling at the person-to-person level and the people-related skills of the sales staff are critical in the success or otherwise of the operation.

1.3.2 Technical

The primary role of the **technical function** is **technical innovation**. For the most part, this involves product-related research, development and design but some of the work may relate to the product creation process itself. The function has a central role in every technology-based business. It is the interface between the marketing and production functions.

The majority of the technically qualified people in a business, be they engineers, scientists or mathematicians, start their industrial careers in this function and most of them remain in it during their industrial employment. A substantial fraction of this book is about the technical function. It covers the jobs it has to do, how it is organized and how it is managed.

1.3.3 Production

In this book the production function is defined to include the product **manufacturing operation** and a set of **manufacturing support services**. The manufacturing operation is where inputs are converted into finished products. It is the central wealth-creating heart of the business.

Manufacturing support services

The principal supporting service activities are now briefly described.

(1) **Facilities maintenance** The performance of all physical machines deteriorates as they are used and they are always vulnerable to failure. Facilities maintenance aims to sustain (economically) the performance of the manufacturing machinery at, or above, some pre-defined quality level. It includes inspection, servicing, preventive maintenance and repair.

(2) **Industrial engineering** This focuses on the efficiency of systems which comprise human operators and machines with the objective of achieving the best possible output for the least possible cost. It includes the study and specification of working methods and procedures, the measurement of work and the determination of work standards.

(3) **Production engineering** This activity is concerned with manufacturing technology in all of its many facets. At the overall level, production engineers

make their specialized contribution to such issues as capacity planning, the introduction of new manufacturing technologies and the evaluation of new machines. At the product level, they work with the development and design engineers of the technical function. This work involves the introduction of new products into production, enhancements to current products, and problems arising with established products. Another major concern is product cost. Activity in this arena involves both day-to-day cost control and reduction, and more structured **value analysis** and **value engineering** studies.

(4) **Production planning and control** The central feature of production planning is the scheduling of the individual sub-operations which make up the manufacturing operation. This is not a trivial problem, particularly in a multi-product/multi-customer batch manufacturing situation. One plan objective is to maximize the utilization of the available resources (people and machines) so that the costs that they represent are used to the best effect. However, this economic ambition is invariably compromised by the need to meet specifications on product delivery time, cost and quality. Production control can also be made more challenging than it needs to be by the capricious nature of some external suppliers.

(5) **Purchasing** and **quality assurance** Either or both of the purchasing and quality assurance activities may reside within the production function as supporting services to manufacturing. The trend, however, is to promote these activities to functions in their own right, reporting to the 'top line'. This arrangement is assumed here.

1.3.4 Finance

The activities of the **finance function** permeate every facet of a business, because all business activities have financial consequences. Its major tasks are, in summary:

(1) **Cash control** This is a company level activity aimed at the optimum management of cash, and near cash, resources. It includes, for example, arranging short-term credit in times of temporary cash famine (pay-day, say), short-term lending in times of temporary cash excess, negotiating long-term loans, and the currency exchange transactions required by international trading.

(2) **Accounting** In its many forms accounting is the most visible and pervasive aspect of finance. It is about financial planning, control and reporting. The three reasonably distinct types of activity are:

(a) **Bookkeeping**, which is the identification, classifying and recording of financial transactions to provide data for the two other major activities.

(b) **Management accounting**, which concerns financial planning, results analysis and reporting to assist business managers at all levels with their own duties. Generally, each distinct business function is treated as a separate financial entity with its own set of **budgets**. Budgets are financial plans. Their preparation, monitoring and control is the focus of management accounting.

(c) **Financial accounting**, which involves the preparation of formal accounts and reports to meet the legal requirement to publish specified financial information at regular intervals.

(3) **Investment planning and evaluation**   This relates to the financial aspects of the many investments that a company might consider. Examples include the purchase of new manufacturing machinery, major new product creation projects, and the acquisition of other businesses.

(4) **Tax collecting**   This is a duty which governments impose on companies to harvest various taxes. Examples include corporation tax on company profits, income tax on employee remuneration, and value added or sales taxes on product sales.

(5) **Payroll**   The task here is to calculate the remuneration of individual employees and pay it to them at the appropriate intervals.

1.3.5 Personnel

The **personnel function** is responsible for the people resource within the company. There are two major aspects. First, ensuring that the resource matches what is required in skills, numbers and location, and second, ensuring that the employment environment is such that the people within it can give of their best. The responsibility extends across the whole spectrum of people, from top management to that small army of cleaners which keeps the manufacturing area habitable.

In many cases, this function is best regarded as a group of people with a common professional skill. This is because the majority of its members are normally dispersed, in small teams, among the other functions. These teams provide a specialist, advisory, 'staff' role assisting the local 'line' managers who are responsible for the business purpose of the function that employs them. In structures of this sort, there is invariably a small senior team at company headquarters which retains some overall personnel responsibilities, such as management remuneration policy and graduate training.

The major tasks of the personnel function are as follows:

(1) **Resource planning** is required at all levels in the hierarchy because increasing or decreasing the size of teams *in an orderly fashion* is always a slow process.

(2) *Increasing* the 'headcount' by internal transfer or external recruiting. Both mechanisms involve search and selection.

(3) *Reducing* the headcount by internal transfers, encouraging voluntary redundancies or terminating employments.

(4) Defining and implementing **remuneration policies** at all levels.

(5) Providing facilities for **training and career development**.

(6) 'Refereeing' the operation of the **grievance and disciplinary** procedures at all levels.

(7) Negotiating with employee representatives, who are often trade union officials, on the working conditions and terms of employment enjoyed by the 'organized' section of the work-force. This arena is usually described as **industrial relations** and, for the most part, relates to the shop-floor workers in the manufacturing operation.

1.3.6 Purchasing

All manufacturing companies make purchases from **external suppliers** and most of these are the **direct materials** that get built into their products. These inputs can comprise some sixty per cent, say, of product cost. Manufacturing schedules depend critically on the delivery of these items in the right quantities, at the right time and to the right specification. Efficient **purchasing**, therefore, is a central element in efficient manufacturing. An important contribution in this area is the concept of **materials management** which has developed over recent years. This brings some form of overall planning and control to the use of externally purchased items, replacing the more traditional dispersion of this task.

Purchasing may be incorporated into the production function as a support service to the manufacturing operation. However, all of the other business functions need supplies of some sort from outside the company and the trend now is to elevate purchasing into a business function in its own right.

The focus of the purchasing task is the identification and cultivation of satisfactory suppliers who habitually deliver the ordered items on time, in the ordered quantities, to the specified functional and quality specification, *and* who do all these things at a competitive price. Achieving this ideal is no small challenge to which is added, usually, an overriding requirement for continuity of supply. This latter problem may be solved for standard items by establishing multiple sourcing arrangements.

1.3.7 Quality assurance

In an industrial context, product **quality** is defined as the degree to which the product meets the needs of its user. In other words, quality is a measure of the fitness of the product for its user-defined purpose. **Quality assurance** is defined here as all activities aimed at achieving and maintaining defined levels of product quality at an economic cost. (This is a simplified version of the definition in Chapter 10.) It includes management activities such as quality planning and quality control.

Achieving and maintaining adequate quality levels is now recognized as a survival issue by most European and North American manufacturing companies, although their Japanese rivals acted on this conviction as long ago as the early 1960s. Usually, quality assurance concepts are first introduced in the production function since product quality is clearly dependent on both the quality of the manufacturing process and the quality of the inputs (materials, operator effort and management) to that process. In some cases this has proved to be an unsatisfactory arrangement because, in times of crisis, quality might take second place to delivery schedules. For this reason the quality assurance activity is now increasingly treated as a distinct business function reporting on the top line. This arrangement, which affords the function an independent status, is frequently a mandatory precondition for the award of government contracts.

There is also a perceptible trend towards the **total quality** approach. This recognizes that *all* the activities of the company, without exception, have an impact on product quality, so they should all be subject to quality assurance. Implementing such a policy is generally made easier if the quality assurance expertise is in a separate function.

1.3.8 Information services

Efficient information handling is increasingly recognized as an essential competitive weapon and many medium and large companies now focus that activity in a distinct **information services function**. Names for this function vary quite a lot. Typically, the old 'EDP (Electronic Data Processing) Department' has become the 'Information Processing Division' or some such similar title, and has taken over responsibility for voice and data communications inside the company. A vast range of information concerning products, customers, competitors, suppliers, stocks, personnel, physical resources, finance, and so on is stored, updated, analysed and communicated. **Management information systems** offering facilities of this nature are becoming progressively more useful and important.

1.3.9 Legal

The laws of the country in which a company resides, and those of the countries in which it operates, have a pervasive influence on every aspect of business activity. In recognition of this, most substantial companies have their own **legal function**, although they may still employ external legal firms for particularly specialized work. Some examples of the legal constraints applying to company operations are now listed.

(1) The minimum requirements for statutory financial reporting (in terms of frequency, methods and content) are defined by the Companies Act in Britain and by the Securities and Exchange Commission in the USA. Most other countries, but not all, have similar provisions. One purpose is to provide a measure of protection against fraud for company shareholders, customers, suppliers and lenders. Incidentally, the law does not penalize company directors for innocent stupidity but is less forgiving of (detected) fraud.

(2) A growing body of legislation in both Europe and the USA is designed to protect customers from unfair, deceitful or dangerous business practices. Examples from Britain are the Trade Description Acts and the Fair Trading Act. Product liability legislation, which provides for sanctions against suppliers of products that damage people, is becoming increasingly prevalent, especially in the USA. In a similar vein but more broadly applicable is 'social' legislation, such as that relating to environmental pollution, and health and safety at work.

(3) The minimization of company taxation is a fruitful field of endeavour for specialist lawyers and accountants. As with personal taxes, corporation (company) tax avoidance is not illegal but tax evasion is. This situation perpetuates the long-standing conflict between enthusiastic tax collectors and reluctant tax payers which absorbs much creative effort on both sides.

(4) All companies enter into a variety of contracts, such as those with customers to supply products, those with suppliers to purchase components and services and those with people to employ them. All of these situations are covered by one facet or another of the law of contracts.

1.3.10   Board of directors

The directors of a company are its most senior managers and they are responsible to the shareholders (owners) for its performance. A board of directors usually comprises a chairman, a managing director and a number of other directors. Most company boards also include a number of non-executive directors, who are usually senior business executives in non-competing industries. Their role is to assist the board by bringing an informed *external* perspective to its deliberations.

Typically, a company board meets each month to discharge its duties, which are summarized as follows:

(1) Establishing longer-term business policies, setting the corresponding objectives and defining, in broad terms, ways of achieving them.
(2) Ensuring the availability of the resources needed to achieve the objectives.
(3) Assessing current results in relation to current plans and initiating corrective action when necessary.
(4) Selecting managers to fill posts one and (possibly) two levels below the board.
(5) Motivating managers and others to give their best performance.

1.3.11   Company organizations

There are many different ways of organizing companies but structures based on functional partitioning are normally used at the level nearest to the markets. Higher-level structures are typically based on product (range) or geography but subdivision by customer is also used.

Organization by function

Typically, small to medium-sized manufacturing businesses are organized on a functional basis. Figure 1.3 illustrates the arrangement and summarizes the major responsibilities of the various functions.

This particular business is a company and, therefore, it has a board of directors. Here, the board comprises a chairman, a number of non-executive directors, a managing director reporting to the chairman and *some* of the functional directors reporting to the managing director. Note that four of the functional directors are not board members. In their case the 'director' title is a courtesy indicating 'top line' seniority. The other directors would probably be referred to as 'main board' directors when the distinction needed to be made.

The board structure shown in Figure 1.3 is a typical British arrangement in which the managing director and the functional directors form the executive team which runs the company on a day-to-day basis. In contrast, the company chairman normally devotes more attention to the longer-term aspects of company affairs. The company secretary is responsible for the formal administration of the board but is not necessarily a member of it. The post usually carries other duties, such as those indicated in the figure.

The business might be an independent private or public limited company or it might be wholly owned by a larger company. In the latter case, it would be a private limited company and its chairman would probably sit on the board of the parent company.

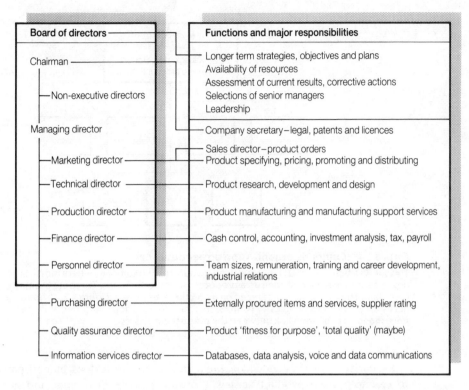

Figure 1.3   **Company organization on a functional basis.**

Small to medium-sized manufacturing companies are commonly organized on a *functional* basis, as in the typical (British) structure shown here. The functional directors report to the managing director, who reports to the chairman. The right-hand side of the figure summarizes the most important duties and responsibilities of the the various business functions. Note that not all the functional directors are on the main board, so their 'director' title is a courtesy recognizing top management status. The chairman bears ultimate responsibility for the whole company but (usually) tends to concentrate on the longer-term issues, delegating day-to-day management to the managing director.

In practice, there are many variations on the basic theme of Figure 1.3, but all of the major functions shown are normally present whatever detailed arrangements are employed. The functions also have their own internal hierarchy. A very small company would contain all these functions in the sense that all of the corresponding activities need to be performed. However, the functions might not all be separately identified and the hierarchy would probably be less formal, with some senior people fulfilling more than one role.

Organizational charts of this nature are a traditional way of depicting a business. They illustrate the *formal* authority and decision-making structure, but they do not reveal much about how the business works.

Organization by product

Figure 1.4 shows a medium- or large-sized manufacturing company in which the top level is partitioned primarily on a product range basis.

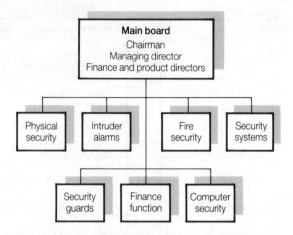

Figure 1.4 **Company organization on a product basis.**
This shows a typical medium to large-sized manufacturing company where most of the second-level organizations are distinguished on a *product* (market sector) basis. These are businesses in their own right. They are usually organized on a functional basis, as in Figure 1.3, although they are not necessarily distinct companies. A 'professional' finance function is included at the second level, since money is a common link between the product businesses.

A security company (endeavouring to prove that crime does, indeed, pay) is used as an example. Each product area is a business in its own right and is (typically) organized on a functional basis. Note that a finance function is included in the top-line structure since financial matters are a common link between the technologically diverse product businesses. Note, too, that one of these businesses, security guards, is a service business.

Organization by geography

An alternative arrangement for a medium- or large-sized company is depicted in Figure 1.5. Here the top level is partitioned primarily on a geographic basis, but it also includes a finance function as in the previous scheme. Each regional area is a business in its own right.

A large company organization

The three partitioning techniques outlined in the preceding discussion are complementary rather than competitive. Figure 1.6 illustrates the point. It shows a fragment of the organization of a large (and hypothetical) security company.

The first-level structure is based on geographic regions (as in Figure 1.5), the second-level structure is based on products (as in Figure 1.4) and the third-level structure is based on functions (as in Figure 1.3). Here, though, the physical security product area business is a **trading division** of British Security Ltd rather than a company.

Figure 1.6 represents one possible version of the business hierarchy illustrated in Figure 1.2 – where Global Security PLC is the *large* business, British Security Ltd is one of the *medium* businesses and the physical security division is one of the *small* businesses.

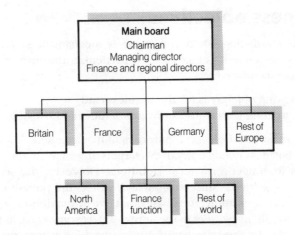

Figure 1.5   Company organization on a geographic basis.
This is an alternative structure for a typical medium to large-sized manufacturing company to that of Figure 1.4. Here, the distinct businesses at the second level are distinguished by geographic *location* rather than by product type. A second-level finance function is included, as before.

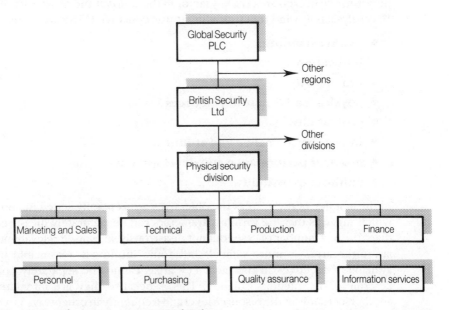

Figure 1.6   A large company organization.
The three business partitioning techniques (functional, product type and geographical) are complementary rather than competitive. This figure illustrates the point. The first-level structure is based on geography (as in Figure 1.5), the second-level on products (as in Figure 1.4) and the third-level on functions (as in Figure 1.3). Here, though, the physical security product area business is a trading division of British Security Ltd, rather than a company. The figure represents a version of the business hierarchy shown in Figure 1.2, in which Global Security PLC is the large business, British Security Ltd is one of the medium businesses and the physical security division is one of the small businesses.

1.4	# Business objectives

A business is distinguished from a purely mechanistic system because the people it contains influence its behaviour. In particular, the managers of a business aim to determine its future by:

(1) setting objectives for the business, and
(2) directing its resources towards achieving those objectives.

Indeed, these are the central purposes of management.

So, a business needs objectives (targets at which to aim) as markers on the path towards its longer-term term ambitions. However, the search for a single 'right' business objective is unrewarding and, worse, the pursuit of a single objective can prove fatal. For example, the single objective of 'maximum profit' is easily achieved by eliminating all investment in the future. But, at some stage in this future, the products become obsolete and the manufacturing machinery decrepit beyond further repair – so the business dies. What is required is a set of balanced objectives and a process which periodically reviews them as the business and its environment changes. Drucker (1989), in one of his early management classics, identifies eight **critical performance areas** where objectives should be set. He argues, convincingly, that performance in each area is a key factor in the survival and prosperity of the business. His analysis is as valid today as when it was conceived. The areas are:

- **market standing**
- **innovation**
- **productivity**
- **physical and financial resources**
- **profitability**
- **worker performance and attitudes**
- **manager performance and development**
- **public responsibility**.

In the first five of these areas the objectives are generally stated in numerical terms, which suggests that the various parameters can be accurately measured. This is less than true in a number of cases but not disastrously so. Stating relevant numbers in the last three areas is more difficult but some intuitively reasonable indicators are available. Objectives in the eight key areas cannot be separately considered and determined in splendid isolation. This is because they are interactive, one with another, certainly at the resource level and frequently in other ways as well. Obtaining a balanced set of realizable objectives is no more than a milestone on the road to achieving the strategic aims. Each objective must then be compared with the corresponding present position. This identifies the **planning gap** and is the start of the detailed planning process in that area.

1.4.1 The critical areas

Each of the critical areas for objective setting is now explained in a little more detail, but no attempt is made to define any specific objectives.

Market standing

Market standing is some index of relative importance as a product supplier in the market or markets in which the business operates. The percentage market share captured in a defined period is the normal measure. Clearly, this can only be assessed if the total market size in that period is known. There are real dangers in being a marginal supplier holding a much smaller share than that of the major competitors. Under these circumstances, a price war among the major players may destroy the minor participants operating on fragile profit margins. But the position of a dominant supplier is not without its problems, although there is little doubt about which of the two extremes is to be preferred. There are two major vulnerabilities in a dominant market position. These are, first, legal constraints aimed at protecting customers from exploitation and, second, complacency. Complacency is probably the more lethal, especially in product areas susceptible to dramatic shifts in technology.

Innovation

Innovation is one path to better market standing (acquisition of other businesses is another) so innovation objectives must align with those in the marketing area. There are two rather different sorts of innovation. One is aimed at enhancing the profit contribution of current products and at creating new ones. The other is more broadly directed towards improving the efficiency of the whole business process. The first of these involves technological innovation and is very much the concern of the technical function.

It is not, of course, sufficient merely to innovate. It is also necessary to choose the right innovations. This requires forecasting the future in both market and techno-logical terms. The fundamental difficulty with forecasting the future is that nobody actually *knows* what is going to happen. The level of this uncertainty increases rapidly with the time-span of the forecast, and mistakes are inevitable. Choice is just one of the problems with innovation. Another turns on the conflict, which is unavoidable in the normal resource-limited situation, between the needs of the present and those of the future. The costs of innovation are investments made in anticipation of returns substantially greater than the costs. But the costs, being closer in time, are more visible and certain than the returns, which are necessarily speculative. Investment costs are most prudently accounted for as a charge against profit as and when they occur. Thus the future is paid for in the present. In times of profit famine, investments in the future may be cut back so as to secure the present. Such action is conventionally justified by arguing that there is no point in investing in the future if there is not going to be one. The argument has merit. But the danger of a downwards spiral to oblivion is inherent in this situation, since 'innovate or die' is a fundamental choice for all businesses operating in competitive markets.

Productivity

Productivity is some measure of how efficiently a business uses its resources. One critical resource is people, and two monetary measures of other resources are **total assets** and **capital employed**. The first of these puts a value on all the things that belong to the business. Capital employed is (most usefully) defined as the sum of the owners' investment in the business and its long-term borrowings.

Productivity is the only way to compare different businesses operating within the same market sector, different businesses within the same company and businesses operating in different market sectors. It measures management competence since, by and large, all businesses have access to the same resources so the factor that distinguishes one business from another is the quality of the management teams. Productivity is always measured over a defined period, usually one year. A number of different measures are used in practice, and some popular variants are:

$$\text{Labour Sales Productivity} = \frac{\text{Sales Revenue}}{\text{Number of Employees}} \tag{1.6}$$

$$\text{Labour Profit Productivity} = \frac{\text{Operating Profit}}{\text{Number of Employees}} \tag{1.7}$$

$$\text{Return on Assets} = \frac{\text{Operating Profit}}{\text{Total Assets}} \tag{1.8}$$

$$\text{Return on Capital Employed} = \frac{\text{Operating Profit}}{\text{Capital Employed}} \tag{1.9}$$

Physical and financial resources

In one sense, obtaining adequate financial resources is *the* most critical objective, since investment is a necessary prerequisite to achieving all the other objectives. There are only three ways of obtaining finance to invest in a company: by retaining some profit, by borrowing, and by selling more shares. The relative merits of these options are not considered here, but the optimum choice is a matter that does demand careful attention.

Profitability

Profitability is variously defined. Return on assets and return on capital employed, at Equations 1.8 and 1.9, respectively, are two productivity measures which indicate profitability. The ratio of operating profit to sales revenue (return on sales or sales profitability) is a third common measure. One function of profit and profitability is, therefore, to describe business and management performance. But the **role of profit** is wider than this. To survive and prosper a business must be sufficiently profitable to finance, directly or indirectly:

- maintenance and growth of its physical facilities
- its innovation objectives
- adequate rewards for its owners.

Thus, if management chooses to retain some profit for direct investment there must still be enough left for the owners, where 'enough' is determined by what their investment could earn elsewhere at comparable risk levels. Similarly, if some of the profit is used to service loan capital, the earnings on that capital must do more than just pay its interest costs. Equally, the promised rate of return must be competitive if investment money is to be raised by selling additional shares.

Worker performance and attitudes

The term 'worker' is generally understood to mean those employees who, actually or potentially, are members of a trade union. It generally includes the manual workers in the manufacturing operation, clerical staff and, perhaps, staff with professional qualifications in low-level management or non-management positions. These employees make an essential contribution to the business and the quality of their performance is a critical element in its progress. It is now accepted that worker attitude, which depends on how they feel about the business, is a factor in worker performance. But 'attitude' is an intangible thing not easily measured. Some indicators which can be measured include absenteeism, sickness, inter-union and union–management disputes and, of course, strikes.

The days of 'donkey-management', based on the assumption that workers are motivated simply by monetary carrots and loss-of-job sticks, are now passing and more enlightened worker-management methods are being employed. These include schemes whereby workers are encouraged to participate in the ownership of the business, enhanced job satisfaction by job enrichment and positive steps to inform the work-force of the status of the business on a regular basis.

Manager performance and development

As noted earlier, because competing businesses have access to much the same resources (though resource unit costs may differ between businesses), **management quality** is the single factor which tends to distinguish one competitor from another. Measuring manager performance in a defined management job is not difficult, but developing management talent is less easy. Many businesses now recognize this requirement as a survival issue and have introduced mechanisms for identifying potential managers. Conventionally, these are then developed by means of a range of graded training courses. The more enlightened of these businesses realize that these courses are no substitute for real-life practice and have the courage to back this conviction.

Public responsibility

This responsibility demands that a business accepts, and acts upon, the fact that it is part of a social and economic situation at least locally and, usually, on a much broader front. There are then the obvious neighbourly duties of not polluting the environment, producing products that do not damage customers, providing a physically safe and healthy work-place, and so on. There are also less obvious contributions such as the provision of training places for young people and participation in community projects. Sadly, not all businesses voluntarily accept this responsibility to the public, and legislation is increasingly being used to enforce the appropriate actions.

1.5 About management

Management competence has been cited as the critical factor determining the health of a business. This section examines, albeit briefly, the **nature of management** and identifies some of the **personal qualities** that managers require.

1.5.1 Management tasks

Management embraces four distinct, but related, tasks:

(1) **Planning** Setting objectives, and defining an economic way of achieving them.

(2) **Organizing** Mobilizing resources, people and other, to implement the plans.

(3) **Controlling** Assessing deviations from plan and taking corrective actions when required.

(4) **Leading** Motivating people to deliver their best performance.

There is a body of systematic knowledge in each of these task areas which suggests that management can be taught and learnt. To the extent that management is represented by skill in applying that knowledge base the suggestion is true. But read on.

1.5.2 Personal qualities

Real management ability goes beyond technical skill to include inborn talents which can be developed only if they first exist. These facets of **personality** include:

- A high level of creativity and analytic skill – because management is about solving problems. (Management is also about choosing which problem to have, because solving one invariably creates another.)

- Selling and political abilities – because management is about persuasion. But, in contrast with engineering, the shortest distance between two management points is not always a straight line.

- Communication skills – because the way in which a message is presented is as important as its content.

- Good judgement – to select what matters from a mess of trivia.

- Courage – to do what must be done when the consequences will be unpleasant.

- Mental and physical endurance – because the work is hard and the hours can be long.

- Confidence, optimism, zest, competence and a trust in people – because these are the infectious qualities of leadership.

Thus a good manager has both skills in 'management technology' and the right personality.

1.5.3 The management hierarchy

This discussion has identified factors which are common to all management jobs and desirable characteristics for all managers. There are two major factors which distinguish management jobs. Firstly, the extent to which a particular non-management professional skill enters into the job and, secondly, the level of the job in the management hierarchy. There is a correlation between the factors. Figure 1.7 illustrates the typical hierarchy of jobs within a company and indicates some factors which separate management jobs at different levels in the hierarchy.

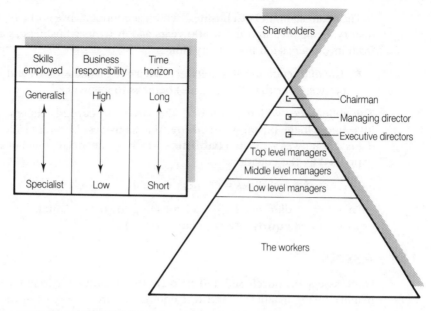

Figure 1.7 **The typical job hierarchy.**
The job hierarchy in a company can be represented as a pyramid structure, as shown here on the right-hand side of the figure. The shape emphasizes that the number of jobs available diminishes sharply as the level and scope of jobs increases. Some factors which distinguish management jobs at different levels in the hierarchy are indicated on the left-hand side of the figure. Managers at the lower levels (technical project leaders, say) mostly use the specialist skills developed in their initial training and early experience. To progress upwards, they must develop and use ever broader 'business' skills to cope with increasing responsibilities. This is accompanied by the need to look further and further ahead.

Most managers are first trained in a non-management professional skill such as law, accountancy, marketing or engineering. Their first few industrial jobs generally relate to this early training. As they progress up the management ladder, their business and management experience is broadened such that, at director level, they are generalist managers first, and lawyers, accountants, marketeers or engineers second. Having said that, the finance director is invariably qualified in finance, and the technical and production directors in technology. This rule seems not to apply with the same force in the case of the other functional directors.

1.6 A financial model of a business

The chapter now concludes with a more searching examination of how a business works than that covered in the opening section. It absorbs this section and the two that follow it. The financial business model presented here is used, in the next section, to develop the earlier (very) basic model depicted in Figure 1.1. This new model is exercised, by means of an extended example, in the final section. The material shows how business operations can be described in terms of a few simple, but powerful, financial concepts.

The financial model of a business which accountants use is one of the great ideas in history, being invented about 500 years ago. It treats a business as an entity distinct from its owners such that, at any time:

- The difference in value between what the business *owns* and what it *owes* (to parties other than the owners) belongs to its owners.

The difference, which is termed the **owners' capital**, represents the owners' investment in the business. The *things* that a business owns are called **assets**, and the *debts* that it owes are called **liabilities**. The basic financial model of a business is then expressed by the equation:

$$\text{Assets} - \text{Liabilities} = \text{Owners' Capital} \tag{1.10}$$

(A number of different terms, all meaning 'owners' capital', are in use. **Owners' equity**, or just **equity**, are popular variants.)

1.6.1 Assets

Some assets are purchased and held by the business for long-term use. Buildings, manufacturing machinery and test equipment are examples in this category. Such items are termed **fixed assets**. They are the 'tools', using the word very broadly, which a business uses in its various activities. Cash, on the other hand, is a **current asset**. Such assets are relatively short-term items in the sense that they are either cash or destined to become cash in the near future. Current assets include:

- **Materials** and **components** purchased from external suppliers and held in stock prior to incorporation into a product.
- The **finished product** itself while it is still held by the business.
- The customer's *promise to pay* for it when it is sold on credit.

A promise to pay the business is a **debtor** asset. Note that assets can be tangible items, such as computers or steel bars, or intangible items like debtors. A valuable patent is another example of an intangible asset. Normally, tangible assets are initially valued at their cost.

'**Long-term**' (fixed) and '**short-term**' (current) are defined in relation to the normal **accounting period** of one year. (This interval is chosen because companies have a statutory duty to publish formal **accounts**, which report on the financial health of the business, at least once a year.) An asset is classified as 'fixed' if it is expected that it will still be useful more than one year after its purchase. Non-cash assets with shorter anticipated 'lives', and cash itself, are classified as current assets.

1.6.2 Liabilities

Liabilities are promises to pay made *by* a business, so they are intangible items. A **current liability** is a debt due for payment within a year of it being incurred. For example, suppose that some components (current assets) are ordered from an external supplier. It is a credit transaction and a credit period of 30 days from receipt of order applies. When the components are delivered a **trade creditor** liability is created, which represents the promise made by the business to pay the supplier. This current liability is removed after 30 days by payment of the debt. Other debts are classified as **non-current liabilities**. A long-term bank loan is in this category, as is any debt which is due for repayment more than one year after being incurred.

Note that the owners' capital is also a liability because the business owes it to its owners. However, the term 'liabilities' is generally used to mean debts owed to parties other than the owners.

1.6.3 The model as a balance

Equation 1.10 can now be rewritten in terms of fixed assets (FA), current assets (CA), current liabilities (CL), non-current liabilities (NCL) and owners' capital (OC) as:

$$(FA + CA) - (CL + NCL) = OC \qquad (1.11)$$

This equation describes the relationships between the *five fundamental elements* in the financial model of a business. It is the basis of **balance sheets**. These principal business accounts are periodic reports on the financial status of the business. They illustrate the 'balance', at a specific time, between the excess of total assets over total liabilities (called the **net assets**) on the left of Equation 1.11 and the owners' capital on the right. Equation 1.11 is sometimes called the **balance sheet equation** for this reason. So, too, is Equation 1.10 – which is the earlier form of Equation 1.11.

Compensating changes

Many business transactions 'occur' only on the left-hand side of Equation 1.11. In other words, they involve only **mutually compensating transactions** among the FA, CA, CL or NCL elements such that the value of OC is not changed by the transaction. Some examples will make this more clear:

(1) A new computer is purchased for £5,000 in cash. The computer is a fixed asset, so FA is *increased* by £5,000. But cash is a current asset, so CA is *decreased* by the same amount.

(2) Components costing £10,000 are ordered on credit from an external supplier. When the components are delivered (and accepted) they become current assets, so CA is *increased* by £10,000. At the same time, however, the promise to pay the supplier (after the credit period) becomes a current liability, so CL is also *increased* by £10,000. Note that the act of accepting a delivery marks a change in the ownership of the delivered items. At that time, the accepting business **recognizes** both the asset that they represent and, when credit is involved, the corresponding liability that they represent. In this context, 'recognize' means 'enter into the accounts'.

(3) A bank loan of £20,000, repayable in three years' time, is negotiated and paid into the business bank account (where it counts as 'cash'). The loan is a non-current liability, so NCL is *increased* by £20,000. But cash is a current asset, so CA is *increased* by the same amount.

Non-compensating changes: profit and loss

Some business transactions involve changes in the four elements on the left-hand side of Equation 1.11 which are **non-mutually compensating transactions**. Such transactions do change the value of OC. The most important are product sales. Suppose that a finished product, which cost £1,000 to make, is sold for £2,000 in cash. Just prior to its sale, the product is a current asset valued at its cost of £1,000. The sale transaction 'changes' the *product* current asset into a *cash* current asset valued at £2,000. The net change in CA is an *increase* of £1,000, being the difference between the sale price of the product and its cost. Equation 1.11 requires that this increase in CA, which is the profit on the sale, is balanced by an equivalent *increase* in OC. In other words, *profit accrues to owners' capital*. Of course, the same arithmetic applies to losses. For example, suppose that the product is sold for only £750 in cash. In this case, the net change in CA is a decrease of £250 and OC suffers the same loss. There are some important messages here:

(1) Every uncompensated change on the left-hand side of the balance sheet equation, formulated either as:

$$\text{Assets} - \text{Liabilities} = \text{Owners' Capital} \qquad (1.10)$$

or as:

$$(\text{FA} + \text{CA}) - (\text{CL} + \text{NCL}) = \text{OC} \qquad (1.11)$$

causes an identical change in the owners' capital.

(2) Profit is an increase in owners' capital and loss is a decrease in owners' capital.

(3) Changes in owners' capital are recorded in **profit and loss accounts**.

(4) Messages (1), (2) and (3) emphasize the *link* between balance sheets and profit and loss accounts. Thus, the profit or loss achieved over an accounting period is the difference in owners' capital between the closing and opening balance sheets for the period.

1.7 A manufacturing business model

Manufacturing businesses creating high technology tangible products, and ranging in size from small upwards, are the primary focus of this book. Most engineers are employed in this sort of business. Normally, these businesses will either be companies in their own right and/or parts of a company in the pattern of Figure 1.2. Their operation is examined, in broad terms, in this section and in the one that follows. The overall aim is to attach some reality to the preceding, rather abstract, discussion of the financial business model. This section introduces a model of a manufacturing business. It is exercised in the next section by means of an example concerning the manufacture and sale of a single product.

1.7.1 Overview of the model

A particular model of a manufacturing business, in its environment, is depicted in Figure 1.8. It combines the simple vision of a business illustrated in Figure 1.1 with the financial model of Equation 1.11. This perspective may not be obvious at first sight.

The business, which is a company in this case, is represented by a structure of assets and liabilities placed at the nodes of a network. The nodes are 'stores' where the assets and liabilities may accumulate. The *solid* paths in the network represent connections between pairs of associated nodes. There are 'gates' on some of these paths. The gates

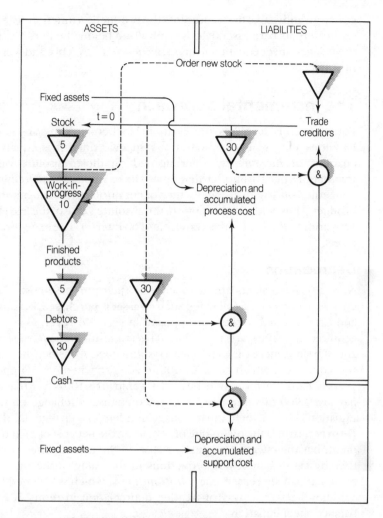

Figure 1.8 **A manufacturing business in its environment.**

This figure is based on the balance sheet equation (Equation 1.11). It models a manufacturing business as a network of assets (at nodes on the left) and liabilities (at nodes on the right). The nodes are temporary stores connected by the solid network paths. Flow along some paths is restricted by closed gates, which can be briefly opened by a control signal. The control signals move along the dotted paths. The sequence of events in the network is determined by time delays, shown as triangular boxes, on some paths. The outer (solid path) loop is the trading cycle corresponding to the processing loop in Figure 1.1. Section 1.8 traces this loop in some detail.

are normally closed but they open, briefly, on receipt of a control signal. Control signals move along the *dotted* paths. A number of paths include time delays which determine the sequence of events in the network. Delays are shown as triangular boxes containing, in most cases, a number signifying delay time in days. The numbers relate to the forthcoming example.

The model is divided vertically, with assets on the left of the partition and liabilities on the right. A horizontal partition is located at the level of the cash asset. The structure above this line represents the production function. The rest of the business, reduced to its bare essentials, is symbolized below the line. The model incorporates the balance sheet equation in an *incremental* form. This, and some other matters, are now explained.

1.7.2 The incremental approach

Equation 1.11 describes the relationship between the absolute values of assets, liabilities and owners' capital at any specific time. It is equally applicable to any changes, or *increments*, superimposed on those absolute values as a result of transactions occurring after that time. The example considered in the next section is concerned *only* with changes which occur during the manufacture and sale of a single product. Thus, with one exception, the absolute value of the five elements of Equation 1.11 prior to the start of this activity is of no interest. The exception concerns the fixed assets.

Depreciation

Normally, fixed assets are first valued at their purchase cost. This produces no net change in owners' capital when such an asset is purchased, because the changes in FA and CA are equal in size but opposite in sign. However, as soon as a fixed asset is acquired, its value starts to decline. This is a result of the normal wear-and-tear of use and, possibly, increasing technical obsolescence. Consider the case of a small item of test equipment which costs £1,000 to acquire when new. Suppose that, after three years of hard use, it can only be sold as scrap for £100. Over that three years the item has lost £900 of value. This is an uncompensated change on the left-hand side of Equation 1.11, which must cause an identical change in the owners' capital. **Depreciation** is the technique of spreading the net cost of a fixed asset over its useful life. It has the effect of gradually reducing the balance sheet value of the asset and thereby causing matching reductions in the value of the owners' capital. For this reason, it may be regarded as a *notional* cost which is 'charged' against profit. Table 1.1 shows a typical way of treating depreciation in terms of Equation 1.11 – the balance sheet equation.

The table adds detail to the 'small item of test equipment' case outlined above. It records only those changes in the elements of Equation 1.11 which arise from that case, which has no impact on liabilities. The item is purchased with cash at the end of Year 0, which is the beginning of Year 1. At that time, fixed assets increase and current assets decrease by the same amount (£1,000), so there is no change in owners' capital. It is then assumed that the item depreciates at the uniform rate of £300 per year. Its annual loss of value, which is the annual depreciation, is mirrored by the changes in owners' capital. However, the item is sold at the end of Year 3 for £100 in cash. This action is shown separately in the Year 3 column to make matters more clear. The sale of the item removes its depreciated value (£100) from the fixed assets, but this is exactly compensated (here) by a corresponding increase in current assets. So there is no net effect on owners' capital arising from the sale. Note that this treatment spreads the effects of depreciation evenly over the useful life of the asset. Note, too, that when a fixed asset is sold the price obtained is not necessarily equal to its depreciated value at the time of the sale. The depreciated value of a fixed asset is called its **book value**.

End of Year	0	1	2	3	3	Totals
	Buy	Depreciation	Depreciation	Depreciation	Sell	
Change in fixed assets	1000	−300	−300	−300	−100	0
+						
Change in current assets	−1000	0	0	0	100	−900
=						
Change in owners' capital	0	−300	−300	−300	0	−900

Table 1.1 **Illustrating depreciation of a fixed asset.**
Depreciation is the technique of spreading the net cost of a fixed asset over its useful life. The table illustrates its application to an item of equipment which costs £1,000 to acquire at the end of Year 0 (that is, at the beginning of Year 1). It assumes that the item will be used for three years and then sold as scrap for £100. The table uses a linear depreciation algorithm. It shows that, for this isolated situation, the change in owners' capital is the sum of the changes in fixed and current assets at every stage – as required by the balance sheet equation.

Assumptions

For the purposes of the forthcoming example, the model shown in Figure 1.8 incorporates three simplifying (but not essential) assumptions:

(1) That no fixed assets are purchased or sold during the period covered by the example.
(2) That there are no changes in non-current liabilities during that same period.
(3) That all sale and purchase transactions are made on credit (which is the normal situation).

The incremental balance sheet equation

Assumptions (1) and (2), together with the earlier considerations, reduce Equation 1.11 to:

$$(\delta FA + \delta CA) - \delta CL = \delta OC \tag{1.12}$$

where δFA, δCA, δCL and δOC represent *changes* in fixed assets, current assets, current liabilities and owners' capital, respectively, and δFA arises because of depreciation of the fixed asset base.

1.7.3 The trading cycle

The outer (solid path) loop in the upper part of Figure 1.8 is commonly termed the **trading cycle**. It is traced here, starting at the top left corner, as a preliminary to the more detailed analysis in the next section.

(1) **Stock** – which comprises raw materials, components and sub-assemblies destined for incorporation into products – moves from an input store into the manufacturing operation, where it is termed **work-in-progress**.
(2) Work-in-progress is transformed, during the manufacturing process, to **finished products**, which are delivered to an output store. Finished products

are complete, tested items which are packaged ready for distribution to customers.

(3) Finished products are sold to customers *on credit* and so become **debtors**.

(4) Debtors pay the amounts that they owe and so become **cash**. (Strictly, the term 'cash or near cash' is more correct, because most of this fund is normally held in a current bank account.)

(5) Cash is used to pay **trade creditors**, and so underwrite *credit orders* for new stock.

(6) New stock is delivered to the input store, thereby creating new trade creditors, and the cycle is repeated.

The trading cycle largely corresponds to the basic model of a business introduced earlier in Section 1.1.1, and illustrated in Figure 1.1.

Interfaces with the external environment

Note that the debtors asset and the trade creditors liability 'connect' the business with customers and suppliers, respectively, in its external environment. The nodes where these two elements reside can be regarded as external interface nodes. The two nodes where costs accumulate, on the liability side of Figure 1.8, are also external interface nodes. This is because the day-to-day running costs that they 'store' are periodically released as cash movements out of the business into its external environment. The liabilities at these nodes are discussed in more detail in the next section.

1.8 │ An example exercising the model

As noted earlier, the example concerns the manufacture and sale of a single product. It absorbs a 'sample' trading cycle, which is deemed to start when stock destined for incorporation into the product is delivered. The delivery defines zero time in Figure 1.8, where it is labelled 't = 0'. This same time is taken to occur at the beginning of a 30 day month. The timing of subsequent events is determined by the path delays. The numbers assigned to the various quantities in the example have no special significance. They are chosen so as to expose significant points.

1.8.1 Sequence overview

The event sequence is illustrated in Table 1.2. Table 1.2(c), which is examined later, is derived from Tables 1.2(a) and (b). Those tables record changes, as time increases, in the 'start' values of the various assets and liabilities of Figure 1.8. They are based on Equation 1.12, which is reproduced here for convenience:

$$(\delta FA + \delta CA) - \delta CL = \delta OC \tag{1.12}$$

Table 1.2(a) records the sequence of changes in the upper part of Figure 1.8. It includes the trading cycle and relates, primarily, to the production function of the business. The combined effect of these changes is summarized in net assets at row 11. The same row is reproduced in Table 1.2(b). This also records the sequence of

(a)

Row	End of Day	0	5	10	15	20	30	50
1	Stock	100						
2	Work-in-progress		100	350				
3	Finished products				600			
4	Debtors					1000	1000	
5	Cash (T)						−500	500
6	Current assets (T)	100	100	350	600	1000	500	500
7	Trade creditors (T)	100	100	100	100	100		
8	Accumulated process cost (Rev)			200	400	400		
9	Fixed assets depreciation (T)			50	100	100	100	100
10	Liabilities (T)	100	100	350	600	600	100	100
11	Net assets (T)					400	400	400

(b)

Row	End of Day	0	5	10	15	20	30	50
11	Net assets (T)					400	400	400
12	Cash (S)						−300	−300
13	Total assets					400	100	100
14	Accumulated support cost (Rev)		50	100	150	200		200
15	Fixed assets depreciation (S)		5	10	15	20	30	50
16	Liabilities (S)		55	110	165	220	30	250
17	Net total assets		−55	−110	−165	180	70	−150

(c)

Row	End of Day	0	5	10	15	20	30	50
18	Sales revenue					1000	1000	1000
19	Cost of products sold					600	600	600
20	Gross profit					400	400	400
21	Operating cost		55	110	165	220	330	550
22	Operating profit		−55	−110	−165	180	70	−150
23	Memo: Total cash						−800	200

Table 1.2 **A manufacturing business: sample trading cycle. (a) A trading cycle; (b) the whole business; (c) profit and loss accounts.**

This table describes, in monetary terms, the sequence of events during a sample traverse of the trading cycle loop of Figure 1.8. It is based on the incremental version of the balance sheet equation at Equation 1.12. (a) and (b) illustrate sequential changes in the net assets (left-hand side) of that equation. (c), which is derived from (a) and (b), shows the same information in profit and loss account terms. In particular, note the equality, at every stage, of rows 17 and 22. This illustrates that a change in net assets = a change in owners' capital = profit. The central principles of business accounting are encapsulated in this sentence.

changes in the lower part of Figure 1.8, which arise from the support activities. Thus, Table 1.2(b) summarizes the situation for the whole business in net total assets at row 17. The labels (T) and (S) are used to distinguish between similar changes arising in the trading cycle and in the support activities, respectively. In particular, note that cash changes, at rows 5 and 12, are distinguished in Table 1.2. This is purely a matter of analytical convenience, because the cash asset is shared by the whole business.

The changes are measured in pounds sterling but this has no bearing on the operation of the model. The row numbers in the first column of the table are used to link it to the commentary in later sections. However, the liability elements at rows 8, 9, 14 and 15 must be examined first.

Revenue costs

Revenue costs are the day-to-day running costs of a business. The benefits that they provide are normally completely 'delivered' within a year of purchase, and usually much sooner. Examples include salaries and wages, rent, rates, insurance premiums, and the costs of heat, light and power. Revenue costs are generally accumulated for a short period before being paid, and they are liabilities while in the accumulated form. For example, monthly salaries are normally paid in arrears, and the salary account which accumulates during a month is a liability until it is paid. The entries at rows 8 and 14 of Table 1.2 assume that *all* revenue costs are accumulated for payment at the end of each month. Row 8 in the table is that *part* of the accumulated revenue cost, associated with the manufacturing process, which is assigned to the single product in the example. Row 14 is that *part* of the accumulated revenue cost, associated with the support activities, which is assigned to the single product.

Fixed assets depreciation

There are a number of different ways of including depreciation in an analysis such as that of Table 1.2. Perhaps the most obvious is to include a fixed asset row with progressively more *negative* entries representing increasing loss of fixed asset values. This has been rejected here in favour of treating depreciation as an increasing liability. This allows associated items, such as those at rows 8 and 9, to be placed alongside each other in the table. Row 9 is that *part* of the depreciation, associated with the manufacturing process, which is assigned to the single product. Row 15 is that *part* of the depreciation, associated with the support activities, which is assigned to the single product.

1.8.2   A trading cycle

The sequence of events recorded in Table 1.2(a) is considered first. Rows 1 to 5 are current assets which are summed at row 6. Rows 7 and 8 are current liabilities, and row 9 is treated as a liability. Rows 7 to 9 are summed at row 10. Net assets, at row 11, is the difference between current assets at row 6 and liabilities at row 10. It relates only to that part of the business represented in the upper part of Figure 1.8. The event sequence is now described.

End of Day 0

The end of Day 0 is the beginning of Day 1. At this time, a quantity of stock (ordered earlier on credit) is delivered to the input store. It is valued at its cost of £100. Both the stock asset (1) and the trade creditors liability (7) increase by this amount. The liability is due for payment in 30 days. Net assets (11) do not change.

End of Day 5

The stock (1) becomes work-in-progress (2) at the beginning of the product manufacturing process, which absorbs the next 10 days. Net assets (11) do not change.

End of Day 10

This is half way through the manufacturing process. The work-in-progress (2) is valued at £350, being the sum of its input value (£100) and the value of the work done, at this stage, on the input. The value of the work done (£250) is made up of two parts. These arise from the revenue costs of the manufacturing process and the depreciation of the fixed assets that it uses.

The revenue cost (8) assigned to the product starts accumulating at £40 per day from the time when the stock becomes work-in-progress. The depreciation (9) assigned to the product starts accumulating at £10 per day from the same time. They build to £200 and £50, respectively, by the end of Day 10. Net assets (11) do not change.

End of Day 15

This marks the end of the manufacturing process. The work-in-progress emerges as the finished product (3) which is valued at £600. This reflects the additional £250 of work, recorded in rows 8 and 9, done on the work-in-progress during the last half of the manufacturing process. Net assets (11) do not change.

End of Day 20

At this time the product is sold, on 30 days credit, for £1,000. The finished product asset (3), valued at £600, is replaced by a debtors asset (4), valued at £1,000. This is an uncompensated transaction on the left-hand side of Equation 1.12. Net assets (11) increase by £400.

End of Day 30

Day 30 is the last day of the month. The time has come to use cash (5) to pay the trade creditors (7) and the accumulated revenue cost (8). Together, these two liabilities cost £500 to remove and cash becomes −£500. Depreciation (9) is a notional item which cannot be paid off. It remains on record at the value it attained at the end of the manufacturing process. Net assets (11) do not change.

End of Day 50

This is the end of the credit period allowed to the product customer. The debtors asset (4) becomes a cash injection of £1,000, which leaves cash (5) at +£500. Net assets (11) do not change.

This transaction concludes the manufacture and sale (to the point of receiving cash) of the single product. Note that the further stock needed to keep the cycle going could have been ordered at any time. A reasonable time, perhaps, is at the end of Day 5. No further stock has been ordered in the example.

1.8.3 The whole business

The sequence of events recorded in Table 1.2(b) is considered here. Row 11 summarizes the changes recorded in Table 1.2(a), and row 12 records cash changes arising from the support activities. They are summed at row 13 to yield total assets. Row 14 is a current liability, and row 15 is treated as a liability. They are summed at row 16. Net total assets, at row 17, is then the difference between total assets at row 13 and the liabilities at row 16. It relates to the whole business. The event sequence is now described.

Up to the end of Day 15

The revenue cost (14) of the support activities starts accumulating at £10 per day from the beginning of Day 1. The corresponding depreciation (15) starts accumulating at £1 per day from the same time. Their combined effect sets net total assets (17) to −£165 by the end of Day 15.

Note that these costs relate to benefits which are consumed as the costs are incurred. They do not contribute to a future benefit and so are uncompensated changes on the left-hand side of Equation 1.12. This contrasts with the corresponding costs at rows 8 and 9 of Table 1.2(a). Those costs contribute directly to the finished product, which is a future benefit. This situation is recognized in Table 1.2(a) by the inclusion of the work-in-progress and finished product assets which compensate the costs which contribute to them.

End of Day 20

This marks the sale of the product. Net assets (11) become £400 and net total assets (17) swings positive to £180.

End of Day 30

Here cash (12) is used to pay the accumulated revenue cost (14) which has reached £300 at this time. This is a compensated transaction on the left-hand side of Equation 1.12. As before, depreciation (15) is a notional item which cannot be paid off. Net total assets (17) become £70 because of the increase in the costs at rows 14 and 15 over the preceding ten days.

End of Day 50

The costs at rows 14 and 15 have continued to increase and combine to offset total assets (13) by £250 at the end of day 50. Net total assets (17) become −£150.

1.8.4 Profit and loss accounts

Profit is the excess of sales revenue over corresponding costs. A profit and loss account reports these parameters at the end of a specific period. Table 1.2(c) shows six such accounts, corresponding to the periods terminating at the end of Day 5, Day

10, and so on. Gross profit (20) is earned by the buying, manufacturing and selling activities in the trading cycle. Operating profit (22) relates to the whole business. It is obtained by subtracting the operating cost (21) from the gross profit (20).

The revenue (18) arising from the sale of the product, and the matching cost of making it (19), are recognized (that is, entered into the account) as soon as the product is sold. This is at the end of Day 20, when the revenue of £1,000 is in credit form, at row 4 in Table 1.2(a). The matching cost is £600 in liability form, at row 10 in Table 1.2(a), so the gross profit (22) becomes £400. This value is retained in the subsequent accounts because the revenue (18) and its matching cost (19) are not affected by subsequent transactions recorded in Table 1.2(a).

The operating cost (21) relates to the sum of the support cost and the depreciation at rows 14 and 15, respectively, of Table 1.2(b). However, it is not affected by transactions recorded in that table and thus increases uniformly at £11 per day. This is reflected by increasingly negative values of operating profit (22), indicating losses, until the end of Day 20. At this time the advent of gross profit (20) allows the operating profit (22) to swing positive. It then remains positive until a few days beyond the end of Day 30.

Note that the gross profit (20) equates with the net assets (11). The net asset entries arise because of an uncompensated transaction on the left-hand side of Equation 1.12. A similar equality exists between the operating profit (22) and the net total assets (17). Uncompensated transactions on the left-hand side of Equation 1.12. create corresponding changes in the owners' capital. The equalities demonstrate that profit (and loss) accrue to owners' capital.

Cash-flow

Row 23 in Table 1.2, which is the sum of rows 5 and 12, shows the overall **cash-flow** at the specific times. That is, it records the changes in the total (incremental) cash position. The table illustrates that cash-flow can be *negative* when profit is *positive*, and can be *positive* when profit is *negative*. The effect arises because of the various delays in the system, shown in Figure 1.8, which models the business.

1.8.5 Section end note

The example considered in this section has traced a sequence of events related to the manufacture and sale of a single product. In practice, an established business is likely to be concerned with a multitude of products which 'move' through it in an unsynchronized fashion. This sort of situation can be analysed simply by aggregating the changes arising from the individual products and/or synchronous groups of products. This is a routine accounting activity.

The example produced a balance sheet, and a profit and loss account, at the end of each significant day. In practice, these accounts are likely to be produced only at monthly intervals for management information and control purposes. The monthly 'management' accounts then form the basis of the formal accounts which all companies must publish at least once a year.

1.9   Concluding summary

This chapter provides the background scenery for the chapters that follow. Equipped with this material, readers with no previous business knowledge should be able to cope with the rest of the book. It is also commended to more experienced readers because it illustrates the underlying approach to the whole topic of engineers in business. This is the inherently simple view that a business, and each distinct function within it, is a system for transforming information inputs to information outputs with a higher value. (The notion that a product, which is a business output, is a form of information may come as as shock. But think about it – it is perfectly valid.) This is an engineering perspective and engineers are now on familiar ground. They know how to approach systems. A system is analysed (and designed) by finding out:

- what outputs it must provide
- what inputs are available to it
- how to change, economically, those inputs to the required outputs.

This, then, is the methodology of the whole book. It is easier to describe than it is to deliver, and some aspects are intellectually demanding. But most engineers are arrogant enough to believe that they can take apart things that others have put together.

The chapter opens with a general 'why–what–how' analysis of businesses, which introduces the basic financial concepts. Some ways of classifying businesses are then considered before attention turns to the technology-based manufacturing businesses which are at the focus of this book. These are viewed as systems of cooperating functions. The purpose of each major function is examined and some basic organizational structures introduced. The critical areas where business managers should strive towards specific objectives are then identified, and the nature of management and the demands it places on managers are briefly analysed.

Sections 1.6, 1.7 and 1.8 comprise a more searching examination of how a business works than that of Section 1.1. A basic financial model applicable to all businesses is introduced, which is then combined with earlier ideas to yield an improved model for a manufacturing business. This model is exercised over a trading cycle in Section 1.8. The material, which has a financial bias, is a little more demanding than that presented earlier. It may be omitted at first reading. But it provides a first insight into the stark beauty of business accounting which, in fact, is a genuine engineering topic.

REFERENCES

Channon D. F. (1973). *Strategy and Structure of British Enterprise*. London: Macmillan
Drucker P. F. (1989). *The Practice of Management*. London: Heinemann

SUGGESTED FURTHER READING

The opportunity is taken here to list a small selection of texts which will assist engineers to extend their management and business knowledge. Armstrong (1990) and Kempner (1987) are management 'manuals' with contrasting styles. The first is a series of essays which examine (and usually find wanting) many traditional solutions to traditional business problems. Kempner's book records a wide range of management concepts in the form of an extended glossary. The Lock (1989) handbook is expensive but still good value. Both Rees (1991) and Lawrence and Lee (1984) are valuable (and intensely non-mathematical) 'overview' texts which emphasize practice rather than theory. Hellriegal and Slocum (1986) provides a comprehensive treatment of current USA thinking and contains much case study material. Chapman *et al.* (1987), Johnson (1989) and Twiss (1988) are aimed specifically at engineers. The first is a challenging and wide-ranging textbook written from an accounting and management science perspective which makes few concessions, in style or content, to its target readers. The Johnson and Twiss contributions are more selective volumes, authored by practising engineers, in the very readable IEE Management of Technology series. These texts are probably best appreciated by engineers with some years of industrial experience and/or those involved on MBA studies. Waters (1989) is pitched at the right level for engineers (embryonic and hatched) and exactly matches its title. Barrow (1988) and Wilson (1990) share the same title, and cover much the same ground in an attractive way. The latter is slightly cheaper and more formal. The 'small businesses' emphasis does not limit their introductory value. Droms (1990) is in the same tradition, but ranges rather more widely and is based on US practices. The cited IEE journal covers management issues of interest to engineers at all levels. Finally, Peters and Waterman (1982) and its 'sequel', Peters (1988), should be required reading for all engineers and managers. Handy (1989) is in the same category. These authors share the *'change is here to stay'* theme, questioning conventional business wisdoms and pointing out future directions.

Armstrong M., ed. (1990). *The New Manager's Handbook*. London: Kogan Page

Barrow C. (1988). *Financial Management for the Small Business* 2nd edn. (A *Daily Telegraph* Guide) London: Kogan Page

Chapman C. B., Cooper D. F. and Page M. A. (1987). *Management for Engineers*. Chichester: John Wiley

Droms W. G. (1990). *Finance and Accounting for Nonfinancial Managers* 3rd edn. Reading, MA: Addison-Wesley

Handy C. B. (1989). *The Age of Unreason*. London: Business Books (Century Hutchinson)

Hellriegal D. and Slocum J. W. (1986). *Management* 4th edn. Reading, MA: Addison-Wesley

IEE (Bimonthly from February 1991). *Engineering Management Journal*. London: Institution of Electrical Engineers

Johnson D. L. (1989) *Management for Engineers* 2nd edn. London: Peter Peregrinus (for the IEE)

Kempner T., ed. (1987). *The Penguin Management Handbook* 4th edn. Harmondsworth: Penguin

Lawrence P. A. and Lee R. A. (1984). *Insight into Management*. Oxford: Oxford University Press

Lock D., ed. (1989). *Handbook of Engineering Management*. London: Heinemann

Peters T. J. (1988). *Thriving on Chaos*. London: Macmillan

Peters T. J. and Waterman R. H. (1982). *In Search of Excellence*. New York: Harper & Row

Rees W. D. (1991). *The Skills of Management* 3rd edn. London: Routledge

Twiss B. C. (1988). *Business for Engineers*. London: Peter Peregrinus (for the IEE)

Waters C. D. J. (1989). *A Practical Introduction to Management Science*. Wokingham: Addison-Wesley

Wilson P. (1990). *Financial Management for the Small Business*. (A Barclays Guide) Oxford: Blackwell

QUESTIONS

1.1   A manufacturing business can be modelled as a production function for transforming inputs to higher value outputs which is supported by a number of other business functions. Use this model to explain the meaning of the following terms:

- sales revenue
- input cost
- added value
- process cost
- gross profit
- operating cost
- operating profit

1.2   During a particular year, a business receives a total income of £1,000,000 from product sales. The cost of these sales is £600,000, of which £350,000 is accounted for by processing externally purchased materials and components into the products sold. The processing operation is supported by a number of other activities which cost £300,000 over the year.

Calculate, as percentages of sales revenue, the added value, the gross profit and the operating profit achieved by the business during the year in question.

1.3   Explain how manufacturing businesses differ from service businesses. In which category is a retail shop?

1.4   Distinguish between sole-trader, partnership and limited liability company businesses. Why have companies become the dominant form of business organization?

1.5   A business may be regarded as a system of distinct cooperating functions. Describe, briefly, the major tasks of eight such functions which support the production function in a manufacturing business.

1.6   The boundaries of the production function in a manufacturing business can be drawn to include a number of service activities which support its manufacturing activities. Describe, in this context, the roles of:

- facilities maintenance
- industrial engineering
- production engineering
- production planning and control
- purchasing
- quality assurance

Why are the purchasing and quality assurance activities sometimes organized as separate functions in their own right?

1.7   A company is usually structured as a hierarchy of subsidiary organizations, with the company board at the top. Describe three distinct ways of choosing the second level organizations which report directly to the board. Show how a large multinational company may use all three basic structures in its overall organization.

1.8   (a) What is the meaning of the term 'market share'? Why are companies with a very low or a very high market share in a potentially unstable situation?
(b) Efficient innovation is one way of increasing market share. How might 'efficient' be defined in this context? What are the two basic problems faced by all innovative companies which are in a resource-limited situation?

1.9   (a) What is 'productivity'? Why is it important? How can it be measured?
(b) In a particular year, a company employing ten people makes an operating profit of £100,000. The average capital employed during the year is £2,000,000. Calculate its productivity. On the basis of this (limited) evidence, would you be willing to buy shares in the company? If not, why not?

1.10   'Operating profit must be sufficiently positive if the business is to stay in business.' Why?

1.11   'Everybody is a manager.' Discuss the validity of this claim by:
(a) Describing the duties of a company director in terms of the four basic

management tasks.

(b) Describing the duties of a university student in terms of the four basic management tasks.

1.12 What is meant by the terms:

- fixed assets
- current assets
- current liabilities
- non-current liabilities
- owners' capital

What is the relationship between these business parameters?

1.13 (a) Describe the depreciation technique for valuing fixed assets.

(b) A company has adopted a policy of depreciating fixed assets uniformly to zero over their anticipated life. At the beginning of a particular trading year, it purchases a desktop computer for £4,000. It is anticipated that the useful life of this machine will be four years. Under these planned circumstances, what will be the effect of the purchase on annual operating profit in each year of its anticipated life?

(c) Sadly, the computer disintegrated on the last day of the third year and the remains were thrown away. Under these actual circumstances, what is the effect of the purchase on annual operating profit in each year of its actual life?

1.14 (a) What is meant by the terms:

- stock
- work-in-progress
- finished products
- debtors
- cash
- trade creditors

(b) Show how these parameters 'participate' in the trading cycle.

1.15 A manufacturing company completed the following list of transactions on the same day:

(a) Purchased a new machine tool for the manufacturing operation at £30,000 on credit.

(b) Sold the old machine tool, which has no book value, for £500 in cash.

(c) Purchased £5,000 of stock on credit.

(d) Paid wages of £3,000 in cash.

(e) Received a cash payment of £12,000 for products previously sold on credit. These products had cost £7,000 to make.

(f) Sold products for £20,000 on credit. These products had cost £12,000 to make.

(g) Borrowed £15,000 from a bank and paid it into the company bank account. The loan is due for repayment in two years.

At the end of the day, the owners' capital has increased by £5,500. Why is this?

Business Strategy and Technology

The best laid schemes o' mice an' men
Gang aft a-gley.

Robert Burns 1759–1796

2.1	The strategic role of technology	45
2.2	About planning in general	48
2.3	Business planning	52
2.4	Technology and strategic position	68
2.5	Building a technological strategy	73
2.6	Concluding summary	81

 Advanced material   While this chapter is properly placed in Part I, readers new to business ideas may find some of the material too demanding for comfort. Sadly, this is most likely to occur at the focus of the chapter in Sections 2.3 and 2.4. However, none of the subsequent chapters *depend* on this one – although it illuminates all of them. It is reasonable, therefore, to omit it entirely at first reading or merely absorb its flavour from Sections 2.1 and 2.2. The case study at Section 2.5 has a 'stand-alone' quality which allows it to be understood, if not fully appreciated, with only a sketchy knowledge of the earlier material.

The overall objectives of this chapter are to demonstrate the critical role of technology in ensuring the survival and prosperity of a business and to equip engineers, as custodians and practitioners of technology, with the means to contribute to the formulation of technological strategy. Objectives by section follow:

2.1 To introduce the concepts of strategy, tactics and corporate planning.

2.2 To present the basics of planning.

2.3 To examine the strategic aspects of business planning, culminating in an extension of the conventional growth-share matrix.

2.4 To develop the concept of technological vectors as forces representing the opportunities and threats which technology offers to a business.

2.5 To illustrate the creation of a technological strategy for a sample business.

2.6 To identify its salient points and summarize its major messages.

2.1 The strategic role of technology

Modern technology-based manufacturing businesses operate in a complex environment of political, economic, competitive, legal and social factors. This chapter introduces the use of **corporate planning** to determine the **strategies** needed to succeed in that environment. Basic concepts and terminology are introduced in this first section, which concludes by demonstrating the critical role of technology in business survival and prosperity. The next two sections review planning in general and business planning in particular. This material supports the subsequent examination of strategic technological planning, which is the principal purpose of the chapter.

2.1.1 Strategy and tactics

A **strategy** is a course of action intended to achieve a **strategic objective**. 'Strategic' is an adjective much used in business circles to describe objectives, plans and issues when they exhibit most of the following features:

- They relate to the *long-term* survival and prosperity of the business, and decisions about them require a speculative view of the future embracing a multiplicity of factors.
- They involve changes in the purpose, activities and structure of the business which will be difficult to undo.
- They are characterized by incomplete information, high levels of uncertainty and substantial risk.

- They demand long-term resource commitments to achieve, implement or resolve.
- They can lead to tragic consequences if badly managed.

Strategic matters are the concern of top management because only they have the authority to make the necessary far-reaching decisions. Once the strategic objectives have been set, and the corresponding strategies decided, **tactics** come into play. These are the means by which a strategy is implemented. They are characterized as follows:

- They have more limited (tactical) objectives and shorter time-scales.
- They demand smaller resource commitments.
- They involve less risk.
- They have less severe failure penalties.

Tactical objectives are usually set by less senior managers and they are the targets of tactical plans. On occasion, the more detailed analyses of tactical planning demonstrate that the parent strategy is not viable in some respect and must be reconsidered.

A hierarchy of objectives

The notion of a strategic objective being broken down into its constituent tactical objectives mirrors the conventional management structure of a business. Thus, the first-level managers set a strategic objective for their immediate subordinates. The second-level managers partition it into a set of tactical objectives for their immediate subordinates. This process then propagates down the management hierarchy. In this way, the 'big' top-level strategic objective is decomposed into a hierarchy of ever 'smaller' objectives at the successive management levels. A consequence of this partitioning process is that 'strategic' and 'tactical' are often used in a relative rather than absolute way. This is because managers perceive the objectives that they are given as strategic, but those that they give to their subordinates as tactical.

An example

The following example illustrates the concept of strategies and tactics. Suppose that, following an analysis of a set of strategic factors, the top management of a particular company decides to market a new (to them) product range – desktop computers, say. This is a *strategic objective*. Next, they decide to achieve this objective by internal development rather than by purchasing another company already offering that product range. This is a *strategy*. Implementation of this strategy involves (mostly) marketing, product design, manufacturing and selling activities. Accordingly, the second-level managers responsible for those business functions agree a set of compatible *tactical objectives* in each of their areas. Further work translates these objectives into a set of tactical plans which, together, equate to the parent strategy. Thus, the broad strategy is split up into a number of more detailed but individually smaller *tactical plans* which, when implemented, (should) deliver the strategy. Note that the risk inherent in the original strategic objective and the chosen strategy is not reduced by this partitioning technique. However, the tactical activities are isolated from the strategic uncertainties and, individually, are relatively low risk affairs.

2.1.2 Corporate planning

Corporate planning is the process by which strategic objectives and strategies are determined for a complete business, company or corporation. The term 'corporate' distinguishes this high-level activity from planning at lower levels. A classic text by Ansoff (1965, 1987) sets out the basic concepts. Corporate planning became widely accepted (if not exactly popular) during the late 1970s, and is now well established in most large and medium-sized businesses. There is a substantial body of literature supporting the topic, which is a mandatory component of all management science courses. However, most authors and many businesses neglect the role of technology in strategy formulation. Within a business, the omission implies either that technological issues are treated solely in tactical terms or, worse, are delegated in their entirety to the technologists. These talented scientists and engineers are surprisingly tolerant of top-management foibles, and they will cheerfully make strategic technological decisions in the absence of guidance from above. Sadly, it is unlikely that such decisions will align with the overall business strategy, but the technologists will have a lot of fun before disaster strikes. The 'suggested further reading' cited in the chapter bibliography by Ansoff and Stewart (1967), Parker (1985) and Twiss (1986) *do* recognize the proper place of technology in corporate planning.

2.1.3 What is technology?

Strictly, a 'technology' is *any* organized body of knowledge which is applied in a field of human endeavour, such as industry. So all the different flavours of engineering (mechanical, civil, electrical, electronic, computer, production, chemical and so on) are distinct technologies. Engineering technologies are science-based. They are built on the solid foundations of the laws of nature. In common parlance, the word 'technology' means a science-based technology, which is a body of engineering knowledge. But 'management', 'design', 'marketing' and 'accounting' exemplify some other organized bodies of knowledge which are also applied in industry. So these, too, are technologies. They are not, however, science-based. They have no recourse to some well-understood laws of nature. The phrase 'management science', for example, is a widely accepted terminological contradiction.

This chapter is primarily concerned with the science-based technologies and their *strategic* role in those businesses which aim to exploit them. As engineers are the custodians and practitioners of these technologies, this chapter also introduces, by implication, their role in such businesses. Other less rigorous, but *not* less demanding, technologies inevitably enter into the discussion. However, from now on, the unqualified word 'technology' is used here to mean a science-based technology.

2.1.4 Why is technology important?

An important factor in the **competitive status** of a business is the degree to which its products are differentiated from those of its competitors. For example, the introduction of 'executive' cars with anti-lock braking systems gave the pioneering manufacturer a competitive edge over its rivals, who then had to follow its lead. This illustrates the use of technology to provide a product *performance* differentiation, because all cars provide a braking *function* but the anti-lock system performs that function more efficiently.

Technological innovation and competitive status

There are three major ways in which **technological innovation** can be used to improve the competitive status of a business through **product differentiation**:

(1) By providing distinctive and attractive product *functions*, which leads to greater product sales.

(2) By providing distinctive efficiency in *performing* the functions offered by the product, which leads to greater product sales.

(3) By reducing the cost of manufacturing the product. This distinguishes it from competing products in *economic* terms, which allows more unit profit or lower unit price (and thus greater sales) or some combination of these advantages.

The three sorts of competitive advantage are not necessarily mutually exclusive. For example, in pursuit of manufacturing economy, several standard integrated circuits in an electronic product might be replaced by a single 'special to purpose' integrated circuit. Typically, this innovation also leads to improved performance in terms of size, weight, power consumption, operating speed and reliability. The special integrated circuit might also allow new operational functions to be introduced at little extra cost.

Opportunities and threats

Technology, therefore, offers opportunities to improve competitive performance to those businesses which use it wisely. Equally, it can pose threats to the survival and prosperity of those businesses which fail to match the successful technological innovations of their competitors. Acquiring and extending a new technology is always a time-consuming and expensive exercise. The decision to do so is likely to have a profound effect on the business, and it will probably be costly in time and money to reverse if this becomes necessary. There are severe (possibly fatal) consequences, therefore, of making the wrong basic decisions about technology. It is a high risk area at any time, and the more so in markets where the rate of technological change is high. Technology is a strategic factor. The formulation of appropriate strategic techno-logical objectives, and of the best strategies for achieving them, is an important part of business planning. This is the purpose of strategic technological planning.

2.2 About planning in general

Planning is the management process of setting objectives and defining the optimum way of achieving them. Its fundamental aims are to ensure that the target objectives are the 'right' objectives and that they are achieved with the least possible expenditure of time, money and other resources. A **plan** describes an (intended) orderly progression from a defined start position to a defined end position, which is the plan objective(s). It is an instrument for implementing change while maintaining stability and a sense of purpose. Planning and plans have other virtues:

- Problems are analysed during planning and a range of different solutions explored and evaluated before valuable resources are committed to a particular course of action.

- The time, money and other resources required are estimated *before* the planned activity is started. This allows the resource cost of the plan to be compared with the benefits it should provide.

- A plan motivates the team charged with implementing it, and enables the individual tasks of each team member to be defined.

- A plan provides a reference statement of *anticipated* progress for comparison with *actual* progress. This allows control action to be taken to correct serious deviations from plan.

2.2.1 The basic planning process

The basic techniques of planning are well covered in Lorange (1980), and a more comprehensive treatment of the subject is contained in Hellriegal and Slocum (1986). The fundamentals are described here with reference to Figure 2.1. This is an outline plan of the planning process!

Planning conventions

There are two basic ways of presenting plans in graphic form. These are often termed the **activity-on-node** and the **activity-on-arrow** formats. Both are discussed in detail in Chapter 6. Figure 2.1 is a simple activity-on-arrow diagram. It employs some conventions commonly used in that format:

- The circles (boxes or ellipses are also used) represent **events**. These are verifiable happenings which occur at an instant in time.

- The *solid* arrows represent (real) **activities**. These connect pairs of events. They represent what has to be done to move from the event at the tail of the arrow to the event at the head of the arrow. Activities consume resources – time always and, usually, money and effort as well.

- The *dashed* arrows are called **dummy activities** or just dummies. They represent logical connections between events. They impose constraints on the occurrence of events. Dummies take no time and consume no other resources.

- An event is not complete until *all* the activities, real *and* dummy, leading into it have been completed. Thus the circles (boxes or ellipses) behave as logical 'And' gates. By the same token, an activity cannot start until the event that precedes is complete.

The planning environment

An important event in Figure 2.1 is labelled **planning environment**. It represents information relevant to the planning process, and its role in that process emerges as this discussion proceeds. The planning environment is periodically updated as a result of activities not shown in the figure but, in principle, it remains constant during the planning process. The process itself is represented by the sequence of numbered events.

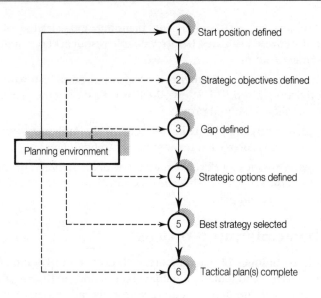

Figure 2.1   **The basic planning process.**

This is an outline 'activity-on-arrow' diagram of the strategic planning process. It shows an orderly sequence of analytical activities applied to a body of information called the planning environment, which contains everything that is known about the business and its operational situation. Event 1 is a description of the business position to be changed by implementing the plan, and Event 2 is a description of the planned changes. The difference between these two descriptions is the 'gap' which the plan aims to close. Its magnitude is defined at Event 3, together with estimates of the maximum acceptable amounts of time and money which can be spent on closing it. Event 4 is then a description of all reasonably tenable ways of closing the gap. This allows the relative merits of these gap-closing strategic options to be evaluated, leading to selection of the best (perceived) strategy at Event 5. The tactical plan(s) aimed at implementing the chosen strategy are then created and described at Event 6. The tactical planning process follows much the same pattern as that for strategic planning.

The planning sequence

The steps in the planning process sequence correspond to the events. These are:

(1) *Start position defined*   This is a description of the situation which is to be changed by implementing the plan. It is derived from an analysis (which is an activity) of the planning environment. Completion of this analysis signals the occurrence of Event 1 which allows the next activity, that of defining strategic objective(s), to start.

(2) *Strategic objective(s) defined*   This event specifies the target end position of the plan. Its achievement is conditioned by an input from the planning environment, because the plan objective(s) must be chosen with respect to certain constraints or criteria. This logical connection with the planning environment is a dummy activity. The occurrence of Event 2 allows the next activity, that of defining the gap, to start.

(3) *Gap defined*   This event comprises *three* statements about the difference between the target end position and the start position. This difference is the **planning gap** which the plan aims to close. The first statement measures, in some way, the magnitude of the gap. A forty per cent increase in profit is one example, and the 500 miles between Canterbury and Edinburgh is another. Time will elapse and costs will be incurred in closing the gap. The other two statements define the maximum acceptable size of the gap, measured in time and cost, respectively. These two parameters are constraints on planning freedom derived from the planning environment. Typically, there is a limited 'see-saw' relationship between time and cost, in that raising one lowers the other.

For example, suppose the plan concerns the need for a manager to travel from Canterbury (the start position) to keep an appointment, at a specific time, in Edinburgh (the end position). The gap is about 500 miles. The maximum acceptable time to close this gap is the difference between the appointment time and the latest time that the manager can leave Canterbury. This latter figure is obtained from the planning environment. The maximum acceptable cost to close the gap comes from the same source, because the manager has a restricted allowance for business expenses. Now, if the manager travels by hired helicopter the cost will be high but the time will be short. If the public intercity coach service is used the cost will be low but the time will be long.

The occurrence of Event 3 allows the next activity, designing the gap-closing options, to start.

(4) *Strategic options defined*   This event lists and details a number of different ways, or strategies, for closing the gap. The activity leading into it is of a design nature. It examines a number of ways in which the available resources can be used to create gap-closing options. An input from the planning environment is therefore required. No attempt is made, at this stage, to distinguish the relative merits of the options, although only those which are reasonably tenable are included in the final listing. The occurrence of Event 4 allows the next activity, selecting the best strategy, to start.

(5) *Best strategy selected*   The activity leading into this event is again of a design nature. It evaluates the relative merits of the different options in the light of the factors comprising the planning environment, including the maximum allowable time and cost criteria. A great deal of judgement is normally involved in the analysis; evaluating relative risk, for example, is an exercise in speculation. Another common problem arises from the sheer volume of (frequently conflicting) factors which must be considered. A conscious search for a single dominant factor is always helpful, since it will at least identify the most critical factors.

A situation may arise where there is no apparent way of closing the gap within the maximum allowable time and/or cost. In this case, and if the start position is immutable, there are just three possible actions:

(a) Reduce the gap to an acceptable level by making the target end position less ambitious. This involves reworking the plan and, probably, negotiating concessions from higher authority.

> (b) Increase (or ignore) the maximum allowable time and/or cost criteria, which increases the risk of plan failure.
>
> (c) Abandon the plan.
>
> The occurrence of Event 5 marks the end of the strategic planning phase and allows the next activity, which is tactical planning, to start.
>
> (6) *Tactical plan(s) complete* The occurrence of this event signals the completion of the tactical plan(s) which implement the selected best strategy. The corresponding tactical planning activity is conditioned, as always, by factors in the planning environment. In procedural terms, tactical planning is just the same as strategic planning. That is, a tactical plan is developed by a sequence of events and activities identical, in principle, to those outlined for strategic planning. In the tactical planning case, however, the objectives are 'smaller', better defined and less risky because the 'big' strategic plan is partitioned into a series of smaller tactical plans. These tactical plans may run in parallel or in series, or in some combination of these two modes.

2.3 | Business planning

The term **business planning** embraces both corporate (strategic) planning and tactical planning. The procedures involved follow the pattern outlined in the general discussion of Section 2.2.1, but these must be extended to cope with the complexity of the planning environment. Justis *et al.* (1985) provide an excellent text on the subject. This section emphasizes corporate planning and shows how its complexity can be handled. Tactical planning is covered in some depth in Chapter 6.

2.3.1 The major strategic objective

All business managers share one overriding strategic objective. This is that they wish to survive and prosper. Companies operating in competitive environments can only achieve this objective by providing *competitive* rewards, over an extended period, for their shareholder owners. This requirement, which is at the heart of the corporate planning problem, is now explained.

On the one hand, owners hope for a steady stream (dividends every six months) of ever-improving returns on their investment in the company *and* growth in the capital value of this investment over the longer term. The owners of a company which persistently fails to meet their reward expectations will start to desert it for more attractive situations. The share price then declines and the company ultimately disappears into take-over or bankruptcy. On the other hand, the passage of time brings deterioration in the physical resources of the company, product obsolescence, and the advent of new technologies and competitors. The inevitable consequences (decline and death) of these facts of business life can only be avoided by continuous re-investment in the company.

There is, however, only one source of funds to provide *both* the rewards for the owners and the investment in the company. This source is **profit**, which is the surplus of company income over company costs. (The fact that profit may be employed directly or indirectly, through servicing loans, in its investment role must not be allowed to obscure this basic message.) There is, then, an enduring conflict within all companies between the demands of the present (rewards to owners) and the demands of the future (investment). Achieving an at least **adequate profit** becomes, therefore, the paramount strategic objective.

The meaning of 'adequate' for a particular company depends, mostly, on three time-dependent circumstances:

(1) The shareholder rewards available from other companies at similar risk levels to those associated with the market(s) of the particular company. This circumstance influences the **profit distribution policy** (or dividend policy) that the company adopts to provide returns to its owners.

(2) The rates of innovation and growth in the market(s) of the company. This circumstance is an important factor in determining the **investment strategy** which the company chooses to follow.

High innovation rates (in, say, marketing, product technology, products and manufacturing technology) are generally associated with dynamic, unstable and growing markets. Such markets demand high levels of investment to achieve and retain a competitive position. The investment needed to retain a satisfactory position in more mature and stable markets are less demanding (although the *price of entry* to such markets may be prohibitive).

(3) The competitive status of the company within its market(s). This is another important circumstance in determining the investment strategy which the company chooses to follow. Depending on its competitive status, the company must decide whether to develop, consolidate, or abandon its position in each market sector of interest. Each option demands a different level of investment funding (and, of course, spending it wisely).

Profit distribution policy

At first sight, setting a profit distribution policy looks easy since it seems only to require an examination of the financial press to establish the current competitive reward level for shareholders. In practice, the matter is not quite so simple. For example, a company might choose to re-invest most or all of its profit in growth, and promise its owners future riches rather than immediate, but unexciting, returns. One well-known computer company successfully followed a 'nil dividend' policy for the first decade of its life. Alternatively, a company might choose to pay dividends at a level much higher than the competitive rate, so as to retain shareholder loyalty. This policy can go beyond rationality when companies are threatened by take-over. Profit and profit distribution promises are then frequently made which may cripple the company if they ever have to be delivered.

Investment strategy

Profit distribution policy is certainly one facet of corporate planning, but that activity is more usually associated with achieving an optimum investment strategy. The purpose of investing in a business is to change something; investment is about innovation. Innovation comes in many forms. Some examples from a long list of possibilities are:

- The extension, renewal and/or updating of physical resources.
- Developing skills in new product or manufacturing technologies.
- Specifying, designing and introducing a new product range.
- Modifying an organizational structure.
- Introducing modern information technology into business communications.

To get the investment strategy right, the right strategic investment objectives and implementation plans must be selected. It can be argued that this is more important than a proper profit distribution policy, because the absence of a proper investment strategy is soon followed by an absence of a profit. That sad situation makes any profit distribution policy irrelevant. This particular defence of vested interest is commonly used by those who are concerned primarily with the longer term future of the business. Scientists and engineers involved in technological innovation are in this category. Their perspective is invariably countered, by those more concerned with the short-term future, with the observation that unhappy owners will rapidly arrange the absence of a future. That sad situation makes any investment strategy irrelevant. Both arguments have merit, but each fails to recognize that keeping the owners happy and investing in the future are opposite sides of the same coin. Debating their relative importance is analogous to comparing the relative merits of the two wings of an aeroplane. A proper balance of both are needed to stay in the air as, indeed, are some other things.

2.3.2   The dimensions of the problem

Achieving adequate profit, which is the paramount strategic objective, is a simple target. The problem lies in choosing the best strategies to achieve it from the available options. The selection process is complicated by the large number of strategic factors which together comprise the planning environment in which competing businesses operate. Strategic factors can be classified as either internal or external.

Internal strategic factors

Some important **internal strategic factors**, assembled into major categories, are:

- *Financial*   Profit, dividends and investment policy, debts, productivity, cash-flow.
- *Markets*   Sales volumes, product ranges, product pricing, product promotion and distribution arrangements.
- *Technical*   Product technology, research capability, development and design capability.
- *Production*   Manufacturing costs, technology, capabilities and quality, supplier relationships.
- *People*   Manager performance, worker performance, industrial relations, motivations, remuneration policy, training.
- *Organization*   Structure, geography, physical resources.

There are dependencies *within* most of these major categories. Within financial, for

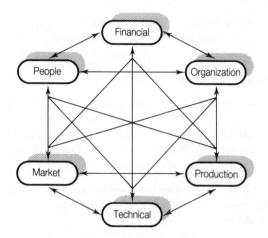

Figure 2.2 **Linking of major internal strategic factors.**
The planning environment in which a business must determine its 'survive and prosper' strategies is
a complex and dynamic situation comprising many internal and external strategic factors. The most
important types of internal strategic factor are identified in the figure, which also emphasizes their
mutual dependencies. This complicates strategic planning by preventing independent planning in
each factor area.

example, dividends and investment are linked by profit. Similarly, sales volumes
clearly depend on the balance of the other market factors and, within production, low
manufacturing costs tend to be incompatible with high product quality.

At any one time, therefore, strategic objectives and strategies should exist for each
of these major internal strategic factors. In other words, innovation directed at
improved and/or less costly (though not necessarily less pricey) products should be a
constant theme in each of these areas. Only in this way can a business survive in a
competitive market, because its competitors are on the same treadmill. (Of course,
one strategic option which is always available is 'do nothing now'. This is entirely valid
provided it has been consciously chosen for good reasons. It corresponds to the well-
known engineering maxim 'don't mend it if it isn't broken'.)

Dependencies also exist *between* all the major internal strategic factors. These links
are shown in Figure 2.2, which illustrates another level of complexity applying to
consideration of internal strategic factors.

The most active linkages are those involving the financial factor, since all activities
incur costs. An example is a market innovation – the introduction of a new product
range, say. Typically, this demands costly developments in both product and
manufacturing technology. Another example is the introduction of profit-sharing
incentives for manufacturing workers, which links the people, production and
financial factors.

The existence of this intricate web of interdependencies both within and between
the major internal strategic factors is an inescapable fact of business life. It complicates
strategic planning by preventing (in a rational approach to the problem) independent
innovation in each factor area. A compatible set of factor-level objectives and
strategies aggregating to the pursuit of a limited number of corporate objectives and
strategies is what is really needed. This may seem to be an obvious requirement. It is

not unknown, however, for the production engineers to be developing improved assembly techniques for a product range which the marketeers are phasing out, while extensions to that same range are happily being pursued by the product design team.

External strategic factors

The internal strategic factors are that part of the total planning environment which is, to some degree, controllable by the business managers. The other part of the environment comprises a set of **external strategic factors** which are largely outside their control, although they might have some influence on them. Some important external strategic factors, assembled into major categories, are:

- *Markets*   Total sales volumes in each relevant product sector and geographical area, market growth rates, customer data, competitor data, technologies employed.
- *External stakeholders*   Owners, customers, suppliers, competitors, debt holders, unions, the environmental lobby, the general public, government and government agencies.

   'Stakeholders' (Stewart, 1982) are groups, institutions or organizations who have vested interest in the performance and behaviour of the business *and* who are able to apply pressure in pursuit of that interest. The employees of a business are *internal* stakeholders.
- *Legal constraints*   Product liability, minimum wage, and health and safety at work legislation.
- *Economic constraints*   General health of the economy in countries of interest, taxation, interest rates, inflation, currency exchange rates, fiscal barriers to international trade.
- *Social constraints*   Language and cultural barriers to international trade, educational levels, the relative status of wealth-creating as opposed to wealth-consuming and wealth-manipulating activities, various perceptions of non-ethical as distinct from non-legal trading, such as selling cigarettes, animal skins and weapons.

Summary

In summary, the planning environment in which private sector businesses operate is a complex dynamic situation comprising very many interdependent internal and external strategic factors. It must be continuously monitored, and periodically analysed in depth, to underpin proper corporate planning. Its complexity highlights the need to partition the corporate planning problem into manageable sub-problems. 'Divide and conquer' is one standard attack on complexity.

2.3.3   The corporate planning model

The first partitioning, into time-frames, of the business planning problem has already been described. This is its separation into the strategic (corporate) and tactical phases. It has also been established that the individual strategic factors should not be treated separately, because of their mutual dependencies. This leaves structural

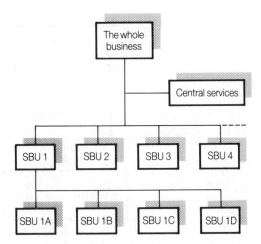

Figure 2.3   **A business as a structure of strategic business units (SBUs).**
A 'divide and conquer' technique commonly used in the management of corporate planning complexity partitions the whole business into an investment portfolio of SBUs. The concept is illustrated here. Note the similarities between this figure and Figure 1.2. Each SBU can plot its own future within a restricted set of strategic factors, subject only to the imposition of investment and market constraints from business headquarters.

partitioning as the second step in the management of corporate planning complexity. In this widely used approach a whole business is viewed as an 'investment portfolio' of so-called **strategic business units** (SBUs).

Strategic business units

SBUs are largely independent and (often) semi-autonomous business operations in their own right. Notionally, subject only to the imposition of investment constraints, each SBU can plot its own future with respect to its more limited set of strategic factors. The partitioning concept is illustrated in Figure 2.3.

Ideally, the SBUs coincide with the trading divisions or subsidiary companies which comprise the whole business, but this goal cannot always be met. SBUs are generally selected on the basis of one or more of the following criteria:

- They address a well-defined and distinctive product market segment, such as spreadsheet software packages, 'fancy' telephones, process control sensors, modems or beach buggies.

- They have a well-defined and distinctive customer set, such as domestic consumers, civilian airport operators, other manufacturing businesses or government departments responsible for national defence.

- They operate in a well-defined and distinctive geographical area, such as the north of England, Norway, southern France or California.

Clearly, the SBU portfolio notion is capable of further extension where required. For example, a large first-level SBU called 'defence products' might be further subdivided into second-level SBUs called 'army products', 'navy products' and 'air force products'.

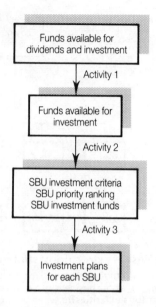

Figure 2.4 **Outline of the whole corporate planning process.**
When the strategic business unit (SBU) concept is used, a corporate investment plan becomes an amalgam of individual SBU investment plans. The figure shows a planning sequence which creates such a corporate plan. When the total fund available for investment (in a given period) has been determined, it is partitioned among the SBUs according to their investment needs and relative importance as contributors (actual and potential) to the whole business. The sequence culminates in a set of SBU investment plans which, together, make up the whole business investment plan.

A corporate planning sequence

Once the level of the total corporate fund available for dividends and investment has been established, structural partitioning into SBUs splits the whole corporate planning problem into three smaller problems. These are then tackled sequentially as outlined in Figure 2.4.

The three problem solving activities are:

(1) Deciding the maximum investment fund available for the whole business. This depends, first, on the level of the total fund available for dividends and investment in the relevant period and, second, on the fraction reserved for dividends. This decision is the prerogative of top management.

(2) Deciding the amount of investment funding, and the investment criteria, to be applied to each SBU. These twin constraints are applied to an SBU as inputs to its business planning process. The critical decisions derived in this activity depend on the investment needs of the individual SBUs, and on an assessment of their relative importance. They are again the prerogative of top management. An analytical technique which provides guidance for such decisions is discussed in Section 2.3.4.

(3) Preparation of a set of business plans at the SBU level.

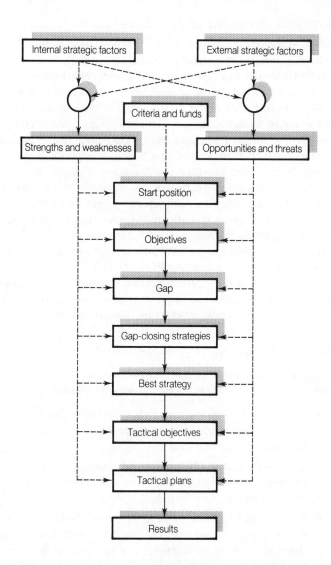

Figure 2.5   **Business planning at the strategic business unit (SBU) level.**

This illustration of business planning at SBU level is a development of the procedure outlined in Figure 2.1. The events labelled 'internal strategic factors' and 'external strategic factors' correspond to the 'planning environment' of the earlier figure. The initial planning work compares corresponding internal and external strategic factors to reveal the competitive strengths and weaknesses of the SBU (left-hand side) and its market opportunities and threats (right-hand side). These factors, together with a general 'wish-list' of criteria applied to all business investment situations, then condition the SBU planning process as shown in the figure.

Business planning at SBU level

A procedure for business planning at the SBU level is shown in Figure 2.5. This figure is a development of the basic planning process illustrated in Figure 2.1. The events labelled 'internal strategic factors' and 'external strategic factors' together represent the planning environment of the SBU at the time of plan preparation.

The first activities in the procedure are to compare some corresponding internal and external strategic factors. The purpose of these comparisons is to assess the *competitive* internal strengths and weaknesses of the SBU and the external opportunities and threats presented to it. Some examples will make this more clear. A status comparison of the product technologies available to the SBU with those of its competitors reveals its technological strengths and weaknesses. Similarly, manufacturing costs or marketing competence might be identified as either a strength or a weakness. In terms of threats and opportunities, the comparisons could reveal an opportunity to exploit a particular niche in the product market. In addition, a looming threat from the entry of a powerful new competitor or, perhaps, from some pending product liability legislation could be detected.

Note that the specific SBU investment criteria and its assigned amount of investment funding are inputs to the start position event, as are a number of more general criteria for the selection of strategic objectives and strategies.

General investment criteria

The general investment criteria are not specific to any particular SBU. They are a set of universal guidelines applying in all cases. The following list is a typical set:

- *Low risk with high return*   This feature is sought by investors the world over. Observation and experience suggest that it must contravene some natural law, because it is rarely found.

- *Economy*   Viable objectives and strategies which can be achieved relatively cheaply are usually favoured since they allow a limited total investment fund to be more widely distributed.

- *Internal and external 'matching'*   The aim here is a high level of compatibility with the internal and external business environment. For example, proposals to enter the ice-cream business are unlikely to be approved in an electronics business, however hot the weather. Equally, toys covered with lead-based paint do not appeal to most customers (parents) whatever enthusiasms the end users (children) might demonstrate.

- *Minimum 'lock-in'*   This criterion expresses a reluctance to enter into situations that will commit (lock-in) resources for extended periods, or are otherwise difficult to reverse.

- *Synergy*   A synergetic objective or strategy is one which contributes to some other independent objective or strategy, such that the combination is substantially more attractive than either one alone. Synergy is often parodied as the '2 + 2 = 5' effect.

It is unusual to satisfy all the items on this list. The remaining features of Figure 2.5 align closely with those of the basic planning process shown in Figure 2.1.

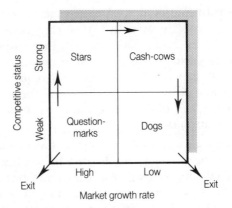

Figure 2.6   **A Boston Consulting Group matrix.**
Most techniques for selecting SBU-level investment criteria are based on an approach introduced by the Boston Consulting Group (BCG), summarized in the two-by-two matrix shown here. It combines the growth rate of the total market with the competitive status (equated with market share) of the SBU in that market. This 'positions' the SBU in one of four matrix segments. Each segment is associated with a distinctive set of investment criteria.

The model

Figures 2.3, 2.4 and 2.5 together encapsulate what is termed here 'the corporate planning model'. The question of investment criteria for the SBUs is now considered.

2.3.4   Investment criteria for the SBUs

The most widely used techniques for selecting SBU-level investment criteria are based on an approach introduced by the Boston Consulting Group (BCG) (Henderson, 1973; Hedley, 1977).

The BCG strategic position matrix

This approach assumes that the SBUs are based on product market sectors, as is usually the case, and it uses only two parameters. One of these is the growth rate of the whole market sector, and the other is the proportion of the market sector which is claimed by the SBU. This is assessed by comparing the sales volume achieved by the SBU with the sales volume of the whole market sector. Provided that these two quantities are measured over the same reasonable period, such as one year, their ratio is the fractional **market share** held by the SBU. Market share is then regarded as an indicator of the **competitive status** of the SBU in its product market. A low ratio indicates a weak competitor and a high ratio a strong competitor. This approach also favours high, rather than low, whole market growth rates. The results of a BCG analysis are normally summarized by positioning the SBU on a simple two-by-two **strategic position matrix**. Figure 2.6 shows an empty BCG matrix.

The BCG terms used to describe the four segments of the matrix lack elegance but have a memorable descriptive power. Their interpretations are:

- **Question-marks** are weak-to-average competitors in high growth rate markets. Such markets are normally in their early development stage and all competitors may be in a similar position because there are so many of them. It is unlikely that such SBUs will be able to follow or outstrip the market growth rate using only internally generated cash. So they will require additional investment to succeed. Those that do succeed become *stars*. Those that fail are normally terminated, becoming part of the **shake-out** of weak competitors that often characterizes growth markets.

- **Stars** are average-to-strong competitors in high growth rate markets. They are likely to be profitable but also cash-hungry because of the investment needed to sustain the high growth. **Cash-flow** may be negative. (It will be recalled, from Chapter 1, that profit and positive cash-flow are not the same thing.) Stars are good news because of their long-term growth, profit and cash-generating potential. As the market matures its growth rate declines and stars should develop into *cash-cows*.

- **Cash-cows** are strong-to-average competitors in low growth rate (or even declining) markets. These, too, are good news because manufacturing and other costs are likely to be low with only minimal investment needed for innovation. Thus cash-cows can be 'milked' to generate high levels of positive cash-flow for their parent business. Performance relative to their market must be tightly managed to delay their descent into the *dog* segment for as long as possible.

- **Dogs** are average-to-weak competitors in low growth rate or declining markets. Such markets are often characterized by fierce price-cutting as the competitors react to protect their investments. It may not be possible to sustain a viable position under such circumstances. On the other hand, fortune does sometimes favour the brave (or stupid) who persist long enough into the twilight of a declining market, as they garner residual sales abandoned by their competitors.

The arrows in Figure 2.6 indicate the normal progression of an SBU from one classification to another.

Traditional investment criteria

A set of traditional SBU investment criteria exists for the four BCG categories. These are described with reference to Figure 2.7, which shows a portfolio of four SBUs plotted on the *same* BCG matrix. This is allowed, but it must be remembered that each SBU is operating in a different market. The SBUs are represented by circles. The size of the circles indicates the relative size (in sales volume) of the SBUs. This is a popular convention in diagrams of this sort. The sample portfolio consists of:

(1) A relatively small but well-positioned question-mark SBU.
(2) A substantial star SBU which is also well positioned in its market.
(3) A large cash-cow SBU positioned in about a mid-range situation.
(4) A substantial dog SBU positioned towards the weak end of the range.

The traditional investment criteria are:

- *Question-marks* Invest heavily in well-positioned question marks in an attempt to turn them into stars. Poorly positioned question marks of long

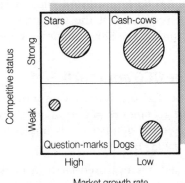

Figure 2.7 **Boston Consulting Group matrix with strategic business units (SBUs).**
This figure shows a portfolio of four SBUs plotted on just one BCG matrix. This is allowed, but it must be remembered that each SBU is operating in a different market. The SBUs are represented by circles, whose relative area describes the relative size (measured as annual sales volume) of the SBUs. The traditional investment criteria for SBUs in each of the four segments are described in the text.

standing should be eliminated in a manner which (if possible) generates cash, such as by selling them. Weak to mid-range question marks of recent vintage should, on balance, be encouraged by further investment but each case needs careful investigation.

- *Stars*   Generally, stars should be encouraged to grow by further investment if this strategy is compatible with the competitive situation. If competition is very fierce it might be better to invest at a level which merely maintains the present position pending developments in the market.

- *Cash-cows*   Investment in cash-cows should be no greater than that required to sustain the current position and should emphasize cost reduction activity so as to improve cash generation.

- *Dógs*   Investment should be reduced to the absolute minimum compatible with generating as much cash as possible. If this is not possible, dogs should be eliminated; preferably (and obviously) in a way which generates rather than consumes cash.

The BCG approach to setting SBU investment criteria (as a preliminary to strategic planning at the SBU level) illustrates another general 'rule' for the management of complexity. This might be termed 'the dominant constraints theory'. It claims that in all complex planning (and design) situations there exists a very limited number of *critical* constraints which, if identified, eliminate a great number of apparent options. These critical constraints are of great value since progress in planning (and in design) can be equated with the elimination of non-viable options.

In the BCG technique, the selected constraints are the growth rate of an SBU market and the competitive status of the SBU in that market. The combination of these two constraints positions the SBU on the BCG matrix and, hence, suggests appropriate investment criteria for it. There is also, of course, the third critical constraint noted earlier. This is the (entirely normal) limited availability of investment funds. The funding constraint requires that the investment requirements of all the SBUs are ranked in priority order. The SBUs can never be totally independent for this reason (and some others).

Criticisms of the BCG approach

There is no doubt that the Boston Consulting Group has made an outstanding contribution to the techniques of corporate planning. The two-by-two BCG matrix has an appealing logic and simplicity. It is, however, perhaps too simplistic and can be criticized (Coate, 1983) because:

- Competitive status is measured solely by market share. This is a fair measure of a current position but does not recognize trends in either direction. The inclusion of other factors into the assessment, such as relative manufacturing costs, would improve on this weakness.

- High growth rate markets are not necessarily attractive markets, as the BCG approach implies. Such markets are always highly competitive, unstable and risky. Mature, low or zero growth markets with substantial volumes and employing low technology are not exciting – except in their profit earning potential. The traffic-separation cones business is one example, and funeral directing is another.

- The BCG approach suggests that high market share is a good thing because it implies high profits. This implication is not always valid. For example, market share can usually be purchased at the expense of profit by reducing product price. This might be a potent growth (investment) strategy, provided that profit levels can be recovered later.

Despite these reservations, most modern corporate planning schemes are based on the BCG contribution. A number of extensions have emerged which go some way towards eliminating its weaknesses. This applies to the technique presented in the next section.

2.3.5   An extended BCG approach

The horizontal dimension of the strategic position matrix shown in Figure 2.8 indicates the 'rate of sales' status of the specific market in which the SBU operates. Its vertical dimension indicates the competitive status of the SBU within that market.

In this approach each of these dimensions is partitioned into three bands, yielding a three-by-three matrix (in contrast to the two-by-two BCG matrix). In reality, of course, both matrix parameters are continuous functions (within their boundaries) and the partitioning is purely a matter of analytical convenience.

The status of a product market sector

The fact that the rate of sales in a specific product-based market varies with time was hinted earlier. This characteristic is commonly termed a **life cycle**. Figure 2.9 illustrates the idealized form of a life cycle, which is divided here into three phases, labelled **growth**, **maturity** and **decline**.

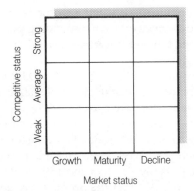

Figure 2.8 **A three-by-three strategic position matrix.**

This is a small extension of the BCG matrix shown in Figure 2.7. The horizontal market status axis can now be aligned with the characteristic phases of a product market, and this increased precision is matched by the vertical competitive status axis. In fact, both matrix parameters are essentially continuous, and the partitioning used is a matter of analytical convenience.

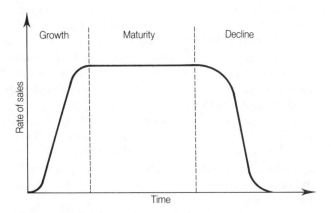

Figure 2.9 **Life cycle of a specific product-based market.**

The total rate of sales (measured in product units per month, say) of a specific product generation is a function of how long the product generation has been on the market. A somewhat idealized diagram of the typical sales life cycle is shown here. Reasons for this form of variation are discussed in the text, and those relating to technology are of special interest to engineers. The growth, maturity and decline phases align with the market status divisions in the strategic position matrix of Figure 2.8.

Note that the figure is a plot, against time, of the *rate* of sales (measured in product units sold per month or per year, say). *Total* sales volume over a period is obtained by integrating the life cycle curve over that period. It is total sales volume which is shared between the competitors operating in the market sector. In this discussion, the plot includes all the individual product variants comprising the product range available in the market sector; such as a **product generation** of multi-function telephones, or motor bikes, or spreadsheet software packages. A product generation is an aggregate of a class of competing products (motor bikes, say) which have broadly similar features and performance at corresponding points in the price range. It generally represents (at and beyond maturity) a well-defined stage in product and manufacturing technology.

Individual products within a range also exhibit life cycles whose timing does not necessarily coincide with that of the whole range. The range life cycle is the aggregate of the individual product life cycles.

In the *growth* phase, the rate of sales increases only slowly at first. A number of factors conspire to bring this about. Some customer reluctance to commit to the new products (which may have been rushed to the market), no history of product promotion and, possibly, product shortages and inefficient distribution can all play a part. However, provided that the products are acceptable to customers, a period of rapid growth then follows with (usually) more competitors entering the market which has now been proved by the pioneers. Eventually, the rate of sales slows down as the pent-up demand is satisfied. The life cycle then enters the *maturity* phase in which the rate of sales is relatively constant. Ultimately, however, the *decline* phase is entered and the rate of sales starts to fall away. This usually occurs slowly at first and then more rapidly. The rate of decline then normally slows somewhat before reaching zero, corresponding to the death of the product generation.

There are two fundamental reasons which can lead to the decline of a specific product-based market. The first, and least usual, is that customer demand for the functions offered by the product range evaporates for some reason. Hula-hoops are a classic example of a 'fad' market which emerged, flourished and faded in the absence of any rational explanation for its birth, life or death. More logically, the need for nuclear weapons may disappear if peace really does break out (and more certainly and suddenly if it does not).

The second, and more common, reason for a decline is that customer demand remains but a major technological innovation allows an improved generation of products to be created. Typically, these offer more functions and/or better performance – aggregating to better value for money. The effect of technology on the rate of sales status of a market is a central issue in this chapter. It is examined in some detail in Section 2.4.

The age status of a market can be estimated by evaluating a number of indicators:

- *Rate of total sales*   A comparison of this parameter, and *its* rate of change, with historical data can locate a point on the life cycle plot. The technique works best during the growth and decline phases.

- *Technological stability*   The growth phase is usually characterized by instability in product technology which is still immature. During the maturity phase both product and manufacturing technology are relatively stable. The start of the decline phase is normally signalled by a radical innovation in product and/or manufacturing technology.

- *Competitive activity*   The growth phase is often characterized by instability in price levels and the number of competitors. Thus, in the early stages, the pioneers may enjoy premium prices which must be reduced as 'follow-my-leader' competitors enter the market. Later, there may be a shake-out of the weaker competitors as the growth rate increases, because some will be unable to sustain the high investment levels required. During the maturity phase, the number of competitors is relatively stable, and market shares and prices are often substantially constant also. This effect may arise from unspoken agreements between the competitors not to disturb a comfortable situation. The decline phase is likely to be unstable; first in price levels, as competitors reduce prices in an attempt to retain market share, and then in the number of competitors as some withdraw from the market.

- *Scope of the product range* The number of offered product variants usually increases in the growth phase as competitors seek function-based and performance-based product differentiation (as opposed to price differentiation in the decline phase). The number of variants tends to a constant in the maturity phase, but may drop off sharply as the market declines, indicating selective withdrawal of less profitable products.

The competitive status of an SBU

Competitive status is the vertical dimension of the strategic position matrix illustrated in Figure 2.8. It is partitioned into three bands, labelled strong, average and weak. In itself, this represents only a trivial extension to the BCG approach. It will be recalled, however, that BCG equates competitive status with market share. This is an over-simplification. Improving on this measure is not easy but the effort is worthwhile.

A better measure of competitive status can be obtained from comparative assessments in each of the six internal strategic factor areas previously identified (in Section 2.3). The analysis yields sets of SBU competitive strengths and weaknesses (one set per area) which must then be combined, in some way, to indicate overall competitive status. However, there is a danger of 'paralysis through analysis' in a non-selective attack of this sort. This can happen because of the huge volume of data, much of it highly speculative, which is involved. A preferred technique restricts the analysis to a limited number of dominant factors in each major area. This works well provided, of course, that the right dominant factors are selected. A typical list is:

- *Financial* Profit, productivity, cash-flow.
- *Market* Sales volume, scope of product range, distribution arrangements.
- *Technical* Product technology, development and design capability.
- *Production* Manufacturing costs and technology.
- *People* Management quality.
- *Organization* Structure, physical resources.

Within this list, relative sales volume (market share), the technical factors and manufacturing economics are crucial. But a powerful case can be made for placing management quality in pole position.

There is one further problem in assessing competitive status which cannot be ignored. Clearly, the assessment requires adequate competitive data and an objective evaluation of the relative strengths and weaknesses of the SBU in question. Acquiring the competitive data calls for hard work and intelligent analysis, which should be no problem. But the *comparative* evaluation often does present a problem. This arises in achieving acceptance of its conclusions by top management, rather than in doing it.

Successful business managers are successful entrepreneurs. A necessary personality trait for entrepreneurs (and politicians) seems to be a level of optimism which can lead to a refusal to face unpalatable facts and a tendency to overemphasize the tasty ones. (This outlook on life is sometimes mistakenly called 'positive thinking'. It is an excellent thing in its proper place. But it was positive thinking of this sort that sunk the *Titanic*.) Good business analysts and engineers are not generally so gifted, and this can lead to conflict. The outcome of the conflict tends (sadly) to be that internal strengths are overstated and internal weaknesses understated.

2.4 Technology and strategic position

The point was made earlier that technology is a weapon which may be used to improve competitive performance. It therefore offers *opportunities* to those businesses that exploit it properly, and poses *threats* to those businesses that neglect or misuse it.

In fact, this is the case for all categories of technology. For example, companies have been known to 'improve' their financial performance by the use of entirely legal but not entirely ethical accounting procedures, thereby exploiting accounting technology. (The term 'creative accounting' is sometimes used to describe these practices.) On the other hand, a company which does not minimize its tax liability by all legal means is clearly failing in its duty to its owners.

However, this section is concerned only with the opportunities and threats presented by science-based engineering technology. It considers this sort of technology from a non-technical point of view. It is the last step on the road leading to a technique for building a technological strategy.

2.4.1 The drift towards oblivion

Now, the initial location of an SBU somewhere within the framework of its strategic position matrix represents a judgement made at a specific time. As time increases from that instant (and there is no way of stopping it) the SBU appears to move within the matrix. This is because the factors which determine its location are time-dependent. The natural tendency (that is, the tendency in the absence of action to counter it) is movement towards the unattractive bottom right-hand corner of the matrix. This is the weak competitor in a declining market situation. This natural drift towards oblivion is not just one more example of Murphy's Law ('anything that can go wrong will go wrong at the most inconvenient time'). It is an inevitable consequence of market ageing and competitive pressures. However, it can be countered, to some extent, by management action. The aim of this action is profitable deferment of the inevitable for as long as possible, followed by a graceful exit with honour and, better, as much cash as possible.

Technology is a potent competitive weapon and it may be safely assumed that it is wielded by most of the serious competitors in the market. Indeed, technological change is arguably the most powerful influence in the scenario just sketched in. The aim now is to justify and explain the statements that the sketch contains by focusing on the impact of technology on market status and on competitive status.

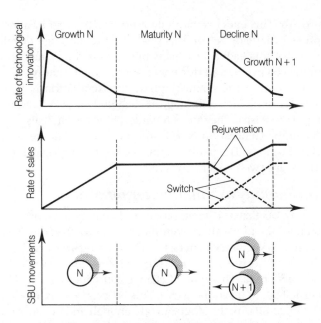

Figure 2.10 **Rate of technological innovation and market status.**
The rate of technological innovation varies during the sales life cycle of a specific product-based
market. The upper graph depicts this situation. The labels 'N' and 'N + 1' refer to successive product
generations. Growth Phase N is triggered by the advent of a radical change in technology. The rate
of technological innovation then declines and is at a relatively low level during the maturity phase.
The end of the maturity phase for generation N products is (usually) triggered by a second dramatic
technological change, which signals the start of the growth of Phase N + 1 and the corresponding
decline of Generation N. The second technological innovation is either a market terminator or a
market rejuvenator. In the first case, a complete technological switch is involved (from mechanical
to electronic, say), which can destroy a whole market and the SBUs participating in it. More usually,
the change is a dramatic advance in current technology which the stronger SBUs can follow if they
choose to do so. Changes of this nature usually rejuvenate the market by enabling new product
features with good value for money. The lower graph represents the inevitable drift of an SBU
towards oblivion as its market ages under technological and competitive pressures. But this drift
can be reversed by an SBU which properly exploits a radical technological change of the market
rejuvenator type.

2.4.2 Market status

The rate of technological innovation varies during the sales life cycle of a specific
product-based market and, to some extent, determines the duration of its different
phases. Figure 2.10 depicts the situation, in which the labels 'N' and 'N + 1' refer to
successive product generations.

The first growth phase (labelled 'Growth N') is triggered by a rapid increase in the
rate of technological innovation. This is the advent of a radical change in product
technology. In this phase, the technology is unstable – comprising a sequence of
hesitant advances and retreats. However, following its sharp initial increase, the
aggregate rate of technological change decreases as the growth phase progresses. As
the technology stabilizes, those customers who have postponed (wisely, perhaps)
their purchasing decisions come into the market and temporarily accelerate its

growth. This effect reduces pent-up demand and hastens the arrival of the maturity phase ('Maturity N'). In this phase, the technology develops only slowly through a series of small advances, many of which will be aimed at cost reduction rather than improved product performance and/or functionality.

The end of the maturity phase for Generation N products is brought about by another dramatic technological change. This is indicated in the figure by the second rapid increase in the rate of technical innovation. It also signals the start of the growth phase for Generation N + 1 and the corresponding decline in the rate of sales of Generation N. The nature of this second technological innovation is of great interest. There are two cases to consider.

Technology as a market terminator

It may be that the technological change is a complete *switch* from one form of technology to another; from mechanical to electronic watches, say, or from carpet beaters to vacuum cleaners. Usually, the **market terminator** technology that enables the switch is not novel in itself; the innovation lies in its application in a different product arena. This type of change can wipe out a whole market and the SBUs that participate in it (an industry). This is because only rarely can the 'old' SBUs conquer the unfamiliar technology quickly enough and cheaply enough to survive. Thus, the market held by the Swiss watch industry mostly migrated to Japan in the early 1970s. Similarly, mechanical typewriters have been largely replaced by word processing software and computer-driven printers, and slide-rules by calculators.

Technology as a market rejuvenator

The second type of technological change is more usual and less dramatic. In this case the change, while still a substantial advance, is a *natural extension* of the technology currently employed. One example of this phenomena is the development of a popular microprocessor family from 8-bit through 16-bit to 32-bit designs, leading to three distinct generations of desktop computer. The SBUs operating in such a market can normally follow, if they choose to do so, this type of technological change. It is termed a **market rejuvenator** technology because, by enabling the creation of a new product generation based on the technology of the previous generation, it breathes new life into the original market.

Technological change and market demand

The two types of technological change, the market terminator arising from a technology switch and the market rejuvenator arising from a technology extension, are distinguished in Figure 2.10 by their effect on the rate of sales plot. Note that market rejuvenation is often accompanied by market expansion. This reflects a broader range of applications for the new, enhanced, product generation – television sets able to receive, store and display electronic mail, say.

In summary, therefore, technological innovation is an enabling factor in the creation of product generation markets and is also a powerful influence on the 'shape' of those markets.

Horizontal SBU movements

Figure 2.10 also shows SBUs as circles located in each of the three market phases. The arrows attached to the circles indicate horizontal 'movement' of the SBU along the market status axis of the strategic position market. Generally, and not surprisingly, the drift is towards the right as the market ages under the influence of the technology. But, in the decline phase, the direction of the drift can *reverse!* In fact, this is the most usual situation. The reversal occurs when the technological change triggering the product range decline is a market rejuvenator rather than a market terminator. Rejuvenators present the opportunity for a fresh start to the SBUs, rather than almost inevitable oblivion. Note that this drift reversal is really an analytical convenience which allows the multi-generation picture shown in the upper parts of Figure 2.10 to be accommodated within the more restricted dimensions of the strategic position matrix.

2.4.3 Competitive status

Product and manufacturing technology are also major determinants of competitive status, because of the product design and manufacturing options that they make available. As discussed earlier, the principal opportunities relate to product differentiation in terms of functions, performance and manufacturing costs.

Vertical SBU movements

The competitive status of SBUs which neglect technology or do not exploit it wisely must decline. Those SBUs which keep up with the general development of technology in the market should at least retain their competitive status. SBUs that invest more heavily and wisely in technology should improve their competitive status. Technology, therefore, can cause vertical 'movement', either down or up, of an SBU within its strategic position matrix.

2.4.4 Technology vectors

The term **technology vector** is used here to express the combined effect on SBU location (within its strategic position matrix) of technology-induced market changes and competitive status changes. Figure 2.11, in which the vectors are shown as solid arrows operating on an SBU, summarizes the concept.

Market regimes

In Figure 2.11(a), the vertical centre line separates two market regimes. To the right of the line, the market goes through a normal growth, maturity, decline sequence but it is not rejuvenated in the decline phase. This is the case where the technological change which triggers market decline is a radical departure from current technology, or the decline is brought about by the disappearance of customer need (as with hula-hoops). The regime to the left of the vertical line is restricted to the decline phase. It is the case where the market is rejuvenated in that phase. Here, the technological change which triggers market decline for the 'old' product generation is a radical extension of current technology.

Status regimes

The horizontal centre line separates two SBU competitive status regimes. Above the

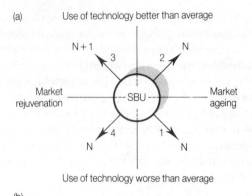

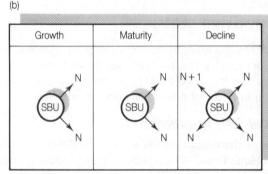

Figure 2.11 **Technology vectors and SBU location.**

This summarizes the combined effects of market ageing and technological policy in changing the position of an SBU within its strategic position matrix (as in Figure 2.8). In (a), segments 1 and 2 apply to the situation where the market goes through a normal growth–maturity–decline sequence but is not rejuvenated in the decline phase. SBUs in segment 1 lose competitive status as the market moves towards decline, because they use technology less effectively than the average competitor. This contrasts with the improving competitive status of SBUs in segment 2, which use technology more effectively than the average competitor. When the decline phase is triggered by a technological switch, SBUs in both these segments are likely to fail. Those in segment 2 may generate serious losses as their investment in outmoded technology becomes worthless. Segments 3 and 4 apply only to a decline phase where the market is rejuvenated. Happily, this is the rule rather than the exception and SBUs in segment 2 are well placed to move into segment 3, where they continue to prosper. But SBUs in segment 1 are usually unable to exploit the radical extension to current technology which rejuvenates the market. Most move into segment 4 and then withdraw from the competition. The same processes are illustrated in (b) in a rather different way.

line, the SBU is exploiting technology more effectively than the average competitor. Below the line, the SBU is exploiting technology less effectively than the average competitor.

Vector segments

The vectors, which combine the effects of technology on the market and on SBU competitive status, then fall into one of four vector segments:

(1) Vectors in this segment represent the almost inevitable drift of an SBU towards oblivion when its market declines due to a technology *switch*, which is the

advent of a superior and radically different technology. This was the fate of the Swiss mechanical watch industry.

(2) In this segment, vectors indicate the movement of an SBU which is using technology aggressively to improve its position in the market growth and maturity phases. If the subsequent decline is then brought about by a technology *switch* the SBU drops into segment 1. It might then sustain heavy losses due to its heavy commitment to an outmoded technology.

(3) Vectors in this segment represent the more usual progression of an SBU from segment 2, where it is well placed to exploit the radical *extension* to current technology which has rejuvenated the market.

(4) In this segment, vectors indicate the descent to oblivion of an SBU which has failed to use current technology properly and is then overtaken by a radical *extension* to that technology.

Figure 2.11(b) illustrates the technology vector concept in a slightly different way. It emphasizes that the (analytically convenient) left-pointing vectors associated with market rejuvenation are only possible in the decline phase.

2.5 Building a technological strategy

The arguments developed in Section 2.4 illustrate the critical nature of technology in determining SBU strategy. Technology is a major, perhaps *the* major, competitive weapon. The aim now is to explore the nature of that weapon in more detail in order to clarify its strategic role. The vehicle for this exploration is an extended example in which a particular (hypothetical) SBU is analysed from a technological point of view.

2.5.1 An SBU and its products

The SBU in the example is in the telephone business. There are presently four distinct products within its range, and these are distinguished (mostly) by 'special' functions, cost and price. Of course, all the products incorporate the basic functions for receiving incoming calls and making, by way of a keypad, outgoing calls. The special functions currently available are:

- *Last number recall*   The number last called can be called again by pressing just one key. This is useful when the number called is engaged at the first attempt.

- *Auto last number recall*   The number last called is automatically recalled, periodically, until connection is established (or the attempt is abandoned).

- *Memories*   These can store frequently used numbers which can then be called by pressing only one or two keys.

- *Battery back-up*   Numbers stored in the memories (and other stored data) may be lost if the telephone is disconnected. Battery back-up largely eliminates this hazard.

- *Display*   A display for showing the number called, the numbers in the memories or other data, such as the time of day.

- *Clock*   The display shows the time when not being used for another purpose.
- *Alarm*   The clock has an alarm facility.
- *Hands-free operation*   The telephone base-unit has a separate microphone and a loudspeaker so that the handset need not be used, and more than one user can participate in a call.
- *Conversation record*   Both sides of a conversation can be automatically recorded on a built-in magnetic tape cassette.
- *Cordless*   Communication between the telephone handset and its base-unit is by radio (rather than by wires) such that the handset is usable within a local area of, say, 50 metres radius of its base-unit.
- *Intercom*   Two-way conversation is possible between the base-unit and handset of the cordless telephone.

The four products in the range of telephones are described in terms of these special functions in Figure 2.12.

Product T1 is a cheap and primitive 'keys on handset, one piece' telephone, with very few special functions, aimed at domestic users. Product T2 is a mid-range domestic or business 'keys on handset, two piece' telephone with a few more functions. T3 is equipped with an extensive function set including the relatively unusual (and expensive) hands-free and conversation recording facilities. It is a 'keys on base-unit, two piece' telephone which sells well in the financial services industry, which is its target market. The cordless telephone, T4, is a relatively conventional product of its kind aimed primarily at domestic users.

The technological investment programme which resulted in these products has been allowed to run down in recent months while effort (and funds) have been concentrated on product promotion and improving the product distribution arrangements. The SBU has just established a tenable position in the market and its directors now intend to consolidate and develop that position with a further investment in technology.

2.5.2 Blends of technologies

Up to now, the term 'technology' has been used as a portmanteau word to embrace a multitude of individual technologies. This simplification is now discarded because, in strategic analysis, it is useful to view a product as a *blend* of a number of separate and distinct *technologies*. Henceforth, therefore, the word 'technology' is more sharply defined. It now means:

- A distinct body of technical knowledge applied in that specialized environment of requirements and constraints which is characteristic of a product and its market.

This interpretation of 'technology' is central to what follows. The crucial point is the combination of a distinct knowledge with a distinct environment. For example, 'power supplies' is a distinct technology. 'Telephone power supplies' is a distinct and specialized subset of that technology employed in telephone products. When defined

Special features	Products			
	T1	T2	T3	T4
Last number recall	●	●	●	●
Auto last number recall		●	●	
Number of memories	1	10	30	10
Battery back-up			●	●
Display		●	●	
Clock		●	●	
Alarm			●	
Hands-free			●	
Conversation record			●	
Cordless				●
Intercom				●

Figure 2.12 **A range of telephones distinguished by special functions.**
A particular SBU markets four distinct products (T1, T2, T3 and T4) in its current product range. The figure shows the special features belonging to each of the four products. T1 is a cheap and primitive 'keys on handset, one piece' telephone aimed at domestic users. T2 is a mid-range domestic or business 'keys on handset, two piece' telephone with a few more functions. T3 has an extensive function set, including the relatively unusual (and expensive) hands-free and conversation recording facilities. It is a 'keys on base-unit, two piece' unit. The cordless telephone, T4, is a relatively conventional product of its kind, aimed primarily at domestic users.

in this way the **constituent technologies** of a product can often be directly equated with the distinct sub-units which, together, make up the product.

Step 1: Identify the technologies

The first step, therefore, in determining a technological strategy is to identify the distinct technologies which are blended together to create the products offered in the market. The analysis must cover *all* the products available in the market, embracing those offered by the SBU in question *and* its competitors. Thus, it may reveal gaps in the technological armoury of the SBU.

The technologies exploited in the telephone product market are:

- *System interface*   The nature of the physical, speech signal and control signal relationships between the telephone unit and the telephone network.

- *Speech electronics*   Speech frequencies signal processing.

- *Digital electronics*   Control, data storage and display functions realized with digital integrated circuits.

- *Enclosures*   Mechanical and ergonomic aspects of the product 'boxes' fabricated, mostly, in plastic extrusions.

- *Power supplies*   All aspects of power provision for the products.

- *Printed circuit boards*   Used to support and connect the electronic and mechanical components (such as switches).

- *Magnetic recording*   All aspects of speech recording and play-back using magnetic tape cassettes.

Technologies	Products			
	T1	T2	T3	T4
System interface	•	•	•	•
Speech electronics	•	• •	• • •	• •
Digital electronics	•	• •	• • •	•
Enclosures	•	•	• •	• •
Power supplies		•	• •	• • •
Printed circuit boards		•	• • •	• • •
Magnetic recording			•	
Radio				•
Microprocessor software				
Volume manufacturing	•	• •		
Batch manufacturing			•	• •

Figure 2.13 **Telephone products as blends of technologies.**
This shows how a product can be viewed as a blend, or 'recipe', of distinct product technologies. Note that some technologies appear in all products but the use of others is more patchy. The number of 'bullets' indicates the scope and depth of knowledge in a particular technology that is required by the different products. The technological blend concept is important because some technologies have a greater impact on competitive status than others.

- *Radio* All aspects of cordless communication between a handset and its base-unit.
- *Microprocessor software* Control programs for microprocessors, themselves a facet of digital electronics.
- *Volume manufacturing* 'Continuous' large volume assembly and test of moderately complex electronic equipment.
- *Batch manufacturing* Intermittent assembly and test of more complex electronic equipment in 'batch' quantities.

Telephone products as technological recipes

Figure 2.13 shows the **technological recipe**, or **technological blend**, of each product in the present product range of the example SBU. Note that some of the technologies are used in all of the products but others are not. For example, magnetic recording and radio are each used in only one product. Microprocessor software is not currently used by the SBU. Some of its competitors, however, offer 'smart' telephones with data processing functions. One such product is able to display the accumulating cost of a call while it is in progress, and it can be used as a calculator when not otherwise employed.

Note, too, that the relative level of a particular technology may vary between products. Here the term 'level' is used to express the scope and depth of knowledge required in a particular technology. It is indicated, rather crudely, in the figure by the number of bullets. The same level of system interface technology, for example, is required in all the products whereas the level of the two electronic technologies is greater in the more complex products.

2.5.3 Competing with technologies

As noted previously, technology can influence competitive status in three basic ways: through product function and performance differentiation, and through its impact on manufacturing costs. But not all the distinct technologies that blend into a product are equally important in determining competitive status.

Relative importance of technologies

In terms of relative competitive importance three types of technology can be distinguished:

- **Foundation technologies** These are some of the technologies which are common to most of the products in a range and are used by most of the competitors in the market. They are essential constituents of the products but have no significant effect on competitive status. This is because they are relatively stable with limited potential for further development, and all competitors are about equally competent in their use.

- **Critical technologies** Those in this category have the greatest *current* impact on competitive status because of their potential for product differentiation. Such technologies are usually still developing in their own right or in their application to the particular product and market sector. Competitors are not equally competent in the critical technologies. Relative competence is, therefore, a major determinant of competitive status.

- **Looming technologies** These technologies *may* have the potential to become critical technologies, probably by displacing one of the current techno-logies. However, when assessed, they are still either in an earlier stage of development in their own right, or their application to the particular product and market sector is not yet significant.

(Note that technologies have life cycles just as products do. Foundation technologies are mature in the sense of having almost reached the limit of their development potential, and they are widely understood and exploited. Critical technologies are well into their growth phase, but with substantial development potential yet to be exploited. Looming technologies are in their early growth phase, with only patchy distribution among the competitors.)

Step 2: Classify technologies and competence

The second step, therefore, in determining a technological strategy is to assess the relative competitive importance of the product market technologies, and the relative competence of the SBU in each such technology.

Figure 2.14 illustrates the results of these analyses in the example case. Here, the number of bullets is used to indicate relative importance *within* the technology classifications (foundation, critical and looming). The relative competence of the SBU in each technology is assessed on a three level (strong, average, weak) scale.

Technologies	Type			SBU competence
	Foundation	Critical	Looming	
System interface	●			Average
Speech electronics		●		Strong
Digital electronics		● ● ● ● ●		Average-to-strong ?
Enclosures	●			Average
Power supplies	●			Average
Printed circuit boards	●			Average
Magnetic recording		●		Strong
Radio		● ●		Average
Microprocessor software			● ?	Weak
Volume manufacturing		● ● ●		Strong
Batch manufacturing		● ● ●		Weak

Figure 2.14 **Competitive assessment of telephone technologies.**
This shows how the relative competitive value of product technologies can be evaluated to provide critical data in formulating SBU technological policy. The product technologies are first classified as 'foundation' (no effect on competitive status), 'critical' (greatest impact on competitive status) or 'looming' (may become critical). The number of bullets then indicates relative importance *within* such a category (so, here, digital electronics is super-critical). Finally, an assessment is made of the relative competence of the SBU in each product technology. The one in this example has a severe problem with its batch manufacturing technology, and may be in difficulties with microprocessor software.

Note that six of the eleven market technologies have been assessed as critical, which is a substantial proportion. This suggests that the market is still in its growth phase. The diagnosis is confirmed by a still increasing rate of total sales, frenetic competitive activity and a wide range of product variants on the market.

2.5.4 Step 3: Product strategy

The third, and penultimate, step in determining a technological strategy is to analyse the data obtained from the assessment of the technologies with a view to identifying areas for investment in new or enhanced products. The analysis should take into account the current market situation and the anticipated more immediate developments in it. The relevant data for the example SBU is summarized in Figure 2.14.

Foundation technologies

The four foundation technologies are deemed to be equally important and the SBU has average competence in each one. This is a satisfactory position and there is little to be gained by investing to improve it. This is because the technologies are both mature in their own right and well established in their application to the particular product and market environment. The investment/return ratios in these technologies, therefore, are likely to be small and uninteresting.

Critical technologies: Opportunities

The ranking of speech electronics and magnetic recording as critical technologies reflects their role in the 'hands-free' and 'conversation record' functions of product T3 (see Figure 2.12). But products offering these two functions are expensive specialized items aimed at a relatively small market segment. This accounts for their 'low' (one bullet) importance ranking in Figure 2.14. The directors rate SBU competence in these two technologies as 'strong' but they recognize that these hard-won positions are under-exploited. They decide to invest further in these technologies by:

(1) Creating a new product incorporating the 'hands-free' function aimed at bridging the substantial function, cost and price gap between products T2 and T3, which is exploited by a number of their competitors.

(2) Exploiting both technologies in a new low cost, low price automatic telephone answering machine for the domestic market segment, where there is evidence of developing demand for such products.

The decisions to launch these product development and design projects are aimed at synergetic opportunities, since the enabling critical technologies have been largely paid for by the T3 product. In the first case it is anticipated that a premium price can be obtained for the relatively low cost addition of the desirable 'hands-free' function to the T2 product. With regard to the answering machine, it is assumed (perhaps optimistically) that the technical work involves little more than rearranging the relevant technologies to provide the automatic answering and play-back functions.

Critical technologies: Threats

Radio is ranked as a moderately important critical technology since it is central to the cordless telephone product, T4. SBU competence in this technology is ranked as only average. Sales (and earnings) of the T4 product have been disappointing in a slowly expanding segment of the market. It has been overshadowed by similar, but lower-priced, competitive products. A significant price reduction aimed at boosting sales is not an immediately viable solution to the problem. This is because T4 is made, as is T3, in the SBU's own batch manufacturing facility, which is rated as a weak technology of major importance. This reflects the price-sensitive nature of the market and the comparatively high costs of the facility, which are dominated by local labour rates. In contrast, most of the competitors subcontract all product manufacturing to low cost specialist assembly companies in Taiwan or Hong Kong. The SBU has already adopted this approach for manufacturing its volume products T1 and T2, which accounts for the 'strong' competence rating of 'their' volume manufacturing technology. The directors decide to investigate upgrading SBU competence in batch manufacturing technology by sub-contracting T4 production to a low cost overseas specialist company. If this does prove to be a viable option, the market performance of the T3 product might be similarly improved. Pending resolution of this matter, it is decided to retain the current positions on radio technology, and on the T4 product, since it is probable that they can be profitably enhanced at a later stage.

The remaining critical technology is digital electronics. This is ranked as the most important of the critical technologies because of its potential for enabling new product functions, improved performance, *and* (through higher levels of circuit integration) reduced product cost. SBU competence in this super-critical technology is rated 'average' to 'strong'. The uncertainty reflects another uncertainty concerning the future role of microprocessor software. This is shown as a possible looming technology in Figure 2.14. It will be recalled that a number of competitors are using microprocessor hardware and software to provide data processing functions such as call-cost monitoring and 'off-line' calculator facilities. Smart telephone products of this nature are recent entries onto the market and it is too early to assess their long-term significance. However, the SBU has no recent microprocessor experience. If microprocessor technology becomes important its digital electronics competence must be ranked as only average, since microprocessor hardware skills are lacking. There would also be a serious weakness in microprocessor software.

In response to this situation the SBU directors consider the option of specifying a smart telephone product and subcontracting its development and design to a specialist company. However, they are reasonably sure that smart telephones will never attain more than a small 'gimmick' niche in the market. They choose, therefore, not to take urgent product action in this market segment. The engineering director, who is fascinated by the flexibility offered by microprocessor technology, argues against this decision but is overruled by her colleagues.

Strategy before tactics

It is emphasized here that the product-related decisions just outlined are strategic decisions. Each one is the starting point for the creation of a tactical plan aimed at implementing the decision. It is possible that the work involved in creating this plan will demonstrate that the strategy is not viable. For example, it may be that the answering machine plan will indicate that the return on the investment needed to create the product and to launch it onto the market is too low. In cases of this sort the strategy must be reconsidered. In this sense, strategic decisions are decisions in principle only and are subject to scrutiny in a more detailed analysis.

2.5.5   Step 4: Research strategy

The fourth, and final, step in determining a technological strategy is to analyse the data obtained from the competitive assessment of the technologies with a view to identifying areas for investment in *new* technologies. This necessarily requires a longer term, more speculative, survey of technological and market possibilities. It may lead to the identification and launch of research projects which are aimed at extending new technologies and building skills in their application. Generally, research projects relate to a product range rather than to a specific product.

Technological and market outlook

In this context, the example SBU is in a particularly interesting situation with regard to its cordless telephone product, T4. This is a local area device because the handset can only operate in the vicinity of a single specific base station. (In fact, all the current SBU products are local area devices but T4 can operate over a wider local area than the others.)

However, there is also an active market in wide area cordless telephones. These products, known generically as 'cellular telephones', can communicate by radio with a wide area network of base stations, each of which is linked to the conventional 'wired' telephone network. The network of base stations defines a pattern of overlapping local cells. This allows the handling of a call to be transferred from cell to cell as the telephone (user) moves inside the network. Due to power and weight limitations, most of the cellular telephones presently on the market are car phones. However, reasonably satisfactory hand-portable products are increasingly available. All the products are expensive to buy or rent, and to operate. There is also some customer irritation arising from limited network cover and overload, lost calls, and poor speech quality.

A looming technology threat?

The advent of cellular telephone technology presents the SBU directors with a dilemma. Currently, the market it has created appears to be quite separate from the market in which the SBU operates. The products do not compete. But this may not always be the case since, in principle, a wide area telephone can perform all the functions of a local area telephone as well as being portable. Indeed, the prospect of individuals routinely carrying their own telephone, much as they now carry a watch, could be on the horizon. Perhaps, from the perspective of the SBU, cellular telephone technology is a *looming technology* which could trigger the decline of their current market. The SBU directors are sufficiently disturbed by these speculations to authorize a research programme aimed at establishing a competence in cellular telephone technology. The engineering director points out that system interface technology for cellular telephones is more complex than that to which they are accustomed. It demands expertise in microprocessors. It is agreed that acquiring this expertise shall be part of the research programme.

2.6   Concluding summary

Following a discussion of planning in general and business planning in particular, this chapter concentrates on the strategic role of technology in the longer-term survival and prosperity of a business. The analysis shows that:

(1) Technology is a major strategic factor which presents both opportunities and threats to a business. It deserves serious attention from top management.
(2) It is no more difficult to formulate the technological element of an overall business strategy than it is for any other strategic element. Because of this, the relative neglect of technology in the teaching, literature and practice of corporate planning is particularly disturbing.

Engineers are the custodians and practitioners of technology within a business. It is important that they understand its strategic implications, and that they can contribute to the formulation of technological strategies.

However, technology is but one of six major strategic factors. In many situations, technology is the dominant factor but this is not always the case. The principles embodied in Sections 2.4 and 2.5 can be equally well applied to those other strategic factors.

REFERENCES

Ansoff H. I. assisted by McDonnell E. J. (1987). *Corporate Strategy*. Revised edn. Harmondsworth: Penguin (Update of a classic text first published in 1965)

Coate M. B. (1983). Pitfalls in portfolio planning. *Long Range Planning*, **16**(3), 47–56

Hedley B. (1977). Strategy and the 'business portfolio'. *Long Range Planning*, **10**(2), 9–15

Hellriegal D. and Slocum J. W. (1986). *Management* 4th edn. Reading, MA: Addison-Wesley (Chapters 6–9)

Henderson B. D. (1973). The experience curve reviewed. IV. The growth-share matrix of the product portfolio. *Perspective*, (135), The Boston Consulting Group, Boston, MA

Justis R., Judd R. and Stephens D. (1985). *Strategic Management and Policy: Concepts and Cases*. Englewood Cliffs, NJ: Prentice-Hall

Lorange P. (1980). *Corporate Planning: An Executive Viewpoint*. Englewood Cliffs, NJ: Prentice-Hall

Stewart R. (1982). *Choices for the Manager*. Englewood Cliffs, NJ: Prentice-Hall

SUGGESTED FURTHER READING

Parker (1985) is a wide-ranging account of the strategic aspects of technological innovation in manufacturing industries. Twiss (1986) is also directed at the broader issues of technological innovation, treating it (very properly) as an integral component of the whole business operation. Both texts provide illuminating insights, but the Twiss approach aligns most closely with this book.

Ansoff H. I. and Stewart J. M. (1967). Strategies for a technology-based business. *Harvard Business Review*, November/December 1967

Parker R. C. (1985). *Going for Growth*. Chichester: John Wiley

Twiss B. C. (1986). *Managing Technological Innovation* 3rd edn. London: Longman

QUESTIONS

2.1   How do strategies differ from tactics? How do strategies resemble tactics? What is the relationship between strategies and tactics?

2.2   'Technology is a strategic factor.' Is it? Why?

2.3   You are a business executive based in Canterbury, Kent. One Thursday in November, at 15.30, you are summoned to meet your boss in Edinburgh, Scotland, at 14.30 on the following day. Edinburgh is about 500 miles from Canterbury, and there is an established weather pattern of early morning fogs.

List five different, but reasonably tenable, strategies for getting to Edinburgh by the appointed time. Then explain how you will choose the best strategy from this list.

2.4   Why is earning an at least adequate profit the paramount strategic objective of most company directors? What is an 'adequate'

profit? How can its size be estimated?

2.5 The corporate planning environment can be regarded as an assembly of strategic factors. These may be classified as either internal or external. How is this distinction made? List and describe the principal types of strategic factor in each of these classes. Identify the most important type of factor in each list and justify the selections.

2.6 (a) Explain, in the context of business planning, the concepts of:

- internal strategic factors
- external strategic factors
- strengths and weaknesses
- opportunities and threats
- criteria and investment funds

(b) Outline a business planning sequence which is based on these concepts, and is directed at achieving a strategic objective by means of a set of tactical plans.

2.7 Describe the original Boston Consulting Group (BCG) 'growth-share' technique for determining an appropriate investment strategy for a strategic business unit. What are the particular advantages and disadvantages of the BCG approach to this problem?

2.8 Describe, briefly, how the 'age' of a product

market sector and the relative competitive strength of a strategic business unit (SBU) can be estimated. Show how these two parameters may be combined to place the SBU within a three-by-three strategic position matrix. What is the purpose of such an exercise?

2.9 Discuss the role of technology in the time-dependent variation of the total rate of product sales in a product-based market sector. How may technological innovation create, destroy or rejuvenate such markets?

2.10 Show how the opportunities and threats which technology presents to a strategic business unit (SBU) may be represented as 'vectors' which cause it to move within a strategic position matrix.

2.11 Should the directors of a company always be striving to achieve and maintain a high level of technological innovation? If not, why not? If so, why?

2.12 Describe how a motor vehicle can be considered as a configuration of a number of distinct product technologies. Show how this notion can be combined with the concepts of foundation, critical and looming technologies to indicate the broad outlines of a technological investment policy for a motor vehicle design and manufacturing business.

The Role of the Technical Function

*He that will not apply new remedies must
expect new evils;
for time is the greatest innovator.*

Francis Bacon 1561–1626

3.1	Introducing innovation	85
3.2	The primary tasks	89
3.3	Innovation is investment	102
3.4	Secondary tasks	106
3.5	Software innovation	112
3.6	Concluding summary	114

 Repetitions The product sales life-cycle concept was introduced in Chapter 2 at Section 2.2.5. In that chapter, the potent influence of product technologies on its shape and duration was examined in detail. Other important factors are emphasized in this chapter in Section 3.3.1.

The overall objectives of this chapter are to describe the purpose and relationship of the technical function of a technology-based manufacturing business by examining the product innovation duties and other tasks which are assigned to it. Objectives by section follow:

3.1 To introduce a relatively distinctive view of technological innovation in industry. This partitions the process into four distinct tasks.

3.2 To establish the nature, dependent relationships and distinguishing features of these four primary tasks of the technical function.

3.3 To examine an important concept which perceives the whole product creation process as an investment/return situation.

3.4 To identify and explore a number of secondary, but important, tasks which are commonly assigned to a technical function.

3.5 To review some factors which illuminate the special difficulties of software product creation.

3.6 To identify its salient points and summarize its major messages.

3.1 Introducing innovation

The technical function has a special role in a technology-based manufacturing business. It also has a special place in this book, because most newly qualified graduates in the science and engineering disciplines start their industrial careers in the technical function. The purpose of this chapter is to examine the nature of the tasks which are assigned to the function. It is *not* about how these tasks are selected, organized, planned or controlled. Those topics, and other delights, are covered elsewhere.

The primary role of the technical function is **technological innovation**, which can be crudely defined as doing new things with technology. So this chapter is mostly about technological innovation. But, because the technical function is a centre of technical expertise, a number of secondary tasks are also assigned to it. These, too, must be considered in a comprehensive description of its role in a business.

The term 'technology-based manufacturing business' conjures up images of hardware products, where the term 'hardware' is broadly interpreted. But businesses creating software items, either as stand-alone products or as parts of other products, are also of this type. Unfortunately, the software innovation process is not (yet) as mature, well-understood or manageable as the corresponding hardware process. The chapter concludes with an exploration of the problem area of software innovation.

3.1.1   About technological innovation

In most management texts, in industry generally, and in government circles techno-logical innovation is called **research and development**, or simply R&D. This traditional jargon conceals two fundamental problems for those seeking to under-stand what it is about. Firstly, there is no generally agreed definition of what the words 'research' and 'development' mean. They are differently interpreted in different businesses within the same industry, as they are also in different industries. There is a general acknowledgement that R&D refers to innovation, but figures published by government and industry often seem to assume that all scientists and engineers who are exercising their professional skill are innovating. This view certainly makes the figures bigger and, perhaps, better. But it ignores the facts. Many government scientists, for example, are employed in the analysis and testing of materials (food, chemicals, and so on) which are important tasks but nothing to do with innovation. Secondly, and more seriously, the jargon suggests there are just *two* phases in the technological innovation process. For industrial management purposes further subdivisions are desirable.

In this book, these twin problems are resolved in a way which has served the author (and others) well over many years in a number of different industries. It hinges on a relatively distinctive view of the technical innovation process. The process is partitioned into five phases called **pure research**, **basic research**, **applied research**, **product development** and **product design**. Industry does not indulge in pure research (by definition) so the emphasis here is on the other four activities. In principle, these activities are simply defined as everything that has to be done to progress from a defined start position to a defined end position. Much of this chapter is about these four different activities and the relationships between them. They comprise the technical aspects of a broader innovation process which creates new and enhanced products for sale. Figure 3.1 illustrates the major elements and communication paths in this *whole* **product creation process**. The technical function has a pivotal role.

There are three major sequential stages in the whole product creation process. Referring to the figure:

(1) Market data is analysed by the marketing function to yield the specification of a new product, or enhancements to a current product. This defines the product features required and sets an upper limit on product cost. It is passed to the product development and design team in the technical function.

(2) That team transforms the specification into proven product definition data, which specifies how the product is to be made and tested. This data is passed on to the production function.

(3) The new or enhanced product is then built and tested, in pre-determined quantities, by the manufacturing operation within the production function. The product is then available for sale.

The marketing and sales functions (which are usually part of the same organization within a business) interface the business to its market. Marketing conditions the market to expect and accept the new product with its longer-term promotional activities. Sales, on the other hand, manages the day-to-day interaction: selling, order

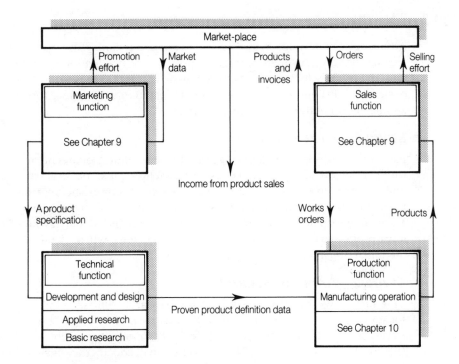

Figure 3.1   **Major elements in the product creation process.**
The technical function has a pivotal role in the whole new product creation process illustrated here. The marketing function transforms market data into a new product specification. The product development and design team in the technical function transforms the specification into proven product definition data. The production function transforms this data into products for the sales function to sell. The product development and design activity in the technical function is the interface between the marketing and production functions. It is supported by the applied and basic research activities.

processing, and product dispatch and invoicing. The production function manufactures the products defined by the technical function to schedules (time and quantity) defined in 'works' orders from sales. The marketing and sales function is discussed in Chapter 9, and the production function in Chapter 10.

The product development and design activity in the technical function is the interface between the marketing and production functions. It is supported by the applied research and basic research activities. These activities also have links with marketing and (to a lesser extent) with production. These links are not shown in Figure 3.1.

Research, development and design are not invariably directed at products for sale, as suggested by the figure. They can be concerned with improving, in some way, the product creation process itself. The in-house development of computer-aided-design (CAD) tools is an example of **method-oriented technical innovation**. It is of the same nature as product-oriented technological innovation, but the customer for the product is the parent business.

3.1.2   The treasure-hunting analogy

An analogy which yields an instructive insight into technical innovation is found in the treasure-hunting business. Strangely, this esoteric occupation has a lot in common with the primary technical activities of basic and applied research, development and design. The analogy is used here as an introduction to the more formal explanation and definition of those activities in Section 3.2.

Stage 1: 'Basic research'

Basic research is like the first stage of a treasure hunt. Documents must be located, sifted, analysed and correlated. Nebulous clues must be evaluated and various uncertainties investigated and resolved. A wary eye must be kept on competitors. Eventually, the *possible* location of some *perhaps* valuable treasure *may* be identified. More often than not, however, the search will be abandoned in favour of a seemingly more promising prospect. In, say, two cases out of ten it will be deemed wise to pursue the initial dream to the next stage.

Stage 2: 'Applied research'

This next stage corresponds to applied research. Initially, this concentrates on locating the treasure more precisely so as to minimize the area for subsequent excavation. This data then allows the technical feasibility and cost of digging holes in that location to be assessed. The assessment will specify the digging tools required. Most of these will already be available to an established team of treasure-hunters, but others may not. (Treasure is not now found in easy places. Such places have already been explored, and any fruits of the endeavour sold to grateful customers.) While all this is going on, marketing colleagues seek a more precise valuation of the treasure. The results of, maybe, half of these projects will be judged worthy of further investment.

Stage 3: 'Development'

The development activity is directed at completing the kit of required digging tools. Technical failure is still possible at this stage, but is unlikely if a proper job has been done in applied research. Development is not always necessary because the existing tool-kit may be adequate. When it is necessary, it should precede the next stage, which is digging. Otherwise, the completion of the hole could be held up, leaving marks in the sand to guide competitors to the treasure.

Stage 4: 'Design'

The final stage of digging up the treasure is the design activity in this analogy. If all the earlier work has been done properly technical success, which is retrieving the treasure, is virtually assured. It then remains to be seen if it can be sold at a price which both pays for the costs of liberating it *and* provides an acceptable surplus to reward the hunters.

Analogies: Handle with care

No analogy is perfect. The major imperfection of this one lies in stage 2, where the shortfall to be rectified in stage 3 is identified as items missing from the kit of required digging tools. In product-oriented applied research, this shortfall is items missing from the kit of required product piece-parts, and it is these that are the subject of development. Other than this detail, the analogy is satisfactory and some further points are worth noting.

There is a stage 0, which is pure research, before stage 1. It is carried out, mostly by scientists, in universities and sometimes in government research establishments but seldom, if ever, in industry. It is motivated by curiosity, hopes of fame, career ambitions or for providing benefits to humanity. The prospect of commercial gain is rarely a factor. Pure research progresses, very slowly, in a general direction rather than towards sharply defined objectives. It is the basis of both modern treasure-hunting and modern industry. However, connections between specific treasures or products and specific basic research programmes are often tenuous and clouded by the passage of a very long time.

Note that, in the analogy, only about ten per cent of the stage 1 projects actually yield a worthwhile return in the end. This is about right for the success rate of research in industry. Note, too, that two factors enter into the overall success equation. These are technical success and commercial success. Thus, even if the treasure is retrieved it still has to be sold at an adequate profit before the whole project can be deemed successful.

3.2 | The primary tasks

The primary tasks of staff involved in technological innovation are product-oriented basic research, applied research, development and design. Before these tasks are discussed, a particular way of regarding products must be explained.

3.2.1 Products as configurations

A complete product can be viewed as:

- A unique configuration (or arrangement) of **sub-units** about which everything that needs to be known is known.

This **configuration view of a product** is central to the perception of applied research, product development and product design which is presented in this book. It is a *recursive* view. Thus, first-level sub-units can be regarded as configurations of smaller second-level sub-units — and so on. Ultimately, the **basic product elements** are identified. This point is reached when further decomposition would yield non-functioning parts. Figure 3.2 illustrates the concept.

The building analogy

The building industry provides a useful introduction to understanding the nature of applied research, product development and product design. A particular building is a configuration of building sub-units. There is a vast range of *proven standard* building sub-units available. For example, bricks, concrete preformations, window frames, doors, electrical fittings, plumbing fittings and the like. All come with detailed specifications which describe their important features, such as shape, dimensions,

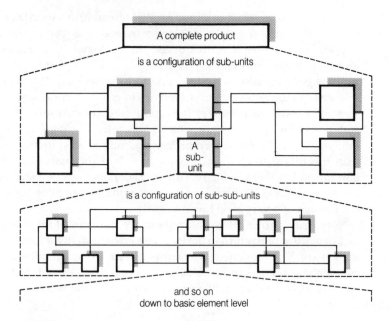

Figure 3.2 **The configuration view of a product.**
The recursive configuration view of a product, illustrated here, underpins the definitions of applied research, product development and product design which are featured in this book. A product (type) is regarded as a unique configuration of 'big' sub-units. Each big sub-unit is a unique configuration of 'small' sub-units. Each small sub-unit is a unique configuration of 'smaller' sub-units, and so on. Ultimately, the decomposition process yields a unique configuration of basic product elements.

colour, load-bearing capacity, recommended interfacing techniques and price. Many new buildings are constructed solely from the proven standard building sub-units available. Their design novelty resides only in the mixture of standard sub-units used and their unique configuration or arrangement. But some new buildings also incorporate *novel* sub-units which have not been used before in a practical, real-life, situation.

Conceptually, the only difference between synthesizing new products in the buildings industry and in any other industry lies in the technology of the sub-units employed. Every new product is a new configuration of proven standard and, sometimes, novel sub-units. The primary nature of the product is determined by the dominant sub-unit technology – electrical, electronic, mechanical, software or whatever. The technical aspects of product innovation are, therefore, largely concerned with:

- standard sub-units
- novel sub-units
- novel configurations of sub-units.

Sub-units are *functional* entities which may be progressively decomposed into ever smaller sub-units until the basic element level is reached.

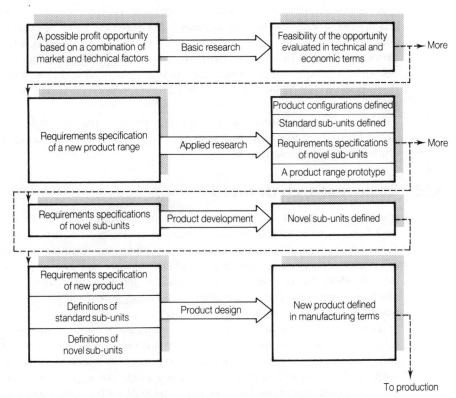

Figure 3.3   A simplified view of the technical innovation process.
This is a somewhat idealized overview of industrial technical innovation, showing its four distinct
activities (as arrows) in a sequential arrangement. The boxes describe the start and end positions for
each activity. Basic research is generally aimed at enhancing a specific product technology, whereas
applied research is concerned with a specific product range. Both product development and
product design focus on a single product in that range. Note that both types of research may lead to
more than one 'next phase' project.

The concept of a product family, commonly termed a **product range**, is implicit in
the configuration view. Particular sub-units bestow particular features on the
complete product. A range of similar products with marginally different costs, prices
and features may then be synthesized, relatively economically, by choosing various
recipes of sub-units. The motor-car industry provides a familiar example of this
marketing strategy.

3.2.2 Serial product innovation

The primary tasks of basic research, applied research, product development and
product design may be regarded as contiguous projects in an essentially serial
process. This is a valid approach under certain circumstances and it is the one initially
adopted here. Figure 3.3 shows a simplified view of the technical innovation process
in this form. The figure is expanded with further detail as the discussion proceeds.

A process sequence is started by the recognition of a combination of technological and market possibilities which, together, offer a possible profit opportunity. This may lead to the launch of a basic research project. The desired end result of the whole process is **proven product definition data** for the production function. This is the output of a product development and design project. It is a complete and verified description which defines how to manufacture and test a particular new or enhanced product.

In the task descriptions that follow, it is assumed that the input of a successor project is derived from the output of its predecessor project, as in Figure 3.3, which complements the descriptions.

3.2.3 Basic research defined

A basic research project arises from the recognition of a possible profit opportunity based on a combination of technological and market factors. It is that activity which aims to move from that position to a position where the feasibility of the opportunity has been evaluated in both technical and economic terms. The emphasis is generally on extending the boundaries of a particular *technology*, rather than on specific products employing that technology. It includes studies of potentially useful new materials, processes, components, sub-units and techniques.

If the new concept does appear to be technically feasible at an economic cost (in relation to its possible applications) it may spawn several applied research projects. For example, the advent of a new low-cost material which does not conduct heat could lead to applied research work on a new range of compact fire-resistant cabinets. This, of course, is just one possible application of such an attractive material.

Basic research is carried out in university engineering departments, government establishments, contract research organizations and, principally, in large businesses. It can involve engineers but scientists predominate.

3.2.4 Applied research defined

A product motive is introduced in applied research. It is that activity which aims to extend the technical position established in basic research to that where the technical capability exists to meet the requirements specification of a new *product range*. These requirements include cost targets as well as performance targets. Applied research is concerned with the resolution of a variety of potentially conflicting issues such as technical limitations, reliability considerations, ease of use, physical characteristics and cost boundaries.

The activity culminates in the working demonstration (or simulation) of a product range prototype, and a report which evaluates the project results in a product development and design context. The prototype comprises a configuration of sub-units chosen to prove the technical and economic feasibility of a typical product in the range. It includes preliminary versions of any novel sub-units which appear to present demanding technical problems. However, in the interests of economy, it may omit those features (novel or not) where there is high confidence that they are not problem areas.

Two critical specifications are included in the project report. These are:

(1) An **implementation specification** of the target product range which defines the different sub-unit configurations of the individual products within the range. It includes a target maximum cost for each such product. It also defines the standard sub-units and identifies the novel sub-units which, together, are required to create the range. The target maximum cost for each sub-unit is included.

(2) A **requirements specification** of all the novel sub-units identified in the target product range specification. For those novel sub-units which have been implemented in some form this data is accompanied by reports on their preliminary design, test and cost results. These reports emphasize areas where the initial versions fail to meet specification and suggest, ideally, ways in which the problems might be resolved.

Applied research is virtually confined to industry and is usually staffed by engineers, although some scientists do become involved.

3.2.5 Development and design defined

A development and design project is aimed at a single *product* within the range. The specifications from applied research refer to the whole product range and, therefore, they provide launch data for a number of product development and design projects. Only one such project is illustrated in Figure 3.3.

Product development and design is that activity which aims to extend the technical capability established in applied research to deliver a verified description, in manufacturing terms, of a particular product which meets pre-defined performance and cost specifications. When it is feasible to do so, the project includes the manufacture of one or more prototypes so as to prove the output data. The activity is partitioned, as shown in the figure, into two sub-projects called product development and product design. Note that product development is shown as preceding product design.

Product *development* is defined as the process of defining and proving novel sub-units destined for incorporation into a pre-determined configuration of proven sub-units, some (probably most) of which will be standard.

Product *design* is defined to complement the product development definition. It is the process of defining a novel configuration of well-understood and proven sub-units to meet the pre-determined requirements specification of a complete product. (Strictly, this defines only the technical aspects of product design. A more comprehensive definition of product design is contained in Chapter 8.)

The subject of product development is the appropriate subset of the second specification from the applied research project, which refers to novel sub-units. The aim is to design, and prove, those novel sub-units so as to meet their technical specifications within their specified cost boundaries. The output of this phase then feeds into the product design phase, where it joins the appropriate subset of the first specification from the applied research project.

Product development and design is essentially an engineering occupation, and it is virtually all carried out within industry.

The distinction between development and design

In this analysis, the distinction between development and design depends on the position of the observer. This is a consequence of the recursive nature of the configuration view of a product. To illustrate the point, consider the technical innovation of a new car which is to incorporate, among other novelties, a new engine. From the perspective of the design team concerned with the whole product (the new car), the new engine is a novel sub-unit which must be developed. But the team concerned with the new engine is charged with the task of providing proven sub-unit (the new engine) definition data. They will perceive this (rightly) as a design task at the sub-unit level. This design task might also have subsidiary development tasks relating to engine sub-units, such as a new cam shaft.

Why then, given this duality, is the distinction made between development and design? The answer is 'to minimize the risk of technical failure'. Product design is the process of defining a novel configuration of well-understood and proven sub-units to meet the pre-determined specification of a complete product. If a design project is attempted in terms of sub-units which are not well-understood and/or not adequately proven, the probability that it will overrun its time and cost budget is greatly increased. It is also more probable that the resulting product will not meet its original performance specification and will prove unreliable in service. So, when the product incorporates novel sub-units, it is wise to define and prove the novel sub-units in development before launching into the design of the complete product. In other words:

- Development should precede design. This is why the distinction between development and design is important.

In any complex operation a step-by-step approach, with testing at each step, is the safer course. 'Divide and conquer' wins most battles and many wars.

3.2.6   Practical considerations

The perception of the technological innovation process summarized in Figure 3.3 is idealized in a number of respects. This section aims to show how that simplified concept is modified by practical considerations.

Project outlines, planning and reviews

A more detailed (and realistic) version of Figure 3.3 is contained in Figures 3.4 (research) and 3.5 (product development and design). These show the innovation projects within a management framework aimed at obtaining the optimum return on the resources invested in the product innovation work.

In these two figures, a box represents a particular **event**, which occurs at an instant in time. A solid arrow represents an **activity**, which absorbs time and incurs cost. A dotted arrow is a **dummy** activity. This is a logical connection between two events which does *not* absorb time or money. A critical 'rule' of this notation is that an event cannot occur until all the activities leading into it are complete. Similarly, an activity cannot start until its predecessor event has occurred. (Readers may recognize these conventions as belonging to the PERT project planning and control technique. PERT is examined in Chapter 6.)

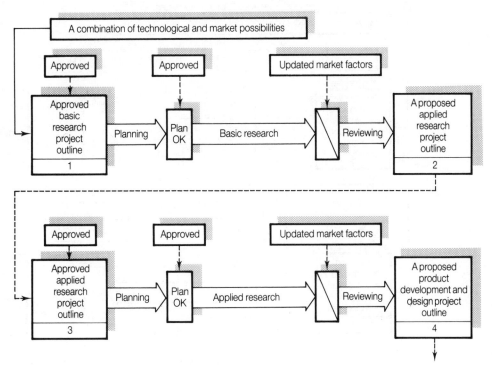

Figure 3.4   Basic and applied research.
This is a more detailed version of the research aspects of Figure 3.3, which recognizes the
management framework of the research organization. It now contains project planning and
results-review activities and shows the need for management approval at important milestones.
Note, too, that the reviews take the updated market situation into account, and that project plans
are based on an approved project outline.

In Figure 3.4, the recognition (an event) of an interesting set of technological and
market possibilities is developed into a proposed basic research **project outline**. If
this proposal is accepted (perhaps after some modifications) it becomes an approved
basic research project outline at event 1 in the figure. The occurrence of this event
allows the project planning activity to start. This terminates when a proposed **project
plan** becomes an approved project plan at the next event, labelled 'Plan OK' in the
figure. The basic research project is then launched, and completion of this activity is at
the following event. While all this has been in progress, it is quite likely that the market
situation has changed in some way. The next activity, therefore, is to review the
results of the basic research project in the light of the updated market factors. This
leads, at event 2, to a proposed applied research project outline.

The sequence of events and activities for the applied research follows much the
same pattern as for basic research. Thus, in Figure 3.4, the proposal of event 2
becomes the approved applied research project outline of event 3 which leads,
through project planning and project work, to a proposed product development and
design project outline at event 4.

This same pattern is largely reproduced in Figure 3.5, which deals with the product
development and design project.

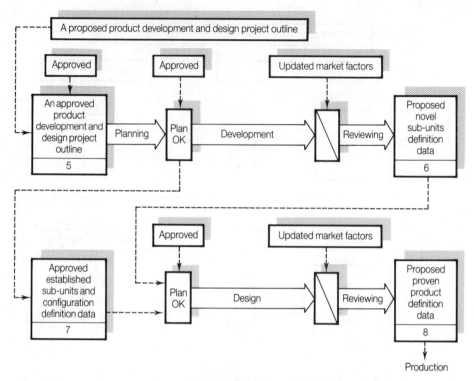

Figure 3.5   **Product development and design.**

The management framework introduced in Figure 3.4 also appears in this figure, which is a more detailed version of the product development and design aspects of Figure 3.3. Note that the plan arising from event 5 (which is derived from an applied research project) is in two parts. The first relates to any novel sub-units, and it defines the development sub-project. The second part becomes event 7, which is concerned with the established sub-units and product configuration definition data.

Event 5 is an approved product development and design project outline which leads to an approved project plan. Here, though, the plan is in two parts. The first relates to any novel sub-units specified in the applied research project, and it defines the development sub-project. The second part, at event 7, is concerned with the established sub-units and product configuration definition data. The development sub-project leads to the proposed novel sub-units definition data at event 6. This data is combined with that at event 7 to obtain an updated and approved plan for the design sub-project. The output of this project is reviewed in the light of the market factors applying at that time to yield the proposed proven product definition data. This data is subject to a further approval stage before being used, in production, as instructions defining the product manufacturing process.

Figures 3.4 and 3.5 are distinguished from their parent illustration (Figure 3.3) by the inclusion of project outlines, the planning and **review procedures**, and the need to obtain the approval of higher management at critical stages. As noted earlier, the purpose of this management framework is to obtain the best possible value from the resources (money, time and people) invested in the innovation work.

A project *outline* is a relatively brief document which seeks to justify the project in commercial terms. It describes its objectives (technical and commercial) and gives a rough estimate of the time and cost of achieving these objectives. A project *plan* is a detailed description of the objectives of the project and the way in which it is intended to achieve them. It evaluates the type and amount of all the required resources, and indicates when these are needed during the project. More accurate estimates of the total required time and cost are also given. They may differ significantly from those made at the outline stage. A project plan must also be approved before the project that it defines is started. When this occurs, the project plan becomes a **control document** against which project progress is subsequently measured. Thus, a project is periodically reviewed while in progress. These intermediate reviews are not shown in Figures 3.4 and 3.5. They are concerned, principally, with progress towards technical objectives, but the commercial context of a project may also be reviewed if circumstances merit it.

The purpose of the two-stage approach (outline and plan) to project definition is to minimize abortive project planning work. Project planning is a critical but relatively effort-hungry activity. In contrast, a project outline can be produced relatively quickly and cheaply. Project planning effort is not then wasted on project proposals which are rejected at the outline stage.

A project can fail while in progress either because a technical objective proves unattainable (within acceptable time and cost extensions) or because of some dramatic change in its commercial context. Basic research projects most frequently fail on technical grounds.

At the notional end of a project, its results are always reviewed in the context of the market situation as it applies at that time. This review is critical because a market environment is never static. In the extreme case, the market situation may have so changed that the whole project is invalidated and must be abandoned. More usually, however, only minor corrections are needed and these are accommodated in some minor rework during the review period.

The level of management involvement and the nature of the documentation required in the outlines, plans and reviews depends on the type of project. In a given industry, a typical product development and design project is rarely less than ten times more costly than the typical basic research project. Cost ratios of one hundred to one are not unknown. Inevitably, therefore, it is the product development and design projects that receive more attention from top management. Happily, such projects are also more susceptible to detailed project planning and control. Applied research projects lie somewhere between these two extremes.

Subject to the caveat entered under the next heading, Figures 3.4 and 3.5 are more representative of industrial reality than the earlier Figure 3.3. Even so, these two figures are still simplifications in that they omit the unplanned **iteration loops** which do occur within projects. Even less desirable loops can occur between projects.

Recognition of the four phases

The four distinct activities denoted by the terms basic research, applied research, development and design can be detected in all industrial technological innovation work. However, it is a sad fact that the four phases are not always adequately distinguished in practice. Too often, both varieties of research are lumped together and no distinction is made between development and design. The four phases are sufficiently different to justify distinctive treatment, and failure to recognize this situation is a serious weakness. This point is expanded in Section 3.2.7, which considers further distinguishing features of the four phases.

The project sequence

Figures 3.4 and 3.5 illustrate the case of a speculative profit opportunity being successfully pursued through basic research, applied research, and product development and design. It culminates in proven new product 'how-to-make' data, which is passed to the production function. A complete traverse of this path is a rare event in practice. One reason for this lies in the inherent uncertainties of research. On average, only about one in five basic research projects succeeds to the extent of triggering at least one applied research project. Only about half of those projects trigger at least one product development and design project. The other reason is more subtle. Superficially, it appears that the great majority of new and enhanced products are launched by businesses without any prior basic research and, very often, without any applied research either. Indeed, many small and medium-sized businesses regard research as an unaffordable and, fortunately, unnecessary luxury. This position is tenable so long as the business can survive and prosper with products that do not incorporate leading-edge technology. The majority of businesses are in this happy position. They do not need to worry that only one-tenth of their research costs achieves positive results. They are concerned only with product development and design. But they are still relying on research which someone else has paid for in the past, because all technology starts in a research laboratory. This observation is not in any way a criticism of those businesses which can survive and prosper without their own research activities. In fact, quite the reverse. There is no business merit in taking unnecessary risks.

This discourse illuminates three important points:

(1) It is not necessary for the basic research, applied research, product development and design sequence to be traversed inside the same business. It is getting the information from these projects that matters. Provided that there are people available in the business who can evaluate and exploit this information then the work can be done outside the business. This opens up the possibility of cost-sharing among interested parties. This is commonly done in those areas where research is very expensive and the parties can adequately protect their commercial interests.

(2) It is not always necessary to go through the whole sequence. Provided that the information from a predecessor project is available, the sequence can be started at the successor project.

(3) Both basic research and applied research can, potentially, trigger more than one successor project.

Proving the novel sub-units

Both Figure 3.3 and Figure 3.5 illustrate sequential positioning of development and design. This is preferred so as to avoid (so far as possible) designing with non-proven sub-units. There are situations where the practice of 'fully' proving the novel sub-units is not followed, either by choice or because it is not feasible to do so.

In some cases, where time is at a premium, design is advanced to overlap with development in the belief that this action alone will reduce the overall project time. There is no reason why this should be so, because the amount of work to be done is not changed. However, when development and design are mingled in this way the need to test and prove the novel sub-units is less obvious and this critical requirement may not receive the attention it deserves. This amounts to relaxing the development dependency constraint on the start of the design phase. The extent to which this can be done without seriously compromising the future varies from case to case. There are no general rules and experience is the best guide. If the gamble comes off, overall project time is reduced. But there is no escaping harsh reality. Businesses which do not distinguish between development and design are exposed to disasters stemming from designing with, and using, non-proven sub-units.

Unfortunately, it is not always feasible to carry out exhaustive testing of the novel sub-units. This is generally the case with complex software sub-units, since there is rarely enough time to do more than explore the most obvious subset of all possible tests. A similar difficulty arises with only moderately complex, by current standards, integrated circuit chips.

3.2.7 More distinctions

It was noted earlier that basic research, applied research, and product development and design are sufficiently different to justify distinctive treatment. The essentially different nature of the activities has already been described, but there are some other features which illustrate contrasts in the management problems presented by these activities. These are compared in Figure 3.6.

Clarity of objectives

The highly speculative nature of basic research is generally reflected in a relatively fuzzy, non-numeric and flexible expression of project objectives. The situation is much improved in applied research, because of the clarified technical position and (hopefully) better market insight. A prerequisite for successful product development and design is near total clarity and rigidity of the technical objectives. Given competent applied research and clear perception of the market, this ideal is readily achievable.

The relative clarity of technical objectives largely sets the feasible levels of project planning and control. Product development and design projects represent major resource commitments. The great majority of these projects must succeed if the business is to survive. At this end of the spectrum, therefore, detailed and meticulous planning followed by tight project control is both possible and essential. This approach is hardly applicable to basic research where a 'broad-brush' approach to planning followed by relatively relaxed control is more productive. The optimum approach for applied research lies between these extremes, but techniques closer to those appropriate to product development and design are usually, and properly, employed.

	Basic research	Applied research	Product development and design
Clarity of objectives	Low	Medium	High
Probability of technical success	About twenty per cent	About fifty per cent	About ninety-five per cent
Relative costs	1	5 to 20	10 to 100
Optimum staffing strategies	Thinly spread over all topics of interest	Concentration	Concentration

Figure 3.6   **Other distinguishing features.**
The discussion so far in this section has demonstrated the essentially different natures of the basic research, applied research, and product development and design activities. This figure shows some other distinctive features of the activities. It emphasizes an earlier point regarding the need to manage (plan, organize, control and lead) the activities rather differently.

Probability of technical success

The percentage figures quoted in Figure 3.6 are generally accepted as about right in well-managed organizations. The overall success rate for attempts to traverse the whole technical innovation sequence (about ten per cent) is dominated by the low basic research figure. This figure has not substantially varied, in either direction, since it was first assessed in the mid 1950s.

Relative costs

There are wide variations in relative costs, as is suggested by the ranges quoted in Figure 3.6. As a rule, project costs are dominated by people costs and team sizes tend to increase sharply as the profit opportunity becomes more assured.

Optimum staffing strategies

The different optimum staffing strategies for basic research, applied research, and product development and design are a consequence of the other distinguishing factors, rather than being intrinsic factors in their own right.

Basic research is more likely to fail than succeed. The chances of making a major breakthrough are small, and not much increased by concentrating large forces on any one of the large number of only vaguely visible opportunities. The correct staffing strategy is, therefore, to devote limited effort to all the more promising possibilities. Just enough, say, to keep abreast of the field and to monitor the competition. Some lateral thinking is required in identifying the opportunities (or threats). For example, a basic research programme on adhesives is a wise precaution for a business which manufactures sewing machines. If an acceptable method of gluing cloth together were to emerge from somewhere then sewing machine sales could go into sharp decline. Forewarning of this trauma should be welcome, and might even allow the new technology to be exploited to minimize the shock.

Technical objectives, and the manner in which they can be achieved, are each more clear in applied research. The chances of technical success are correspondingly improved. Market visibility is also better, enabling tentative time-scales to product launch to be stated and early projections on cost and price to be considered. So reasonable plans can be formulated, progress monitored and control exercised. Taken together, these factors justify the assignment of a more substantial effort and other resources.

When the development and design stage is reached both the technical and the commercial objectives can be seen with great clarity. Optimum ways of achieving them should also be known. Precise planning is both feasible and mandatory to allow the requisite tight control of the major resources which will be committed. The objective must be to get to the market (dig up the treasure) as soon as possible, otherwise competitors may get there first and take the cream.

Concentration of forces is the key in product development and design. As much effort as is available should be invested, consistent with not falling foul of the law of diminishing returns, to achieve this aim. A simple example, based on some fascinating arithmetic, will make this more clear.

Suppose that there are two development and design projects, project A and project B, which must be completed as soon as possible. The projects are similar in that each requires the same sort of skills. It is estimated that project A needs 24 engineer-months of effort to complete, whereas project B needs 36 engineer-months. There are only four suitably qualified engineers available.

Broadly speaking, there are just two possible staffing strategies, dispersion or concentration. In the first case, dispersion, the two projects are launched simultaneously with, say, two engineers assigned to each project. If everything goes as planned project A will be completed in 12 months and project B in 18 months, because 24/2 = 12 and 36/2 = 18. Alternatively, concentration could be used. The four engineers are initially assigned to project A, say, which should be completed in 6 months. The team of four is then switched to project B. This should then be completed in a further 9 months, making up 15 months in all. The concentrated, 'serial', staffing strategy has paid-off handsomely. (Note that the overall time cannot be less than 15 months, because 60/4 = 15. Note, too, that project B could be completed in 15 months when both projects are launched simultaneously, by assigning all four engineers to do its last 12 engineer-months of work.)

A number of assumptions are made in the example. The most important is that project completion time varies as the direct inverse of the number of people assigned to it (twice the people yields half the time, and so on). For large and small team numbers this assumption fails. But there is an approximately linear regime for mid-range numbers. This minor criticism does not invalidate the basic message which, incidentally, is applicable in all fields of human endeavour. (The complex relationship between project completion time and team size is discussed in Chapter 6.)

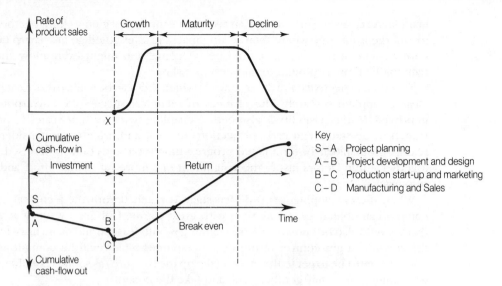

***Figure 3.7* The product sales life cycle and cash flow.**

This key figure illustrates how a new product creation project can be regarded as an investment/return project, by treating it as an isolated activity within the business. Project cash initially flows out of the business in the investment phase, before starting to flow into the business as profitable product sales begin in the return phase. The concept is important because, unless most new products can more than pay for their own creation costs (at point C), the business must ultimately fail.

3.3 Innovation is investment

The purpose of every business cost is to generate, directly or indirectly, an income greater than the cost. Business survival and prosperity depend on total income being sufficiently greater than total cost over some reasonable period of time. Expenditure on basic research, applied research, and product development and design is no exception to this rule. Innovation costs are an investment in the future which, hopefully, will be returned many times over. But technical innovation is only one part of a larger innovation process. It is instructive to consider this *new product creation process* as an investment/return situation. This perspective illuminates the critical relationships between the key business functions of marketing, technical, production and sales.

Expenditure on basic and applied research is not (as a rule) specifically identified with a particular product. Here, therefore, the new product creation process is assumed to start when an approved product development and design project outline is available. This corresponds to event 5 in Figure 3.5. Figure 3.7 then illustrates important milestones on the route from that point of product 'conception', through gestation, and subsequent birth, life and death. The figure is in two parts, the **sales life cycle** and the associated cumulative **cash-flow**.

3.3.1   The sales life cycle

The product sales life cycle concept was introduced in Chapter 2 at Section 2.2.5. In that chapter, the potent influence of product technologies on the shape and duration of product life cycles is examined in detail. Some other important factors are emphasized in the following commentary.

It is convenient to ignore, temporarily, the product gestation period and move forward to where the product is actually born. This is the point labelled X in Figure 3.7. It is the time when product units first emerge from the manufacturing operation and become available for sale. The so-called sales life cycle is the (idealized) diagram in the upper part of the figure. It describes the variation in the rate of product sales with time. This pattern of **growth**, **maturity** and **decline** applies to the majority of products. However, some do seem to defy this 'natural' law. A well-known chocolate bar is one classic non-conformer and the ordinary wooden pencil is another. It may be, of course, that such products are still in an extended maturity phase. There are wide product-type dependent variations in the shape and duration of life cycle curves. For example, the sales life of a civil airliner may extend over thirty years, whereas that of a desktop computer might be no more than one year. Note that it is the *rate* of product sales which is plotted in the diagram. It might be measured, say, in the number of product units sold per week or per month. The *total* number of product units sold in a given period is obtained by integrating the rate curve over that period.

Growth

The rate of sales increases only slowly at the start of the growth phase due (usually) to a combination of limited manufacturing volume, customer caution and, perhaps, distribution limitations. However, assuming a good product which is well promoted, the sales rate then accelerates as customer demand develops. The growth slows down towards the end of the phase. This may be because of approaching satisfaction of the early pent-up demand in the target market. Alternatively, the advent of competitive products which absorb some share of the demand can have the same effect. It is quite normal for both factors to be operating at the same time.

Maturity

The growth phase then shades into the fairly stable maturity phase where the total rate of sales is virtually constant for a relatively long period. Typically, in this phase, the total demand is shared by a number of competing businesses offering similar products. These market shares are not necessarily equal and are subject to change as the competitors vie with each other using pricing, promotion and distribution weapons. The diagram in Figure 3.7 assumes that the business concerned retains a constant market share during the maturity phase.

Decline

Eventually, the sales rate starts to decrease. It then falls away more rapidly to a low value, where it may pause for a while before becoming zero. This phase can be triggered by a number of factors acting alone or in combination. Some products (hula-hoops, for example) just go out of fashion. The need for others simply disappears, as may yet happen to nuclear weapons. Commonly, however, the demand remains but current products are rendered functionally obsolete and/or too costly by a major technological innovation. Thus, the internal combustion engine replaced the horse, bow and arrow businesses succumbed to rifle makers, and slide-rules have given way to calculators. Note that the business may choose to withdraw from the market before the rate of sales reaches 'natural' zero.

3.3.2 The cumulative cash-flow

The financial implications of the product creation and sales process are illustrated in the lower half of Figure 3.7. This is the time variation of the *cumulative* cash-flow out of and into the business arising solely from the particular product under consideration. Conventionally, cash-flow *out* (cost) is shown as *negative* and cash-flow *in* (income) is shown as *positive*.

The point S in the figure corresponds to event 5 in Figure 3.5. This is the start of the development and design project planning activity by the technical function. The cumulative cash-flow is taken to be zero at this point. This means that prior costs which could be assigned to the specific product are ignored. These include any relevant basic and/or applied research costs. (Ignoring such costs is just a convenient artifice to simplify matters a little. They are commonly ignored in practice but it is not essential to do so.)

As the work of the planning team proceeds, cash flows out of the business because of the costs of their employment (salaries and so on), and because of the operating cost of the facilities that they need. The time and money consumed in planning are comparatively small, and an approved project plan exists at point A in the figure. It signals the start of the product development and design project. This also consumes time and money, not only because of its people-related costs but also because various external purchases are made. The project terminates at point B (event 8 in Figure 3.5) with the delivery of proven product definition data to the production function.

Cash continues to flow out of the business in the period between points B and C in the figure. This arises from two parallel activities. First, production must prepare to make the product in the requisite quantities. This 'start-up' work involves planning, machine preparation, and the purchase of components and other piece-parts for the initial manufacturing run. Second, while all that is going on, the marketing function prepares the market to expect and accept the product by means of advertising and other promotional activities. In fact, marketing may have started product promotion during the development and design project. But it is generally considered unethical to encourage orders for products before a firm delivery date can be honestly quoted. Not all businesses conform to this practice. At point C, which corresponds to time X on the sales life cycle diagram, the first product units emerge from the manufacturing operation and selling starts.

Manufacturing and sales continues in the period bounded by points C and D. The manufacturing operation continues to incur costs during this period – arising from the people that it assigns to making the products, the use of the facilities that they need, and the external purchase of product components and piece-parts. Other costs, such as those due to marketing, selling and product distribution, also arise during this period. Fortunately, however, cash now also starts to flow into the business from product sales.

Important assumptions

The shape of the cash-flow curve in Figure 3.7 during the manufacturing and sales period assumes that:

- The sale price of a product unit is *greater than* the sum of the cost of manufacturing it and of its share of the other costs (marketing, selling, distribution and so on).

- Products are sold as they are made. In other words, products are not stored ('stocked') before sale.

- All sales are made on a cash basis, rather than on credit.

Under these circumstances each product sale generates a net cash-flow *into* the business as it is sold. In other words, the *net incremental* cash-flow becomes positive at point C.

Only the first of the three assumptions is critical. If this assumption is not satisfied, manufacturing and selling the product is merely encouraging closure of the business since the incremental cash-flow remains negative. This invariably upsets top management who, generously, will then share their grief with those responsible for it. Generally, the other two assumptions do not apply in practice. The effect of product stocking, and of credit sales, is to shift the positive-going segment of the cumulative cash-flow curve forward by the appropriate time. Point C then occurs later than point X. The delay in positive cash-flow is wholly undesirable but it has to be tolerated.

Provided that price and cost levels remain constant over the period (which is unlikely), the shape of the positive-going segment of the cumulative cash-flow curve follows that of the total sales curve. This is obtained by integrating the rate of sales curve.

Evaluating the cash-flow performance

In Figure 3.7, the cumulative cash-flow becomes increasingly negative until point C, marking the start of product sales, is reached. The period from S to C is the *investment* phase of the product creation and sales process. In this period, the business is spending money in the hope of getting it back later several times over. The maximum investment is at point C, where the cumulative cash-flow is most negative.

The period bounded by points C and D is the *return* period. Here, the incremental cash-flow becomes positive as (net) cash flows into the business, and the cumulative cash-flow curve becomes positive-going. The point where it crosses the horizontal (zero cumulative cash-flow) axis is labelled **break even** in the figure. At this point, the investment has been 'recovered'. In other words, the product has paid for its own gestation costs. Beyond this point the cumulative cash-flow continues to increase until, at point D, the product dies. The product makes a contribution to the financial health of the business while the cumulative cash-flow is positive. It is tempting, but wrong, to call this positive cumulative cash-flow 'profit'. Profit is an accountancy concept and it is not the same as positive cash-flow, as is discussed in Chapter 1.

Questions now arise as to whether or not the product venture has proved to be a good investment:

- Was it worth spending that money to get that return?

- Or could the same investment have yielded a better return if spent in some other way?

Superficially, the investment does seem to be a good one. The positive cumulative cash-flow at point D is about twice the maximum investment at point C. So, over the sales life cycle, the product has earned about three times the sum invested in it. That is, it has paid back the investment and provided a further two hundred per cent return! But appearances may deceive. In fact, there is not enough information in Figure 3.7 to determine whether the example product is a good investment or not. No information is given about the time-scales of the various cash-flow segments and, without this, a proper evaluation of the cash-flow cannot be made. For example, if the cash-flow of Figure 3.7 absorbed just one year (from point S to point D) then its investment performance borders on miraculous. On the other hand, the same result achieved over twenty years is less exciting.

A business usually has more options for investment than resources to invest. Evaluating the relative merits of *forecast* cash-flows then becomes an important part of the broad topic of project evaluation and choice. It is covered in Chapter 11.

A warning

It is emphasized that the diagrams of Figure 3.7 are illustrations only. The shapes, relative amplitudes and time-scales shown are a compromise between the need to show specific features and the limitations of drawing size. In practice, the corresponding diagrams conform to these overall patterns but there are wide variations in relative amplitudes and timings.

3.4   Secondary tasks

A number of tasks are assigned to the technical function which are only marginally related to its main work of product innovation. This occurs because the function is the focus of technical expertise in a business. There are a substantial number of such secondary tasks, which tend to distract attention from the primary tasks. Their management demands frequent review of priorities, since the resources needed will usually be committed elsewhere. However, they do form part of the overall role of the technical function. The following list identifies the main secondary tasks, but it is not exhaustive:

- analysis of non-company products
- licences and patents
- assistance to other functions
- preparation of project proposals
- project evaluation and choice
- wider commercial objectives
- access to clubs.

These tasks are now considered in turn.

3.4.1   Analysis of non-company products

The need to investigate the products of other companies can arise for a number of reasons:

(1) *As part of product innovation*   The early technical analysis of competing products is always a wise precaution in creating new or enhanced products. There is no monopoly on good ideas. A hallmark of good engineers is a willingness to adapt other people's ideas to their own purposes. However, rejection of such ideas for 'not invented here' reasons is (sadly) quite common, although the motive is often expressed in the guise of more rational thinking.

(2) *For other business functions*   Work of this nature may also be undertaken for, say, marketing colleagues as a contribution to their collection of **competitive intelligence**.

(3) *As part of 'supplier-rating'*   No business makes all the sub-units required to manufacture its products. Businesses normally maintain a list of **'approved' suppliers** of those items which they habitually purchase externally. Potential suppliers are evaluated against a range of criteria and only survivors of this supplier-rating process receive approval. The topic is outside the scope of this chapter, but technical evaluation of the offered items is a necessary part of the process. (Supplier-rating is examined, briefly, in Chapter 10.)

(4) *As part of 'buy-or-make' decisions*   The need for a **buy-or-make** decision arises when a required sub-unit can be purchased or, alternatively, can be designed and made inside the business. A technical evaluation of the alternatives is one necessary prerequisite of the decision.

3.4.2   Licences and patents

Technical evaluation, on a larger scale, is often required when the parent business is offered a **licence** by another business. Typically, this is an agreement allowing the parent business to manufacture and sell (or perhaps just sell) a product range which is proprietary to the other business. Another example is the right to use a proprietary manufacturing process – an integrated circuit process, say. The **licensor** business offering the licence is attracted by exploitation of its 'know-how' in markets which might be otherwise difficult for it to penetrate. The potential **licensee** benefits from a quick and economical entry into new areas.

Licence negotiations may also involve some sort of **patent** situation but the topic of patents is a minefield outside the present scope. Technical staff, particularly the researchers, are likely to become embroiled in the preparation of patents. The process is generally conducted by patent agents. They have special skills in establishing the likely validity of the possible patent, and in the arcane language of writing it. The defence or attack of a patent in a court of law can be a lengthy and expensive exercise with no certainty of a satisfactory outcome (except for the legal profession). In recognition of this, many large companies regard their collection of patents as an investment portfolio for judicious 'rights-to' swapping with their competitors. Occasionally, however, a case of alleged patent infringement does involve litigation. A member of the technical function might be summoned as an 'expert witness' for the defence or prosecution, as the case may be. Comparative technical evaluation of the competing claims will be required.

3.4.3   Assistance to other functions

A frequent demand is for assistance by the marketing, sales and production functions in relation to 'own' products. It usually involves the technical staff concerned with product development and design. Activities of this nature may be termed 'technical assistance to sales' (TAS), or 'technical assistance to manufacturing' (TAM).

Technical assistance to sales

Generally, this takes one of two forms. In the first, applying especially to complex products, the technical staff are responsible for explaining (selling) the technology of the product, or product proposal, to the target customer. The work involved can be very demanding, as the customers are likely to field their own technical experts. In these situations the technical staff involved behave as part of the marketing team. Generally, it is better for marketing to call up these people as required, rather than to employ a technical team of their own. In this way they are able to present the customer with knowledgeable enthusiasts who have been involved in creating the item offered for sale. The alternative arrangement, that of marketing employing **sales engineers**, works well with relatively straightforward standard products. The method may be extended to include an applications service for customers, aimed at showing them how best to use such products. Such a mechanism can be a potent aid to sales, but it becomes less effective as product complexity increases.

The other manifestation of TAS needs to treated with caution by technical management. Some less responsible sales staff, motivated solely by the desire for a signed order form (and the rewards that flow from it), habitually offer product modifications and/or demonstrations to potential customers. Salespeople who fill their order book with one-off 'specials' are just as damaging, to others, as those who consistently miss their sales targets. For the technical function the irresponsible salesperson is a potential time-waster and problem-maker. Rarely do the rewards justify the problems that they generate. Problems of this sort emphasize the need for good relationships across functional boundaries.

Technical assistance to manufacturing

Unfortunately, one aspect of TAM is a task which, too often, comes the way of the development and design staff. This problem arises in the communication of product (or product sub-unit) data from the design or development phase into the manufacturing phase. In principle, the 'how-to-make' information passed over at this stage is proven, and compatible with the capabilities of the manufacturing operation. In some cases this is simply not possible, and in others it just does not happen. A reasonably clear distinction can be drawn between the cases of complex 'one-off system' products, and those targeted at a volume market.

In the first case, such as that of an air-traffic control system, the final configuration must, perforce, be assembled on the manufacturing shop-floor. Design prototypes of complex one-off products, even if time allowed, are usually unaffordable luxuries. Thus, even if the sub-units have been exhaustively tested, the final stage of design proving with technical personnel is a special sort of manufacturing operation. The term **commissioning** is normally used to describe this (hopefully) final stage of the complex product gestation process. All this is normal and acceptable in that sort of business. For the sub-units, provided that they are defined at a sufficiently low level, the **proven compatible data theory** *should* work.

This same optimism applies to the case of less complex volume products. That it so often proves unfounded is a measure of human frailty. The technical staff and the manufacturing staff can be expected to have different perspectives on incidents of this sort. Manufacturing will claim that they have been asked to make the unmakable which, by virtue of their dedication and superhuman skills, they have still managed to do. Only to prove that it does not work. The technical people, faced with this situation, will take refuge in citing the well-known inability of manufacturing to make even clothes-pegs to specification. A pointless, and perhaps acrimonious, discussion is then virtually assured. A similar situation is familiar to all involved in the creation of real-time computer-based systems. Here, the hardware and the software are intimately linked in a time-sensitive relationship. Both elements must be right at the same time if the system is to work. Obscure faults are invariably diagnosed as due to software failings by the hardware team. In their diagnosis, the software engineers express similar faith in the hardware. In reality, both parties are probably at fault for not having communicated properly.

While there is no known way of ensuring complete freedom from these problems, they can be minimized quite easily. The approach recognizes that, although hard boundaries between the product creation phases are invaluable management aids, hard boundaries between the people responsible for them are not. In the case of the dissent between design and manufacturing, for example, the problem could have been avoided by involving some manufacturing people in the design project. Similarly, temporary secondment of technical staff to manufacturing smooths the hand-over of the manufacturing data.

There is, in fact, some powerful psychology at work here. Involvement usually brings with it a personal commitment. Team involvement leads to the formation of friendships. It is harder to quarrel with friends, especially about something which incorporates a common effort. This happy position can be reinforced by the design team making a conscious effort to build some ideas from their manufacturing colleagues into the product, even if they believe (rightly or wrongly) that this might detract from it a little. Better a less than perfect product that works than no product at all. Note that selling, by all parties to all other parties, is an essential part of this human interaction. The most successful way of selling ideas demands suppression of some ego factors by the seller. It occurs when an idea originally proposed by one individual is played back to its originator by another. Restraint and enthusiasm will result in a successful sale.

A partial solution along the same lines can be used in the real-time computer-based system situation. The hardware team should contain a software engineer with special responsibility for the software–hardware interface. The software team should be similarly equipped. Obscure faults at this interface are then less frequent and, when they occur, are perceived as a common problem.

3.4.4 Preparation of project proposals

The responsibility for the finishing touches to significant project proposals, and their presentation to potential sponsors for approval, normally rests at the more senior levels. The early stages of proposal preparation, however, are often delegated to the lower levels.

Project proposals may be classified in many ways. Classification by sponsor (customer) is considered here, because different types of sponsor require different proposal formats. Basically, there are only two types of sponsor: those inside the business and external agencies. In the first case, a proposal is a plan to spend money belonging to the parent business. This type of money is usually called PV, for **private venture**. It is a 'charge' against profit. In other words, if it is not spent the business profit will be correspondingly larger. In the second case, a proposal is a plan to spend money belonging to an external agency.

Sources of project funds

Project funds may be provided by a number of different types of sponsor, or customer:

- **Central or corporate PV**   This is charged against profit at the total business level. It is usually reserved for the more speculative 'blue-sky' basic research, but it may support applied research.

- **Own divisional PV**   Here, costs are charged against the profit of the trading division 'owning' the technical team assigned to the project. It is commonly used for applied research, and development and design.

- **Other divisional PV**   This is a charge against the profit of some other trading division in the business. It, too, is commonly used for applied research, and development and design.

- **Contract funding** or **contract development (CD)**   This term is used to describe funding by an external agency. Support for basic research, applied research, and product development and design is available from such sponsors. The 'contract development' terminology is used without regard to the nature of the project work. That is, the term is used in connection with research, and with development and design projects.

- **Joint funding**   This may refer to some mixture of the different types of PV funding or, more commonly, to a mixture of PV and CD funding. In Europe, a joint venture between several different companies and, perhaps, the European Commission is an example. This cost-sharing approach is relatively common in expensive high technology areas. Knowledge-based computer systems and aerospace are examples.

It might be expected that the requirements set for profit-consuming PV proposals would be the more demanding. In fact, this prize invariably goes to government and similar agencies. This may reflect a triumph of bureaucracy over common sense but, in fairness, there is a genuine requirement to take every care in spending taxpayers' money. In contrast, the severity of project progress monitoring after approval is commonly the other way round.

Note that PV money is rarely approved for longer than one (financial) year. One rather odd consequence of this is the astonishingly large number of PV research projects which are planned to last for exactly that time period. There is certainly a message here about the validity of such plans. Of more significance is the need to seek annual re-approval for PV projects planned to last longer than this.

3.4.5 Project evaluation and choice

This fascinating subject presents a constant dilemma, because there are normally more project ideas than resources to prosecute them. The fundamental aim of this analytical work is always to ensure the best use of these limited resources. The topic, which cannot be covered here, absorbs the whole of Chapter 11. Technical personnel are necessarily involved, as are also members of a wide range of the other business functions.

3.4.6 Wider commercial objectives

The technical function is likely to be party to a range of commercial objectives above and beyond those implicit in the technical innovation work. These can include a direct profit requirement, certainly with respect to external contracts (CD funding) and, sometimes, on PV work also.

Profit requirement

Of course, PV 'profit' merely involves moving money from one pocket in the parent business to another pocket in the same business. However, it provides a useful motivation and is often allowed where the trading divisions are under no obligation to use the services of the in-house technical teams. The teams may be allowed to 'keep' any sums earned in this way to spend in any reasonable way.

   The profit earned on external contracts is not likely to be a significant fraction of the total profit achieved by a manufacturing business, but it may be a critical source of income for the technical function.

Adjunct to marketing

More significant is the technical function role as a marketing tool. An ability to mount impressive demonstrations and exhibit sundry advanced technologies can have a potent influence on prospective customers. The effect may be enhanced by providing all this in a country-house environment, with facilities for the proper entertainment and accommodation of important visitors. The central research laboratories of large companies are often located in this way, and the decision to do so is not entirely altruistic. Prestige also plays its part in this strategy.

3.4.7 Access to clubs

The chance of a basic research team making, unaided, a major technological break-through of commercial significance is vanishingly small. For example, the invention of something as important as the transistor is a very rare event. A fundamental strategy for basic research, therefore, is to maintain a world-wide awareness of research progress in all fields of possible interest. This is done by studying the literature, establishing rapport with relevant university departments and, above all, joining various 'clubs'. These are communities of common interest crossing business and international boundaries and comprising industrial and university researchers in particular fields. The entry qualification is to be making a significant contribution to progress in the field. This is evidenced by the publication of refereed papers in respectable journals, participation in conferences and seminars, and a willingness to cooperate in various ways with other club members. This **openness of basic research** is very necessary for progress, but poses problems of business confidentiality and, hence, for management. Gaining and keeping membership of relevant special interest groups is an additional task, principally for the basic research teams. It is one that they usually tackle with enthusiasm.

3.5 Software innovation

The manufacturing aspect of software product creation is relatively trivial, involving little more than copying magnetic media and printing documentation. In all other respects the software product innovation process mirrors, in terms of what has to be done, that for hardware products. It is tempting to suppose, therefore, that software creation is really no different from hardware creation, except that a different specific technology is involved. But the sad history of a typical large software project is still characterized by:

- overrun of time and cost budgets
- failure to meet specification
- failure to meet 'ready for service' promises
- unreliability in service.

The fact that the development and design of software products is a relatively new occupation undoubtedly contributes to this disturbing scene. But there is a more subtle influence than mere novelty at work. This is a human weakness in coping with a particular form of complexity, coupled with a lack of adequate tools to ease the problem. The major facets of this problem area are now reviewed.

3.5.1 Software complexity

Complexity is easier to recognize than it is to define, but it may be thought of as a measure of the number of possible interactions between the distinct elements making up a system of cooperating elements. This measure grows rapidly as the number of elements increases, even if only the deliberate interactions that contribute usefully to the system purpose are counted. Thus, a highly-connected system soon becomes beyond the detailed comprehension of any one individual. It may then be termed 'complex', and a complete understanding of it can only reside in a group of people. In the software case the elements or sub-units concerned are typically relatively small software modules and data structures. Each of these, of course, may also be divided into smaller sub-units.

This interpretation of complexity does not, in itself, distinguish software systems from other systems. For example, a building, a microprocessor chip and an aeroplane are also complex when measured in this way. But the complexity of a large software system usually has another dimension. In the building, the aeroplane, and in hardware systems generally most of the sub-units are not novel entities. They are well-understood standard parts. This happy circumstance is much less true of the software industry, which has yet to mature in this sense. Achieving this maturity is confounded by three more factors: software flexibility, burgeoning applications and the salient characteristics of some, maybe most, software creators.

3.5.2 Software flexibility

Software is almost infinitely flexible. A software module is simply an algorithm, or recipe, for solving a particular problem. It reflects the thought processes of its creator at the time that it is created. So software approaches the flexibility, in its problem solving potential, of the human mind.

A software module is not inherently unique in the manner in which it is implemented. The same creator, facing the identical problem at different times, may produce a series of satisfactory solutions each in a radically different way. This is the nature of algorithms and recipes, as experience of other forms of cooking will testify. The probability of two individuals producing identical software solutions as the answer to the same problem is small, except in the most trivial cases. This 'non-uniqueness' consequence of flexibility is encouraged by the relative freedom which the software development environment provides for rampant creativity (unless positive steps have been taken to constrain it). For software, the time-lag between concept and reality is tiny in comparison to the corresponding gap in the hardware case. The complexity equivalent of, say, an electronic band-pass filter can be running in software just one hour after the design is complete. At that time the electronic engineer would have just found out that the parts needed for the filter were out of stock.

Flexibility also allows an ever increasing range of new software applications, and there is continuous pressure to enhance existing applications with new features and greater speed. It is often deemed better (that is, more fun) to write new modules rather than modify the old tried and tested ones: 'Understanding the old ones, which are so obviously inefficient, will take as just as long writing new ones.' Standardization takes another knock.

3.5.3 Software people

The opportunities for speedy creativity seem to attract a special breed of people to software innovation. They may lack many basic engineering instincts, such as a reluctance to re-invent the wheel and the ability to see their work in a wider context. Strangely, because they practise a logical trade, they tend to reject the order and discipline which is mandatory for project success; and regard management as a boring and plebeian activity unworthy of their attention. They frequently graduate from an early background in amateur computing and may revert to childish bad habits under stress, or out of boredom. A propensity to develop software at the keyboard rather than at the desk is one symptom. 'Spaghetti' code and poor documentation are others. These hardly matter in a trivial program of 100 statements but spell trouble when incorporated into 100,000+ statements of serious software.

3.5.4 Fuzzy system definition

As if all this was not enough there is an even more serious disease which can fatally infect a software project long before any code is written. This sickness again turns on complexity and flexibility. It is simply that it is extremely difficult to create a complete and unambiguous specification for *any* large system, and the more so for one that incorporates software flexibility. **Requirements definition**, that mandatory first step for success in any development and design project, is discussed elsewhere (in Chapter 8). But there is a tradition of launching into the code-writing stage of a large software project while its specification remains clouded with uncertainties. This demonstrates an optimistic disregard for the mathematics of probabilities. Consequently, the pious hope that lies behind it is normally rewarded with the disaster it so richly deserves.

3.5.5 Software engineering

It may be safely, but sadly, concluded that software creation does differ in a number of critical ways from hardware creation, which itself is no easy task. The 'software crisis' was recognized in the late 1960s, and it has received continuous attention over the intervening years. This effort still continues.

Back in those early days the term **software engineering** was coined to describe a set of then primitive techniques aimed at mitigating the software crisis. Substantial progress, made principally by adapting techniques borrowed from the hardware environment, has been made in this field since those early years. Macro and Buxton (1987) provide a good introduction to the topic which reviews of a variety of software design methods. However, at this time, software engineering remains more of an ambition than a fact. But, interestingly, it is highly probable that recent developments in the field will have an increasingly beneficial influence on the more mature engineering disciplines.

3.6 Concluding summary

The majority of the scientists and engineers employed by a technology-based manufacturing business work in its technical function, usually on some facet of technological innovation. This is the focus of the chapter. It is commonly (and confusingly) termed 'research and development' or just R&D.

- A relatively distinctive view of industrial technological innovation is introduced which permeates the rest of the book.
- It divides the process into four phases, termed basic research, applied research, product development and product design.

The subsequent discussion aims to build a deeper understanding of the nature of these four primary tasks. It shows that they are sufficiently different to require different management treatments.

Technological innovation is an investment in the future of the business which conducts it. This view provides further insight into the role of the technical function in relation to the other critical business functions. It is developed by analysing the whole product creation process from conception to death.

The technical function is the centre of technical expertise in the business and, because of this, a range of secondary tasks are assigned to it. These form part of the overall technical environment and the most important are identified and discussed.

Finally, software innovation is contrasted with the more mature process of hardware innovation, and differences are detected. Some reasons for the continuing problems with software creation are presented.

REFERENCES

(Note: The limited number of references reflects the relatively distinctive partitioning of the technological innovation process which is introduced in this chapter, and which is then employed throughout the remainder of the text.)

Macro A. and Buxton J. (1987). *The Craft of Software Engineering*. Wokingham: Addison-Wesley

SUGGESTED FURTHER READING

Monds (1984) is another text in the IEE Management of Technology Series providing, in this case, an experienced-based management perspective of electronic development and design. Oakley (1984) covers rather more of the same ground, but penetrates less deeply, in a technology-independent treatment. The Roy & Wield (1986) book comprises a series of review articles which furnish interesting background material of a somewhat philosophical nature. Twiss (1986), while mainly concerned with the strategic issues of technological innovation, still yields useful insights into the more tactical matters discussed in this chapter. Pugh (1991) is a book of a rather different character to all of these. It propounds a powerful approach to product design which recognizes the business ramifications of the whole process, and it is cited here for that reason.

Monds F. (1984). *The Business of Electronic Product Development*. London: Peter Peregrinus (for the IEE)

Oakley M. (1984). *Managing Product Design*. London: Weidenfield & Nicolson

Pugh S. (1991). *Total Design*. Wokingham: Addison-Wesley

Roy R. and Wield D., eds. (1986). *Product Design and Technological Innovation*. Buckingham: Open University Press (reprinted with additions 1991)

Twiss B. C. (1986). *Managing Technological Innovation* 3rd edn. London: Longman

QUESTIONS

3.1   (a) Describe, with the aid of a diagram, how the marketing, technical, production and sales functions of a manufacturing business cooperate to create and sell new products.
(b) What fundamental condition must this process satisfy if the business is to stay in business?

3.2   A system may be defined as *an arrangement of cooperating systems*. Is a product a system? Illustrate your answer with references to one tangible and one intangible product.

3.3   Describe, in the context of a manufacturing business, the technical aspects of product innovation by partitioning that process into four distinct stages.

3.4   (a) Explain your understanding of the terms *basic research*, *applied research*, *product development* and *product design*.
(b) Show how the technical aspects of product innovation may be represented as a simple sequence of these four distinct activities.
(c) How and why is this simple sequence likely to be modified in practice?

3.5   (a) Show how the concept of a product as an assembly of 'smaller' products enables *product development* to be distinguished from *product design*.
(b) Why is this distinction important?

3.6   The term 'research and development' is commonly used to signify the technical aspects of product innovation. It suggests that it is a two-stage process. Why is this view a dangerous over-simplification?

3.7   'Product innovation is investment.' Is it? Why?

3.8   (a) Describe the concept of a *product life cycle* in terms of its associated *cash-flow*.
(b) What features of the cash-flow performance determine the value of the product to the business which creates and sells it?

3.9   Explain, in the context of a manufacturing business, five duties of the technical function which are only marginally related to technological innovation.

3.10   'Creating good software products is no more difficult than creating good hardware products.' Is this a valid statement? Justify your answer.

About People at Work

There's nowt so queer as folk.

Traditional Yorkshire contribution to
behavioural science

4.1	Organization: Why and what	118
4.2	What about the workers?	119
4.3	Organization design: Overview	131
4.4	Organization design: Company level	135
4.5	Speculations on the future	142
4.6	Concluding summary	149

 Repetitions   The material under *The attributes of a good manager* heading in Section 4.2.3 was introduced in Section 1.5. This is an expanded treatment.

The material in Section 4.4.3 provides the rationale underpinning the organizational structures presented, with little explanation, in Section 1.3.11.

The overall objectives of this chapter are to explore why people behave are they do; and to examine, from a design perspective, how they may best be organized in a working environment. Sections 4.1 to 4.4 are recommended background reading for Chapter 5. Objectives by section follow:

4.1 To show that a business is defined by its people, and to consider the nature and purpose of organizations.

4.2 To examine some people characteristics which influence their behaviour and job performance at work.

4.3 To establish the basic principles of organization design.

4.4 To consider, from a design perspective, the major factors which should determine the organization of a company.

4.5 To contemplate the future of industrial organizations and people at work in the light of postulated discontinuous change in the working environment.

4.6 To identify its salient points and summarize its major messages.

4.1 Organization: Why and what

As soon as a business contains more than just a few people some form of task partitioning and work specialization is usually adopted to make more efficient use of resources. The resources in question are normally the people themselves, because specialization eases the development of job knowledge and skills. The success (from the business point-of-view) of the traditional mass manufacturing line is a classic example. However, when task partitioning occurs the need for task coordination also arises and so **management** becomes essential to provide a focus of direction and authority. In large groups of non-equals this is traditionally exercised in a multi-level hierarchical organization structure.

Occasionally, the major concern is the efficient use of non-people resources, such as space, machines and data, with the human element somewhat discounted. But, in a competitive business environment, all the competitors have access to essentially the same non-people resources (although the cost of these resources to different businesses may vary). Such resources, therefore, are largely non-differential. In contrast, no two people are the same. People are **differential resources**. In the long run, it is people and how efficiently they work together that distinguishes one business from another. Empires are built and retained by those businesses which organize people properly.

Organizing may be defined as partitioning people into activity groups, each with a specific sub-task, and providing coordination within and between the groups so as to achieve the whole task. An **organization** is any group, or a set of related groups, established with such a structure and purpose.

Organizations, therefore, are designed to minimize human frailties and to maximize human strengths. They are needed to cope with the constraints that people impose on business objectives, systems and procedures. A study of industrial organizations must start with a study of people at work.

4.2   What about the workers?

This section reviews some of the theories that help to explain human behaviour in work situations. The term 'behavioural science' is used to describe this field.

4.2.1   Theory X and Theory Y

In the bad old days, the management of human resources was too often based on the **Theory X** (McGregor, 1960) assumptions that the average person:

- Dislikes work and will try hard to avoid it.
- Must be manipulated, coerced or threatened to deliver adequate effort.
- Is motivated simply and exclusively by money, and the physical security that it can provide.
- Prefers straightforward repetitive jobs requiring the minimum of thought and involvement.
- Prefers to be directed, has no ambitions beyond shorter hours and better pay, will shun responsibility, and regards working only as an unpleasant, unavoidable, penalty for life outside work.

Students will, no doubt, reject these assumptions as inapplicable in their own case, but they may recognize them in the behaviour of others. They lead to 'donkey-management' based on sticks and carrots. In other words, a mixture of monetary threats and rewards. The approach, based on the human need for physical security, initially worked well. This is largely because treating people in accordance with the Theory X assumptions encourages them to behave in that way. Thus, the pyramids were built and the first Industrial Revolution was launched. But increasing business prosperity, together with developing trade unionism, led to the average person achieving a **comfort threshold** of security. Theory X techniques then started to fail, because the average person wanted more of something. The 'something' was initially misdiagnosed since, sadly, the flawed Theory X view of human nature appeared to explain the failure. Bigger threats and better rewards were employed, and industrial decline set in.

A more enlightened, and certainly more correct, perception of the human animal is now beginning to prevail, called **Theory Y** (McGregor, 1960). This suggests that the average person:

- Is not inherently idle and, in the right working environment, will derive satisfaction from the work and deliver good performance.
- Will exercise self-direction, self-control and self-criticism in jobs relating to objectives to which the person is committed.

- Will have a level of commitment depending on the rewards, which are not just money, for effort and achievement.

- Will accept additional responsibility in the right environment, and may actively seek it.

- Has a greater intellectual capacity than is commonly supposed for organizing, managing and problem solving.

The validity of this insight is now widely accepted and conscious attempts are made to apply it in modern organizations. This is particularly so in relation to non-routine jobs, where some measure of discretion and autonomy is demanded of the job holder. It is less easy to use in routine and repetitive work and has yet to make much impact on this aspect of, say, labour-intensive mass manufacturing.

The quality of individual performance

A prime purpose of any organization is to encourage optimum job performance, both from individual members and from the whole group. The factors involved in the quality of the performance of individuals include:

- Their understanding of the job requirements and the performance standards expected.

- Their ability to deliver those requirements to the required standards.

- The degree to which the necessary tools and facilities are available.

- Their motivation to give their best performance.

It is a management duty to provide an environment with all of these factors. This first involves understanding the total mission of the organization, and then dividing it into clearly defined jobs with achievable but demanding standards. The wise selection of people able to do those jobs is the next step, together with the provision of the necessary facilities. Finally, the selected individuals must be motivated to give of their best. All this is no small challenge, but providing the **motivation** is probably the most demanding aspect.

4.2.2 Motivation theory

Motivation has been defined by Mitchell (1982) as the degree to which an individual wants, and chooses, to engage in certain specified behaviour. The definition poses the question 'why do people behave as they do?' This is a big question which has exercised philosophers, and parents, from the beginning of time. It continues to do so. A broad but rational answer is 'because they are seeking to satisfy some human needs, as a reward for the effort they expend and the results obtained'.

It is not unreasonable to suppose that these needs are shared by the human race. But the response to a given set of circumstances varies widely between different individuals. This suggests that each individual evaluates the common needs differently, with some ranking higher than others in a very personal priority list. Further, since an individual may react differently at different times to the same circumstances, it appears that priority rankings on this personal list of values can vary from time to time.

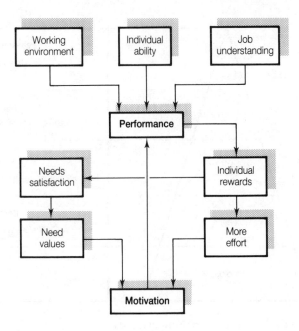

Figure 4.1 **Job factors and the motivation loop.**

Individual job performance depends on the working environment, ability to do the job, understanding what has to be done, understanding how well it has to be done, and motivation. Motivation measures how strongly the individual wants to deliver good job performance. This depends on how well the rewards for doing the job meet the different needs of the individual, and the relative importance of those needs to the individual.

The concept of an individually unique, but time-sensitive, value ranking of a common set of human needs is central to motivation theory.

This view of the role of motivation in job performance is proposed by Porter and Lawler (1968), and others. It is summarized in Figure 4.1. This illustrates a feedback situation. Job performance depends on the working environment, individual ability, understanding of the job and motivation. It leads to rewards, which result in further efforts and the satisfaction of some valued needs, which together contribute to motivation.

Hierarchy of human needs

Maslow (1943) has proposed a **hierarchy of human needs**, where lower level needs must be largely satisfied (to an extent determined by the individual) before satisfaction of the next higher level needs is sought. This needs hierarchy is shown in Figure 4.2.

The lower level physiological, security and social needs are probably shared by all animals but the esteem and self-actualization levels are claimed, perhaps arrogantly, only by man. (Cats might dispute this claim if they thought it mattered.)

Thus, in common with other animals, the first human priorities are the physical needs. These include food and drink, warmth and shelter, sex, and sleep (often in that order). Next comes the security requirement. Here, personal safety, lack of worry, an

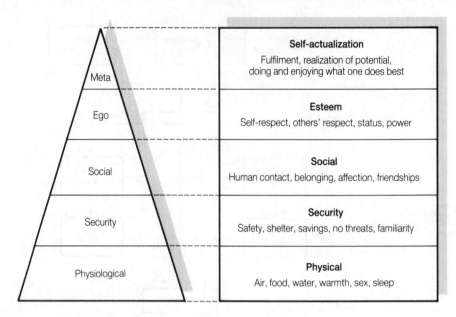

Figure 4.2   **A hierarchy of human needs.**
Maslow argued that human needs can be partitioned into five priority levels, as labelled in the
pyramid structure on the left of the figure. This shape indicates that it becomes progressively
harder to satisfy the higher level needs. Examples of specific needs are on the right. Individuals seek
adequate satisfaction, for them, of lower-level needs before investing any surplus energy in pursuit
of higher-level satisfaction.

orderly life and a preference for familiar things become important. When these needs
have been adequately satisfied, social needs dominate. These include the desire for
human contact and affection, belonging to a family and/or organization (tribal
instincts) and the seeking and acceptance of authority (a dog with no master is an
unhappy dog). Then comes esteem, including self-respect, seeking respect from
others, achievement, recognition and status. Finally, at the highest level, self-
actualization becomes a requirement. This need embraces satisfaction of the wider
ambitions, fulfilment, realization of potential: that warm glow of satisfaction which
arises from completing a difficult job properly, or solving a seemingly intractable
problem.

Motivators and hygiene factors

Maslow's analysis has appealing logic and consistency. It provides a framework
supporting the earlier concept that motivation depends on individual perceptions of
need priorities. On its own, however, it too simplistic to explain the whole range of
human reactions in a particular environment.

   An extension to Maslow's work is provided by Herzberg (1968). His research into
human behaviour (based on a sample of accountants and engineers) suggested that
motivation factors could be classified into two *unidirectional* categories. Herzberg
called these categories **motivators** and **hygiene factors**. The hygiene factors may be
considered as de-motivators. The unidirectional nature of motivators and hygiene
factors is described as follows:

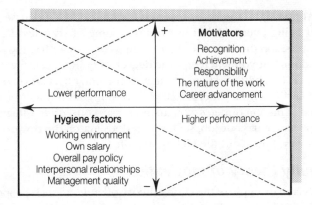

Figure 4.3 **Herzberg's unidirectional twin-factor theory.**
Herzberg recognized that higher-level needs tend to be 'unidirectional'. If an individual sees a motivator factor (top right of the figure) as positive then job performance improves. But job performance does not always worsen if the same factor is seen as negative. Reaction to a hygiene factor (lower left of the figure) is the other way round. If it is seen as negative then job performance worsens. But performance does not always improve if the same factor is seen as positive. The self-esteem need and perceptions of 'natural justice' go some way towards explaining such behaviours.

- *Motivators* If these are perceived as positive then increased job satisfaction and job performance does occur. But if they are perceived as negative, the converse behaviour does not always occur. That is, job satisfaction and performance does not necessarily diminish. Motivators include such elements as achievement, recognition, the challenge of the work, responsibility and career progress.

- *Hygiene factors* If these are perceived as negative then reduced job satisfaction and job performance does occur. But if they are perceived as positive, the converse behaviour does not always occur. That is, job satisfaction and performance do not necessarily increase. Hygiene factors include such elements as overall company remuneration policy, the quality of management, own remuneration package, personal relationships and the physical working conditions.

Figure 4.3 illustrates Herzberg's twin-factor theory. Note that the motivators relate to the two higher levels in Maslow's hierarchy of needs. To some extent, these factors are controllable by individuals because they may choose whether or not to pursue them. But the hygiene factors, which approximate to Maslow's lower level needs, are largely outside individual control. They describe aspects of the overall working environment that the company provides.

A personalized example will make the twin-factor theory more clear. Suppose that you believe your pay is too low in relation to the demands and importance of your job. A progressive de-motivation then occurs, which leads to reduced job satisfaction and job performance. This reaction seems entirely reasonable: the maxim 'pay peanuts, get monkeys' has some merit. But suppose that you believe that your pay is too high (it can happen). In this case, it is unlikely that you will feel increased job satisfaction and your job performance will probably not improve.

At first sight, the latter reaction is rather odd. Of course, you might take the view that being overpaid merely confirms some of your less flattering views about your masters; and then smother your feelings of guilt with smug satisfaction with your own wisdom. But you will feel some degree of guilt, because we all have a innate sense of justice. (A child's first coherent, and correct, observation on the world is usually 'it's not fair!') On the other hand, your odd reaction might be explained by the esteem need. This encourages you to increase your *own* valuation of the demands and importance of your job, such that it does match the reward you get for doing it. And, this way, you avoid the feeling of guilt.

Equity theory of motivation

This is an example of the equity theory of motivation. It proposes that people react to a perceived mismatch in the **natural justice equation**:

$$\text{Effort} + \text{Achievement} = \text{Reward} \tag{4.1}$$

by adjusting their behaviour to create a perceived balance. So, workers who believe themselves to be underpaid may attempt to reduce the perceived inequity by reducing the effort put into the job. Workers who believe that they are overpaid have two ways of achieving perceived equity. They may increase their valuation of the job (which enhances achievement) or reduce their valuation of the reward, or do both of these things. There is considerable scope for self-deception here, but the need for self-esteem is very potent.

Most large modern companies provide good hygiene factors. This recognizes that proper attention to those factors provides a platform on which job satisfaction and performance can be genuinely improved. It also suggests that further organizational developments in such companies should emphasize the motivator factors. There are, of course, numerous examples of situations where the hygiene factors are still badly lacking. Many of the so-called 'vocational' professions suffer such circumstances with varying degrees of serenity, as do many unskilled and semi-skilled employees in large organizations.

Individual characteristics

Motivation theory, which has been outlined in this section, provides some valuable insights into human behaviour. However, it is cast very much in terms of the average individual while, at the same time, denying the existence of such an individual. This ambiguity is answered, in the theory, by the concept of an individually unique, but time-sensitive, value ranking of a common set of human needs. In other words, each individual has a unique set of distinguishing characteristics, a **personality**, which reflects some innate personal set of values. This includes individual perceptions of the value of different rewards in the natural justice equation. Some attributes of personality seem to change only slowly with time, or not at all. Given the right stimulus, other attributes can change dramatically and suddenly. Personality, in the context of work, is the next topic for discussion.

4.2.3 Personality

Everybody exhibits a mixture of good and bad traits in their working environment. The former are aspects of personality which make a positive contribution to the mission of the organization. The latter are those which detract from it. On balance, therefore, some people are contributing to solving the problem whereas others are part of it.

The distinction between positive attributes and negative attributes depends on the nature of the job. Thus a jolly, irrepressible, outgoing personality may be entirely suitable for a trader in the local market but could lose a funeral director a lot of business. Engineers are most likely to be employed in the non-routine, less programmed, situations where there are real opportunities for self-actualization. The three facets of personality reviewed here:

- management attributes
- creativity
- conservatives and revolutionaries

are examined from an engineering perspective, but the messages have a much broader relevance.

 The attributes of a good manager

The material under this heading was introduced in Chapter 1 at Section 1.5 (About management). This is an expanded treatment.

All workers (and students) are managers at some level, even if all that they manage is their own time and effort. So, the management job is an appropriate place to start considering personality. It has four elements:

- **Planning**   Setting objectives and defining ways of achieving them.
- **Organizing**   Mobilizing resources, human and other, to implement the plans.
- **Controlling**   Assessing deviations from plan and taking corrective actions when required.
- **Leading**   Motivating people to deliver their best performance.

Good managers think first in terms of plan end-objectives and intermediate targets, rather than activities – *what* comes before *how*. In other words, they concentrate first on defining proper destinations rather than on how to get there. Problem-solving ability, which demands a high level of creativity, is prerequisite for effective planning (and for the other job factors). They can handle the inner conflict between their fascination with order and the chaos in which creativity can flourish. Commercial acumen sets their priorities. They know that time and quality are often mutually exclusive and can recognize and accept those occasions when time must prevail.

Skilful organizing demands both selling and political abilities because resources are always in short supply and keenly sought after. Communication skills, both verbal and written, are potent weapons in this arena. How a message is transmitted is, perhaps, even more important than the message itself. Good salesmen are genuine enthusiasts for what they are selling, and enthusiasm is infectious.

A good controller has a sharp sense of priorities. No plan ever devised is totally followed in its implementation phase. This should come as no surprise because planning involves predicting the future, and no one really knows what is going to happen. So, while plans try to shape the future, some of their forecasts always fail. But some deviations from plan are less important than others, and these may be ignored to conserve resources. The correct choice of such deviations demands good judgement. When corrective action must be taken, then the relative merits of the range of available options must be evaluated. Options *always* exist. Doing nothing is always an option, and claims that 'there is no alternative' are always wrong. Usually, a manager is presented with the choice between several evils, since solving one problem will normally create another one. Resource limitations are often responsible for this dilemma.

For example, suppose an important project has slipped well behind schedule, and further suppose that an injection of additional effort will (it is believed) recover the situation. The requisite effort is employed in the business, but it is currently committed to another project. The manager's decision on whether or not to switch the effort will be influenced by the relative importance of the two projects and (perhaps) the possibility of any adverse impact on the staff involved. If the effort is switched, a problem is created with the second project. Alternatively, the manager may choose not to switch internal resources, and seeks to solve the problem by bringing in subcontract effort from outside the business. This action may create a budget overspend problem!

All of the preceding management tasks demand intellectual processing capacity of a high order for their successful prosecution. This attribute also enters into the next requirement, that of leadership. But, in this case, something beyond a powerful and disciplined mind is needed.

Leadership qualities, which can be equated with the ability to motivate, are of paramount importance. There is more to this than just operating the mechanics of motivation as discussed, albeit briefly, in Section 4.2.2. Good leaders radiate an indefinable, but instantly recognizable, message which includes confidence, optimism, zest and competence. They have an unforced empathy with their co-workers, not only with those above and below them in the organization but also sideways with colleagues at the same or similar level. Loyalty to their staff, and integrity in dealing with them, are an intrinsic part of this empathy. Another characteristic, stemming from confidence, is the ability to bring order out of chaos. In their tactical (day-to-day) duties, good leaders move coolly from crisis to crisis as the priorities dictate, creating an aura of calm all about them.

All of this amounts to a very demanding job specification which, in summarized form, can be found in the management appointments section of any of the heavier Sunday newspapers. It lacks, perhaps, only the requirement to walk on water to round-off the description of these obviously non-human specimens. Be not dismayed – few managers meet the whole specification, but they are still gainfully employed.

Good managers are motivated principally by Maslow's esteem and self-actualization needs, provided, of course, that the lower levels are adequately satisfied. So they are normally at, or above, their comfort threshold. It is worth noting, however, that comfort needs tend to expand and more than absorb the comfort available, which is an interesting variation of Parkinson's Law. This states that work expands to fill the time and space available. Computer files exhibit a similar tendency.

Other desirable personal attributes for managers include self-starting ability, and mental and physical endurance – because the work is hard and the hours may be long. But good managers do not confuse activity with progress. If any human activity is pursued for long enough there is the danger that the activity becomes its own purpose to the detriment of real achievement.

A further essential is courage. This is often required in communicating both upwards and downwards. On occasions, unwelcome messages must be transmitted upwards and radical, even security-threatening, proposals made. Carriers of bad news are rarely popular. History confirms an alarming assumption that removal of the messenger will also remove the message. In fact, such action merely provides an interesting diversion for those involved in it. The prospect of carrying bad news poses a needs conflict for the messenger manager. On the one hand, self-esteem demands that the perceived duty must be done; on the other, security may be at risk. A wise manager will always assess the chances of winning any particular battle before initiating the fray, and will often choose discretion rather than valour. But there will be occasions when duty must be done. This will be in the certain knowledge that the distinction between a brave act (that is, a success) and a stupid act (that is, a failure) is normally adjudicated after the event.

Equally daunting problems will arise with respect to a manager's own staff. Commonly, the most difficult of these is when an employee must be discharged. This is easier when the employee is at fault but traumatic under other circumstances. Again, an inner conflict is involved since the action is always an attempt to correct a failure of management.

Creativity and the technical function

The technical function within a business is concerned principally with the techno-logical aspects of product innovation. This process has two, somewhat overlapping, elements which involve problem solving. Firstly, there is the application of existing knowledge, experience, reflexes and habits to problems susceptible to such things. Some problems, however, do not yield to this attack but *may* do so to the second, less predictable, approach involving new insights, and original and imaginative concepts.

The creation of new wire-based telecommunications systems using established electronic signal processing techniques is an example in the first category. Such systems have inherent limitations including, for example, low bandwidth, noise, and susceptibility to electromagnetic and human interference. These problems stimu-lated the advent of optical fibre-based systems using laser technology and optical processing. The new product technologies greatly extend the innate performance boundaries of the traditional systems. Radically new concepts were required for this achievement.

Solving both sorts of problem demands creative ability, but that associated with the second type of problem is traditionally accorded higher status, especially by its aspirants and practitioners. The absurdity of this notion is manifest: both forms of creativity are required for progress, just as an aeroplane needs two wings to get off the ground. But it does reflect a set of values under the esteem heading.

Good development and design engineers have much in common with good managers. They share, for example, the same sort of analytical talent, creativity, problem-solving ability and temperament. They can make the transition into management without difficulty. All of this is generally less true of research scientists, for whom the thrill of the chase is a major motivation. Thus, in the technical function, seekers after knowledge can be distinguished from those more interested in the synthesis of something novel from what is already known. Creative problem-solving ability is required of both classes. There are those who excel in exploration, those who perform better in synthesis, and those who are notable for doing both things well. The latter, however, are comparatively rare and highly prized. Creativity is considered again in Chapter 5.

Conservatives and revolutionaries

Finally, any reasonably sized group of people will contain some mixture of **conservatives** and **revolutionaries**. The former believe that the way forward lies in maintenance of the status quo! Revolutionaries are fundamentally bored and dissatisfied with the status quo (often without regard to what it is) and seek to change it. It is a sad fact that all the great changes in the human condition, for good or ill, have been stimulated by the rebels and often achieved by violence. A propensity in one direction or the other is a personality trait of interest not only in the technical function. The right organizational balance of these two conflicting tendencies is essential for survival. If an organization is dominated by conservatives it will eventually wither away. If the rebels hold sway, the end will be more spectacular but no less certain.

4.2.4 Management styles

Just as every company exhibits a distinct culture so, too, does each organization within it. A company culture derives principally from the way in which its top managers react to the more subjective ethical and political issues. The culture of a constituent organization necessarily reflects that of its parent, but this is modified to some extent by the style of its local management.

At the extremes, there are two very different management styles called here (with no pretence to originality) **democracy** and **dictatorship**. The Athenians invented democracy about four thousand years ago. Dictatorship arrived very much earlier. Both, of these management styles, in various guises, are in operation today so it is reasonable to assume that they have some merit.

Democracy and dictatorship

Democracy, in its most pure form, assumes that all of the people are equally capable of objective situation analysis, logical decision making, and rational actions based on the decisions. It also assumes that everybody is equally interested in these matters. Dictatorship, in its most pure form, makes quite the opposite assumption. It assumes that all wisdom and executive ability reside in just one individual at each authority level in a very tight, elitist, hierarchy. An emphasis on democracy leads to flat, non-hierarchical, organizations (as in universities), whereas an emphasis on dictatorship yields the multi-level company structure which is so typical today. But, not only are the assumptions underlying both democracy and dictatorship clearly absurd, they are also potentially lethal. Yet a pronounced emphasis on one extreme or the other can be observed in even the most cursory survey of organizations. Organizations are human systems for defining and achieving missions. These are problem-solving activities. So, solving problems is the fundamental management task. It encapsulates all the problems of planning, organizing, controlling and motivating. What, then, is the ideal approach to solving management problems?

The ideal approach?

Management problem solving has three sequential stages, give or take some looping:

(1) **Justification**   Analysis aimed at understanding why the problem is a problem and exploring options for solving it. This is the *debate* stage.

(2) **Specification**   Choice and detailing of the best solution. This is the *decision* stage.

(3) **Implementation**   Putting the decision into effect. This is the executive *action* stage.

Perhaps the ideal approach, or style, for managing this process combines the principles of democracy and dictatorship in a way which exploits their strengths and minimizes their weaknesses:

- The debate should include all those willing and able to make a rational contribution to it, and those likely to be most affected by its outcome. These two groups are rarely identical. Certain circumstances may preclude inclusion of the second group. In such cases, an advocate of their likely views should be involved. With the guidance of a good chairman, the range of possible solutions soon emerges, together with a vision of their good and bad points.

- In straightforward cases, the correct decision will probably be obvious and the second stage, decision, flows from the debate. More complex decisions are best delegated to a smaller expert group charged with making the final decision, and planning its implementation.

- Finally, the executive action should be firmly placed in the hands of a very limited group, perhaps just one individual, which has the authority and ability to enforce the decision.

Note that the initial debate is essentially democratic, but democracy shades into dictatorship as the process develops. Note, too, that conventional hierarchical organization charts reveal only the executive action structure, not the equally critical debating and decision-making parts of the process.

Leadership models

The idealized recipe for management problem solving suggests that different management styles are appropriate in different situations. It also suggests that a single manager can adopt contrasting styles. Current thinking about leadership, which is manager behaviour aimed at motivating subordinates, supports these propositions. This people-oriented section now concludes with a brief survey of ideas about leadership.

Traditional notions of leadership quality focused on **personality traits**, as discussed earlier in Section 4.2.3. These are useful indicators, but are difficult to measure and have no proven predictive value. Further, they aggregate to a superhuman requirement specification which is clearly only partially satisfied by most obviously competent leaders.

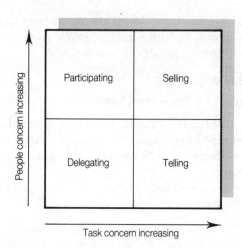

Figure 4.4   **A management style matrix.**
A management or leadership 'style' can be equated with a position on a plot of concern for the task versus concern for the people doing the task. Exclusive concentration on the task is the absolute dictator or *telling* style. Exclusive concentration on the people is the absolute democrat or *participating* style. The extreme *selling* style is the maximum possible concern for task and people. Extreme *delegation* is a total lack of concern for either. Modern thinking suggests that the best style depends on the nature of the task and of the people assigned to it.

In the 1960s, Blake and Mouton (1965) explicitly recognized two dimensions of leadership as 'concern for people' and 'concern for task'. Plotting these parameters along the axes of a ten-by-ten matrix yields their **managerial grid** for classifying different management styles. Managers positioned close to the plot origin show little concern either for the task or the people assigned to it. Blake and Mouton rank managers at the diagonally opposite corner of their grid as 'best'. These individuals show great concern both for the task *and* for the people assigned to it.

More recently, Hersey and Blanchard (1988) have expanded the grid concept (but simplified the grid) by introducing subordinate characteristics as a third parameter. Their approach typifies the **contingency** notion of an ideal management style, so called because it recognizes that 'ideal' depends on the interplay of subordinate and task characteristics. It is illustrated in Figure 4.4.

Four basic management styles are recognized:

(1) **Telling** blends high task concern with low people concern. It is regarded as best suited to subordinates who are not dedicated to the task and not willing (or not able) to seek more responsibility and job interest.

(2) **Selling** blends high task concern with high people concern. This style is seen as particularly appropriate for subordinates who respond positively to esteem and self-actualization motivators. Most people are probably in this group.

(3) **Participating** blends low task concern with high people concern. It is most effective with subordinates who seek active involvement in task management and are effective in those roles. The manager is then able to concentrate on the personal relationships, secure in the knowledge that the subordinates will achieve the task.

(4) **Delegating** blends low task concern with low people concern. This is the extreme logical extension of the participating style, where the manager is able to delegate virtually all responsibility to highly competent, dedicated, subordinates. Achieving this situation, on a task by task basis, should be the ambition of all managers. It is the best possible way of employing people.

An important part of the Hersey and Blanchard leadership perspective is its emphasis on the management duty to develop subordinate staff, where possible, 'towards' the delegation quadrant.

4.3   Organization design: Overview

It was stated earlier that organizations are designed to minimize human frailties and to maximize human strengths. Section 4.2 then explored the people dimension. This illustrated that the old view of people as emotionless cogs in a money-making machine is yielding to wiser insights. It is now appropriate to consider organization *design* in broad general terms. Opportunities to design organizations from a clean start are rare, but an understanding of the basic design principles is useful in the analysis of existing organizations and essential if they are going to be changed.

4.3.1   The background

The **traditional organizational hierarchy** is a pyramid-like structure of authority levels and superior–subordinate relationships. The supreme source of authority at the top of the hierarchy sets overall objectives, and delegates sub-objectives and matching authority to the next lower level. These second-level authorities behave in a similar way, and so on, such that the whole organization spreads out downwards like an upside-down tree. Thus, the big management tasks of company-level planning, mobilizing, controlling and motivating are assigned to the company directors. The corresponding sub-tasks are deemed to get progressively smaller at each subsequent level until the lowest level is reached. This level involves entirely routine, rule-based, tasks. This classic structure is still the most common situation and it will absorb most of the subsequent discussion.

Traditional business structure

The format of the traditional business hierarchy is largely determined, at least in theory, by a number of **classic organizational principles**. These were first stated by Fayol, the managing director of a successful French coal-mining group. They can be found in many management books, and the following list is typical:

- *Unity of purpose*   The structure must encourage individuals to contribute to the overall mission of the organization.
- *Span of command*   The number of subordinates that can be properly supervised by one individual is limited to, say, six.
- *Linearity*   Defined lines of authority must run from the highest level in the organization to the lowest level in the organization.

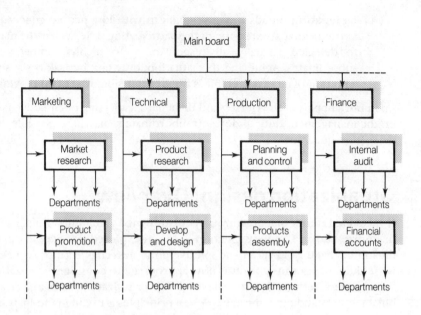

Figure 4.5 **A typical manufacturing company.**

The prevalent form of business organization arranges people into a hierarchy of authority levels, with sequences of superior–subordinate relationships. The first four levels in such a structure are outlined here. In this case, the whole business mission (creating and selling products for profit) is partitioned into successive layers of cooperating activities or functions. This partitioning principle places people with similar tasks in the same organization. It is a form of partitioning commonly used at levels close to a specific market, but other forms are possible.

- *Responsibility and authority*   The responsibility delegated by a superior to a subordinate must by matched by a delegated matching authority.
- *Indivisible authority*   Superiors are completely responsible for their subordinates, and subordinates are completely responsible to their superior.
- *Unity of command*   Each subordinate should have only one superior.

A typical organization for a manufacturing company structured on these principles is outlined in Figure 4.5. It shows the first four levels in a repetitive pattern.

At first sight, the traditional principles make a good deal of sense. Everyone has a boss (the board of directors are responsible to the owners of the business); duties are well-defined at each level; each level has the authority and ability discharge its duties; no manager is required to supervise an excessive number of subordinates; and so on. And it works! Or, at least, it has done in the past.

But it is important to remember that, in a competitive business environment, it is *relative* performance that matters. There are no absolute standards. If all the competitors are organized in the same way, relative performance is not a test of organizational structure. It merely tests the relative competence of different managements in making that structure work. The earlier discussion suggests that there must be a better way. If this is the case, those businesses which adopt it will use their human resources more efficiently and will beat the competition. Already there is some evidence of change. Some speculations about the future of people at work and industrial organizations are included in Section 4.5.

4.3.2 The growth requirement

Properly managed **business growth** can be one ingredient of survival and prosperity, and most top managers set growth as a basic objective. Exceptions include some small privately-owned concerns where the owners have achieved a satisfactory life style and choose to avoid the problems inherent in becoming bigger. Publicly-owned businesses do not have this option. The pressure from their shareholders, always seeking the best return on their investment, obliges them to strive constantly for a greater and more profitable share of their markets.

Company organization should change as a company grows. Indeed, failure to develop the organization as a company develops is one of the main reasons why companies fail. A structure which is suited to a small company could be the kiss of death to a large one, and vice versa. In fact, the nature of the organization of a successful company is one (unreliable) way of assessing its size.

The life cycle of an organizational structure

The concept of an **organization life cycle** is analogous to the notion of a product life cycle, which is discussed in Chapters 2 and 3. Thus, a particular organizational structure can grow with the company until a maturity phase of high efficiency sets in. For a period, this relatively stable format is able to accommodate more growth but, eventually, its effectiveness begins to decline. Hopefully, as with products, an enhanced organization is ready to take over and company growth continues under the new regime. Salter (1970) and Channon (1973) have explored this concept. Figure 4.6 outlines a typical sequence of growth-induced changes in company structure.

Table 4.1 describes some characteristics of the company at each stage of its development. The four stages correspond to the tiny, small, medium and large descriptors introduced in Chapter 1.

The options for achieving business growth include:

- obtaining a larger share of current markets
- penetrating existing markets which are not currently exploited
- creating new markets
- geographic diversification
- acquisition of other businesses.

All of these pursuits put increasing demands on management, and on the organizational framework in which it operates. Company growth which stems directly from investment in its own resources is termed **organic growth**. **Growth by acquisition** is also a popular strategy, often in concert with organic growth. This involves the purchase (or **take-over**) of another company, usually one operating in the same or related markets. Thus, the purchasing company achieves increased market share and eliminates a competitor at one stroke. Genuine **mergers** also occur. Here, the end result is a larger operation in which neither of the original managements teams dominates. This is a rare event – most so-called mergers are really take-overs.

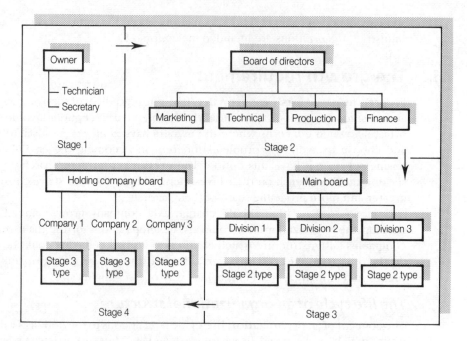

Figure 4.6 **A possible sequence of company growth.**

A company organization should grow as the company grows. One possible sequence of different structures is shown here. The simple arrangement of the start-up business, at stage 1, develops into a structure of cooperating sub-process functions at stage 2. Further growth is accommodated by creating, at stage 3, a number of trading divisions, each structured as in stage 2. Finally, at stage 4, a large company is formed to 'hold' a number of stage-3-type subsidiary companies. Some options for achieving business growth are listed in the text.

Some companies concentrate almost exclusively on acquisitions, which they then regard solely as investments. When a company is acquired, it is usually reorganized in some way (which may be painful for its employees) to improve its performance and, hence, that of its purchaser. Subsequently, the constituent parts of the investment portfolio are encouraged to grow in their own right. Activities of this sort can result in a very mixed bag of constituent parts. A **holding company** which owns a large number of largely unrelated, in market terms, other companies is termed a **conglomerate**. Some have a very impressive record.

Small companies

Organizational structure in small companies is generally informal. A detailed discussion of the problems of starting a small company and growing it into a larger one is not included here. The major difficulties relate to:

- obtaining adequate capital
- the lack of some specialist skills
- engendering confidence in potential customers and suppliers
- vulnerability of the limited product range

Stage	Organization type	Product(s) and market(s) characteristics	Management structure	Performance measures
1	One trading unit and one owner	Single product range, single market, limited distribution channels	Owner does everything	Limited, not formal. Set by owner
2	One trading unit and a few owners	Limited product ranges, limited markets and distribution channels	Team of functional managers	Functional operating budgets
3	A few trading units and more owners	Diverse product ranges each with own market and distribution channels	Unit managers reporting to main board	Trading budgets and investment criteria
4	Holding company with several subsiduary companies. Many owners	Subsidiary companies have own distinctive product ranges, each with distinct markets and distribution channels	Semi-autonomous companies report to holding board	Mostly investment criteria

Table 4.1 **Typical characteristics at different stages in company growth.**
This table supports Figure 4.6. It compares some distinctive features of the business shown in that figure as it grows from a tiny beginning, at stage 1, into its final form at stage 4.

- limited markets and distribution channels
- the massive work-load on the budding entrepreneurs.

Small companies do, however, enjoy some advantages over their larger companions. These include:

- a high level of management motivation
- flexibility
- speed of response
- creative tension
- the potential rewards.

Sadly, however, only a very few of those that are launched survive to tell the tale. The material that follows concerns the larger businesses. However, it should be of interest to those contemplating starting out on their own. This step is not recommended to new graduates.

4.4 Organization design: Company level

This section reviews the major factors which should determine the nature of a particular organizational structure at the company level. The material owes much to Drucker (1989), who reveals timeless principles in this area with his usual clarity. A design approach based on **why–what–how** or, more formally, justification, specification and implementation is used as an analytical tool to present the material.

4.4.1 Justification

A company organization is a human mechanism for determining and achieving the objectives of that company. These twin purposes state *why* an organization must exist. This glimpse of the obvious is the first design step – justification.

4.4.2 Specification

Specification of *what* the organization has to do must start with an analysis of the business that it is designed to serve. This must cover both the current status of the business and its ambitions. The analysis can divided into three areas:

- *Activities*   Establishing what distinct activities are required in the business, how much of each is needed and where they should be located.

- *Decisions*   Defining what sort of decisions are required to achieve the business objectives and who should make them.

- *Relationships*   Determining who has to work with whom and where these cooperating parties stand in the hierarchy.

(Connoisseurs of job descriptions will be familiar with this list.)

Activities are functions

Traditionally, a **business function** is defined as a group of people with similar professional skills. This classic definition suggests that people with common professional skills are always organized into a single group with a unique business purpose. For example, it implies that the production function contains only people who specialize in making things. This definition may, or may not, apply to a function in a real company.

The preferred approach defines a function as a separate and distinct *activity* contributing to the business process. This makes no assumptions about the organization of a function within the company. The people carrying out the activity may, or may not, be contained within a single organization and may, or may not, have the same professional skills. This activity-based rather than skill-based definition is what is meant by 'function' in this book. The technical function at its focus is one example, marketing and production are two more. Functions are treated in more depth later on.

Decisions

Analysis of the decisions that must be made in the business is important because it indicates the sort of top management structure required, and the nature of authority and responsibility that can be delegated to the lower levels. The majority, perhaps eighty per cent, of decisions that must be made in an established business concern familiar situations which have occurred before. The organization must be primarily shaped to deal efficiently with those routine decisions, and allow the remainder to be handled on an exception basis. So, the analysis must identify:

- the different kinds of decision
- the management levels at which they be safely taken

- the individuals who must participate in making them
- which functions will be affected
- who should be informed after the decision has been made.

This daunting task is made easier by classifying decisions by major feature, as follows:

(1) *Longevity*   Measures the time that the decision will commit the company to some particular course of action. Generally, critical decisions with long-term implications should be taken at the higher levels.

(2) *Reversibility*   Measures how hard or how damaging it will be to reverse the decision if the need arises. Difficult to reverse and potentially damaging decisions should be retained by the higher levels.

(3) *Scope*   If only one function is affected a decision might be regarded as a low-level matter, rising only to higher levels if more than one function, or the future of many people, is involved.

(4) *Qualitative content*   If substantial value judgements (on such factors as ethics, conduct, social responsibility, politics, and so on) are involved in a decision then it is a high-level matter. On the other hand, purely quantitative decisions should be relegated to the lower levels.

(5) *Routine recurrent*   Decisions of this nature are susceptible to a rule-based approach and, as such, should be delegated to the lower levels.

(6) *Rarity*   It is obviously difficult to define rare decisions in advance, and impossible for the unique ones. Decisions of this sort must be handled on their merits as the need arises. The more significant, as determined by the preceding factors, must be handled at a high level.

These features are not, of course, mutually exclusive. Also, one might override another. For example, a company manufacturing and selling steel central-heating radiators is periodically faced with a purchasing dilemma. The alternatives are either to purchase sheet steel to match forecast product sales or to exploit forecast cost fluctuations through a futures contract. The first choice should result in an advantageous cost as bulk purchase discounts are available. The latter choice removes the need for an immediate cash outlay and might allow a series of smaller, phased, purchases with even better economy. This is a significant problem involving the analysis of many complex factors. But sheet steel can always be resold if necessary, and a futures contract is also a saleable asset. So, even though significant money may be involved, there is no long-term commitment and the decision should be delegated to the lowest competent level. However, the decision to bid for a major fixed-price design, supply and support contract is a different matter. If the bid is successful, substantial company resources will be 'locked' into the contract for a number of years, and the penalties for poor performance are not only financial. Decisions of this sort should be taken at a high level.

Decisions demanding difficult qualitative value judgements are more common than might be supposed in the orderly world suggested by the conventional organization chart. They must be taken at a high level. Decisions relating to the future of people are always in this class. As noted earlier, every company has its own unique culture or ethos, which is rapidly absorbed by its employees. This culture is largely determined by the value judgements of the senior management team.

Some decisions may be regarded as totally quantitative, such that they can be safely taken solely on the basis of the numbers involved. One example is routine stock reordering action when a pre-determined threshold is reached. Another is 'chasing' debtors when their time allowance for credit is exceeded by some margin. If some measure of risk is accepted (or not recognized) then such decisions are very common in some businesses. They should be delegated to the lowest competent level, perhaps even to a computer program. However, it should be a good program: more than one menacing letter demanding money for services rendered has been automatically dispatched to a Mrs H.M. Queen at an address in Norfolk.

Decisions should always be made at the lowest competent level, and as close to the point of immediate impact as is sensible. The 'sensible' qualifier is important. For example, nothing is gained by asking dishonest staff whether or not they should be fired without compensation, because the answer is both predictable and irrelevant.

Relationships and communications

The next facet of the specification of what the organization has to do concerns personal relationships and communications. With the exception only of those at the lowest level in the hierarchy, everybody needs to cooperate with colleagues above, below and alongside them in the structure. Establishing the optimum pattern of these relationships is vitally important. The same need applies to functions. For example, the technical function is often a separate entity, on a par with the other major functions, such as finance, production, marketing and so on. However, because marketing has a major role in product creation it can be argued that the technical function should be part of that function. The production director might make a case of equal probity. In some circumstances, either one of these structures could be an efficient arrangement.

For an individual, the upward relationship with the boss is critical in terms of the strategic (longer term) health of the business. But job specifications (produced by bosses) tend to emphasize downwards relationships. These, and the sideways relationships, are certainly critical in tactical (shorter term) matters. There is no contradiction here. Strategy shades into tactics, with the time horizon of decisions shortening, as objectives are passed downwards through the hierarchy. The conventional organization chart shows only the formal, vertical, reporting relationships. Whether or not an organization works satisfactorily depends greatly on the informal lines of communications and relationships, especially the sideways ones. No one business function is an island unto itself, all depend on others for support of one kind or another. The same situation holds for individuals. Thus, a high priority for a newly-joined graduate engineer should be to establish good rapport with the canteen staff, the storeman who guards needed components and equipment, and the boss's secretary. The recruit's immediate bodily welfare and future career are then probably assured.

4.4.3 Implementation

This material provides the rationale underpinning the organizational structures presented, with little explanation, in Chapter 1 at Section 1.3.11 (Company organizations).

When the organizational specification has been derived (or, more correctly, when it is believed that this is the case), the question of *how* to implement it arises. How to arrange the optimum partitioning of the whole business mission is the central issue. The first task is to identify the **constraints** which restrict freedom of action. Many of these will be special to the particular case under consideration. Others, discussed here, are generally applicable.

General constraints

Three people-related constraints always apply. They are listed here as organizational requirements:

(1) *Business performance*   The structure should encourage good business performance. This requires that managers are able to behave as business managers as distinct from bureaucrats. That is, more should be demanded of them than just administrative competence and a professional skill. The challenge and opportunity to extend themselves should also be present.

(2) *Minimum levels*   The structure should contain the least possible number of management levels. Each additional level in an organization tends to dilute its common purpose and distort communications. It restricts opportunities for the development of managers and encourages the development of specialists rather than generalists. Further, it may provide comfortable accommodation for passengers rather than challenging accommodation for crew. There is a conflict here with the span of command constraint, noted earlier, because there *is* a real limit to the number of subordinates that a manager can supervise effectively. The conflict must be resolved.

(3) *Manager development*   The structure must allow for the training and testing, in real situations, of the next generation of managers. Note that training on its own is not enough, even when supported by simulations of reality. Real-life testing is needed and it should be non-destructive, for the business and the individual under test. (Despite persistent attempts to prove otherwise, there is little merit in forcing square pegs into round holes. But pegs can be shaped to some extent, and square holes do exist.)

Two conventional solutions to these 'mission-partitioning' constraints are commonly employed. They are termed (here) **functional partitioning** and **divisionalization** respectively. North American practice favours the equivalent **functional decentralization** and **federal decentralization** terms. These structures are supportive and complementary rather than competitive.

Functional partitioning

As noted earlier, functional partitioning may be implemented in either of two ways, although the two arrangements may co-exist. Grouping by shared professional skills is the traditional way, and grouping by common activity is the alternative, where the activity is a distinct sub-process within the whole business process.

For example, a **technical professional function** contains, in a single organization, all the scientists, mathematicians, engineers and technically qualified supporting staff in the company. In the alternative scheme, these individuals are dispersed among, say, the research, marketing, development and design, production, and sales functions.

These functions are **stage functions**. They form a sequence of sub-processes comprising the primary business process: that of creating products and selling them to customers. Each such function is a mixed-skills group dedicated to a common activity and purpose.

An overall professional technical function may co-exist with the stage function structure. This would have some central, high-level, responsibilities for all the technical staff and technology. Typically, these include:

- performance standards
- staff remuneration policy
- graduate recruiting policy and the early stages of that process
- career development and training
- overall technological strategy
- administration of the central research fund (if any)
- (perhaps) overall coordination of major projects which cross organizational boundaries.

Organizations of this sort are termed **staff functions**, rather than **line functions**. The term implies that they do not wield direct authority in the vertical line-reporting chain of the hierarchy, being 'set off' to the side. Their role is more advisory and consultative. However, because such functions report at high level and have a broad overall vision, they can exert a powerful influence on the line operations.

Functional partitioning has been illustrated by reference to the technical function. The same principles can, of course, be applied to the other functions. All the finance personnel, for example, may be grouped into a single professional finance function or dispersed, as the need arises, throughout the stage functions. A central professional finance staff function would almost certainly exist in the latter case. Its duties would include monitoring overall financial performance, maintenance of professional standards and internal auditing. Figure 4.7 is a modified version of Figure 4.5. It illustrates a manufacturing company organization with a mixture of staff and line functions.

Divisionalization

Divisionalization, when applied, tends to overlay the functional technique. A divisional structure partitions the total company operation into a set of semi-autonomous, largely self-contained, separate businesses. Each such business is assigned its own markets, product ranges, and profit and loss responsibility. They may be either trading divisions of the parent company, or private limited (subsidiary) companies wholly (usually) owned by the parent. The businesses may themselves be structured internally on a divisional basis, or on a functional basis, or be some mixture of the two.

Note that *total* autonomy cannot be awarded to the separate businesses, because this would destroy the parent company. The parent retains, therefore, some elements of control over its constituent businesses. This always includes setting financial targets and 'hire-and-fire' rights over senior staff. Other prerogatives, such as the provision of capital and market definition, may also be retained. The parent company may also provides some central services. The use of such functions by the dependent divisions

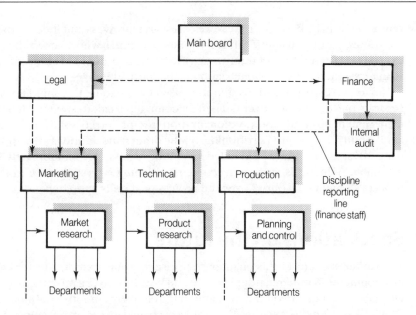

Figure 4.7 **A typical manufacturing company with staff and line functions.**

Business functions can be either stage (sub-process) functions or professional functions. Stage functions are activity-based, where the activities contribute to the whole business process. A professional function relates to a body of people with a common professional skill. The two forms can co-exist. This figure is developed from Figure 4.5. It shows three second-level line functions, which are activity-based stage functions. Two staff functions, legal and finance, are also present at the second level. These retain some duties and authority with respect to the corresponding professionals who work in the line functions. Their presence compromises, to some extent, the classic 'only one boss' principle.

can be mandatory or optional. A central research function is one example, and central legal, data-processing and publicity departments are others.

The essential element of divisionalization is delegation of profit and loss (P&L) responsibility. This requires each unit to have its own defined market. It may be defined in a variety of ways. Definition by product range or geographical region, occasionally by both, are the most common.

Functional partitioning and divisionalization compared

Divisionalization puts managers into a near-autonomous business situation and, hence, provides substantial esteem and self-actualization motivating opportunities. This is significantly less so in the functional arrangement where total profit and loss responsibility is not possible. In this case, motivation must relate to performance measured against the function budget or in terms of professional standards. But function performance against budget is critically dependent on that of cooperating functions, so results are always ambiguous. A motivation policy based on performance against professional standards is also flawed. One problem is to determine who will set the standards, and what they should be. Another, more serious, difficulty is that easily determined standards do not always align with the best interests of the business. For example, researchers might be motivated and rewarded on the basis of publications in refereed journals. This is one measure of research prowess, but it does not necessarily contribute to the business. Similarly, sales personnel who exceed their targets by excessive price-cutting extract their reward from a diminished profit. Of the two structures, therefore, divisionalization is the more effective.

However, divisionalization cannot be used below some threshold level where the separate businesses, however defined, become too small to support their own viable management structure. So divisionalization, the preferred solution, is limited in its applicability. Functional partitioning, on the other hand, is universally applicable, and dangerously so. It should be avoided for as long as possible, but ultimately its advent is inevitable. When this stage is reached, partitioning by major stage in the business process should be favoured over the professional skills approach.

4.5 Speculations on the future

The earlier sections of this chapter comprise, to some extent, a historical review of developments in understanding people and how best to organize them. Mostly, these changes have been evolutionary, implying relatively smooth continuous transition from one situation to the next. Evolutionary change is reasonably comfortable, barely perceptible, change. It allows moderately accurate prediction of the future by extrapolation from the past, the basis of traditional planning down the centuries. This approach, however, does not always work. If it did, the betting industry, on horses, football teams, and so on, would not exist. In those cases it fails because there are too many variables, of varying degrees of uncertainty, influencing the end result.

Extrapolation also fails when, for some reason, change becomes discontinuous rather than evolutionary. Many events can trigger discontinuous change: warfare and technological breakthroughs are two examples. The 1939–1945 war, for example, changed more than the map of Europe: it also brought women into the job market, radar to civil air transport and a multitude of other new good or bad situations. On the other hand, the first Industrial Revolution was stimulated by the ability to replace muscles with cheaper machines, a technological step forward yielding better business economics and an overall increase in prosperity.

Today, in the early 1990s, the first indicators of another period of discontinuous change may already be present. Handy (1989) argues cogently that this is inevitable – that irreversible discontinuous change is already in progress. He foresees dramatic changes in business organizations and patterns of work. This book is particularly aimed at those generations whose working lives would embrace such a drama. This section, therefore, steps back from the minutiae of the earlier discussion and takes a broad speculative look into the future of organizations and people at work. The emphasis is on Europe and North America, that is, on the relatively well-developed Western nations. Note first that *discontinuous change* is, of course, a comparative term. It can happen overnight, as when war is declared, but here the time-scale is some twenty to thirty years, about one or two generation gaps.

4.5.1 Portents of change

Discontinuous change happens when a constrained pressure for change is released by the coming together of some set of factors which removes the constraint. The pressure can always be traced back to the human urge to satisfy the basic needs discussed earlier in Section 4.2, but it usually coagulates into an economic–political problem at world, national, business or individual level. For example, many people now accept that there is no future (literally) in rapidly depleting the world of its non-renewable resources and poisoning it in the process. They get together and create a pressure. The pressure-releasing agent is not primarily technological, because technical solutions are more or less available. Nor is it a (voluntary) return to a caveman economy, because that solution is unacceptable to the great majority. So the pressure releaser is money, and the primary pressure translates into an economic problem of major proportions. Big economic problems are also big political problems.

Pressures for change

Some of the primary pressures for change which are creating problems at the present time are now listed.

- *Demographic*: changing age distributions within defined populations, particularly an increase in the proportion of older people in the well-developed nations and explosive birth-rates in the less developed nations.

- *Global competition*: all major industries now operate world-wide and protection of individual national markets is diminishing.

- *Nuclear technology*: while the possibility of a major East–West nuclear confrontation seems to have sharply declined, the capacity for nuclear conflict and contamination is now widely distributed across the world.

- *Pollution*: of the whole human environment with life-threatening by-products of industry and conflict, either deliberately or accidentally.

- *Poverty*: particularly in the less developed nations, but also elsewhere. The poor have seen affluence and want their share; not all the affluent are willing to share it with them.

Note that the root cause of the pressure created by each of these factors is the human drive to maintain (at least) a satisfactory life style, or to achieve one. But they all reduce to economic–political problems: economic because money is needed to solve them and political because finding the money and then solving the problem creates other problems.

Discontinuous change seems to occur when the pressure-creating factors and pressure-releasing agents feed on, and reinforce, each other. Multiple loops of cause and effect are built into the system. Positive feedback takes over and the system becomes unstable. It goes sharply from evolution to revolution. Predicting the precise direction and rate of the change defies analysis: the available algorithms and the computers are just not up to the job.

There is merit in the view that all this summarizes the present world-wide scene. Technology is a villain of the piece.

The role of technology

Technology plays two parts in the system. On the one hand, it can be the instrument that leads to a pressure; on the other hand, it can provide, at an economic–political cost, a means of relieving the pressure. A few examples illustrate the dual role of technology:

- *Information technology*: the convergence of communications and computers, in both technical and market terms, resulting in new competitive pressures on established industries. But it also provides new ways of doing old things in those industries, and a vast range of new, knowledge-based industries.
- *Medical technology*: has resulted in an increase in the average age of populations, even in the less developed nations. But has also made birth control safer, cheaper and a matter of female choice.
- *Nuclear technology*: in its civil or military applications is a potential killer. But, properly used, it could solve most of the energy problems, and many of the pollution problems, that now abound.
- *Satellite communications*: has brought pictures, which transcend language barriers, of affluence to the starving, and of the starving to the affluent. But it could carry education, and training in self-help, to the poverty-stricken.

4.5.2 Forecasts with numbers

It is always instructive to put numbers into forecasts even when, as here, only crude estimates are possible. The numbers that Handy (1989) provides are as good as any available. He concentrates on trends in working and population patterns for Britain. The figures included here have been adapted from his to include continental Europe and North America on a 1988 datum. There are seven main trends:

(1) A shift from mostly full-time to mostly part-time work.
(2) A shift from mostly manual to mostly intellectual jobs.
(3) A decline in the birth-rate.
(4) An increasing proportion of older people.
(5) A decline in hours of work.
(6) An increase in job-type swapping.
(7) An increase in leisure.

Each of these changes is now considered.

Full-time to part-time work

There is a trend from mostly full-time to mostly part-time work. Currently, about sixty-six per cent of people in work are employed full-time by companies. The remainder are either self-employed, or in temporary full-time or part-time work. In the year 2000, it is predicted that less than fifty per cent will be employed full-time by companies, with a corresponding growth in the other sectors. Part-time work (self-employed or otherwise), rather than full-time work, will become the norm. The fundamental reason supporting this trend is that it makes more economic sense to the employing companies. It is cheaper and less vulnerable to the vagaries of the market-place, trade cycles and global economics.

It was noted earlier (in Section 4.1) that the principal factor which distinguishes a company from its competitors is the quality of the people that it contains. People are (expensive) differential assets. But not all the people are equally critical. A company is really defined by its irreducible central core of dedicated professionals, with their specialist skills and knowledge. If the work that the *other* people supply can be supplied efficiently (that is, competitively) then, crudely, these other people are less important. Indeed, subject only to their services being competitively available, they do not need to be part of the company.

The only penalty for this economic flexibility is that a new management problem is acquired, because a critical resource is now externally owned. This is a minor matter when weighed against the advantages. The contracted-out services are provided by a second tier of competing companies, who vie with each other for the business. They have to be competitive. If the primary business activity declines, the external suppliers can be 'turned-off' at comparatively short notice. The excess capacity problem is then theirs, rather than that of the erstwhile customer. This is already a common way of handling seasonal trade variations. The use of temporary staff in the retail trades at Christmas is an example.

The concept is not new. The building industry has been organized in this way for many years. Typically, marketing and design are retained in the company, but the buildings are assembled by specialist bricklayers, plumbers, carpenters, electricians and the like. These subcontractors may be either self-employed individuals or companies. The structure is also common in the microcomputer industry. Integrated circuit chips are manufactured by one group of specialist companies and assembled, together with other components, into the finished product by yet another specialist company. System software comes from another specialist supplier. Even design is sometimes subcontracted.

What is new is the rapid growth of this business strategy in both the private and public sectors. It requires a new (perhaps) type of skill for managing relations with the external contractors. The emphasis shifts to a precise specification of *what* is required, *when* it is required and for *how* much. How it is done, within reason, barely matters. This approach removes the need for several layers of management in the primary company. The costs thus avoided more than compensate for the profit requirements of the contractors.

Handy calls companies operating in this way an **industrial 'shamrock' structure**, by analogy with the Irish national emblem – a small three-leafed plant. One leaf of the shamrock is the professional central core employing mostly intellectual workers. The second leaf is the specialist contractors, both companies and individuals. The company contractors may be substantial organizations in their own right and they, too, adopt the shamrock philosophy. The third leaf is the army of potential part-timers who do not want, or cannot take, or cannot get a full-time job. But they are available to meet peak labour requirements when these occur.

So, the trend is towards a shamrock work-force serving shamrock organizations. Individuals may move from leaf to leaf of the shamrock during their working lives. In addition to the workers in paid employment, there will still be a substantial fraction of the potential work-force not employed, and a large group in domestic 'unpaid' employment, the housewives and househusbands.

Manual to intellectual jobs

There is a trend from mostly manual to mostly intellectual jobs. In the 1950s, employ-ment was mostly in full-time skilled, semi-skilled or unskilled manual jobs. These needed muscles and dexterity rather than brains, and some seventy-five per cent of all jobs were in this category. By the year 2000, the proportions are forecast to reverse, with seventy to eighty per cent of all jobs demanding specialist professional knowledge, and the energy and intellect to use it.

There are two factors driving this trend along. The first is business economics again. It is now cheaper to operate *labour-intensive* manufacturing in the less well-developed countries than in the well-developed countries. This has two conse-quences: manual jobs are exported and their results are imported. Salvation, in a sense, comes (hopefully) from the second factor.

This second factor is technological progress, particularly in electronics, computing (hardware and software) and communications. These three have come together to create information technology. This is breaking down barriers of language, time and distance to turn the world into a village. It gives power to those who create it and, even more so, to those who know how to use it. It is an enabling technology, allowing new things to be done and old things to be done better. Already, there is hardly any facet of industrial or domestic life which is untouched by this new technology. But it is an intellectually demanding taskmaster, and is primarily for the young, brave, energetic, highly educated and trained professionals. Many of the older generation, nowadays anyone over fifty, will not be able to keep up. There are substantial educational and training problems implicit in this trend, which might be particularly severe in Britain.

Birth-rate

Most of the important decline in the birth-rate has already happened, in the late 1960s and early 1970s, but its impact in the job market is only now being felt. The initial reduction was of the order of twenty-five per cent, and the trend is still slightly downwards. Thus the younger, more energetic and more educable part of the work-force has declined and continues slowly to do so. (Other trends, such as longer potential working lives and more women in employment, may numerically com-pensate the total work-force for the reduction at the younger end.)

Lower birth-rates are usually associated with the more affluent societies. The urge to breed as an insurance against impoverished old age is diminished, and infant mortality is also reduced. There is evidence, too, that the affluent choose not to compromise their life style with the economic burden of a large family. Technology again plays its part in this trend.

Proportion of older people

There is an increasing proportion of older people. Some fifty years from now, if current trends continue, about twenty per cent of the total population will be pensioners. Many, perhaps most, of them will be largely dependent on those able to work (sixty per cent, say, of the total population) for their costs of living. And, as they get older, they become more costly to keep alive! Advances in medical and, to a lesser extent, nutritional technology lie behind this situation.

Hours of work

The hours of work in the average working life are declining. In the 1950s, individuals entering the job market could expect to deliver about 100,000 hours of work over their working lives, largely irrespective of the type of job. Nowadays, the average figure is down to about 50,000 hours.

The 100,000 hour pattern was about 47 hours per week, 47 weeks per year, for 47 years. The 47 hours per week would probably include paid or unpaid overtime (depending on the job) and holidays were less than now, although time-off because of illness was higher. The 47 years of working life represents a start at about 18 years of age and retirement at 65. It will be recalled that manual rather than intellectual jobs prevailed at this time.

The anticipated job-life now is more like 37 hours per week, 37 weeks per year, for 37 years, making up the 50,000 hours. The reductions in hours per week and weeks per year represent the workers getting a share of the fruits of large gains in labour productivity (based on improved technology). For example, a hundred years ago the average worker needed to work for about two hours to pay for a loaf of bread. Today, some four minutes is long enough. Technology (machines and chemistry) has allowed the real price of bread to be reduced by thirty times.

The expected reduction in the number of working years arises for two reasons. Firstly, more education and training will be needed to meet the requirements of the increased fraction of intellectual jobs. So individuals will, on average, start their first real (productive) job later in life than previously. They may also need to participate in (non-productive) retraining during their working life. Secondly, they are likely to retire sooner, voluntarily or otherwise, because they are no longer able to cope with the intellectual jobs (or so it will be assumed). This second factor is already reasonably well established.

Job-type swapping

There is an increasing rate of job-type swapping. When the 100,000 hours job-life prevailed, most individuals could expect to hold a progression of full-time jobs throughout their working lives. That is, employment was essentially continuous for most people. But full-time jobs are in increasingly short supply, and their average duration is also reducing. So, voluntarily or otherwise, people who wish to work will have to move between the full-time and part-time sectors.

The full-time sector includes both employment by companies and, in principle, self-employment. The part-time sector embraces continuous employment at less than full-time hours and intermittent jobs of full-time hours (such as seasonal employment). It may be that the general pattern will be one of initial full-time employment followed by a period in the part-time sector, but wide variations will occur between individual cases.

Leisure

Many of the previous trends create, as a side effect, increasing leisure time for the majority of the population. This may or may not be welcome in individual cases. Substantial leisure time is already established and it is becoming more prevalent. Leisure, like most activities, costs money. It can also earn money for the providers of leisure services. But it is non-productive in the sense that it does not add value to material or intellectual resources. It must, therefore, be subsidized by such value-adding activities. This, again, presents an increasingly severe economic–political problem.

4.5.3 Summary: The way ahead?

This final section summarizes the visible trends in industrial structure, company organizations and the likely consequences in job terms. It comprises a speculative look at the way ahead for organizations and people.

Industrial structure

Here, three main trends are visibly in progress. There is continuing decline in labour-intensive manufacturing, and increasing volumes of both service-type subcontracting and information-based industrial activity.

Labour-intensive manufacturing is being replaced by **smart manufacturing** based on the use of 'intelligent' machines and elaborate information communication and processing. The terms used to describe this new era include 'computer-aided design, manufacture and test' (CAD/CAM/CAT), 'computer-aided engineering' (CAE), 'computer-integrated manufacturing' (CIM) and 'flexible manufacturing systems' (FMS). These illustrate the application of information technology to do old things in new ways, and more efficiently. One significant aspect of the approach is the increasing integration of the design and manufacturing functions.

The service sector includes more than just 'body-shopping', such as industrial cleaning services and security guards. Specialist marketing, 'R&D', programming and manufacturing companies increasingly co-exist with the more traditional accountancy, legal and consultancy suppliers in the developing professional services segment. Service companies of all types have a problem which distinguishes them from their customers, who sell tangible physical products. Those companies can, if they choose, stockpile their output during periods of low demand. For example, if a company makes only Christmas toys then it must make stock for about ten months of the year. Service companies, on the other hand, sell skills, and these cannot be stocked in anticipation of future sales. The service companies will increasingly handle this problem by themselves subcontracting to the flexible full-time and part-time labour market to smooth over the peaks and troughs in demand.

Increasingly, all surviving industries might be regarded as knowledge-based. Indeed, the purist must classify virtually all human activity in this way. But it is a matter of degree. The all-pervasive nature of information technology means that the communication and processing of information will be increasingly critical in all businesses. The maxim 'work smarter, not harder' will no longer ensure survival. Perhaps 'work smarter and harder' will do so.

Organizational structure

The changes in overall industrial structure imply corresponding changes in the structure of industrial organizations. The roots of the still prevalent multi-level hierarchical structure lie in labour-intensive manufacturing. But this will soon be no more than a race memory in the highly-developed nations. The intellectual cores of the shamrock companies will be smaller and populated by professionals very conscious of their rarity and worth. They need not, and will not, tolerate more than just a few levels between the lowest and the highest. Nor will they accept an overly dictatorial management style. The end of the era of the multi-level highly authoritarian organizations is in sight. Probably, the most prevalent type of future organization will be based on **matrix structures** (described in Chapter 5), with the majority of the work packages, but not marketing, design and management, being subcontracted to specialist service companies.

Job structure

Arising from all this, a wide range of job-type options will be available for all sections of the work-force. Individuals are likely to move between the various job options throughout their working lives. The term 'options' is perhaps a misnomer, as moves from one job-type to another will often be a matter of necessity rather than choice. The options will include:

- *Full-time in a company core*   This is a minority option, confined mostly to young professionals, offering an exciting and rewarding life style followed by, for many, 'retirement' in early middle-age.

- *Self-employed, part-time or full-time*   This is not generally a viable option for young people, but increasingly a possibility for them as experience develops. It is a feasible option for some of the professionals retiring from the full-time employed core.

- *Part-time contracting*   This sector overlaps with the self-employed sector and includes both part-time continuous employment and intermittent full-time employment. All age bands will participate in this type of job, but women and/or professionals retired from full-time employment will probably predominate.

The self-employed and part-time workers comprise a flexible work-force. Rewards for this type of work will be increasingly based on the satisfactory performance of the assigned task. In other words, there will be an increasing emphasis on payment for results, rather than for the time absorbed in producing results.

4.6   Concluding summary

People are differential assets. It is the quality and effectiveness of the people it contains that differentiates one business from another. This chapter is concerned with the optimum organization of people in industry. An industrial organization is a system of people working on a specific business mission. Its structure is, necessarily, a compromise between the needs of the mission and the needs of the people it contains. The topic is analysed at company level and from a design perspective, which allows the compromise to be examined.

   An essential prerequisite to understanding organizations is some understanding of how people are likely to behave within them. Human needs, motivation, personality and management style all enter into this equation. Other vital background lies in the rules that shape the still-dominant multi-level hierarchical organization structure and the nature of its typical growth pattern.

An organization can be specified in terms of the activities which comprise its mission, the types of decisions involved and the requisite working relationships. The central issue is then how to partition the mission to obtain the best overall performance. To this end, the structure must encourage good business performance, minimize the number of management levels and provide for manager development. A blend of functional partitioning and divisionalization is commonly employed.

Currently, there are some omens of forthcoming major changes in industry structures, organizations and patterns of work. The chapter concludes, therefore, with a section which takes a broad speculative look into the future of organizations and people at work.

Sections 4.1 to 4.4 are recommended background reading for Chapter 5.

REFERENCES

Blake R. R. and Mouton J. S. (1965). *The Managerial Grid*. Houston: Gulf

Channon D. F. (1973). *Strategy and Structure of British Enterprise*. London: Macmillan

Drucker P. F. (1989). *The Practice of Management*. London: Pan

Handy C. B. (1989). *The Age of Unreason*. London: Business Books (Century Hutchinson)

Hersey P. and Blanchard K. H. (1988). *Management of Organisational Behaviour: Utilising Human Resources*. Englewood Cliffs, NJ: Prentice-Hall

Herzberg F. (1968). One more time: how do you motivate employees? *Harvard Business Review*, 46(1)

Maslow A. H. (1943). A theory of human motivation. *Psychological Review*, **50**, 370–96

McGregor D. (1960). *The Human Side of Enterprise*. New York: McGraw-Hill

Mitchell T. R. (1982). Motivation: New directions for theory, research and practice. *Academy of Management Review*, 7(1)

Porter L. W. and Lawler E. E. (1968). *Managerial Attitudes and Performance*. Homewood: Irwin/Dorsey Press

Salter M. S. (1970). Stages of corporate development. *Journal of Business Policy*, **1**(1)

SUGGESTED FURTHER READING

Highly readable and recommended specialist texts in this chapter area are provided by Handy (1981), Baron & Greenberg (1990) and Huczynski & Buchanan (1991). The last two are comprehensive textbooks; Handy ranges less widely but more quickly. Chapter 13 of the text by Hellriegal and Slocum (1986) covers leadership, as does Chapter 3 of the slimmer volume by Lawrence and Lee (1984). These two books are people-oriented texts covering a wide range of management topics. Pugh (1990) traces development of the subject in a series of classic essays, which provides a fascinating background.

Baron R. A. and Greenberg J. (1990). *Behaviour and Organizations* 3rd edn. Needham Heights: Allyn and Bacon

Handy C. B. (1981). *Understanding Organisations* 2nd edn. Harmondsworth: Penguin

Hellriegal D. and Slocum J. W. (1986). *Management* 4th edn. Reading, MA: Addison-Wesley (Chapter 13)

Huczynski A. and Buchanan D. (1991). *Organisational Behaviour* 2nd edn. Hemel Hempstead: Prentice-Hall

Lawrence P. A. and Lee R. S. (1984). *Insight into Management*. Oxford: Oxford University Press (Chapter 3)

Pugh D. S., ed. (1990). *Organizational Theory – Selected Readings* 3rd edn. Harmondsworth: Penguin

QUESTIONS

4.1 What are organizations, and why are they needed?

4.2 'McGregor's Theory X and Theory Y assumptions about human behaviour are self-fulfilling prophesies.' What are these assumptions? Why have they been described as 'self-fulfilling'?

4.3 What part does motivation play in job performance? Outline the contributions to motivation theory made by Maslow's hierarchy of human needs and Herzberg's motivator and hygiene factors.

4.4 'Pay peanuts, get monkeys.' To what extent does motivation theory support this observation on the likely consequences of a parsimonious remuneration policy?

4.5 Leadership quality, or management style, has been analysed in terms of personality traits, management grids, and on a situational or contingency basis. Explain and compare these different approaches.

4.6 'The structure of a traditional business organization is largely determined by a number of classic principles.' What is this traditional structure, and what are the principles that shape it?

4.7 The first objective in one approach to designing a company organization is to define:

- *why* the organization is needed
- *what* it has to do
- *how* some people-related constraints restrict design freedom.

Describe, briefly, appropriate topics for analysis in each of these three areas.

4.8 (a) Describe, with the aid of diagrams, the techniques of functional partitioning and divisionalization for defining the levels in an organizational hierarchy.
(b) Which of these structuring techniques is to be preferred, and why? Is the preferred technique generally applicable? If not, why not?

4.9 (a) Identify, and explain, three important trends which are modifying the overall structure of industry in the 'well-developed' Western nations.
(b) In what ways might the changes in industrial structure affect the nature of industrial organizations and employment opportunities?

PART 2

Technical Management

Chapter 5 Technical Organizations and People

Technological innovation, which is the process of creating new things with technology, is the primary task of the technical function within a business. This chapter is about the organization of technological innovation in industry. It is considered from a design perspective. In fact, the opportunity to design a technical organization from scratch occurs only rarely. But the approach used exposes the problems and limitations of various organizational structures in a way which assists the understanding of how they work. Chapter 4 is a broader introduction to the organization of people at work and provides a background for the more specialized material in this chapter.

Chapter 6 Technical Project Planning and Control

Normally, the first significant step towards management for engineers with that ambition is elevation to the post of project manager. A major facet of project management is project planning and control. Proper attention to this activity is one of the few low-risk high-return investments available to modern businesses but, strangely, not all of them give it the priority that it deserves. This (long) chapter concentrates on important planning and control techniques which are suited to technical innovation projects. But all projects share a common set of critical features, so the material is applicable to all types of project.

Chapter 7 About Costs and Costing

The subject of business costs and costing is sometimes regarded as the exclusive domain of financial staff. But the cost aspects of technical projects and of products are critical engineering issues which are too important to be left entirely to the accountants. The approach adopted here treats these facets of the whole subject as fundamental engineering topics. The chapter opens with a justification of this perspective (which is not universally accepted, despite its clear rational). But the purpose of costing is to inform internal users of cost information, so it falls within the orbit of management accounting. Because of this, the chapter can also be regarded as an excursion into the accounting arena.

Chapter 8   Structured Product Design

Businesses operating in competitive markets face disaster unless they can create products which provide good value for money to their customers *and* are sufficiently profitable. Business survival and prosperity, therefore, is critically dependent on excellence in product design. This chapter introduces a relatively informal, but tightly structured, approach to product design which provides a foundation on which excellence can be built. It is totally technology independent, so it can be applied to any and every sort of product. In fact, it is a general purpose methodology for solving a broad range of management problems, of which the problem of product design is just one example. Appendix A provides an illustration of the methodology in practice.

Technical Organizations and People

... for Art and Science cannot exist but in
minutely organized Particulars.

William Blake 1757–1827

5.1	Introduction	156
5.2	Technical function: Role summary	157
5.3	Profiles and objectives	161
5.4	Design constraints	166
5.5	Design implementations	177
5.6	Concluding summary	191

 Repetitions   Sections 3.2 and 3.4 comprised a detailed description of *what* the technical function has to do. This chapter is about the organizational aspects of *how* it does it. A summary of the Chapter 3 material appears at Section 5.2 as a necessary preliminary to the subsequent discussions.

Funding sources for technical projects were identified in Section 3.4.4. The treatment here, at Section 5.4.5, expands the initial summary into a perspective of funding sources as organizational and management constraints.

Section 3.5 sought an understanding of the special problem of software innovation. Section 5.5.7 summarizes that problem analysis as background to a brief discussion of an organization for software creation.

The overall objectives of this chapter are to examine, from a design perspective, a number of organizational structures which are suited to the different phases of technological innovation activity relating to both hardware and software products. Chapter 4 gives a broader introduction to organizational issues, and provides a background for the more specialized material in this chapter. Objectives by section follow:

5.1 To emphasize the importance of employing competent people in appropriate organizations, and to focus the chapter on the technical function of technology-based manufacturing businesses.

5.2 To review the primary and secondary tasks of the technical function.

5.3 To introduce technological profiles as a tool to aid the analysis of technical organizations, and to derive a set of design objectives for technical functions.

5.4 To identify the principal people-related and other constraints which should be recognized in the design of technical organizations.

5.5 To discuss the relative merits and most appropriate applications of five distinct types of technical organizations, and to introduce an appropriate structure for software innovation.

5.6 To identify its salient points and summarize its major messages.

5.1 Introduction

The most important single factor which determines the future of any business is the quality of the people it employs. But survival and prosperity is not ensured simply(!) by acquiring high-quality people. They also have to be organized to give of their best. This challenge is examined in general terms in Chapter 4. A more focused analysis continues in this chapter. It is about the organization of the **technical function** in technology-based manufacturing businesses. The topic is considered from a *design perspective*, because that approach exposes the positive and negative aspects of different organizations in a way which assists the understanding of how they work. The term 'technical function' is used in the sense of a stage, or sub-process, in the primary business process of creating and selling products to customers. It encapsulates, therefore, all those activities within a business relating to **technological innovation**.

The function normally employs most of the technically qualified staff in the business, be they scientists, engineers, mathematicians or supporting staff. Most of these people also start their industrial careers in this area, because their first few industrial jobs relate directly to the specialist skill derived from their initial education and training. They will start by joining an organization based on one or other of the structures discussed in this chapter.

5.2 | Technical function: Role summary

The role of the technical function is detailed in Chapter 3 at Section 3.2 (The primary tasks) and at Section 3.4 (Secondary tasks). A summary of that material follows immediately at Sections 5.2.1 and 5.2.2. It is a necessary preliminary to the later sections.

5.2.1 Technological innovation

Technological innovation is about creating new things with technology; it is the technical aspect of the **product creation process**. The work is generally focused on new and enhanced products to be offered for sale, but it may also be aimed at improving, in some way, the product creation process itself. In this book, the activity is partitioned into four primary tasks (or phases) which are termed **basic research**, **applied research**, **product development** and **product design**. In many texts, and in industry generally, these activities are lumped together under the broad heading of **research and development** (R&D) or, perhaps, **engineering**. This traditional jargon is now too well established to change, but it is misleading and potentially dangerous:

- There are very real differences between the four primary tasks. These differences should be recognized in their organization, staffing and management.

The technical aspect of the new product creation process can be visualized, somewhat idealistically, as a sequential flow of **product definition information** through four project phases. The concept is illustrated in Figure 5.1.

As each phase is traversed the quality of this information, in terms of its completeness, integrity and value, improves. Finally, the idea investigated in the basic research project becomes incorporated, usually in greatly modified form, in proven 'how to make and test it' information passed from the product design project to the production function. The provision of this expression of product definition data, in a high quality form which is compatible with the manufacturing capabilities of production, is the ultimate purpose of technological innovation.

Basic research

Basic research is about assessing the technical and economic feasibility of some new technological concept. One or more applied research projects may then be launched if this feasibility is judged sufficiently promising.

Applied research

In applied research, the aim is to resolve the uncertainties (technical and economic) carried over from the basic research, and to specify a **product range** based on the now more precise initial concept. Preliminary product cost estimates are also produced at this stage. These are one critical input to the commercial re-evaluation which occurs at the end of every phase (and, possibly, also at intermediate 'milestones').

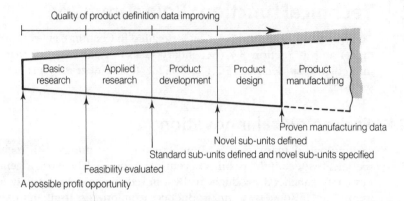

Figure 5.1   **A simplified view of the product creation process.**
This combines and condenses Figures 3.4 and 3.5 to show the *technical* part of the new product creation process as a sequential flow of product definition information through four project phases. The completeness, integrity and value of this information increase as each phase is traversed. Ultimately, proven 'how to make and test it' information is passed from the product design project to the production function. Achieving this is the end objective of technological innovation.

Product development and design

The distinctive features of product development and product design are important, but quite subtle. To explain them, the **configuration view** of a complete product must be reiterated. This perceives:

- A complete product as a unique configuration of sub-units, about which everything that needs to be known is known.

Some new products are designed and constructed solely from **established sub-units**. These are sub-units which are easily available, well-understood and proven. In such cases, product novelty resides only in the sort of established sub-units used and the manner in which they are interconnected. But other new products also incorporate some **novel sub-units**. These are sub-units which have not been used before in practical, real-life, situations.

(The building analogy, cited in Chapter 3 at Section 3.2.1, will clarify these concepts – and those immediately following – for readers meeting them for the first time.)

So, in the general case, creating a new product involves creating a unique configuration of established and novel sub-units. But the novel (new) sub-units must themselves be created in exactly the same way as the new product which is their ultimate destination! This observation leads directly to the perspectives of product development and product design which are presented here. The two activities are distinguished by their different purposes and positions in time, rather than by their nature.

Product *development* is the process of creating well-understood, proven, novel sub-units which are destined for incorporation into the pre-determined configuration of proven sub-units comprising the complete product.

Product *design* is the 'matching' activity. It is the process of creating the novel configuration of well-understood and proven sub-units to implement the pre-determined specification of the complete product. Established sub-units usually dominate (numerically) the novel configuration, but it may contain a significant proportion of novel sub-units.

From a purely technical point of view, product development (when it is needed) should precede product design, rather than be in parallel with it. However, a saving in the cost and time of the combined phases often occurs if parallelism is adopted. This is usually achieved (unwisely, perhaps) by inadequate proving of the novel sub-units. But the probability of product failure, sooner or later, is then greatly increased. The fact that buildings, and other products, sometimes fall over bears witness to this. Less dramatic problems can also occur. A fruitful source of such incidents is designing with non-proven sub-units. (Software products seem to be particularly vulnerable to this disease. That problem is examined, briefly, in Section 5.5.7.) In any complex operation a step-by-step approach, with testing at each step, is the safer course. This is why the distinctions between product development and product design are important.

The phases compared

Basic research is about exploring the unknown. Project objectives can be firmly defined but the paths to their achievement tend to be speculative, fuzzy and changeable. Predicting the time and cost which will be absorbed in completing such projects is difficult and the answers are unreliable. The work is best carried out by scientists who are motivated by a thirst for knowledge, since most basic research projects fail in the (limited) sense that they do not spawn an applied research project.

At the other extreme, product development and design is about creating something novel from what is already largely known. Project objectives, and the time and cost available to achieve them, are invariably sharply defined. The vast majority of these projects succeed in the sense that they meet their technical objectives more or less to plan. This is work for engineers.

Applied research is the intermediate case, with some of the characteristics of its predecessor and successor phases. However, clarity of objectives and probability of technical success are each much higher than for basic research. It is more akin to development and design for these reasons.

Phase boundaries should be imposed by management, but some 'people-overlap' should occur in practice. This reduces NIH (not invented here) problems, and eases information flow between successive phases. Some iteration around the phases is inevitable – 'right first time' is a worthy but unreachable target. It is not, of course, necessary for all four phases to be carried out within the same business, because it is getting the information that matters and any (legal) way will suffice.

Failure to distinguish adequately between the phases is a sad fact in many cases where the whole process is contained within one business. The fault should be corrected. It is no more difficult to manage technological innovation properly than badly, and the rewards are greater.

5.2.2 Secondary tasks

Some other tasks, as well as those directly associated with technological innovation, are normally assigned to the technical function. These are generally regarded as secondary to the main task, but they must be taken into account because they are part of the total technological innovation environment. The major items are identified here, but the supporting detail is limited. More illumination is provided in Section 3.4 of Chapter 3.

- *Analysis of non-company products*, relating to:
  - own new product development and design
  - competitive intelligence for the marketing function
  - supplier ratings for the purchasing function
  - 'make or buy' decisions.
- *Licences and patents*, involving:
  - evaluation of technologies or products offered on licence
  - preparation, defence or attack of patents.
- *Assistance to other functions*, in relation to own products:
  - technical assistance to sales (TAS)
  - technical assistance to manufacturing (TAM).
- *Preparation of project proposals* aimed at:
  - internal sponsors with **private venture** (PV) funds
  - external sponsors with **contract development** (CD) funds
  - joint sponsors with a mix of PV and CD funds.
- *Project evaluation and choice (technical aspects)*, because:
  - project proposals must compete for limited project resources.
- *Wider commercial objectives*, such as:
  - a profit requirement on externally sponsored projects
  - 'capability marketing' directed at potential customers.
- *Access to 'research clubs'*, which:
  - transcend company and national boundaries
  - ensure the necessary openness of pure and basic research.

Private venture funds 'belong' to the business launching (or proposing to launch) the venture, or project. The crucial point is that they are a *charge against profit*, which means that they are paid for out of profit. In other words (words which are important for later in the chapter), if they are not spent the profit is correspondingly larger. The term 'venture' has connotations of gamble or risk. This is a feature shared by all projects: money, time and staff effort are all spent in the hope, not the certainty, of a worthwhile reward.

The 'secondary tasks' problem

With a few exceptions, the secondary tasks have one characteristic in common. This is the mostly unpredictable nature of the extent, timing and frequency of their incidence, although history suggests that they will continue to arise. One management job is to do everything possible to minimize this uncertainty. This is relatively easy in some cases. For example, the time for preparing PV proposals, aimed at internal sponsors, is fixed by the business annual budget cycle. But the general problem remains. It is evidenced by frequent crises demanding reconsideration of current priorities, because the resources needed will usually be committed elsewhere.

5.2.3   Summary so far

It is useful to summarize the preceding summary (!) at this point. This is followed by a section which aims to shape the material into a framework of organizational objectives. Subsequent sections, about organizational **design constraints** and design implementations, are then built on this framework.

Why have a technical function?

The only justification for the existence of a technical function within a business is its contribution to the business process of creating new and enhanced products. Technological innovation, crudely defined as doing new things with technology, is its primary role in the business. The ultimate purpose of technological innovation is to supply high quality 'how to make and test it' data to the product manufacturing operation.

What does it have to do?

The scope of technological innovation is reviewed in Section 5.2.1. A particular view of a finished product (the configuration view) allows the process to be divided into four relatively distinct activities: basic research, applied research, product development and product design. The distinctions are important because they highlight the need to organize and manage the four activities in different ways.

The technical function is a centre of technical expertise in the business. Because of this, secondary tasks are normally assigned to it which are only marginally related to its main task of technological innovation. The most important are summarized in Section 5.2.2. The secondary tasks are an integral part of the technical function, and the special problems that they present must be recognized in its organization and management.

5.3   Profiles and objectives

The aim of this section is to rationalize the information and views of Sections 5.2.1 and 5.2.2 into a coherent structure for subsequent development.

5.3.1   Technological profiles

No two businesses are identical and no two solutions to the overall problem of technical function design are the same. But businesses within the same industry frequently adopt similar technical organizations. This suggests that common technical factors do exist within an industry. Ansoff and Stewart (1967) have developed this insight into the concept of the **technological profile**. This is:

- A set of technology-related factors which are characteristic of an industry at a particular stage in its development and, to some extent, of the individual businesses within that industry. In other words, each industry has an 'average' technological profile, to which the businesses comprising that industry conform to a greater or lesser extent.

The discussion that follows is adapted from the Ansoff and Stewart contribution. It provides a useful analytical tool and underlines some of the different organizational requirements of the four phases of technological innovation.

The major profile factors

The major factors making up a technological profile are:

(1) The **primary activities mix**. Technological innovation can be sub-divided, as shown earlier, into the four primary activities of basic and applied research, product development and product design. The relative proportions of these activities are important because they need different organizational and management techniques. This is less marked at the product development and design end of the process.

(2) The **secondary activities mix**. This expresses the relative proportions of the secondary tasks assigned to the technical function. The fraction of the total activity absorbed in this way is also critical. The factor is important in matters concerned with the most efficient use of resources, budgeting and project control.

(3) The **degree of coupling** with other business functions. This factor is an indicator of predominant project type. Development and design activity usually has busy links with the marketing, production and finance functions. Research tends to be relatively isolated in this respect. Interaction with the other business functions such as legal, personnel, purchasing, and so on also occurs.

(4) The **typical duration of the product life cycle**. Short product life cycles, measured (say) in months rather than years, generally indicate a high rate of technology change in markets that are intensely competitive and unstable. (The product life cycle concept is discussed in Chapter 3 at Section 3.3.1.)

(5) The **R&D investment ratio**. Conventionally, this is the ratio of total techno-logical innovation costs to sales revenue, both measured in the same year.

(6) The **degree of 'state-of-the-art'**. When most of the products are based on technology close to the frontiers of current knowledge a high-risk, high-reward business strategy is implied.

Clearly, the factors making up a technological profile are not all totally independent. It provides, however, a set of convenient headings for assessing the extent to which an *existing* technical organization matches that required for efficient operation. The underlying factors which link the profile factors are market conditions and the rate of relevant technological change. Because an organizational change rarely occurs before the need for it is well established, a technical function organization is likely to be less than ideal at any given time. In the rare event of designing a totally *new* technical organization, the profile approach enhances the probability of a good result.

The major profile factors are now examined in a little more detail.

A note on the primary activities mix

There are two built-in traps for the unwary analyst here. For some reason, particularly in Britain, 'research' (as distinct from 'development') has an aura of academic respect-ability and high status. The other side of this counterfeit coin is that product develop-ment and design are often regarded as relatively lowly occupations. As such, they are best left to those unfortunate individuals whose technical aspirations are not, sadly, matched by their technical prowess. An industrial consequence of this myth is that the term 'research' can be used to describe activities which are manifestly not in that category – because this elevates the perceived status of the work or of the establishment concerned.

There is another situation, also in Britain, which can result in the misuse of the research category. This one makes more business sense. Businesses which conduct a high proportion of government-funded contract development argue (correctly) that their capability to do the work stems largely from their PV activities in the relevant field. These activities are paid for out of profit. The government ministries concerned accept the argument to the extent that some fraction of agreed PV expenditure on research can be included within the costs of the CD contracts. Here, then, is an assured mechanism for recovering some part of business costs! Not surprisingly, businesses in this happy position are inclined to take a liberal view of what constitutes research. Equally, the ministry officials tend to have a more narrow outlook in this respect. A compromise has been reached in which the term 'research' is defined in a way compatible, in fact, with the definitions in this book. These still present ample opportunities for debate, especially between accountants.

It is largely irrelevant if the term 'research' is abused for either reason, unless it leads to product development or product design being organized in ways more appropriate to research. But the message for the analyst is plain: it is the true research activities which must be identified, irrespective of what they are called within the business.

A note on the secondary activities mix

The secondary activities present a management problem for two main reasons. First, as indicated earlier, they are largely unpredictable in timing and extent. Second, they are mostly **indirect** activities which do not directly contribute to the primary purpose of the function. But a substantial part of the work they entail must be assigned to the **direct** staff: those whose principal role *is* the primary purpose of the function. This combination of circumstances can present budgeting difficulties. Faced with the problem, there is a temptation to 'lose' the time and cost of the secondary activities within the primary activities. The ethics of this practice are, at least, debatable. It also results in excessive costs and extended time-scales for the primary projects which bear the burden, and confuses their monitoring and control. Another side effect is that the true extent of the secondary activities may never become apparent.

There is no doubt that proper budgeting is the only satisfactory answer to the problem. But it has to be admitted that it can be difficult, on occasions, to persuade higher management that such a budget is both realistic and justified.

A note on the degree of coupling

Typically, the marketing, production and finance functions are heavily involved only once a year with the research activities. This occurs when the PV research project proposals are being evaluated. At the other end of the spectrum, development and design projects need constant communication across interfunctional boundaries. This fact is significant in deciding the optimum location of those technical activities which are close to the market-place.

Two major barriers to good human communication are geographical and organizational boundaries. These should be avoided, where possible, in the case of product development and design. This is a strong argument in favour of **divisionalization** (a topic which is discussed in Chapter 4 at Section 4.4.3). On the other hand, basic research might benefit by the presence of at least one such barrier. A degree of detachment from the frenetic activity at the coal-face can create an atmosphere more conducive to longer-term thinking. And the research staff are less likely to be drafted into the front line in times of crisis. This solution, however, does carry with it the danger of too much detachment from the business. Applied research is (as usual) an intermediate case. Equally convincing arguments can be made, in theoretical terms, for association with or separation from the business it serves. Existing situations are often easily resolved by leaving them alone.

A note on the life cycle duration

When the rate of technological change is high and the market very competitive, the organization of the technical function should encourage close coupling with both marketing and production. Rapid and innovative product development and design is needed, especially for product enhancements. The major businesses in such industries usually maintain substantial research activities which, in association with a potent marketing function, spearhead growth in new business areas. Their smaller competitors will observe these activities with great interest, aiming to follow selected initiatives as quickly and cheaply as possible.

In the more mature, slower changing, industries the competitive pressures are much reduced and a fairly lethargic approach generally prevails. Relative isolation of the technical function, especially of its most innovative part, is the accepted norm in these industries. It is not suggested that this is a good thing, it merely indicates that tight business function interaction is considered unimportant.

A note on the R&D investment ratio

There is, of course, usually no direct connection between the two elements of the ratio: the level of technological innovation in any one year is unlikely to affect sales in that same year. But the ratio is a useful 'normalized' measure of the relative level of technological innovation activity in different businesses. The relative status of the technical function with respect to the other functions within the same business is also indicated. A high ratio implies a high status, absorbing substantial top management attention, close alignment with major business objectives and, probably, an efficient organization. Conversely, low ratios imply low status and, possibly, neglect by top management. The technical functions in these latter businesses are not exciting operations. Ratios range from as high as thirty per cent in exceptionally fast-moving market sectors, or where the technology is inherently expensive (nuclear power generation, for example) to figures of less than one per cent in ponderous and, perhaps, dying industries.

There is a prestige value associated with a high ratio, since it suggests (sometimes correctly) dynamic management. Herein lies another trap for the unwary in assessing published figures. It is common practice to advertise ratios which include externally funded activities in the calculation. The ratio expressed in purely PV terms is generally of greater interest, and some minor research may be required to extract it. Another problem is that expenditure on the secondary technical activities is invariably included in the total sum. It is virtually impossible to undo this confusion without an intimate knowledge of the business concerned.

A note on the degree of state-of-the-art

Typically, businesses with a high rating on this factor either blossom as product innovators or fade into obscurity soon after birth. A fast-moving, flexible, highly creative technical function closely coupled to the other major functions is one critical requirement for initial success. The organization of the technical function in such a business is likely to be very informal in its early stages. Few of these businesses sustain their initial launch strategy into an era of significant growth; some sort of management or money crisis usually intervenes. If they survive this, reversion to more conventional behaviour and organization generally follows.

5.3.2 Organizational objectives

A number of high-level organizational objectives for the technical function can be distilled from the discussion so far. These are:

(1) Alignment of technical activities with business objectives
 – to achieve profitable exploitation of all relevant technologies.
(2) Recognition of the four distinct phases in technological innovation
 – because the organizational and other management requirements of these four phases are not identical.
(3) Efficient communication
 – of high-quality product definition information from phase to phase in the technological innovation process
 – when and where appropriate, with other business functions, especially marketing, production and finance.
(4) Efficient data selection and assimilation
 – by the organization from sources inside and outside the business.
(5) Provision for the efficient discharge of other tasks
 – which are assigned to the technical function, but which also tend to distract attention from its primary purpose.

It might be considered, initially, that these organizational objectives are all fairly obvious, and there is merit in this view. But longer reflection indicates some internal conflicts within the listing. For example, the need for 'efficient communication' suggests co-location of all four primary technical activities with (at least) marketing, production and finance. This may be physically impossible, and would probably result in an unwieldy overall organization even if it were possible. So the organization design problem is (as always) to achieve some acceptable compromise of the objectives while, at the same time, satisfying (or avoiding) various constraints, or boundary conditions.

The word 'efficient', used with some abandon in the list of objectives, can be interpreted as 'in a way which delivers good value for money'. Money and time are always in short supply: they are always constraints. Often, even more severe constraints are buried in the nature of technical people. Typical constraints applying to technical function design are now considered.

5.4 | Design constraints

Design constraints, which are factors restricting freedom of manoeuvre in a design exercise, always exist. They should be specifically identified before design implementation is tackled. Organizational design constraints are discussed here under the broad headings of *people-related* and *other*. But, first, a (perhaps surprising) message about design constraints in general.

Design constraints are good news!

The term 'constraints' suggests bad news but this is rarely the case. Initially, in all but the most trivial design projects, there always seems to be a large number of different ways of achieving the design aims. The proper identification of design constraints can knife through this early confusion by closing down most of these false design options. Progress on a design project can be equated with the emergence of design options and the rejection of most of them.

For example, consider the use of an 'application-specific integrated circuit' (ASIC) to provide a specific feature in a particular electronic product. Its purchase cost is well below that of the twenty standard integrated circuits that are needed to provide the feature in the 'old-fashioned' approach. It is also less costly to incorporate into the finished product. So, an ASIC-based design yields the lowest manufactured cost for the product. But the ASIC is a non-standard sub-unit (by definition). It has to be designed to meet its specific application. And it is very much more expensive to design an ASIC to provide the feature than it is to design a configuration of twenty standard integrated circuits to do the same job. In the absence of other decisive constraints (relating to physical size, say) the proper choice of implementation technique then turns on the volume of anticipated product sales and net earnings per product sale. There is no virtue in achieving a low manufactured cost for the product if the corresponding design costs compromise its profitability.

(This example illustrates a common business situation involving **fixed** and **variable** costs. A straightforward application of these notions, relating to vehicle ownership, is included in Chapter 7 at Section 7.5.2. It is labelled the **break-even concept**.)

5.4.1 People constraints

The most critical part of the technical function is the body of qualified scientists, mathematicians and engineers that it contains. Provided that these individuals are at, or beyond, their personal **comfort thresholds** their principal motivations are likely to be focused on **self-esteem** and **self-actualization** needs (all discussed in Section 4.2.2). Engineers, as they mature, tend to develop rather different needs of this sort than scientists and mathematicians, who seem to be more stable in this respect. This is one way in which technical people can be differentiated.

The conflict between university and industry cultures

In their early formative years, many qualified technical people are exposed to a university-type culture in which research prowess is highly valued and a belief in a set of **research norms** prevails. Management, as the term is used in industry, is neither well understood nor widely employed. Commercial targets, when present, are frequently rejected. In practice, as distinct from theory, these organizations tend to be 'flat' rather than hierarchical and their government is democratic rather than authoritarian.

Inevitably, students in the university-type ambience absorb some of this culture. The effect is most marked in those individuals who do postgraduate work. The reality of sharply contrasting university-type and industry environments suggests that graduates joining industry will be poorly equipped to handle the resulting culture shock. (Some speculations about the future of industrial, organizational and job structures are included in Section 4.5. These suggest that industrial organizations will become more like universities, and that universities will become more like business organizations.)

Parker (1985) discusses the conflict between the beliefs comprising the **scientific norms** and some **business norms** (which are expectations rather than beliefs). Here, the term **research norms** is preferred, because the original scientific norms now permeate all academic disciplines. The research norms are summarized by the following traditional beliefs:

- **Universalism** Professional judgement of research contributions should be based on impersonal, objective criteria relating to novelty, repeatability of results, and their explanation in terms of established principles.
- **Communality** Knowledge gained from research should be made universally available.
- **Disinterestedness** The advancement of knowledge should take precedence over individual reward.
- **Research scepticism** Research results should be valued, by independent peer review, on the basis of their contribution to knowledge.
- **Autonomy** Researchers should be free to choose their own fields of endeavour.

It is the research culture expressed by these beliefs that has shaped the whole university system. It encourages individual behaviour patterns in stark contrast to those expected in industry. Included amongst the business norms are:

- **Business loyalty** Staff are expected to serve the business that employs them, rather than to owe their loyalty to a professional discipline or community.
- **Conformity** Staff are required, and expected, to follow established business rules and procedures, and they will have little influence on the choice of projects to which they are assigned.
- **Hierarchical structure** Staff must accept a hierarchical status structure of authority, responsibility and discipline which may bear no relationship to professional expertise.
- **Confidentiality** Commercially sensitive information created by a staff member is regarded as the property of the business and should be kept confidential.
- **Rewards** Individual rewards depend primarily on ranking in the management hierarchy.

In general, management expertise is more highly rewarded than technical status measured against the research norms. However, a number of businesses have now adopted a purely technical hierarchy which parallels the management hierarchy. Access to it is usually restricted to exceptionally productive individuals. But the quality of a piece of technical work is still likely to be judged solely on its potential commercial value. Any contribution that it might make to wider knowledge, if considered at all, will usually be a matter of some indifference to the judges.

It is difficult and, usually, unrewarding to attempt to change the value perceptions of a committed scientist or mathematician. Thus, the management team in charge of the research activity, which is where most of these people reside, has a motivation problem of a rather special sort. The solution must recognize the nature of the research staff and pay more than mere lip service to the business expectations. A compromise is inevitable. Whatever this is, some measure of occasional dissent can be confidently predicted from levels both above and below in the hierarchy.

Usually, engineers are less troubled by this awkward, in industrial terms, set of values. This is mostly a matter of native temperament reinforced, hopefully, by some insights into industrial reality absorbed in their early professional education and training. In this sense, engineers are easier to manage in industry and they will most frequently start their careers in product development or product design. This observation does *not* suggest that management of that end of technological innovation is easier than management of the research aspects. The greater commercial pressures in product development and design at least counterbalance the benefits of a more acquiescent staff.

Having made this distinction between the scientific and engineering temperaments, a caveat must be entered: the distinction is often not very great. As a broad generalization, to which honourable exceptions exist, technical people tend to reject the normal business culture with its paramount commercial motivations and exhibit strong discipline loyalties. This factor seems to be an organizational design constraint chiefly confined to technical people. (It is a personality trait which, on balance, damages the individuals and the businesses that employ them. It is something that this book aims to change.) Technical management generally, therefore, carries with it the special burden of compromising between two very different cultures, which puts great emphasis on sensitive leadership.

Creativity and its problems

Creativity is an ability shared by good scientists and engineers. Encouraging it presents some organizational design constraints and management problems. But it must be encouraged because creativity is the life-blood of innovation and a business must innovate or die. There are no plateaux in the business world: a business is either getting better or getting worse.

The **creative process**, which solves novel non-routine problems, is not well understood. It always involves a flash of insight which knits together some already understood ideas or concepts into a new relationship. It is now generally accepted that four sequential steps are involved:

(1) *Preparation*   This is where the real problem (often not the same as the one

first posed) is recognized, and a number of abortive attempts at its solution are explored.

(2) *Incubation* A subconscious element of the process during which it appears that the mind, now steeped in the problem, continues to explore different possible solutions. Incubation seems to be most productive when the conscious attack on the problem has been temporarily abandoned, and when the conscious mind is relaxed, even to the extent of being asleep.

(3) *Illumination* This is the sudden conscious flash of insight previously cited. It may reveal a 'finished' solution (as in the obviously correct answer to the obscure crossword puzzle clue) or only suggest a new line of attack, often by an analogy with some other problem. In these cases, the process loops back to the preparation phase.

(4) *Verification* Here the 'finished' solution is tested against the criteria posed by the problem. It is a non-trivial phase in many situations. Failure at this stage is not necessarily a total disaster. Looping back to the preparation phase, armed with the flawed new concept, may well produce the desired result.

A systematic, logical approach is entirely appropriate for the preparation stage but, if pursued too far, may inhibit the incubation and illumination stages. This may be avoided by consciously avoiding early decisions – even when they seem very obvious and pressures for progress are developing. When initial saturation with the problem has been achieved, and a good solution remains elusive, then the effort should be temporarily abandoned. This requires courage on occasions, both by the potential problem solver(s) and by their managers. But it is the wisest course, because, in fact, the problem has not been abandoned. It has been passed over to the subconscious mind(s) where processing continues. Ross (1977), in his seminal design methodology papers, offers a different expression of the same advice. He counsels deferment of design implementation decisions for as long as possible, to avoid confusing problems with solutions.

This brief excursion into the nature of creativity illuminates a conflict between the process mechanism (insofar as it is understood) and some typical management aims. 'Go and solve it by tomorrow' is a challenging, but unrealistic, command. Predicting the duration of the creative process borders on impossible. Its outcome is uncertain and success cannot be guaranteed. How, then, can the process be planned, timed, costed and controlled? The answer, which is 'it cannot', is bad news for managers. But they must learn to live with it. They must also come to accept that apparently irrational thought processes, as in a 'brainstorming' session, can be potent problem solving tools.

Further to all this, exceptionally creative people often have their own set of behavioural norms. Frequently, these do not align with business conventions on appearance, hours of work, overt respect for management, and so on. There is no malice in such behaviour: its practitioners are merely absorbed with more important (to them) things. The effective management of these stars is no small challenge. Exciting their interest in a relevant problem and shielding them from less perceptive higher management are the keys to success.

Compared with people-derived constraints, the other constraints considered in the remainder of this section are relatively straightforward. Note, though, that many of these can be traced back to an origin in human nature.

5.4.2 Location constraints

First, there is the question of the optimum location of a particular technical activity. The word *'location'* is used here in both its geographical and its organizational sense.

Apart from cost, there are two major constraints on the suitability of a particular location for a particular technical activity. These are its attractiveness to people with the requisite skills and business communication factors. Both the required skill mix and the required communication structure depend on the nature of the technological innovation activity concerned. For example, it might be advantageous to establish a basic research operation near to a major university, even if this geographically isolates it from the rest of the business. On the other hand, the optimum siting of product development and design activities is dominated by the need for good communication with their 'customer' businesses.

The bonds and barriers concept

The concept of **bonds and barriers** to communication is useful in debating the location of technological innovation activities. All technical projects funded by the 'parent' business have an in-business customer (sponsor) who is, usually, also the source of the PV funds. The project team may be co-located or geographically isolated from that customer. So relative geography with respect to the customer can be a bond or a barrier. Equally, the team may be part of the same organization as the customer or part of another organization (both are within the same overall business). So relative organization with respect to the customer can also be a bond or a barrier.

The matrix of Figure 5.2 shows the four possible combinations of these bonds and barriers. In principle, each of these four **bond/barrier constructs** can be used with each of the four distinct phases of technological innovation, yielding sixteen basic options. There are also several (five, say) choices for the detailed substructure within each of the four high-level constructs. So, in theory, there are about eighty organizational options! Happily, most of these are not practical business propositions. In a large business, for example, the **two-bond** construct for basic research and the **two-barrier** construct for product design, even if they are geographically feasible, come into this category. A selection of detailed organizational structures is discussed in the next section. Here, the emphasis remains on establishing some broad general principles by evaluating the bond/barrier constructs in the light of various constraints.

The **two-barrier** case is commonly used for basic research. Many large businesses have a 'central' research laboratory which reports directly to headquarters and is separately sited in attractive surroundings. It sells its services to the rest of the business (and, usually, to a variety of external customers). This organizational and geographic isolation encourages an academic atmosphere which appeals to many of the staff and allows the 'capability marketing' role to be emphasized. Because of the long-term nature of the work, and because of its inherent uncertainties, continuous interaction with the other major business functions is not needed. Indeed, it is not even desirable as it might divert the focus from long-term aims onto a current crisis.

However, there are intrinsic dangers in the scheme. One of these is too much isolation from the parent business. Scientists, naturally enough, prefer to work on the things that interest them. These are not necessarily the things that interest the business. Also, translating basic research outputs into applied research inputs is hard

Type	Location	Organization
Two barriers	Different	Different
One bond One barrier	Same	Different
One bond One barrier	Different	Same
Two bonds	Same	Same

Figure 5.2 **Communication bonds and barriers**

A technical team working on private venture (PV) projects may, or may not, be co-located with its company customers. So team location is a helpful bond, or a restricting barrier, in communicating with its customers. Equally, the team may, or may not, be part of the same organization as its company customers. So organization is a helpful bond, or a restricting barrier, in communicating with its customers. The matrix shows the four possible combinations in this 'communication bonds and barriers' concept. It is a useful notion which highlights communications as a potent factor in debating the best location and organization of the four different types of technological innovation activity.

work, which includes some tedious administration. The temptation to extend basic research projects well beyond their pre-defined boundaries may prove irresistible. A side effect is that further 'evidence' supporting the flawed theory that basic research cannot be planned or controlled accrues, to the great satisfaction of its advocates.

It is quite usual to co-locate applied research activities with basic research work in the same organization. Some economies of scale may flow from this, and the change from basic to applied research is certainly eased. But the case for two-barrier applied research is less strong: close interaction with the customers is frequently required.

Perhaps the ideal solution to the location problem of the research activities is to use the two-barrier arrangement for basic research and one or other of the **one-bond, one-barrier** schemes for applied research. There are two cases to consider. In the first, the applied research team is co-located with the basic researchers, but 'belongs' (organizationally) to the trading division that it serves. In the second case, the applied research team is co-located with its customer trading division but belongs to the overall research organization. Figure 5.3 outlines the three cited possibilities.

Note that, in both one-bond, one-barrier schemes, the managers of the applied research units are in a *dual* reporting situation. On the one hand, they are responsible to their line manager for the satisfactory conduct of the applied research work. On the other hand, they are responsible to their site manager for the acceptable conduct of the applied research team. There is a conflict here with the 'one boss only' principle of classical organization theory (discussed in Section 4.3.1). In practice, such arrangements usually work satisfactorily.

Product development activity, as the term is used in this book, is sometimes organized in a one-bond, one-barrier scheme. This may be justified when the sub-units that are developed are stand-alone products in their own right or economies of scale are thereby achieved.

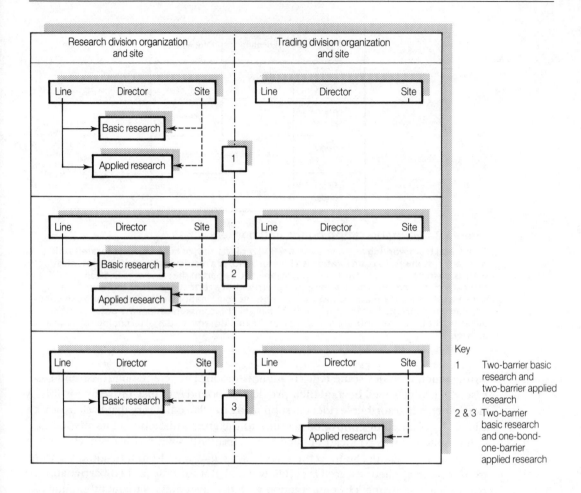

Figure 5.3   **Three possible research structures.**
Based on the bonds and barriers concept, this shows three possible ways of arranging research activity in a large company. The research headquarters and location are on the left, and a single (in-company) trading division research customer is shown on the right. Note that research team managers are responsible to a line (own organization) manager for the satisfactory conduct of research projects, and to a site manager (possibly as a tenant on the site) for the acceptable conduct of the research team. Basic research is commonly arranged in two-barrier format, as in all three structures here. The applied research case for this approach is less convincing and one of the one-bond–one-barrier schemes is often used, as in 2 and 3 here.

The intimate association of product design with the business that it serves demands the **two-bond** scheme of co-location in the same organization whenever possible. If this ideal is not available for some reason (space limitations, perhaps) then the **location-barrier, organizational-bond** arrangement is the next best option.

In a sense, product development has product design as its customer. Both activities require strong links with their customer business. This observation forms a strong case for associating product development with product design in the two-bond format.

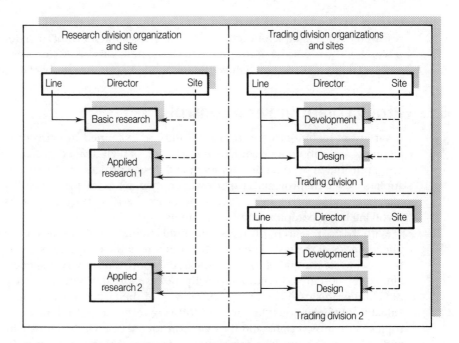

Figure 5.4 **A possible technical function organization.**
This is also based on the bond/barrier principles. It outlines *one* possible organization for the whole
technical function in a large business. The research arrangement is discussed in the text associated
with Figure 5.3. The intimate association of product design with the business that it serves demands
the two-bond scheme of co-location in the same organization whenever possible. In a sense,
product development has product design as its customer. So, there is a strong case for associating it
with product design, as shown here.

Figure 5.4 is based on the bond/barrier principles. It outlines one possible
organization for the whole technical function in a large business. The structure
emphasizes the role of applied research as the transition phase between the longer-
term speculations of basic research and the immediate realities of product development and design.

The discussion on bonds and barriers is centred around ways of coping with the
rather different 'communication with the customer' constraint of the four distinct
activities which comprise technological innovation. This factor is one critical
constraint. Skills availability is another.

Expensive technical facilities

Just occasionally, the ownership of a very expensive technical facility is regarded as
the dominant constraint, demanding that all of the people who need such a thing be
co-located with it. An example is where an integrated circuit process *research* team is
placed alongside the integrated circuit *manufacturing* process-line, so that they can
share this costly facility. Schemes of this nature should be regarded with deep
suspicion, since they rarely work in practice. Top management (rightly) award very
different short-term priorities to manufacturing and research, because manufacturing

earns profit but research spends it. This would, almost certainly, ensure frustrated research in the example quoted (which underlines the merit of a barrier scheme for research). Those who have attempted to create new software systems on a computing service facility will also recognize the unfounded optimism of this false economy.

5.4.3 Project planning and control

A variety of techniques are available (and are examined in Chapter 6) to aid the planning, and subsequent control against plan, of well-defined projects. These tools are applicable to product development and design projects and, to a lesser extent, to applied research projects also. However, two types of project still present real planning and control difficulties. These are basic research projects and those involving large, complex, software systems.

With basic research projects the fundamental problem lies in the inherent uncertainties of the task. The activity is not unlike the early stages of a treasure hunt because, while the end objective is clear, the route to get there is speculative and the clues often obscure. This is not normally the case with the large software projects. The difficulty in this case lies in the complexity of the target software product and the valuable, but dangerous, flexibility of software technology. Both of these subjects are topics in their own right, and they are considered elsewhere (mostly in Chapter 3). Suffice it here to note their presence constraining the organization and management of such projects.

5.4.4 Performance measurement

Performance measurement, indicating how efficiently the technical activities are carried out, is a distinct topic related to project planning and control. It is an essential part of **quality assurance** applied to technical function activities. It seeks answers to questions like:

- Could it have been better planned?
- Are the control techniques adequate?
- Could it have been better implemented?
- Could the results have been more useful?
- Why did it go wrong?
- Why did it go right?
- Could it have been completed more quickly and/or more cheaply?

One approach to questions of this sort lies in the maintenance of project records and the frequent comparison of records for similar projects. Performance trends can then be detected and corrective action (**quality control**) taken if necessary. This technique is satisfactory for well-defined projects and then the performance measurement requirement hardly counts as a constraint. Basic research projects, again, pose a problem. Of course, the cited technique will yield some data on the more simplistic questions about project times and costs. But the more important quality assurance questions to be levelled at basic research are, for example:

- Are all the relevant technologies adequately covered?
- Is effort being wasted on irrelevant technologies?
- How many of our successful products started their life cycle in 'own' basic research?
- How does the effectiveness of the operation compare with that of our major competitors?

Sadly, because of the long product gestation time between basic research and the acid test of the product market-place, questions of this sort can only be answered retrospectively. The time lapse can amount to several years. Even then, faults are not necessarily due to flawed basic research. There are very many links in the tenuous chain between basic research and related product sales (or the absence of such sales). So, the major constraint on the organization of basic research remains encapsulated in the single big question:

- How should it be structured and managed to ensure optimum value for money?

At the present time there appears to be no good answer to this question, because about eighty per cent of basic research expenditure ultimately proves abortive. It may be, of course, that this does represent optimum value for money. But that is a hard thing to accept.

5.4.5 Sources of project funds

This topic was introduced, in relation to the secondary task of preparing project proposals, in Section 3.4.4. The treatment here expands an initial summary into a perspective of the topic as an organizational and management constraint.

Finally, in this survey of organizational design constraints, the means by which project funds flow into the technical function must be considered. In summary, the four principal sources in a large business are:

(1) **Central PV** (also termed **corporate PV** or **company PV**). This source is a private venture fund held at the top level in the business. It is sometimes derived from a small levy (one per cent of sales, say) on the trading activities of the business divisions.

(2) **Own-division PV** (also termed **intra PV**). This refers to a private venture fund held by the trading division owning the project team.

(3) **Other-division PV** (also termed **inter PV**). Here the source is a private venture fund held by a trading division not owning the project team.

(4) **Contract development** (also termed **customer-funded**, and abbreviated to **CD** or **CF**). These are funds obtained from project customers outside the business. The contract development (CD) terminology is potentially confusing, because external customers may sponsor basic research, applied research, product development or product design.

(Divisional funds are clearly not available in small to medium-sized businesses which lack a divisional structure.)

All of the PV funds are a charge against profit at one level or another in the business.

All of the PV project sponsors are committed to a profit target. If, at any time, it appears that the achievement of such targets is in doubt the sponsors concerned will seek to minimize their costs to ease, or remove, the problem. One of their costs is PV expenditure. Hence, all of the PV funds are vulnerable to profit pressure on their sources. This means that they are liable to be withdrawn at relatively short notice. When this happens, that fraction of a technical team assigned to affected projects is deprived of financial support. This is a serious technical management problem. The technical function is not supposed to make a loss (more correctly, its costs are supposed to be contained within a pre-determined budget). Its own profit earning capacity is likely to be too small to solve the problem, because making a substantial profit is not their primary role.

A wise technical manager will have a contingency plan for this crisis. This will include, if possible, a number of CD projects waiting for effort to become available before they can be launched. So, a normal reaction to the PV shortfall problem is to switch the vulnerable teams to CD work, either by increasing the effort on current contracts or by starting new ones.

While this might resolve the immediate problem, it is a ploy with inherent dangers (although, in justice, these are no fault of local technical management). The dangers include:

- *'Stop–go' policy on the PV work* This has a detrimental effect on the work and on the staff involved.

- *Irrelevant CD work* That is, choosing to do CD work for the wrong commercial reasons.

- *CD lock-in* When the PV funds are reinstated, the required teams are committed to CD contracts of less commercial interest.

So long as profit pressures and cost priorities exist, PV vulnerability will remain a constraint on the management and organization of the technical function. The impact can be minimized by following some 'rules of thumb':

(1) *Basic and applied research* Use central PV to fund all basic research, and as much applied research as possible. This puts the lowest priority (from top management perspective) work under the umbrella of the most secure PV fund. The teams involved are also likely to be the least flexible.

(2) *Product development and design* Use divisional PV to fund both activities. Divisional customers are likely to be cautious when it comes to cutting back work closely aligned with their immediate commercial interests. Choose own-division PV rather than other-division PV where possible, because charity begins at home.

(3) *CD work* This should satisfy one or more of the following selection criteria:
    (a) The work has a positive commercial value to the business, either directly or via some 'spin-off'.
    (b) It is deemed necessary so as to achieve or maintain good relationships with a valued external customer.
    (c) It is absolutely necessary to 'save' a valuable technical team.
    (d) A very substantial profit can be obtained.

(4) *Technical function budget* Aim at an overall technical function budget

which supports the staff on a one-third central PV, one-third divisional PV, one-third CD basis. This is generally not easily achieved but the closer the better to minimize PV vulnerability.

But note that, if external customers are willing to pay for work that is of commercial value to the business, it is usually a rational business decision to take their money. Exceptions occur when resource priorities dictate otherwise or, for some reason, there is no wish to get involved with a particular customer.

Note, too, that some trading divisions within a large business may be principally concerned with major **turnkey contracts**. That is, their business is the development, design, commissioning, supply and ongoing support of large 'one-off' systems funded by external customers. Examples include air-traffic control systems, military command and control systems and telephone switching systems. The mild caveats regarding CD work, expressed earlier, clearly do not apply in such cases.

5.4.6 Section end note

This section has reviewed some of the people, location and management constraints which apply to the design of technical organizations. It also illustrates a feature common to all management decisions. This is that compromise is always involved: there are no totally right solutions, but some solutions are better than others. Design work has this same characteristic. Management and design have a lot in common.

Some well-established, and less than perfect, solutions to the problem of technical function design are now considered in some detail.

5.5 Design implementations

Some years ago, Stanley and White (1965) published an analysis of technical function organizations covering some forty large American companies. They identified four types of basic structure. These are still found today, either alone or in combination, in both America and Europe. One particular combination is becoming increasingly popular. All of this is on the agenda for discussion here. Typical structures are illustrated, and their good and bad features explored. The analysis suggests both areas of application and, as emerges later, some further extensions. The section concludes with a brief excursion into the special problem of software creation. The four basic structures are considered first.

5.5.1 Professional discipline focus

This arrangement imitates the traditional university pattern of grouping broad disciplines into faculties and specialist disciplines into faculty departments. It is most commonly employed in industry for basic research and, less frequently, for applied research. An indicative structure, here cast in terms of basic research for a security company, is shown in Figure 5.5.

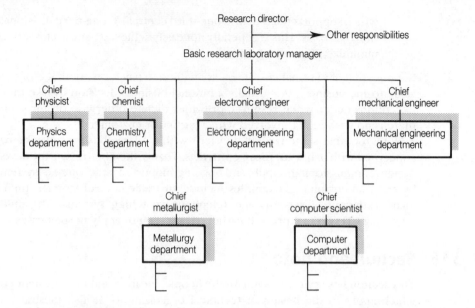

Figure 5.5   **Research laboratory organization by professional discipline focus.**
The type of structure shown here is commonly employed in industry for basic research and,
sometimes, applied research also. It imitates the traditional university pattern of grouping by
professional discipline (skill). The arrangement is attractive to many scientists and is well suited to
the advancement of knowledge in the individual disciplines. But projects which cross
interdisciplinary boundaries often run into difficulties, and staff easily lose touch with commercial
motivation and realities.

Advantages: Professional discipline focus

The structure is entirely appropriate for the advancement of knowledge in the disciplines. It encourages the evolution of closely knit, increasingly expert, specialist teams,
and the individual development of professional skills. New graduates are attracted to it
because of the familiarity of the university-like structure. Projects which are confined
to a single discipline can be handled effectively.

Disadvantages: Professional discipline focus

Simulation of the university environment can be damaging. Discipline loyalties, more
crudely described as 'tribal instincts', may be regarded as all important and the
underlying commercial motives then suffer. All professional groups exhibit a
tendency to believe that their part of the broader mission is the most important,
difficult, least appreciated and poorly rewarded. As a consequence, each discipline
seeks an ever-larger share of the limited resources available, leading to acrimonious
debate and interdiscipline rivalry. The situation is not improved by an elitist emphasis
on the quality of the research assessed in scientific terms. In turn, this encourages a
relaxed view on cost and time-scale targets which, in industry, are always important
factors.

Projects which cross the boundaries of the specialist disciplines often run into difficulties. The reasons for this are implicit in the sketch outlined above. Rational,

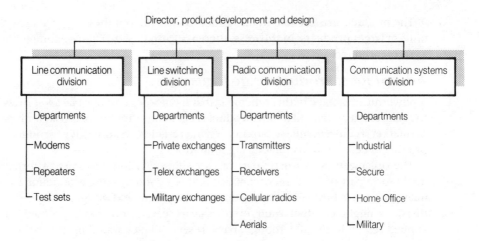

Figure 5.6 **Organization by product range focus.**
Here, the partitioning mechanism applied to the whole mission is based on products rather than
professional discipline. Each division, which is concerned with a broad class of similar products,
comprises a number of departments focused on an individual product range. The structure is well
suited to product development and design (as shown here) and it is usually part of its trading
division customer organization. It usefully enforces commercial awareness among the staff. But
their professional expertise may suffer from lack of contact, because of the internal boundaries,
with colleagues in their own discipline.

business-oriented, communication across the boundaries may be virtually non-
existent in extreme cases. Relative priorities also enter into the equation. Large single-
discipline projects are seen as more important than minor (in effort terms)
contributions to interdisciplinary projects. Yet those 'minor' contributions are often
the critical input to such projects. This structural weakness with interdisciplinary
projects is the most serious criticism of the organization. The reason is simple. It is
because, potentially, the most valuable innovations arise from a judicious amalgamation of concepts from the different disciplines.

Finally, the professional discipline environment does not encourage the nurturing
of generalist managers. Exposure to wider business issues is severely limited, as are
opportunities to test management expertise. This factor, together with some others,
poses career development problems for the staff.

In view of all these reservations, it is surprising that such organizations do survive in
industry and, on balance, work quite well. That this *is* so is a tribute to the quality and
patience of their managers. Clearly, the professional discipline approach is totally
unsuited to product development and design. These activities demand strong
commercial orientation and no disciplinary boundaries.

5.5.2   Product range focus

In this scheme, each second-level unit is concerned with a distinct product range,
rather than with a distinct professional discipline. Figure 5.6 illustrates such a
structure in a communications company. The second-level units are called 'divisions'
in this particular case. They each comprise a number of 'departments'.

The products are saleable items in their own right, but they might also be the sub-units of larger products. In this case, there will also be a division relating to the larger 'system' products.

Advantages: Product range focus

A powerful advantage of this scheme is that it enforces commercial awareness among the staff, albeit restricted to one product range. They rapidly absorb an understanding of market requirements, customer characteristics, competitive products, viable prices and costs, and manufacturing limitations.

The organization is usually part of its trading division customer. Alternatively, it might form part of a central organization. It is a good training ground for embryonic managers and is best suited to product development and design. The product range divisions might conduct their own basic research and, more probably, relevant applied research. Usually, though, basic research is separated by at least one barrier from this organization.

Disadvantages: Product range focus

But nothing is perfect. Each product range division must cover a wide technical area and a particular technical expertise, such as digital electronics, can become thinly spread over many divisional departments. Thus, individuals may lose the stimulus of contact with colleagues in their own discipline, from whom they are separated by structural boundaries. Sadly, there is likely to be little movement of highly-regarded personnel between divisions, even when work loads are unbalanced. This is partially due to tribal reasons, as in Section 5.5.1, but also because of the narrow commercial knowledge acquired. Cross-fertilization of technical developments between divisional departments is reduced by the same effects. In extreme cases, the divisions degenerate into groups of technically-outdated former experts, whose commercial acumen does not compensate for the obsolescence of their technical output. Top management can minimize this danger, provided it is recognized in time, by enforcing circulation of personnel around the organization. The action also encourages career development. Some excessively parochial divisional managers will resist these assaults on their empires, citing short-term business reasons as an excuse.

5.5.3   Project focus

Positive encouragement of staff movements between the product range divisions of the previous organization lead to another distinct structure, which is focused on projects. Here, the second-level units are a set of individual project teams. The leaders of these teams report directly to the organization manager. It is inherently a time-varying arrangement whose 'shape' changes as projects come and go. A 'snapshot' of such an organization is shown in Figure 5.7. A communications company is again used as the example.

Advantages: Project focus

The staff involved clearly need to be flexible, but this talent rapidly develops and tribal attitudes are much reduced. The dissolution of old teams and the formation of new ones provides the desirable contacts between like-minded specialists. Another

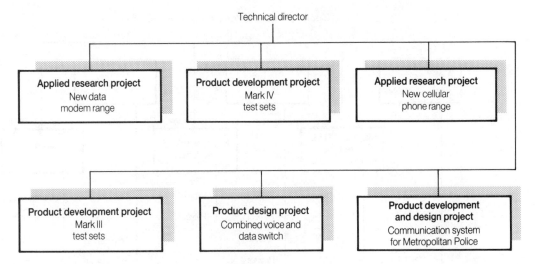

Figure 5.7   **Organization by project focus.**

In this organizational structure the second-level units are current technical projects whose leaders report directly to the organization manager. It is a time-varying arrangement because of the dissolution of old teams and the formation of new ones as projects come and go. This feature provides a good staff development situation, because there are no organizational barriers to staff mobility, and opportunities for commercial experience and project management abound. But there is a limit to the number of project leaders, and hence projects, that the top manager can effectively supervise. Six (as shown here) is a typical figure.

feature, not intrinsically present in the previous scheme, is that individual specialists mix with a wide range of other specialists, to their mutual benefit. It is a good management training ground, even more so than the previous product-focused variant. The structure fits in well with the requirements of product development and design, where it is most commonly used. In principle, it is also well suited to research of both varieties but it is not so often employed at that end of technological innovation. This may be because of an overriding discipline orientation in scientists as distinct from engineers.

Disadvantages: Project focus

There are some disadvantages. The most important arise from human limitations. First, there is a definite limit to the number of project leaders, and hence projects, that the top manager can effectively supervise. The limit depends on the nature of the projects, and on the quality of the project leaders and their manager. But six is a typical figure. This problem is resolved by introducing another management layer, as shown in Figure 5.8.

This (costly) extension of the basic principle only marginally reduces another difficulty. Many people derive great satisfaction by exercising authority, and they measure their importance by the number of staff they control, the fraction of the budget they command and their job title. Such people are valuable and the typical industrial reward system specifically encourages them. And this facet of human nature does ensure that divisional and project leader jobs are much sought after. But there will not always be enough project leader posts to go round, because projects come

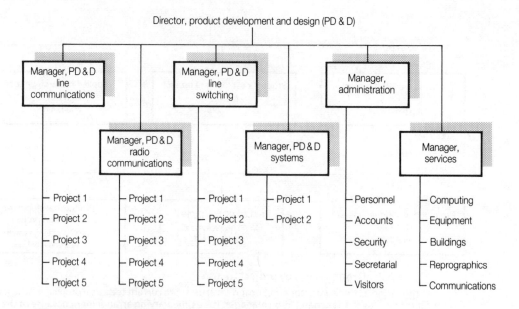

Figure 5.8 **An extended organization by project focus.**
The management capacity problem exposed by the project focus organization of Figure 5.7 is resolved in this extended version by introducing another management layer (the traditional response to this limitation). Note, too, that administration and site services are now managed quite separately from the projects, which is a more tidy and efficient scheme.

and go. Not all individuals who have tasted the project leader role are able to accept, with good grace, temporary 'demotion' to project team member. This situation can be conquered by good leadership. The project focus approach is popular in consultancy businesses, where it usually works well. Commonly, a critical factor in this success is direct top management participation in some projects as ordinary team members. A situation in which a director is responsible to a junior staff member for part of a project is not uncommon! This 'example-setting' is a powerful disincentive to prima donnas in the body of the organization. It is reinforced by the directors taking good care always to deliver high-quality work on schedule (even if they have to change the schedule to do so).

An inescapable disadvantage, because it stems from the built-in flexibility of the structure, is that staff are less likely to develop an acute commercial sensitivity for any one particular product area. On the other hand, they will develop some commercial insight into a number of related areas, which might be even more useful.

5.5.4 Organization by phase

Finally, in this review of basic structures, comes organization by phase. The scheme brings together basic research, applied research, development and design into one organization on, possibly, one site. Figure 5.9 outlines the arrangement. It may be employed in small to medium-sized companies or within the major trading divisions of large businesses. Sheer size and diversity, apart from any other considerations, render it unsuitable for use at the top level in a large business.

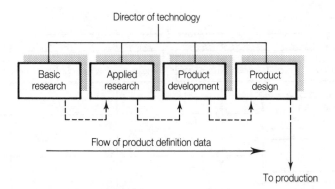

Figure 5.9   **Organization by technological innovation phase.**
The scheme brings together the four different types of technological innovation into one organization and, possibly, one site. It is used by some small to medium-sized businesses, but it is too unwieldy for large companies. It allows staff to concentrate on the work they find most satisfying and do best, but it takes no account of the preferred twin-bond arrangement for product development and design.

Advantages: Organization by phase

The arrangement allows staff to concentrate on the work they find most satisfying and, therefore, that which they do best. This is a potent advantage, because there is no doubt that individual temperament varies in this respect. Subject only to this, there is also the flexibility to move staff between phases, as loading demands, without the intervention of an organizational barrier.

Disadvantages: Organization by phase

Apart from the size-related constraints on its applicability, the scheme has two significant flaws. One is that it takes no account of the preferred twin-bond arrangement for product development and design. The problem might be reduced by co-locating those activities with their trading division customers. The other difficulty springs from that human arrogance which arises from inexperience. It convinces people that no other job is as difficult or demanding as their job. Thus, researchers frustrated by the prospect of their work being destroyed by sundry incompetents further along the innovation chain know how to solve the problem. It merely requires that they are awarded total responsibility for the whole product creation process including (when they know about such things) product marketing, manufacturing and sales. Similarly, engineers who find fault (and it is rarely difficult to do so) with the research outputs that fall to their lot are quite clear about what should be done. It would clearly be better, if they must repeat the research, for them to have done it in the first place. There are many other variations of such egotism.

Illusions of this sort are hard to dispel. Both research and engineering are demanding intellectual tasks, as are marketing, manufacturing and selling. But they are all different tasks requiring different temperaments, skills and management expertise. Despite the obvious nature of this fact there remain those who are unconvinced by it. No doubt experiments would change their minds, but this medicine is more dangerous than the disease it cures.

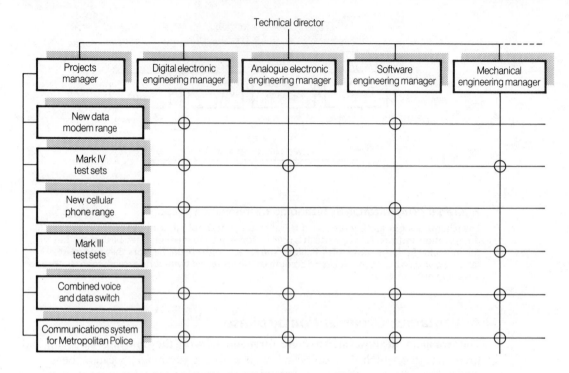

Figure 5.10   **A simple matrix organization.**
This widely-used structure is a combination, in a matrix arrangement, of the by-discipline and by-project schemes of Figures 5.5 and 5.7, respectively. Project reporting forms the horizontal lines of the matrix, and professional discipline resource reporting forms the vertical lines. A project team is formed by assignment of staff at the appropriate matrix cross-points, shown here by circling specific cross-points in the figure. Matrix organizations combine most of the merits of the parent structures and minimize their disadvantages; and they demonstrate that some rules of classical organization theory are not well founded.

5.5.5   Matrix organization

The **matrix-type of organization** is a relatively modern development of the project-oriented basic structures discussed in Section 5.5.3. It is sometimes found in association with the older forms. The structure is a combination, in a matrix arrangement, of organization by discipline and the project focus organization. It can provide the best features of both of those more elementary schemes. Figure 5.10 shows a typical arrangement, and retains continuity with previous figures by using a communications business as the example.

Project reporting forms the horizontal lines of the matrix, and professional discipline reporting forms the vertical lines. A project team is formed by assignment of the requisite staff at the appropriate matrix cross-points. Specific resource assignments are shown by circling cross-points in the figure. The new feature introduced in the matrix structure is the clear distinction between **project management** and **professional discipline management**. The former role is self-explanatory. The responsibilities of the **resource managers** (the discipline managers) are less obvious. They include:

- *Professional standards*   The maintenance and enhancement of professional standards and expertise within the staff resource under their command.
- *Staff welfare*   The welfare and career development of their staff.
- *Special facilities*   The development of any special tools and techniques aimed at improving the effectiveness of their staff.

Advantages: Matrix organization

The matrix format is a powerful technique. It is a natural extension of the more simple project focus scheme, retaining all of its advantages and reducing some of its disadvantages. For example, the number of senior posts is not as dependent on the number of projects. It is suited to all phases of technological innovation, but is not widely used in basic research. Of course, limits remain on the supervisory capacity of the organization manager and, as before, growth is accommodated by introducing another management layer. Figure 5.11 illustrates a larger and more developed matrix organization. It includes a number of **service departments** (in non-matrix format) which manage various shared facilities. One example is the computing services department. It provides networked facilities for computer-aided design, project planning and control, project accounting, and so on.

Disadvantages: Matrix organization

In terms of classical organization theory, matrix structures are fundamentally flawed. Traditional theory requires each subordinate to have only one superior. But project staff, other than project managers, have two masters. Horizontally, they report to their project manager; vertically, they report to their discipline (or resource) manager. This ambiguity can cause problems, but they are generally not serious. This may be because the day-to-day pressures arise from project responsibilities, whereas the vertical interactions are likely to concern longer-term matters and occur less frequently. However, the dual reporting situation *can* cause difficulties when a matrix structure is imposed on a long-standing professional discipline structure, like that commonly used for basic research (and in universities). Discipline loyalties can be very strong and sensitive leadership is needed by both project and discipline managers to make the system work.

The project managers are in a different, more subtle, situation which also contravenes traditional thinking. Thus, while they carry responsibility for the satisfactory conduct of their project, they do not have total formal authority over all the requisite project resources. In other words, their responsibility and authority do not equate. In the real world of industry this is not at all uncommon. The project managers must negotiate mutually satisfactory deals with the resource managers. Negotiating ability is a required management skill. Many engineers realize this for the first time when elevated to the project management peerage.

(In passing, the fact that matrix organizations are generally satisfactory directs some questions at classical organization theory and illustrates that most people delight in solving problems when motivated to do so.)

The discipline, or resource, manager role is less specific and more strategic than the

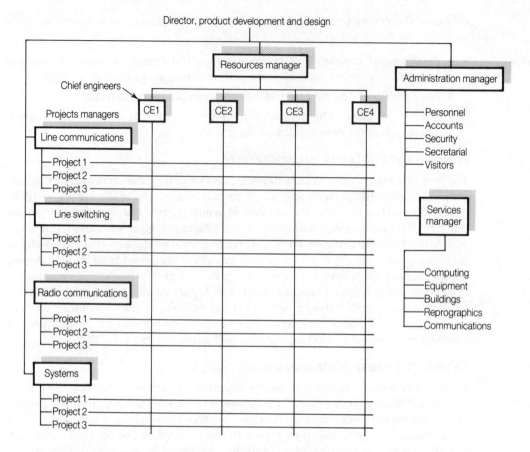

***Figure 5.11*   A more complex matrix organization.**
This is an extension of the simple matrix structure shown in Figure 5.10. It accommodates growth (in the usual way) by introducing another management layer. The developed scheme includes a number of *service* departments (in non-matrix format) which manage various shared facilities.

essentially tactical project manager role. The immediate pressures, crises, successes, failures and enthusiasms tend to accrue to the projects rather than to the professional skill departments. Some departmental heads are not comfortable with this situation. They may suspect that their value is not fully appreciated in status and/or other terms. Others will welcome isolation from such transient excitements and derive great satisfaction from the resolution of longer-term issues particular to their situation. Clearly, therefore, individual personalities are a central factor in the choice of departmental heads. The role is critical in the matrix structure. The positions are best filled by mature and competent engineers who are able to discharge their management duties with competence and zeal.

5.5.6   An extended matrix organization

The principles of matrix structuring are applicable to all projects. Projects comprise a substantial part of total activity in progressive businesses. Hence, the matrix approach is becoming increasingly prevalent and dispersed throughout many businesses. Figure 5.11 shows its use within a single company. It is equally applicable, across company boundaries, to implement **joint ventures**. Projects which cross organizational boundaries are sometimes called **venture projects**. This is a good generalized descriptive term (although all projects are ventures). However, in the following illustration of an extended matrix organization, the precision of the term **business creation project** is preferred.

Conceptually, a trading division in a large company can be regarded as a set of **mini-businesses**, each based on a distinct product range. These will generally be in different stages of their life cycles. The products within a range are saleable units in their own right and, for the concept to be most useful, the great majority of such sales should be to customers outside the trading division. In this case, the conditions for **divisionalization** *within* the division apply. So, the mini-businesses can each have their own profit and loss account, together with the responsibility and authority which that implies. (Divisionalization is explained in Section 4.4.3 of Chapter 4.)

The project in this illustration reflects the discussion of the investment aspects of technological innovation in Section 3.3 of Chapter 3. It concerns the creation of a new mini-business based on a new product range. Its launch is signalled by the issue of two documents. The first of these is an approved **new business brief**, probably prepared by the marketing function. It describes the new business opportunity in terms of product specifications (including acceptable price and cost), customer characteristics, competitive situation, total market and accessible share, market timing, and so on. The second document is a top management instruction to prepare a **business plan** aimed at exploiting the opportunity. This is backed by authority to spend a relatively small amount of money on preparing the plan. The plan, which may cover several years, comprises sub-plans for technological innovation, production, marketing, sales and the financial aspects of all of these. To receive approval, it must (credibly!) demonstrate that the initial investment in launching the business is recovered, through product sales, in a sufficiently short time; and that adequate positive **cash-flow** contributions are assured well beyond that point. Other, non-financial, criteria are also set. The technological innovation sub-plan involves only product development and product design, because the uncertainties of research are too significant to meet the credibility requirement. (If research is necessary, it should be satisfactorily completed before the business plan is even contemplated.) Subsequently, if the business plan receives top management approval, substantially more money (as defined in the plan) is released to implement it. Then, hopefully, actual events largely conform to the plan and the new mini-business eventually starts to make satisfactory cash-flow contributions to its parent organization. The business creation project terminates at a pre-defined point when the new mini-business is genuinely self-supporting and profitable in its own right. The new mini-business then joins the other established mini-businesses as a relatively routine operation.

It will be seen that several business functions are involved in the business creation process outlined above. There are powerful motivation factors to be derived by

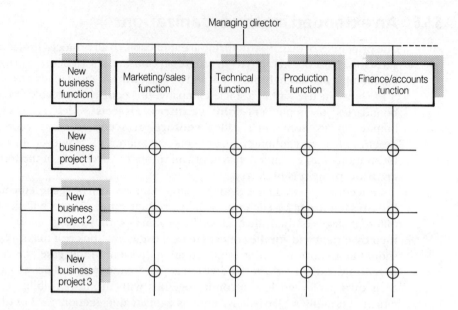

Figure 5.12 **A matrix organization for a business creation project.**

A trading division in a large company can be regarded as a set of mini-businesses, each based on a distinct product range. Generally, these will be at different stages of their growth, maturity and decline cycle. New mini-businesses must be created as old ones die to ensure that the whole division stays in business. This figure illustrates how a matrix organization can be used to implement the multidiscipline mini-business creation projects. The scheme lays the project structure across the functional structure of the trading division. A project team is shown here reporting to the director of the new business development function. Alternatively, if that function is not present, it might initially report to the technical director, because product development and design are the principal early tasks.

treating it as a single overall project, and it is a near-optimum way of developing future business managers with relatively low risk.

A possible organization for such business creation projects is shown in Figure 5.12. This lays the project structure, matrix-style, across the functional structure of the trading division. The project management team is shown here reporting to the director of the new business development function. Alternatively, if that function is not present, it might initially report to the technical director – because product development and design are the principal early tasks. The management reporting arrangements might then be changed, to match the functional emphasis, as the project progresses through its various phases. This is less likely when a new business development function exists as a separate entity.

The project management task may be focused on one individual (often an engineer with management potential), or a small team may be formed with an assigned leader. Ideally, whatever the arrangement, it should persist until the defined end of the project. This ensures project management continuity, provides true business motivation (and pressure), and exposes the staff involved to a broad range of problems, people and experience. Others members of the project team will come and go, as circumstances dictate, by secondment from the other business functions. These people are also broadened by the experience.

The project structure discussed here is just one example of the more general **venture project management** matrix technique. It is an approach which flies, normally very comfortably, in the face of much classical thinking about organizations. The principles that it embodies are likely to find even wider application in the future.

5.5.7 Software organization

The special problem of software innovation, as distinct from the innovation of any form of hardware, is explored in Section 3.5. That investigation concentrates on understanding the problem. It cites the relatively new discipline of software engineering, but does not examine it. The software-related material presented *here* focuses on an organizational facet of software engineering. It starts, however, with a background summary based on Chapter 3.

Summary: The dimensions of the problem

The development and design of non-trivial software products and sub-units dates back to the mid-1950s. But, sadly, the typical history of a large software creation project is still characterized by:

- overrun of time and cost budgets
- failure of the product to meet its specification
- failure to meet promised 'ready for service' dates
- unreliability in service

The (somewhat controversial) problem analysis in Chapter 3 suggests that its source is a human weakness in managing a type of complexity inherent in the software situation. It also implies that the weakness has more to do with lack of discipline than lack of intellect. This provocation is softened by noting that the lack of good tools to aid the creation process is also significant. The analysis examines four factors which contribute to the problem. In summary, these are:

(1) *Software complexity* Managing the creation of complex hardware products (such as buildings, aeroplanes, computers and integrated circuits) is considerably eased by a design strategy which emphasizes the use of standard, well-understood and proven sub-units. This concept of **reusable designs** at sub-unit level is not widely employed in the software creation process. In that process, the design strategy often seems to emphasize the use of novel sub-units, each of which represents a product vulnerability.

(2) *Software flexibility* A software module transforms its inputs to its outputs using an algorithm which mirrors the thought processes of its designer. The module is nearly as easy to change as the human mind it reflects. And it can always be 'improved': that is, redesigned to go faster, or to use less memory, or to provide additional features, or to work as first specified. This sort of easy flexibility is the fundamental beauty of software. But it is a seductive beauty carrying the seeds of its own destruction, which blossom when it becomes the vehicle for rampant creativity. It works against the simplifying notion of reusable software and encourages proliferation of non-standard novel sub-units.

(3) *Software people*　The scope for speedy creativity attracts some exceptionally creative people to the software arena. This is as it must be – they are essential to the process. But, typically, a characteristic of these individuals is that they are motivated by the activity itself, rather than by achieving the purpose of the activity. (This is a personality trait which also tends to distinguish scientists from engineers and managers.) So, there is a natural tendency towards overrun of time and cost budgets – because many of the travellers enjoy the journey more than the destination.

(4) *Fuzzy system definition*　It is extremely difficult to create a complete and unambiguous specification for any complex system, and the more so for one which offers the temptations of software flexibility. But it is not possible to develop and design a product without prior knowledge of what it is supposed to do. Too often, in the software creation business, the simple truth of this observation is either not recognized or it is ignored. (In many real-life situations, product development and design must start while the system specification remains blurred, because the alternative is to lose the business. This is acceptable *if* the project plan adequately recognizes the inherent risks and these risks are accepted by all concerned.)

Software engineering

The 'software crisis' stemming from this software creation problem was recognized in the late 1960s. The term 'software engineering' is used to describe a broad collection of insights, tools and techniques aimed at eliminating the problem. This effort continues. Macro and Buxton (1987) survey the whole field in a very readable text.

Chief programmer team organization

Software engineering includes the organizational issues associated with software project teams. The topic has survived many traumas, but an approach termed the **chief programmer team** (CPT) is now a widely accepted norm. It is derived from the early work of Mills (1971), Brooks (1979) and many others. Brooks uses an analogy with a surgical team to illuminate the idea: skilled assistants support the chief surgeon who performs the highly specialized work. Macro and Buxton (1987) provide an excellent commentary on CPT.

CPT comes into play, or should do so, when an acceptable system specification exists and the overall functional architecture of the system has been determined. It is concerned, principally, with the detailed product development and design stages comprising sub-unit design, coding, test and integration; and the final system commissioning. The basic concept, however, is equally applicable to the initial analytical work. The principles underpinning modern CPT organizations are:

(1) *Team size*　This should be small enough for efficient control and communication, and large enough to provide diverse insights and experience. A number in the range of, say, three to six is about right. More than one team is usually required. This implies proper initial partitioning of the total project into its natural sub-tasks (or **work-packages**) and coordinated team control.

(2) *Team composition*　The skill mix of the team should match the natural structure of the task. This is critical: task definition should not be distorted to

suit a particular team. All the team members should be professional software engineers, although variation in experience levels is acceptable (and inevitable). This principle removes the old hierarchy of 'analyst', 'designer', 'coder', 'tester' and so on. These sub-tasks are no longer seen as distinct tasks in a status structure, but as less distinct tasks in a semi-equity structure. (As in cabinet government: all team members are equal, but some are more equal than others.)

(3) *Careful choice of chief programmer* Substantial relevant technical experience, and mature management and leadership qualities are the prime considerations. An appropriate management style, in view of the likely characteristics of the team members, is vitally important.

(4) *Inclusion of a deputy chief programmer* To act on behalf of the chief when the chief is elsewhere, and as an insurance policy. The same qualities as for the chief are required, but a lower experience level is acceptable.

(5) *Formation of 'experts'* Some team members should be required to become expert in facets of the task which apply to the whole team. Task and task-interface specifications, local rules on documentation, coding style and testing criteria, and the use of complex tools are typical examples.

(6) *Task administration* One team member (not the junior!) should be assigned to the necessary 'housekeeping' chores, such as document archiving, task accounting and progress recording.

(7) *Training* Provision should be made to associate relatively inexperienced individuals with the team, both for training in software engineering and for continuity purposes. The consequential reduction in team productivity must be specifically recognized in plans and budgets.

(8) *Design reviews* A central feature of task control (and of the total project) should be the periodic **peer group review** of individual sub-tasks. (**Design reviews** are a powerful quality assurance technique, but their management is not entirely straightforward. This major topic is not considered further here.)

The CPT structure has been used, in one form or another, for some twenty years. It is increasingly popular. While further development of the approach is required, as in software engineering generally, the validity of the basic concept is apparent. It fits in well with matrix-type organizations. The principles of CPT are based on the rare commodity of common sense. They are clearly applicable to the more mundane situations discussed earlier in this section.

5.6 Concluding summary

The chapter examines, from a design point of view, the organization of industrial technical functions, where the primary task is technological innovation. This is a specialized aspect of a larger topic concerning the organization of people at work, which is reviewed in Chapter 4. The design of any industrial organization is a complex exercise, because it must find the right compromise between the often conflicting constraints of business objectives and human nature. It is this author's (maybe parochial) view that the complexity is particularly severe in the case of the technical function.

The analysis attempts to simplify the issues. It identifies a number of distinct organizational structures which may be applied to technical activities. In the real world of industry, these are only rarely found in their pure form. Mixtures and compromises of variable effectiveness are much more common.

An industrial organization is a human mechanism aimed encouraging the people within it to work efficiently in the best interests of the business that employs them. No organization is perfect, as has been seen. But some structures are better than others for particular tasks. Good management will make almost any arrangement work after a fashion. There is, however, little virtue in making management more difficult than it has to be, and still less in frustrating 'the workers'. This is the real message of the chapter. Aim for an organizational structure which best suits the task in hand.

REFERENCES

Ansoff H. I. and Stewart J. M. (1967). Strategies for a technology-based business. *Harvard Business Review*, November/December 1967

Brooks F. P. (1979). *The Mythical Man-Month*. Reading, MA: Addison-Wesley

Macro A. and Buxton J. (1987). *The Craft of Software Engineering*. Wokingham: Addison-Wesley

Mills H. (1971). Chief programmer teams, principles, and procedures. *IBM Federal Systems Division Report FSC-5108*

Parker R. C. (1985). *Going for Growth*. Chichester: John Wiley

Ross D. T. (1977a). Reflections on requirements. *IEEE Transactions on Software Engineering*, 3(1), 2–5

Ross D. T. (1977b). Structured analysis (SA): A language for communicating ideas. *IEEE Transactions on Software Engineering*, 3(1), 16–35

Ross D. T. and Schoman K. E. (1977). Structured analysis for requirements definition. *IEEE Transactions on Software Engineering*, 3(1), 6–15

Stanley A. V. and White U. K. (1965). *Organizing the R&D Function*. American Management Association

SUGGESTED FURTHER READING

(Note: The texts listed here largely coincide with those listed in the Chapter 3 bibliography, illustrating a continuity between the two chapters.)

Monds (1984) is another text in the IEE Management of Technology Series providing, in this case, an experienced-based management perspective of electronic development and design. Oakley (1984) covers rather more of the same ground, but penetrates less deeply in a technology-independent treatment. The Roy & Wield (1986) book comprises a series of review articles which furnish interesting background material of a somewhat philosophical nature. Twiss (1986), while mainly concerned with the strategic issues of technological innovation, still yields useful insights into the more tactical matters discussed in this chapter.

Monds F. (1984). *The Business of Electronic Product Development*. London: Peter Peregrinus (for the IEE)

Oakley M. (1984). *Managing Product Design*. London: Weidenfield & Nicolson

Roy R. and Wield D., eds. (1986). *Product Design and Technological Innovation*. Buckingham: Open University Press (reprinted with additions 1991)

Twiss B. C. (1986). *Managing Technological Innovation* 3rd edn. London: Longman

QUESTIONS

5.1   The industrial process of technological product innovation can be usefully partitioned into four distinct technical activities, denoted by the terms *basic research*, *applied research*, *product development* and *product design*.
(a) Describe the four activities, with special attention to their distinguishing features and the relationships between them.
(b) Why is it 'useful' to partition the process of technological innovation in this way?

5.2   The role of the technical function in a manufacturing business can be divided into primary and secondary tasks.
(a) How are these two categories of task distinguished?
(b) Briefly describe six different types of secondary task.
(c) Why do the secondary tasks pose a special problem for local management, and what can they do about it?

5.3   A large, technology-based, manufacturing company contains a technical function which is responsible for all the technical aspects of product innovation.
(a) List and briefly describe four primary tasks and seven secondary tasks which are commonly assigned to such a technical function.
(b) Why does the presence of the secondary tasks complicate the management of the primary tasks?

5.4   (a) Explain the concept of *technological profiles* in the context of a group of companies trading within the same market sector. Why is this concept useful?
(b) Briefly describe six major factors which can be evaluated to form a technological profile.

5.5   (a) In the context of designing a technical function, *what* does a technical function organization have to do and *why* does it have to do it?
(b) Why does design usually involve compromise?

5.6   University and industrial cultures differ in a number of ways. Show, by comparing these two cultures, how the distinctions between them present challenging problems to industrial technical managers.

5.7   The concept of *bonds and barriers* to communication is useful in considering the optimum location of technical innovation activities in industrial companies.
(a) Explain this concept.
(b) A large, technology-based, manufacturing company comprises a number of semi-autonomous trading divisions reporting to company headquarters. The company conducts product research, development and design. Illustrate, and justify, a practical organization based on the bonds and barriers concept for the technical function within this company.

5.8   'The:
● need for project planning and control,
● the need for technical function performance measurement, and
● the various ways in which technical projects can be funded

all impose constraints on the design of a technical function organization.' Do they? Why?

5.9 Describe four basic and distinct organizational structures which are commonly employed, alone and in combination, in industrial technical functions. The descriptions should be supported by diagrams and emphasize advantages, disadvantages and appropriate applications.

5.10 (a) Describe a simple matrix organization for conducting three design projects. Each project requires access to no more than three distinct engineering disciplines.
(b) In what ways do matrix organizations contravene traditional organization theory?
(c) Show how the simple matrix organization can be extended to cover twenty-four design projects, each of which may require access to six engineering disciplines and to a range of local services. The organization must satisfy the constraint that no manager can have more than six subordinates.

5.11 Describe and illustrate a possible matrix organization for the development of new product business opportunities in a technology-based manufacturing company. In what ways do matrix organizations contravene the 'rules' of traditional organization design theory?

5.12 'The problems of creating large software systems are no different from those associated with creating large hardware systems.' Discuss this statement.

5.13 (a) Explain what is meant by the term 'software engineering'.
(b) Describe the principal features of the 'chief programmer team' organization commonly used in software engineering.

Technical Project Planning and Control

'If seven maids with seven mops
Swept it for half a year,
'Do you suppose,' the Walrus said,
'That they could get it clear?'
'I doubt it,' said the Carpenter,
And shed a bitter tear.

Lewis Carroll 1832–1898

6.1	The context	196
6.2	Bar charts and resource tables	201
6.3	Flow diagrams	208
6.4	The PERT network technique	219
6.5	Task time versus task effort	248
6.6	Project control	259
6.7	Concluding summary	264

 Advanced material The material in Section 6.3.1 which begins at the *A two-loop example* heading is, perhaps, pitched at a slightly higher level than is appropriate for undergraduate courses in this area. It may be omitted at first reading.

This comment applies also to the material in Section 6.4.3 which begins the *Activity starts, finishes and floats* heading.

PERT novices may find Section 6.4.5 somewhat puzzling. It is more rewarding when familiarity with the basic PERT concepts has been achieved.

The introduction to the time-to-complete mythology contained in Section 6.5 up to the end of Section 6.5.1 is straightforward, and it contains valuable messages for embryonic engineers. Section 6.5.2 develops a 'solution' to the problems underlying the myths. The material is quite challenging.

 Repetitions   The purposes of plans and planning were introduced in Section 2.2. They are reiterated at Section 6.1.1 under the *Projects, project plans and planning* heading.

The overall objectives of this chapter are to examine important management techniques for the planning and control of basic research, applied research, and product development and design projects. Objectives by section follow:

6.1   To define the language of technical project planning and control and to expose the basic concepts and problems of the topic.

6.2   To describe an elementary project planning and control technique, based on bar charts and resource tables, which is suited to most basic research projects.

6.3   To describe a network technique for project planning which explicitly recognizes path length uncertainty due to looping. It is a flow diagram approach which is suited to many applied research projects.

6.4   To describe, in some detail, the PERT network technique for planning well-defined projects, such as those concerned with product development and design, and some applied research programmes.

6.5   To illuminate the largely unresolved problem of relating task completion time to assigned effort, and to introduce a technique for minimizing the difficulty.

6.6   To describe the basic purpose and mechanism of project control, and to introduce a simple approach which is applicable to any and every sort of project.

6.7   To identify its salient points and summarize its major messages.

6.1   The context

The primary task of the engineers and scientists who work in the technical function of a technology-based manufacturing business is technological innovation. In conventional terminology, this activity is called **research and development** or, perhaps, just **R&D**. This established jargon obscures the wide variety of different meanings which are attached to the words and hides a great deal of confusion about the technical innovation process. That topic is covered in some depth in Chapter 3, which describes a relatively distinctive view of the technological innovation process in industry. It divides the process into separate phases labelled **basic research**, **applied research**, **product development** and **product design**. Technical activity in each of these four areas is invariably project oriented. This chapter is about the planning and control of such technical projects. The material, however, is equally applicable to any sort of project.

Technological innovation projects are generally part of a broader strategy determined by top management. A cluster of related basic research projects, for example, might be aimed at enhancing the level of silicon integrated circuit process technology available to the business. At the same time, the marketeers could be orchestrating entry into a new product arena through a major investment project involving marketing, product development and design, production and sales. Thus, basic research, applied research, and product development and design projects are tactical projects aimed at implementing parts of broader strategies. Tactical planning is directed at more sharply defined, shorter term and 'smaller' objectives than strategic planning. It demands deeper and more detailed analysis. Strategic planning is considered in Chapter 2.

6.1.1 Some words and concepts

A number of important words and concepts are reviewed here. Sections 6.1.2 and 6.1.3 consider the problems and feasible levels of project planning and control.

Technological innovation projects

The meaning of the terms *basic research*, *applied research*, and *product development and design*, as they are used in this book, is detailed in Chapter 3 (Sections 3.1 and 3.2) and summarized in Chapter 5 (Section 5.2.2). The differences between these activities are such that they call for different project planning and control techniques. This topic is examined in Section 6.1.3.

Projects, project plans and planning

A **project** is an activity with a (or some) pre-defined objective(s). It absorbs time and other resources, such as effort and money. The word 'project' suggests that the activity and its target objective(s) have some degree of novelty. It is likely to be a 'one-off' exercise. In contrast, the word **process** suggests an activity or a sequence of events which is repetitious. For example, designing and building a tunnel under the English Channel is a project, whereas operating the trains that use it is a process.

A **project plan** is a model (that is, a representation) of a project created before the real project is launched. **Project planning** is the process of creating project plans. Its fundamental aims are to ensure that the target objectives are the 'right' objectives and that they are achieved with the least possible expenditure of time, money and other resources.

Since the real project will absorb time, a project plan embodies a forecast of future events. The four basic elements of a project plan are:

(1) A defined start position in time and relevant knowledge.
(2) A defined end position consisting of one or more objectives. The difference

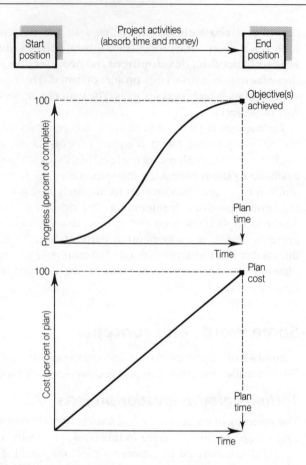

Figure 6.1 **The basic elements of a project plan.**
A project plan is a model of a project created before the real project is launched. The diagram at the top of the figure is a simple but universal model for all projects. It illustrates that specific project activities, which will take time and cost money, are planned to close the 'gap' between the project start position and its target end position. The graphs show how plan progress and plan cost (shown as increasing linearly here, for simplicity) vary with time.

between the defined end and start positions is sometimes termed the **planning gap** or, perhaps, just the **gap**.

(3) A defined activity (or set of activities) for advancing from the start position to the end position; that is, for closing the gap.

(4) An estimate of the time and resource cost required to complete the project activity; that is, to advance from the start position to the end position. This element is usually called the **project budget**.

Figure 6.1 shows the relationships between these basic elements. The diagram at the top of the figure comprising two 'event boxes' and an 'activity arrow' is a simple but universal model for all projects. The graphs illustrate how planned project progress and planned project cost might vary with time.

Note that the plot of progress (measured here as a percentage of project completion) is an S-shaped curve. This is reasonably typical: a slow start followed by a period of rapid advance which then slows as project completion is approached. The cost plot is shown as linear but wide variations in the form of this curve occur in practice.

A generalized approach to planning is described in Chapter 2 and this is not repeated here. But it is worth reiterating the purposes of planning and of plans:

- The disciplines of the planning process have intrinsic merit. This is because problems must be analysed, and a range of different solutions explored and evaluated, before valuable resources are committed to a particular course of action.

- The process enables the amounts of time, money and other resources needed to achieve the end objective(s) to be estimated before the plan is launched. This allows the resource cost of the plan to be evaluated with respect to the plan benefits (plan objectives) it is intended to provide. Project plans are (generally) approved or rejected on the basis of this evaluation.

- Plans provide motivations for the teams charged with implementing them and enable the individual task of each team member to be defined. Ideally, the planners should involve the implementation team in the planning process because this encourages 'ownership' of the forthcoming tasks.

- Finally, during plan implementation, the plan provides a reference baseline with which actual project performance can be compared. This allows control action to be taken aimed at correcting serious deviations from plan. At this stage, the value of the plan is wholly dependent on the quality and timeliness of the 'feedback' information.

Project control

Project control is the management task of detecting differences between the planned and actual performance of a project, and then taking corrective action to ensure, so far as is possible and sensible, that the performance of the project does conform to its plan. A project plan, therefore, is a necessary prerequisite of project control. The plan defines an intended relationship between three **project parameters**: progress, time and cost. The plan links these parameters such that specifying any one of them defines unique values of the the other two, as Figure 6.1 illustrates.

The first step in a project control sequence is to align one particular plan parameter (progress, time or cost) with the corresponding actual parameter. The differences between the plan and actual values of the other two parameters are then measured. These differences are called **deviations**. Normally, plan time is aligned with actual time and the progress and cost deviations are measured. One possible situation is illustrated in Figure 6.2. This shows that progress is less than planned at project review time, although project cost is running ahead of plan!

The second step in a project control sequence is to assess the magnitude and direction of the deviations and determine what, if any, corrective action should be taken. The close relationship between project planning and project control is invariably recognized at the planning stage by arranging that the plan documentation also serves as the control documentation.

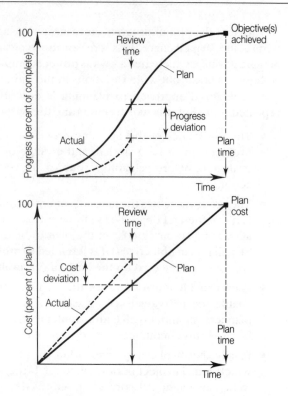

Figure 6.2   **Deviations from a project plan.**

Project control is the management task of detecting deviations between planned and actual progress, and then taking action (if possible and sensible) to correct the deviation. In the figure, progress is less than planned at project review time, although project cost is running ahead of plan. This is just one possible (though not unusual) situation.

6.1.2   Problems of planning and control

The central problem with planning is forecasting the future, because nobody actually knows what is going to happen! So good planning demands knowledge of the techniques, relevant experience, good judgement and a measure of luck since it all turns on balancing probabilities. The problem first arises in estimating the time and cost needed to complete the project activities.

No project ever launched has totally conformed to its initial plan, so it is quite normal for deviations to arise between plan and actual performance. The three linked parameters of performance are progress, time and cost. Measuring them is a necessary prerequisite to control. Measuring elapsed time is easy and measuring cost is not much more difficult. But measuring project progress is never straightforward, particularly if the measurement must be made at regular intervals, and therein lies one major problem of project control.

The most usual situation requiring intervention by management is when project progress falls behind schedule: a *negative* progress deviation. If the magnitude of the deviation is significant the need to correct it might arise, together with the problem of how to correct it. A common response is to increase the effort assigned to the project. In a badly-structured project this 'common sense' approach will probably make the situation worse, and it does not always work with a well-structured project. The difficulty is another facet of the time and cost estimating problem mentioned earlier. It turns on how **human effort** is measured.

Human activity clearly absorbs human effort, and this is measured as the product of people numbers and time, such as people-months, people-years, people-hours. Now, suppose a particular project activity is estimated, during planning, to require 12 people-months to complete. It is then but a short step to assume that 1 person will complete the activity in 12 months, 2 people in 6 months, 3 people in 4 months, and, ultimately, 250 in about 1 day. Assumptions of this sort can prove wildly wrong. Similarly, the assumption that progress slippage can be corrected by increasing the number of people applied to the task is, too often, the first step towards a disaster. There is no generally applicable easy answer either to activity estimating or to progress recovery. Section 6.5 is assigned to an examination of these related problem areas of project planning and control.

6.1.3 Levels of planning and control

Basic research is like the early stage of a treasure hunt. It is concerned with the resolution of various uncertainties and the target objective(s) should be somewhat flexible, since exploration into unknown areas is involved. Individual projects are generally relatively inexpensive. But most fail, in the sense that they demonstrate that a speculative concept is not technically feasible or, at least, not economically so. Quite often, however, exploration launched in one area uncovers clues suggesting a more rewarding exploration in a different area. For these reasons, a relatively broad brush approach to the planning and control of basic research projects is appropriate, feasible and necessary. At the other extreme, product development and design projects are (or should be) characterized by sharp objectives, critical time-scales, substantial resource commitment and limited technical uncertainties. Such projects demand meticulous planning and tight control because the penalties for failure are severe. Thus, the feasible and useful level of planning, and of control, depends on the nature of the project. The characteristics of applied research lie between those of its neighbours but they are closer to those of product development and design. Planning and control techniques appropriate to that type of project are, therefore, preferred for applied research projects.

A number of different project planning and control techniques are described in the immediately following sections. Each approach is particularly appropriate for a particular type of project, but aspects of each one can be usefully applied to any type of project. They are complementary rather than competitive techniques.

6.2   Bar charts and resource tables

The use of **bar charts** (also known as **Gantt charts**) to represent work plans and delivery schedules goes back many years. The technique, which was developed by

Henry L. Gantt during World War I, is still alive and well-employed in a variety of formats. Bar charts, and similar forms of pictorial project models, are frequently combined with **resource tables** which detail planned and actual resource consumption. In some project planning and control systems, these tables are supported (or replaced) by a graphical presentation of the same information. The basic techniques of presenting resource data, and of the administration behind it, are examined in this section in the context of a typical bar chart model of a sample project.

6.2.1   Bar charts

Bar charts are a particularly simple and visually appealing method of representing projects. An example is shown in Figure 6.3, which is a plan and control summary document for a typical small basic research project (called Project BR1).

The bar chart comprises the upper part of the document. The project is scheduled for completion in six months, and the total activity has been partitioned into six sub-activities. The plan start time, completion time, and duration of each of these sub-activities is indicated by a solid black bar on the chart.

The results of a status review of the project conducted at the end of month 03 are shown by a **progress wavefront** (or **progress profile**). At review time, the amount of progress towards completion is evaluated for each sub-activity. These values are then marked onto the appropriate bars and the wavefront is constructed by connecting the markers. Here, the wavefront indicates that the literature study is behind schedule but the experimental equipment is ready ahead of plan time. Similarly, the work on resolving the first uncertainty is on time but that on the second uncertainty is lagging.

The wavefront method of showing actual progress compared with plan progress is just one of many ways of doing it. In another method, the activity bars are initially 'empty', and are subsequently filled in to indicate progress.

The rows labelled 1, 2 and 3 in the lower part of the document are not, strictly, part of the bar chart. This is a resource table which records (in this case) the plan and actual cumulative cost of the project as elapsed time increases from zero at the beginning of Month 01. (**Cumulative** figures include all the earlier incremental figures and thus show the total expenditure at the end of each period.) In this case, the anticipated total cost of the project is £80,219 but it is underspending at the end of Month 03: compare the plan cost of £40,125 with the actual cost of £31,145. Row 3 of the table shows the deviation of actual cost from plan cost. A financial deviation is usually called a **variance**. Here the variance is normalized by expressing it in percentage terms using the formula:

$$\text{Cost Variance} = [(\text{Plan} - \text{Actual})/\text{Plan}] \times 100\% \qquad (6.1)$$

Note that, as defined, the **cost variance** will be positive if the plan cost is greater than the actual cost, and negative if this situation is reversed. This is the normal convention for cost variances. A positive variance is regarded as good news (actual cost less than plan) and a negative variance as bad news (actual cost greater than plan). From an isolated financial viewpoint, this interpretation of good and bad cannot be faulted. But

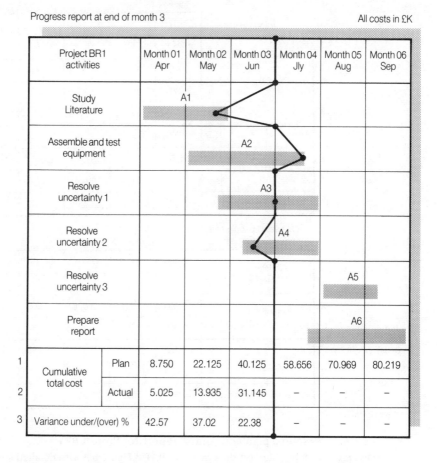

Figure 6.3   **Bar chart for basic research project BR1.**

Bar charts are a simple and visually appealing method of modelling projects. The example in the upper part of figure is a plan and control document for a small basic research project. The bars define the planned start and finish times of the various project activities and the results of a progress review (conducted at the end of Month 03) are shown by the wavefront (or profile). The lower part of the figure is a (summary) resource table, which records the plan and actual cumulative cost of the project as project time increases from zero at the beginning of Month 01. The variance row of the table shows that the project is underspending, with respect to plan, by about twenty-two per cent at the end of Month 03 (see Equation 6.1 in the text).

the project in the example is, on balance, falling behind its progress schedule. This has to be bad news and it *may* be connected with the underspend situation. However, the cost variance simply indicates the magnitude and direction of the difference between plan and actual cost at a specific time. It does *not*, as defined here, give any information about the progress status of the project.

Incidentally, negative financial figure and variances are usually shown in parentheses. The labelling of the variance row in Figure 6.3 as 'Variance under/(over) %' reflects this common accounting convention.

Project BR1 Headcount table			Month 01 Apr	Month 02 May	Month 03 Jun	Month 04 Jly	Month 05 Aug	Month 06 Sep
4	Scientist h/c	P	2.00	3.00	4.00	4.00	2.00	1.00
5		A	1.00	2.00	3.50			
6	Drawing office h/c	P				0.25	0.50	1.00
7		A						
8	Cumulative h/c	P	2.00	5.00	9.00	13.25	15.75	17.75
9		A	1.00	3.00	6.50	–	–	–
10	Variance (under)/over %		(50.00)	(40.00)	(27.78)	–	–	–

Cost table (1 people-month @ £4.125 K)   All costs in £K

11	Cumulative effort cost	P	8.250	20.625	37.125	54.656	64.969	73.219
12		A	4.125	12.375	26.813			
13	Cumulative other cost	P	0.500	1.500	3.000	4.000	6.000	7.000
14		A	0.900	1.560	4.332			
15	Cumulative total cost	P	8.750	22.125	40.125	58.656	70.969	80.219
16		A	5.025	13.935	31.145	–	–	–
17	Variance under/(over) %		42.57	37.02	22.38	–	–	–

Key: h/c = headcount; P = plan; A = actual

Table 6.1   Resource plan and control report for Project BR1.

These resource tables support the summary table in Figure 6.3 with detailed information. Note that the plan rows of these tables constitute the detailed project budget. The headcount table shows the planned and actual allocation of human resources to the project. The cumulative effort shortfall with respect to plan is signalled by a negative effort variance. Note that the cost underspend variance (at row 17) is positive. The Month 03 figures confirm that the effort shortfall (partially compensated in cost terms by 'actual other costs' running ahead of plan) has caused the project underspend. It is a reasonable assumption, but not an absolute certainty, that the effort shortfall is also responsible for the progress slippage.

6.2.2   Resource tables

More detailed information about the sample project, BR1, is revealed in the resource tables of Table 6.1. These tables are, again, just examples of their kind.

In Table 6.1, rows 4 to 10 inclusive comprise the **headcount table** which shows the plan and actual assignment of project staff to the project. This table is considered before the **cost table**, which is at rows 11 to 17 inclusive.

The headcount table

Rows 4, 6 and 8 of the headcount table together make up the **headcount plan** for the project. In this case only scientists and drawing office personnel are required. Rows 4 and 6 show the anticipated number of these staff assigned to the project in each month. Row 8 is the cumulative headcount plan.

As project elapsed time increases, the actual staff assignments to the project are recorded in the appropriate rows (5, 7 and 9). The entries show the situation at the end of Month 03. Note that the plan number of scientists has not actually been achieved in any month up to, and including, that month. This shortfall in the anticipated scientific effort, which has accumulated to 2.50 people-months at the end of Month 03, is highlighted by the negative figure of some twenty-eight per cent in row 10. Here the **effort variance** is defined by the formula:

$$\text{Effort Variance} = [(\text{Actual} - \text{Plan})/\text{Plan}] \times 100\% \tag{6.2}$$

This rearrangement of the conventional cost variance formula ensures that bad news (actual effort less than plan) is flagged by a negative figure. A positive value of effort variance (actual effort more than plan) usually indicates the assignment of extra staff in an attempt to recover from a progress slippage situation.

Note that the effort variance only indicates the magnitude and direction of the difference between plan and actual effort at a specific time. It does *not*, as defined here, give any information about the progress status of the project.

The cost table

The people who work directly on projects (scientists and drawing office staff only in this case) cost the business money. The cost is substantially greater than just the cost of their salaries. This is not only because of employment benefits that they might receive but also, and more significantly, because of the various support services and facilities that they need. For example, the project staff must be accommodated in a fully serviced building, be provided with any necessary 'tools of the trade', have access to a range of secretarial and communication services, and be organized and supervised in their endeavours.

In the cost table of Table 6.1 (rows 11 to 17 inclusive) effort has been costed at £4,125 per person-month. (This corresponds to £49,500 per person-year or about £30 per person-hour. The way in which the cost of effort is determined is covered in Chapter 7). Rows 11 and 12, which are derived from rows 8 and 9 respectively, show the cumulative plan and actual effort cost.

The plan **other costs** (non-people costs) directly attributable to the project are entered in row 13 on a cumulative basis. These relate to such items as the purchase of experimental materials, the use of expensive special test gear (a scanning electron microscope, say), computer time, travel and subsistence expenses for project staff, and so on. The corresponding actual costs are entered in row 14. Rows 15, 16 and 17 then provide the total cumulative plan, actual and cost variance data which is reproduced with the bar chart of Figure 6.3.

Inspection of the Month 03 data in Table 6.1 confirms that the cumulative effort shortfall (only partially compensated in cost terms by actual other costs running ahead of plan) has caused the project underspend. It is a reasonable assumption, but still only an assumption, that the effort shortfall is also responsible for the progress slippage.

6.2.3 Project administration

Before the real project is launched, Figure 6.3 and Table 6.1 contain only plan information. They might form part of the project proposal submitted to the potential project customer (the source of the project funds) for approval. The plan figures in the resource tables comprise the **phased project budget** illustrating how the total anticipated resources spend of 17.75 people-months and £80,219 is built up over the anticipated 6 months of elapsed project time.

As discussed earlier, when the project is launched these same documents become part of the project control system. This is based on deviations between actual and planned performance. The wavefront of Figure 6.3 shows progress deviations. Cost and effort deviations are shown by the variance entries in that figure and in Table 6.1. Variances are derived by comparing corresponding plan and actual values. A project accounting mechanism is provided to obtain the actual values. This mechanism assigns a unique **charge code** to each current project and collects individual project costs against these codes. As part of this system, each member of the project staff is usually required to complete a weekly **timesheet** which records the number of hours 'spent' on each project.

It is important to compare like with like when calculating variances. As a rule, therefore, 'actual' is interpreted as 'actual + committed'. For example, suppose that some materials costing £500 are ordered, in Month 01, from an outside supplier. Assume that this is a credit purchase such that the materials will not be paid for until 30 days (say) after their delivery, which is scheduled for the middle of Month 02. If the delivery does occur on time the £500 becomes a real actual in the middle of Month 03. However, the £500 is committed to the purchase from the time the order is placed and is treated as an actual cost in Month 01. This avoids incorporating the potential confusions of credit and delivery delays into the cost figures. However, delivery delays must still be recognized in the activity planning.

6.2.4 Advantages and disadvantages

The principal merit of bar chart project models is their simplicity and visual appeal. For this reason, they are frequently used to summarize more complex project models, particularly in 'overview' presentations to senior managers. The common association of bar charts with resource tables is entirely compatible with this usage. Bar charts are also often used as the primary model for basic research projects, where the depth of analysis needed for the more rigorous planning techniques is not justified by the project cost, activity dependencies and clarity of objectives.

As primary models for large and complex projects bar charts suffer from two disadvantages. These are that there are no provisions for showing and analysing either **precedence relationships** between activities or **mutually exclusive alternative activities** (with or without **activity looping**). Figure 6.3 can be used to illustrate these shortcomings.

Precedence relationships

Suppose, first, that the activity A5 (directed at resolving uncertainty 3) requires the results of the activities A3 *and* A4 (directed at resolving uncertainties 1 and 2, respectively) as input data. A precedent relationship is implicit in this supposition. It requires that both of the activities A3 and A4 must be completed (satisfactorily) before activity

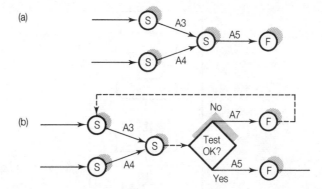

Figure 6.4   **Representation of activity precedents and alternative activities.**
This figure illustrates some real-life project situations which are not explicitly shown on
conventional bar charts. Here, activities are represented as solid arrows connecting start and finish
events, shown as circles labelled S and F, respectively. The event symbols have the properties of
logical 'and' gates (that is, they hold up progress until *all* their inputs are complete). This allows
precedence relationships to be modelled. Thus, (a) shows that A5 cannot start until both A3 and A4
have finished. A more complex situation is shown in (b). If the combined result of A3 and A4 is 'OK'
then A5 is started, as before. But, if the decision diamond yields 'not OK', then A7 must be
completed before A3 is repeated. This construct illustrates mutually exclusive activities, selected by
testing, and activity looping.

A5 can start. This relationship between these three activities might be surmised from
their relative positions in the bar chart but it is not explicitly shown. In the absence of
this explicit linking it might be assumed (dangerously) that activity A5 is so
positioned simply for headcount economy. If that were the case, the assignment of
additional scientists would allow A5 to be started sooner and the progress slippage
thereby recovered.

One way of representing this precedence type of situation is shown in Figure 6.4(a).
Here the activities are represented by solid arrows connecting activity start events
and activity finish events, shown by the circles labelled S and F, respectively. A
topological rule, which is:

- an activity cannot start until its preceding event has happened, and no event can
  happen until all the activities leading into it are finished

then allows precedence relationships to be built into the model. Note that the circles
in this model have the properties of **logical 'and' gates**: that is, they hold up progress
until all their inputs are complete.

Mutual exclusion and activity looping

Now, further suppose that the combined result of activities A3 and A4 may be either
satisfactory or not satisfactory (a binary variable). If the combination is satisfactory
then activity A5 can be started as previously. If, however, the combination is not
satisfactory then something must be changed before activity A3 is repeated. This
situation is represented by Figure 6.4(b). Here, a **decision diamond** is introduced to
check the binary variable and the new activity, A7, is concerned with changing the
'something'. The dashed (non-solid) arrows are not activities, they merely represent
logical connections which consume no time, money or effort.

This type of situation, involving a branching decision and a loop, is quite common in

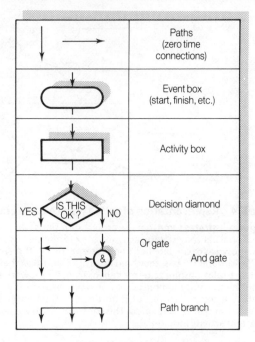

Figure 6.5   **The elements of research planning diagrams (RPD).**
RPD is a particular 'activity-on-node' flow charting technique designed for modelling the larger and more complex research projects (where bar charts are too limited). This figure shows the basic elements and notation used. An 'and' gate remains closed until all its inputs are present, whereas an 'or' gate simply merges two or more inputs.

practice, particularly in applied research. It substantially complicates project time and cost estimating because of the looping possibilities.

The complexities of activity precedence, mutual exclusion and looping are not explicitly shown in conventional bar charts although they might be taken into account during planning. Flow diagram models do recognize and show all of these realities.

6.3   Flow diagrams

The use of **flow charts** to develop and illustrate software algorithms seems, sadly, to have gone out of fashion. However, the technique remains of great value in technical project planning and plan analysis. A popular version, called **research planning diagrams** or just **RPD**, is due to Davies (1970, 1982). The elements and notations used in RPD are shown in Figure 6.5. As explained earlier, the 'and' gate remains closed until all its inputs are present. The **'or' gate** simply merges two or more inputs.

The utility of the RPD method is not confined to the research arena. This is demonstrated by Figure 6.6, which illustrates the basic concept in a plan for coping with weekends. The diagram is largely self-explanatory, which is one advantage of the technique.

In summary, the plan is to stay in bed if the weekend is wet but to go fishing if it is fine. The start of the possible fishing trip may be delayed by a standing request from

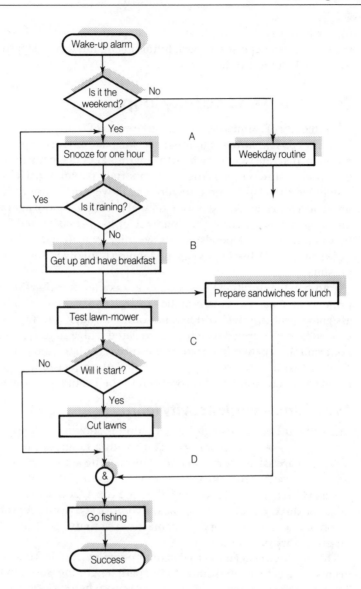

Figure 6.6   **Weekend planning.**

This figure is an example to illuminate the RPD technique. It is a plan for enjoying weekends. The objective is to stay in bed if the weekend is wet but to go fishing if it is fine. The start of the possible fishing trip may be delayed by a standing request from higher authority to cut the lawn before departure. Happily, this delay does not occur if the lawn-mower refuses to start. In this event, however, departure might be delayed by the lack of sandwiches for lunch. Plans in this format can be analysed by assigning durations to the activities and probabilities to alternative paths (as in Question 6.6).

higher authority to cut the lawn before departure. Happily, this delay does not occur if the lawn-mower refuses to start. In this event, however, departure might be delayed by the lack of sandwiches for lunch.

6.3.1   Estimating and activity loops

The difficulty of estimating the resource costs of individual plan activities has already been noted. The flow diagram format for plan models exposes another estimating problem, that due to uncertain path lengths. It occurs in the domestic drama of Figure 6.6, where elapsed time is the most important parameter. There is no certain way of predicting the elapsed time required to move from point A to point B, despite the unusual fact that activity duration between A and B (snoozing) *is* tightly defined. The uncertainty arises because the number of loop transits, and hence the path length between A and B, depends on the weather. A path length uncertainty also occurs between C and D, but in this case no looping is involved and only two path lengths are possible.

Path length (duration) uncertainty is a common estimating problem in technical project planning, particularly at the research end of the spectrum. It may be tackled by assigning probabilities to different routes through the plan network. This allows estimates to be derived which are associated with a stated level of risk or confidence. For example, a plan might state that project cost has a ten per cent risk of exceeding £1M or that it is ninety per cent certain that project time-scale will be less than or equal to fifteen months. This approach to the problem is now explored.

Estimating a single activity loop

The general case of a single activity loop is shown in Figure 6.7(a). Typically, the activity A_S is of an exploratory nature with a range of possible outcomes. Not all outcomes are satisfactory. On completion of the activity its outcome is tested. If the outcome is satisfactory the exit event is achieved. If the outcome is not satisfactory, a 'feedback' activity, A_F, is completed before the A_S activity is repeated. The activity A_F might be directed at modifying the outcome of activity A_S. A probability, P, is assigned to obtaining a satisfactory outcome from activity A_S. Thus, the probability of an unsatisfactory outcome is $(1 - P)$.

The resource cost (measured in time, effort and money) between the enter and exit events is directly proportional to the path length measured in completed activities. The minimum path length of $(A_S + T)$ occurs when no looping takes place, and this is increased by $[A_F + (A_S + T)]$ for each loop transit.

The probability of no loops occurring is P, so the probability that some loops will occur is $(1 - P)$. However, the *confidence* that there will be no more loops increases as the number of loops increases. Equally, the *risk* of more loops decreases as the number of loops increases. This mechanism, and its interpretation, is best explained by means of an example.

Assume first that the initial value of P ($= P_0$) is 0.4 (forty per cent) and that it does not change as a result of loop transits. Figure 6.7(b) then shows how confidence and risk change (in steps) as the number of loops increases. The results indicate, for instance, that an estimate of three loops is associated with a risk (that there will be three loops or more) of about twenty-two per cent. Alternatively stated, an estimate of

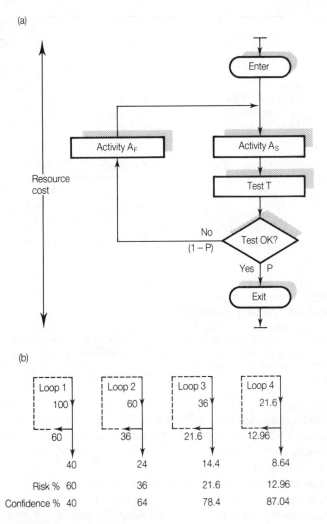

(a)

Resource
cost

(b)

Figure 6.7   A single activity loop.
Path length (duration) uncertainty arises in project planning whenever alternative paths are
chosen as result of a test. Activity looping may, or may not, be involved. (Both situations are present
in Figure 6.6.) The general case of a single activity loop is shown in (a). The probability of no loops
occurring is P, so the probability that some loops will occur is (1 − P). However, the *confidence* that
there will be no more loops increases as the number of loops increases. Equally, the *risk* of more
loops decreases as the number of loops increases. This mechanism is traced in the example in (b),
where P remains constant at forty per cent.

three loops is associated with a confidence (that there will be three loops or less) of
about seventy-eight per cent. Note that confidence plus risk is one hundred per cent.

   The assumption that the initial value of P does not change as a result of loop transits
is not usually valid in practice. Generally, the purpose of the feedback activity A_F
(Figure 6.7) is to modify some factor in the activity loop so as to increase the value of
P. This more realistic situation presents no analytical difficulties, although it does

Number of loops	Resource cost	Probability of exit	Probability of more loops = risk
			Simple loop
0	$1\,(A_S + T)$	P_0	$(1 - P_0)^1$
1	$2\,(A_S + T) + A_F$	P_0	$(1 - P_0)^2$
2	$3\,(A_S + T) + 2A_F$	P_0	$(1 - P_0)^3$
3	$4\,(A_S + T) + 3A_F$	P_0	$(1 - P_0)^4$
.	.	.	.
.	.	.	.
N	$(N + 1)\,(A_S + T) + NA_F$	P_0	$(1 - P_0)^{(N+1)}$
			Accelerated loop
0	$1\,(A_S + T)$	P_0	$(1 - P_0)$
1	$2\,(A_S + T) + A_F$	P_1	$(1 - P_0)(1 - P_1)$
2	$3\,(A_S + T) + 2A_F$	P_2	$(1 - P_0)(1 - P_1)(1 - P_2)$
3	$4\,(A_S + T) + 3A_F$	P_3	$(1 - P_0)(1 - P_1)(1 - P_2)(1 - P_3)$
.	.	.	.
.	.	.	.
N	$(N + 1)\,(A_S + T) + NA_F$	P_N	$(1 - P_0)(1 - P_1)\ldots\ldots(1 - P_N)$

Table 6.2 **Activity loop analysis.**
In activity looping situations, like that shown in Figure 6.7(a), the usual purpose of the feedback activity (A_F) is to modify some factor in the loop so as to increase the value of P. This table builds the algorithms relating risk (defined as the probability of more loops) to loop number. In the simple loop case the initial value of P is unchanged by loop transits. The accelerated loop algorithm is more general, because it can handle the variation of P with loop number.

introduce further assumptions relating successive values of P to the loop number. Table 6.2 builds the algorithms for both the simple case in which the initial value of P is unchanged by loop transits, and for the general case where this condition is not necessarily true.

The general case algorithm is employed for 'accelerated' loops by choosing appropriate figures for the successive values of P. Figure 6.8 shows that even gentle acceleration is effective in diminishing the number of loops required to achieve a given risk level.

The initial value of P ($= P_0$) is set at twenty per cent for both the simple and accelerated loops. In the accelerated loop, successive values of P are increased by the addition of ten per cent ($P_1 = 30\%$, $P_2 = 40\%$, and so on until $P_8 = 100\%$). Note that the simple loop needs ten transits to meet a ten per cent risk level. The accelerated loop meets this level comfortably at four transits and is down to a risk level of less than five per cent at five transits. Note, too, that the acceleration algorithm is purely illustrative, practical algorithms could be quite different. ('Markers' have been placed on the risk curves to emphasize that the figure is illustrating sets of discrete loop and risk numbers.)

A two-loop example

This example, which involves two activity loops, is loosely based on material supplied by GEC–Plessey Research (Caswell) Ltd (Myers, 1990, private communication). Figure 6.9 is an outline RPD model of an applied research project directed at a new

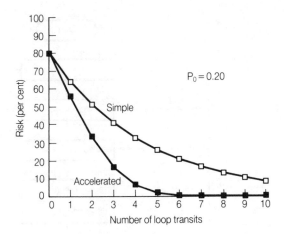

Figure 6.8   **Simple (□) and accelerated (■) loops.**
This illustrates the algorithms of Table 6.2. P_0 is set at twenty per cent for both the simple and accelerated loops. In the latter case, successive values of P are increased by the addition of ten per cent at each loop transit, until $P_8 = 100\%$. Note that even this gentle acceleration is very effective in diminishing the number of loops required to achieve a given risk level.

range of integrated circuit digital logic chips. These are to be fabricated on a recently enhanced silicon processing facility.

Specifically, the project is concerned with adjusting the circuit design, mask making and silicon processing parameters to obtain an economic yield of good chips from each slice of silicon. A typical product from the new range has been chosen as a research prototype.

Each silicon processing step (A_3 in the figure) is followed by a test A. This is an examination for gross defects based on a visual inspection and a limited 'zero frequency' functional test of individual chips. If the test A pass criterion is met, the surviving chips are subjected to high-speed switching in test B. The pass criterion for this second, more severe, test is somewhat less demanding than that for test A, and survival signals a successful end to the project.

If test A is not passed the diagnosis A activity is entered, which determines whether the defect is due to faulty circuit design (A_1), mask making (A_2) or silicon processing (A_3). Relative probabilities of P_X, P_Y and P_Z, respectively are assigned to these three possibilities, where $P_X + P_Y + P_Z = 1$. Similarly, if test B is not passed, the diagnosis B activity is entered to determine the source of the fault. The relative probabilities are P_U, P_V and P_W in this case, where $P_U + P_V + P_W = 1$.

Probabilities of P_A and P_B, respectively are assigned to passing test A and test B. The probability of achieving the minimum path length, which is ($A_1 + A_2 + A_3 +$ test A + test B), between the enter and exit events is ($P_A \times P_B$). Even if an estimating risk level as high as ten per cent is acceptable (ninety per cent confidence) then the initial values of both P_A and P_B will need to be about ninety-five per cent to achieve this 'zero loops' minimum path length. These initial values are unrealistically high in practice, so some looping is virtually inevitable.

The first step in the analysis of the model of Figure 6.9 is to deal with the

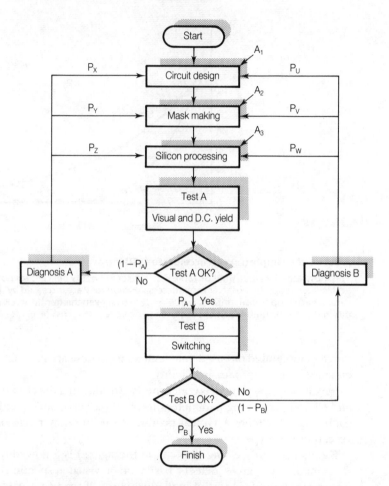

Figure 6.9 **An applied research project with two loops.**
The figure is a research planning diagram (RPD) model of an applied research project directed at a new range of integrated circuit digital logic chips. The project aim is to adjust the circuit design, mask making and silicon processing parameters so as to obtain an economic yield of good chips from each slice of silicon. The model contains two activity loops, and the path duration inside each loop is dependent on a diagnostic activity which determines its re-entry point. Its analysis is started by simplifying the loops, using the probability structure, to yield the reduced model of Figure 6.10.

probabilities inside the loops. This is done by defining three new activities:

- $A_0 = A_1 + A_2 + A_3$
- $A_4 = P_X A_1 + (P_X + P_Y)A_2 + A_3$
- $A_5 = P_U A_1 + (P_U + P_V)A_2 + A_3$

and redrawing Figure 6.9 in the simplified form of Figure 6.10.

The analysis of this more simple model is then based on the single loop algorithms of Table 6.2. A set of illustrative results is shown in Figure 6.11. In this figure, the initial values of P_A and P_B in case 1 are each set at forty per cent. Both loop A and loop B are

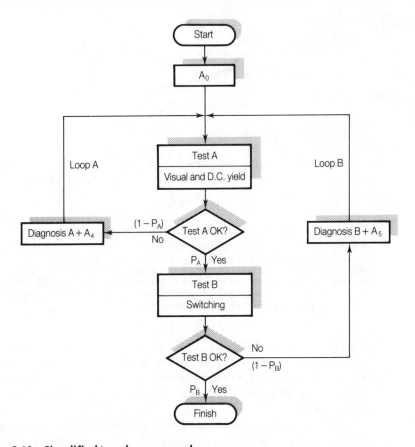

Figure 6.10   **Simplified two-loop example.**

This is a simplified version of Figure 6.9 (in which the activities A_1, A_2 and A_3, and the probabilities P_X, P_Y, P_U and P_V are all defined). Here:

$$A_0 = A_1 + A_2 + A_3$$
$$A_4 = P_X A_1 + (P_X + P_Y)A_2 + A_3$$
$$A_5 = P_U A_1 + (P_U + P_V)A_2 + A_3$$

and the subsequent analysis is based on the single loop algorithms of Table 6.2.

accelerated by adding five per cent to the values of P_A and P_B at each successive loop transit. A risk criterion of better than five per cent is set for exit from loop A. The conditions for case 2 are identical except that the accelerator is fifteen per cent rather than five per cent.

Note that this discussion has made the implicit assumption that the resource cost of the individual activities A_1, A_2 and A_3 does not change as a result of looping. It is not necessary to make this assumption, but it does simplify the total resource cost calculations which should follow the loops versus risk analysis.

Contract bids

Suppose that the estimating procedure just outlined relates to the preparation of a bid for a research contract. A major factor in determining the success or otherwise of this

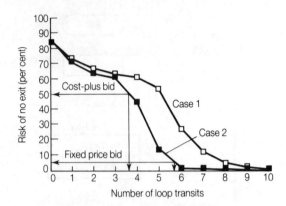

Figure 6.11 **Two-loop example: illustrative results.**
The graphs are sample results obtained by analysing the project model of Figure 6.10. In Case 1 (□), the initial values of P_A and P_B are forty per cent and both loop A and loop B are accelerated by adding five per cent to the values of P_A and P_B at successive loop transits. A risk criterion of better than five per cent is set for exit from loop A. The conditions for Case 2 (■) are identical except that the accelerator is fifteen per cent rather than five per cent. Note the relevance of this type of analysis in preparing bids for research contracts.

exercise will be the bid price. Typically, a bidding situation arises when an external organization issues an **invitation to tender** (ITT) to a number of competing research organizations. The ITT specifies (among many other things) the research objective(s) and the type of contract on offer. This is usually a **cost-plus** or a **fixed price** arrangement.

In the cost-plus case, prospective contractors bid a price which represents a project cost estimate plus an agreed percentage of this cost as profit. If actual project costs exceed the estimate, then these actual costs plus the agreed percentage are still paid. With this scheme the contractor cannot lose (financially). The risk is carried by the customer. For this reason cost-plus bids at cost risk levels as high as fifty per cent might be considered reasonable.

In the fixed price case, prospective contractors are required to bid a price (including cost and profit) which, once accepted, is fixed until the contract objectives are delivered. This remains so irrespective of how much it actually costs or how long it actually takes. Here, then, the risk is carried by the contractor. There is, therefore, the opportunity to make a substantial profit or a substantial loss. Under these circumstances, the risk associated with the cost element of a fixed price bid is normally set at a comparatively low figure, such as five per cent.

The fixed price situation, which is increasingly common, emphasizes the critical need both for good estimating and some insight into the relationship between cost and risk. For example, assume that previous experience of similar situations suggests that the case 2 profile of Figure 6.11 applies. The most competitive cost-plus bid at fifty per cent cost risk corresponds to between three and four loop transits. However, the most competitive fixed price bid at about five per cent cost risk corresponds to between five and six loop transits. (Actual costs, of course, will correspond to a whole number of loop transits). Customers for contract research have noted an increase in bid prices as the trend from cost-plus towards fixed price contracts has developed.

Figure 6.11 illustrates why this has happened. Ultimately, of course, the cost (and the price) of a research project is likely to be much the same whether it is launched under a fixed price or a cost-plus contract. The fixed price mechanism, however, establishes the maximum customer liability at the beginning of the contract and places the financial risk on the contractor.

Another two-loop project

The following example (Cather, 1991, private communication) illustrates that two-loop applied research projects are not confined to the electronic product technologies. Researchers in a metal pipe manufacturing business are investigating a new forging process aimed at forming tight radius bends in unusually thin material. Such a process, if economic, would allow the development and design of a new range of products for the air-conditioning ducts market. The process involves heating a 'starting' tube, of smaller outside diameter than the finished bend, and then forming the bend by feeding the tube over a shaped tool, or mandrel. The success of the operation depends on the characteristics of the starting tube, the heat input, mandrel design (especially its expansion gradient) and forging speed. The project consists of a series of controlled experiments on a range of different starting tubes. Its structure is shown in Figure 6.12.

Bend radius, outside diameter of the formed tube and its twist are checked, after each forging operation, at test A. If this test fails in some respect, one of the control parameters is adjusted and the procedure is re-entered with a new starting tube. Success at test A leads into a second, more exhaustive, examination of overall wall thickness at test B. This final test allows the process parameters to be 'fine tuned', such that process yield is high enough to deliver acceptable product cost. The structure of Figure 6.12 is much the same as that of Figure 6.9, and it can be analysed in the same way as that figure.

6.3.2   Advantages and disadvantages

The principal merit of flow diagram models for project planning is the explicit display of activity precedence and path uncertainty situations. A useful technique, based on probabilities, is also available to assist estimating when path uncertainties exist. The mathematics involved is more tedious than difficult and is easily handled by a spreadsheet program.

The technique is most commonly applied to applied research projects with limited dependencies between the activities. It is sometimes claimed that it is particularly suited to research because it mirrors the way in which research staff think about their work. Researchers do seem to think in terms of activities rather than events. Whether or not this is a point in favour of RPD and similar approaches is debatable. It might be more productive to persuade researchers to become event oriented. Sadly, it is all too common for research project objectives to be stated in activity rather than event terms (for example: '. . . the objective of this project is to *investigate* . . .'). This does nothing to assist project control, because it is difficult to measure progress along a road with no milestones.

The estimating procedure for coping with path uncertainties depends on the assignment of relative probabilities to alternative routes through the network. The

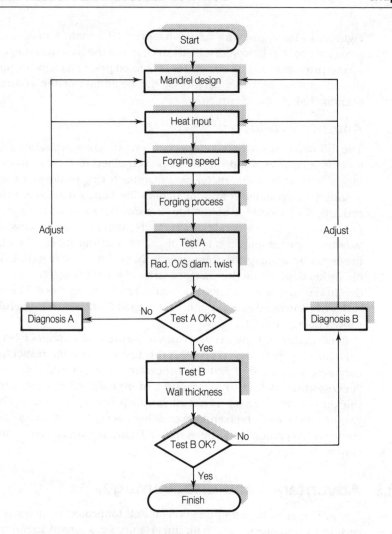

Figure 6.12 **Plan of another two-loop project.**
The figure is an RPD model of an applied research project aimed at forming tight radius bends in thin-walled metallic tubes. The model contains two activity loops, and the path duration inside each loop is dependent on a diagnostic activity which determines its re-entry point. The structure of this project model is virtually identical to that shown in Figure 6.9, and its analysis follows the pattern described for that figure.

subsequent application of high-precision arithmetic to these probabilities does not improve the degree to which they reflect reality. Yet delusions of certainty easily arise as a result of confusing calculation accuracy with input data accuracy. This problem is highlighted by the technique but it is, perhaps, unfair to cite it as a disadvantage. The problem is present in all methods which profess to improve visions of the future by massaging dubious numbers. As always, good estimating depends primarily on experience of similar situations.

6.4   The PERT network technique

When the term **network technique** is used in a project planning and control context it normally refers either to the **critical path method (CPM)**, to the **program evaluation and review technique (PERT)**, or to one of their derivatives. However, the term could be equally well applied to the RPD approach discussed in Section 6.3, which is also a network technique.

CPM and PERT are independent developments which first surfaced, in the USA, in the late 1950s. They are remarkably similar in all important respects and the discussion here is confined to PERT, which has achieved broader industrial acceptance (possibly because of its defence industry ancestry). The first publication on PERT appeared in 1959 (Malcolm *et al.*, 1959) and a comprehensive list of PERT references would now contain several thousand entries. Weist and Levy (1977) is a deservedly popular American text. Recommended books by British authors are Battersby (1978) and Woodgate (1977). British Standard 6046 (British Standards Institution, 1984), published in four parts, is a comprehensive reference for network planning and control techniques in general.

PERT is best suited to projects with well-defined objectives involving, say, ten or more major events with a significant degree of event connectivity. This (deliberately) loose description covers virtually all product development and design projects, and a large proportion of applied research projects. It uses an **events-on-nodes** format, in contrast with the **activities-on-nodes** format of RPD. The initial application of PERT to assist the preparation of a project plan always relates to the elapsed time parameter, using the basic PERT/Time method. It is this method which is considered in this section.

6.4.1   PERT basics

An example PERT network is shown in Figure 6.13. The network is a model of a product design project and it is used throughout most of this section as a the reference example for the exploration of PERT. The product is a typical microprocessor-based electronic item and this fact is used later to illuminate the reality of the network model. But PERT is totally independent of any particular technologies.

Events, activities, dummies, paths and conventions

The circles (boxes and ellipses are also used) in Figure 6.13 represent **events**. Each event has a unique number and they are referenced here as E01, E02, and so on (where 'E' means 'event' but is not shown in the figure). An event is a verifiable happening which occurs at some specific instant of time. For example, E01 is 'functional architecture specified and authority to proceed received' and E06 is 'software architecture designed'. Events must be uniquely identified but the inclusion of a descriptive label within the circle (or whatever), while desirable, is optional. E01 is a **start** event and E20 is an **end** event. It may be that this network is a detailed part (a **subnet**) of a larger network. In that case, its start and end events are also termed **interface** events and they would be reproduced, with the same event number, on the larger network.

The solid arrows in Figure 6.13 represent **activities**. An activity is uniquely defined

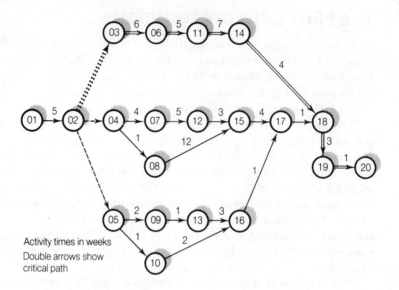

Figure 6.13   **An example of a PERT network.**

PERT is an 'events-on-node' planning and control technique best suited to projects with well-defined objectives and a significant degree of event connectivity, such as those concerned with product development and design. The network shown here models a real-life example of such a project. It illustrates a number of important PERT features: events, activities, activity times, dummies, paths (forward, backward and critical) and the precedence rule which is central to the whole concept. This states that an event does not happen until all the activities which lead into it are finished, *and* an activity does not start until the event that precedes it has happened.

by its **predecessor event** and its **successor event**, because no more than one activity can connect any two events. Thus, an activity can be uniquely identified by the numbers of the only two events that it connects: its predecessor at the arrow tail and its successor at the arrow head. The notation used here is of the form 'A09.13' (where 'A' means 'activity'), which signifies the activity between E09 and E13. Activity identifiers can be included in the network but they are not necessary. Activities always absorb time and, usually, effort and money as well. Activities are where the project resource costs (time, effort and money) are incurred. For example, A06.11 is 'design software modules' and A08.15 is 'wait for delivery and inspection of bought-out electronic components'. Note that A08.15 absorbs project time but does not absorb project effort or cost project money. But A06.11 does absorb project time, effort and money. The estimated activity times (durations), measured in weeks in this case, are shown centred over the activity arrows.

The dashed arrows in Figure 6.13 represent **dummies** (or **dummy activities**). They are identified here in the same way as activities, A02.04 for example. Dummies are like activities in the sense that they connect events but they absorb no time or any other resource. Their principal uses are to clarify a network and to circumvent some topographical dilemmas to be discussed later. Normal activities which do absorb time are sometimes called **real activities** to further distinguish them from dummies.

A **path** is a connected sequence of events in the network. Every event, except the start event, has at least one path leading into it. The paths of most interest are those which connect the start event to the end event. Both **forward paths** (traced forward from the start event) and **backward paths** (traced backwards from the end event) paths are considered in network analysis. There are five different forward paths between E01 and E20 in Figure 6.13. There is no prize for calculating, from that observation, the number of different backward paths between E20 and E01.

A number of conventions (as distinct from rules) are commonly employed in constructing PERT networks. These are that:

- Time is assumed to flow from left to right, and events are also numbered in that direction.

- The event number at the tail of an activity arrow is less than the event number at the head of an activity arrow.

- The start event is assigned the number 01 but, with this exception, event numbers have no positional significance.

- The length of the activity arrows is not proportional to activity duration.

Conventions can be ignored when it is deemed necessary to do so. The only penalty is that of provoking some irritation in other network readers. But the networks are subject to some **topographical PERT rules** which cannot be ignored. The central rule is now examined.

The precedence rule

This simple rule states that:

- No event can occur until all the activities which lead into it have been completed, and no activity can start until the event that precedes it has occurred.

In Figure 6.13, for example, E06 cannot occur until A03.06 has been completed and A06.11 cannot start until E06 has occurred.

Note that a number of events in the figure require two activities to have been completed before they occur. E17 is a case in point: both A15.17 and A16.17 must finish before it can occur. This illustrates that the circles (or whatever) representing events have the logical and-gate properties previously explained. They hold up progress until all their inputs are complete.

Precedence relationships are shown naturally and clearly in PERT networks and the precedence rule is the basic principle underpinning the technique.

6.4.2 Network synthesis

The first decision to be made when synthesizing (designing) a PERT network is whether to work primarily in terms of events or in terms of activities. Convincing arguments can be made favouring each alternative so the choice becomes a matter of personal preference. Here, the view is taken that events are pre-eminent because they define *what* has to be done whereas activities define *how* to do it, which is clearly a secondary consideration.

The design steps involved are:

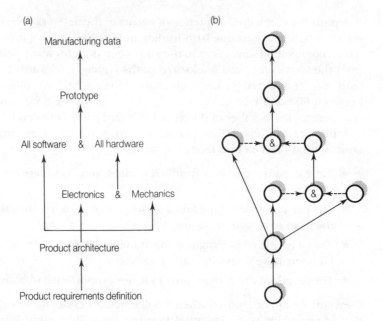

Figure 6.14   **The example PERT network: Stage 1 design.**
The initial design of a PERT network should contain only limited detail. The exercise should start with the required outputs and work back towards the available inputs, as in the early stage of all design tasks. Network (a) is constructed in this way, using an informal event-oriented PERT shorthand. It is a true PERT network. This is confirmed by network (b), which is its equivalent drawn in conventional PERT notation. Note the use of dummies to clarify (b). Figure 6.13 was developed from (a), and the structural similarities between the two networks should be observed.

(1) Define the events.
(2) Establish their precedence relationships.
(3) Draw the network to reflect the precedence relationships.
(4) Verify the network.

Experience indicates that an iterative series of small loops around this sequence of steps is more productive than attempting to completely resolve one step before moving on to the next.

Stage 1 design: Outline – a PERT shorthand

The initial network design should contain only limited detail. It should focus first on the required outputs and work back towards the available inputs, as in the early stage of all design tasks.

Figure 6.14(a) illuminates this advice. It is the initial design from which the more complex network of Figure 6.13 was developed. It uses an entirely informal **event-oriented PERT shorthand** notation which has proved useful in PERT planning over a number of years.

It was noted earlier that the reference example of Figure 6.13 is a model of a product design project directed at a typical microprocessor-based electronic item. This factor should not be allowed to obscure the generality of the following explanation of Figure 6.14.

The required output of a product design project is proven data describing, for the manufacturing operation, how to make the product. This event is simply called 'manufacturing data' in the shorthand and it is placed at the top of the figure. (The shorthand only labels events, so there is no merit in elaborate descriptions which emphasize their event-like nature. These can come later.)

The available technical input to the project (in this discussion) is a verified **product requirements definition (PRD)**. The derivation of such documents is described in some detail in Chapter 8. It comprises two separate but related items: a **functional architecture** and a set of **design constraints**. The functional architecture is a description of the product in terms of the functions that it must provide. It makes no reference to implementation details. The design constraints restrict, in some way, the way in which the product can be designed. Constraints may be of a technical, economic or operational nature.

The purpose of the project is to transform the PRD input into the manufacturing data output. Working downwards (backwards in time) from this output the intermediate 'markers' (events) are:

- A working prototype must be built to prove the manufacturing data. It must provide all the functions called for by the functional architecture and satisfy (or avoid) all the design constraints, including those relating to maximum product cost. The prototype is made up of:

- A distinct software sub-unit which can be designed, built and tested as a separate item,
  AND

- A distinct hardware sub-unit which can be designed, built and tested as a separate item. The hardware sub-unit is made up of:

- A distinct electronics sub-unit which can be designed, built and tested as a separate item
  AND

- A distinct mechanical sub-unit which can be designed, built and tested as a separate item.

- A product architecture which is derived by applying the design constraints to the functional architecture. It describes the product in terms of three distinct technological architectures: software, electronic and mechanical.

- The product requirements definition, which is the data input to the project.

(As an aside, note how this list illustrates the algorithmic structure of the product; indeed, of all products.)

The PERT shorthand diagram of Figure 6.14(a) is a true PERT network, albeit somewhat unconventionally drawn. This is confirmed by Figure 6.14(b) which is drawn beside it for comparison. Note the use of dummies to clarify this network.

Stage 2 design: Detail

The level of detail established in the stage 1 design of the network is not sufficient for activity estimating and project control purposes. Accordingly, the same design process is applied to each of the major activities represented by the arrows in Figure

Label	Activity description	Estimated activity time (weeks)
01.02	Design product architecture	5
02.03	Dummy	0
02.04	Dummy	0
02.05	Dummy	0
03.06	Design software architecture	6
04.07	Design electronic architecture	4
04.08	Order bought-out electronic components	1
05.09	Design mechanical architecture	2
05.10	Order bought-out mechanical components	1
06.11	Design software modules	5
07.12	Design printed circuit boards	5
08.15	Wait for delivery and inspection of bought-out electronic components	12
09.13	Design mechanical piece-parts	1
10.16	Wait for delivery and inspection of bought-out mechanical components	2
11.14	Code and test the software modules	7
12.15	Make and test the printed circuit boards	3
13.16	Make and test the mechanical piece-parts	3
14.18	Assemble and test software architecture	4
15.17	Assemble and test electronic architecture	4
16.17	Assemble and test mechanical architecture	1
17.18	Integrate electronic architecture and mechanical architecture	1
18.19	Assemble and prove the product prototype	3
19.20	Prepare manufacturing data	1

Table 6.3   **The example PERT network: activity table.**
This records the description and estimated duration (time) of the activities in the network of Figure 6.13. (Estimating the activity times in relation to the effort assigned to them is considered in Section 6.5.) Note that the activity identifier labels (left-hand column) form a complete topographical description of the network, which could be manipulated in a computer.

6.14(a). In this case, stage 2 design leads directly to the network of Figure 6.13. The level of detail in that figure is about right both for activity estimating and *overall* project control.

Activity times

The final step in synthesizing a network is to estimate the elapsed time which each of its activities will absorb. The nature of this estimating problem was noted earlier and its discussion is deferred to Section 6.5. (Note that the approach to estimating the duration of an activity loop considered in Section 6.3.1 assumes that the duration of the activities within the loop has already been estimated.)

Table 6.3 shows the estimated duration of the activities in the reference example network of Figure 6.13. (These are the times that are inscribed above the activity arrows in that figure.)

The network dictionary

It is normal PERT practice to provide a **network dictionary** as part of the supporting information for a complex network. This provides precise definitions of each activity and event because, even if these are labelled in the network, abbreviations must often

Label	Event description
01	Project start (= verified product requirements definition *and* authority to proceed received)
02	Product architecture designed
03	Software architecture specified
04	Electronics architecture specified
05	Mechanical architecture specified
06	Software architecture designed
07	Electronics architecture designed
08	Bought-out electronic components ordered
09	Mechanical architecture designed
10	Bought-out mechanical components ordered
11	Software modules designed
12	Printed circuit boards designed
13	Mechanical piece-parts designed
14	Software modules coded and tested
15	Printed circuit boards made and tested *and* bought-out electronic components received and inspected
16	Mechanical piece-parts made and tested *and* bought-out mechanical components received and inspected
17	Electronic architecture assembled and tested *and* mechanical architecture assembled and tested
18	Hardware assembled and tested *and* software assembled and tested
19	Product prototype assembled and tested
20	Proven manufacturing data available

Table 6.4 **The example PERT network: event table.**

The table here complements Table 6.3 by describing the events which define the start and finish of the activities in the earlier table. Note that this label column contains no precedence or connectivity information. Tables 6.3 and 6.4 comprise the network dictionary for Figure 6.13. It is instructive to compare the phrasing of activity and event descriptions in the two tables. It is chosen to emphasize the different nature of the network elements: activities have a continuity flavour, whereas events are instants in time.

be used. Here the network dictionary comprises an **activity table** and an **event table**, shown in Tables 6.3 and 6.4, respectively.

Note that the label (identifier) column in the activity table is a complete topographical description of the network. This is not the case in the event table, which contains no precedence or connectivity information.

6.4.3 Network analysis

Network analysis can start as soon as the network is verified and the estimated activity times are available. Its primary purpose is to establish the likely duration of the whole project. If this is acceptable, the next step is to review the planned resource allocations to the project. The aim of this review is to determine whether the planned resources can be reduced while still maintaining an acceptable total project duration. It may be, of course, that the first estimate of project duration is not acceptable. In this case, it may be necessary to reconsider both the design of the network and the resource allocations.

The reduced version of the example PERT network

The full network of Figure 6.13 comprises twenty events and twenty (real) activities. This level of detail is appropriate for estimating its activity times, but is more than is strictly required for the preliminary network calculations. It is convenient and permissible, therefore, to **reduce the network** to a more simple form by retaining only certain **key events** which determine the logic of the network. These key events include:

- The start and end events (E01 and E20 in this case).

- Events which launch more than one activity, because forward paths diverge at such events (E02 launches three (dummy) activities, and E04 and E05 each launch two real activities).

- Those events which may be reached from the start event by more than one forward path, because paths converge at such events (E15, E16, E17, and E18 here).

- Events that must be retained to avoid the ambiguity of different activities connecting the same pair of events, because an activity must be uniquely distinguished by its predecessor event and successor event (at least one of E07, E12 and E08 must be retained to avoid this ambiguity with respect to E04 and E15, and at least one of E09, E13 and E10 must be retained for a similar reason).

The reduction process yields the network of Figure 6.15. This uses a **stacked box structure** to represent events, each of which is now associated with three numbers. The central number in a box stack is the event number and the significance of the other two emerges as the discussion progresses. The events are numbered to correspond with the full network.

It was decided to retain E08 and E10 to avoid the ambiguities. E03 is also retained as a significant project marker (corresponding to E04 and E05) but it is not strictly required. The estimated activity times have been entered above the activity arrows. These times are extracted from Table 6.5, which shows the correlation between the activities of the full and reduced networks.

The reduced network of Figure 6.15 comprises twelve events and twelve (real) activities. It represents a significant simplification of Figure 6.13.

The critical path

The time absorbed by any particular path in a network is obtained simply by summing the individual times assigned to the activities making up the path (because, conceptually, events take no time). It is conventional to define network time as zero at the start event.

Generally, one of the paths connecting the start event of a network to its end event will be 'longer', in elapsed time, than the others. This path is called the **critical path**, since its duration determines the elapsed time for the whole project.

In the reduced network there are five different paths between the start event and the end event (as, of course, there are in the full network). The paths, and path times, are:

(1) 01.02.03.18.20   31 weeks.

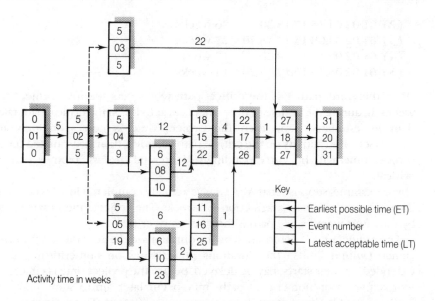

Figure 6.15 **The reduced version of the example PERT network.**

The network of Figure 6.13 has twenty events and twenty (real) activities. Its structure is such that this is more detail than that required for preliminary analysis. This network is a reduced version, containing only twelve events and twelve (real) activities, suitable for analysis. It is achieved by retaining certain key events, including the start and end events, those which launch more than one activity, those which terminate more than one activity, and those that must be retained to avoid the ambiguity of different activities connecting the same pair of events.

Label	Equivalent in full network	Estimated activity time (weeks)
01.02	01.02	5
02.03	02.03	0
02.04	02.04	0
02.05	02.05	0
03.18	03.06 + 06.11 + 11.14 + 14.18	22
04.15	04.07 + 07.12 + 12.15	12
04.08	04.08	1
05.16	05.09 + 09.13 + 13.16	6
05.10	05.10	1
08.15	08.15	12
10.16	10.16	2
15.17	15.17	4
16.17	16.17	1
17.18	17.18	1
18.20	18.19 + 19.20	4

Table 6.5 **The reduced network: activity table.**

The table shows the correlation between the activities of the full and reduced networks in Figures 6.13 and 6.15, respectively. It is similar to Table 6.3.

(2) 01.02.04.15.17.18.20   26 weeks.
(3) 01.02.04.08.15.17.18.20   27 weeks.
(4) 01.02.05.16.17.18.20   17 weeks.
(5) 01.02.05.10.16.17.18.20   14 weeks.

Here, therefore, path 1 is the critical path which sets the total project time at 31 weeks. If, during the course of the project, an activity on the critical path takes longer than its estimated time then the project time is correspondingly increased. Conversely, if an activity on the critical path takes less than its estimated time then the project time will be correspondingly decreased, *unless* another path becomes critical.

For example, suppose that A03.18 was actually completed in 17 weeks rather than the estimated 22 weeks, a reduction of 5 weeks. The project time, however, is reduced by only four weeks since path 3 then becomes critical.

The project time is determined by the durations of the activities on the critical path. Hence (within limits) the durations of activities on non-critical paths may be extended, or their starts may be delayed, before the project time is effected. In other words, events on non-critical paths may occur later, up to some limit, than their earliest possible time before the project time is effected. This restricted 'freedom of movement' for events on non-critical paths is called **slack**. It is an important parameter for consideration when determining the planned resource allocation to a project, and during its subsequent control.

Event times and slack

The **earliest possible time (ET)** that an event can occur is the longest forward path, measured from the start event, leading into the event. In Figure 6.15, for example, the ET for E08 is 6 weeks, obtained by summing the activity times along the only forward path (01.02.04.08) leading into it. But two forward paths lead into E15:

(1) 01.02.04.15   17 weeks.
(2) 01.02.04.08.15   18 weeks.

The ET of E15, therefore, is 18 weeks because an event cannot occur until all the activities leading into it are complete.

The ET (in weeks) for each event in the figure is the upper number in the event box stack. It is suggested that the reader verifies these numbers to become familiar with the concept of earliest possible time. Note that the ET calculations can be done incrementally (forwards) from event to event. The general case is illustrated in Figure 6.16(a).

Using P and S subscripts to denote predecessor and successor events respectively, as in the figure:

$$ET_S = Max[ET_{PI} + T_{P.SI}] \text{ where } I = 1, 2 \dots N \tag{6.3}$$

In Figure 6.15, the critical path (01.02.03.18.20) is, of course, the longest forward path leading into the end event – the ET for E20 is 31 weeks.

The **latest acceptable time (LT)** that an event can occur is the latest time it can occur without increasing the overall project time. LT is calculated in a similar way to ET, but by tracing backward paths through the network. In PERT jargon, the network

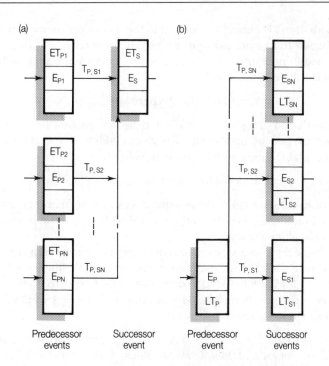

Figure 6.16 **Earliest possible time (ET) and latest acceptable time (LT) for events.**
The earliest possible time that an event can occur is the *longest forward* path, measured from the
start event, leading into the event. It is calculated by tracing forward paths from the start event. The
latest acceptable time that an event can occur is the latest time it can occur without increasing the
overall project time. It is calculated by tracing backward paths from the end event, such that LT +
longest backward path = project time. The calculations can be done (most quickly) incrementally
from event to event. The general case is shown here, in terms of the stacked box event symbol used
in Figure 6.15.

In (a): $ET_S = Max[ET_{PI} + T_{P.SI}]$
In (b): $LT_P = Min[LT_{SI} - T_{P.SI}]$, where $I = 1, 2 \ldots . N$

is 'anchored' on the end event and the project completion time is noted (31 weeks in
the example case). The LT for an event is then calculated by subtracting the length of
the longest backward path, measured from the end event, leading into that event from
the project completion time. (This calculation is just another way of expressing: LT +
longest backward path = project time.)

In Figure 6.15, for example, the length of the longest (and only) backward path
leading into E15 (20.18.17.15) is 9 weeks, so the LT for E15 is 22 (= 31 − 9) weeks.
On the other hand, there are two backward paths leading into E04 (a launching
event). These paths are:

(1) 20.18.17.15.04   21 weeks.
(2) 20.18.17.15.08.04   22 weeks.

The LT for E04 is, therefore, 9 (= 31 − 22) weeks.

The LT (in weeks) for each event in the figure is the lower number in the event box
stack. It is (again) suggested that the reader verifies these numbers to become familiar

with the LT concept. Note that the LT calculations can be done incrementally (backwards) from event to event. The general case is illustrated in Figure 6.16(b). Using P and S subscripts to denote predecessor and successor events respectively, as in the figure:

$$LT_P = Min[LT_{SI} - T_{P.SI}] \text{ where } I = 1, 2 \dots N \tag{6.4}$$

The ET and LT figures for an event define the earliest and latest time boundaries on the occurrence of that event. An **event slack** is the difference between its latest acceptable time and its earliest possible time, that is:

$$\text{Event Slack} = (LT - ET) \text{ for that event} \tag{6.5}$$

The event slack figure defines the 'freedom' that an event has to move inside its LT and ET boundaries. Events on the critical path, of course, have no such freedom – their slack values are zero.

Note that, because every event (except the start event) has at least one predecessor event, a slack change may propagate forward. To illustrate this effect suppose that, in Figure 6.15, it is decided to defer E04 from Week 5 to Week 7. This can be done, in the network, by making A02.04 a 'waiting activity' of 2 weeks. The relevant 'before and after slack' values are:

	E04	E08	E15	E17	E18
When A02.04 = 0, slack values:	4	4	4	4	0
When A02.04 = 2, slack values:	2	2	2	2	0

Thus the slack reduction at E04 is propagated forward to E08, E15 and E17 because their ET values are arithmetically related. But the propagation stops at E18 because the ET of E18 is set by the ET of E03 and the duration of A03.18.

Activity starts, finishes and floats

Slack values, which are associated with events, are less interesting than the consequences of slack on activities. There are several parameters associated with activities, all of which depend on the ET and LT values of the events which define them. Figure 6.17 shows an activity, $A_{P.S}$, of duration $T_{P.S}$, with its predecessor and successor events, E_P and E_S, respectively.

The activity $A_{P.S}$ is bounded by E_P and E_S and has, therefore, a range possible start (and finish) times defined by:

- the earliest possible time of its predecessor event, ET_P
- the latest acceptable time of its successor event, LT_S
- its duration, $T_{P.S}$

The activity start and finish parameters are:

Earliest start	$ES_{P.S} = ET_P$	(6.6)
Latest start	$LS_{P.S} = LT_S - T_{P.S}$	(6.7)
Earliest finish	$EF_{P.S} = ET_P + T_{P.S}$	(6.8)
Latest finish	$LF_{P.S} = LT_S$	(6.9)

The maximum range is between the latest and earliest starts (or, equally, between the

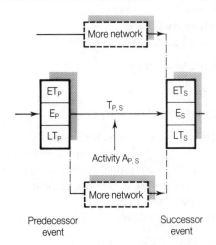

Figure 6.17   **An activity with its predecessor and successor events.**

The ET and LT for an event set the earliest and latest time boundaries on its occurrence. Event slack, which is (LT − ET), is the 'freedom' that an event has to move inside its LT and ET boundaries. The corresponding parameter for activities is float. This diagram shows the general case. There are four different types of activity float, because there are four possible pairings of ET_P or LT_P with ET_S or LT_S:

(1) Total float = $TF_{P.S}$ = $(LT_S − ET_P) − T_{P.S}$ is the amount by which an activity can be delayed or extended without increasing the total project time;

(2) Free float early = $FFE_{P.S}$ = $(ET_S − ET_P) − T_{P.S}$ is the amount by which an activity can be delayed or extended without delaying the earliest start of a successor activity;

(3) Free float late = $FFL_{P.S}$ = $(LT_S − LT_P) − T_{P.S}$ is the amount by which an activity can be delayed or extended without advancing the latest start of a predecessor activity;

(4) Independent float = $IF_{P.S}$ = $(ET_S − LT_P) − T_{P.S}$ is amount by which an activity can be delayed or extended without effecting any other activity.

latest and earliest finishes). This maximum range is called the **total float**, $TF_{P.S}$, for the activity:

$$TF_{P.S} = (LT_S − ET_P) − T_{P.S} \qquad\qquad (6.10)$$

where Equation 6.10 is obtained by subtracting Equation 6.6 from Equation 6.7. Note that the quantity $(LT_S − ET_P)$ is the maximum possible time gap between E_P and E_S. Total float measures the amount by which an activity can be delayed or extended without increasing the total project time. As an illustration, the possible start times and the corresponding total floats for a few selected activities in Figure 6.15 are:

Activity	03.18	04.15	05.16
Earliest start	5	5	5
Latest start	5	10	19
Total float	0	5	14

(The corresponding finish times are determined, of course, simply by adding the activity duration to the start time.) Note that the total float for activities on the critical path is zero. By the same token, as the total float of an activity is used up (voluntarily or otherwise) the path containing that activity becomes increasingly critical.

In fact, there are four float parameters associated with an activity; because there are four possible pairings of ET_P or LT_P with ET_S or LT_S. Total float, defined by Equation 6.10, is one parameter. Returning now to Figure 6.17, the other parameters are:

- **free float early** (FFE)
- **free float late** (FFL)
- **independent float** (IF)

Free float early is defined by:

$$FFE_{P.S} = (ET_S - ET_P) - T_{P.S} \tag{6.11}$$

It measures the amount by which an activity can be delayed or extended without delaying the earliest start of a successor activity. For example, in Figure 6.15, the FFE of A03.18 is zero because it is on the critical path. But the FFE of A04.15 is 1 week. This indicates that it could start at Week 6, or be extended from 12 to 13 weeks, without delaying the earliest start of A15.17.

Free float late is defined by:

$$FFL_{P.S} = (LT_S - LT_P) - T_{P.S} \tag{6.12}$$

It measures the amount by which an activity can be delayed or extended without advancing the latest start of a predecessor activity. For example, in Figure 6.15, the FFL of A03.18 is zero because it is on the critical path. But the FFL of A04.15 is 1 week. This indicates that it could start at Week 6, or be extended from 12 to 13 weeks, without advancing the latest start of A02.04. Free float late is generally of less interest than free float early (which is often just called 'free float') and then only in the planning stage.

Finally, independent float is defined by:

$$IF_{P.S} = (ET_S - LT_P) - T_{P.S} \tag{6.13}$$

It measures the amount by which an activity can be delayed or extended without affecting any other activity. It is a fairly rare commodity and not usually very interesting. It is not present (in a positive form) in Figure 6.15. However, if A04.15 were reduced to less than 9 weeks it would acquire an independent float.

Incidentally, the concept of activity float originated in CPM rather than in PERT, where it is still sometimes called **activity slack**. The terms **primary slack** and **secondary slack** are also sometimes used in PERT, rather than total float and free float early, respectively.

Squared, calendar or schedule presentation

When all the calculations are complete, it is usual to redraw the network on a calendar or schedule basis. This is sometimes called a **squared network**. The duration of the critical path sets the time-scale and real dates may be inserted. This type of presentation provides an illuminating insight into the project plan. Figure 6.18 shows the example PERT network in this format.

In this case, the events have been positioned at their earliest possible times so that visible float appears prior to those events where two (or more) paths converge. (This illustrates the preferred approach to project implementation. For example, in the figure, it is better to wait at E18 for the software to be ready than to start E04 and/or E05 late; and possibly miss the appointment with the software.) Alternatively, the events can be placed at their latest possible times so that visible float appears at the beginning of some activities.

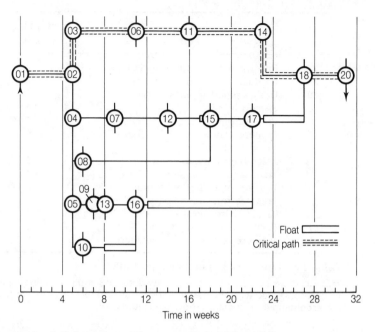

Figure 6.18 **A scheduled version of the example PERT network.**
This shows the example network redrawn in the squared, scheduled or calendar form against a real
timescale. Here, the events have been positioned at their earliest possible times so that float (free
float early) appears prior to events where two (or more) paths converge. This mirrors the preferred
approach to project implementation.

A pipework project

As a diversion from the central example in this section, a simple pipework project
(Cather, 1991, private communication) is now considered. It employs a marginally
different presentation technique to that shown in Figure 6.18 and, more importantly,
emphasizes that project completion time depends on the availability of resources.
Table 6.6 is the activity table for this project, which is concerned with the design,
fabrication and test of a pipework installation. The table also shows the precedent
relationships. Completion of activity S (which is more of an event than an activity)
launches the project. The corresponding project network plan is shown in Figure
6.19(a). This is drawn as a bar (or Gantt) chart, but the precedence information from
Table 6.6 is built into it in the form of links between related activities. Activities are
shown starting at their latest allowable dates, so that float appears before the start of
some activities on non-critical paths. This technique contrasts with that shown in
Figure 6.18. The critical path is C-F-G-J-K-L-M, which sums to 35 (working) days.

But this plan assumes that resources are instantly available when required. This is
unlikely in a real situation. For example, suppose that the support designer already has
a (priority) workload of 15 days when the project is launched. In this case, the earliest
possible start of activity B is at Day 15. This is 2 days later than the latest allowable start
needed to meet the 35 days completion time for the project analysed in isolation. The
situation is illustrated in Figure 6.19(b), which shows that the critical path under
these circumstances is *other work*-B-H-K-L-M. This sums to 37 (working) days.

	Activity	Working days	Precedent activity
S	Receive pipework layout drawing	–	–
A	Produce shop-floor drawings	2	S
B	Design pipe supports	7	S
C	Procure pipes	10	S
D	Procure pipe fittings	7	A
E	Procure valves	15	S
F	Cut and prepare pipes	5	A, C
G	Assemble individual pipes	12	D, F
H	Manufacture pipe support bases	10	B
I	Procure pipe support fittings	5	B
J	Pressure test individual pipes	3	G
K	Transport to installation site	2	E, H, I, J
L	Final assembly on site	2	K
M	Pressure test whole installation	1	L

Table 6.6 **Pipework project: activity table.**

This lists the activities, estimated activity durations and precedence relationships for a small project concerned with the design, fabrication and test of a pipework installation. The corresponding project plan is shown in Figure 6.19.

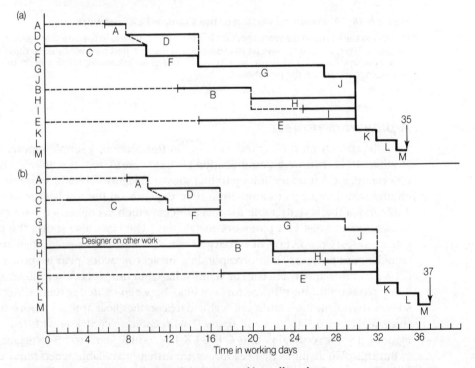

Figure 6.19 **Pipework design, fabricate and install project.**

The project model illustrated here combines bar chart and PERT techniques to produce a network, in (a), not unlike Figure 6.18. It differs from that network by showing activities starting at their latest acceptable times, so that float appears before the start of some activities on non-critical paths. This plan assumes instant availability of needed resources when required. The assumption may not be realistic. The lower half of the figure shows, at (b), the effect on estimated project completion time of the late availability of the pipe support designer.

Tuning the network

The primary purpose of network analysis is to establish the likely duration of the project, which may or may not be acceptable. If the total project time is acceptable, the next step is to consider if the planned resources allocated to the project can be reduced (so as to reduce project cost) without increasing the project time beyond its acceptance limit.

In Figure 6.18, A16.17 has an FFE of 10 weeks; indicating that a more relaxed approach can be taken to the activities between E05 and E16 without putting undue pressure on E17. These activities, therefore, are candidates for a cost saving investigation. On the other hand, the FFE at A17.18 is only 4 weeks, which is about thirteen per cent of total project duration. This might well be regarded as too small to risk reducing the resources assigned to the activities between E04 and E17.

Of course, it may be that the maximum permissible project time is pre-set by some external, non-project, consideration, such as a promised date to a customer. In such cases, the network may be 'anchored' on the pre-set time and the event slack parameters calculated by first working backwards through the network. If the pre-set time is less than the 'natural' first estimate of total project time, *negative* value of slack and float will arise. In Figure 6.18, for example, suppose that the total project time is pre-set at 28 weeks. The critical path will then exhibit a slack of −3 weeks! Under these circumstances it may be necessary to reconsider both the design of the network and the resource allocations. This re-planning work must clearly start with the most critical path. There are four valid options for consideration:

(1) Change series activities to parallel activities. For example, start A11.14 (code and test the software modules) before A06.11 (design software modules) is complete. There is usually, as here, a technical risk associated with this approach.

(2) Reduce the duration of appropriate activities by applying additional resources and/or improving the productivity of the assigned resources. Not all activities are susceptible to this approach. It is sometimes possible, when the skills match, to transfer people from high float activities to the more critical activities.

(3) Delete or restrict some activities. For example, by eliminating or reducing some specified product features or by not implementing complete testing schedules. This is another high risk option. In particular, no liberties should be taken with the product specification which are not endorsed by the project customer.

(4) Negotiate a more realistic project time-scale with the customer.

These options are not mutually exclusive. Very often, investigation of the first three options provides the ammunition needed to convince the customer that the fourth option is the wisest course. A fifth option is merely to reduce activity estimates until events on the critical path shows zero rather than negative slack. It is not recommended. This is a soft answer which does *not* turn away future wrath.

The matrix calculator

A substantial amount of calculation is required to analyse even quite modest networks, and this must be repeated every time a parameter is changed during network

From/to	E01	E02	E03	E04	E05	E08	E10	E15	E16	E17	E18	E20	ET
E01		5	–	–	–	–	–	–	–	–	–	–	0 E01
E02	–		0	0	0	–	–	–	–	–	–	–	5 E02
E03	–	–		–	–	–	–	–	–	–	22	–	5 E03
E04	–	–	–		–	1	–	12	–	–	–	–	5 E04
E05	–	–	–	–		–	1	–	6	–	–	–	5 E05
E08	–	–	–	–	–		–	12	–	–	–	–	6 E08
E10	–	–	–	–	–	–		–	2	–	–	–	6 E10
E15	–	–	–	–	–	–	–		–	4	–	–	18 E15
E16	–	–	–	–	–	–	–	–		1	–	–	11 E16
E17	–	–	–	–	–	–	–	–	–		1	–	22 E17
E18	–	–	–	–	–	–	–	–	–	–		4	27 E18
E20	–	–	–	–	–	–	–	–	–	–	–		31 E20
ET LT	0 0	5 5	5 5	5 9	5 19	6 10	6 23	18 22	11 25	22 26	27 27	31 31	ET LT
Slack CPath	0 * E01	0 * E02	0 * E03	4 E04	14 E05	4 E08	17 E10	4 E15	14 E16	4 E17	0 * E18	0 * E20	Slack CPath

Figure 6.20 **Matrix calculations for the reduced version of the example PERT network.**
A matrix representation of a network can ease analytic tedium. This figure is the reduced version of the example PERT network (Figure 6.15) in a matrix format. Event numbers label (in numerical sequence here) both the columns and the rows of the matrix. Each matrix cross-point, other than those on the top left to bottom right diagonal, represents a possible activity. The forward direction through the network is from rows to columns. The calculation algorithms for ET and LT (based on Equations 6.3 and 6.4) are a little obscure. They are explained in the text.

design. A matrix representation of the network can go some way towards easing this tedium. Figure 6.20 shows the reduced version of the example PERT network (Figure 6.15) in a matrix format.

The event identifiers are used to label (in numerical sequence here) both the columns and the rows of the matrix. Each matrix cross-point, other than those on the top left to bottom right diagonal, then represents a possible activity. The forward direction through the network is taken to be from rows to columns.

The estimated activity times are entered at the appropriate cross-points. Thus A01.02 is represented by the 5 (weeks) at the intersection of the E01 row with E02 column, and so on for the other activities. The earliest possible time (ET) and the latest acceptable time (LT) for each event are then calculated using algorithms based on Equations 6.3 and 6.4, which are reproduced here for convenience:

$$ET_S = Max[ET_{PI} + T_{P.SI}] \tag{6.3}$$
$$LT_P = Min[LT_{SI} - T_{P.SI}] \qquad where\ I = 1, 2 \dots N \tag{6.4}$$

and the P and S subscripts denote predecessor and successor events, as before.

The earliest possible times are calculated first. The ET for E01 is 0 which is entered in the E01 row in the ET column on the right of the matrix. The E02 column is then inspected. Entries in this column are $T_{P.S}$ (where $S = 02$) figures for the activities which terminate at E02. When such a figure is encountered it is added to the ET figure in its row, as required by Equation 6.3, to yield a set of $[ET_{PI} + T_{P.SI}]$ values. The largest of these values is then entered as the ET for E02. This algorithm is repeated for the remaining events. Note that the first time there is more than one $T_{P.S}$ figure in a column occurs at E15. The ET for E15 is, therefore, $18 (= 12 + 6)$ weeks rather than 17 $(12 + 5)$ weeks. Note, too, that ET and LT are identical for end events (E20 here). The LT for the end event is then entered into the LT row at the bottom of the matrix.

A similar algorithm is then employed to calculate the remaining latest acceptable times in reverse order. There are two differences. Firstly, the backward paths being considered lie along rows rather than columns. Secondly, it is Equation 6.4 that is being exercised so the smallest $[LT_{SI} - T_{P.SI}]$ values are sought. For example, the LT for E18 is $27 (= 31 - 4)$ weeks, but the LT for E05 is $19 (= 25 - 6)$ weeks rather than $22 (= 23 - 1)$ weeks.

When the ET and LT values for all the events have been calculated it is a simple matter to derive the event slack and activity float parameters. Slack values are shown in Figure 6.20, which also indicates those events on the critical path (for which slack $= 0$). Table 6.7 lists the important float values derived from the ET and LT rows. It also indicates those activities on the critical path (for which total float $= 0$).

A 'manual' approach to the matrix calculator has been described but it is not difficult to construct a spreadsheet program for this purpose. In fact, Figure 6.20 is adapted from a printout from such a program.

Activity	CP	Est[a]	TF	FFE	FFL
01.02	*	5	0	0	0
02.03	*	0	0	0	0
02.04		0	4	0	4
02.05		0	14	0	14
03.18	*	22	0	0	0
04.15		12	5	1	1
04.08		1	4	0	0
05.16		6	14	0	0
05.10		1	17	0	3
08.15		12	4	0	0
10.16		2	17	3	0
15.17		4	4	0	0
16.17		1	14	10	0
17.18		1	4	4	0
18.20	*	4	0	0	0

Est[a] = Estimated activity time.

Table 6.7 **Float table for the reduced version of the example PERT network.**
This table is from the same spreadsheet program that produced the matrix of Figure 6.20. It lists the important activity float values derived from the ET and LT values shown in that figure. It also indicates those activities on the critical path (for which total float = 0). All times given are in weeks.

One final point: note that all the activity times entered into Figure 6.20 lie above the blocked diagonal. This arises because the events have been numbered in **topological sequence** and ordered sequentially along the sides of the matrix. In a topological sequence, predecessor events have a lower numbers than successor events. This is a tidy, but not necessary, way of doing it. It makes no difference to the calculation algorithms embodied in the matrix.

6.4.4 Topological rules

PERT methodology lays down a number of rules which must be obeyed to achieve topological integrity in network design. Additionally, some of the rules affect the level of detail shown in a network. All of them affect the quality of the final plan.

Rule 1: Predecessors and successors

This rule concerns what comes before and after both events and activities. Events are considered first:

- With the exceptions of the start event and the end event, each event must have at least one predecessor and one successor activity. But events may have more than one predecessor and/or more than one successor activity.

For activities the rule is:

- Each activity must have just one predecessor event and just one successor event, and only one activity may connect a pair of events. In other words, each activity must be uniquely defined by connecting a unique pair of events.

The network of Figure 6.15 illustrates both facets of this rule.

When a number of activities converge on the same event, the definition of that event should recognize the completion of all those activities. For example, the definition of E15 in Figure 6.15 is 'printed circuit boards made and tested, and bought-out electronic components received and inspected'. Only two activities converge on 'logic' event E15, but the definition of such events becomes increasingly diffuse as more activities converge on them. The problem can be eased by arranging that each real activity has its own unique successor event. Figures 6.21(a) and (b) show alternative representations of the same network logic.

In Figure 6.21(b) the real activities converging on the event 'S' each have a unique successor event. This has been achieved by introducing new events and dummies. This type of construction should be used very selectively, because the additional events and dummies that it introduces clutter up the network and increase analysis time. Dummies also enter into float calculations in a mildly disturbing way, as is discussed later.

Rule 2: The precedence rule

This rule was introduced earlier because it is central to the whole PERT concept. It is restated here for convenience:

- No event can occur until all the activities which lead into it have been completed, and no activity can start until the event that precedes it has occurred.

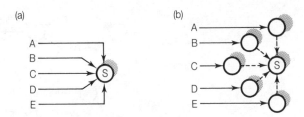

(a)   (b)

Figure 6.21 **Rule 1: the use of unique successor events.**
PERT Rule 1 concerns what comes before and after both events and activities and is stated in the text. This figure illustrates one application. An event description becomes increasingly diffuse as the number of events that converge on it increases. For example, in (a), the description of event S must recognize the completion of the five activities A, B, C, D and E. The problem is eased in (b), which represents the same logic, by arranging that each *real* activity has a unique successor event.

The rule requires that the circles, boxes or whatever that represent the events have logical and gate properties, holding up progress until all their (activity) inputs are complete. This rule is responsible for the inherent pressure that PERT exerts on its users for careful analysis to reveal real project constraints, and for the clear definition of events and activities.

Rule 3: Dependent and independent activities

While this situation is commonly cited as a rule, it is more of a warning and illustration. Suppose a situation exists where an activity 'C' cannot start until activities 'A' and 'B' are finished, and an activity 'D' cannot start until 'A' has finished. Figure 6.22(a) shows one common, and incorrect, expression of such situations.

This logic indicates that both 'C' and 'D' are dependent on 'A' and 'B'. In fact, only 'C' is dependent on 'A' and 'B'. Activity 'D' depends only on 'A' and is independent of 'B'. The correct logic is shown in Figure 6.22(b), which uses a dummy both to separate and to combine the completion of activities 'A' and 'B'.

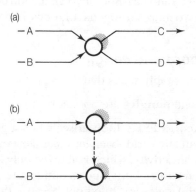

Figure 6.22 **Rule 3: dependent and independent activities.**
Suppose activity C cannot start until activities A and B are finished, and activity D cannot start until A has finished. A common expression of this situation is shown in (a). It is wrong, because it indicates that the starts of both C and D are dependent on the completion of both A and B. The correct logic is shown in (b), which uses a dummy both to separate and to combine the completion of activities A and B.

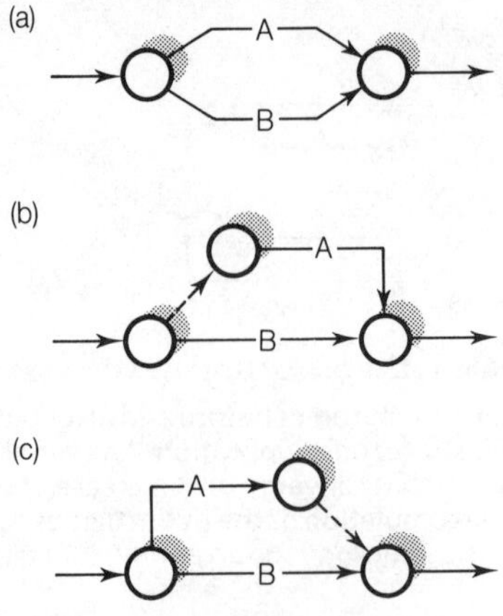

Figure 6.23 **Rule 4: representation of parallel activities.**
Sometimes two (or more) activities effectively exist in parallel between the same predecessor and successor events. The wrong way of expressing this is shown in (a). It breaks a facet of Rule 1, aimed at avoiding the ambiguity of two or more activities sharing the same predecessor and successor event. Alternative correct expressions are shown in (b) and (c). Both involve the introduction of a dummy and a new event.

Rule 4: Parallel activities

This so-called 'rule' is in the same category as rule 3. There are occasions where two (or more) activities effectively exist in parallel between the same predecessor–successor event pair. The situation can arise, for example, when two different approaches aimed at the same target are launched from the same event. Figure 6.23(a) is the incorrect way of showing this logic. It breaks a facet of rule 1, aimed at avoiding the ambiguity of two or more activities sharing the same predecessor and successor event numbers and definitions. Two possible solutions to the problem are shown in Figures 6.23(b) and (c). Both involve the introduction of a dummy and a new event. (There are two more analogous solutions, obtained by interchanging activities A and B.)

Rule 5: Loops and dangles

This final rule simply states that:

- Loops and **dangles** are not allowed.

In this context, a **PERT loop** arises when a given event is followed by an activity which (eventually) leads back into that same event. A dangle is an event which is not followed by an activity, which is allowed only for end events. The network shown in Figure 6.24 fractures both aspects of this rule.

Loops and dangles are ruled out because they spoil the mathematics of network analysis, which is encapsulated in Equations 6.3 to 6.13. Dangles can always be avoided by the judicious use of dummies, but loops are a different matter.

In project terms, a loop may be an entirely justified sequence of events. The applied research project illustrated (in RPD format) in Figure 6.9 is one example. The planned rework of faulty units during a construction phase is another. Of course, in practice, all

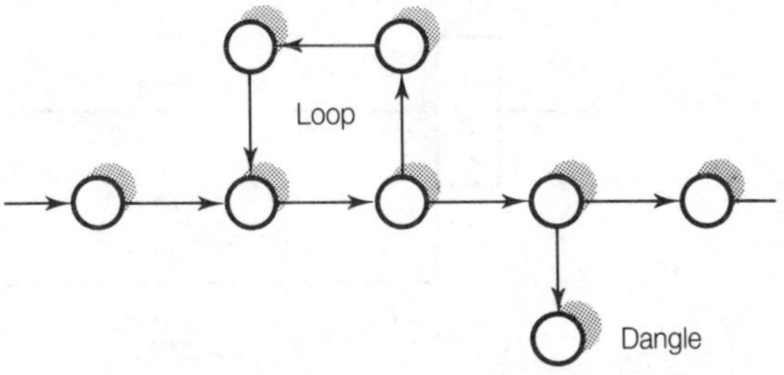

Figure 6.24 **Rule 5: loops and dangles.**

Loops and dangles are not allowed in PERT, because they spoil the mathematics of network analysis. The meaning of the terms is illustrated here. Dangles can always be avoided by the judicious use of dummies, but a loop may be a valid sequence of project events. It must be condensed (somehow) to a single activity before inclusion in the PERT network. This usually involves some probability-based estimating exercise, such as that discussed in Section 6.3.

project loops include an exit mechanism. This construction is not available in PERT: if a PERT loop is entered the activities it contains are then repeated indefinitely!

The answer to the loop problem is to exclude them from the PERT network. This means that legitimate project loops must appear in the network as a single activity. The loop that this single activity represents can be estimated and analysed by some other technique such as RPD (see Section 6.3), possibly in combination with the 'three times' approach to be discussed shortly (see Section 6.4.5).

Free float and dummies

The solutions offered to many of the network construction problems outlined in the discussion of the topographical rules involve the introduction of dummies. Under certain circumstances dummies can confuse free float calculations. The problem is exemplified in Figure 6.25.

In Figure 6.25(a) an event and a dummy (E03 and A03.04) have been introduced to distinguish two essentially parallel activities connecting E02 and E04 (a rule 4 situation). The results of the float calculations are shown on the network. Note that A02.03 has no FFE. The FFE which properly belongs to A02.03 has been acquired by the dummy! This suggests that A02.03 cannot be delayed or extended, which is not the case.

The solution usually advocated to avoid this oddity is illustrated in Figure 6.25(b). This merely transfers the problem to the FFL parameter, as the figures show. It also demands a different definition for E03, which may be inconvenient. Despite these quibbles the construction of Figure 6.25(b) is preferred, because FFL is a less useful measure than FFE.

These situations only arise on paths which have free float. This glimpse of the obvious presents the optimum solution, but it is not always available. In Figure 6.25, for example, the new event and dummy could have been inserted into the A02.04 activity whose duration sets the E02 to E04 time gap. In this case both the FFE and the FFL for the dummy are zero.

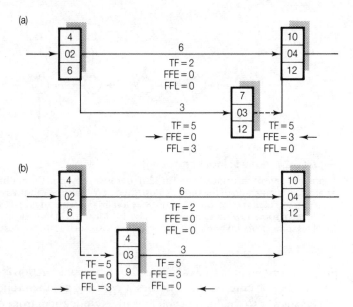

Figure 6.25 **Free float and dummies.**
Many network construction problems are solved by introducing dummies, but they can spoil free float calculations. In (a), for example, E03 and A03.04 have been inserted to distinguish two essentially parallel activities connecting E02 and E04. The float calculations demonstrate that A02.03 has no free float early (FFE). That which properly belongs to it has been acquired by the dummy! This suggests that A02.03 cannot be delayed or extended, which is not the case. The arrangement shown in (b) is preferred. This transfers the problem to the free float late (FFL) parameter, which is a less useful measure than FFE. Problems of this nature only arise on paths which have free float, so they can be totally avoided by inserting the new event and dummy into a zero float path, if one is available.

6.4.5 Probability and PERT

A single time value has been used for the duration of each activity in the whole of the preceding discussion on PERT. This is reasonable when experience with near-identical activities allows durations to be estimated with great certainty. But these circumstances are fairly rare, especially in technological innovation work, and time estimates must frequently be made under conditions of some uncertainty.

One approach to this problem simply ignores it! The project plan is based on single value 'best guess' times for each activity, and the project is launched in the pious hope that fortune really does favour the brave. However, natural optimism, and time and cost pressures from above usually conspire to frustrate this hope. Consequently, the project overruns its time and cost budget. Another 'cure', which might be worse than the original disease, is to conceal a **contingency time allowance** (more commonly called **padding**) in each activity time estimate. Projects planned on this basis rarely overrun their budgets. But not all that many of them even get launched, because they promise to spend too much money over too long a time-scale. **Three-times estimating** is a probability-based technique which aims to strike a rational middle course between these two extremes.

Three-times estimating was part of the original PERT system and it is still particularly associated with PERT. Within its limitations, however, it is applicable in all network planning methods. As the name suggests, it is based on three time estimates for each activity.

The three times defined

The three time estimates for an activity assume the same level of assigned resources and are defined as:

(1) The **optimistic time** is an estimate of the minimum time that the activity will absorb assuming unusual good luck and 'right first time' resolution of technical uncertainties.

(2) The **most likely time** is an estimate of the normal time that the activity will absorb assuming average luck and the usual 'win some, lose some' situation with technical uncertainties. This is the time which would occur most frequently if the activity could be repeated a large number of times under these circumstances.

(3) The **pessimistic time** is an estimate of the maximum time that the activity will take assuming unusual bad luck, and substantial technical surprises which require some measure of rework. 'Natural' disasters, such as fire, flood, strikes, power cuts and the like, are discounted unless there is realistic probability that they will occur.

The three times combined

These three times, labelled here as T_O, T_M and T_P, respectively, are assumed to be connected in a unimodal probability density distribution with the most likely time, T_M, as its modal (most frequent) value. A skewed, or 'beta', distribution is employed because the optimistic and pessimistic times are not necessarily symmetrically disposed about the modal value. The skew can be to the left or to the right, as shown in Figure 6.26.

Then, using some rather dubious mathematics and assumptions, it can be shown (though not here) that the mean or **expected time**, T_E, is given by:

$$T_E = (T_O + 4T_M + T_P)/6 \qquad\qquad (6.14)$$

while the **standard deviation**, s, and the **variance**, s^2, are:

$$s = (T_P - T_O)/6 \qquad\qquad (6.15)$$
$$s^2 = [(T_P - T_O)^2]/36 \qquad\qquad (6.16)$$

The expected time, T_E, differs from the model time, T_M, because the distribution is skewed, rather than symmetric, about the modal value. It is located on the time axis such that it divides the area under the curve into two equal parts. In other words, the probability of the actual activity time being more than, or less than, T_E is fifty per cent. The standard deviation, s, indicates the dispersion (or 'sharpness') of the distribution curve. The amount by which an actual time differs from T_E at other probability levels increases as the standard deviation increases: that is, as the **range** $(T_P - T_O)$ increases.

The relationships expressed in Equations 6.14, 6.15 and 6.16 can be used (in conditions of substantial estimating uncertainty) in a variety of ways, including:

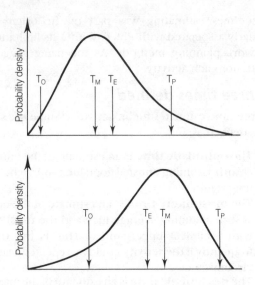

Figure 6.26   **The assumed three times probability distribution.**

The three-times activity estimating technique may be used to improve on single time estimates in conditions of great uncertainty. Optimistic (T_O), mostly likely (T_M) and pessimistic (T_P) activity times (defined in the text) are estimated. These are assumed to lie on a unimodal probability density distribution, as in the figure. (The distribution is usually skewed left or right, because T_O and T_P are not necessarily symmetrically disposed about T_M.) This assumption, and some others, leads to Equations 6.14, 6.15 and 6.16 for calculating the activity expected time (T_E), standard deviation and variance.

(1) Obtaining improved single time estimates for individual activities.

(2) Assessing the probability of a project actually completing in a specific target time.

(3) Assessing the completion time vulnerabilities presented by non-critical paths.

The first two of these applications are now explored in an extended example. It is based on the example PERT network of Figure 6.13.

An example of three-times estimating

Table 6.8 lists the three-times estimating calculations for the critical path of the example network of Figure 6.13. In the table, the previously used single-time estimates for the seven (real) activities on the critical path have been retained as the individual T_Ms. However, estimates have also been made of the optimistic and pessimistic times for each activity. The individual expected times are then calculated using Equation 6.14. Note that most of the T_Es are greater than the corresponding T_Ms because most of the assumed distributions are biased towards pessimism, which is often the case. But the differences are not dramatic (here) since T_M is heavily weighted in the calculation. Note also that, in view of the nature of the input data, the T_E calculations have been rounded to one decimal place.

It is now assumed, quite reasonably, that the individual T_Es are better single-time estimates for the activities than the corresponding T_Ms. It is further assumed:

Label	T_O	T_M	T_P	T_E	s	s^2
01.02	4.0	5.0	7.0	5.2	0.50	0.25
02.03	0.0	0.0	0.0	0.0	0.00	0.00
03.06	5.0	6.0	7.0	6.0	0.33	0.11
06.11	3.0	5.0	8.0	5.2	0.83	0.69
11.14	6.0	7.0	12.0	7.7	1.00	1.00
14.18	3.0	4.0	6.0	4.2	0.50	0.25
18.19	2.0	3.0	5.0	3.2	0.50	0.25
19.20	0.6	1.0	3.0	1.3	0.40	0.16
Critical path	–	31.0	–	32.8	1.60	2.72

***Table 6.8* Critical path calculations for the example PERT network.**
This shows the three-times calculations for the critical path of the network of Figure 6.13. The earlier single-time estimates are retained as T_M, and are combined (using Equations 6.14, 6.15 and 6.16) with new T_O and T_P to obtain a T_E, standard deviation and variance for each activity. Some important assumptions (principally that the whole path time obeys a normal distribution, see text) then allow the corresponding parameters for the whole path to be calculated.

- That there are enough activities on the critical path for the Central Limit theorem to apply. This is equivalent to assuming that the total path time will obey a normal (as distinct from a beta) distribution. A normal distribution is symmetric about its mean (and modal) value, and is completely defined by its mean value and standard deviation.

- That the expected times for the individual activities are *not* correlated. This allows the mean time and the variance for the whole path to be obtained simply by summing the corresponding values for the individual activities. The mean time for the whole path is also its expected time. The standard deviation for the whole path is obtained by taking the square root of the whole path variance (and rounding to one decimal place).

The calculations for the example, contained in Table 6.8, indicate that the normal distribution of the critical path length is symmetric about a mean of 32.8 weeks with a standard deviation of 1.6 weeks. (This compares with the figure of 31.0 weeks previously obtained for the critical path).

It is now possible to assess the probability of the actual critical path length being less than or equal to particular targets, because the normal distribution curve is well documented. The first step is to convert the normal path distribution into standard form. Figure 6.27 illustrates the process.

This shows, in the upper half of the diagram, the form of the critical path distribution with a particular **target path time (TPT)** greater than the mean of 32.8 weeks. The probability that the actual path length will be less than or equal to this TPT is equal to the area under the curve to the left of TPT. (Thus, the probability that the actual path length will be less than or equal to the mean, 32.8 weeks here, is fifty per cent.)

The standard normal distribution, in the lower half of the diagram, is symmetric about zero with a standard deviation of unity and a total area of unity. A **standard target path time (STPT)** is shown corresponding to the TPT on the critical path

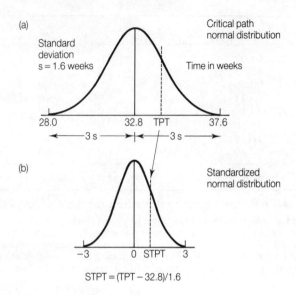

Figure 6.27   **Standardizing a normal distribution.**

The critical path calculations for the network of Figure 6.13 (Table 6.8) assume that the path time obeys the normal distribution shown in (a). The normal distribution curve is well documented, so the probability of the actual critical path length being less than, or equal to, particular targets can be assessed. The first step is to convert the normal path distribution into the standard normal form, as is shown in (b). The upper curve is mapped onto the lower curve by measuring target path times as differences from the mean, and normalizing these differences by dividing by the standard deviation. That is, here: STPT = (TPT − 32.8)/1.6 weeks. This allows values of STPT to be obtained which correspond to selected values of TPT.

distribution. This latter distribution is mapped onto the standard curve by measuring target path times as differences from the mean, and normalizing these differences by dividing by the standard deviation. That is:

$$STPT = (TPT - Mean)/s \qquad\qquad (6.17)$$
so, here $STPT = (TPT - 32.8)/1.6$

which allows values of STPT to be obtained which correspond to selected values TPT. The STPT values are then entered into published statistical tables for the standard normal distribution to obtain the corresponding probabilities. The relationship between probability and target path time for the critical path in the example is shown in Figure 6.28.

Note that the probability of the actual path time being less than or equal to the 31 weeks originally estimated is only about thirteen per cent! On the other hand, there is nearly an eighty per cent probability of the path time being within 34 weeks, which is about ten per cent more than the original path time estimate.

At this stage in a probability analysis, it would be wise to investigate marginally sub-critical paths in the network. The investigation may reveal a path which, while shorter than the notional critical path in T_E terms, has a finite probability of becoming the critical path because its distribution curve has a large dispersion. This exercise is not pursued here.

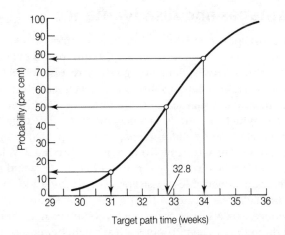

Figure 6.28   **The probability of target path times.**
The graph (which is subject to some important assumptions) shows the relationship between
probability and target path time for the critical path in the network of Figure 6.13. It is obtained by
entering STPT values derived from Equation 6.17 into published statistical tables for the standard
normal distribution to obtain the corresponding probabilities. The probability of the project being
completed within the 31 weeks originally estimated is only about thirteen per cent! But it is nearly
eighty per cent probable that it will be completed within 34 weeks.

Probability and PERT: For and against

The application of probability theory to PERT has been, and remains, an area of some
controversy. Consider, first, the three-times estimating technique. The three times are
not precisely defined and the mathematics which underpins the technique is somewhat dubious. It can also be argued that planners cannot make the three estimates
with either accuracy or consistency. Indeed, it might be better to use single-time
estimates modified by some factor which calibrates the estimator for undue optimism
or pessimism. These arguments against three-times estimating have merit. But there
can be no doubt that requiring three estimates does cause conscientious estimators to
explore the problem more deeply. Equally, the approach can largely eliminate the use
of hidden 'padding' in estimates, because it exposes uncertainties quite explicitly. But
the most potent factor in its favour is the observed fact that it usually gives better
results for activity estimating than the single time alternative!

    Several assumptions are also employed in using the results of three-times estimating
to assess the probability of target path lengths. These include the assumption that
individual activity times are not correlated and that whole path time obeys a normal
distribution. This latter assumption is reasonable if there are enough (more than five,
say) non-correlated activity times on the path for the Central Limit theorem to apply.
But, while non-correlation may be valid in the planning stage, it can fail in practice due
to shared resourcing problems. Once again, however, experience often triumphs over
these seemingly valid objections. This extension of the three-times technique is, on
balance, a worthwhile weapon in the planning armoury. It is particularly useful for
exploring the vulnerability of a forecast project completion time to uncertainties on
paths which are marginally sub-critical.

6.4.6 Advantages and disadvantages

PERT is most appropriate for well-defined projects of significant size and complexity, where these factors are measured by the number of events and their dependencies. PERT is characterized by demanding a sharp distinction between events and activities. This is a powerful planning discipline not as clearly manifest in activity-on-node network techniques such as RPD. PERT networks provide a clear and natural model of the project which encourages management to focus their attention on critical areas, both in initial planning and in the subsequent project control.

Extensions to the basic PERT technique have been developed which go beyond the elapsed time application to cover project cost, effort and risk. A number of software packages are also available to assist project planning and control with PERT. Typically, these offer facilities for network drawing, analysis and rapid updating, with management reports available in a variety of levels and formats. Some can handle networks of several thousand distinct events, such as might be required for an oil-rig construction project. The analysis of more elementary networks (up to about fifty events, say) can be handled quite comfortably with the aid of a standard spreadsheet.

The probability aspects of PERT should be approached with some caution but, used wisely, make a useful contribution to the whole method. The earlier warning that mathematical contortions do not improve numerical predictions of the future also applies here.

The criticism most often levelled at PERT (and any other related network technique) is that it is an expensive tool in both the planning and control phases. This is true: properly used, PERT planning and control generally contributes a few per cent (rarely as much as ten per cent) to total project costs. However, as with many other activities, the cost of doing it should be compared with the cost of *not* doing it. A proper analysis of this sort places the value of PERT in its true perspective. Assessing the cost of not using it (or its equivalent) must take into account the consequential higher rates of project budget overrun and complete project failure.

6.5 Task time versus task effort

Apart from a dire warning early in the chapter, all discussion of activity estimating so far has avoided a central issue. This issue concerns the relationship between the time to complete a particular activity and the amount of (people) effort assigned to it. Effort is measured in units of the number of people multiplied by their active time: people-months, people-years, people-hours and so on. People costs are proportional to effort. It is commonly, *and wrongly*, assumed that activity progress is also proportional to effort.

Suppose, for example, that a careful estimate of a particular activity indicates that that four engineers can complete it in 6 months, so the effort needed to complete the activity is $(4 \times 6) = 24$ engineer-months.

> *Question*: But $(4 \times 6) = 24 = (2 \times 12) = (8 \times 3)$, yes?
> *Answer*: Yes, splendid!
> *Question*: Therefore two engineers will complete it in 12 months and eight
>   engineers in three months, right?
> *Answer*: Wrong, probably. At the best, a firm 'maybe'.

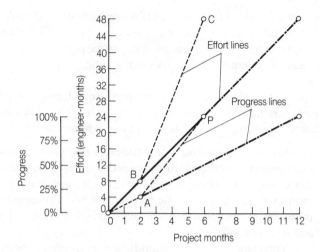

Figure 6.29   A straight line is the shortest distance between a problem and a disaster.
The human effort needed to complete a project task is PT, where P = number of people assigned to the task and T = task completion time. It is commonly assumed that, for a given task, PT is constant or (equivalently) that T is inversely proportional to P. The task planning and re-planning history summarized in the graphs is based on this 'linear' assumption. Line OP is the initial plan that the effort consumed and the progress achieved increase linearly, over 6 months, to 24 engineer-months and one hundred per cent respectively. But, at the end of Month 2, actual progress (point A) is half that planned while actual effort is on schedule (point B) at eight engineer-months. This suggests that the (total) effort really needed to complete the task is 48 engineer-months, not the 24 engineer-months first planned. So, at the end of Month 2, 40 engineer-months must be spent over four months to complete the task on schedule. Line BC is the new effort plan corresponding to line AP, which is the new progress plan. The original task team of four engineers must be increased to ten engineers to provide the required effort. (But when this was done the task took a *further* 12 months to complete! See text.)

The basic flaw in the 'linear' reasoning is the implicit assumption that the effort needed to complete the activity is independent of the rate at which effort is expended. The error can compound a small 'slip' problem into a project disaster. This observation is now illustrated by an example which yields some clues about activity estimating.

6.5.1   Straight lines to disaster

A particular task was planned to take 6 months and four engineers were assigned to it full-time. It was a sub-project on the critical path of a product design project. Figure 6.29 is a summary plan and control document for the task. It plots, using linear assumptions, effort spent and progress made against elapsed time.

The line OP summarizes the initial plan that the effort consumed and the progress achieved will each increase linearly from zero, over 6 months of elapsed time, to 24 engineer-months and one hundred per cent respectively.

Progress was reviewed at the end of the first month and at the end of the second month. Each of these reviews indicated that the rate of progress was only about half of that planned. The progress deviation detected at the end of the first month was ignored because 'the team needs a bit of learning time to get familiar with the task and, anyway, there are another five months in which to catch up'.

Point A indicates the actual progress at the end of Month 2. This was about seventeen per cent, rather than the thirty-three per cent anticipated. Point B indicates the actual effort consumed at that same time, which was (of course) 8 engineer-months.

At the end of Month 2 it was accepted, reluctantly but wisely, that the original estimate was flawed. The extent of the error was unknown but optimistic and pessimistic cases were suggested from the evidence available:

- *Optimistic*   This assumed that the rate of progress would immediately revert to that originally planned. In other words, it assumed that the amount of work remaining to be done was 20 (= 24 − 4) engineer-months, needing 5 more months to complete by the four engineers. The activity would be complete, therefore, at the end of Month 7 with a total effort spend of 28 engineer-months. So, optimistically,
  Time slip   = 1 month (about seventeen per cent)
  Effort overspend = 4 engineer-months (about seventeen per cent).

- *Pessimistic*   This assumed that the rate of progress would remain at about half of that originally planned. In other words, it assumed that the amount of work remaining to be done was 40 (= 48 − 8) engineer-months, needing 10 more months to complete by the four engineers. The activity would be complete, therefore, at the end of Month 12 with an effort spend of 48 engineer-months. So, pessimistically,
  Time slip   = 6 months (one hundred per cent)
  Effort overspend = 24 engineer-months (one hundred per cent).

There was no good reason for believing the optimistic view, but pessimism was supported with some solid evidence. This vision of the future was, therefore, adopted and bravely reported to the project management. They took the view that the consequential delay of 6 months to the whole project could not be tolerated. An edict was issued: 'this task must not slip – do whatever is necessary to complete it on time'. This edict required that progress move along the line AP in the figure. The problem of how to bring about this alarming increase in the rate of progress then arose.

It is the obvious, incorrect, and (sadly) entirely conventional response to this type of problem which is explored here. This merely notes that there are 40 more engineer-months of work still to do and 4 months in which to do it. Ten engineers are therefore required, so six more must be added to the existing team. The line BC in Figure 6.29 expresses the new effort plan corresponding to line AP, which is the demanded new progress plan.

Armed with the authority of the project manager, the task leader then borrowed six engineers (from other tasks within the project) and launched into the new plan. But the progress review one month later revealed some deterioration in the rate of progress. In fact, this then remained about constant until the task was finally completed at the end of Month 14, at a total effort cost of 128 engineer-months. The new product was launched onto the market 8 months later than originally planned. It then failed to capture a viable market share. The disaster was directly attributable to the assumed linear relationship between progress and effort.

This case history, which has a foundation in fact, is an illustration of **Brooks's 'Law'** (Brooks, 1975) which, when slightly modified to broaden its application, states that adding people to a late project makes it later. The statement should be treated with caution, but it is supported by a great deal of evidence.

What went wrong?

The first thing that went wrong was that the original estimate was flawed. It probably understated the effort required to complete the activity but, just possibly, the error was in the other direction. The second mistake was to ignore the early warning of trouble at the first progress review. Time is a non-renewable resource: once lost it is gone forever. Many problems do wither away from neglect, which is fortunate or no manager could manage. But this one did not.

The edict from project management, which followed the commendably honest problem report, was an abdication of responsibility. There is no evidence that they made any attempt to understand the problem. Nor, it seems, did they explore any other possible problem solutions: such as reconsidering the other activities on the critical path or reducing the size of the problem task. When corrective action was demanded the simple arithmetic employed required that six engineers be added to the current team. This was the kiss of death, because three consequences flow from such an action:

(1) The task organization and work partitioning arrangements must be changed to accommodate the new team members. Not only will implementing these changes take time and absorb effort, but they will also modify the roles of the original team. The original team will need time to learn these new roles.

(2) The new team members will need time to understand their new roles, and the way in which they fit into the overall task structure. The people best qualified to assist their learning are the members of the original team. Every engineer-hour that they spend educating their new colleagues is at least two engineer-hours lost to the sub-project.

(3) The volume of necessary communication and interactions between members of the team will increase from a level appropriate to four engineers in the original structure to a level appropriate to ten engineers in the new structure. The volume multiplier is a nonlinear function of the number of engineers. It might be as high as (about) 6 if the new task structure is unfavourable!

So, adding more people to increase the rate of progress also increases the amount of work to be done. Conceivably, the additional effort will not compensate for the additional work, and the rate of progress will diminish rather than increase. Brooks's Law strikes again!

The reader is counselled that the comedy of errors outlined in this little story is not just a fanciful tale. It actually happened, although details have been blurred to protect the guilty. Worse, it continues to happen. And it does so because of the deceptive simplicity of statements like:

• 'It is estimated that the effort required to complete this task is 24 engineer-months.'

The estimate may or may not be accurate. What is certain is that it is dangerous illusion as stated, because it is incomplete. It starts to make sense when modified to:

● 'It is estimated that the effort required to complete this task is 24 engineer-months spread over 6 months.'

It is then clear that the estimator envisages an average of four engineers working on the task for the 6 months. Changing the number of engineers assigned to it also changes the nature and the size of the task. There is, therefore, no reason to suppose that two engineers will do it in 12 months or twenty-four in 1 month. Two engineers might do it in 9 months. If 24 engineers are assigned to it, then it will probably never finish.

6.5.2　Curves to salvation?

The principal message to emerge from the cautionary tale describing how to ruin a perfectly good project is that:

● The effort required to complete a defined task is a function both of the nature of the task and of the number of people assigned to it.

This observation is the basis of an approach to task estimating which recognizes that people and time are not usually interchangeable. The PERT network of Figure 6.13 illustrates typical task levels and types. It shows the estimated (most likely) time for each of the tasks (activities) comprising that network. The aim now is to introduce a general technique for deriving such times.

The nature of tasks

The tasks in the network are described in Table 6.3. They can be classified into three categories:

(1) **Indivisible**　These are tasks with completion times which are independent of the number of people assigned to them beyond a certain minimum, which might be zero.

(2) **Divisible**　A task in this category can be partitioned into a number of smaller sub-tasks which may then be assigned to different people. Within limits, therefore, the task completion time will decrease as the number of people assigned to it increases.

(3) **Partially divisible**　These tasks are separable into indivisible and divisible sub-tasks. Such tasks are the general case. They are estimated by the simple addition of the estimates for the indivisible and divisible tasks which they contain.

Referring now to Figure 6.13 and Table 6.3, the most obvious examples of indivisible tasks are the delivery delays A08.15 and A10.16. The corresponding ordering tasks, A04.08 and A05.10, are also indivisible because these represent fairly mechanistic actions by the purchasing department whose response time (here) is determined by a fixed data processing schedule.

　　The various design tasks are divisible, because they can all be partitioned on some rational basis. For example, A01.02 is concerned with translating a purely functional specification (the product requirements definition) into an outline product design employing three different technologies. This task, therefore, divides quite naturally into software, electronic, mechanical and coordinating sub-tasks. Similarly, A04.07 defines several electronic circuit modules which are then to be designed, and accommodated on printed circuit boards, in A07.12. This latter task is highly divisible on the basis of the several defined modules. The situation with A06.11 is much the same but in terms of software modules.

Testing things, be they electronic, mechanical, software or whatever, tends to be a serial process and this introduces an indivisible element into most of the remaining tasks which then fall into the partially divisible category.

It is only necessary to consider estimating indivisible and divisible tasks, since the general case of a partially divisible task is handled by summation of its indivisible and divisible parts.

Estimating indivisible tasks

In many cases estimating indivisible tasks is straightforward, because the time-to-complete is set by some reasonably well-defined, non-effort dependent, serial process. This might be a delivery delay, the limited throughput of a machine, restricted access to some necessary facility, or other constraints of a like nature. In other cases, the task completion time is virtually independent of the number of people assigned to it beyond a certain (and normally fairly obvious) minimum. Any and every sort of testing seems to exhibit this characteristic: it is essentially a sequential process with little scope for parallel action. But it is susceptible to overtime and/or shift working in an emergency. There is no magic formula for estimating indivisible tasks, but a combination of experience and step-by-step analysis generally yields acceptable results.

Estimating divisible tasks: The f factor method

Achieving good estimates for the divisible tasks is the most important *and* the most difficult part of the whole job. It is important because only such tasks offer opportunities for interchanging time and people, which is one way of adjusting project completion time. It is difficult because it contains the twin problems of estimating the individual sub-tasks and of assessing the relationship between time and people. Again, there is no magic available for estimating the sub-tasks: a combination of experience, careful analysis and a degree of pessimism are essential elements of the recommended approach.

Forecasting the relationship between the completion time of a divisible task and the number of people assigned to it is a demanding, and not entirely resolved, problem. The approach to it that is now described has served the author well over a number of years. However, as with some other aspects of project management, its assumptions can be challenged and its results are supported by experience rather than by unassailable theory or extensive empirical research.

The first requirement is to make a **sparse estimate** of the divisible task. A sparse estimate is one which assigns the absolute minimum number of full-time people to the task, by considering only the different skills that its completion requires. It is not important, at this stage, if the completion time estimated under these circumstances is unacceptably large. The aim is to achieve an estimate which measures, as closely as possible, the **intrinsic work content** of the task. This should recognize the whole context of the task, including internally and externally imposed constraints, and the skill level and experience of the personnel likely to be involved. It is a 'minimum people' estimate, which reduces the effort dispersed in learning-time and in person-to-person communication to its inescapable minimum.

By way of illustration, consider the task A01.02 (Figure 6.13 and Table 6.3) that was previously cited. This requires a minimum of three, or possibly four, different people because it embraces three different technological sub-tasks and a coordination task. Task A04.07 might require at least two different people, one for the electronic design and one for the printed circuit board design. But a sparse estimate for task A06.11 could well involve just one person, unless there is some special application-related skill implicit in the specification of the software modules.

The steps involved in achieving a sparse estimate for a particular task are:

(1) Partitioning it into several divisible sub-tasks on some rational basis, such as different technologies and/or modules with different functions. Ideally, the sub-tasks should be the same size (in effort terms) and totally independent. The greater the independence the less time lost on person-to-person communication.

(2) Obtaining credible, experience-based, time and people estimates for each sub-task treated as a stand-alone, fully understood, independent item. Ideally, for reasons already explained, a sub-task estimate should relate to the time required for *one* (qualified) person to complete the task. 'Part-timers' (people sharing their time with other commitments) should not be assigned to the task, if this can be avoided. Their efficiency is limited by the need to re-climb learning curves each time they switch from one task to another.

A limited amount of iteration around these first two steps may be necessary.

(3) Summing the individual sub-task estimates to yield an effort subtotal and a **sparse people total**, called Ps here.

(4) Adding, to the effort subtotal, allowances for effort 'lost' in necessary learning and interperson communication. This yields an effort total and, hence, a **sparse time total**, called Ts here. The magnitude of the allowances will depend on the people total, the complexity of the task and its sub-tasks, and on the degree of coupling between the sub-tasks.

Nothing in what follows does anything to improve the accuracy of the sparse estimate encapsulated in the Ps and Ts numbers. It should be prepared with some care by experienced estimators.

Then, for any combination of people numbers (P) and completion time (T):

$$PT = PsTs + F(P) \qquad\qquad (6.18)$$

where F(P) is some function of the number of people, P.

F(P) represents the incremental effort required to complete the task when P is not equal to Ps. Two factors contribute to F(P):

- The learning effort arising from the need for people to understand the task and sub-tasks.
- The need for communication between the people.

These factors are already accounted for, at the Ps level, in the sparse estimate, so F(P) must be zero when P is equal to Ps, negative when P is less than Ps and positive when P is greater than Ps.

The magnitude of the effort increment due to learning depends on the nature of the task and sub-tasks (unfamiliarity, complexity, and so on) and on the number of people. Each person involved will spend some time in learning. So, this increment is assumed to be proportional to the number of people, P.

The magnitude of the effort increment due to the need for communication between the people depends on the degree of coupling between the sub-tasks and on the number of people. If the sub-tasks are totally independent the communication increment will be zero. This ideal is rarely achieved because the separate targets at which the sub-tasks are directed are carved out of the same whole task objective. Suppose that the names of the P people assigned to the task are used to label the P rows and P columns of a matrix of P^2 boxes. Each box in the matrix represents a person-to-person communication opportunity. If a communication from a row to a column is regarded as a different transaction to that from a column to a row then there are $P(P - 1)$ such opportunities between different people. If people are allowed to communicate with themselves (a reasonable concession which allows thinking to happen) then the number of communication opportunities rises to P^2. Each person involved will spend some time communicating. This increment is assumed, therefore, to be proportional to P^2.

These arguments allow Equation 6.18 to be rewritten as:

$$PT = PsTs + (LP + CP^2) \qquad (6.19)$$

where F(P) has been replaced by the expression in the parentheses, and L and C are constants. The constant L is some measure of the need for learning and C is an indicator of the degree of coupling between the sub-tasks. This equation is now recast in the form:

$$T = (PsTs)/P + (L + CP) \qquad (6.20)$$

If L and C were both zero, the equation expresses the simplistic (and wrong) view that task time-to-complete varies inversely with the number of people assigned to the task. (In other words, that the effort required to complete a task is a constant.) When L and C are not zero, the equation shows that the time derived from the simplistic view is increased by an amount (positive, zero or negative) which varies linearly with P.

Now, bearing Equation 6.20 in mind, suppose that:

if   P = 2Ps
then T = Ts/2 + fTs/2

where f is a numerical factor greater than zero. In other words, suppose that when P = 2Ps the value of T is (1 + f) times larger than that suggested by the simplistic view (which is Ts/2).

In this case:

$$L + 2CPs = fTs/2 \qquad (6.21)$$

and, as previously argued:

$$L + CPs = 0 \qquad (6.22)$$

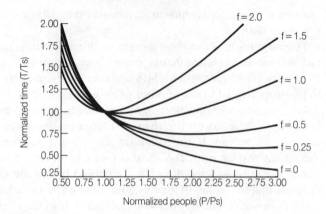

Figure 6.30   **Task completion time versus number of assigned people.**

The human effort needed to complete a project task is PT, where P = number of people assigned to the task and T = task completion time. It is commonly assumed that, for a given task, PT is constant or (equivalently) that T is inversely proportional to P. This assumption is wrong, because the effort required to complete a given task depends on the nature of the task and, importantly, on the number of people assigned to it. This observation is developed, in the text, into Equation 6.23:

$$T/Ts = 1/(P/Ps) + f/2(P/Ps - 1)$$

where Ts, Ps and f are constants depending on the nature of the task. It is plotted here for various values of f. The f = 0 curve is the (usually) flawed PT = PsTs assumption. The other curves demonstrate that T initially decreases as P increase from a low value, but this trend reverses as P is further increased. The reversal becomes more severe as the value of f increases.

Solving the simultaneous Equations 6.21 and 6.22 yields:

$$C = (f/2)(Ts/Ps) \text{ and}$$
$$L = -(f/2)Ts$$

Equation 6.20 then becomes:

$$T/Ts = 1/(P/Ps) + f/2(P/Ps - 1) \tag{6.23}$$

where (T/Ts) is the time-to-complete the task normalized with respect to Ts, and (P/Ps) is the number of people assigned to it normalized with respect to Ps.

(It will be appreciated that this development of the form of the F(P) function makes some breath-taking simplifications. Other formulations of F(P) are possible. The one employed here has the merit of stark simplicity and it appears to be a reasonable approximation of reality.)

The relationship between (T/Ts) and (P/Ps) expressed in Equation 6.23 is shown, for various values of the factor f, in Figure 6.30. The curve for f = 0, which describes the discredited 'constant effort' theory, is included for comparison purposes only.

Whatever the imperfections of the theory behind Equation 6.23, the form of the curves for f greater than zero does align with practical experience. In particular, they show that there is a point beyond which increasing the number of people assigned to a project increases rather than decreases its completion time. Thus, when time is the essence, there is an optimum value of (P/Ps) which gives a minimum value (T/Ts) for any value of f.

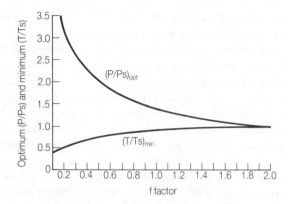

Figure 6.31   **Staffing for minimum task completion time.**
The graphs in Figure 6.30, which illustrate Equation 6.23, show that there is a point beyond which increasing the number of people (P) assigned to a task increases rather than decreases its completion time (T). So, for a given task, there is an optimum value of P which gives a minimum value T. These task parameters are functions of the f factor (see Equations 6.24 and 6.25), which is task dependent. This figure shows how corresponding values of $(P/Ps)_{opt}$ and $(T/Ts)_{min}$ vary as f increases (that is, as the task becomes less divisible). These curves demonstrate that increasing P to reduce T is an increasingly poor strategy as the value of f increases.

It is not difficult to show that (T/Ts) is a minimum when:

$$(P/Ps)_{opt} = +(2/f)^{1/2} \tag{6.24}$$

and, from this, that:

$$(T/Ts)_{min} = +2(f/2)^{1/2} - f/2 \tag{6.25}$$

Corresponding values for $(P/Ps)_{opt}$ and $(T/Ts)_{min}$ as functions of the f factor are plotted in Figure 6.31. These curves demonstrate that increasing the number of people assigned to a task in order to reduce its completion time is an increasingly poor strategy as the value of the f factor increases.

The value of Equations 6.23, 6.24 and 6.25 as estimating tools turns on the extent to which they represent reality, and the ability to choose appropriate values of factor f. The validity of the equations is not susceptible to rigorous proof, there are too many imponderables. There is, however, a great deal of widely distributed (and distressing) evidence which confirms their general 'shape'. Choosing reasonable values for factor f, which reflect subjective views on task complexity and the degree of sub-task coupling, is a skill that can be acquired with practice. The question to be answered is:

• If P is (2Ps), by what percentage will T be greater than (Ts/2)?

For example, consider again the tasks A01.02 and A06.11 (Figure 6.13 and Table 6.3).
The first of these divides into four tightly-coupled sub-tasks, which have little scope for independent progress. An f factor of one hundred per cent (1.0) is appropriate. Increasing the number of people assigned to this task beyond Ps by, say, fifty per cent reduces T by only about eight per cent (see Figure 6.30). This represents poor value for money.
On the other hand, task A06.11 can be partitioned into as many sub-tasks as there

are distinct software modules. Provided that these have been specified properly (in A03.06), and that there is no sharing of a limited resource, these sub-tasks are virtually independent. An f factor of ten per cent (0.1) is appropriate. Equation 6.24 suggests an optimum value for (P/Ps) of about 4.5 under these circumstances. But fractional people are not efficient. Setting (P/Ps) = 4 in Equation 6.23 yields a value of 0.4 for (T/Ts): a sixty per cent reduction for a four hundred per cent increase in the number of assigned people. This might be worthwhile. The best (f = 0) that could be obtained with this increase in effort is a seventy-five per cent reduction.

It is instructive to apply, albeit retrospectively, Equations 6.23, 6.24 and 6.25 to the sample disaster outlined in Section 6.5.1. The early progress reviews suggested that a good estimate for the whole task was four engineers for 12 months. This was in sharp contrast to the original estimate of four engineers for 6 months. The forecast time slip of 6 months proved unacceptable. The 'straight line' sums then indicated that six more engineers were required to recover the time slip. These were drafted into the task team, which eventually completed its work after a total of 14 months.

The task was moderately complex with substantial coupling between the sub-tasks. An f factor of 1.0 is deemed appropriate. Equation 6.23 can be rewritten as:

$$T = Ts[Ps/P + f/2(P/Ps - 1)] \tag{6.23a}$$

Then, setting Ts = 12 months and Ps = 4 engineers (as the sparse estimate), the predicted completion time when ten engineers (P = 10) are assigned to the task is:

$$T_{10} = 12[0.4 + 0.5(2.5 - 1)] = 13.8 \text{ months}$$

which compares favourably with the actual outcome. Equations 6.24 and 6.25 suggest that the optimum staffing level and minimum completion time are:

$$P_{opt} = 4 \times 2^{1/2} = 5 \text{ engineers (rounding down) and}$$
$$T_{min} = 12(2 \times 0.5^{1/2} - 0.5) = 11 \text{ months (rounding up)}$$

These results (which could be extracted from Figure 6.31) indicate that the task completion time is not very sensitive to increased staffing. More importantly, they confirm that piling effort onto the task was a waste of money which could have been better spent on a more intelligent approach to reducing the duration of the project critical path.

The cost of completing a task is often dominated by the people cost. This cost is proportional to the required effort-to-complete the task, that is, to the product of people numbers and time. Equation 6.26 is the expression for the normalized effort derived from Equation 6.23.

$$(PT)/(PsTs) = 1 + f/2(P/Ps)(P/Ps - 1) \tag{6.26}$$

This equation is plotted in Figure 6.32.

Note that the required effort-to-complete increase rapidly for values of P greater than Ps, especially at high factor f values. This is due to the presence of P^2 in the equation.

Large software projects

The 'f factor' expression of the relationship between the completion time of a divisible task and the number of people assigned to it seems to work well enough for hardware

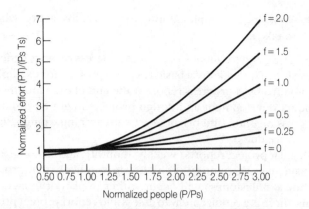

Figure 6.32   **Task completion effort versus number of assigned people.**

The human effort needed to complete a project task is PT, where P = number of people assigned to the task and T = task completion time. The cost of completing a task is often dominated by the people cost, which is (generally) directly proportional to PT. Derived from Equation 6.23, Equation 6.26:

$$(PT)/(P_sT_s) = 1 + f/2(P/P_s)(P/P_s - 1)$$

shows how PT varies with P. It is plotted here for different values of the f factor. Note that PT, and hence task completion cost, increases rapidly for values of P/Ps greater than 1. The effect becomes more marked as f increases (that is, as the task becomes less divisible).

tasks and small software tasks. This writer has no experience of applying it to large software projects, which are notorious for overrunning their time and cost budgets, often by very substantial factors. There is a body of active research aimed at creating and proving techniques for estimating completion effort and time-scales for such software projects. Macro and Buxton (1987) provide an interesting survey of this work in Chapter 5 of their treatise on software engineering. They conclude that the results to date do more for exposing the problem than actually solving it. They favour an effort–time relationship of the form:

$$(\text{Effort})(\text{Time})^z = \text{constant}$$

with values of z between 2 and 4 and a tightly restricted range of applicability. Outside this (not very useful) range, the expression can yield results which strain credulity, even for large software projects. For example, suppose that z = 4. Then a project first estimated to need 20 people-years to complete in 2 years is predicted to need 320 people to complete it in 1 year, but only 4 people-years to complete it in 3 years.

6.6   Project control

Project control is a management activity aimed at ensuring that the conduct of a project conforms (so far as is possible and sensible) to its plan. There are three basic steps:

- Measurement of the magnitude and direction of deviations from plan.
- Evaluation of the deviations to assess if corrective action is required.

- Choosing and implementing the corrective action when it is deemed necessary to take it.

The nature and frequency of project progress reviews generally depends on the type of project. The leader of a basic research project, for example, might only be required to submit a brief progress report at the end of each month. But commercially critical product development and design projects might be discussed at a weekly projects progress meeting, and be subject to a searching examination when major milestone events are due.

Regular project reports (weekly, monthly, and so on) are required to align with the management accounting cycle. But it is unlikely that project events (the auditable technical milestones) will occur, either in plan or in fact, at these regular intervals. Thus, there is a requirement to assess and report project progress while the work is in transit between events. Figure 6.18 shows the typical situation where project events do not occur at regular intervals. The figure also illustrates another facet of project progress reporting. The progress status of the project at any particular time is some amalgam of the progress status of the activities planned to be in progress at that time. But not all of these activities are critical, so the progress report must also recognize the structure of the project. A recommended technique for assessing and reporting project progress is now described. It is called **delta analysis**.

6.6.1 Delta analysis for deviations

A project plan defines an intended relationship between the three linked project parameters of technical progress, time and cost. Time and cost are easy to measure but technical progress is relatively difficult, especially between milestones. Delta analysis circumvents this problem by measuring technical progress in terms of time and cost.

In the upper half of Figure 6.33, project progress is measured as a percentage of target achievement. The plots show the planned progress of a hypothetical project against elapsed time and the actual progress achieved at a project review time. Actual progress does not coincide with planned progress at that time so a progress deviation exists. In this case, actual progress is less than planned progress.

In delta analysis, the shape of the progress curves and the absolute units of technical progress are irrelevant: the only thing that matters is measuring the deviation between planned and actual progress.

Four progress-related quantities, which are all measured from zero at project start, are positioned on the graph:

(1) **Plan time**   (PT)   The total planned elapsed time to achieve the project objective.
(2) **Plan cost**   (PC)   The total planned cost to achieve the project objective.
(3) **Actual time** (AT)   The actual elapsed time at the progress review.
(4) **Actual cost** (AC)   The actual project cost at the time of the review (including committed costs).

The time and cost deviations

At the time of each progress review, the project leader is required to answer two questions:

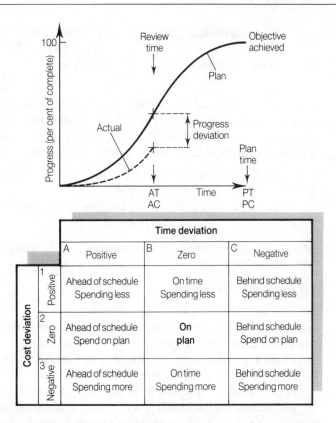

Figure 6.33   **Project progress, time and cost: delta analysis.**

A project plan is an intended relationship between project progress, time and cost. Measuring progress is always difficult, especially between project 'milestones'. Delta analysis avoids the problem by measuring progress in terms of time and cost. The upper half of the figure shows a typical situation, and defines the project parameters of plan time (PT), plan cost (PC), actual time (AT) and actual cost (AC). These are combined with forecast time-to-complete (FT) and forecast cost-to-complete (FC) (measured from AT and AC, respectively) to yield a time deviation (DT) and a cost deviation (DC), where:

$$DT = PT - (AT + FT) \text{ and } DC = PC - (AC + FC)$$

Both DT and DC can be either positive, zero or negative. So a project can be in any one of *nine* different progress situations at any particular time. These are shown in the three-by-three matrix in the lower half of the figure. The magnitude of the deviations is another factor to be considered. The delta technique reduces complex progress report situations to just two (signed) numbers. It is applicable to every sort of project.

- How much more time, *from now*, is needed to complete the project? The answer is the **forecast time** (FT).

- How much more cost, *from now*, is needed to complete the project? The answer is the **forecast cost** (FC).

Time and cost deviations, which are measures of project progress at the review time, can then be calculated in accordance with Equations 6.27 and 6.28:

Time deviation (DT): $DT = PT - (AT + FT)$ **(6.27)**

$\qquad\qquad = \{[PT - (AT + FT)]/PT\} \times 100\%$ **(6.27a)**

Cost deviation (DC): $DC = PC - (AC + FC)$ **(6.28)**

$\qquad\qquad = \{[PC - (AC + FC)]/PC\} \times 100\%$ **(6.28a)**

Note that both DT and DC can be either positive, zero or negative. Note, too, that the quantities have been defined such that a negative deviation indicates trouble: a time slip or cost overspend. As an illustration, the project involved in the sample disaster discussed in Section 6.5.1 was reviewed after 2 months yielding:

$$DT = 6 - (2 + 10)\ \ = -6\ \text{months}$$
$$= -100\%$$
$$DC = 24 - (8 + 40) = -24\ \text{engineer-months}$$
$$= -100\%$$

where it is assumed that project costs track exactly with project effort (which actually understates the reality).

The deviation matrix

Because both DT and DC can be either positive, zero or negative a project can be in any one of *nine* different progress situations at a particular time. The magnitude of the deviations adds an extra dimension to these situations, which are summarized in the matrix shown in the lower half of Figure 6.33. This diagram illustrates one reason why project management can be such a complex matter.

There is a sad tendency for honest project progress reports to favour situations in column C ('behind schedule') and row 3 ('spending more'). Perhaps the double negative of cell C3 is the most usual (though certainly not the most popular) choice.

Advantages and disadvantages

Delta analysis is a powerful (though strangely neglected) technique for project progress reporting. It can be applied to any type of project at any level. For example, a delta progress report for the project illustrated in Figure 6.18 would be constructed from delta reports for the individual activities or tasks. The technique is well suited to the rapid scanning of a large number of projects, because it encapsulates intricate situations in just two figures. It lends itself to computer-aided project monitoring and encourages **management by exception**. On the other hand, it does depend on 'technical honesty': the willingness of task and project leaders to tell their masters what they should hear, rather than what they would prefer to hear. But this is true of any reporting situation. Perhaps the most serious criticism of the technique is that it imposes an additional estimating burden on task and project leaders. This is a small price to pay for the beauty, simplicity and utility of this particular management tool.

6.6.2 Corrective action

When a progress deviation is detected the question of what, if anything, to do about it arises. Evaluation of the deviation indicates a 'do nothing' response in many cases, as is now illustrated.

Action or no action?

As a general rule, projects showing a combination of positive and zero delta deviations (cells A1, A2, B1 and B2 in Figure 6.33) should be left alone, because progress is either ahead of or on plan by both measures. Exceptionally, this rule might be broken by transferring resources (people or money) to rescue another project or task which is in trouble. Action of this nature should always be approached with caution, especially if the transfer of people is involved. Removing people from a project can only disturb it in some way, perhaps even to the extent that it then needs restructuring. Adding people to a project does not always correct a progress problem. There is a finite chance, therefore, of turning one problem into two problems with this approach to problem solving.

Projects which are repeatedly reported as 'on plan' (cell B2 in Figure 6.33) should be regarded with suspicion. A pattern of this sort usually indicates either a casual approach to progress monitoring by an immature project leader, and/or a faith in providence which is rarely justified by subsequent events.

Projects showing at least one negative delta deviation (those on column C and row 3 in Figure 6.33) are normally candidates for management attention and, possibly, corrective action as well. However, each case must be treated on its merits. It does not always matter, for example, if projects are behind their time plan. A case in point, at the task level, is shown in Figure 6.18. Here it is of no consequence if activities on the mechanical engineering sub-project are somewhat delayed because of the large amount of free float available. Similarly, projects which are ahead of, or on, time plan while being ahead of cost plan (cells A3 and B3 in Figure 6.33) may merely be reflecting the happy result of earlier corrective action. Also, as a general rule, small deviations are best noted rather than acted on. Experienced gardeners know that too frequent excavation to inspect progress hinders rather than encourages root development. The same is true of high-level intervention in projects.

Types of action

When it has been decided that some corrective action must be taken, the first step is to establish the reason for the progress problem. There is a vast range of possibilities, including those now listed:

(1) Faulty initial estimate.
(2) Flawed project structure, such as inadequate or inappropriate task partitioning, too few people or too many people.
(3) Poor project organization, such as inappropriate delegation of responsibility (too much or too little) or inadequate role definition.
(4) People problems, such as unsuitable technical background, temperamental incompatibilities, 'carrying passengers', managerial or technical incompetence, and so on.
(5) Lack of project facilities, such as funding, test equipment, computer-aids and computer time.
(6) Lack of support services, such as project administration, technician and secretarial.
(7) Supplier difficulties, such as unanticipated delays in component deliveries or the delivery of faulty items.

(8) Customer problems, such as inadequate initial project specification or frequent changes to specification while the project is in progress.

With this rich field of potential hazards, and no mutual exclusivity between the major items, it is only feasible to offer general guidance to problem solving.

The first principle is that the number of people assigned to the project should only be increased as a last resort; and then only if there is total certainty that it will accelerate progress. The preferred approach aims to increase the productivity of the existing project team by removing, where possible, the inhibiting factors in the foregoing list. Failing success with this ploy, the context of the project should be investigated. Just as an activity (or task) is part of a project so a project is, usually, part of a larger programme. It may be that the predicted extended time-scale of the project in question can be accommodated by accelerating some other project or projects.

If all else fails and the planned project completion time cannot be relaxed, there is only one option left. This is to reduce the project objective, quite deliberately, to a level which can be achieved within the available time and effort equation. This is no more than making the best of a bad job. Because, if the planned time-scale is still demanded in impossible circumstances then the job will be trimmed anyway, by its staff: typically by the omission of 'minor' requirements and by inadequate testing. If the job *is* going to be trimmed it is better to control the process, so that the knock-on effects can be anticipated and minimized.

6.7   Concluding summary

Planning is not a fun occupation for most people. Many will seek every reason, from the merely specious to the plain wrong, to avoid doing it. This is unwise. Planning is one of the few low-risk, high-return investments available to a business and it should not be neglected. It is also a necessary prerequisite to control. Attempting to control the conduct of anything without knowing what is supposed to happen is a form of 'management by surprise' which often leads to a well-deserved disaster.

This chapter has considered three tactical project planning and control techniques, principally in the context of technical innovation work. Purely from the planning point-of-view there is, perhaps, a preferred technique for each type of technical innovation project. Bar charts are quite adequate for most basic research projects and the research planning diagram approach suits many, but not all, applied research projects. PERT is recommended for larger, well-defined projects with significant coupling between their activities. It is entirely appropriate for product development and design projects and many applied research projects also. But the various techniques should not be regarded as distinct stand-alone entities, blends are frequently useful. Project control is a matter of measuring progress deviations from plan, assessing these deviations, and then, perhaps, taking corrective action. The control sequence is the same irrespective of the type of project and planning technique employed. Delta analysis is a powerful and universally applicable technique for measuring progress deviations.

REFERENCES

Battersby A. (1978). *Network Analysis for Planning and Scheduling Studies in Management* 3rd edn. London: Macmillan

British Standards Institution (1984). *Use of Network Techniques In Project Management. Parts 1 to 4.* (BS 6046) London: BSI

Brooks F. P. (1975). *The Mythical Man-Month*. Reading, MA: Addison-Wesley

Davies D. G. S. (1970). Research Planning Diagrams. *R&D Management*, **1**(1), 22–9

Davies D. G. S. (1982). R&D Tactics: Applications of RPD decision analysis. *R&D Management*, **12**(2), 73–80

Macro A. and Buxton J. (1987). *The Craft of Software Engineering*. Wokingham: Addison-Wesley

Malcolm D. G., Roseboom J. H., Clark C. E. and Fazar W. (1959). Application of a technique for research and development program evaluation. *Operations Research*, **7**(5), 646–70

Weist J. D. and Levy F. K. (1977). *A Management Guide to PERT/CPM* 2nd edn. Englewood Cliffs, NJ: Prentice-Hall

Woodgate H. S. (1977) *Planning by Network* 3rd edn. London: Business Books

SUGGESTED FURTHER READING

Meredith and Mantel (1989) is a specialist text which looks well beyond the mechanistic aspects of project planning and control. Most books on operations management include material on project planning. Waters (1991) and Wild (1989) are no exception, and each considers some extensions not covered in this chapter. So, too, does the more general text offered by Chapman *et al.* (1987).

Chapman C. B., Cooper D. F. and Page M. A. (1987). *Management for Engineers*. Chichester: John Wiley (Chapter 29)

Meredith J. and Mantel S. J. (1989). *Project Management – A Managerial Approach* 2nd edn. New York: John Wiley

Waters C. D. J. (1991). *An Introduction to Operations Management*. Wokingham: Addison-Wesley (Chapter 9)

Wild R. (1989). *Production and Operations Management* 4th edn. London: Cassell Educational (Chapter 13)

QUESTIONS

6.1 Explain the meaning of the terms:

- project
- project plan
- project progress
- project progress deviation
- project control

6.2 Identify and explain four distinct business benefits obtained from project planning.

6.3 (a) Describe the bar chart technique of representing a project plan, and explain two different ways of showing project progress deviations from plan.

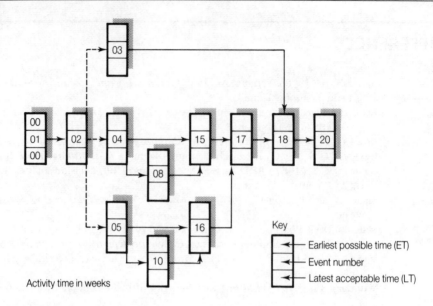

Activity time in weeks

Key

Earliest possible time (ET)
Event number
Latest acceptable time (LT)

Figure 6.34   **A PERT network.**

(b) Show how a resource table relating project cost, elapsed time and progress can be associated with the bar chart.

(c) What are the advantages and disadvantages of bar charts?

6.4   Table 6.1 is the detailed table comprising the resource plan and control report which supports the bar chart in Figure 6.3. The following data is reported at the end of Month 04:

- actual scientist headcount = 4.00
- actual drawing office headcount = 0.00
- actual cumulative other cost = £5.200K.

(a) Complete the (end of) Month 04 control report by calculating:

- the actual cumulative headcount
- the effort variance
- the actual cumulative effort cost
- the actual cumulative total cost
- the total cost variance.

(b) What does this report reveal about the technical status of the project at the end of Month 04?

6.5   Conventional bar charts do not show:

- precedence relationships between activities
- choice of one of a pair of alternative activities
- activity looping.

Illustrate each of these three situations in a flow diagram using RPD notation.

6.6   The following data applies to Figure 6.6:

Activity times in minutes:

snooze for one hour	$t_1 = 60$
get up and have breakfast	$t_2 = 45$
test lawn-mower	$t_3 = 15$
prepare sandwiches for lunch	$t_4 = 30$
cut lawns	$t_5 = 60$

Probability:

of any day falling at the weekend	$P_1 = 0.286$
of rain at any time	$P_2 = 0.200$
of the lawn-mower starting	$P_3 = 0.400$

(a) What is the minimum elapsed time between the wake-up alarm and going fishing? What is the probability of going fishing at this time after the wake-up alarm on *any* day?

(b) Assuming that it is a weekend, and

Activity	T_O	T_M	T_P
01.02	3.0	4.2	4.8
03.18	14.5	16.0	18.1
04.08	1.8	2.5	3.2
04.15	6.8	7.8	10.0
05.10	1.5	1.8	2.1
05.16	7.9	9.2	10.5
08.15	9.8	11.0	11.6
10.16	1.2	1.5	1.8
15.17	1.6	3.4	4.0
16.17	0.8	1.0	1.2
17.18	0.6	0.8	1.0
18.20	4.4	6.0	6.4

Table 6.9 'Three-times' activity estimates (weeks).

measuring time in minutes from the wake-up alarm, show that the probability of finishing breakfast at:

time = 105 is   0.800
time = 165 or less is   0.960
time = 225 or less is   0.992

(c) Hence, calculate the sequence of the first *six* possible times for going fishing and their associated probabilities.

6.7 In the context of the PERT project planning and control technique, explain the meaning of the following terms:

- event
- activity
- dummy
- path

and state the precedence rule which governs PERT networks.

6.8 Describe, in summary form, the process of synthesizing (designing) a project plan in PERT format. The description should cover the basic design steps, outline design, detail design, network labelling, activity times and network dictionaries.

Note: Questions 6.9 to 6.15, which follow, are concerned with analysis of the PERT network in Figure 6.34. The question sequence follows the normal course of such an analysis. For this reason, Questions 6.9 and 6.10 are not in chapter order.

6.9 In PERT, the technique of three-times (activity) estimating is most commonly used to obtain improved single-time estimates for individual activities in conditions of substantial estimating uncertainty.
(a) Describe this particular application of the technique.
(b) State two of its other applications.

6.10 Use the technique of three-times estimating to obtain expected time (T_E) estimates for the individual activities in the PERT network of Figure 6.34. The estimated optimistic time (T_O), most likely time (T_M), and pessimistic time (T_P) for the (real) activities in the network are shown in Table 6.9.

6.11 (a) Explain, with the aid of a diagram, the meaning of the PERT terms:

- critical path
- earliest possible time for an event
- latest acceptable time for an event
- event slack

(b) Why are these parameters useful in PERT network analysis?

6.12 Use the expected activity times (T_Es) derived in answering Question 6.10 (and shown in Table 6.11, p. 650) to determine the expected values of the following parameters of the PERT network of Figure 6.34.

- the duration of all paths between event 01 and event 20
- the duration of the critical path
- the earliest possible time for every event
- the latest acceptable time for every event
- the slack for every event.

6.13   (a) Explain, with the aid of a diagram, the meaning of the PERT terms:

- total float
- free float early
- free float late
- independent float

(b) Why are these parameters useful in PERT network analysis?

6.14   (a) Using the data derived in answering Question 6.12 (and shown in Table 6.13, p. 650), determine the:

- total float
- free float early
- free float late
- independent float

for activities not on the critical path in the PERT network of Figure 6.34.
(b) What are the corresponding float values for the activities on the critical path? Explain why these latter values are so easy to calculate.

6.15   (a) Using the data derived in answering Question 6.10 (which is shown in Tables 6.11 and 6.12, p. 650) and making the 'usual' assumptions, calculate the standard variation of the critical path *and* of next most critical path in the PERT network of Figure 6.34. Hence, estimate the probability that:

(i)   the critical path will terminate at, or before, the expected time of the next most critical path, and
(ii) the next most critical path will terminate at, or before, the expected time of the critical path.

(b) What are the usual assumptions referenced above? Comment on their likely validity in this case.

6.16   In the context of task (activity) estimating, the 'constant effort' theory claims that task completion time is inversely proportional to the number of people assigned to completing the task. The theory is flawed. Why? (Note: this is an invitation to explain why 'Effort = Constant' is wrong, *not* to produce another theory.)

6.17   (a) Producing a 'sparse estimate' is the first step in the *f factor method* of assessing the relationship between assigned effort and likely completion time for a 'divisible task'. Explain, in this context, the meaning of the terms:

- divisible task
- sparse estimate

(b) Let the sparse (effort) estimate to complete a particular divisible task in time = Ts be PsTs, where Ps is the number of people assigned to the task. Assume that, for any combination of people numbers (P) and completion time (T):

$$PT = PsTs + F(P) \qquad (6.18)$$

where $F(P)$ is some function of P. It arises because of the learning effort needed for the people to understand the task and its sub-tasks, and the need for communication between the people. These factors are already accounted for in the sparse estimate, so $F(P)$ is zero when P = Ps.

Now show, by making reasonable assumptions, that Equation 6.18 can be developed into:

$$T/Ts = 1/(P/Ps) + f/2(P/Ps - 1) \qquad (6.23)$$

which relates the normalized task completion time (T/Ts) to the normalized number of people (P/Ps) assigned to it; and f is a positive factor which increases as task complexity and the degree of sub-task coupling increase.
(c) Show, too, that an appropriate value of f can be obtained from a correct answer to the question:

- By what proportion will T exceed Ts/2 when P = 2Ps?

6.18   The variation of task completion time (T) with team size (P) of tasks A, B and C are to be estimated using the f method. It turns out that the sparse estimates for these three different tasks are identical, being Ps = 4

Task or project		Plan Time (PT) Months	Plan Cost (PC) £K	30–08–91 Actual Time (AT) Months	30–08–91 Actual Cost (AC) £K	Forecast from now Time (FT) Months	Forecast from now Cost (FC) £K	Deviations Time (DT) Months	Deviations Cost (DC) £K	Deviations Time (DT % of PT)	Deviations Cost (DC % of PC)
A1	Times	6.0		4.0		1.5					
	Costs		60		36		15				
B2	Times	22.0		20.0		2.0					
	Costs		1,100		1,000		100				
C3	Times	18.0		3.0		18.0					
	Costs		450		90		540				

Table 6.10 **A delta project report.**

engineers for Ts = 6 months in each case. But task A is totally divisible, task C is divisible to only a very limited extent and task B is an intermediate case. It is decided that the appropriate f values are 0.0, 0.5 and 1.0 for tasks A, B and C respectively.

(a) Estimate the completion time for each task when the team assigned to it is two, four and eight engineers (yielding nine results in all). Calculate the difference between the estimated completion times for task C when the team size is four engineers and eight engineers respectively, and explain the result.

(b) Show that there is an optimum value of P which gives a minimum value T for any value of f greater than zero. What are the values of these parameters for task C?

6.19 (a) Describe how the delta technique enables the progress status of a task or project to be assessed at any time, and show how that status can be in any one of nine different situations.

(b) What are the advantages and disadvantages of delta progress reporting?

6.20 Table 6.10 is an incomplete delta projects progress report. It was prepared at the end of August 1991 from information supplied by the leaders of three projects. The projects are called A1, B2 and C3.

(a) Complete the report by calculating the delta deviations for the three projects.

(b) Discuss the completed projects report from the perspective of the technical manager in overall charge of the projects. This manager is new to the job and is not familiar with the projects.

About Costs and Costing

Truth is rarely pure, and never simple.

Oscar Wilde 1854–1900

7.1	Introduction	272
7.2	Why is cost important?	272
7.3	Cost and costing problems	277
7.4	Budgets: An overview	281
7.5	Cost categories	287
7.6	Cost behaviours	296
7.7	Project costs and costing	301
7.8	Product costs and costing	310
7.9	The profit equation revisited	318
7.10	Concluding summary	331

The overall objectives of this chapter are to present an overview of the whole topic of business costs and costing (in the first five sections), and a more focused analysis of aspects which relate particularly to technological innovation (in the remainder of the chapter). This is a long chapter which contains no advanced material. In view of this, it has been structured so that it can be reasonably approached in any one of three ways:

(a) As a continuous sequence of sections which, together, form a solid foundation for a deeper (and later) study of the vast subject of cost and costing.

(b) As a sequence of Sections 7.1 to 7.6 and, optionally, Section 7.9. This provides a broad overview of the topic pitched at business level.

(c) As a sequence of Sections 7.1, 7.2, 7.7, 7.8 and, optionally, Section 7.9. This provides a selective view of the topic focused on two critical engineering issues.

Clearly, approach (c) minimizes the material to be absorbed and it is a feasible (but limited) option. Some referring back to ideas first exposed in Sections 7.3 to 7.6 may be required. The glossary and table of contents will assist in this. Objectives by section follow:

7.1 To introduce the chapter and describe its structure.

7.2 To explain why costs are important and to demonstrate that cost and costing is a fundamental engineering topic.

7.3 To show why estimating and judgement play such large parts in the costing process.

7.4 To view a large company as a hierarchy of financial plans and projects, in order to set costs and costing in the framework of a whole business.

7.5 To introduce some cost-related concepts and terminology by classifying business costs into a set of categories. This (mostly) excludes classification according to any possible variation with activity level.

7.6 To examine different ways in which some costs do vary with activity levels, and to introduce the break-even concept.

7.7 To show how a technical project can be costed by treating it as a component of a technical department budget. (The principles apply to any sort of project.)

7.8 To examine product cost and costing by analogy with the project case, and to introduce the concept of standard costing.

7.9 To exercise the earlier material by considering its impact on the profit equation, and to introduce the notions of demand curves, marginal theory and contribution to fixed costs.

7.10 To identify its salient points and summarize its major messages.

7.1   Introduction

This chapter is about the concept of cost. A first reaction to this promise of delights to come might be that cost is a totally familiar and uncomplicated topic. It hardly deserves elevation to the status of a concept. Cost, surely, is a simple everyday experience. Indeed, it is such a simple matter that it can only be of interest to accountants, and other unfortunates, whose training has not equipped them to participate in the excitements of technology. This naive view of cost is shared by most unenlightened science and engineering students, too many of their teachers, and some so-called managers. But a million accountants cannot be wrong. They know that cost is like truth (rarely pure and never simple) but more important. In fact, cost is too important to be left entirely to the accountants. It is a fundamental *engineering* topic, and is treated as such in this chapter. Cost and costing is also a battleground where engineers and accountants often exercise their flawed perceptions of each others' jobs and difficulties. Hopefully, the chapter will bring some peace to that arena.

Section 7.2 examines the critical importance of business costs and shows why costs and costing is a fundamental engineering topic. The fact that estimates and judgements form such a large part of costing comes as a shock to many engineers. The following section describes the origin of these uncertainties by exploring major costing problems. This is followed by a section which presents an overview discussion of budgets and budgeting. Budgets are financial plans. An appreciation of their purpose and preparation is useful background for the rest of the chapter. The next two sections examine, in turn, different types of costs and the manner in which some costs vary with activity level. This partitioning is not entirely satisfactory, but it does help to break up quite a large body of material into digestible pieces.

The focus then switches to technological innovation as the discussion concentrates on two critical engineering cost topics. A section is devoted to each one. The first, at Section 7.7, concerns project cost and costing, which is approached by building a budget for a typical technical department. Attention then turns to product cost and costing, in a treatment which emphasizes standard costing.

The penultimate section is a re-examination of the profit equation in the light of the earlier material. Demand curves and marginal theory are introduced. These are exercised in worked examples which illuminate some important issues and introduce the contribution concept. The economies and diseconomies of scale are briefly reviewed. The chapter concludes with a brief summary of its main messages.

A book by Knott (1988) on cost and management accounting extends many of the ideas introduced in this chapter. Other, more specific, references are cited in the text. (Chapter 12 emphasizes financial accounting.)

7.2   Why is cost important?

Business life is dominated by just one deceptively simple equation:

$$\text{Profit} = \text{Revenue} - \text{Cost} \tag{7.1}$$

This is the **profit equation**. It expresses the relationship that profit is the excess of the revenue (income) obtained from selling the products of the business over the total cost incurred in creating and selling those products. To make sense, revenue and cost must be measured over the same period. This is never more than one year and it may be less. The profit equation was introduced in Chapter 1 and it is explored further in this chapter.

7.2.1 The profit objective

Businesses which do not make adequate profits cannot survive in the long run. Profit is required to maintain and renew the resources used by the business in creating and selling its products. It provides the reward (in the form of dividends and capital growth) to the owners of the business for their investment in it. It is the key to obtaining injections of investment capital from outside the business by paying interest charges on loans. Adequate profits, therefore, are a prerequisite for business survival; better than adequate profits promise prosperity.

Most industries are dominated by public limited companies, in which ownership is usually separated from control. In effect, the business owners (investing institutions and members of the public) elect paid managers to run the business for them. These managers are encouraged to identify their own survival and prosperity with that of the business. Not surprisingly, therefore, the managers have a consuming interest in profit. This interest is often reinforced by the inclusion of a profit-related element in their remuneration package. For such businesses, which are at the focus of this book, it can be assumed that longer-term profit maximization is an important objective. (This is not always true of smaller private businesses, where owner–managers may choose a comfortable life style rather than a comfortable profit and loss account.) Equation 7.1 shows how profit can be maximized. The simple recipe merely blends the highest possible revenue with the least possible cost (of obtaining the revenue). So:

- Cost is important because profit is critical, and cost is an essential ingredient of the profit equation.

Management attention is (or should be) always aimed at minimizing cost, although the aim can be more positively phrased as 'seeking the best return for money spent'. (A somewhat dubious exception to this general rule arises when a business is holding a **cost-plus contract**. It is then in the happy position of receiving a profit which is a percentage of the contract costs, irrespective of the level of these costs and for how long they continue. These situations would test the business rectitude of a saint. Sadly, not all business managers qualify in this respect.)

7.2.2 A cost structure

So far, the term 'cost' has been used as a portmanteau word which encapsulates the summation of a multitude of distinct cost items. There are many different ways in which these items can be separated and classified. Several of these emerge as the discussion progresses. But a first separation of cost into constituent parts is shown in Figure 7.1. This partitioning and terminology reflects 'cost' as it appears in the profit and loss equation (Equation 7.1). It also aligns with the concept of a business as a system of cooperating **functions** which is developed in Chapter 1. The cost structure

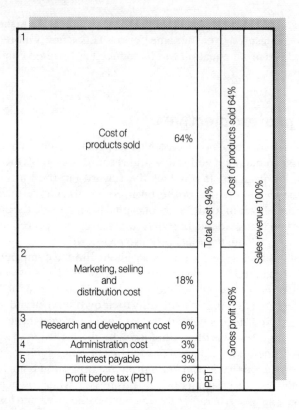

Figure 7.1 **A typical cost structure for a manufacturing business.**
The partitioning and terminology used here reflects 'cost' as interpreted in the profit and loss
account of a manufacturing business (and reflecting the profit equation, Equation 7.1). The total
cost is subtracted from the sales revenue to yield profit before tax. It is made up of the major items
numbered 1 to 5 on the left. The cost of (manufacturing the) products sold is easily the largest cost.
The percentages are reasonably typical of a large company, although the profit is uncomfortably
low. An alternative view of the diagram treats it as the price–cost structure of the average (but non-
existent) product.

applies to a typical manufacturing business. The **total cost**, which is subtracted from
the **sales revenue** to yield **profit before tax** (PBT), comprises five major items:

(1) The **cost of products sold** or **cost of sales**. This cost is incurred by the
production function in making and testing the products which are (hopefully)
to be sold. It is otherwise called the **factory cost** or the **works cost**, especially
when applied to individual products.

(2) **Marketing, selling and distribution cost**. Costs in this category are those
incurred by the marketing and sales function, assuming that the function
incorporates the product distribution operation. In some organizations,
product distribution is managed by the production function. Even if this is the
case, distribution costs are included here rather than under the cost of
products sold heading.

(3) **Research and development cost**. This is the conventional term for the costs

incurred by the technical function. It is not a good description for reasons that are discussed in Chapter 3, but the jargon is now too well established to change. It covers expenditure by the technical function on technological innovation (its primary task), but it also includes the costs of the many other secondary tasks which are assigned to the function.

(4) **Administration cost**. This uninformative heading embraces the costs of *all* the other business functions, such as:

    (a) the board of directors

    (b) finance

    (c) information services

    (d) personnel

    (e) purchasing

    (f) quality assurance, and so on.

(5) **Interest payable**. Costs in this category represent interest payments on any loans, usually from banks, used to help finance the business activities. They are **financing costs**, which relate to funding the **operating costs** identified at 1, 2, 3 and 4 above. Some businesses own investments which earn interest. For example, a company might own shares in another company and so receive dividend payments. Another example is that of a company which is building a 'cash mountain' in a bank deposit account, in preparation for acquiring another company. In such cases, the entry under this heading is the net of interest payable minus **interest receivable**. Conceivably, this is a negative figure indicating that more interest is earned than paid out. It then just counts as a negative cost, offsetting, to some extent, the other positive costs.

The **gross profit** or **gross margin** is defined by the relationship:

$$\text{Gross Profit} = \text{Revenue} - \text{Cost of Products Sold} \tag{7.2}$$

It measures the difference between the sales value of the products and the costs of making them. Gross profit is the major source of income to the business. It (usually) has to pay for all the other costs and provide the profit. There is an important point here. The production function is the only business function which is a net money earner. All the other functions cost money. There may be other sources of income, such as interest received and profit on externally-funded technical function projects, but these are usually quite insignificant in comparison with the earnings of the production function.

The profit earned before interest payable and tax are subtracted is called the **operating profit**, since it relates to the activities of the business. Subtracting the interest payable from this yields the **profit before tax** (PBT). Once a business has declared a profit, it is liable to tax before the residue, termed the **profit after tax** or the **net profit**, can be used for other purposes. These other purposes are normally re-investing in the business and paying dividends to the owners. In some circumstances, however, there may be **extraordinary costs** (arising, say, from reorganizing the business) which must be paid before residual profit is applied to its more usual purposes.

The structure as a profit and loss account

As a whole, Figure 7.1 can be viewed in either of two ways. At the overall business level, it may be regarded as a typical **profit and loss account** for a particular year. The *illustrative* percentage figures assigned to its major elements reflect this view: indeed, the figure is based on the published accounts of a large and real electronics and communications company. The percentage figures are included to indicate reasonably typical comparative levels for that sort of company. Different companies show rather different proportions in the same year, and the example company shows quite wide year-on-year variations. Note that the major cost item, by a handsome margin, is cost of products sold; and the marketing, selling and distribution cost is remarkably high. The level of research and development cost is somewhat less than is typical for European companies in the electronics and communication industries, and some would argue (this author for one) that it is too low for long-term comfort. The interest payable is on the high side of normal and the profit before tax is less than exciting. In fact, the company is in some difficulty, primarily because the cost of products sold is a few points too high, and because of the level of interest payable.

The structure as the average product

The alternative (but equivalent) perception of Figure 7.1 views it as the price–cost structure of the average (but non-existent) company product. This is an attractive and useful interpretation. It does not imply, however, that there is some mathematical connection between **product price** and **product cost**. The price of a product is what a purchaser is willing to pay for it. This has nothing at all to do with what it costs to make it available to purchasers.

7.2.3 Engineering and cost

Figure 7.1 allows the earlier statement that 'cost and costing is a fundamental engineering topic' to be justified. Engineers are directly involved with two of the five cost segments. In each case, there is a major impact on the cost of products sold segment, which is invariably the largest part of total cost.

Engineers within the technical function who are assigned to product development and design projects must provide the production function with 'how to make' data relating to new and enhanced products. This data defines the product in terms of:

- its basic materials and components
- the configurations into which these must be assembled
- the physical format of the various sub-assemblies
- the way it should be tested at intermediate and final stages.

Each of these distinct factors has a bearing on the cost of the finished product. A demanding requirement in the development and design of competitive products is to provide the specified functional and performance features within the specified works cost target. The maxim that recognizes an engineer as one who makes for five bob (25 pence) something any fool can make for a pound is dated but still true.

Production engineers are (or should be) obsessed with extracting the best possible value from money spent in the production function. Their twin objectives of cost reduction and cost avoidance are attacked both at the overall manufacturing system level and at the individual product level. At the overall level, for example, a machinery maintenance strategy is required which minimizes the sum of maintenance costs and machine out-of-service costs; because, within limits, increasing the first reduces the second, and conversely. Achieving a satisfactory answer to this problem is an exercise in engineering economics demanding insight, delicacy and finesse. At the other end of the spectrum, production engineers are (usually) responsible for accepting or rejecting the product definition data created by the technical function. In this respect, their role is often to curb the wilder excesses of their development and design colleagues. This they do by minimizing the use of rare and exotic components offered by dubious suppliers and ensuring, so far as possible, that the defined products can actually be made and tested with the available facilities. This task is best discharged by working alongside the product engineers in the critical creative phase. Success, or otherwise, has a major impact on finished product cost.

Good engineering, therefore, is about manipulating technologies in a cost-effective way. So engineers must understand something of the language, problems and techniques of costing. This understanding is one factor which tends to distinguish engineers from scientists and mathematicians, who often prefer to extend the depth rather than the breadth of their knowledge. For engineers, areas of special interest and concern are the cost of technical projects, and the works cost and **life cycle costs** of products.

The following sections treat cost and costing as a fundamental engineering topic. Some of its basic problems are explored first.

7.3   Cost and costing problems

Perhaps the most pernicious problem with costs is their tendency to increase with time. This feature is not restricted to business costs, it is a characteristic of all income versus expense situations. A form of reverse gravity seems to apply to costs. The problem has its roots in that human pleasure which is derived from spending money, especially other people's money. Managers need to be conscious of this human foible. While, of course, it is no part of their job to deny their subordinates the simple pleasures of life, this indulgence must stop well before the business is damaged.

At a more rational level, determining the cost of something is always a critical issue: be it a technical project, a product component, a finished product or an item of production machinery. Only if the cost of the something is known can its economic merit be assessed, because its cost must be compared with the benefits that (should) flow from that cost through the medium of the something. But there are some inherent problems in the costing process. These conspire to turn it into an exercise of some complexity which delivers inexact results. These problem areas are now examined.

7.3.1   Which cost matters?

This is quite an alarming question in its own right, because it implies that more than one cost can be associated with an item. Unfortunately, this is true. Suppose, for example, that the 'how to make' data for a particular new product specifies the use of a particular component which is already stocked in the production stores. The cost of the component (it might be an integrated circuit, a computer or an engine, say, depending on the product) contributes to the works cost of the finished product. A number of different costs might be assigned to the component. But which of the following list of different costs is the right one to incorporate into the cost build-up for the product?

(1) The cost originally paid to the component supplier, called the **historical cost** or the **past cost**.

(2) The cost of restocking the production stores, called the **current cost** or the **replacement cost**.

(3) The cost likely to apply during manufacture and sale of the product, called the **anticipated future cost**.

(4) The amount of money which could be obtained by selling the component as a single stand-alone item, called the **realizable value**.

(5) The net amount of benefit *sacrificed* (measured, somehow, in money terms) by not using the component in its best other use, called the **opportunity cost**.

An economist would probably choose the opportunity cost, because that is what 'cost' means to economists. Opportunity cost is a nice idea which is explored later in this chapter (at Section 7.5.8). An accountant might hesitate between current cost and anticipated future cost. A usual assumption is that the price of the product can be increased during its sales lifetime in line with product cost inflation. This biases the choice towards replacement cost. (Because if both price and cost increase by the same percentage so, too, does their difference. This is one force that drives the inflationary spiral.)

7.3.2 Relative timing

There is only one rational reason for a business to incur any particular cost. This is that the cost will lead to some revenue (an income) that both repays the cost itself and leaves a net surplus. But, generally, the cost is incurred before the return is obtained. In other words, the income is an anticipated rather than a certain reward for the cost.

The time gap between a cost and the benefits that flow from it presents a measurement problem. This arises because the only certain thing about the future is that nobody knows what is going to happen. All of life, business and otherwise, is conducted on the basis of a balance of probabilities. Business, therefore, is about taking risks. In many cases, business managers are taking risks with other peoples' money. This is one reason why there is a statutory obligation for companies to publish statements of their financial performance and status at relatively frequent intervals. In Britain, all limited companies must publish **audited accounts** every year. Public limited companies must report their results at least twice a year. Furthermore, these published statements must be prepared using **accrual accounting**. In this method, the items of cost and revenue which determine profit are **recognized** (entered into the accounts) in the period in which they are incurred (committed) or earned, rather than in the period when they are paid or received. For example, the revenue figure declared at the end of an accounting period probably contains a fraction which is promised but not received, due to sales made on credit. Similarly, the cost declared at the end of the period probably contains a fraction which is committed but not paid, due to purchases made on credit.

Accrual accounting makes it easier to match a cost with the revenue that it earns by bringing them together in the same accounting period. **Matching** is an important accountancy principle. It allows the merit of a particular cost to be assessed by comparing it with the revenue that it earns. The rationale underpinning this splendid ambition is flawless. But it is achieved only by creating an uncertainty problem, because accrual accounts generally contain some proportion of estimates. Estimates are forecasts of the future. They can be wrong and usually are, to some extent. However, this problem must be tolerated. The twin needs of frequent reporting and matching are paramount.

One consequence of accrual accounting is that there can be dramatic differences between the profitability of a business and its **cash-flow** position. Cash-flow is the net amount of money actually received by a business in a specific period: the factual difference between the money received and the money spent in that period. A business can be profitable but **bankrupt** (unable to pay its debts) because its customers have not paid for the products sold to them on credit. This is a well-established failure mechanism in small businesses.

The matching principle requires that, if a cost is not **written-off** (entered as a cost) in the period when it is incurred, then it must be carried forward as an **asset** of the business. This is dangerous if the carry-forward option is applied to costs with benefits which are highly speculative and scheduled far into the future. Research costs are a case in point. Most research projects fail in the sense that they demonstrate that some speculative idea is not practical. The benefits which flow from research projects that do succeed tend to occur some years after the research, when the connection is attenuated by the passage of time and many other factors. For research, therefore, matching is sacrificed on the alter of prudence: the cost is written-off as it is incurred. Product development and design is (or should be) substantially less speculative than research. In this case, companies may choose either to write-off such costs, or to carry them forward. Most opt for the less dangerous course of writing them off.

Prudence is another accountancy principle. Under conditions of uncertainty, it requires that revenue should be understated and cost overstated, so that profit is understated. Accountants believe, and they are right, that it less dangerous to understate a profit than to overstate it. The approach also minimizes the rate of unpleasant surprises. But it pollutes the purity of the profit equation:

$$\text{Profit} = \text{Revenue} - \text{Cost} \tag{7.1}$$

because some fraction of the cost does not relate to the revenue, despite earlier claims that revenue and cost were an exact match. Perceptive readers may have noticed this anomaly in Figure 7.1, which shows technical function costs as part of the total cost structure. It is more accurate, therefore, to regard the cost term in Equation 7.1 as the cost of being *and* staying in business, since it includes costs relating to both reported and future revenues.

7.3.3 Fixed and variable costs

Some types of cost do not vary as the level of activity associated with them varies. Building insurance premiums and rents are examples of such **fixed costs**. They remain the same whether the building is being used or not. Other costs are classed as **variable costs**, because they do vary with their associated activity, such as rate of sales or production. For example, the monthly cost of components purchased for incorporation into products clearly increases as the monthly rate of product production increases. There are many different forms of variation: linear, nonlinear, continuous, discontinuous and combinations thereof. Accounting is not a branch of higher mathematics and linear approximations are commonly employed to cope with the more exotic functions (which, in any case, rarely conform to an analytic expression). Both fixed and variable costs are subject, of course, to variation with time. Insurance premiums, for example, are generally 'reviewed' (increased!) annually and component costs usually increase periodically in line with inflation.

7.3.4 Cost allocation

It is a relatively straightforward matter to calculate, on an accruals basis, the total cost incurred by a self-contained business during a specific period. It is less easy to decide how the various activities which make up the business contribute to this total cost.

For example, consider the task of costing a technical project which is active in this period. Clearly, the **labour cost** (mostly salaries) of the engineers assigned to the project is part of the project cost. So, too, is the cost of any items and services that they purchase from outside the business for purposes exclusive to the project. Costs like these which are wholly attributable to the project are called **direct costs**. But the engineers must be accommodated in a suitably equipped laboratory which keeps them warm, dry and secure. They need access to a range of internal services, such as secretarial, communications, reprographic and computer-aided design. And they must be supervised in their endeavours. All of these items, and many more, cost money. But the services provided by these support costs are shared by all the engineers who work on all the projects in the laboratory. They are termed **indirect costs**, because they are not wholly attributable to any one project. The question then arises of how best to **allocate** (that is, share) the indirect costs between the various projects. One technique spreads them 'over the heads' (that is, allocates them in proportion to numbers) of the project engineers. Hence the term **overheads** to describe shared costs of this nature. There is always some degree of arbitrariness in allocating overheads to different activities.

The problem of costing a product is analogous to that of costing a project. All the same factors are involved: direct labour and material costs which are attributable exclusively to the product, plus an allocation of the total indirect cost which represents (or purports to do so) the consumption of other services and facilities used in making the product.

7.3.5 Section summary

In summary, the message that emerges from this preliminary skirmish with the concepts of cost and costing is that costs are not pure and costing is not simple. But the earlier discussion demonstrated the importance of cost in all aspects of business, and its special significance for engineers.

7.4 Budgets: An overview

A **budget** is a financial plan: that is, it is a statement of objectives expressed in revenue and/or cost terms. Businesses use budgets both to define their immediate intentions in financial terms, and as 'baseline' documents against which actual financial perform-ance is measured. Usually, the word 'budget', when unaccompanied by a qualifying adjective, refers to a particular **financial year** (also termed a **fiscal year**) which rarely coincides with the calendar year. But a **project budget**, for example, is the cost plan of a project and it relates to a period which, in principle, is not related to a financial year.

Budgets are **tactical plans** covering a relatively short time. In the larger companies, the current budget is often (the financial aspects of) the first year of a **rolling** long-term plan. In other words, the company maintains a **strategic plan** which always looks five (say) years ahead, so that the current budget aligns with the longer-term policies of the business. Of course, the clarity of forward vision declines sharply as time increase, and the later years of a five-year plan become increasingly speculative and less detailed. Some companies feel more comfortable if they always have the next 12 months mapped out in some detail. This may be done by applying the rolling principle on a monthly basis. In this scheme, as one month ends another is added to the budget twelve months 'downstream'.

The central problem with budgeting, at any level in any business, is determining the optimum way in which to spend the available, always limited, resources. Preparing budgets in a large company is no small task. It can absorb much of the time of those managers most closely involved, perhaps over a period of several months. The aim is to have the new budgets prepared, and approved, before the start of the new (financial) year. The target is usually achieved but it can be disturbing experience. The mechanics of the process are now outlined.

7.4.1 Budgeting in a large company

The large company model on which this discussion is based is a composite fiction called Global Widgets PLC, a public limited company based in Britain. Its organiza-tional structure is typical of a large and diversified manufacturing company operating on a world-wide basis. It happens to be concerned mostly with electrical, electronic, communications and computer-based products but this does not spoil the generality of what follows.

The organizational model

The structure comprises a number of **trading divisions** reporting to group head-quarters: a central organization which is essentially the (main) board of directors of the company and their immediate supporting staff. The Company Research Laboratory reports directly to group headquarters, which also includes a **corporate** (whole business level) finance function. The organization is outlined in Figure 7.2.

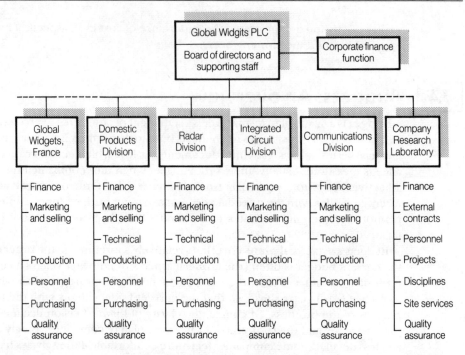

Figure 7.2   **The basic structure of the large company model.**
The discussion of company-level budgeting is based on this typical organization of a large manufacturing company which operates world-wide. The second-level 'trading' organizations are semi-autonomous units with distinct budgets and profit and loss accounts. They are made up of business functions (assigned to different stages of the product creation and selling process). These third-level units also have distinct budgets and profit and loss accounts. So budgets and accounts at the second level combine budgets and accounts from the third level. Similarly, the company budgets and accounts combine budgets and accounts from the second level. The combining arithmetic is slightly complicated by the need to 'net out' internal trading. The process is called 'reconciliation'.

The trading divisions are so called because they sell products. In a manufacturing company, as here, the divisions usually develop, design and make most of the products that they sell. But they may also be licensed to sell the proprietary products, which they may or may not make, of other companies. Trading divisions concerned only with marketing and selling also exist. Divisions of this sort are usually outposts of the company operating in an overseas market.

The divisions are relatively autonomous organizations with profit responsibility for their own activities. Usually, each division within the overall structure is assigned a distinct segment of the total market addressed by their parent company. Segmentation can be based on product technology (the Integrated Circuits Division, say), customer type (the Domestic Products Division is an example) or geography (such as Global Widgets, France). Some of the divisions may be companies in their own right. In such cases, the parent company (Global Widgets PLC here) holds the majority of the shares (usually all of them) and the subsidiary company is of the private limited variety, or its overseas equivalent.

The role of a research laboratory is discussed in Chapters 3 and 5. In this case it is assigned two principal tasks. One is the longer-term, technology oriented, basic research. The divisions, with their short-term profit focus, do not usually (voluntarily) support this work, because it is too speculative and far from the market-place. The other task is applied research involving critical technologies which transcend divisional boundaries and underpin a substantial fraction of the total trading activity. In the Global Widgets case, the silicon integrated circuit and systems software technologies are examples. An aerospace engineering company, on the other hand, might have a equally broad interest in composite structural plastics and high-temperature tolerant materials.

A typical division is organized into a number of business functions, each of which is responsible for a specific part of its total activity. The functions identified in Figure 7.2 are reasonably universal, although there is no fixed formula which covers all manufacturing companies. Purchasing and/or quality assurance, for example, might be part of the production function. Note that most divisions have their own technical function, and that this is distinct from the Central Research Laboratory (although all are part of the whole company technical function). The structure illustrates a common separation of research from product development and design. The latter activities are of immediate interest to the divisions, and are usually included within divisional boundaries.

The functions that make up the Company (or 'Central' or 'Corporate') Research Laboratory reflect the role of this unit and the way in which it is organized. This particular laboratory happens to be organized on a 'matrix' basis, but its precise structure is irrelevant at this stage. (The organization of technical functions is covered in Chapter 5, and the topic also has some bearing on the discussion in Section 7.7).

The budgets structure

The (top level) whole company budget is an amalgam of the budgets of all the trading divisions and other second level units, such as the Central Research Laboratory, which report into group headquarters. In turn, a second level budget is an amalgam of the budgets of all the third level units which report into that second level unit. There may also be fourth and lower levels but this possibility is ignored here. Thus, the budgets structure reflects the organizational structure of the company. In budgetary terms, the company may be regarded as a configuration of relatively small low-level budgets which are then amalgamated into a series of higher-level budgets defining operating units of ever increasing size. The mechanism delegates profit and business responsibility to the successive layers of management in a way which allows objectives to be set and monitored at each level. Each unit with its own budget is commonly called a **profit centre**, a **P&L centre**, a **cost centre** or a **budget centre**. P&L is an acronym for profit and loss.

The whole structure is not unlike an upside-down tree, rooted in group headquarters, with a main trunk, substantial limbs, branches, twigs and leaves. A less arboreal analogy is that of a structure of files organized into directories, subdirectories, sub-subdirectories and so on by a computer operating system.

In principle, the budget of each P&L centre has two separate but related parts. These are the **profit and loss budget** and the **capital budget**. (Logically, these two parts of a whole budget should be termed sub-budgets. But they rarely are.) The P&L budget is concerned with the revenue from product sales in the period covered by the budget, and the cost of the resources used in that period. This cost includes:

- labour cost
- the cost of outside purchases which are either transformed into products or consumed in other ways
- a cost which depends on the facilities (such as buildings, equipment and tools) which are used by the centre.

The 'facilities cost' is called the **depreciation charge or cost**. Depreciation is an arithmetical ploy used by accountants to allocate part of the purchase cost of those resources which are only *partially* used up in a budget period to that period. The part allocated equates, supposedly, to the part used up. Depreciation is discussed in more detail in Section 7.5.1.

The capital budget is concerned with the purchase of new **capital items** (and, possibly, with the sale of old capital items). A capital item is some resource which the budget centre needs, but which is not wholly used up in a single budget period. A building, for example, might last for fifty years and a machine-tool for ten. Their costs are spread over their (estimated) life by means of depreciation charges. **Depreciation**, therefore, is a device which links the P&L and capital budgets.

Revenue-earning product sales are budgeted in only a limited number of budget centres. In Figure 7.2, the centres initially budgeting revenue are the marketing and sales functions in the divisions and the Central Research Laboratory. Revenue is also budgeted at the divisional and top levels through the amalgamation process. Thus, most P&L budgets are really cost budgets relating to cost centres rather than to P&L centres. But the profit concept is still useful even in these cases.

For example, a personnel function has a budget which shows how its total annual cost is composed of its staff costs, external purchases and use of facilities. This cost is **recovered** by charging it against a fixed allowance in a higher-level budget. The profit notion is applied in this situation by regarding the people-related services that the personnel function provides as the products which it sells within its parent division. Cost recovery is then equivalent to revenue; and profit and loss are over-recovery and under-recovery, respectively, of actual compared with budget cost. This common convention is used to set financial objectives for cost centres. Clearly, in this example, there is no merit in requiring the personnel function to over-recover its costs. But there is every reason to require it not to under-recover them: that is, not to incur costs in excess of budget.

The budgeting process

The budgeting process for a particular financial year is launched by a series of meetings between the top- and second-level managers which culminate in 'agreed' budget targets for the second-level budget centres. The extent to which these targets are mutually agreed, as opposed to unilaterally imposed, is rarely revealed to the lower echelons. However, there is a natural tendency for the top managers to set **hard budgets** with demanding targets. There is an equally natural tendency for the divisional managers to favour less demanding **soft budgets** (which they call 'realistic'). The targets will generally be expressed in financial terms, such as:

- achieve better than a fifty per cent share of a particular market
- deliver a profit before tax of more than fifteen per cent of revenue
- attain a return on capital employed of at least twenty-two per cent.

Targets of this nature effectively set the boundaries for budgeted revenue, cost and (net) new capital investment at divisional level.

The divisional targets are then used to set the targets for the third-level budgets that will eventually come together to form the divisional budget; and so on for the budgets (if any) at lower levels. (The construction of a sample budget for a 'second-level' technical department is described in Section 7.7.) So, the targets for individual budgets trickle down from the top of the management hierarchy. The budget approval part of the whole process develops in the opposite direction. The lower-level budgets are approved first, and these build upwards until, eventually, approved divisional level budgets are amalgamated to form the whole company budget. Managers are required to approve the budgets for all centres within their responsibility.

Novice managers soon realize that the possession of an approved budget is not, in fact, a license to start implementing it on Day 1 of the new financial year. They find that individual projects still require the formal approval of the project sponsors (that is, the project customers and/or source of project funds) prior to launch. Similarly, the approval of local top management is required prior to the purchase of financially significant capital items and they, too, may need to seek higher-level approval. In fact, budgets are only ever 'approved in principle'. Cynics have claimed that phrases like 'agreed in principle' and 'approved in principle' are really only less provocative ways of saying 'go away until I have thought of a reason for saying no'. Realists know that this is sometimes the case. But the real reason is that budgets are necessarily prepared and approved some considerable time, in business terms, before they come into effect. Circumstances can, and do, change in the intervening period. Knowing this, wise managers do not commit their resources until the latest possible time.

Note that the 'approval to proceed' routes for P&L budget items and capital budget items do not necessarily coincide. This is because the former approvals relate to profit, whereas the latter relate to cash-flow and profit (through the depreciation mechanism). Guarding the cash-flow is, of course, sound business sense but the separate approval routes can create some odd situations. Thus, it is not unknown for a project team to be assembled and costing money, while the purchase of the equipment that they need to discharge the task remains unapproved. The reciprocal problem also occurs. There are occasions in business when the right hand neither knows nor cares what the left hand is doing, if anything.

Reconciliation

Throughout the preceding discussion of budgets and budgeting the words 'amalgam' and 'amalgamation' have been used to describe the process of combining subsidiary budgets into a single larger budget. This is because the process involves more than just simple arithmetic.

Referring again to Figure 7.2, suppose that the Radar Division has budgeted to purchase components at a *cost* of £1,000,000 from the Integrated Circuit Division. Similarly, the Integrated Circuit Division has budgeted the *sale* of components to the Radar Division for a revenue of £1,000,000. The figures match because the divisional accountants have discussed the planned transaction and they have a mutual interest in budget accuracy. The components are destined for incorporation into sundry air-traffic control systems for various Radar Division customers. To the Radar Division, the Integrated Circuit Division is just one of its many suppliers and the planned purchase is just one of the many routine purchases that it will make. To the Integrated Circuit Division, the Radar Division is just one of its many customers and the sale is just one of the many routine sales that it will make. In other words, the two divisions have a normal and satisfactory trading relationship.

But, from the perspective of the whole company, the budgeted transaction is illuminated by a different light: because the money that will change hands is company money simply moving from one company pocket to another company pocket. The components only bring 'real' revenue into the company when the air-traffic control systems are sold to the external customers. This revenue accrues in the Radar Division. Similarly, the 'real' cost to the company of the components is incurred in the Integrated Circuit Division. So, when the divisional budgets are combined to form the whole company budget, the internal trading transactions in the divisional budgets must be recognized and 'netted out' to avoid double counting of both revenue and cost items.

The process of first matching internal trading transactions between budget centres and, subsequently, adjusting combined budgets to avoid double counting is called **budget reconciliation**. It has been described in terms of amalgamation of the divisional budgets into the whole company budget. But it might also be required at lower levels, because internal trading relationships are quite common between the functions of a division. These must be reconciled in the divisional budget before it is made available for amalgamation into the whole company budget. The need for reconciliation substantially complicates and protracts the budgeting process.

Budgeting in a small company

Budgeting has been reviewed in a large company context because this allows its full horror to be exposed. The principles of budgeting in a small company are identical but the magnitude of the task is, of course, proportionally reduced.

7.4.2 Basic cost sources

The costs that appear in any budget, set of accounts, project cost report or product cost build-up are invariably some blend of costs arising from just four basic sources. These sources are:

(1) *Labour* This is the cost of employing people. It is made up of wages or salaries, payroll taxes such as the employer's national insurance contributions, and any employee benefits like employer's contributions to pensions and the provision of company cars. There are also additional costs incurred in administering the payroll, and in collecting payroll and employee income tax on behalf of the Government. These latter costs are a (badly) hidden tax imposed on businesses.

(2) *Materials and services* This cost source is broadly defined to include all external purchases of a tangible and of a service nature which are expected to

be wholly used up within a year of purchase. Such items are sometimes called **consumables**. They include items as diverse, say, as mechanical fasteners and management consultancy.

(3) *Facilities* These are the buildings, machinery, equipment and tools which the people need to carry out their duties efficiently. They are generally (but not always) purchased from outside the business and distinguished from consumables by not being wholly used up within a year of purchase. The purchase cost of these capital items is handled in P&L budgets and accounts by the depreciation mechanism discussed earlier.

(4) *Finance* The most obvious example of this cost source is the interest paid on bank loans used in the business. But this is only one of a number of ways in which businesses might raise money, so other types of financing cost can arise. The underwriting fee associated with an issue of new shares illustrates the point.

The following two sections discuss, in turn, different categories of costs and the manner in which some costs vary with activity level. This particular partitioning of this more detailed examination of costs is not entirely satisfactory, but it breaks up quite a large body of material into digestible pieces. Alternative treatments can be found in Chapman *et al.* (1987) and White *et al.* (1989).

7.5 Cost categories

Costs are conventionally grouped into a number of distinct categories on the basis of criteria other than their variation with activity level. In this approach, the classification criteria that are applied to a particular cost mostly concern its position in time, and/or the extent to which it is attributable to a specific activity or product. (The concept of opportunity cost does not conform to this pattern). This structure of cost categories forms part of the language of costs and costing. It provides a verbal and written shorthand for accountants to communicate with each other. It is also a jargon (all professions have them) which can confuse engineers and others who must communicate with accountants. The aim of this section is to provide an antidote to confusion of that sort. In this sense, it is an extended glossary of cost-related terms. For completeness, there is some deliberate repetition of revelations made earlier in the chapter. Coverage of the related topic of fixed and variable costs is deferred to the next section.

All of the costs cited in the discussion that follows are some mixture of costs arising from the four basic sources of labour, materials and services, facilities and finance.

7.5.1 Depreciation charges or costs

The concept of depreciation was introduced in Section 7.4.1, in the discussion about budgeting. Some of the resources employed by a business are held for its long-term use. They are not converted directly into products, and thence into cash, but are needed to aid that conversion process. Resources of this nature are called capital items or, more usually, **fixed assets**. They include:

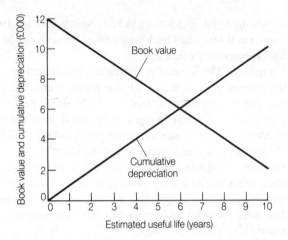

Figure 7.3 **A depreciation example.**

Some resources belonging to a business are held for *long-term* use in business processes, such as manufacturing. These 'fixed assets' are paid for on purchase, but they are not wholly 'used up' (or 'consumed') in one accounting period. Depreciation is an accounting ploy which allocates fractions of the net purchase cost of such items to the successive accounting periods covering their useful life. The mechanism is illustrated here. It is anticipated that an item of equipment, costing £12,000, will be used for ten years and then sold for £2,000. So the anticipated net cost (taking a simple view) is £10,000. It is unfair to set all of this against profit in Year 1, and equally unfair not to set something against profit in Years 2 to 10. So a depreciation charge of £1,000 is set against profit in each of the ten years. Note that the cumulative depreciation plus the 'book value' of the item is always equal to the purchase cost.

- land and buildings
- plant, machinery and equipment
- tools
- vehicles
- fixtures and fittings.

A distinguishing feature of fixed assets is that, although they are paid for on purchase, they are not wholly consumed during one accounting period. Depreciation is a mechanism which allocates fractions of the net purchase cost of such items to the successive accounting periods covering their useful service life. An example will make this more clear.

Suppose that, at the beginning of a particular financial year, an item of equipment is purchased for £12,000. There is an immediate cash outflow of this amount when the purchase invoice is paid. The estimated useful life of the equipment is ten years, and it is anticipated that it can then be sold for a net sum of £2,000. So the net purchase price (in simplistic terms) is £10,000. It is clearly unreasonable to burden the P&L account of the year of purchase with the whole of this cost, and equally unreasonable not to burden the subsequent nine years. So a depreciation charge against profit of £1,000 is made in each of the ten years. The mechanism is illustrated in Figure 7.3.

This shows the **book value** of the equipment (its value as an asset recorded in the 'books' of the business) declining linearly from the purchase cost to the estimated salvage value over its estimated useful life. The annual depreciation charges accumulate linearly from zero such that the loss of value is recovered as the equipment is 'used up' or 'consumed'. Note that book value plus cumulative depreciation is always equal to purchase cost. Note, too, that the mechanism takes no account of inflation: it assumes, probably incorrectly, that pound or dollar purchasing power will remain constant over a substantial period. In this example, a linear depreciation algorithm is used and this is frequently employed in practice. However, more complex algorithms are sometimes used. These might, for example, accelerate the depreciation in the early years of asset life.

It will be appreciated that a depreciation charge (a cost) is really a piece of convenient fiction (although an accountant may take a contrary view). There is no change in the cash position when the charge is made, it is a paper transaction. Depreciation is one more reason why the financial position of a business as assessed by accrual accounting is likely to be different from its cash-flow position.

7.5.2   Historical and sunk costs

Historical costs, also called **past costs**, are costs that have already happened. **Sunk costs** are those parts of a past cost which are not recoverable.

An example will make this more clear. Suppose, as earlier, that an item of (production) equipment was purchased for £12,000. It was estimated that its useful life would be ten years, and that it could then be sold for a net sum of £2,000 (the proceeds of the sale less the cost of selling it). Thus, the net cost of the equipment was assumed to be £10,000. Recovery of this cost was planned through a series of £1,000 per annum depreciation charges (costs) over the estimated lifetime of the equipment. In other words, the cost of each product that the equipment helped to make would include a fraction (maybe a very small fraction) of the annual depreciation charge. This is recovered (repaid) when the product is sold. This, then, was the plan.

But, sadly, the item of equipment fell irreversibly to pieces after just five years and the remains were sold as scrap for a net sum of £200. The arithmetic of this small drama is shown in Table 7.1.

The sunk cost of £6,800 is a capital loss which reflects the original estimating error. At the time of its collapse, the equipment had a book value of £7,000 (= £12,000 − £5,000) but events have demonstrated that its actual value, in a collapsed condition, is only £200. There is no way of recovering any of the sunk cost. It has gone for ever. Its only certain value is as an expensive reminder either to look after equipment better or to buy from a different supplier in the future.

Sunk costs are the subject of a well-known fallacy, the fallacy being that they matter! They are, of course, bad news and should be avoided. But when they do occur, that sad event must not be allowed to influence any subsequent financial decisions. To personalize the point: the fact that you have invested £100 over the last ten weeks in a series of vain attempts to scoop a football pool is not a good reason to carry on investing. There is no memory and less sympathy in that system. Each week presents an independent decision whether to invest or not. To take note of the past is to be tempted to throw good money after bad, which is the sunk cost fallacy.

A fairly common sunk cost situation in business is that of a project which goes seriously wrong for some reason. Perhaps an anticipated product market fails to

	£	£	
Past cost:		12,000	(Purchase cost)
Recovered cost:			
	5,000		(Depreciation charges)
	200		(Sale of the remains)
		5,200	
Sunk cost:		6,800	

Table 7.1   **An example of past and sunk costs.**

'Past' (or 'historical') costs have already happened. 'Sunk' costs are those parts of a past cost which are not recoverable. The table illustrates such a situation based on the depreciation example of Figure 7.3. That figure refers to an equipment item costing £12,000 which is uniformly depreciated to its forecast salvage value of £2,000 over its anticipated 10 years of useful life. But it failed to conform with this plan, being sold for £200 as scrap after 5 years. At that time only £5,000 of its past (purchase) cost had been recovered by depreciation. So the unrecovered cost is £7,000 − £200 = £6,800. This is a sunk cost, because it has gone forever.

materialize or some totally unexpected technical snag destroys a whole product concept. Once it has been determined (beyond reasonable doubt) that the project has no future it should be stopped. Its costs to date should then be recognized as sunk and its staff transferred to more rewarding activities. Too often, however, such projects are merely wounded by management dithering and left to fade slowly and painfully away.

7.5.3   Replacement or current cost

The purchase cost of a specific item can be different at different times, even though the item itself remains unchanged in every other respect. The **replacement cost**, or **current cost**, of an item to the business that buys it is, of course, the current *price* of that item to the business that sells it. There are three main reasons why the selling business (the supplier) might vary the offer price of an item. These are:

(1) The price normally reflects the competitive situation in which the supplier operates. If this becomes more severe prices may be reduced to retain market share. Conversely, prices may be increased if the competitive supply situation becomes less fierce.

(2) Most pricing structures offer reduced unit prices as the number of units purchased increases. This is the so-called **volume discount** mechanism which is a central feature of trading between businesses. It is made possible by **the economies of scale**, which is a topic for later discussion (at Section 7.9.5).

(3) Cost inflation affects suppliers and encourages them to increase prices to retain profit margins. Passing on cost inflation to customers is the easy way of dealing with the problem and it is, therefore, the most favoured solution. It is not unknown for suppliers, especially those in a monopoly or near-monopoly position, to more than compensate for cost inflation in their prices.

Some manufacturing businesses make periodic volume purchases of the multiplicity of different materials and components which are destined for conversion into their products. The policy takes advantage of available volume discounts, minimizes the cost impact of local administration on unit costs and reduces the risk of delivery delays disrupting production. Items purchased in this way are held in a local store – that is, they are **stocked** and fed out to the production function on demand. ('Just-in-time' methods of procuring consumable items are based on a different approach. They are discussed in Chapter 10, Section 10.5.2.)

This purchasing policy presents two linked costing problems. At any one time, the stock of a particular item is likely to consist of a number of these items distinguished only by the range of different costs at which they were purchased. This stock is a business asset, and one of the problems concerns how it should be valued. There are at least five different solutions to this problem, and this fact alone indicates that none of them is entirely satisfactory. Fortunately, stock valuation is not a concern here but the second problem cannot be avoided in this dismissive fashion.

This second problem concerns the most realistic cost to assign to an item from stock in the cost build-up of a product incorporating that item. Choosing a cost that is too low will result in profit being overstated, choosing a cost that is too high produces the opposite effect. It seems to be generally accepted that the best choice is the current or replacement cost of the item, since this offers the best chance of replenishing the stock without compromising the profit in either direction. Of course, this answer assumes that production will continue to use the item in question. 'Replacement' costing may well be the best theoretical answer to time variations in purchase costs (if only because it is difficult to think up a better one) but it is not always the pragmatic answer. Practical considerations which can work against it include:

- The need to maintain constant awareness of the current cost of a very large number of different items, which is an expensive routine in its own right.

- The fact that these current costs are volume dependent often adds an 'order level' dimension of uncertainty to cost assessment.

- In times of rampant inflation, current costs may be changing too quickly for acceptable accuracy to be maintained.

Many businesses adopt a practice known as **standard costing** which, when properly designed and managed, provides a reasonably satisfactory system for cost determination and control. Conceptually, it embraces all costs, not just those associated with the purchase of consumable materials and services. For this reason discussion of standard costing is deferred at this stage. (It is examined in Section 7.8.2.)

7.5.4   Realizable value

When a capital item (a piece of equipment, a machine-tool or a vehicle, say) has come to the end of its useful life, it might still have a market value. However, the process of selling it will generally incur some **disposal costs**, such as advertising, dismantling, safety precautions, transport and so on. The net return from the proceeds of sale after the disposal costs have been paid is called the **realizable value** or **salvage value**. A similar situation arises when consumable items held in stock become redundant. This can happen when production of the products for which they were purchased is terminated before 'stock out', and the items are not needed for other products. In some cases, a supplier will purchase such items (at a substantial discount on original cost) if they are still in demand elsewhere.

One final point on realizable values. The net return on the sale of assets depends greatly on the circumstances of the sale. For example, if the business concerned is known to be in financial difficulty (such that it desperately needs the cash) then only relatively low values will be obtained. Such are the laws of the business jungle.

7.5.5 Future costs

There is nothing very subtle about the term **future costs**. Any cost of any other sort which is yet to happen can be termed a future cost. It is always associated with some level of uncertainty. In other words, a future cost is always an estimate.

7.5.6 Direct and indirect costs

A direct cost is a cost which is easily measured and directly attributable to a specific activity, project or product. For example, the cost of employing the engineers and other staff assigned to a product development and design project is the **direct labour cost** of that project. The project team will incur various **other direct costs** during the course of the project, a term which covers the cost of any item or service which is purchased exclusively for project purposes. It includes, for example, materials, components and expenses incurred by members of the project team when working away from the 'home' base.

In the case of a product, the attributable labour cost of transforming the materials and components that it contains into the finished item are termed its **direct labour** and **direct materials** costs, respectively. Together, these two cost elements are called the **prime cost** of the product. This is less than the **factory cost**, or **works cost**, of the product because a proportion of various indirect costs are also assigned to it. Similarly, projects must also carry a share of the indirect costs that benefit them.

An indirect cost is a cost which is not easily (that is, cheaply) attributed directly to a specific activity, project or product. The term covers both **indirect labour costs**, **indirect material costs** and a host of other cost elements. In the technical project context, for example, the employment cost of those managers responsible for many projects or for project services such as a library, computer network or mechanical workshop, are classified as indirect labour costs. The labour costs of the secretaries, telephonists and cleaning staff come into the same category. Indirect materials typically include stationery and computer supplies; and small components, such as nuts and bolts, which are too expensive to track as direct materials.

In product production, all the employment costs associated with production planning and control, production engineering, operator supervision and so on count as indirect labour. Indirect materials include such items as machinery lubricating and cooling oils, and the solder and fluxes used in wave soldering equipment.

Other indirect costs include such items as rent, rates, insurance premiums, facilities maintenance and repair, heat, light, power, communications, reprographics, postage, training and very many more. Depreciation is generally treated as an indirect cost but, in some circumstances, it can be regarded as a direct cost.

Indirect costs are also called **overhead costs**. Strictly, this term indicates an indirect cost which is shared amongst the projects or products that it benefits in proportion to the amounts of direct labour used by those projects or products. In other words, the indirect cost is 'spread over the heads' of the direct labour force. However, this is just one (very common) way of allocating indirect costs. Alternatively, for example, the depreciation cost of a machine tool could be shared between the products that it helps to make on a 'machine usage' basis. Despite this possibility, and others like it, indirect costs are commonly referred to as overhead costs or simply as 'overheads'.

7.5.7 Life cycle cost

The **life cycle cost** of an item is the summation of all the costs attributable to that item, measured from when it is first identified as a separate entity to when it becomes of no further economic interest to the business. The types of separate element which make up a life cycle cost depend on the nature of the item. For example, the life cycle cost of a new product could include:

- the cost of the relevant product development and design project
- the cost of production start-up, including production engineering and any special machines, jigs and tools
- the cost of launching the product onto the market
- ongoing production, marketing, selling, and distribution costs
- the cost of product repairs and/or replacements under warranty
- the cost of design enhancements, as required, to sustain the sales of the product.

On the other hand, the life cycle cost of an item of production machinery could include:

- the initial purchase cost (known as the **first cost**)
- the cost of site preparation, installation and operator training
- the cost of any safety precautions and environmental protection against noise, dust and vibration
- cleaning, inspection, maintenance and repair costs
- operating costs such as fuel, power, lubricants and so on.

The **economic worth** of an item, be it a new product, a machine-tool or whatever, is determined by comparing its cost with the benefits which it provides. The merit of the life cycle cost concept is that it emphasizes the total cost implications of the item. The first cost of a machine-tool, for example, is but the first of a long list of consequential expenses which flow from its ownership and operation. Motor cars, washing machines and other domestic items exhibit this same feature.

In cost–benefit analysis, misleading results arise from a simple comparison of costs and benefits which occur at widely different times. For example, a new product creation project which returns twice its costs in two years is probably worth more than one which returns four times its costs in twenty years. But simple arithmetic, which ignores the time parameter, suggests otherwise. The **time value of money** is considered in Chapter 11.

7.5.8 Opportunity cost

The opportunity cost of a resource which is used in a particular way is the amount sacrificed by not using it in its best other (economic) way. Conceptually, the resource is of any sort: people, materials and components in stock, facilities, owners' capital, cash or whatever.

An economist regards the cost of using a resource as its opportunity cost. In contrast, accountants and engineers generally view the cost of using a resource as its replacement cost. Of course, this is not always the case and the appropriate perspective depends on the circumstances. For example, an accountant will be properly concerned with the amount of money (a resource) 'tied up' in stock. This is idle money which might be better employed elsewhere, such as on marketing or engineering or even just earning bank interest. This concern is based on opportunity cost concepts and results in a great deal of attention being given to minimizing stock costs.

Opportunity cost is the basis of all rational thinking about mutually exclusive investment decisions. Consider, for example, the position of a business which is contemplating its new products investment strategy. It is evaluating the relative merits of two proposed projects, called A and B, which are mutually exclusive, because funds are available to pay for only one of them. In fact, the business has three options. These are to launch Project A, to launch Project B or merely to leave the funds in the bank to earn interest. An analysis based solely on financial criteria will usually indicate the best economic option quite clearly. Whether or not this is the best option in a total business context is a wider question. Again, matters of this sort are covered in Chapter 11.

The significant differences between the accountancy and economic perceptions of cost and profit are illustrated in Table 7.2. This shows, at Table 7.2(a), a summarized version of the Year 1 P&L account for the small business (Adastra Ltd) which is discussed in Chapter 12 at Section 12.4. This is constructed in accordance with normal accounting conventions. It shows a small 'accounting' profit of £4,359 after the owner-manager, a Mr Arthur Starr, has paid himself a salary for the year of £20,000.

Mr Starr originally invested £7,500 of his own money (owner's capital) in the business which partially funded its start-up costs. A bank loan provided a further £2,500. Mr Starr was previously employed by a large electronics and communications company at a salary of £40,000 per annum.

Table 7.2(b) shows the same P&L account modified by an economist to include opportunity costs. It shows a loss rather than a profit. (Note that the negative figure is shown in parentheses. This is a common accounting convention.) The first 'economic' adjustment relates to Mr Starr as a resource. He has exchanged a salary of £40,000 per annum for a salary of £20,000 per annum, a net opportunity cost of £20,000. Similarly, while interest (included in 'accounting costs') is paid on the bank loan, the accountant takes the view that the owner's capital of £7,500 is 'free' money and it receives no

(a)

		£	£	£
Revenue				
Sale of products				67,500
Costs				
Direct labour		13,357		
Direct materials		8,550		
	Sub-total		21,907	
General overheads		21,234		
Salary – A. Starr		20,000		
	Sub-total		41,234	
	Total cost			63,141
Profit/(loss)				4,359

(b)

		£	£	£
Revenue				
Sale of products				67,500
Accounting costs				
Direct labour		13,357		
Direct materials		8,550		
	Sub-total		21,907	
General overheads		21,234		
Salary – A. Starr		20,000		
	Sub-total		41,234	
Opportunity costs				
Re: A. Starr		20,000		
Re: Owner's capital		750		
	Sub-total		20,750	
	Total cost			83,891
Economic profit/(loss)				(16,391)

Table 7.2 **Accountancy (a) and economic (b) perceptions of cost and profit.**
The opportunity cost of a resource which is used in one way is the amount sacrificed by not using it in its best other way. These accounts illustrate two ways of treating a resource cost. Table 7.2(a) is the Year 1 P&L Account for a small company prepared under normal accounting conventions, which do not recognize opportunity costs. It shows a small profit after the owner-manager, Mr Starr, has received a salary of £20,000. He originally invested £7,500 (owner's capital) in the business. Mr Starr was previously employed by a large company at a salary of £40,000 per annum. Table 7.2(b) is the same account modified to include opportunity costs: (1) Mr Starr has exchanged a salary of £40,000 for a salary of £20,000, a net opportunity cost of £20,000, (2) an opportunity cost of £750 is 'attached' to the owner's capital because it would have earned this interest in a saving account if it had not been invested in the business. Note that the 'accounting' profit is turned into an 'economic' loss by the modifications.

interest. But the economist attaches an opportunity cost of £750 to this sum. This is based on the argument that, if it had not been invested in the business, it could have earned ten per cent per annum interest in a building society saving account.

Mr Starr was modestly pleased with the accountancy version of his first independent P&L account. He was, however, less excited with the economic version, which shows a substantial economic loss. But he accepted that this was an accurate statement of the price he had paid for the privilege of owning and managing his own business, with its prospects of great job satisfaction and, perhaps, future riches.

7.6   Cost behaviours

All costs are associated with one or more specific business activities. This section is concerned with the way in which costs vary in relation to the level of those activities. 'Activity', sometimes called 'volume' in this context, can be measured in various ways, depending on the nature of the cost element of interest. Some commonly used activity measures are:

- direct labour hours
- machine hours
- rate of production, such as product units per month
- rate of sales, such as product units per month
- rate of purchasing, such as components per month
- periodic sales revenue measured in, say, £s per month.

7.6.1   Types of variation

The vast range of different types of cost behaviour can all be considered as some combination of two basic patterns: fixed and variable. *Fixed costs* are essentially independent of the activity variable, whereas *variable costs* change as the activity variable changes. Their behaviour can be linear or nonlinear and continuous or discontinuous. Figure 7.4 illustrates the basic patterns and some common combinations. It contains nine small graphs, labelled (a) to (i), which are now examined. In all cases, the dependent cost variable is measured along the vertical axis and the independent activity variable along the horizontal axis.

(a) This is the basic fixed cost pattern, there being no variation with the activity level. Examples include insurance premiums on the fabric of buildings, business rates or local property tax, and depreciation on production machinery and test equipment. Normally, each of these costs varies only with time and, generally, remains constant for at least one year.

(b) This is the basic variable cost pattern. A linear relationship is shown but nonlinear forms are quite common. Direct labour costs increasing linearly with direct hours is one example, and direct material costs increasing with rate of product production is another. Similarly, electrical power costs rise in proportion to machine hours run, and sales staff commissions in proportion to sales revenue.

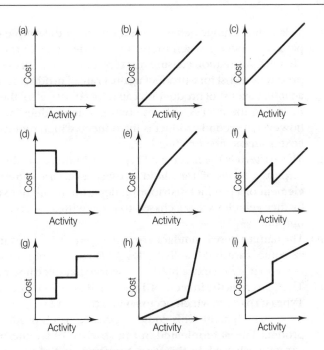

Figure 7.4   **Examples of cost variation with activity level.**

Business costs are always associated with a business activity. Fixed costs are independent of the level of that activity, whereas variable costs change as the level of the activity changes. The figure illustrates some common types of cost behaviour as the associated activity level increases. They are all some combination of the two basic patterns shown in graphs (a) and (b). The simple 'semi-variable' relationship of (c) is important in many business situations.

(c) The relationship shown here is the most simple **semi-variable cost** pattern. It may be regarded as a summation of a Type (a) fixed and a Type (b) variable cost. A cost variation of this form approximates many situations. An important example is that of *total* production costs increasing as the rate of production increases. The fixed element includes such items as machinery depreciation and operator supervision costs, while the variable element corresponds to the direct product costs and variable indirects such as power, lubricating oil and so on. Communication costs also tend to follow this pattern, with fixed leasing costs for equipment adding to variable call charges.

(d) The pattern here is that of a fixed cost which decreases in steps as a series of 'threshold' activity levels are crossed. The typical 'volume discount' price structure provides an example of this form, when the purchase cost *per unit* is plotted against the number of units purchased in a period. The purchase cost of an integrated circuit chip, say, might decrease by five per cent for each additional 1000 purchased.

(e) This is an extension of the basic variable pattern in which the rate of increase decreases at some threshold activity level. Some fuel tariffs structures lead to this type of pattern. For example, a volume discount purchasing agreement for units of electrical power is reflected in a plot of this form for total electrical power against machine hours.

(f) This rather strange behaviour is a variant of the simple semi-variable Type (c) pattern. It occurs when there is a step decrease in the level of the fixed cost element. A situation causing this type of pattern can occur in a plot of the total production cost for a product against rate of product production, when there is an initial excess of production capacity. At first, all of the fixed production cost, including the excess, is borne by the one product. At a certain output level, however, a second product is introduced which removes its share of the fixed cost from the first product.

(g) This pattern is the inverse of Type (d). In this case, the fixed cost increases in steps as a series of 'threshold' activity levels are crossed. The total fixed cost element of a product distribution department might exhibit this behaviour, as further vehicles are purchased to cope with an increasing volume of product output.

(h) The pattern here is similar to that of Type (e), but the rate of increase increases at some threshold activity level. Direct labour costs show this type of behaviour when extra hours are worked at overtime rates.

(i) This pattern is the inverse of Type (f). It is a variant of the simple semi-variable Type (c) pattern which occurs when there is a step increase in the level of the fixed cost element. This could occur in a batch production situation, when a product line is terminated in the absence of another product to absorb the capacity released. In this case, the fixed cost of the excess capacity must be borne by the other products.

The plots of Figure 7.4 illustrate some ways in which costs can vary as a result of changes in corresponding activity levels. All costs are also likely to vary with time. The time-related variations are usually relatively infrequent 'step' changes. For example, building rentals are subject to periodic (upward) review. Similarly, the purchase costs of raw materials and components tends to increase from year to year, or more frequently in times of severe inflation. The cost of labour is subject to the same effect, as salary and wage levels are usually increased at least once per year.

A substantial fraction of the engineering significance of cost and cost behaviours relates to the comparison of mutually exclusive project proposals on the basis of their relative cost effectiveness. This topic is now introduced in terms of the simple semi-variable cost relationship of Figure 7.4(c). This particular type of cost behaviour is of central interest in later sections of this chapter.

7.6.2   The break-even concept

An everyday example of semi-variable cost behaviour is provided by the economic implications of vehicle ownership and use. Some of the annual costs, such as license, insurance and so on, are fixed: they do not vary with usage. Other costs, such as fuel, servicing and the like, are virtually proportional to usage. The total annual cost (T) is then given by:

$$T = F + Vm \tag{7.3}$$

where F is the fixed annual cost, V the incremental cost per mile, m the annual mileage (the usage), and Vm is the annual variable cost.

Now, suppose that Mr Arthur Starr (he of the small business discussed briefly in Section 7.5.8) is contemplating the purchase of a vehicle for use in his business. He has decided that the maximum cash outlay that the business can afford is £5,000. This sum is the purchase cost of a second-hand 'gas guzzler' which, he calculates, will cost £0.20 per mile to run. Alternatively, he has been offered a new diesel van for £10,000 which, he believes, will cost only £0.05 per mile to run. The business is able to borrow money at fifteen per cent per annum and can invest it at ten per cent per annum. Mr Starr sets out to determine which of the two vehicles is the more economic purchase.

The parameters of the problem are set out in Table 7.3. The annual opportunity cost is the same for the second-hand gas guzzler (SHGG) and the new diesel van (NDV). This is the earned interest sacrificed on the £5,000 cash outlay required in either case. A further £5,000 must be borrowed to purchase the NDV, so there is an annual interest cost of £750 in that case. Annual depreciation is estimated at twenty per cent of purchase cost in both cases. Finally, an annual cost of £400 is included for both vehicles to cover licence, insurance and some miscellaneous fixed costs.

The 'best buy' problem is now encapsulated in a pair of simultaneous equations expressing the total annual cost of owning and operating the vehicles. These are:

$$T_{SHGG} = 1900 + 0.20m \qquad\qquad (7.4)$$

for the second-hand gas guzzler, and

$$T_{NDV} = 3650 + 0.05m \qquad\qquad (7.5)$$

for the new diesel van. This is the classic comparison of a low fixed cost but high running cost system with a high fixed cost but low running cost system. Clearly, the best buy depends on the anticipated annual mileage. Below a certain activity (that is,

	SHGG £	NDV £
Purchase cost:	5,000	10,000
Fixed annual costs:		
Opportunity @ 10.00 % p.a.	500	500
Interest @ 15.00 % p.a.		750
Depreciation @ 20.00 % p.a.	1,000	2,000
Licence, insurance and miscellaneous p.a.	400	400
Fixed annual total:	1,900	3,650
Running cost/mile:	0.20	0.05

Table 7.3   **Cost of alternative vehicles.**

A manager needs to determine which of two vehicles is the best (most economic) buy for the business. The alternatives are to spend £5,000 on a second-hand gas guzzler (SHGG) which costs £0.20 per mile to run, or £10,000 on a new diesel van (NDV) which costs £0.05 per mile to run. The business can only afford to spend £5,000 of its own money, but can borrow at fifteen per cent per annum and invest at ten per cent per annum. The table sets out the problem in annual cost terms. Opportunity cost is the same for both vehicles, being the interest sacrificed on the £5,000 cash outlay. £5,000 must be borrowed to purchase the NDV, so there is an interest cost of £750 in that case. Other fixed costs for both vehicles are depreciation at twenty per cent of purchase cost and other items at £400 each.

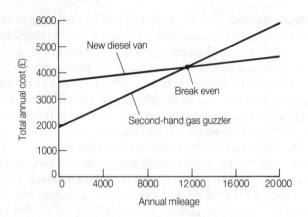

Figure 7.5 **Comparison of vehicle costs: total annual costs.**

The solution to the 'best buy' problem set out in Table 7.3 is obtained by solving the simultaneous equations:

$$T_{SHGG} = 1{,}900 + 0.20m \text{ and } T_{NDV} = 3{,}650 + 0.05m$$

where T is total annual cost and m is the annual mileage. This is done graphically in the figure, demonstrating that the best buy depends on the anticipated annual mileage. Note that the cost variations are the semi-variable pattern of Figure 7.4(c).

annual mileage) level T_{SHGG} is less than T_{NDV}, but the situation reverses above that level. The critical level is obtained by solving the simultaneous equations for the annual mileage, m. This is left as an exercise for the reader, because it is more fun to plot the two equations. This is done in Figure 7.5.

The intersection point of the two functions being compared is generally termed the 'break even' point. A better term in this particular case might be the 'don't care' point, since it defines the annual mileage at which the total cost of owning and operating the two vehicles is the same.

An alternative way of presenting the same information is shown in Figure 7.6. This plots the average cost per mile for each vehicle against annual mileage. The average cost per mile is obtained by dividing the total cost at a particular mileage by that mileage. It declines rapidly from a high value at low annual mileage to become asymptotic to the incremental cost per mile at high annual mileage. This is the **economies of scale** effect. It arises (here) because the fixed costs are spread over more miles as the annual mileage increases. This same effect occurs in product manufacturing, as an increasing number of product units are generated out of the same fixed cost base. The economies of scale lie behind the (now somewhat discredited) 'big is beautiful' approach to industrial organization. But there are also **diseconomies of scale**, of which more later, in Section 7.9.5.

Note that the average cost per mile is different from (and always greater than) the incremental cost per mile. The incremental cost per mile is the factor V in Equation 7.3, which is the gradient of the total cost curve. It is the change in total cost when the annual mileage is changed by one mile. In the worlds of economics and accountancy, this quantity is called the **marginal cost**. Marginal theory is a fascinating topic which is examined in Section 7.9.

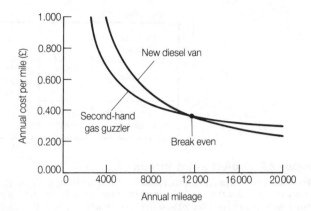

Figure 7.6 **Comparison of vehicle costs: average cost per mile.**
This is another way of presenting the information in Figure 7.5, obtained by plotting the average cost per mile for each vehicle against annual mileage. Note that this declines rapidly from a high value at low annual mileage to become asymptotic to the incremental (marginal) cost per mile (£0.20 for the SHGG and £0.05 for the NDV) at high annual mileage. This is the 'economies of scale' effect. It arises (here) because the fixed costs are spread over more miles as the annual mileage increases.

7.7 Project costs and costing

Cost topics of special interest to engineers are technical project costing and product costing. Project costing is examined in this section, and product costing in the next section.

The cost of a project has three basic elements. Two of these are direct costs: the employment cost of the team assigned to the project, and all the other costs solely attributable to the project. The third element relates to the whole infrastructure which supports the project team. This project cost structure is illustrated in Figure 7.7.

The cost of the whole infrastructure, which is the total indirect or overhead cost, must be shared (in some way) by all the projects which are active at a particular time. The **direct labour cost** also depends on the nature of the organization conducting the projects. Here, therefore, the cost, costing and cost recovery aspects of technical projects are considered in the context of a self-contained technical department conducting a number of such projects.

In order to broaden the discussion, this department is assumed to be a Company Research Laboratory, such as that shown in Figure 7.2. It offers a basic and applied research service to the whole company and to non-company customers. Despite its wide brief, the cost principles involved in this Laboratory are equally applicable to the (probably) smaller and more specialized technical departments that are located within most of the trading divisions shown in Figure 7.2. Normally, such units concentrate on product development and design activities for their parent divisions.

The Company Research Laboratory is treated as a distinct financial entity in the company accounts. This means that it is required to operate in accordance with an

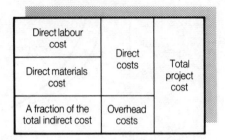

Figure 7.7   **Project cost structure.**
The total cost of a project, illustrated here, has two major elements: the direct costs and the overhead or indirect costs. The direct costs comprise the direct labour cost (which is the cost of employing the project team) and the direct materials cost. This cost includes all other costs solely attributable to the project, and is sometimes termed the 'other direct costs'. The overhead cost element is some fraction of the total infrastructure cost which supports all project work in the projects organization. This cost is commonly shared between the various active projects in proportion to their direct labour content (that is, it is spread 'over the heads' of the project teams).

agreed budget, comprising both P&L and capital sub-budgets. The primary role of the Laboratory concerns the technical aspects of product innovation, so the budget is basically aimed at defining and limiting its operational cost. It might, of course, earn profit on some of its activities. But this is likely to be small in relation to its own costs, and negligible in whole company terms.

A trading concept is built into the financial mechanism by requiring the Laboratory to sell its services (products), which are technical skills and facilities, to project customers. Thus, if all goes well, the costs incurred by the Laboratory in a financial year are completely recovered from its customers in the form of the project costs charged to them. Project costs and departmental budgeting are, therefore, inextricably linked together.

For the most part, the remainder of this section comprises an extended example which illustrates the construction of the trading budget for such a Laboratory. It is this budget which sets the basic parameters for costing the projects conducted by the Laboratory on behalf of its customers.

7.7.1 Definition of terms

The first requirement, in this introduction to departmental budgeting, is to understand the meaning of the terms used. In the definitions and explanations that follow, a conventional and relatively crude approach to technical department budgeting is assumed. In this scheme, total overhead cost is allocated to projects in proportion to the share of the total **project work capacity** (see later) that they absorb.

Direct staff

Direct staff are those individuals whose time is normally spent in working on a limited number (one at a time, preferably) of projects. The **labour plus overhead (L+O/H) cost** (see later) of these staff is 'charged' to the projects on which they work, in proportion to their time spent on each. So, direct staff are required to maintain individual **time-sheets**, which record how their time is distributed among various projects.

Direct costs

Direct costs are those which are easily and solely attributable to a specific project. There are two basic elements:

- The L+O/H cost of the direct staff assigned to the projects.
- Other costs. These are generally called **other direct costs** (ODCs).

Other direct costs (ODCs)

These are non-staff costs which are easily and solely attributable to a specific project. Examples include:

- materials, components and any other purchased items
- machine time on highly specialized and expensive facilities, such as scanning electron microscopes and very high speed computers
- the transport, accommodation and subsistence expenses of direct staff when travelling for project purposes
- outside subcontracts, consultancy fees and so on.

Indirect staff

Indirect staff are those individuals whose work contributes to very many or to all projects, so that that it is either not feasible or not economical to charge their time directly to specific projects. Some examples are:

- management staff
- secretarial and clerical staff
- telephonists, receptionists, canteen staff and cleaners.

Total direct labour cost

Here, and in the definitions that follow, 'total' is used in the sense of a whole department and a whole year.

The **total direct labour cost** is a summation of all the costs associated with the total number of direct staff (called the total **direct headcount**) planned for the financial year. The calculation takes into account:

- The **cost of employment** (COE) of each direct staff member. This comprises:
  - salary, plus
  - **social costs**, such as employer's national insurance contributions (NICs) and employer's contribution to a pension (if any), plus
  - any benefits or 'perks' provided by the employer, such as a company car and private health insurance.

  Note that the cost of employment can be some twenty-five per cent higher than actual salary.
- The total direct headcount, adjusted for any planned gains or losses during the year.
- Any salary adjustments planned to occur during the year.

Total overhead cost

The **total overhead cost** is the cost of supporting the direct staff: that is, the cost of providing the proper environment for their work, supervising their endeavours and selling their services to customers. It includes:

- The cost of employment for all the indirect staff, and their expenses.
- Staff training costs.
- **Waiting time** costs for direct staff. This is a contingency item in case any of the direct staff are temporarily unassigned to a project which covers their cost. This can occur when anticipated project funds fail to materialize or a current project is terminated unexpectedly. The waiting time provision may then be used as a charge point for the unsupported direct labour costs. Its use is generally regarded as a management failure.
- All of the costs associated with accommodation. This includes such items as building rental or depreciation, insurance, maintenance, heat, light, power and so on.
- Equipment depreciation.
- Communication services such as post, telephone, telex, facsimile and electronic mail.
- Site services, including reprographics, library, canteen, security and social facilities.
- Consumables such as stationery, computer supplies, drawing office supplies, cleaning materials, small (and cheap) components and the like.
- Plus a host of other items too numerous to list. (Note that a typical overhead budget, or overhead account, contains 100 to 200 separate headings or **charge codes**.)

Hours per direct (staff member)

Hours per direct is the number of productive hours (that is, project hours) that each member of the direct staff is expected to contribute during the year, excluding **overtime** working. It is estimated by subtracting various allowances from the product of (normal working hours per week) and (weeks in the year). The allowances include:

- annual leave
- statutory holidays
- sickness and training time.

Typical figures for hours per direct are currently in the range 1500 to 1600 per year for professional staff. However, these figures tend to decrease from year to year as working hours per week are reduced and annual leave allowances increased.

Total direct hours (total work capacity)

The **total direct hours** are obtained simply by multiplying the hours per direct (staff member) by the direct headcount averaged over the year. It is a measure of the total project work capacity of the department.

Direct labour rate

The **direct labour rate** is usually measured in £s per hour. It represents the average cost of employment per hour for direct staff and is calculated as:

$$\text{Direct Labour Rate} = \frac{\text{Total Direct Labour Cost}}{\text{Total Direct Hours}} \qquad (7.6)$$

Overhead rate

The **overhead rate** is also usually measured in £s per hour. It represents that part of the total overhead cost which is 'recovered' (that is, paid for by charging to a project customer) in each direct hour of project work. The formula is:

$$\text{Overhead Rate} = \frac{\text{Total Overhead Cost}}{\text{Total Direct Hours}} \qquad (7.7)$$

Labour plus overhead (L+O/H) rate

The **labour plus overhead rate** is simply the sum of the direct labour rate and the overhead rate. For a large company, current rates are typically in the range £20,000 to £60,000 per year, or £1,700 to £5,000 per month, or £13 to £39 per hour. Generally, the overhead rate seems to be about twice the labour rate.

Private venture (PV)

The term **private venture** (PV) is commonly used to denote funds that belong to the company. They are a 'charge' against profit in the sense that if they are not spent the profit is correspondingly higher. PV funds are one source of finance for technical projects.

Contract development (CD)

Conversely, the term **contract development** (CD) denotes funds that belong to some other company or organization. CD funds are a source of finance for technical projects which are conducted for non-company customers. Pedantically, the term can be misleading because it is used in connection with basic and applied research as well as development and design projects.

7.7.2 The departmental budget

The (hypothetical) Company Research Laboratory which is the subject of this example employs some 400 direct staff: scientists, engineers and technicians. About two-thirds of its total project work capacity is employed by the parent company and the remainder by a variety of other organizations. It is planning some £27M of sales in the financial year 1992/93. The sales and cost budgets, which together comprise its trading budget for that year, are now examined.

The sales budget

The Laboratory sales budget for the financial year 1992/93 is summarized in Table 7.4. This shows how the total (planned) revenue of about £27M is built up from sales to a number of individual customers. The vertical structure of the budget is considered first.

Customer	Direct hours	L+O/H £	ODC £	Profit £	Total sales £
CRF	220,120	7,430,566	752,000	–	8,182,566
Communications Division	62,450	2,108,118	525,000	–	2,633,118
Radar Division	57,900	1,954,524	460,550	–	2,415,074
Integrated Cct Division	75,450	2,546,957	686,500	–	3,233,457
Domestic Products Division	22,550	761,218	114,000	–	875,218
Sub-total PV	438,470	14,801,382	2,538,050	–	17,339,432
Communications International PLC	24,280	819,617	210,150	123,572	1,153,339
Wireless and Radio PLC	33,100	1,117,353	255,500	164,742	1,537,595
MOD	143,525	4,844,957	1,325,000	740,395	6,910,352
Sub-total CD	200,905	6,781,928	1,790,650	1,028,709	9,601,287
Grand total	639,375	21,583,310	4,328,700	1,028,709	26,940,719

Table 7.4 **Company Research Laboratory: Sales Budget Summary 1992/93.**
The table is an outline plan showing how the Laboratory intends to sell its products, which are direct hours of project work, during 1992/93. The anticipated cost of a direct hour is the L+O/H rate (which is £33.76 in this case, calculated in Table 7.5). This summary document does not show individual projects – the direct hours set against a customer is the sum of those planned on all projects sponsored by that customer. ODC entries are formed in the same way. Project work for PV (own company) customers is charged at budget cost (in this case), but CD (external) customers are charged a price, comprising budget cost plus profit.

The basic 'product unit' that is sold is a direct hour of project work capacity. Counting from the left, the first two columns list the customers and the number of direct hours that is sold to each one. Generally, of course, a number of different projects are planned for each customer. The budget summary does not show details of individual projects, so the number of hours set against a particular customer is the sum of the planned hours on all the relevant projects. The total number of hours sold (639,375 here) equates to the total project work capacity of the Laboratory over the whole year.

The costs of the hours sold is listed in the next column. This uses the labour plus overhead rate mechanism, discussed earlier, to translate direct hours into money. A brief skirmish with a calculator shows that the budgeted L+O/H rate is £33.76 per hour.

The remaining project cost element, the other direct costs, is listed in the next column. Here, as before, the cost set against a particular customer is the sum of the planned ODCs on all the relevant projects.

The total cost of sales to a particular customer is then the sum of the corresponding amounts in the columns labelled L+O/H and ODC. The revenue value of these sales is obtained by adding a profit element to the cost sum, and it is this figure which appears in the final total column in Table 7.4.

The customers fall into two broad categories: those within the company 'family' and the various external organizations. The in-company customers are the Central Research Fund (CRF), which is controlled at group headquarters, and a number of the trading divisions. These are PV customers. They pay for the projects conducted on their behalf with PV funds charged against profit at whole company (for the CRF) or divisional level.

In this particular case, the Laboratory is required to sell its services at cost to in-company customers. There is no entry, therefore, in the profit column for the PV customers. This requirement is not a universal practice. Some 'central' research laboratories are encouraged to charge their PV customers on a 'cost plus' basis to yield a small profit. Of course, a 'PV profit' merely represents company money moving from one company pocket to another company pocket, but it is real enough at Laboratory level to provide a useful incentive and some measure of price flexibility.

The Laboratory is expected to make a profit on its sales to external customers. This is illustrated in Table 7.4 by the entries in the profit column for the CD customers. Generally, the Laboratory is under no great pressure to make large CD profits: there are other reasons for doing CD work (which are discussed in Chapter 5 at Section 5.4.5). The Laboratory is also in competition for CD work with similar laboratories in other companies, and with some specialist contract research organizations. This factor tends to limit the profit potential because of the need to bid at competitive prices.

The mechanisms by which PV project funds are made available to the Laboratory are a powerful influence on the way in which the Laboratory can be managed and on the policy that it must adopt towards CD-funded work. That topic is also considered in Chapter 5, at Section 5.4.5.

The costs budget

The costs budget is only concerned with the cost of the basic product unit: that is, with the cost of a direct hour of project work. (ODCs are first determined at project level and then brought together within the sales budget.) The cost budget summary corresponding to the sales budget summary of Table 7.4 is shown in Table 7.5. It is divided into two halves, concerned with establishing the labour rate and the overhead rate respectively.

The labour rate calculation on the left-hand side of the budget is quite straightforward. This first estimates the total direct hours (that is, the total project work capacity) by multiplying the average direct headcount for the year by the productive hours per direct staff member. Next, the total direct labour cost is derived by summing the estimated costs of employment for all the direct staff. The labour rate is then obtained by dividing the total direct labour cost by the total direct hours, yielding £12.56 per hour in this case.

The calculation of the overhead rate on the right-hand side of the budget follows a similar pattern. Here, however, it is the total overhead cost (obtained by summing estimates for each individual overhead item) that is divided by the total direct hours to yield the overhead rate. It turns out to be £21.19 per hour in this case.

The L+O/H rate is, of course, merely the sum of the labour and overhead rates. It works out at £33.76 per hour, or £52,323 per year, in the example case.

In passing, note that the average salary per direct staff member is about £16,000 per annum. But it costs more than three times this amount to employ and support the average direct worker in a productive environment! Most of the 'extra' is due to the supporting infrastructure.

Direct labour		Overheads	£
Number of directs	412.5	Employment: management	1,370,512
Hours per direct	1,550.0	Expenses: management	75,550
		Employment: other	402,693
Total direct hours	639,375	Expenses: other	5,500
		Staff training	50,000
	£	Waiting time	70,000
Employment: directs		Accommodation	2,225,490
Salaries	6,638,550	Equipment depreciation	4,522,750
Pensions and NICs	1,062,168	Communication services	242,150
Benefits	331,927	Site services	165,240
		Consumables	93,500
		Other items	4,327,280
Total direct labour	8,032,645	Total overhead	13,550,665
Labour rate £/hour	12.56	Overhead rate £/hour	21.19
Labour rate £/year	19,473	Overhead rate £/year	32,850
L+O/H rate £/year	52,323	L+O/H rate £/hour	33.76

Table 7.5   **Company Research Laboratory: Costs Budget Summary 1992/93.**
The table is an outline plan showing how the Laboratory calculates its anticipated product cost during 1992/93. This quantity is the cost of one direct hour of project work, which is the L+O/H rate. The arithmetic is straightforward. Total direct labour (left-hand side) and total overhead costs (right-hand side) are calculated and divided by total direct hours (work capacity) to yield, respectively, hourly labour rate and hourly overhead rate. These are summed to give the required L+O/H rate. Note, comparing Tables 7.4 and 7.5, that the total direct hours shown on each budget is the same, as is the total (budget) cost of these hours.

Linking the sales and costs budgets

There are two links between the sales and costs budget. These are, first, the total direct hours shown on each budget is the same (639,375 here). Second, the total cost of these hours shown on the sales budget is the sum of the total direct labour cost and the total overhead cost shown on the costs budget. This should come as no surprise, because the direct hours on the sales budget are evaluated at the L+O/H rate.

If the budgets do not provide these equalities then they are said to be **unbalanced**. This term implies that the cost recovery plan embodied in the sales budget either over-recovers or under-recovers the direct labour and overhead costs of the Laboratory. A modicum of over-recovery is a tolerable situation and many managers tend to build 'padding' into cost estimates which biases a cost budget in that direction. The technique is also common in those companies which routinely demand cuts in overhead expenditure during their periodic bouts of profit panic.

Under-recovery of costs is bad news in a budget and a real problem in practice. A budget which initially exhibits under-recovery is usually massaged into balance by reducing cost or by increasing sales revenue, or with some measure of both remedies. There are dangers here, because the adjustments may not be realistic. Many accountants, and some managers, have a strong emotional reaction against budgets showing cost under-recovery and will go to some lengths (contortions, even) to avoid it. All budgets, being plans, must contain assumptions about the future. A budget document which does not explicitly list and evaluate these assumptions is a sloppy piece of work and should be returned to source for correction.

In fact, the budgets as described contain an entirely usual oddity (some would call it a 'fiddle') which, *if* everything goes exactly to plan, will result in a small (about 0.5%) over-recovery of the overhead. The identification of this anomaly is left as a small challenge to the reader.

Real budgets

While no principles have been compromised, the budget summaries presented in Tables 7.4 and 7.5 have been simplified by:

(1) Reducing the number of customers to a level well below that which a Laboratory of the example size would have in practice.
(2) Reducing the number of overhead items somewhat below even that which would normally be included in a summary document.

In practice, of course, there is a great deal more paperwork behind the budget summaries than is shown here. This includes:

- A capital budget itemizing the new equipment purchases (and, possibly, the old equipment disposals) planned for the budget year. This links into the costs budget through a contribution to the depreciation entry.

- Outline plans for all the projects which comprise the customer entries in the sales budget.

- Detailed calculations which support the cost figures entered into the costs budget.

- Current budget and actual performance data which can be extrapolated, to some extent, into the new budget year.

Selected items from this background material will be incorporated into the final budgets 'package', which will also contain a textual commentary on the figures presented and the assumptions on which they are based.

Imperfections in this approach to costing

There are two inherent assumptions within this approach to project costing which fail in practice. The first concerns the direct labour rate. As calculated here, it is an average figure for all the direct staff. But new graduates, for example, are less costly than older staff members with some years of experience and salary increments behind them. Averaging certainly simplifies the sums (and the subsequent administration), but it also distorts project costing. Some companies recognize this situation by operating with a limited number of labour rate 'bands'. The second flaw lies in the calculation of the overhead rate. The method used here implicitly assumes that each member of the direct staff consumes the same amount of overhead resources at a uniform rate throughout the year. This assumption is clearly absurd, and its use further distorts project costing.

But truth is not only impure and complicated, it is also expensive. Most companies (and their customers) accept the imperfections of the system as described rather than paying for improved accuracy. Similar imperfections arise in product costing, which is the next topic for discussion.

7.8   Product costs and costing

As Figure 7.1 shows, by far the largest proportion of the total annual costs incurred by a hardware manufacturing business is the cost of making its products. Comparative inefficiency in this area of just a few per cent, with its consequential profit pressures, spells disaster in a competitive trading environment. So, accurate determination, minimization and control of product costs is a critical factor in business survival and prosperity.

Product costs arise in the production function, which contains the process for converting purchased raw materials, components and other items into finished (and tested) products. The products are the functional expression of the product definition data created by the engineers in the technical function. Product definition data is an interpretation of product specifications created by the marketing function. Thus, the production, technical and marketing functions each bear some responsibility for product costs. The emphasis in this section is on some of the major problems of product cost and costing as seen by the production function. But it is aimed at providing a useful insight for product design engineers.

7.8.1   Product cost elements

The cost of making and testing an individual product is termed its works cost or factory cost. It is a summation of three distinct elements, as shown in Figure 7.8.

The aggregated works cost of all the products sold in a financial year is termed the cost of products sold. Figure 7.1 illustrates that the difference between this major cost and the sales revenue for the year is the gross profit. This is the net income earned by product sales. It has to pay for all the other costs that the business incurs during the year *and* provide the final profit.

There is a clear analogy in the build-up of product cost with the structure of project cost discussed in the previous section: compare Figures 7.7 and 7.8. Similarly, product cost and costing for a particular financial year are based on production volume and cost budgets for that year. Here, 'volume' means products measured both in number of units and in value assessed in cost terms.

Direct labour costs

Direct labour costs are based on the hourly costs of employment for production operatives. These are estimated in exactly the way as was illustrated in the previous section. In the production situation, however, it is usual to define different labour cost rates for different grades of production operative.

Direct materials cost

When the term 'materials' is used in this context it is understood to mean all those easily identifiable and measured items (raw materials, components and whatever) which are purchased solely for incorporation into the product. Items of this nature are

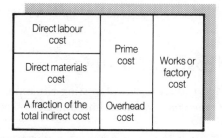

Figure 7.8 **The works or factory cost of a product.**
The cost of making and testing one product unit is called its works or factory cost. It has two major elements, as illustrated here: the prime or direct cost and the overhead or indirect cost. The prime cost comprises the direct labour cost (which is the cost of the human effort 'consumed' in making and testing the product) and the direct materials cost. This cost includes all other costs solely attributable to the product, such as those relating to the raw materials and components consumed in making and testing it. The overhead cost is a fraction of the total infrastructure (indirect) cost which supports the product manufacturing and testing organization. It represents a proportion of the total indirect cost deemed to be consumed in manufacturing and testing the product, and is calculated in a variety of ways (see text).

normally purchased periodically in significant quantities and are stocked (unless 'just-in-time' purchasing is employed) prior to being fed out to production. There is then a significant problem in assigning a 'proper' cost to such items for product costing and production accounting purposes. This problem is discussed in Section 7.5.3. It is particularly acute in times of high inflation.

Indirect (overhead) cost

Estimating the total annual overhead cost for the production function normally presents no special difficulties. But deciding how to share out this total between all the products produced in the year is less straightforward. Two methods are commonly employed.

Sometimes, the total annual overhead cost (or a substantial fraction of it) can be fairly associated with the production, over the year, of a specific (forecast) number of identical product units. In these circumstances, it is usual to set an overhead rate in terms of £s per product unit. For example, if the total overhead cost for the year is assessed at £100,000 and it is forecast that 20,000 identical product units will be produced during the year, then an overhead cost element of £5 is assigned to each product unit. This overhead allocation method is characteristic of 'mass' and high volume production situations. There remains, of course, every opportunity to assess the total overhead incorrectly and also for getting the forecast number of product units wrong.

In other cases, the production operation is concerned with making relatively small quantities of many quite different products periodically throughout the year. This is the 'batch' production situation. Under these circumstances, the total annual overhead cost can be shared among the individual products in proportion to the direct labour hours each consumes in production. This approach, which is based on an overhead rate measured in £s per (direct) hour, is identical to that described earlier for project costing. The 'justice' of the method is debatable but it has the merit of simplicity. It is as vulnerable as any other approach to incorrect assessments and forecasts.

7.8.2   Standard costs and costing

Faced with the product cost and costing situation just outlined, many businesses adopt a costing and cost control technique based on cost 'standards'. This technique is now explored.

Standard costing is a term denoting a technique for planning and controlling costs, usually product costs. It is a vast topic in its own right and it is only possible to introduce the basic principles in this brief exposition. Its main merit is that it separates cost planning from cost control but, at the same time, it provides an orderly mechanism, based on **variances**, for linking these two critical activities together.

The standard cost of a product

The **standard cost of a product** is defined as what it should cost to make the product under normal circumstances. It is established by a careful and realistic evaluation which, generally, includes both theoretical and practical exercises. This necessarily adopts a number of 'normal' assumptions regarding operator and machine efficiency, material quality, scrap rates, volume purchasing discounts and so on. Establishing the standard overhead element may also require that a standard production rate (measured in units per month, say) is chosen. The evaluation leads to a standard cost for each of the three elements of product cost. These are then summed to yield the standard product cost, yielding four cost standards for the product. All of this work is completed (in principle) before significant product production is started. Establishing the standard cost for a product is the planning part of the standard costing technique and the four standards comprise the cost plan for the product.

Variances

'Variance' is a widely used accountancy term which denotes the difference between the plan (or budget) and actual values of a parameter. In this case, actual costs are recorded during production and compared with the corresponding standard (that is, plan) costs to obtain a set of **product cost variances**. Each of these measures the extent to which an actual cost differs from its standard. Variances are normally calculated for:

- the direct labour cost element
- each item comprising the direct materials cost element
- the overhead cost element
- the total product cost, by combining the element variances.

They indicate where corrective action should be taken, if it is economically reasonable and possible to do so, to bring actual product cost closer to the standard.

Each product cost element involves the twin parameters of a unit cost and a unit quantity. For example, the direct labour cost element is obtained by multiplying the direct labour cost per hour (a unit cost) by the number of hours consumed (a unit quantity). If either of these parameters deviates from its standard (that is, from its

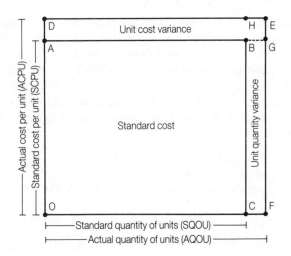

Figure 7.9   **Standard cost elements and variances in product cost.**

The standard cost of a product is what it should cost under normal circumstances. A variance is the difference between the plan and actual values of a parameter. Each element of product cost (see Figure 7.8) is a unit cost multiplied by a unit quantity. Either or both of these can deviate from standard during a period. This figure presents a useful way of illustrating the general case. Area OABC represent the standard cost of a product cost element and area ODEF represents its actual cost. The geometry shows that the difference between these two areas is area ADEG + area CBGF. That is, the cost element variance is the sum of the unit cost variance and the unit quantity variance. This is an unsurprising result, but it conceals the arbitrary (though conventional) assignment of area BHEG to the unit cost variance.

planned level), there will be a corresponding product cost element variance. In the general case, both the unit cost and unit quantity parameters deviate from their standard during the period of interest.

A way of illustrating this general case is shown in Figure 7.9, where the rectangular areas represent a particular product cost element. In the figure, the vertical dimension of the area OABC is **standard cost per unit** (SCPU), and the horizontal dimension is **standard quantity of units** (SQOU). This area, therefore, represents a standard cost. SQOU is simply the number of standard units contained within the standard cost, but the way in which SCPU is measured depends on which cost element is involved. For example:

- In the case of the direct labour cost element, SCPU is typically measured in £s per hour.

- In the case of the direct materials cost element, SCPU is measured in a manner appropriate to the materials concerned, such as cost per unit area or cost per unit length. Alternatively, SCPU may be the unit cost of a specific component or sub-assembly.

- In the case of the overhead cost element, SCPU is typically measured in £s per hour or £s per product unit, depending on the way in which total overhead is shared across all the products. In the latter case, the SQOU number is 1, because of the way in which the overhead element is defined.

A variance is conventionally defined as the difference between the actual value and the standard value of the parameter. The (large) area ODEF in Figure 7.9 is defined by a vertical dimension of **actual cost per unit** (ACPU) and a horizontal dimension of **actual quantity of units** (AQOU). Each of these parameters is greater (in this case) than the corresponding standard, so the cost element in question is subject to two 'bad' variances. The **total cost variance** is the difference between the areas ODEF and OABC (which is the area in the figure shaped like an inverted L). Expressing this mathematically:

$$\text{Standard Cost} = \text{SCPU} \times \text{SQOU} \tag{7.8}$$
$$\text{Actual Cost} = \text{ACPU} \times \text{AQOU} \tag{7.9}$$
$$\text{Total Cost Variance} = \text{Actual Cost} - \text{Standard Cost}$$
or
$$\text{Total Cost Variance} = (\text{ACPU} \times \text{AQOU}) - (\text{SCPU} \times \text{SQOU}) \tag{7.10}$$

Now, Equation 7.10 does not reveal how much of the total cost variance is due to **unit cost variance** and how much is due to **unit quantity variance**. But, however these two contributory variances are defined, the relationship:

$$\text{Total Cost Variance} = \text{Unit Cost Variance} + \text{Unit Quantity Variance}$$

must be valid.

The definitions of unit cost variance and unit quantity variance do present a problem (if matters are to be kept simple) due to the overlap area BHEG which should, strictly, be shared between them. However, the conventional, and entirely arbitrary, solution to this problem defines the contributory variances as:

$$\text{Unit Cost Variance} = (\text{ACPU} - \text{SCPU})\text{AQOU} \tag{7.11}$$

which is the area ADEG, and

$$\text{Unit Quantity Variance} = (\text{AQOU} - \text{SQOU})\text{SCPU} \tag{7.12}$$

which is the area CBGF. The geometry of Figure 7.9 confirms that these definitions do satisfy the required relationship:

$$\text{Total Cost Variance} = \text{Unit Cost Variance} + \text{Unit Quantity Variance}$$

Standard costing and variances: An example

The standard costing technique is not as complicated as it might appear at a first reading of the preceding summary. The following example aims to demonstrate the validity of this claim.

Table 7.6 is a simplified version of the standard cost build-up for Product X. It happens to be an electronic product but this has no significance beyond the fact that it determines, to a large extent, the items on the direct materials list.

Tables of this sort are sometimes called **cost cards**. The sample shown here has been simplified by reducing the list of direct materials (number 2 in the left-hand column) to just a few items. The abbreviations SQOU and SCPU mean standard quantity of units and standard cost per unit, respectively, as before. In accountancy jargon, quantity of units is often termed **usage**, and cost per unit is often shortened to just 'cost'.

Product X		Standard costs			1 off
Period: FY 1992/93					
Weeks: 01–48			£	£	£
	Units	SQOU	SCPU	Item	Total
1.　Direct labour:					
	hours	9.30	5.15		47.90
					———
2.　Direct materials:					
Chips type A	–	120	0.95	114.00	
Chips type B	–	15	4.50	67.50	
PC board	sq cm	22.30	0.45	10.04	
					191.53
					———
3.　Overheads:					
Variable	hours	9.30	1.26	11.70	
Fixed	hours	9.30	2.81	26.16	
					37.86
					———
			1 product units		277.29
					═══
Note:		Var £	Fx £	Hours	
Budget weeks 01–48		30,200	67,500	24,000	

Table 7.6 **Standard cost build-up for Product X (simplified).**
This is a simplified cost card showing the standard cost build-up for Product X. An extract from the production budget (bottom of card) shows that the anticipated production overhead cost for the year is £67,500 fixed plus £30,200 variable, which supports a total work capacity of 24,000 direct hours. Note that the SCPU fixed and variable overhead values on the card align with the budget figures. That is, in £s per hour:

$$2.81 = 67,500/24,000 \text{ and } 1.26 = 30,200/24,000 \text{ (very nearly).}$$

As presented, the cost card applies to the 1992/93 financial year which comprises **48 production weeks**. This implies that the production operation concerned is not active during the whole year. It probably closes over the Christmas to New Year period, and also for a period during the summer. The remaining productive time is divided into production weeks each containing about the same production capacity. Production weeks do not necessarily coincide with calendar weeks.

Some relevant information, extracted from the production budget, is included at the bottom of the card. This shows that the budgetary estimate for variable (Var) part of the production overhead is £30,200, and is £67,500 for the fixed (Fx) part. A productive capacity of 24 000 direct hours is also budgeted. These figures, of course, apply to the whole year of 48 'weeks'. The budget is **phased** (spread out over time) so as to assign about equal fractions of these figures to each production week.

Note that the SCPU values for the variable and fixed parts of the overhead cost element align with the budget figures. That is, in £s per hour:

$$1.26 = 30,200/24,000 \text{ and } 2.81 = 67,500/24,000 \text{ (very nearly)}$$

Product X Period: FY 1992/93 Weeks: 21–24	Units	Actual costs			90 off	Standard costs			90 off	Variances (£s)		90 off
		AQOU	£ ACPU	£ Item	£ Total	SQOU	£ SCPU	£ Item	£ Total	Unit Cost	Unit Quan'ty	Total
1. Direct labour:	hours	925	4.82		4,459	837	5.15		4,311	(305) F	453 A	148 A
2. Direct materials:												
Chips type A	–	11,880	0.90	10,692		10,800	0.95	10,260		(594) F	1026 A	432 A
Chips type B		1,260	4.95	6,237		1,350	4.50	6,075		567 A	(405) F	162 A
PC board	sq cm	2,230	0.45	1,004		2,007	0.45	903		0 F	100 A	100 A
					17,933				17,238	(27) F	721 F	694 A
3. Overheads:												
Variable	hours	925	1.44	1,331		837	1.26	1,053		167 A	111 A	278 A
Fixed	hours	925	2.88	2,667		837	2.81	2,354		65 A	247 A	313 A
					3,998				3,407	232 A	358 A	591 A
		90 product units			26,389	90 product units			24,956	Total variance:		1,433 A
Note: Total weeks 21–24		Var £ 2,770	Fx £ 5,550	Hours 1,925		Var £ 2,517	Fx £ 5,625	Hours 2,000		Var £ 253 A	Fx £ (75) F	Hours 75 A

Table 7.7 Actual costs, standard costs and variances for Product X.

This is a variance report on the manufacture and test of 90 units of Product X (see the standard cost card of Table 7.6) over a four week period. Note (bottom of report) the actual and standard information relating to overhead costs and direct hours. Variances are labelled with A (adverse) or F (favourable). Adverse variances dominate the report. The larger ones are investigated first.

The cost build-up is then merely a matter of simple arithmetic. But note that each element of the total standard cost, of £277.29 per product unit, involves a quantity of units and a cost per unit.

Now, during the course of the year, a requirement arises to produce 100 units of Product X. This is scheduled to occur over the four week period from weeks 21 to 24 inclusive, which is one of the twelve **production month** accounting periods in the year. In fact, only 90 product units are made during that period.

The figures presented by the accountants in their report to management on this (routine) situation are shown in Table 7.7. (This table employs the accounting convention which encloses negative figures in parentheses.)

The format of the table is similar to that of the standard cost card (Table 7.6), but it contains separate sections for actual costs, standard costs and variances.

Note first (at the bottom of the table), the actual and standard information relating to overhead costs and direct hours. The figures in the (middle) standard section are obtained by dividing the corresponding budget figures by 12. Those in the (left) actual section report what happened! The variable part of the overhead appears to be running ahead of budget (bad news), but less fixed overhead cost than budgeted has occurred (good news). Actual direct hours are less than budget (bad news). The actual variable and fixed overhead costs yield, when divided by the actual direct hours, the ACPU values for the overhead rates (in the body of the table).

The unit quantities entered into the actual and standard cost sections correspond to the 90 product units made in the period. This ensures that the variances tabulated in the variance section are based on comparable actual and standard figures. The variances are calculated in accordance with Equations 7.11 and 7.12. The reader may care to confirm these results as an exercise in manipulating the equations.

It will be observed that the variance equations are arranged such that an **adverse variance** (actual cost greater than standard cost) is positive; whereas a **favourable variance** (actual cost less than standard cost) is negative. This convention is contrary to another accountancy convention which arranges bad news to be negative, and vice versa. However, it is also usual to label each variance as adverse or favourable with an 'A' or 'F' as appropriate. This practice has been followed in Table 7.7.

Adverse variances are in a majority in the Product X report: a situation which, sadly, is all too common. In contemplating such a report, the managers would focus first on the larger adverse variances in the extreme right-hand (total) column. For example, that for 'Chips type A' might repay further investigation. It is a combination of a favourable unit cost variance and an adverse unit quantity variance. Perhaps the cheaper than standard chips are of less than standard quality, leading to a greater than standard reject rate and, hence, greater usage.

7.8.3 Section conclusion

All aspects of product cost and costing are critical within a manufacturing business, since the cost of products sold is invariably the major annual cost incurred by such businesses. This section has concentrated on the structure of product costs and has introduced the technique of standard costing as a means of planning and controlling such costs. Standard costing is not a panacea for all product cost problems, but it is a widely used technique. It can, however, be a source of confusion under some circumstances. These are considered in the next section, which is concerned with the profit equation.

7.9 # The profit equation revisited

The fact that business life is dominated by the profit equation:

Profit = Revenue − Cost   **(7.1)**

was emphasized at the beginning of this chapter. The point was also made that businesses operating in a competitive trading environment must seek to maximize their profit in order to survive and prosper. This section now re-examines the profit equation in the light of some of the ideas about cost discussed in the earlier sections. It also examines the important concepts of marginal theory. This is an approach to problem solving borrowed from the economists. It is developed in all economic textbooks. Those by Begg *et al.* (1984) and Parkin (1990) are particularly recommended. The marginal approach analyses the effect of a small (that is, a *marginal*) change in the current position of a business. If the small change is beneficial then the current position is clearly not the optimum, suggesting that a more significant change should be made. On the other hand, if the effect of the small change is adverse, it may indicate that the current position is the optimum.

The discussion initially focuses on the relationship between the level of product output (and product sales) and profit. This is followed by a comparison of the full (or standard) and marginal approaches to costing. However, the profit equation involves revenue as well as cost. The relationship between revenue and product output is, therefore, considered first.

7.9.1 Demand curves

Consider the case of a business producing a particular product which is competing for sales with other very similar, or identical, products. One of the most obvious and simple ways in which the business can increase the rate of sales of its product is to reduce the product price. The effect is shown in Figure 7.10.

Here, it is assumed that the rate of sales (in product units per month, say) is always equal to the rate of product production. This means that the business sells all the products it makes as it makes them. It achieves this happy position by reducing the unit price according to the output level (and sales level) selected. However, the production operation does have a finite maximum capacity. This is set at 100 in the figure, so the horizontal output rate axis is scaled as a percentage of the maximum capacity.

A relationship between unit price (UP) and rate of sales (r) is called a **demand curve**, where the **demand** is the rate of sales. A linear relationship of the form:

$$UP = UP_0(1 - rD)$$ **(7.13)**

is assumed in the figure, where UP_0 is the initial unit price (at which no products are sold) and D is a discount factor. In this illustration, UP_0 is set at 100 and D at 0.005. This is a discount factor of 0.5% for each 1% increase in output level: that is, the unit

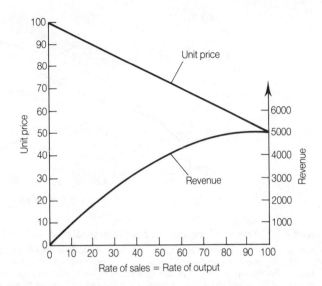

Figure 7.10 **Demand curves: unit price and revenue.**
A business competing with others for sales in a specific product market can generally increase unit sales by reducing unit price. The effect is shown here, where it is assumed that the rate of sales (in product units per month, say) is always equal to the rate of output (product production), so the business sells all the products it makes, as it makes them. It does this by reducing unit price according to the demand curve, which defines the relationship between unit price (UP) and rate of sales (r) for the market. A linear relationship is assumed here. Note that, because the demand curve has a negative gradient, the gradient of the revenue curve declines from its initial positive value as the output level increases. Its value may pass through zero and even go negative at high output levels.

price declines by 50% over the whole available output range. (There is nothing magic or special about these figures, they are used purely to quantify the illustration.)

The revenue curve is obtained simply by multiplying unit price by units sold. That is:

$$\text{Revenue} = UP_0(1 - rD)r \tag{7.14}$$

Note that, because the unit price decreases as the output rate increases, the revenue does not increase in proportion to the output rate. There is an important point here. This is that, because the demand curve has negative slope, the slope of the revenue curve declines from its initial positive value as the output level increases. Its value may pass through zero and even go negative at high output levels. This type of behaviour in the slope of the revenue curve is quite general when the demand curve has a negative slope.

In the illustration developed here, Equation 7.14 can be differentiated to yield an analytic expression:

$$\text{Slope of the Revenue Curve} = UP_0(1 - 2rD) \tag{7.15}$$

which is positive when r is less than $1/2D$, zero when $r = 1/2D$ and negative when r is greater than $1/2D$. Thus, the revenue first increases to a maximum as the output level

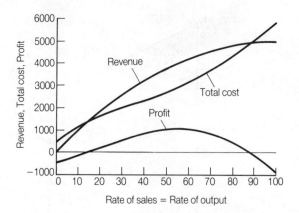

Figure 7.11   The profit equation: revenue, total cost and profit.

A cost curve, of the semi-variable type, is superimposed on the revenue curve of Figure 7.10 to create this figure. The fixed cost element (intercept on the vertical axis) represents costs which do not vary with the output level. A variable cost element, which increases (nonlinearly here) with the output level, is added to the fixed element. The profit curve tracks the difference between corresponding revenue and cost values, as required by the profit equation. Note that there are two break-even points, where revenue and total cost are equal and profit is zero. The profit is a maximum at about fifty-five per cent of maximum capacity. This is the (economic) optimum output level for the business in the illustration. Note, too, that this business is *not* profitable when the sales revenue is at its maximum.

increases and then declines. Here the maximum of 5,000 occurs at the maximum output capacity, but this is just a coincidence of the figures used.

Demand curves usually do have a negative slope. Just occasionally the slope is zero, which indicates that the business can sell all that it produces without reducing the unit price. A small supplier in a large market may be in this position, because its contribution to the total market is too small to affect market price. Demand curves with a positive slope, denoting products which become more attractive to customers as their price is increased, are not unknown. But they are sufficiently rare to be ignored.

7.9.2   Revenue, cost and profit

Cost is also a function of the rate of output. The form of a typical curve, which is of the semi-variable type, is shown in Figure 7.11.

There is a fixed cost element, measured by the intercept on the vertical axis where the rate of output is zero. This represents business costs which do not vary with the output level, and it includes the fixed costs of the production operation. A variable element, which increases with the output level, is added to the fixed element. It includes all the direct costs of production and the variable overhead costs for the whole business. **Cost efficiency** is usually relatively low (shown by a relatively steep slope on the cost curve) at low output levels, but then improves as the output level increases. At higher levels, cost efficiency tends to fall off again as, say, increasing pressure causes machinery faults and overtime working (at overtime rates) becomes the norm.

The revenue curve from Figure 7.10 is also shown in Figure 7.11. The profit curve is then the difference between corresponding revenue and cost values, as required by the profit equation.

Note that there are two break-even points in this figure, where revenue and total cost are equal and profit is zero (compare Figure 7.5, which has just one break-even point). This arises principally because of the shape of the revenue curve. There is a regime of positive profit extending (in this illustration) from about fifteen per cent of maximum output capacity to just less than ninety per cent. Outside this regime, at both low and high output levels, profit is negative: that is, the business is running at a loss.

The profit is a maximum at about fifty-five per cent of maximum capacity. This, therefore, is the (economic) optimum output level for the business in the illustration. It is set by the shape of the revenue and cost curves and their interaction in the profit equation. The shape of the revenue curve depends only on the demand curve. Note that the output rate for maximum profit (about fifty-five per cent) and that for maximum revenue (one hundred per cent) are very different. Thus, there is no merit in striving to achieve maximum revenue unless, of course, the aim is to embarrass competitors by grabbing some of their market share. Clearly, this tactic carries with it a danger of going out of business!

7.9.3 The marginal approach

The slope of the revenue curve is the **marginal revenue** (MR). This is the change in revenue, at a particular output level, arising from selling one more (or one less) unit. Similarly, the slope of the cost curve is the **marginal cost** (MC). This quantity is the change in cost, at a particular output level, arising from producing one more (or one less) unit.

Now suppose, in Figure 7.11, that the business is operating at an output level less than the optimum (which is about fifty-five per cent). It then increases output by one product unit, which is sold. As a result of this small change to the operating point the revenue increases by MR and the cost increases by MC. So the change in profit, which is the **marginal profit** (MP), is given by:

$$MP = MR - MC \tag{7.16}$$

When the output level is less than optimum, MR is greater than MC and the marginal profit is positive: the small change is beneficial. This confirms that the current operating point is not the optimum. So long as marginal revenue is greater than marginal cost the business should increase output and sales because marginal profit is positive, and the profit increases as the output level increases. The optimum operating point is at the output level where marginal revenue and marginal cost are equal, and marginal profit is zero. If the output level is increased beyond this point the marginal profit becomes negative and the profit decreases. The marginal profit is, of course, the slope of the profit curve.

Equation 7.16 above, and the commentary that follows it, is true in general, not just in the case of the illustration used to develop it. The central point is that the optimum output and sales levels occur when marginal revenue is equal to marginal cost.

(At this point it must be pointed out that few, if any, businesses use marginal theory

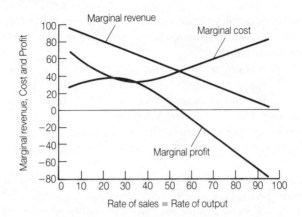

***Figure 7.12*   The profit equation: marginal revenue, cost and profit.**

Marginal revenue (MR), marginal cost (MC) and marginal profit (MP) are simply the slopes or
gradients of the corresponding curves (in Figure 7.11, say). Now, the profit equation is
Profit = Revenue − Cost. So, differentiating both sides of this equation with respect to rate of
output yields MP = MR − MC. The graphs illustrate that expression for the business described in
Figure 7.11. Note that the profit is a maximum when MP = 0 and MR = MC. Thus, the optimum
output and sales levels occur when marginal revenue is equal to marginal cost. Note, too, that the
commentary in the text arrives at the same key conclusion with a (longer) non-mathematical
argument which is more illuminating than this one!

experiments to determine the optimum activity level of their sales and production
operations. But the knowledge that there is an optimum operating point provides a
powerful incentive to strive for it. Those managers who achieve that happy position
seem to do so more by instinct and 'hunch', than by any deep analysis.)

The marginal revenue, marginal cost and marginal profit for the curves of Figure
7.11 are plotted in Figure 7.12. The linear nature of the marginal revenue curve
reflects Equation 7.15. The cost curve of Figure 7.11 is not analytic, so it is
differentiated 'by hand' to yield the marginal cost curve. The marginal profit curve is
then obtained from Equation 7.16.

Full costing and marginal costing compared

The analysis of Section 7.9.2 takes both the fixed and variable elements of total cost
into account. It is termed, therefore, a **full cost analysis**. The **marginal cost
analysis** now developed in this section is just another way of looking at the same
problem. Its emphasis, however, is on the effect of changing situation parameters
which vary with the activity level (which is output rate in this case).

For example, the marginal technique ignores the fixed cost parameter of the
optimum output problem, because it has no influence on the optimum choice of
output level. This observation may be better appreciated by looking at Figure 7.11
again. The fixed cost element of the total cost is its value at zero output level, which is
where the curve meets the vertical axis. If this fixed cost is changed it merely moves
the total cost curve bodily up or down, and has no effect on its shape. Under these
circumstances, it can be readily seen that the optimum output level does not change.
Of course, the maximum profit obtained at the optimum output will vary in 'anti-

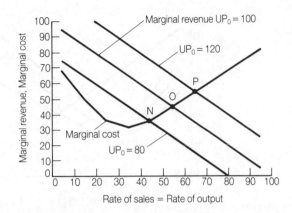

Figure 7.13 **The profit equation: effects of shifts in marginal revenue.**
The linear demand curve assumed in Figure 7.10 can be recast to show that, at a fixed discount rate, the market demand at a given unit price increases as the initial unit price (UP_0) increases. This figure shows the effect of changes in demand on marginal revenue and, hence, on the optimum (maximum profit) operating point. When market demand is depressed (by setting $UP_0 = 80$) the optimum output level is reduced to the point N, whereas it is increased to the point P when the market demand is improved (by setting $UP_0 = 120$).

phase' with variation of the fixed cost element. There is an important point here. Marginal analysis will reveal the optimum output level but it reveals nothing about the value of the maximum profit at that level. So the maximum profit might, in fact, be the minimum loss! The marginal technique is widely employed as a decision aiding tool in many other facets of business and a similar caveat applies to all such analyses. The full costing and marginal costing methods are, therefore, complementary rather than competitive. This relationship will become more clear as further examples are considered later in this section.

Shifts in marginal revenue and marginal cost

Returning now to the illustration of the marginal approach in Figure 7.12, it is instructive to consider the effects of 'vertical' shifts in marginal revenue and marginal cost.

Consider the demand curve of Figure 7.10, which is defined by Equation 7.13:

$$UP = UP_0(1 - rD)$$ (7.13)

This can be recast as:

$$r = \frac{(1 - UP/UP_0)}{D}$$ (7.13a)

to express the market demand (which is the rate of sales), r, as a function of the other parameters. So, keeping the discount rate (D) constant, the market demand at a given unit price (UP) increases as the initial unit price (UP_0) increases. (In other words, the bigger the demand, the higher the price can be set for a given output level.)

In Figure 7.10, the initial value of the unit price is 100. Reducing it to 80, say, reduces the market demand and increasing it to 120, say, increases the market

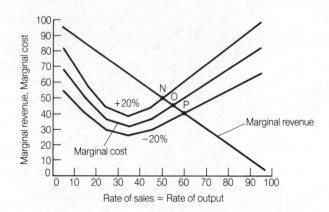

Figure 7.14   The profit equation: effects of shifts in marginal cost.
This figure is similar to Figure 7.13, and point O represents the same conditions in both figures. But here the marginal cost is varied (by +20% and −20%) rather than the marginal revenue. When the marginal cost is increased, the optimum output level is reduced to point N, but it is increased to point P when marginal cost is reduced. Once again, the impact of these changes shows up clearly in the marginal analysis.

demand. The effect of these changes on the optimum output level is shown in Figure 7.13, which plots marginal revenue and marginal cost.

When market demand is depressed the optimum output level is reduced to the point N, whereas it is increased to the point P when the market demand is improved. Thus, the impact of changes in demand and, hence, changes in marginal revenue show very clearly in the marginal analysis. But note that no information is obtained about the level of the profit at either point N or point P.

Suppose now that UP_0 is restored to its initial value of 100, but the slope (not the initial value) of the total cost curve in Figure 7.11 is varied by the same amount at every point. This is equivalent to varying the marginal cost by that amount. Figure 7.14 shows the effect of shifts of plus and minus twenty per cent in marginal cost.

When the marginal cost is increased, the optimum output level is reduced to point N, but it is increased to point P when marginal cost is reduced. Once again, the impact of these changes shows up clearly in the marginal analysis. But no absolute profit information is obtained.

7.9.4   The profit equation: Examples

This section uses a number of worked examples, focused around the profit equation, to further illustrate the complementary nature of full and marginal costing. The first of these examples is based on a simplified version of the optimum output level illustration developed in Sections 7.9.2 and 7.9.3.

Example 1: Revenue, cost and profit
The problem
A business is operating in a competitive environment in which the market price for its product and its total operating costs are related to the rate of product production by

the equations:

$$UP = UP_0(1 - rD) \tag{7.17}$$
$$TC = FC + Kr \tag{7.18}$$

where:

- UP is the product unit price
- $UP_0 = £150$ is its value at zero product output
- r is the rate of product output (in units/month)
- $D = 7.5 \times 10^{-6}$ is the discount rate per product unit
- TC is the total cost
- $FC = £1M$ is the fixed cost
- $K = £37.64$ per unit is the (constant) slope of the cost curve.

The business wishes to know:

(1) The break-even value(s) of product output (r), and the corresponding values of revenue and total cost.
(2) The value of product output for the maximum revenue, and the value of that maximum revenue.
(3) The value of product output for maximum profit, and the value of that profit.

The solution

Now, from Equation 7.17, the revenue (R) is given by:

$$R = UP_0(r - r^2D) \tag{7.19}$$

and the profit (P) is:

$$P = R - TC \tag{7.20}$$

Note that the total cost is linearly related to the output rate by Equation 7.18 (this is a common assumption).

There are two ways of solving the problem from this point: graphically (easy with a spreadsheet) or analytically (easy with a calculator). But both methods are a bit tedious. The graphical solution is quite adequate in view of the assumptions implicit in the problem statement and it illustrates the situation rather well. It is shown in Figure 7.15.

The analytic solution needs some more equations. For the break-even points, the profit is zero when:

$$0 = r^2 - r(UP_0 - K)/(UP_0D) + FC/(UP_0D) \tag{7.21}$$

which yields 9,877 units/month for the low output level and 89,999 units/month for the high output level. The corresponding values of revenue (and cost) are £1,371,758 and £4,387,558, respectively.

Differentiating Equation 7.19 shows that the maximum revenue occurs when:

$$r = 1/(2D) \tag{7.22}$$
$$= 66,667 \text{ units/month}$$

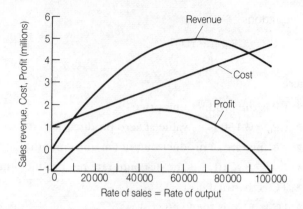

Figure 7.15 **Example 1: revenue, cost and profit.**
The graphs solve the problem presented in Example 1 in Section 7.9.4. The figure is a simplified version of Figure 7.11, because both the (underlying) demand curve *and* the total cost curve are assumed to be linear. The analytic solution allowed by these assumptions is toiled through in the text.

The maximum revenue is then (from Equation 7.19) £5,000,000.

Using the marginal method, the maximum profit occurs when MR = MC, that is when:

$$UP_0(1 - 2rD) = K$$

or when:

$$r = (UP_0 - K)/(2UP_0D) \tag{7.23}$$
$$= 49,938 \text{ units/month}$$

The maximum profit is then £1,805,504.

Example 2: A make or buy decision
The problem
A business makes 100,000 units/month of a particular piece-part for subsequent incorporation into one of its products. The standard works cost of the piece-part is £14.50 per unit. A known and trusted supplier offers to sell the piece-part to the business in the requisite quantities for £13.50 per unit.

Should the business now cease to make the piece-part in favour of buying it from the supplier?

The cost card for the piece-part shows that the standard works cost is made up of:

- Direct labour   £7.00
- Direct materials   £4.30
- Variable overhead   £1.25
- Share of fixed overhead £1.95

If the piece-part is purchased it is estimated that the following additional local costs will be incurred for each unit:

1. Standard (full) costing analysis

	Cost to make			Cost to buy
£s per unit:			£s per unit:	
Direct labour	7.00		Purchasing costs	0.01
Direct materials	4.30		Purchase price	13.50
Variable overhead	1.25		Additional: inspection	0.29
			Storage	0.10
Variable costs	12.55		Transport	0.10
Share of fixed overhead	1.95			
Standard works cost	14.50		Bought-in cost	14.00
Apparent saving by buying	100,000	units per month:		
£s per unit	0.50		£s per month	50,000

2. Marginal costing analysis

	Savings if bought			Cost to buy
£s per unit:			£s per unit:	
Direct labour	7.00		Purchasing costs	0.01
Direct materials	4.30		Purchase price	13.50
Variable overhead	1.25		Additional: inspection	0.29
			Storage	0.10
			Transport	0.10
Marginal cost	12.55		Bought-in cost	14.00
Saving by buying	100,000	units per month:		
£s per unit	(1.45)		£s per month	(145,000)

Table 7.8 **Two ways of analysing a 'make or buy' situation.**
The table relates to the problem presented in Example 2 in Section 7.9.4. It shows a wrong way (upper half) and right way (lower half) of making a 'make or buy' decision. The standard cost build-up of the unit in question includes a share of fixed overhead, because it is compiled on a full cost basis. If the fixed overhead really is fixed, it will not be changed by choosing not to make the unit. In fact, a decision to buy rather than make would 'cost' the business £145,000 per month (fixed overhead cost of £195,000 offset by £50,000 savings) which would have to be recovered on some other product or piece-part.

- Purchasing costs   £0.01
- Inspection   £0.29
- Storage   £0.10
- Transport   £0.10

The solution

Note that the additional local costs add £0.50 to the purchase cost of the piece part, bringing its bought-in cost to £14.00. This is still £0.50 less than its standard works cost. The easy answer, therefore, is 'buy rather than make' because this seems to save the business £50,000 per month.

But this answer is wrong!

	Product Range 1 £	Product Range 2 £	Product Range 3 £	Totals £
Sales revenue:	155,000	200,000	170,000	525,000
Less production costs:				
Variable	52,500	78,250	63,500	194,250
Fixed	22,500	35,550	32,500	90,550
	75,000	113,800	96,000	284,800
Gross profit:	80,000	86,200	74,000	240,200
Less other costs:				
Variable	42,500	56,700	62,500	161,700
Fixed	5,600	8,750	14,250	28,600
	48,100	65,450	76,750	190,300
Profit/(Loss):	31,900	20,750	(2,750)	49,900

Table 7.9   **A portfolio of mini-busineses: total cost format.**
The profit and loss account shown here relates to the problem presented in Example 3 in Section 7.9.4. The right-hand column sums the performance of the three mini-businesses which comprise the whole business. Note that each mini-business has been allocated a share of the total fixed costs incurred by the whole business. The mini-business attempting to earn a living from Product Range 3 is showing a small loss.

The standard cost includes a share of the fixed overhead, because it is compiled on a full cost basis. If the fixed overhead really is fixed, it will not be changed by choosing not to make the piece-part. So it is irrelevant to the make or buy decision, which must be approached on a marginal basis. Table 7.8 shows the detailed working for both methods, wrong and right.

Note that a decision to buy rather than make would actually 'cost' the business £145,000 per month (in fixed overhead which would have to be recovered on some other product or piece-part). The correct answer, therefore, is to continue to make the piece-part.

Example 3: A portfolio of mini-businesses
The problem
A business divides its operations into three mini-businesses, each of which is focused on a particular product range. The year-end profit and loss account is shown in Table 7.9.

Product Range 3 is showing a small loss for the year just ended, and its prospects for the current year are for much the same performance. The management is considering whether to close that mini-business down. Is this the correct decision? A new, and more promising, product range is in development/design but it is at least one year away from market launch.

The solution
If the Product Range 3 mini-business had not existed during the year just ended it is

	Product Range 1 £	Product Range 2 £	Product Range 3 £	Totals £
Sales revenue:	155,000	200,000	170,000	525,000
Less variable costs:				
Production	52,500	78,250	63,500	194,250
Other	42,500	56,700	62,500	161,700
	95,000	134,950	126,000	355,950
Contribution:	60,000	65,050	44,000	169,050
Less fixed costs:				
Production				90,550
Other				28,600
				119,150
Profit/(Loss):				49,900

Table 7.10   **A portfolio of mini-businesses: marginal cost format.**
The profit and loss account shown here also relates to the problem presented in Example 3 in Section 7.9.4. It presents the same information as Table 7.9, but in a way which allows the relative merits of the mini-businesses to be compared before they are assigned shares of the total fixed overhead costs. Here, the variable costs incurred by each mini-business are subtracted from its revenue to yield the 'contribution' it makes to the total fixed overhead. This 'marginal cost' presentation makes it very clear that closing down the Product Range 3 mini-business will remove a contribution of £44,000 to the fixed costs. Unless the closure will be accompanied by a matching (at least) reduction in those costs (unlikely) the idea should be abandoned.

tempting to suppose the other two mini-businesses would have delivered a combined profit of:

$$£31,900 + £20,750 = £52,650.$$

This temptation must be resisted, because it is a snare and a delusion.

The profit and loss account of Table 7.9 is constructed on a full cost basis. Fixed overhead costs of £46,750 (£32,500 production plus £14,250 other) are assigned to the Product Range 3 mini-business. If the Product Range 3 mini-business had not existed during the year just ended, these fixed overheads would have to be charged to the other two mini-businesses. In that case, the end of year profit would have been:

$$£52,650 - £46,750 = £5,900.$$

So, despite the fact that the Product Range 3 mini-business is running at a loss, it *is* making a welcome contribution to the whole business by paying for its share of the fixed overhead. So, unless its share of the fixed overhead can be substantially removed (never easy), closing down Product Range 3 is not a smart move.

Note that the full cost presentation of Table 7.9 is a perfectly valid and, indeed, commonplace way of showing how mini-businesses contribute to a larger business. But the same information can be presented in a marginal cost format which allows the

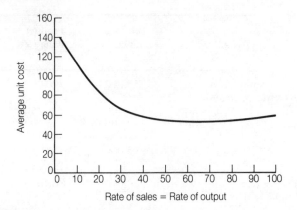

Figure 7.16 **The economies of scale: cost per product unit.**

A typical real-life variation of total cost with the rate of product production is shown in Figure 7.11. The variable element is nonlinear and its slope steepens at high output levels. (The effect is shown more clearly in Figure 7.12.) Here, cost per product unit is plotted as a function of product output rate. Note that unit cost falls rapidly as the output level is increased from zero, goes through a minimum, and then increases at the higher output levels. The initial fall is the 'economies of scale' effect, whereas the subsequent rise is the 'diseconomies of scale' effect. The most important factor causing the fall in unit cost as output increases from a low level is that the fixed costs are spread across an increasing number of units (compare with Figure 7.6). The subsequent rise in unit cost is explained in the text.

relative merits of the mini-businesses to be compared before they are assigned shares of the fixed overhead. This presentation is shown in Table 7.10.

Here, the variable costs associated with each mini-business are subtracted from its revenue to yield a quantity called the **contribution**. This is the contribution each mini-business makes to the total fixed overhead. If the sum of the contributions exceeds the fixed overhead the whole business makes a profit, as happens in this case. Observe that, if the Product Range 3 mini-business is removed from this profit/loss account, then the total contribution is reduced by £44,000. The profit is, of course, then reduced by the same amount to a value of £5,900, as before.

7.9.5 Product unit cost

This section now concludes with a brief examination of the phenomena known as **the economies and diseconomies of scale**. Figure 7.11 shows a variation of total cost with the rate of product production which is typical of most manufacturing situations. This is a semi-variable variation which may be regarded as the sum of a fixed cost element, measured by the intersection with the vertical axis, and a variable element. The variable element is nonlinear, as is usually the case in practice. In particular, the rate at which the total cost increases steepens perceptibly at high output levels. The effect is shown more clearly in Figure 7.12, because marginal cost is the slope of the total cost curve.

Figure 7.16 plots the cost per product unit as a function of product output rate. The cost of a product unit at a specific output level is obtained by dividing the total cost at that level by the output rate at that level. Note that the unit cost first falls rapidly as the output level is increased, goes through a minimum, and then increases at the higher output levels. The decline in unit cost as the output level (or scale of the production operation) is first increased is the **economies of scale** effect, whereas the subsequent rise in unit cost is due to the **diseconomies of scale**.

The economies of scale

The most obvious factor contributing to the fall in unit cost, as output increases from a low level, is that the fixed costs are spread across an increasing number of units. But two other factors often enhance the effect by increasing, to some extent, the efficiency of the variable cost element. The first factor is specialization. As the scale of the operation increases, more production operators will generally be employed. This presents increasing opportunities for individual specialization and skill development, leading to the more efficient use of the people resources. The effect may be further improved by the second factor, which is the introduction of more cost-effective production machinery as the operation becomes profitable. The combined effect of these factors is reflected in the declining slope of the total cost curve at low to mid-range output levels.

The diseconomies of scale

A number of factors contribute to the disproportionate increase in total cost which ultimately causes unit costs to increase at the higher output levels. In terms of the production operation these include, perhaps, the need to pay premium rates to the operators for weekend and overtime working and machinery breakdown problems arising from deferred maintenance.

In a broader context, as the scale of an operation increases it becomes increasingly difficult to manage. There is a definite limit to the number of subordinates that can be properly managed by one individual. As a business becomes bigger, therefore, further layers of management are introduced to partition the whole task into manageable portions. But then the lines of communication become extended and the opportunities for confusion, bureaucracy and politics are much improved. People cease to identify with the mission of the business. Costs begin to increase more rapidly than output.

So 'big is beautiful' works only up to a certain point. Modern businesses do recognize the diseconomies of scale. One way in which they minimize the damage is to subdivide over-large businesses into a number of smaller businesses, in which the economies of scale still prevail.

7.10   Concluding summary

For a business, bigger costs mean smaller profits and smaller profits mean a reduced chance of survival and prosperity. Costs, therefore, are important. The largest fraction of the total costs incurred by a hardware manufacturing business are those incurred in making its products. Product design and product production engineers share substantial responsibility for product costs. Cost and costing, therefore, is a fundamental engineering topic. Good engineering is about exploiting technologies in a cost-effective way.

Cost and costing have quite a lot in common with other engineering topics: the basic concepts are not complicated and the need for judicious estimating abounds. The language of the topic, however, is the language of accounting. This chapter has introduced those basic cost concepts which are likely to be most useful to engineers and, hopefully, has done something to overcome the language barrier. It represents a solid foundation for a deeper study of the vast subject of cost and costing which most engineers must undertake as their careers develop.

REFERENCES

Begg D. K. H., Fischer S. and Dornbusch R. (1984). *Economics*. Maidenhead: McGraw-Hill (A US edition is also available)

Chapman C. B., Cooper D. F. and Page M. A. (1987). *Management for Engineers*. Chichester: John Wiley

Knott G. (1988). *Practical Cost and Management Accounting*. London: Pan

Parkin M. (1990). *Economics*. Reading, MA: Addison-Wesley. A British edition is also available: Parkin M. and King D. (1992). *Economics*. Wokingham: Addison-Wesley

White J. A., Agee M. H. and Case K. E. (1989). *Principles of Engineering Economic Analysis* 3rd edn. New York: John Wiley

SUGGESTED FURTHER READING

Berry & Jarvis (1991) is a particularly attractive text aimed specifically at the users of accounting information rather than intending accountants. It covers both management and financial accounting. This emphasis is less marked in the other texts listed, but all are entirely readable. Sizer (1989) interprets 'management accounting' quite widely and is good value for money.

Arnold J. and Hope T. (1990). *Accounting for Management Decisions* 2nd edn. Hemel Hempstead: Prentice-Hall

Berry A. and Jarvis P. (1991). *Accounting in a Business Context*. London: Chapman & Hall

Horngren C. T. and Sundem G. L. (1990). *Introduction to Management Accounting* 8th edn. Englewood Cliffs, NJ: Prentice-Hall

Sizer J. (1989). *An Insight into Management Accounting*. Harmondsworth: Penguin

QUESTIONS

7.1   Figure 7.1 illustrates the partitioning and terminology of 'cost' as that quantity appears in the profit and loss equation. Table 12.10, which is the 1991 P&L account of a small business, is a numerical expression of a similar cost structure.

Construct a diagram, in the format of Figure 7.1, which is based on the numbers in Table 12.10.

7.2 'Cost and costing is a fundamental engineering topic.' Why is it?

7.3 Why is 'profit', as conventionally defined, generally not the same as positive cash-flow?

7.4 What is a 'budget'? Explain, in the context of budgets and budgeting in a large company, the meaning of the following terms:

- financial year
- P&L centre
- P&L budget
- capital budget
- reconciliation.

Describe four basic types of cost which are likely to appear in a P&L budget.

7.5 A business buys a small item of test equipment for £1,000 cash on the first day of Year 1. It is used for three years and then sold, as scrap, for a net £100 cash on the last day of Year 3.

(a) A depreciation charge of £300 relating to this item is set against the total annual profit earned by the business in each of the Years 1, 2 and 3. Why?

(b) Complete the table below. It is designed to illustrate the profit and cash-flow effects of the purchase and sale of the item as an *isolated* transaction.

(c) Comment on the figures in the 'End Year 3' column.

7.6 Explain the following terms:

- direct cost
- indirect cost
- overhead cost.

7.7 Explain the following terms:

- activity variable
- fixed cost
- variable cost
- semi-variable cost.

7.8 A small business manufactures and sells 63 product units during the year to end of December 1991. The revenue arising from the sales is £70,875 and the total manufacturing cost of the units is £35,005, of which £12,002 is due to fixed production overhead costs.

(a) Assuming that product price remains constant over the year, how many product units must be sold to recover the fixed production overhead costs?

(b) Assuming that products are sold at a uniform rate during the year, when is the fixed production overhead cost recovered?

7.9 In Question 7.8, the cost of manufacturing the 63 product units sold during the year is £35,005, so the product works cost is £556 (to the nearest pound). If 100 units had been manufactured during the year, the product works cost falls to £485. Why?

7.10 In the context of technical departmental budgeting, explain the meaning of the following terms:

- direct staff
- direct costs
- other direct costs (ODCs)
- indirect staff
- total direct labour cost
- total overhead cost
- hours per direct (staff member)
- total direct hours (total work capacity)
- direct labour rate
- overhead rate
- labour plus overhead (L+O/H) rate

	Start Year 1	End Year 1	End Year 2	End Year 3
Incremental profit £				
Cumulative profit £				
Incremental cash-flow £				
Cumulative cash-flow £				

and show how these budget parameters are related.

7.11 The manager of the technical department in the Communications Division of Global Widgits PLC (see Figure 7.2) is discussing the budget for the next financial year with the departmental accountant. Their immediate task is to choose appropriate labour and overhead rates. The manager has come to the view that the department will be asked to deliver 53,190 direct hours of project work to its customers during the year. The accountant has estimated the following figures for the whole year:

- hours per direct engineer   = 1702
- average cost of employing one direct engineer   = £19,600
- total overhead cost   = £1,048,875

(a) Rounding up to the nearest penny, calculate the labour and overhead rates which will just recover the estimated departmental costs in the forthcoming financial year. How many direct engineers must be employed during the year?

(b) Having done these sums, the manager decides to:

- budget for a work capacity of 53,190 direct hours
- accept the estimate of 1702 hours per direct engineer
- build a 'safety factor' into the budget (in case there is difficulty in selling all of the budgeted direct hours)
- do this by increasing the overhead rate calculated in (a) by five per cent.

What is the safety factor, expressed as a percentage of budgeted direct hours, that the budget then contains? What is the effect of the safety factor on the budget cost of one hour of project work?

7.12 Compare and contrast the structure of product works cost with the structure of project cost.

7.13 In the context of standard costing, explain the meaning of the following terms:

- standard product cost
- product cost variance
- product cost element

- unit cost
- unit quantity
- standard cost per unit
- actual cost per unit
- standard quantity of units
- actual quantity of units.

The following parameters are reported for a specific product cost element at a particular time:

Standard cost per unit $= S_C$
Actual cost per unit $= A_C$
Standard quantity of units $= S_Q$
Actual quantity of units $= A_Q$

(a) Show that the total cost variance of the product cost element (TCV_E) is the sum of V_C and V_Q, where

- $V_C = (A_C - S_C)A_Q$ is the unit cost variance, and
- $V_Q = (A_Q - S_Q)S_C$ is the unit quantity variance.

(b) The variance definitions, as expressed here, employ two arbitrary conventions. What are these conventions?

7.14 The variance report of Table 7.11 is similar to Table 7.7. It shows the actual works cost performance of Product X, averaged over the whole of 1992/93, compared with the 1992/93 standard cost card for the product. But the variances have been omitted.

(a) Complete the table by calculating the variances, and label each one as 'favourable' (F) or 'adverse' (A) according to its sign.

(b) What is the most serious issue revealed by the variance report?

Note: Answer Question 7.15 *or* Question 7.16.

7.15 A profitable business is operating in a normal competitive market sector (where marginal demand is negative), and it can control the demand for its products by choosing product unit price. Its costs increase linearly, from a fixed base, as the rate at which it makes and sells products increases from zero. Show that, in general, there is a range of demands over which such a business is profitable, and that it is

Product X Period: FY 1992/93 Weeks: 01–48	Units	Actual costs AQOU Aq	£ ACPU Ac	£ Item	1 off £ Total Aq × Ac	Standard costs SQOU Sq	£ SCPU Sc	£ Item	1 off £ Total Sq × Sc	Variances (£s) Unit Cost	Unit Quantity	1 off Total
1. Direct labour:	hours	9.67	5.34		51.64	9.30	5.15		47.90	—	—	—
2. Direct materials:												
Chips type A	—	122.00	0.94	114.68		120.00	0.95	114.00				
Chips type B	—	15.00	4.45	66.75		15.00	4.50	67.50				
PC board	sq cm	27.50	0.62	17.05		22.30	0.45	10.04				
					198.48				191.53	—	—	—
3. Overheads:												
Variable	hours	9.67	1.41	13.66		9.30	1.26	11.70				
Fixed	hours	9.67	2.70	26.15		9.30	2.81	26.16				
					39.81				37.86	—	—	—
		1.00 product units			289.93	1.00 product units			277.29	Total variance:		

Note: Total weeks 01–48	Var £ 35,637	Fx £ 68,200	Hours 25,222	Var £ 30,200	Fx £ 67,500	Hours 24,000	Var £ 5,437 A	Fx £ 700	Hours A (1,222) F

Table 7.11   Works cost of Product X during 1992/93.

most profitable when marginal revenue is equal to marginal cost.

7.16 (a) What is a demand curve?
(b) A business operating in a particular competitive market sector forms the view that the demand (r) for its products is related to product unit price (UP) by the expression:

$$r = \frac{(1 - UP/UP_0)}{D} \qquad (7.13a)$$

where UP_0 and D are constants and the demand is measured as a rate of unit sales. What parameters are represented by the constants, UP_0 and D, in this expression? Sketch the form of the supposed relationship between UP and r, *taking UP to be the dependent variable*.
(c) By assuming that the business manufactures and sells its products to exactly match the demand, show that the revenue (R) earned from product sales is related to the demand by the expression:

$$R = UP_0(1 - rD)r \qquad (7.14)$$

Sketch the form of this revenue expression, and show that R is a maximum when $r = 1/2D$. What is the value of the marginal revenue (MR) when R is a maximum?
(d) It has been established that the total cost (TC), incurred by the business in manufacturing and selling its products, increases nearly linearly from a fixed base as r increases. The expression:

$$TC = FC + Kr \qquad (7.18)$$

is regarded as sufficiently accurate for practical purposes, where FC is the fixed cost base and K is a constant. How is K related to the marginal (total) cost (MC)? Sketch the total cost expression on the same diagram as that showing the revenue expression, such that R = TC at two points on the diagram.
(e) Sketch the form of the variation of profit with demand on this same diagram, and show that profit (P) is a maximum when MR = MC. What is the value of the marginal profit (MP) when the profit is at its maximum value.

7.17 The business described in Question 7.16 has a maximum manufacturing capacity of 100,000 units per annum, and:

- $UP_0 = £100$ is the lowest unit price at which none are sold
- $D = 7.5 \times 10^{-6}$ is the fractional price discount per unit sold
- $FC = £1.3M$ is the fixed cost
- $K = £37.64$ is the marginal cost per unit.

Calculate:
(a) The break-even value(s) of unit output rate and the corresponding values of revenue and total cost.
(b) The value of unit output rate for maximum revenue, and the value of that maximum revenue.
(c) The value of unit output rate for maximum profit, and the value of the maximum profit.
(d) Sketch the variations of revenue, total cost and profit as unit output rate is increased from zero to its maximum value. (Hint: calculate the maximum profit first.)

Structured Product Design

WHY some feature is needed moulds
WHAT it has to be, which in turn moulds
HOW it is to be achieved.

Douglas T. Ross and Kenneth E. Schoman, Jr

8.1	Motivation and content	338
8.2	Explanation of terms	339
8.3	The product purchasing decision	343
8.4	More about design and designers	346
8.5	Requirements definition: Design	352
8.6	More about functional architecture	362
8.7	More about design constraints	366
8.8	Product design: The whole process	370
8.9	Concluding summary	376

The overall objectives of this chapter are to describe a relatively informal but tightly structured product design methodology which is technology independent and applicable to any and every sort of product. This discourse is the focus of the whole book, because everything that comes before it and after it can be regarded as supporting material. Objectives by section follow:

8.1 To show why product design is important, to outline the characteristics of the featured approach, and to describe the contents of the chapter.

8.2 To define and explain the meaning of various design-related terms as they are used in the chapter.

8.3 To present a simple interpretation of why a customer chooses to buy a particular product from a number of competing products on offer.

8.4 To examine the problems of design and designers, and to demonstrate that the single most important aspect of product design is defining the right product to design.

8.5 To describe, by designing it, a requirements definition methodology which contains the definition of the right product to design.

8.6 To develop the concept of functional architecture as one element of the requirements definition.

8.7 To develop the concept of design constraints as another element of the requirements definition.

8.8 To extend the requirements definition methodology to embrace the whole of product design process, by treating the process as a sequence of model-to-model transformations.

8.9 To identify its salient points and summarize its major messages.

8.1   Motivation and content

Product design is important because, as markets become more competitive, its excellence or otherwise is a factor in business survival. 'We make it, they buy it' is no longer a tenable product strategy. The ability to design competitive products is (or should be) a distinguishing feature of a professional engineer. A broad knowledge base and a wide range of skills is required which include, but go well beyond, the expected competence in a particular set of related technologies. It is largely an exercise in the management of complexity. So management ability is one of the prerequisites, and product design is an excellent training ground for embryonic technical and general managers. The ability to analyse a problem and then synthesize an economic solution to it, which is what product design is about, is a personal attribute in great demand.

This chapter describes a powerful technique for designing products. It is totally technology independent and is applicable to all types of tangible (including software) and service products. But it is more than just a product design methodology. It is also a management tool, because it can be employed to design solutions to management problems. Most management problems are design problems in disguise. Management is about design, and design is about management.

It is a structured methodology. It is not, however, a rigid formal system with firm rules, notations, criteria and conventions. Much recent and current development work on formal design methodologies is directed at large computer-based systems and their software subsystems. Macro and Buxton (1987) survey the recent position in Chapter 7 of their treatise on software engineering. Many of the principles embodied in the specialized methodologies can be exploited on a broader front. But, as formulated, none of them is ideally suited to all stages in the design cycle, nor to all types of product. The purpose here is to introduce an approach of broad utility and, more importantly, to expound a way of thinking about the product design problem. It is a potent weapon in its own right and can serve as an introduction to the specialized methodologies.

The methodology presented in this chapter borrows some of the Ross (1977a), and Ross and Schoman (1977), Structured Analysis and Design Technique (SADT^{TM}) ideas and blends them with a simple marketing concept. This mixture is then seasoned with some penetrating insights into the subject due to Wassell (1979) and Freedman (1981) (private communications). The presentation takes the form of a description of the *design* of the methodology *using* the methodology. This is an exercise in recursion which should appeal to software engineers, and it provides an ongoing example of the technique. This starts at Section 8.5. It is preceded by some necessary background material relating to terminology, product purchasing decisions, the nature of the product design task, and the role of product designers in a business. Appendix A is another example of the methodology in case study format.

8.2 Explanation of terms

Many of the words and phrases used in this chapter mean different things to different people. The terms design, product and system, which have already been used, make the point. So the way in which these terms, and others, are used in this chapter (and elsewhere in the book) is first defined and explained.

8.2.1 About products

Products are tangible artefacts (manufactured things) or services offered for sale by an organization or business. Washing machines, for example, and motor cars, lathes, software packages, computers and telephone exchanges are tangible products. They have a physical presence with the (external) properties of weight, size, shape and colour. On the other hand, management consultancy, education and transport, to mention just a few, are service products. Such products encapsulate a package of specialist skills and facilities which is offered for sale, but has no physical presence in its own right. The acid test which distinguishes a tangible product from a service product is whether or not it can be stored. Tangible products can be made and stored in times of low demand. But it is only worthwhile scheduling undergraduate lectures, for instance, during term-time.

This book is concerned principally with tangible engineering products. Broadly speaking, these are of two sorts:

- **Repeatable products**, also called **high-volume products**. These are manufactured in substantial quantities (high volumes) as exact replicas of each other and sold in the same substantial quantities to, probably, very many different customers. Examples include nuts and bolts, electric kettles, wheelbarrows, standard integrated circuits, television sets and plumbing fittings.

- **Unique products**, also called **one-off products**. These are custom-built products tailored, to some degree, to match the special requirements of a particular customer. An air-traffic control system, a network of cash-points for a bank and a bridge are typical examples.

In fact, these two categories are the extremes of a broad spectrum which extends from high-value complex products sold in low volumes (communication satellites, say) to low-value simple products sold in high volumes (paperclips, say). The relationship between sales volume and complexity is virtually a law of nature. As product complexity increases so do cost, price and specialization, leading to lower demand. However, a variety of marketing ploys can distort this simple picture. For example, a certain popular small car is fundamentally a volume product but it is available (theoretically) in more than one million variations!

8.2.2 About systems

In common parlance, 'system' is one of those general purpose words generally used to denote something which is complicated. There are two problems with this usage. One is that complexity, like beauty, is a matter of individual taste. The other difficulty is that the word 'system' does not, in fact, mean 'complicated'.

Dictionary definitions of 'system' are usually of the form:

- a set of objects with relationships between them
- a collection of interrelated parts.

These are definitions which indicate how systems are constructed. But they carry no message about complexity. Nor are they very useful in contemplating the problems of product design, because they define any two or more related things as a system. Thus, a nut and bolt combination is just as much a system as the motor car it holds together or the world economy which includes them both. But these three systems present design problems which range from the trivial through challenging to impossible (on the evidence to date). The 'how' type definitions are less than helpful in another respect. As the physicists continue their explorations of astronomical and atomic infinities it becomes increasingly clear that everything in the universe is connected, in one way or another, to everything else. This is an awesome idea, but it does not really progress the cause of product design except in one important respect. This is the now self-evident fact that systems come in hierarchies. Figure 8.1 illustrates the point.

Thus no single system is self-sufficient. Every system is part of a larger system and

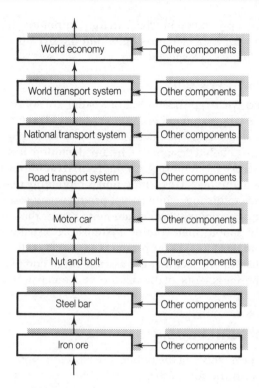

Figure 8.1 **A hierarchy of systems.**
Products are the things that businesses create and sell. All products are systems. All man-made systems are products. A 'how' view of a system describes it as a collection of interrelated parts. Thus, a nut–bolt pair is just as much a system as the motor car it holds together or the world economy which includes them both. So systems come in hierarchies, as illustrated here. A 'what' view of a system describes it as a tool for aiding the achievement of a specific human purpose. This is a better perspective for *product=system* design, because it partitions the hierarchy into manageable pieces. Each piece has a defined role in some overall scheme and interfaces with the other pieces in a defined way.

every system contains a number of smaller systems. (It should be appreciated that this is an engineering view of the universe: that is, it is sufficiently true to be useful.) So another definition of the word 'system' is required to distinguish the various systems within a hierarchy from each other. It is necessary to do this because they cannot be designed if they cannot be separated. This observation may explain some of the difficulties with the world economy.

The key is to focus on the system purpose. In other words, to think first in terms of *what* a system should do, rather than *how* it might do it (which is an important but secondary issue). This leads to a 'what' type definition:

- A **system** is a tool for aiding the achievement of a specific human purpose.

Discounting the arrogance which recognizes only human purposes, this definition is preferred. Its merit is that it suggests how big systems can be separated into smaller systems by distinguishing purposes or functions. It represent real progress in thinking about design. It provides a mechanism for partitioning the universe into manageable pieces, each with a specific mission within the overall scheme and communicating with its neighbours in a specific way.

Products and systems

The 'how' and 'what' type definitions of 'system' are not alternatives. Both are valid and neither makes any statement about complexity. The first illustrates the algorithmic nature of systems and the second shows how to partition the algorithms as a preliminary to detailed design. But, by any definition, it is now clear that all products are really systems. It is tempting, therefore, to treat the terms 'product' and 'system' as synonymous in this text. This temptation is regretfully rejected. Because (illogically), industry tends to distinguish between products and systems on the basis of relative sales volume or complexity, which amount to much the same thing in this connection. So, relatively simple high-volume systems are usually called 'products' whereas relatively complex low-volume products are usually called 'systems'. This confusion is not diminished by the fact that the assessment of complexity varies, of course, from business to business. None of this matters very much provided that the real situation is understood.

8.2.3   About product design

To the average member of the public, the words 'design' and 'designer' are associated principally with the form (shape) and colour of products, with little reference to functional attributes and performance. For example, it is just possible that some 'designer' garments do keep their wearers warm, dry and modest. But they are purchased for reasons to do with status-seeking and mating rituals, rather than as a defence against the environment. This appearance-dominated interpretation of 'design' is entirely reasonable for fashion products. The presentation of many domestic products is influenced by the same obsession: witness the external image of many cheap (and nasty) hi-fi products.

But a different concept is required for the 'engineering' products which are at the focus of this book. The value of such products, as perceived by the customer, is often dominated by functional attributes and performance. To illustrate the point, appearance certainly influences the sales of motor cars in the domestic sector but it has little influence on the purchaser of a fleet of company cars. Considerations of relative reliability, operating economy and terms of purchase will determine the choice under those circumstances.

Definitions of product development and design are given in Section 3.2.5 and are reiterated, in summary form, in Section 5.2.1. Those definitions of *technical* design activity are included within the following comprehensive definition of product design, which is a foundation stone of this chapter.

- **Product design(ing)** is the process of seeking a match between a set of customer-derived product requirements and a way of meeting those requirements, or of finding an acceptable compromise. It embraces everything that has to be done to provide an accurate and proven description of the matching or compromise product in manufacturing terms. It is not, therefore, confined just to the technical aspects of the task.

Competitive product design means performing the above process in a way which leads to products which are as good as or, preferably, better than the corresponding products offered by competitors. Note that the words 'good as' and 'better' suggest that the value of a product can be assessed. This topic is examined in Section 8.3. An analysis of the comprehensive definition of product design, together with the need for it to be competitive, defines the personal abilities required to design competitive products. These are examined in Section 8.4.2.

8.2.4 About structured design

Product design is not made any easier in the electronic and computing arenas by the rapid development of those technologies. They frequently come together in the same product. On the electronic hardware side, advances in integrated circuit chip complexity and/or the speed-power product have now outstripped the design capability available to exploit them properly. The development and design of large software systems remains a black art of dubious probity, despite about twenty years of development work aimed at establishing software engineering (Macro and Buxton, 1987).

But product design is a demanding intellectual activity, whatever the target market and whatever the technologies used. It offers many opportunities for getting it wrong. There are two sorts of attack on the problem:

(1) The increasing use of computer aids in the design process, aimed at increasing the productivity of skilled designers. This is brought about by using the reliable memory of the machine to reduce perceived design complexity and by some automation of the algorithmic design steps. The technique is now well-established in most hardware engineering fields and is making a significant contribution in software engineering.

(2) The development of formal design methodologies aimed at the more efficient management of complexity and 'right first time' designs. These formal methods may or may not be computer-aided.

This chapter is concerned with the second approach: with a (not too formal) methodology which emphasizes the critical non-technical aspects of product design. It is a **structured** approach. At this stage, that term may be interpreted as logical, rational, coherent, methodical, algorithmic, hierarchical, easy-to-communicate and all-embracing. A more concise definition emerges as the discussion proceeds. Interestingly, the provenance of the method owes more to the giants of software engineering than to their hardware-oriented colleagues.

8.3 The product purchasing decision

The definition of product design presented in Section 8.2.3 recognizes (prospective) *customer requirements* as an essential ingredient in the process. This section develops a simple explanation of why a customer chooses to purchase one particular product from a number of competing products on offer. It leads immediately (in Section 8.4) to a deeper understanding of the problems of product design, and of the role of product designers in a manufacturing business.

8.3.1 Product attributes

Consider a situation in which a number of competing products are offered for sale. A potential customer, contemplating the purchase of one or other of these products, will try to obtain the best possible deal. In other words, the customer seeks to obtain the best possible value for the money that is available to purchase one of the products. To identify this best deal, the customer must evaluate (consciously or otherwise) each offered product. The evaluation involves at least six **product attributes**:

- **quality**
- **conformability**
- **availability**
- **delivery time**
- **confidence**
- **price**.

Quality

Product quality is the degree to which the objective and subjective performance features of the product meet the customer requirements. This definition gently expands the conventional 'fitness for purpose' definition of product quality. Observe that product quality is not measured on an absolute scale. It is measured by a customer as a fraction of perfection, where perfection is a complete match with the customer-defined product requirements.

Conformability

Product conformability is the degree to which it *initially* meets its declared quality specification. All products are, to some extent, imperfect because cost and price rise sharply as perfection is approached. Customers have to accept some degree of initial and progressive imperfection.

Availability

Product availability is the degree to which the product maintains its declared quality specification throughout its useful life. Availability measures the operational life of a product as a proportion of its useful life. It is related to reliability and maintainability, and is further examined in Section 8.7.2.

Delivery time

Product delivery time is measured from agreeing the deal. It can range from virtually nothing for simple products purchased 'off the shelf', to many years for complex products.

Confidence

This is the confidence that the customer feels, having agreed the deal, that it will be satisfactorily consummated. Clearly, the importance of this attribute depends on the consequences of failure to the customer. It depends on customer perception of the product supplier, as well as the product.

Price

Product price is not just the first price (that is, the initial purchase price). It is the **price of ownership**. This is the first price plus product operating costs, repair and maintenance costs and any net disposal cost when its useful life has expired.

8.3.2 Product value and benefit ratio

Aggregated together, in some way, the five attributes:

- quality
- conformability
- availability
- delivery time
- confidence

describe the **product value**, as it is perceived by the potential customer in the particular circumstances which apply to that customer.

Suppose that, having assessed the value of each of the competing products on offer, the customer chooses to purchase one specific product rather than any of the others. This purchase decision implies that the customer has, in fact, made two earlier decisions. These are:

(1) That the value of the chosen product is greater than its price, because the customer is willing to exchange the price for the product.
(2) That the ratio of product value to product price for the chosen product is greater than the corresponding ratio for each of the competing products, because the customer believes that the chosen product offers the best value for money (price).

The product **benefit ratio** is defined by the equation:

$$\text{Benefit Ratio} = \frac{\text{Product Value}}{\text{Product Price}} \tag{8.1}$$

and it is a measure of the **competitiveness** of the product. If the customer does make a purchase, then the chosen product should be the one which the customer has evaluated as having the highest benefit ratio.

Warning: Assumptions at work

The explanation of customer purchasing behaviour presented here is a greatly simplified analysis of a complicated situation. It predicts the behaviour of the notoriously unpredictable human system under certain conditions.

The argument employs three major assumptions. Firstly, it assumes that the customer is able to choose freely between a number of competing products. (This is the 'free market' assumption.) Secondly, it assumes the availability to the customer of accurate product and product supplier information which the customer is able to evaluate. Finally, it assumes that the customer behaves in an intelligent and rational way. In practice these conditions are not always met, particularly in consumer (domestic) markets. In industrial markets, where business trades with business, the conditions are substantially satisfied (in the non-monopoly sectors) because professional purchasing personnel are generally employed. Despite the reservations, there are important messages in the analysis. These are explored in Section 8.4.

Aggregating the attributes

A substantial difficulty, for customers who consciously adopt the sort of purchasing strategy outlined in this section, is that of 'aggregating' the first five product attributes. Only two of these (availability and delivery time) are susceptible to objective measurement; subjective evaluation is required for the others. Points-based ranking systems are commonly employed, with varying degrees of satisfaction. (It is, of course, a duty of the marketeers in a product supplying business to guide prospective customers towards a favourable view of the benefit ratio of the products offered by the business.)

8.4   More about design and designers

Every policy and action of those businesses that operate in competitive markets (a category which includes the great majority) is conditioned by the **profit equation**. This expresses the relationship that profit is the excess of revenue over cost:

$$\text{Profit} = \text{Revenue} - \text{Cost} \tag{8.2}$$

In this equation, **revenue** is the income arising from product sales in a specific period and **cost** is the sum of all the costs incurred in that same period. For a hardware (of any sort) manufacturing business, by far the greatest part of cost is due to making products for sale. This is nicely illustrated in Figure 7.1. (Product manufacturing cost is relatively low in business offering software products. The major part of cost in those businesses is usually due to product marketing, design, distribution and support.)

The profit equation was introduced in Section 1.1.1, and is probed in some depth in Chapter 7 at Section 7.9. The critical point is that a business must make an adequate profit if it is to survive, and a more than adequate profit if it is to prosper. So business managers are deeply interested, and rightly so, in obtaining the highest possible price for their products and in creating those products for the least possible cost.

- But, in a competitive market, product price cannot be set too high because this depresses benefit ratio and sales will be lost to the competition.

- Equally, product cost cannot be reduced too low because this reduces product value which also depresses the benefit ratio and, again, loses sales to the competition.

This encapsulates, in two sentences, the central dilemma in managing any business in a competitive environment. It originates in the life or death need for profit. The demands that this critical requirement places on the product design process are now examined.

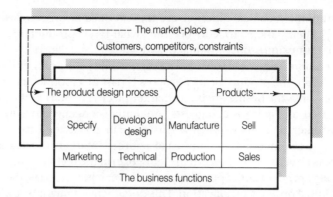

Figure 8.2　**The market, the business and product design.**
This figure illuminates the comprehensive definition of product design given in Section 8.2.3. A business, stripped to its bare essentials, is shown as the four 'stage' functions. These perform sequential sub-processes in the product creation process which (hopefully) turns market knowledge into survival and prosperity. Marketing interfaces with customers and Production makes products. Technical interfaces Marketing to Production. Its development and design teams must transform 'what-type' product specifications from Marketing into 'how to make and test it' specifications for Production. They bear substantial responsibility for product value and product cost.

8.4.1　Profit and product designing

It follows, from the need for profit and the earlier discussion of benefit ratio, that business survival and prosperity requires:

(1) That prospective customers judge the benefit ratios of the products offered by the business to be:
    (a) greater than one (that is, product value to be greater than product price), and
    (b) at least comparable with, but preferably greater than, the benefit ratios of competing products.
(2) That the products are created at a *cost* to the business sufficiently less than the *price* that the customers are prepared to pay for them.

If the first requirement is satisfied the products offered by the business should be sold to the prospective customers. If the second requirement is also satisfied these product sales will result in enough profit to permit survival and prosperity. These twin requirements place onerous demands on the product design process, because the way in which a product is designed has a profound influence on its value (in product attribute terms) and on its cost (in manufacturing terms).

It is now clear that the product design process starts in the market-place (which comprises customers, competitors and constraints) and extends into the manufacturing operation. This is illustrated in Figure 8.2, which shows that the marketing, technical and production functions share primary responsibility for the product design process.

The marketing function interfaces with the market and the production function is responsible for product manufacturing. The product development and design teams, within the technical function, are the interface between marketing and manufacturing. Their task is to convert the 'what-type' product specifications created by marketing into 'how to make and test it' specifications for the manufacturing operation. They bear substantial responsibility for product value and product cost.

In fact, the product design process is part of a loop which, through marketing and sales, links the business with its market-place. The start of the process is rarely as well defined as Figure 8.2 suggests. An initial concept can come from a prospective customer or from within the business. In the latter case, the marketing, sales or technical functions are the usual sources. Market awareness combined with the research activity (not shown in Figure 8.2) in the technical function is a planned route to new product concepts. But, irrespective of how it starts, the first significant event is an initial product specification. This document (it might be called a 'product brief') is considered in Section 8.5.3, and Appendix A contains a sample.

8.4.2 About product designers

It follows, from the critical nature of the product design process, that the product designers employed by a business have a central role in determining its future. They should be skilled, to a range of different levels, in *all* those factors which determine product value (the product attributes) and product cost. A product designer, therefore, has four main tasks:

(1) To assist the **product sponsor** to define the levels of:
   (a) product quality,
   (b) product conformability and
   (c) product availability
   which can be designed and manufactured within a specified
   (d) product delivery time and
   (e) product cost.
       The term 'product sponsor' is used here to signify some organization which is able to describe the product requirements of the prospective customers. This summary description is expanded in Section 8.5. (Note that the designer may well have rational views on product price, but this is primarily the responsibility of the marketing function.)
(2) To seek guidance regarding the required confidence level that must be taken into account during the design process.
(3) To design the product, both conceptually and in detail, against the total product specification derived from Tasks 1 and 2, and to issue proven 'how to make and test it' instructions to the manufacturing operation.
(4) To conduct the whole product design process encapsulated in Tasks 1, 2 and 3 in a manner which is economic, timely and yields a competitive product.

This is a demanding job specification. It requires that designers approach their tasks from (at least) three different **viewpoints**. These are:

- The **technical viewpoint**: that is, in terms of the relevant technologies.

- The **economic viewpoint**: that is, in terms of the relevant time and money aspects.

- The **operational viewpoint**: that is, from the perspective of the prospective customer and/or product end user, as appropriate.

So, the analytic and creative expertise of good product designers goes beyond excellence in the relevant technologies, vital though this is. They also have a solid appreciation of the importance of time and money and are skilled in project and product costing. Added to this is the objectivity which allows them to view their own concepts through the eyes of the prospective product user, and the courage to give this insight the priority that it must have.

8.4.3 Product design revisited

This section takes a closer look at the task of product design. It identifies the basic techniques and the most critical difficulty in the design environment.

Divide and conquer

Product design is about solving problems. A fundamental rule for problem solving is to break down big problems into smaller problems, because smaller problems are easier to solve! But this 'divide and conquer' approach only works if the mechanism used to partition, or decompose, the big problem satisfies two criteria:

- The smaller problems must be essentially self-contained, such that they can be solved, or further partitioned, without reference to their neighbours.
- The solutions to the smaller problems must ultimately join together in a seamless fashion to build the big solution to the big problem.

The earlier identification of the three viewpoints (technical, economic and operational) provides one important partitioning mechanism, or rationale. It is particularly useful in the early stages of the product design process. This approach to divide and conquer is another foundation stone of this chapter.

But this stone only becomes supportive by recognizing that there are links between the three basic viewpoints. These links play a critical role in defining smaller problems and, subsequently, in consolidating their solutions into an answer to the big problem. These links are called **constraints**.

Constraints

In this context, constraints are boundary conditions: factors of some sort which restrict freedom to manoeuvre within a technical, economic or operational design area. Very often, a design consideration arising in one of these areas places a constraint on one or both of the other areas. A constraint of this sort is then acting as a link between the areas. For example, in a particular software system, an operational requirement for high processing speed requires that some software modules be coded in assembler language. This is a technical constraint, which determines the product technology and implementation format to be used in part of the system. Similarly, technical options are often limited by economic factors. The prospective customer, for instance, may not be able to afford some technically feasible and, perhaps, highly desirable product features. Equally, not all customers are prepared to accept the latest high technology, because they believe (often correctly) that it carries an abnormally

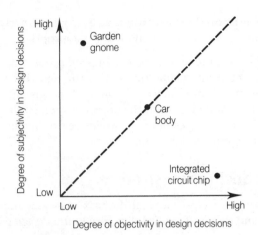

Figure 8.3 **Subjective and objective design decisions.**
The relative proportion of objective and subjective design decisions in a product design process depends primarily on the target market. Thus, the design of fashion products is dominated by subjective considerations, whereas the design of engineering products is dominated by objective considerations. The figure illustrates this way of characterizing different types of design process. The design process for a car body is especially challenging, because subjective and objective design decisions are about equally important.

high risk of failure. This is an example of an operational confidence factor constraining technical design options.

Constraints sound like bad news: things that a designer would rather do without. As it turns out, however, they are generally more helpful than damaging. The constraints concept is yet another foundation stone of this chapter.

Design options and design decisions

A vision of the product design environment, which emerges from this more detailed exploration, is that of a web of largely distinct design areas (the viewpoint areas) held together by a set of constraints. So the creation of **design options**, which are different ways of solving the design problems, is a central part of the design process. Following its creation, each design option is subject to critical evaluation in the light of the relevant constraints. Most are rejected in favour of some more promising option. Ultimately, this iterative process leads to a final (and, hopefully) acceptable compromise. Product design is about compromise.

Both the creation and the evaluation of design options have objective (measurable with numbers) and subjective (not measurable with numbers, or emotional) elements. The relative proportions of objective and subjective design decisions involved in a product design process depends primarily on the requirements of the target customers. This insight provides a way of distinguishing different products, and types of design process, by mapping them onto a design decision framework.

For example, consider the three products positioned in the framework of Figure 8.3. The garden gnome sells chiefly on its winsome appeal, so form and colour (subjective features) are critically important. Thus, the gnome design process is dominated by subjective decisions. Features such as weight, size and durability are important, but less so than appearance. In contrast, the design process aimed at the integrated circuit chip is dominated by objective decisions, relating to the signal processing functions required and the economics of manufacture. Circuit design, surface area, feature size, operating speed and power consumption all interact in a complex way which leads to a classic design compromise. But the appearance of the chip, a subjective feature, is matter of some indifference to all concerned. The car body is a particularly interesting example, because subjective and objective design decisions are about equally important. Fashionable shapes and colours are certainly needed to excite end-user interest. But weight, durability, drag factor, ease of manufacture and repairability also enter into the total equation.

On balance, the design of the engineering products with which this book is mostly concerned is dominated by objective design decisions. But the subjective aspects are still significant. For example, all products should be 'user-friendly' and 'understandable', because they are operated by people with 'ergonomic' needs.

The fundamental aim of the design process

It has been pointed out that an efficient product design process is critically important in ensuring the survival and prosperity of the business.

- The fundamental aim of the process is to ensure that the customer benefits obtained from using the product are substantially greater than the price of designing, making and operating it.

The product and, ultimately, the product supplier will be rejected by the market if this aim is not adequately achieved. So product design and product use are wholly interdependent. The days of designing products without reference to their prospective customers have gone forever, as have those businesses which followed that product strategy.

The fundamental problem of product design

It is now widely recognized that the product design process is most vulnerable to error in its early stages, when the initial specification of the new product is being determined.

- The fundamental problem of product design is specifying the right product to design!

There is no business merit in designing a product which does not sell because the customers do not want it or cannot afford it. This remains true even when it *does* meet its functional and performance specifications within the prescribed cost and delivery targets. Indeed, the seeds of business destruction are sown in such exercises in futility.

Achieving a guaranteed 'right first time' design process remains an elusive target, particularly so for large and complex products. But achieving 'nearly right first time' is achievable even in those cases. This is still worthwhile, because the cost of rectifying mistakes in the design process increases dramatically the longer they remain undetected. Undetected flaws in the initial product specification are the most damaging of all.

The next section describes the design of a structured design methodology aimed, first, at defining the right product to design. The same methodology may also be used, with advantage, in the subsequent phases of the product design process.

8.5 | Requirements definition: Design

'Definition' is both a verb and a noun. The term **requirements definition** is used here (and more generally in the fields of system and software engineering) to denote both the activity and the results of the first phase of the product design process. The aim in this phase is to create a concise and accurate statement of the whole problem that the design of the new product presents to the designer. There are two important points here:

(1) The requirements definition which emerges from this first phase is a problem statement *not* a problem solution.
(2) The requirements that it defines are those of the prospective product customer *and* those of the prospective product supplier.

The requirements definition (problem) statement leads immediately, at the beginning of the second phase of the design process, to a definitive specification of the product. It is that specification which is the basis for planning and (subject to plan approval) implementing the detailed design of the product.

Point 2 above is an essential feature, because some conflict between the needs of customers and the needs of suppliers is inevitable. This conflict must be resolved in a compromise, if the customer is to have the product and the supplier is to stay in business.

8.5.1 Data sources

The data on which a requirements definition is based comes from two sources:

- a description of the new product as it is perceived by its sponsor
- a description of the product design environment in the product supplier business concerned.

Product sponsor

As noted earlier, the term 'product sponsor' denotes some individual or organization which is able to describe the product requirements of the prospective customer for the product. The nature of this proxy customer depends on the type of product.

If the product is a high volume (repeatable) item, such as a 'fancy' telephone or a bicycle, then the product sponsor is invariably the marketing function of the business concerned. Its duty is to obtain, evaluate and represent the product requirements of the multitude of widely dispersed end user customers for such products. They must also take into account the needs of any intermediate customers (typically retail businesses) who will distribute the product. But if the product is a low volume item, such as a network of cash-points for a bank, a railway locomotive or a bridge, the customers are usually few in numbers and not widely dispersed. In these cases, the product sponsor is normally the end user customers and/or some external organization which represents their views. For example, the end user customers of an air-traffic control system are air-traffic controllers and aeroplane pilots. In Britain, their views would represented, in a system procurement project, by the Civil Aviation Authority. The Federal Aviation Authority adopts a similar role in the USA. In the text that follows, the word 'customer' means, unless it is specifically qualified, any sort of customer or proxy customer.

The product design environment

The second input to the requirements definition phase is a description of the product design environment. Generally, this comprises two elements:

(1) The supplier business defines a number of financial and (perhaps) other criteria which new product creation projects must satisfy.

(2) A statement of the resources available, or likely to be available, for marketing, designing, manufacturing and selling the new product and of the costs of using those resources. This is important, because the availability or otherwise of the requisite resources (be they particular skills, machines, money or whatever) and their costs has a profound influence on what can be designed, how much it will cost and how long it will take.

8.5.2 The design approach

As promised earlier, this section describes the *design* of a structured methodology for creating a proper requirements definition of a new product. Here, the term 'proper requirements definition' means a problem statement which contains the elements of the potentially most rewarding compromise between:

- the product needs and limitations of the prospective customer
- the needs and product creation limitations of the prospective supplier business.

Since the concern here is the design of the **requirements definition methodology** (RDM) itself, the customer is a product design team. The design work is divided into three stages:

(1) The **justification** stage, which seeks to answer the question: *why* is the RDM needed by the customer?

(2) The **specification** stage, which seeks to answer the question: *what* should the RDM do for the customer?

(3) The **implementation** stage, which seeks to answer the question: *how* should the RDM do it?

Answers to these critical questions are explored in the next three sections.

8.5.3 Justification of the RDM

All too often, the history of a product creation project (which includes marketing, designing, making and selling) can be summarized as:

- Overspent design budget, in both time and cost.

- Missed delivery and 'ready for service' (RFS) date.
- Product manufactured cost (that is, the works or factory cost) in excess of design target.
- Product failure to conform with its functional and/or performance specification.
- Poor availability in service.

In other words, excessive time and money has been spent on creating a product which has an attribute value less than anticipated, and which costs more than anticipated. Most businesses can survive only a limited number of such experiences.

Of course, the planned time and cost for the project may overrun simply because its planning was flawed, or because of poor project control. Either of these failures can then lead to missed delivery and RFS dates. Technical project planning and control is considered at some length in Chapter 6. It is certainly an area sprinkled with pitfalls for the unwary. But this does not explain the last three items on the tragedy list, which describe a mismatch between product reality and the total product specification.

Clearly, less complex products are less prone to this sad history. But the history is entirely typical of large computer-based systems. In those cases, the largest project budget overrun usually relates to the software. Some of this is due, no doubt, to the nature of software and of software people. (Section 3.5 is a provocative diagnosis of the diseases that can infect software creation, and it is summarized in Section 5.5.7.) But the history frequently applies to complex systems which contain no software and, indeed, to many simple and straightforward products.

What really goes wrong?

The answer to this critical question lies in a coincidence of two specific situations. The first concerns the description of the new product as initially perceived by its sponsor. This is called the **product brief** here, but terms such as **product concept**, **product requirement specification** and **user requirement specification** are also in the literature. Typically, it is a nasty mixture of precision and uncertainty which states:

- Only vaguely what the required functional and performance capabilities of the product are to be, particularly at the more ambitious end of the spectrum.
- More precisely what the product must contain in terms of some specific components and modules. This characteristic is particularly prevalent when the new product is a large and complex system aimed at replacing, or extending, an existing system. This is because the customer seeks compatibility between the two systems to minimize further investment and aggravation. The requirement can apply to hardware, software, spares or operational features.
- Very precisely when (and where) the product must be available.
- With absolute precision what its maximum price can be.

The second situation is the absence of an effective product design methodology, especially one that can handle the early part of the design process. A coincidence of these two situations is a recipe for disaster, as can be seen by reviewing its ingredients:

(1) Uncertainty regarding what the product has to do.
(2) Restrictions on design freedom laid down by the customer.

(3) Limited time in which to complete the design.
(4) Limited funds with which to complete the design. This is set by the maximum price available and the profit requirements of the supplier business.
(5) Inadequate tools to assist the designer in extracting order out of the chaos implicit in the situation comprising items 1 to 4 above.

Sadly, in the euphoria of launching a new project, the brooding presence of this intrinsic disaster is easily ignored, or even forgotten: illustrating yet another triumph of hope over experience.

The fundamental problem lies in the ill-defined initial description of the new product as it is perceived by its sponsor. The problem is not confined to complex systems. It applies, to some degree, to all products.

Customers, real and proxy, will continue to provide these fuzzy descriptions of the products that they are seeking. And they will continue to accompany them with possibly unrealistic restrictions on design freedom, time and money. They know about their compatibility problems. They know how much time and how much money they have got. But they do not really know what they want the new product to do, because there are no limits. Given enough time and enough money it will do anything: even fly to the moon if that is required. Technology is wonderful stuff. But it takes time and it costs money. Product sponsors know this in principle, but they cannot know the current boundaries, times and costs. So the functional and performance capabilities part of their product description is largely a 'wish list' and, usually, a wish list without priorities. It follows that:

● Achieving a precise definition of the product requirements is the first and the most critical task in the product design process.

This is why a good RDM is required and, incidentally, why design is always about compromise.

8.5.4 Specification of the RDM

The specification stage of the initial design phase seek an answer to the question 'what should the RDM do for the customer'? The short answer to this question is 'it should ease the problems of creating the requirements definition'. There are three principal, intrinsic and substantial problems in the requirements definition task:

(1) Communication between the parties.
(2) The supplier margin conflict.
(3) Constraints.

Communications between the parties

There are two principal parties involved in the creation of the product: the customer(s) and the product design team. But they talk marginally different 'languages', because they have different expertise. Thus, the customer understands the application which the product is to serve, but is less expert in the relevant product technologies. Conversely, the design team is expert in manipulating the relevant technologies, but less well equipped in the product application area(s). There are abundant opportunities for misunderstandings, ambiguities and confusion in this situation.

The supplier margin conflict

The prospective customer is seeking the best possible benefit ratio. That is, the customer wants the ratio of product value to product price to be as high as possible, because the benefit of product ownership is that much greater than the price of product ownership. The design team works inside the business aiming to supply the product to the customer. It is seeking to provide the product value required by the customer. But it must do this at a product *cost* which is less than product *price* by a margin acceptable to its parent business. This is how the business stays in business. Thus, the customer and the design team share value-related motives, but their economic motives are, potentially at least, in conflict.

Constraints

Freedom of action by the customer is constrained by some factors which are peculiar to the customer environment. For example:

- Limited budget for product purchase and operation.
- A critical date defining when the new product must be operational.
- A substantial existing investment in application software which must be portable, without modification, to run on the new product. This constraint illustrates a software **lock-in** situation. Lock-ins are not confined to software. Ownership of an oil-fired central heating boiler, for instance, can lock its owner into periodic purchases of heating oil.

Freedom of action by the design team is constrained by some factors which are peculiar to its environment. These constraints are defined in the description of the product design environment cited earlier. They include, for example:

- The minimum acceptable margin between product price and product cost.
- The skill mix and quantity of available product design and production resources.
- The availability, in-house or otherwise, of the requisite cost-effective and proven components and modules from which to build the product.

Constraints are identified as part of the problem of creating a requirements definition, but they are also one key to its solution. There is always a large number of design options in all but the most trivial design tasks. Constraints which cannot be resolved close down some of these options. This is often useful, and it signals real progress in the design task.

The solution: Principal features

Clearly, the principal features of the RDM must be aimed at the three principal problems of the task. This suggests that the methodology must ensure that the designer knows:

- *why* the product is required by the customer   Level 1
- *what* the product has to do for the customer   Level 2
- *how* its design is to be constrained, because   Level 3

    why the product is required will determine

what it has to do, and the various constraints will restrict
how it is able to do it.

These three levels are the principal features of the solution to the requirements
definition problem. There are some secondary features yet to be identified. However,
summarizing specification progress at this stage:

- The first three levels of a structured product design methodology have been
  identified. These comprise the basic structure of the first phase of that methodology, which is the requirements definition phase.

- Three 'magic' questions have been identified:
  why?
  what?
  how?
  which form a natural hierarchy.

- And, as it turns out, this same why–what–how construct can be used in the
  subsequent phases of the design process.

In the requirements definition phase, the result of answering:

- *Why* is the product required?   is the **context analysis**.
- *What* is the product to do?   is the **functional architecture**.
- *How* is its design be constrained?   is the **design constraints**.

This terminology follows that introduced by Ross and Schoman (1977). The term
functional specification is an alternative to functional architecture.

The solution: Secondary features

Context analysis, functional architecture and design constraints comprise the primary
features of the RDM. Some desirable secondary features are:

- universality
- completeness
- unambiguous common language
- implementation independence
- traceability
- conformity with the **six pieces rule**.

Universality means that the methodology should be able to deal with any type of
product; whereas *completeness* requires that it should encompass all the requirements that a product must satisfy: technical, economic, operational or whatever.

The *unambiguous common language* feature allows its results to be read and
understood by customers as well as by designers. Unconstrained natural language is
too rich to satisfy the need for no ambiguity. But it is a talent shared by customers and
designers. Most people absorb and understand graphical information more easily and
quickly than textual information. ('Pictures speak louder than words.') The fact that
the eyes provide a parallel input to the processing mechanism, whereas reading is a
serial process, plays a part in this situation. So some combination of natural language

and pictures, where the pictures restrict the meaning of the words, is a good choice for the design language. This is not a novel thought. For very many years architects, mechanical engineers and civil engineers have employed conventional 'blueprint' technology, which is a 'words and picture' language aimed at the same need. The practice continues to this day, although it is now more often a 'whiteprint' which has been manipulated in a computer as a soft image before emerging as hard copy. A words and pictures language is a powerful medium for expressing ideas and for communicating them between people (Ross, 1977b).

Implementation independence means that the methodology should not exclude any options which may exist for the design of the product. Design options will probably get excluded as a result of the various constraints that apply to the customer and designer situations. This is acceptable and sometimes welcome. But the design methodology should not, of itself, impose any constraints on the design.

The *traceability* requirement demands that the reasoning behind every design decision, made at any level, should be traceable upwards through all the higher levels. This feature allows a complete audit of the design to be carried out. It is aimed at minimizing the impact of a common, and unhappy, experience. This occurs when a change is accepted in one part of the design which later (sometimes very much later) turns out to have damaging consequences in another part of the design.

Conformity with the so-called *six pieces rule* means that the methodology should not require its user to process more than six pieces of information at the same time. Here, the user is the customer, designer or design reader and 'process' means remember, analyse and relate. Ross (1977b) puts this need more succinctly:

> 'Everything worth saying
> about anything worth saying something about
> must be expressed in six or fewer pieces.'

In this context, a 'piece' of information is easier to recognize than it is to define and the rule is not susceptible to absolute proof. However, it is self-evident that most people are limited in the number of pieces of information that they can remember, analyse and relate concurrently. According to Miller (1956), this number appears to be about seven, but six is a safer estimate. There is valuable guidance in this rule about the optimum structuring, including partitioning and presentation, of the information derived from the methodology.

8.5.5   Implementation of the RDM

Section 8.5.3 has established *why* a proper RDM is needed and Section 8.5.4 has specified *what* it should do. This section is concerned with *how* it should do it. It aims to answer two more questions:

(1) How should the methodology be structured?
(2) How may it be further partitioned to ease its use?

The basic structure of the RDM

The basic structure of the RDM must recognize the two parties involved, and the three levels, labelled context analysis, functional specification and design constraints. It

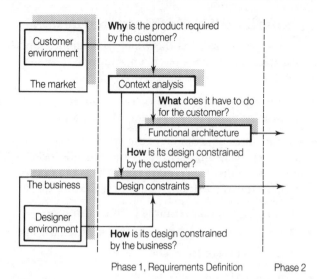

Figure 8.4   **The basic structure of the requirements definition methodology (RDM).**
This figure shows how the specification of the RDM developed in Section 8.5.4 is implemented.
Examination of the customer environment yields the *context analysis*, which provides a statement
for further analysis. This leads to the *functional architecture*, and to the customer facets of *design constraints*. These are completed by adding supplier constraints from the designer environment.
(This is, perhaps, the key diagram in the whole book, since it encapsulates the writer's approach to
management and to structuring this book, as well as product design.)

should do this in a way which incorporates the desirable secondary features or, at
least, does not compromise them. Figure 8.4 illustrates a procedure which achieves
these aims.

At Level 1, examination of the customer environment yields the context analysis
which provides a statement for further analysis. This leads, at Level 2, to the functional
architecture and, at Level 3, to the customer facets of design constraints. These are
completed by adding constraints arising in the designer environment.

Note that the words and pictures of Figure 8.4 capture the most important messages
of Sections 8.5.3 and 8.5.4: the why and what of designing the RDM. Some detail has, of
course, been omitted to assist clarity. Note, too, that (allowing a modicum of poetic
licence) the figure obeys the six pieces rule. It contains five boxes with descriptive
text and one set of connections between the boxes. In relation to the other desirable
secondary features, the figure is:

(1) Universal, because it applies to any and every sort of product.
(2) Complete, because it embraces, in principle, everything that the designer
needs to know about the product at this initial stage.
(3) Expressed in an unambiguous common language of words and pictures in a
format where the pictures limit the meaning of the words.
(4) Implementation independent, because it makes no reference to any specific
technology.
(5) Traceable, because the source of the information in each and every box (topic
and document) is defined.

The 'what' and 'how' of structured design

It is instructive to pause at this point to examine how the description of the RDM encapsulated in Figure 8.4 has been achieved.

Section 8.5.3 demonstrated that:

- achieving a precise definition of the product requirements is the first, and most critical, problem in the product design process

because the initial description of the product derived from its customer(s) is usually unsatisfactory. This analysis posed the big question of how to achieve a precise definition of the product requirements. This big question was examined in Section 8.5.4, where it was partitioned into three smaller questions:

- *Why* is the product required by the customer?
- *What* does the product have to do for the customer?
- *How* is its design to be constrained?

These are the right questions to ask, because:

> *why* the product is required will determine
>> *what* it has to do, and the various constraints will restrict
>>> *how* it is able to do it.

This why–what–how construct is a **partitioning rationale**: a logical mechanism which provides a means of splitting a big question into a set of relatively self-contained smaller questions. Such mechanisms are an essential part of the design process.

Now, provided that there is some rationale to steer it, the initial partitioning can be further partitioned by splitting each of the smaller questions into even smaller questions, and so on. At some point, the questions become small enough to answer. Then the small answers can be amalgamated to make a bigger answer. And so on until, eventually, a big answer to the original big question has been constructed. This is what structured design is really about. It is about building answers to questions by:

- *top-down decomposition* of big questions into successive layers of smaller questions until the questions become small enough to be answered, and then
- *bottom-up construction* of big answers by the amalgamation of successive layers of smaller answers.

Further partitioning of the RDM

Returning to the RDM, there now exists a structure of three levels, labelled context analysis, functional architecture and design constraints. Each of these entities is the answer to a specific question, and they are termed **vantage points** to emphasize the notion of relative height. This is the structure that is depicted in Figure 8.4.

But a rationale also exists which allows *further* partitioning of the three basic questions which relate to these vantage points. The point was made earlier, in Section 8.4.2, that designers must always analyse from (at least) three different viewpoints. These are:

- The technical viewpoint, which relates to the relevant product technologies.
- The economic viewpoint, which relates to the relevant time and money aspects.

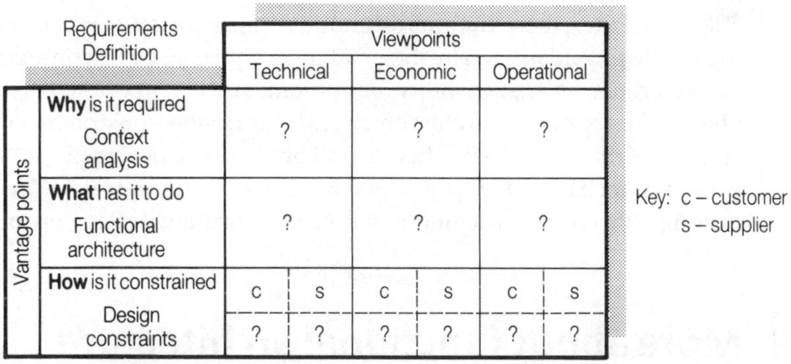

Figure 8.5　**Further partitioning of the requirements definition phase.**

Figure 8.4 expresses the requirements definition methodology (RDM) as a structure of 'vantage point' levels, called context analysis, functional architecture and design constraints. Each contains the answer to a specific question. This figure extends that first picture of the RDM. It adds 'vertical' partitioning to each horizontal level by incorporating the technical, economic and operational viewpoints which designers must bring to their task. Note that the one big question of how to create a proper RDM has been decomposed into twelve smaller questions. This is a good example of an orderly 'divide and conquer' approach to design.

- The operational viewpoint, which relates to the perspective of the prospective customer and/or product end user, as appropriate.

These viewpoints provide a vertical structure to further partition the horizontal structure of vantage points. This extended perspective of the RDM is illustrated in Figure 8.5.

Note that the first big question of how to create a proper requirements definition has been reduced to answering twelve smaller questions. This figure and its companion, Figure 8.4, provide a structure for seeking the answers to these questions in a systematic way which allows the questions to be handled in relative isolation.

A requirements definition example

At this point, all the essentials of the RDM have been described. It is appropriate, therefore, to consider an example of its use. A realistic example is necessarily quite lengthy, because it must first establish the context of the design exercise in terms of a product brief and supplier company data. For this reason, the example is provided at Appendix A. Those readers who wish to consolidate their understanding of the RDM at this stage are referred to that Appendix. Others should read on.

8.5.6　Where from here?

The initial requirements definition phase of the product design process creates three outputs:

(1) The context analysis.
(2) The functional architecture.
(3) The design constraints.

Taken together, these outputs (should) comprise a concise and accurate statement of the whole problem faced by the product design team. The context analysis is retained, as a reference and 'traceability' document, at the end of the requirements definition phase. The functional architecture and the design constraints combine to form the *context* of the next phase. This second phase of the design process is the design of the **product architecture**, and it is considered in Section 8.8. The next two sections examine the concepts of functional architecture and design constraints in more detail.

8.6 More about functional architecture

The functional architecture of a product defines what the customer first perceives that it must do. More formally, it is a rigorous and structured description of that product in terms of its outputs, its inputs and the transformation process it must perform to generate its outputs from its inputs. It includes, therefore, the product transfer function. But, and this is important, it is not concerned with implementation details.

8.6.1 Functional and product architectures

Implementation independence is one critical feature that distinguishes functional architecture from product architecture, which describes the product in terms of a physical implementation using real tangible elements. For example, a motor car would be described as a configuration of body panels, chassis, engine, gearbox, transmission, wheels and so on. In the case of a large computer-based system, the elements would include basic hardware components, software modules, data files, data transmission channels and the like.

Product architecture is determined by 'filtering' the functional architecture through the design constraints. Crudely, therefore, functional architecture is what the customer *wants* and product architecture is what the customer *can have*. There is invariably a gap between ambition and reality. One of the arts of product design is to break this unwelcome news to the customer in a way which provokes confidence rather than hostility.

Sadly, it is quite usual to start the product design process with the design of the product architecture. This approach is unwise, because it tends to:

- close down design options too early
- confuse problems with solutions
- conceal the algorithmic nature of the product.

It is imperative, therefore, to design the functional architecture before the product architecture, because the functional architecture is not compromised by any implementation features.

Functional architecture as a universal concept

The universal nature of the functional architecture concept is best illustrated by means of an example. Suppose an existing 'manual' system for checking-in airline passengers is to be replaced by an 'automatic' system. It is intended that the new

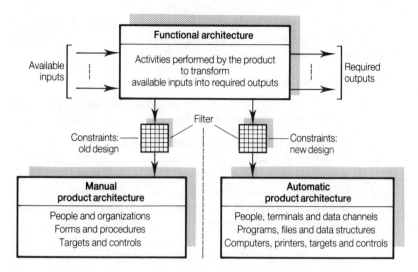

Figure 8.6   **The universal nature of functional architecture.**

Functional architecture is implementation independent and, in this sense, is a universal product model. Product architecture, on the other hand, describes the product in terms of a physical implementation using real tangible elements, and is implementation dependent. A product architecture is determined by 'filtering' the functional architecture through context-dependent design constraints. The figure illustrates all these ideas: the two, very different, product architectures share the same functional architecture. Note that, because of design constraints, functional architecture is what the customer *wants*, but product architecture is what the customer *can have.*

system will provide all the features of the old system, together with some enhancements which flow naturally from the change in technologies.

The first design step is to determine the functional architecture of the existing manual system, since this is shared by the old and new systems. The relationship between the old system and the new system (before any enhancements) is illustrated in Figure 8.6.

Note that, apart from enhancements, the old and new systems differ only because a different set of constraints is applied to derive the product architecture of the new system.

8.6.2 Creating a functional architecture

There are three basic steps in devising a functional architecture:

(1) Specify the required outputs (a 'what' step).
(2) Characterize the available inputs (a 'what' step).
(3) Determine how, in the mathematical, algorithmic or flow chart sense, to transform the available inputs into the required outputs.

The outputs generated by the product are the only way in which it can interact with its environment. Note that the design of the functional architecture must start with an examination of the outputs required, because the nature of the inputs needed by the product cannot be decided until its outputs have been defined.

Step 3 (determining the transfer function) is necessarily iterative, to some extent, with Step 2. It is application dependent and is not considered further here. A general approach to the first two steps is now discussed.

Specification of outputs

Analysis of the product brief and, perhaps, other considerations based on experience, will generally identify three categories of required output:

(1) **Mandatory outputs** which reflect the primary purpose of the product, such as range and azimuth target tracking in an air-traffic control system or controllable mobility in a forklift truck.

(2) **Optional outputs** which add to the attractiveness and value of the product but are not essential to its primary purpose, such as a colour screen on a personal computer or film shows and 'free' champagne on long distance aeroplanes. Normally, it is these optional outputs which are compromised when cost constraints are applied to the functional architecture to yield a product architecture.

(3) **Diagnostic outputs** which warn the user of a potential problem, such as a 'battery low' indicator on a portable telephone or a 'ground proximity' alarm in an aeroplane.

Simply identifying and classifying the required outputs is not enough. A distinct specification for each such output must also be created. Output specifications are inevitably somewhat application dependent. The sample listing that follows applies most specifically to 'real-time' computer-based systems, but it provides a measure of general guidance.

(1) *Identity*   A name which distinguishes the output from all other outputs.

(2) *Information content*   A description of all the information that it must provide.

(3) *Form*   Describing how the information is to be presented. For example, as:
   (a) an electrical signal of a particular sort
   (b) a mechanical movement of a particular sort
   (c) an audible alarm of a specified intensity, frequency and duration
   (d) a visual display in a defined format

(4) *Tolerances*   Indicating acceptable deviations from the perfect presentation defined in 2 and 3 above.

(5) *Stimuli*   Describing the event, or combination of events, which cause the output. For example, a particular combination of inputs or the expiry of a set waiting time (a 'time-out') for an event to occur. Note that some outputs are not stimulated by inputs from outside the product. 'I am OK' messages from built-in diagnostic routines and signals from system load indicators are examples.

(6) *Response time*   The maximum acceptable time that may elapse between the advent of the stimuli and the appearance of the output.

(7) *Freshness*   A parameter which defines how up-to-date the information must be.

(8) *Speed(s)*   Defining how fast the output must be delivered when it appears.

(This is not relevant when response time and freshness refer to the completion of the output.)

(9) *Frequency* Defining how often the output is required in a particular time period or periods.

(10) *Sizes* Specifying the range of sizes of the output when this is a relevant parameter. For example, for output messages to be displayed on a screen.

(11) *Interface* Defining output parameters which interact with the product environment. For example, the source impedance, current capacity and voltage levels of an electrical signal, or the communication protocols for a data channel or the character size, colour and brightness of a message display.

(12) *Variabilities* Describing acceptable variations in any of the above elements of the output specification.

When the product is a complex computer-based system, as in this illustration (and quite often when it is something else), two important questions must be answered under the variabilities heading:

- Can this output be provided at increased response time, or even not at all, when the system is heavily loaded? An affirmative answer can allow very substantial cost savings, by minimizing the computer power that must be built into the system.

- Can this output be provided at an increased response time, or even not at all, under system fault conditions? Meeting tight specifications under fault conditions is generally achieved with additional equipment, which is redundant under normal conditions. It is an expensive solution.

Characterization of inputs

When the product outputs have been specified (by following the sort of process illustrated by the computer-based system example), the product inputs needed for the 'input-stimulated' outputs must be examined. Generally, opportunities to specify these inputs are limited: they are as they are and must be tolerated in that condition. So the emphasis is to define what their condition *is*, rather than specify what it *should be*. The process is termed **characterization**.

The illustration of input characterization that follows also employs the large computer-based example used earlier. It demonstrates that contents of an input characterization are very similar to those of an output specification.

(1) *Identity*
(2) *Information content* ⎱ As for outputs, but in the sense of what is
(3) *Form* ⎰ available rather than what is required
(4) *Tolerances*
(5) *Crisis time(s)* The period(s) when the input is available for capture.
(6) *Recoverability* A statement of the means, if any, of obtaining the input, or other information in lieu of it, in case of failure to capture it when first available.
(7) *Freshness*
(8) *Speed(s)*

(9) *Frequency* ⎫   As for outputs, but in the sense of what is available
(10) *Sizes*   ⎬   rather than what is required
(11) *Interface* ⎭
(12) *Variabilities*

Specifying the required outputs and then characterizing the available inputs are the first two steps in creating a functional architecture. The final step is to design the transfer function which changes the inputs into the outputs, possibly with reference to some stored history. This processing must compensate for imperfections in the available inputs. The final step is application dependent and is not considered here for that reason.

8.7 More about design constraints

Achieving a functional architecture which accurately reflects the product requirements of the prospective customer is a major step towards defining a product architecture. But Phase 2 of the design process (design of the product architecture) cannot start until all the design constraints have been identified. Constraints originate from two major sources, and are of three different types:

- Supplier-imposed constraints:
  - technical
  - economic
  - operational
- Customer-imposed constraints:
  - technical
  - economic
  - operational.

This same structure is shown, in a different format, in Figure 8.5.

8.7.1 Supplier-imposed constraints

A number of typical supplier-imposed constraints were first listed in Section 8.5.4. That list is now extended and its contents considered in a little more detail. The emphasis is on important factors which, whatever their origin, resolve down to technical constraints on the product design.

Financial criteria

The creation of a new product and its launch into the market costs money. Normally, but not always, these funds are provided by the supplier business and they represent an investment in its future. Hopefully, the net income from product sales will repay the investment and provide a substantial surplus beyond that 'break-even' point. From the financial perspective, therefore, the product design process is just one critical element in a **business development** project.

Most companies require that such projects are carefully planned before major resources are committed to their implementation. A business (project) plan serves three basic purposes:

(1) It defines what has to be done to create and exploit the new product to best effect.

(2) It is a reference document for subsequent project progress monitoring and control.

(3) It provides estimates of the investment required, and of the returns that should flow from that investment.

The business plan will (probably) not be approved unless the forecast investment/ return performance of the project meets or exceeds certain minimum standards. These standards are the financial criteria. This topic is covered in Chapter 11. The financial criteria cause three distinct, but related, constraints on the product design:

(1) *Design quality*   The cost of the product development and design project is likely to be a substantial part of the total investment. So it must be kept to a minimum. With this pressure comes the danger of reducing this project cost below the critical level at which design quality is compromised.

(2) *Product value*   The concept of product value as an aggregate of five major product attributes was explored in Section 8.3. These attributes are:
   (a) quality
   (b) conformability
   (c) availability
   (d) delivery time
   (e) confidence.
   Prospective customers compare their perceptions of product value with product price when choosing between competing products. If competing products are offered at similar prices, those with the larger perceived values are likely to achieve the larger market share. This creates a constant pressure on the design team to deliver the largest possible product value. This is entirely normal and reasonable, but too much pressure can be damaging. For example, insistence on meeting an unrealistic delivery time can lead to a loss of product quality because testing is always the easiest activity to omit.

(3) *Works cost*   The difference, called the **gross margin**, between the price obtained for a product and its works cost (its cost to manufacture) is the net income per product unit sold. It is the contribution made by the product sale to the other costs that a business incurs, and to profit. The selling price of a product is set by market considerations and has nothing to do with its works cost. However, businesses often define a minimum acceptable gross margin which, in turn, leads to a maximum acceptable works cost.

Resource limitations

In a sense, all resource limitations are financial limitations because, given the funds (and the time), all other resources can be purchased. But the majority of efficient businesses are deliberately under-resourced with respect to average activity by a few per cent. They choose to operate on the safe side of a thin line between security and disaster in (the normal) times of fluctuating demand. It is a tenable policy because, to a degree, resources can work harder than average when required to do so. So resource limitations are entirely normal constraints applied to the product design. Those most commonly encountered are:

(1) *People*   Limitations here can arise from technical staff deficiencies in quality, quantity or skills. Bringing about an orderly change in the profile of a technical team, in any of these respects, is a slow and expensive process.

(2) *Facilities*   This resource category covers all the 'tools', from buildings to pencils, that the design team needs to exploit their skills efficiently. Alleviating major shortages in this area is also a slow and expensive process. A common error is to underestimate the learning time required to properly assimilate new and complex tools, such as a computer-aided-design package.

(3) *'Building-bricks'*   Efficient product design is dependent on the ready availability of appropriate cost-effective and proven product components and modules (building-bricks). These may be sourced in-house or by purchase from outside suppliers. Competitive pressures, however, require:

(a) The constant development of novel components and modules to provide additional product features.

(b) The occasional technological updating of existing 'own-build' components and modules for cost-reduction purposes (and, perhaps, to provide minor enhancements).

Neglect of these essential development activities can result in the product design process becoming uncompetitive.

Other constraints

Financial criteria and resource limitations are probably the most fruitful sources of the constraints that the supplier company can impose on the product design. But there are many other possible restrictions – too many to consider here. Just two examples are a schedule of mandatory project control meetings (an operational constraint), and the requirement to use 'approved' components purchased from 'approved' suppliers (another technical constraint).

8.7.2   Customer-imposed constraints

A representative selection of customer-imposed constraints was first listed in Section 8.5.4. A more comprehensive list is included here. Each factor is labelled to indicate whether it is primarily a technical (T), an economic (E) or an operational (O) constraint.

(1) *Acceptable first price* (E).

(2) *Acceptable price of ownership* (E,O)   The aggregate of (1) and the costs of operating, maintaining and repairing the product.

(3) *Time scale* (O)   Derived from when the customer requires the product to be operational.

(4) *Environmental* (T,O)   For example, the maximum size, weight and power consumption that are acceptable. Additionally, factors such as the permissible levels of electrical and acoustic noise, portability needs, general appearance and so on.

(5) *Operator parameters* (O)   Ergonomic features, and the qualifications and experience of the staff who will operate the product. Also, the limitations on acceptable staffing levels.

(6) *Maintenance strategy* (O)   There are many possible variations in this area. These include the use of customer or supplier staff, the nature and extent of any spares holding on the product site, and 'fix on site' or 'return to supplier' alternatives for module repairs.

(7) *Enhancement potential* (T,E,O)   Very few large system products remain at their first installed capacity and/or functional capability throughout their useful life. It may be necessary, therefore, to provide 'hooks' in the initial design to accommodate later enhancements to the product functions and/or traffic carrying capacity.

(8) *Security* (O)   These requirements refer to both to physical security and to functional security under fault conditions. Thus, some features may be required to protect the product against, say, fire and unauthorized access. Other features may be necessary to provide an acceptable level of service under particular fault conditions, and 'graceful' recovery after a fault.

(9) *On-site services* (O)   These constraints reflect limitations in customer-provided site services. For example, the available power supply on the product site might be very (electrically) noisy or unreliable or of limited capacity.

(10) *Mandatory design features* (T)   This covers any requirement which infringes the principle of implementation independence in the requirements definition. For example, the mandatory use of customer-approved computers and/or high-level languages.

(11) *Mandatory management features* (T,E)   Any 'project monitoring and control' factors which need to be taken into account when planning the project. Numbers and location of progress meetings, the documentation required and contractual quality assurance procedures are examples.

(12) *Availability* (T,E,O) and *integrity* (T,E,O)   These two constraints deserve a closer examination, which follows immediately.

Product availability and integrity

The concepts of availability and integrity are described here in the context of real-time systems. Analogous constraints can be defined for other types of product. They may be imposed at the total product level or to a limited set of product functions.

Product availability is the extent to which the required outputs are delivered within their specified response times. Availability depends on product reliability in the mean-time-between-failures (MTBF) sense; and on the maintenance strategy and design features which together determine the mean-time-to-repair (MTTR). (Note that, in a properly designed real-time system with adequate capacity to meet its peak load, failure of the outputs to meet their specified response times must be due to a fault.) Even when the required outputs are delivered within their specified response times, they may still be in error (that is, they may fall outside the acceptable tolerance levels). This possibility leads to the concept of integrity. **Product integrity** is the extent to which the outputs, when delivered within their specified response times, are within their specified accuracy.

A simple example will clarify these notions. Telecommunication businesses which offer telephone exchange facilities are not greatly concerned if a few of their customers ('subscribers') are upset by the service provided. But they take great care to reduce the probability of failure of a whole exchange, because this attracts unwelcome publicity and causes substantial loss of revenue. Suppose that a telephone exchange has adequate capacity for its peak load, but it is expected to break down completely once every 30 years (due, say, to catastrophic power supply failure). It is anticipated that it will then take 100 hours to repair. When it is working, 0.1% (on average) of its outputs do not meet the specified accuracy. In other words, they are misconnected, disconnected before release, or are subject to unacceptable noise or cross-talk. The availability and integrity are then calculated as follows:

$$\text{Availability} = \frac{\text{MTBF}}{\text{MTBF} + \text{MTTR}} \tag{8.3}$$

$$= \frac{30 \times 365 \times 24}{(30 \times 365 \times 24) + 100} = 99.96\%$$

$$\text{Integrity} = \text{Percentage of 'good' outputs} \tag{8.4}$$

$$= (100 - 0.1) = 99.90\%$$

Note the significance of the MTTR, which is largely determined by the maintenance strategy, in defining product availability.

8.8 Product design: The whole process

The emphasis up to this point has been on the requirements definition phase (Phase 1) of the product design process. This section now builds a structured perception of the *whole* product design process on that foundation. It also considers Phase 2 in some detail, since it is second only to Phase 1 in importance.

8.8.1 Model-to-model transformations

The product brief which marks the first formal event in the product design process can be regarded as the **initial product model**. At the end of the process, a set of proven (ideally) 'how to make and test it' instructions are delivered to the production function. These can be regarded as the final **delivered product model**. They describe the product in terms which are intelligible to, and compatible with, the product manufacturing operation.

The purpose of the product design process, therefore, is to bridge the gap between the initial product model (the product brief) and the delivered product model (the 'how to make and test it' instructions). It is a substantial gap, with a number of different dimensions:

- *Language* The initial model is expressed in normal human language. The delivered model represents the product as parts lists and drawings, together with instructions for processing, machining, assembling and testing. Even if the textual (as distinct from graphical) content of this model is expressed in normal human language, its terse style contrasts sharply with that of the initial model. More usually, major parts of the delivered model are expressed in machine-readable formats compatible with the manufacturing methods employed.

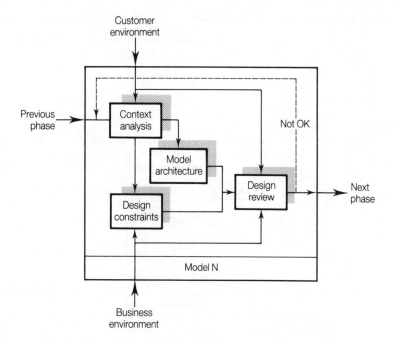

Figure 8.7   **The design process module.**
The product design process can be visualized as a sequence of phases, in each of which a relatively imprecise product model is transformed into a relatively precise product model. This is a is modular concept, where the design activity within each phase follows the same pattern. The figure illustrates the basic 'building-brick' module of the product design process. It is a generalization and development of Figure 8.4. The module output, which provides the context for its successor phase, is subject to a design review. This may require some rework of the phase analyses, as shown by the 'not OK' loop back to the 'previous phase' input. Note that both the (supplier) business and customer environments must be monitored throughout a phase.

- *Precision*   The initial model is usually characterized by flaws, ambiguities and inconsistencies. (A sample product brief for a relatively simple product is included in Appendix A. It illustrates all of those features.) In contrast, the delivered product model must be a totally consistent and unambiguous description of the product which is complete in every significant detail.

- *Supplier compatibility*   The initial model may describe a product which is incompatible with the product supplier business in a number of ways. For example, the price–cost relationship may compromise target profitability or it may require manufacturing resources which are not to hand. The delivered model, on the other hand, must be supplier compatible in all important respects.

The gap between the initial and delivered models is generally too wide to bridge with one span. This leads to the vision of product design as a model-to-model transformation process. In this concept, each successive phase in the process is associated with a product model which satisfies the context of that phase. The big gap between the initial and delivered models is then bridged in a series of comprehensible and manageable stages (phases), with verification at each stage by reference to the context of that stage.

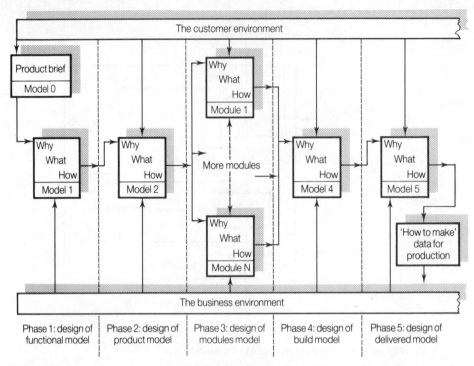

Figure 8.8   **Phase-to-phase linking in the design process.**

This complements Figure 8.7 by illustrating a complete product design process built with the design modules introduced in that earlier figure. Note the phase-to-phase linking mechanisms and the propagation of the basic why–what–how partitioning rationale through all the phases.

The concept has another important advantage: it is modular. In other words, the design activity within each phase follows essentially the same pattern. This pattern is shown in Figure 8.7, which illustrates the basic module of the product design process. It is a generalization and development of Figure 8.4.

The output of the module, which connects it to the next phase, comprises verified statements of the model architecture and design constraints created in the phase. These items are verified, with respect to the customer and business environments, in a **design review**. A variety of review techniques are employed. Senior management are involved at those reviews which commit major resources. A review may require some rework of the phase analyses. This is shown by the 'not OK' loop back to that input which links the module to the preceding phase. Figure 8.4 suggests that only one reference is made to the customer and business environments during a phase. This over-simplifies the real situation because, in practice, both environments are dynamic and must be continuously monitored. This factor is quite general, and it accounts for the other two inputs to the design process module.

Figure 8.8 shows a typical complete design process comprising a structure of the process modules illustrated in Figure 8.7. Note the phase-to-phase linking mechanisms and the propagation of the basic why–what–how partitioning rationale through all phases of the design process.

- *Phase 1* is design of the functional model, also called the requirements definition phase. The functional model is the functional architecture.
- *Phase 2* is design of the product model, also called the product architecture design phase.
- *Phase 3* is design of the modules model. This illustrates a very common 'parallel' partitioning (usually by technology) of the product model into distinct modules. Serial combinations of design modules within the same phase can also be employed.
- *Phase 4* is design of the build model. This model generally corresponds to the product prototype. However, in those cases where prototypes are an unaffordable luxury, the build model is also the real product.
- *Phase 5* is design of the delivered model. It culminates in the verification of the product manufacturing instructions.

8.8.2   Phase 2: Design of the product architecture

The second phase of the design process is design of the product model (or product architecture). It is (of course!) directed at answering three questions:

(1) *Why must it be this way?*   This question is answered by applying the design constraints from Phase 1 to the functional model from that phase. This yields a context analysis which justifies a more realistic definition of the product (and its commercial environment) by eliminating the flaws, ambiguities and unrealistic ambitions in the original concept.

(2) *What must it contain?*   The answer to this question is the product architecture or the product model: a description of the product as a configuration of tangible real elements. It may involve just one technology (software, say) or several technologies (electronics, software and mechanics, say). The fine detail is still absent, except in the most trivial cases. Typically, the major product functions are assigned to modules within the configuration, but module design remains at the specification stage.

(3) *How must it be built?*   This question is answered in the form of a set of design constraints derived from the context analysis of this phase and the environment of the supplier business. Typically, the constraints apply primarily to the implementation of the modules making up the product model configuration.

The definitive product specification

The Phase 2 context analysis reconciles the customer requirements expressed in the original product brief with the harsh realities of some technical, economic and operational limitations. The product that it specifies will differ somewhat from that first conceived by the customer (or product sponsor). It is wise to discuss this first (and most critical) design compromise with the customer before investing further time, effort and money in its development. The dialogue might, of course, lead to the project being abandoned. A more usual outcome is some relatively minor adjustments to the compromise, which then satisfies both parties.

- This agreed compromise becomes the definitive specification of the product.

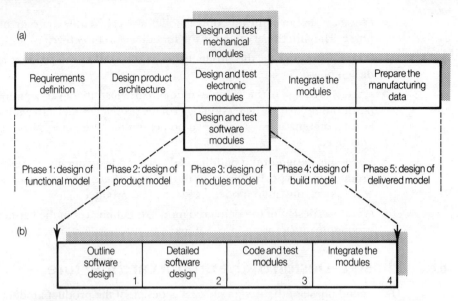

Figure 8.9   **Phase structure of sample product design projects.**

The figure illustrates the flexibility of the product design concept developed in this chapter. In (a), the format of the complete product design process outlined in Figure 8.8 is applied to the small microprocessor-based product analysed in Appendix A. Note that the Phase 3 modules are distinguished by product technologies, which is a partitioning rationale often used at that stage. The diagram at (b) shows how the same basic structure can cope with a larger and more complex product. It is accommodated by expanding the work directed at the Phase 3 modules into a serial structure of basic design modules, as indicated here for the software module.

Critical importance of Phase 2

The Phase 2 documents form an essential baseline for all the subsequent design activity. They also provide crucial data for assessing the commercial viability of the whole venture. The level of detail that should be provided is determined by the need to:

- Demonstrate the degree of matching with the product features described in the functional architecture.
- Establish the technical feasibility of the product model.
- Establish a credible first estimate of the works cost for that model.
- Provide an adequate basis for planning the next phase.

A major design review normally occurs at the end of this phase.

8.8.3   The subsequent phases

There are no fixed rules which determine the number of design phases that follow Phase 2. The product architecture is normally partitioned into a number of modules which can then be tackled essentially in parallel. Probably the most common partitioning rationale is technology but others, such as module function or even geography, are employed. (As illustrated by aeroplane design and manufacture. In

Europe this activity tends to cross national boundaries: wings in Britain, fuselage in France and so on).

A simple illustration is provided by the new product concept examined in Appendix A (A requirements definition example). This is a straightforward microprocessor-based electronic product for a volume market. Figure 8.9(a) shows how the design process for such a product is divided into a series of sequential phases. This 'block structure' corresponds to the example PERT network of Figure 6.12.

Phase 1 is requirements definition and Phase 2 is design of the product model or architecture. This is conceived as a structure of three distinct, but related, modules distinguished by different purposes and technologies. There is a software module, an electronics module and a 'mechanics' module. The latter item comprises the mechanical assemblies and enclosures which support and protect the other modules. The three modules are developed, designed and tested as separate entities in Phase 3 before integration, during Phase 4, into a working prototype. This is tested for conformity with the product specification derived in Phase 2. It becomes the build model of the product on satisfactory completion of these tests. This is used, in Phase 5, to prepare the delivered product model, which is the the manufacturing data.

A more complex example is offered by the case of a large computer-based real-time system. The product architecture is again partitioned into a set of modules comprising, say:

- mechanical hardware
- electronic hardware
- software.

It is important, as always, that the boundaries of these modules are sharply defined and the interfaces between them firmly established. They can be developed, designed and tested as separate entities, as before. In the case of the software, four sub-phases are commonly employed, with labels like:

(1) *Outline software design*, where the whole software structure is partitioned on a functional basis into a configuration of communicating software modules.
(2) *Detailed software design*, where the algorithms for the individual modules are developed and designed, and the module-to-module are interfaces confirmed.
(3) *Code and test*, where the individual modules are coded and tested.
(4) *Software integration*, where the whole software structure is built, in stages, from the individual modules; and is then tested as a distinct entity.

This expansion of the basic structure is shown in Figure 8.9(b). It illustrates a case where serial coupling of the basic design module (Figure 8.7) is employed within the same phase.

The mechanical and electronic modules are subject to analogous activities in parallel with the software sub-phases. On completion, the major modules are brought together in a total system integration and test phase which builds the whole product ready for final acceptance testing.

8.9 Concluding summary

This chapter has described a powerful methodology for designing any sort of product. It is a relatively informal structured approach: as much a way of thinking about general problem solving as a recipe for solving the particular problems of product design. The key mechanism is:

> Big questions are decomposed into successive layers of smaller questions until answers become clear. Big answers are then built from smaller answers.

Rationales are required to decompose the questions. A decomposition process which appears to be universally applicable is encapsulated in the hierarchical why–what–how construct, as in:

> *Why* the product is required will determine
> > *What* it has to do, and the various constraints will restrict
> > > *How* it is able to do it.

In the case of product design, further rationales arise from viewing the product from three distinct viewpoints: technical, economic and operational. Later on in the design process, decomposition by technology and module purpose becomes more useful.

The power of the why–what–how construct remains when the methodology is applied to other classes of problem, but different secondary partitioning rationales must be found. Of course, the mandatory final year project report demanded from engineering students is a product. A report structure based on:

> *Why* this project is important
> > *What* had to be done
> > > *How* it was done

is normally very acceptable. It can also use the technical, economic and operational secondary partitioning rationales with advantage.

Managers, too, can profit from the problem solving technique. Periodic contemplation of their situation based on:

> *Why* are we doing this?   (Justification)
> > *What* are we going to do?   (Specification)
> > > *How* are we going to do it?   (Implementation)

encourages an effective management style which moves calmly from crisis to crisis.

REFERENCES

Macro A. and Buxton J. (1987). *The Craft of Software Engineering*. Wokingham: Addison-Wesley

Miller G. A. (1956). The magical number seven, plus or minus two: Some limits on our capacity for processing information. *Psychological Review*, 63, 81–97

Ross D. T. (1977a). Reflections on requirements. *IEEE Transactions on Software Engineering*, 3(1), 2–5

Ross D. T. (1977b). Structured analysis (SA): A language for communicating ideas. *IEEE Transactions on Software Engineering*, 3(1), 7–35

Ross D. T. and Schoman K. E. (1977). Structured analysis for requirements definition. *IEEE Transactions on Software Engineering*, 3(1), 6–15

SUGGESTED FURTHER READING

Roy & Wield (1986) is a series of broadly relevant articles which yield interesting background material. For the most part, the other specialist texts provide detailed descriptions of particular design methodologies. The general purpose methodology described in this chapter can serve as a useful introduction to any of these. Perhaps the approach presented by Pugh (1991), which is mostly exemplified in terms of mechanical engineering, is closest to it in overall philosophy.

Flurschein C. (1989). *Engineering Design Interfaces: A Management Philosophy*. London: The Design Council

French M. J. (1989). *Conceptual Design for Engineers* 2nd edn. London: The Design Council

Pahl G. and Beitz W. (1989). *Engineering Design: A Systematic Approach* 2nd edn. London: The Design Council (English language version of a German classic published by Springer-Verlag)

Pugh S. (1991). *Total Design*. Wokingham: Addison-Wesley

Roy R. and Wield D., eds. (1986). *Product Design and Technological Innovation*. Buckingham: Open University Press (reprinted with additions 1991)

QUESTIONS

Note: Chapter 8 uses a number of terms which may have marginally different meanings in other texts and, indeed, in common parlance. 'System' is one example. The chapter also develops a specific product design methodology which co-exists (in a compatible fashion) with a multiplicity of other design methodologies. When encountered in the questions that follow, these items should be interpreted as they are defined and/or developed in the chapter.

8.1 (a) Explain the meaning of the following terms:

- product
- repeatable product
- high-volume product
- unique product
- 'one-off' product
- system
- product design
- competitive product design.

(b) What is the difference between a product and a system?

(c) Is the definition of product design in this chapter different from that in Section 3.2.5? If so, why?

8.2 A potential customer must choose just one of a number of similar competing products which are offered for sale.

(a) What is likely to be the principal motivation of such an individual?

(b) Assuming this motivation, identify and define six product attributes that the potential customer should evaluate, for each product on offer, as part of the purchasing decision.

(c) Show how the results of this evaluation

can be used to assess the 'value' of an offered product.

(d) Will a rational customer necessarily purchase the most valuable product on offer? If so, why? If not, why not?

(e) Show how the 'competitiveness' of a product can be measured in terms of the six product attributes referenced in (a) above.

(f) What is an alternative term for 'competitiveness' when it is measured in this way?

(g) Is 'competitiveness', as the term is used here, an absolute or relative measure (of a seventh product attribute)?

(h) Will a rational customer necessarily purchase the most competitive product on offer? If so, why? If not, why not?

(i) What are the most important assumptions underlying this simplified analysis of purchasing decisions?

(j) Are they likely to be valid in practice?

8.3   (a) What is the 'benefit ratio' of a product?

(b) Show, in terms of this concept, how the profit-earning ability of most businesses is constrained by competitive pressures. Hence, derive two product-related conditions, concerning product price and product cost respectively, which must be met if a business is to survive and prosper in the longer term.

(c) What is the role of the product design process in meeting these conditions?

8.4   Write a 'job and person' specification to help a business recruit some product design experts. This should be based on answering, from the perspective of the business that is to employ them, the following three questions:

- *Why* are expert product designers important?
- *What* tasks do they have to do?
- *How* must they be equipped, in terms of skills, to do these tasks?

8.5   Why is 'divide and conquer' a sound basis for product design, and what conditions must be satisfied to make it an effective technique. Explain, in this context, the concepts of:

- partitioning rationales
- constraints
- design options

and show how they can be combined into a powerful design tool.

8.6   Explain the meaning of the terms:

- requirements definition
- product sponsor
- product design environment

and show how the entities that they represent are connected.

Note: Questions 8.7, 8.8 and 8.9 form a why–what–how examination of the structured product design procedure developed in this chapter. It is recommended that they are answered in the sequence offered, because 8.9 builds on 8.8 which builds on 8.7. Together, the three questions provide valuable insights into the problems and solutions of product design. Question 8.10 is designed to cover the same ground in one jump. It is quite a big jump.

8.7   Why is an effective requirements definition methodology the most important design tool?

8.8   The whole problem of creating a product requirements definition contains a communication barrier, an economic conflict and various factors which restrict the freedom of product designing.

(a) Identify and explain these parts of the whole problem. Hence, show that a product requirements definition can be partitioned into a hierarchy formed by the answers to three distinct questions.

(b) The elements of this hierarchy comprise the primary features of the requirements definition methodology. List and explain six desirable secondary features.

8.9   The basic structure of the requirements definition methodology must recognize the prospective product customer, the intended product creator and the hierarchy of primary features identified in Question 8.8. Ideally, it should also incorporates the desirable secondary features referenced in Question 8.8.

(a) Describe, with the aid of a diagram, a

methodology which matches this specification.

(b) Show how this basic structure can be further partitioned, such that the hierarchy formed by the answers to the three original questions becomes a hierarchy of answers to three groups of four questions.

8.10   (a) Explain the concepts listed below as they are construed in the specific structured product design procedure developed in this chapter.

(i) requirements definition
(ii) partitioning rationale
(iii) vantage points
(iv) context analysis
(v) functional architecture
(vi) design constraints.

Show how the entities represented by these concepts are related.

(b) Explain, in the same context, the viewpoints concept. Show how it combines with the other concepts to express the outcome of the first phase of this design procedure as a hierarchical structure of answers to twelve distinct questions. Why is this a useful structure?

(c) How does this first phase of the design procedure link into the second phase, and what is the purpose of the second phase?

8.11   Distinguish between functional architecture and product architecture. Why are these distinctions important?

8.12   'Functional architecture is what the customer wants and product architecture is what the customer can have.' Why?

8.13   List, in time sequence, the three basic analytic steps needed to create a functional architecture. Describe, in relation to some nominated product application, a general procedure for implementing the first two steps.

8.14   (a) What is meant by the term 'design constraint'? Why is the identification of design constraints a critical part of the product design process? How can design constraints be classified into six types?

(b) Show how supplier-imposed constraints might affect the technical aspects of product design.

(c) Show how customer-imposed constraints might affect the technical aspects of product design.

8.15   What is meant by the terms 'initial product model' and 'delivered product model'? Describe, and justify, a standard structure for such models based on the why–what–how partitioning rationale. Hence, show how the whole product design process can be regarded as a modular model-to-model transformation process. Why is this a useful concept?

8.16   The second phase of the design process culminates in the product architecture (or product model). Show how the output of this phase is structured into a hierarchy of three major elements. Why is completion of this phase a major 'milestone' in the product design process?

8.17   *Why* are you studying this chapter?
       What have you learnt from it?
          How can you use this as a planning tool to ensure survival and encourage 'prosperity' at the forthcoming examinations?

PART 3

Interface Topics

Chapter 9   The Marketing and Sales Functions

The marketing and sales functions are usually combined into a single organization within a business. Their common interface with the marketplace provides a rationale for this structure, but it does tend to conceal important differences between the two functions. This chapter provides overview descriptions of marketing and sales in a typical large manufacturing business. The primary purpose is to expose their inner workings and problems at a level of detail appropriate to those engineers outside the functions who must work with them.

Chapter 10   The Production Function

This chapter provides an overview description of the production function in a typical large manufacturing business. As with the preceding chapter, the primary purpose is to expose the inner workings and problems at a level of detail appropriate to those engineers outside the function who must work with it. 'Production' is broadly defined to include the manufacturing operation and a range of ancillary supporting services.

Chapter 11   Technical Project Evaluation and Choice

Choosing the right technological innovation projects for private venture investment is essential for business survival and prosperity. Proposals for such projects are usually competing for limited investment resources. Hence, both their intrinsic quality and the rewards that they promise the business must be evaluated. The chapter covers a number of non-financial and financial evaluation techniques, and provides further insight into business operations. The financial techniques are applicable to a wide range of business situations.

Chapter 12   Basic Financial Accounting

Accounting is a vast topic, and this chapter is an engineering introduction. It is approached by partitioning it into primary and secondary principles, which are described early in the chapter. The primary principles are then explored in some depth by means of an extended example. This is presented in a somewhat different style from the rest of the book. It takes the form of an accounting story about the birth and early life of a new company. The narrative covers the creation of this enterprise and then describes the preparation of its first year accounts. The chapter concludes with an analysis of those accounts which illuminates some of their less obvious messages.

The Marketing and Sales Functions

*If a man write a better book, preach a better
sermon, or make a better mousetrap than his
neighbour, though he build his house in the
woods, the world will make a beaten path to his
door.*

Ralph Waldo Emerson 1803–1882

9.1	Introduction	384
9.2	Marketing, sales and the business	385
9.3	Marketing: The four Ps	394
9.4	Marketing: Mixing the four Ps	400
9.5	More on price and promotion	406
9.6	More on sales	412
9.7	Concluding summary	414

 Advanced material Section 9.5 contains material which is probably best appreciated after gaining some industrial experience. It may be omitted at first reading without significant damage to the basic message.

 Repetitions The chapter includes no significant bulk repetitions, but a number of topics introduced in other chapters are necessarily reviewed. These include the profit equation, economies of scale, the sales life-cycle, product purchasing decisions and the pricing of contract development work. Cross-references are included in the text.

The overall objectives of this chapter are to describe the roles of the marketing and sales functions in a large, technology-based, manufacturing business at a level of detail suited to engineers outside the functions but who work with them. Objectives by section follow:

9.1 To introduce the essentials of marketing and selling, and to describe the structure of the chapter.

9.2 To describe, and contrast, the duties of the marketing and sales functions by examining their part in the profit creation process.

9.3 To analyse marketing in terms of the four Ps concept, which embraces the notions of right product, right price, right promotion and right place.

9.4 To introduce, and illustrate, the marketing mix concept as the particular combination of the four Ps best suited to a defined market sector at a specific time.

9.5 To examine a number of pricing and promotion topics which can be particularly relevant to engineers.

9.6 To review the industrial selling environment, and examine the demands it places on sales personnel.

9.7 To identify its salient points and summarize its major messages.

9.1   Introduction

The Emerson recipe for commercial success (quoted at the chapter head) may have been valid in the nineteenth century, but it is a road to ruin today. Nowadays, only a small number of people are troubled by mice, and they have better things to do than tramp around woods looking for a better mousetrap. They know that an adequate mousetrap, chosen from the many on offer at the local shop, will solve their problem. So how can a contemporary maker of better, or merely adequate, mousetraps survive and prosper in this competitive world? The answer lies in efficient marketing and selling.

A present-day mousetrap maker seeking commercial success must first find those people who have a mouse problem. The nature of their problem must then be understood. Most people do not enjoy killing mice, they just do not want them in the house. Non-lethal mousetraps that just collect mice, later to be released into a neighbour's garden, might be very acceptable. A mouse frightener, which persuades the little beasts to leave voluntarily, would be even more convenient. Understanding the problem leads to a **product**: that is, to a solution to the problem. The potential customers must then be told that there is a mouse-problem solution, that it is easily obtained, and be persuaded that it is better and cheaper than other (competing) solutions. If these messages are believed, some mousetraps will be sold. If the messages are also true, the customers and their infested neighbours will come back for more. But this is still not enough for prosperous mousetrap making, adequate profit must also be made. In other words, the price the customer pays for the mousetrap must be sufficiently more than the sum of all the costs that the maker incurs in getting it into the customer's hands. If this is not so, the maker will eventually go out of business.

This little homily encapsulates the essence of marketing and selling, which are critical activities contributing to business survival and prosperity in competitive markets. They are *different* activities, and the distinctions between them are important. But the differences often go unrecognized, even by their practitioners. So the aim of the next section is to examine these two business functions, and to explore their differences and similarities. This takes the form of an overview of the roles of the marketing and sales functions in the business cycle. Sections 9.3, 9.4 and 9.5 then consider marketing in more depth. This is followed, in Section 9.6, with a brief survey of some aspects of selling. The chapter concludes with a summary of its principal messages.

9.2   Marketing, sales and the business

This section opens with a review of the role of **profit** and goes on to introduce the **market-place** concept. This allows the **profit creation process** to be described, which is the context for the subsequent examination of the roles of marketing and selling in that critical process.

9.2.1   Revenue, cost and profit

Profit is the excess of **revenue** over **cost**:

$$\text{Profit} = \text{Revenue} - \text{Cost} \tag{9.1}$$

This is the **profit equation**. Revenue is the income arising from product sales in a specific period, and cost is the sum of all the costs incurred in that same period. The equation was introduced in Section 1.1.1, is examined in detail in Chapter 7 (especially at Section 7.9) and plays a part in every other chapter. A business operating in competitive markets which does not achieve adequate profit cannot survive in the long run. Profit is needed to maintain and renew the facilities used by the business. It provides rewards to the owners of the business for their investment in it. It pays the interest on loan capital invested in the business. So adequate profits are needed to survive, and better than adequate profits bring prosperity.

It can be assumed (somewhat simplistically at this stage) that the primary business objective is to maximize profit. Profit is achieved by selling products to customers at prices which are greater than costs. The marketing and sales functions of a business are concerned with customers, competitors, products, prices and costs, so they bear substantial profit responsibility. But this is not the whole story, because other businesses also need to make adequate profits. Businesses in the same industry compete with each other to make these profits from the same market. All businesses have access, by and large, to the same technologies and other resources. They can choose which products to create and the prices at which to offer them. If their

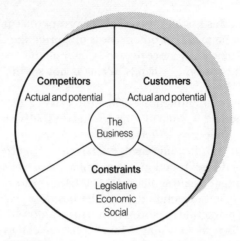

Figure 9.1   **A product market-place.**

This structure represents the commercial environment in which a business operates. It shares this environment, called the product market-place, with its competitors. The business concerned is in the central position in the diagram, where it has interfaces with sets of customers, competitors and constraints. There is also an interface between the customers and the competitors, and both of these parties are also subject to the constraints.

managers are competent, their costs will be much the same as other efficient businesses in the same industry. Success, therefore, must largely depend upon capturing enough customers to make the profit equation deliver a more than merely adequate profit.

9.2.2   The product market-place

The commercial environment in which a business operates is its product market-place. It is a jungle in which the hunters (businesses) stalk their prey (customers) in a steaming environment of barriers to progress and dangers to survival (sundry constraints). Weak or wounded hunters can also fall victim to stronger predators.

A more formal representation of a product market-place is illustrated in Figure 9.1. The business 'owning' this market-place is placed in the central position, with interfaces to sets of customers, competitors and constraints. There is also an interface between the customers and the competitors, and both of these parties are subject to the constraints.

Customers

A **potential customer** is an entity with a need or problem that can be alleviated or removed by a product purchased from one of the businesses operating in the market-place. In fact, this is an incomplete definition of a potential customer. They need two more attributes to qualify. First, they must be able to pay a price for the product which allows its supplier to make an adequate profit. Second, they must be willing to pay that price. There is no shortage of people and organizations with needs and problems. But only some of them qualify as potential customers.

Actual customers are rather different. They 'belong' to the central business, because it has already sold them at least one product. (By the same token, they may also belong to one or more of the competing businesses.) They have proved that they qualify as customers. Their previous need or problem is understood and it will return, because nothing is for ever. Their location is known. Actual customers, therefore, are greatly valued by the businesses that own them, since they represent good prospects for further sales.

Competitors

Competitors are businesses which offer solutions to the same needs and problems as those addressed by the central business, and direct their activities at the same set of customers. Their products are usually similar to those of the central business, but this is not always the case. They may offer **substitute products**, which are aimed at the same customers but use very different technologies. For example, a cat is a substitute product for a mousetrap. It also has additional features which appeal to some customers, despite its much higher price of ownership. Similarly, a word processor substitutes for a typewriter and a calculator for a slide-rule. Threats from substitute product can arise from unexpected quarters, as many makers of typewriters and slide-rules only realized as their businesses disappeared.

Actual competitors are those currently operating in the market-place, offering similar or substitute products. The **potential competitor** category covers those qualified to enter the market with similar products and those who might offer substitute products. The latter are not easily detected.

Constraints

Constraints fall into three broad categories, which overlap to some extent. These are legal, economic and social. (Competitors are also constraints, but of a rather different sort and are treated separately here.)

Many legal constraints are aimed at protecting customers from exploitation or damage by unscrupulous (or ignorant) sellers. The old legal maxim of *caveat emptor* (let the buyer beware) is changing to 'let the seller beware'. Examples from Britain include the Trade Description Acts and the Fair Trading Act. Similar legal provisions apply in many national markets. Additionally, product-liability legislation is becoming increasingly prevalent, particularly in the USA. This provides for legal sanctions against suppliers whose products do harm to customers. Other legal constraints relate to wider social issues. These include such matters as environmental pollution, health and safety at work and minimum wage regulations.

Economic conditions can either constrain or encourage business development. This statement may seem rather obvious, but it does have its subtleties. Suppose, for example, that a national economy is expanding and a particular market is expanding with it. This sounds like good news for all the businesses operating in that market. But the weaker competitors may not be able to raise enough investment capital to expand with the market, although the stronger competitors can do so. Those who invest wisely in additional production facilities then benefit from the **economies of scale**, and may then drive the weaklings out of the market by price-cutting tactics. Thus the rich can get richer and the poor can get poorer even in an expanding market. (The economies of scale concept is discussed quite fully in Chapter 7, particularly in

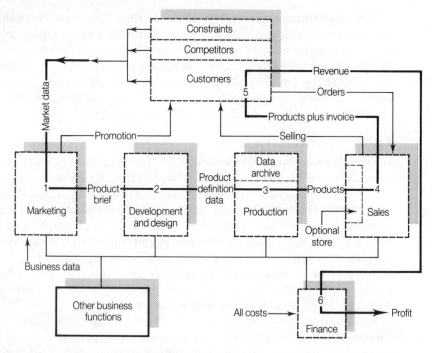

Figure 9.2   A business and its markets.

The marketing and sales functions of a business are its principle interface with the market. The figure illustrates this situation in a typical large, hardware-technology based manufacturing business. The bold path traces the serial process which aims to convert market data (top left) relating to a new or enhanced product into profit (bottom right). The light data paths indicate various parallel interactions with this serial process. The production function holds an archive of product definition data relating to established products. When these are required, the sequence is entered at Stage 4 or Stage 3, according to whether or not the ordered products are stored 'in stock'. Not all businesses maintain a product stock.

Section 7.9.5. It is examined more briefly in Section 9.5.1.)

Social constraints come in many forms. They range from the language and cultural barriers to international trade to the bargaining power of trade unions and the ethics of trading practices not specifically covered by legislation. For example, making cigarettes for sale to consenting adults is not illegal, but it is regarded as wrong by many people.

The term 'level playing field' is now an accepted jargon to describe a situation where the constraints apply equally to all competitors in a market. A great deal of international discussion is devoted to this concept of fair play. The negotiations between the member states of the EEC, destined to become a 'common' market in 1992, illustrate the point. These centre around various constraint-harmonization issues.

9.2.3   The path to profit

The marketing and sales functions of a business are its interface with the product market in which it operates. The term 'interface' is particularly apt, because communication is involved, as is the process of changing data from one form to another. The interface is bidirectional, because both marketing and sales must interact with the market *and* with the rest of the business. Figure 9.2 illustrates the situation in the typical large, hardware-technology based, manufacturing businesses which are at the focus of this book.

The figure shows the main data paths in the system which comprises the business and its markets. The bold path traces the serial process which aims to convert market data (top left) relating to a new or enhanced product into profit (bottom right). The other (light) data paths indicate various parallel interactions with this serial process. In summary, the sequence of activities on the bold path is:

(1) **Product-related market data** is converted, by the marketing function, into a product business plan. Part of this plan is a **product brief**, which defines the objectives of a product development and design project.

(2) The product brief is converted into a product development and design project plan by engineers in the technical function. Implementation of this plan creates the **product definition data**, which describes how to make and test the product.

(3) The product definition data is converted into products by the manufacturing operation in the production function. (Readers who are uncomfortable with the concept of a product as data are asked to forgive this small poetic licence. It is reasonable, because a product is an expression of its product definition data in a particular physical form.)

(4) The sales function associates an **invoice** (which states the price required) with the product(s) and causes the whole package to be dispatched to the customer. The number of product units 'shipped on an invoice' ranges from one upwards, depending on the nature of the market concerned.

(5) The customer retains the product(s) and forwards the price, now termed revenue, to the business.

(6) The revenue is used, in the finance function, to pay costs that the business has incurred and the residue is the profit.

This sequence outlines the process which (hopefully) converts market data relating to a new or enhanced product into profit. In an established business, the production function has an archive of product definition data relating to *established* products. When these are required by the market, the sequence is entered at Stage 4 or Stage 3, according to whether or not the ordered products are in stock. Not all businesses maintain a product stock, and the product store shown in Figure 9.2 is optional.

Practical considerations

In practice, matters are not quite as simple as this summary suggests. As data moves along the path to profit, its value increases incrementally by amounts which can be equated with the cost of processing it at each stage. These costs are incurred before revenue is generated at Stage 5. Generally, there is no way of storing such costs for more than a limited time. For example, wages must be paid weekly, salaries monthly, and external suppliers 30 days (say) after delivering the components needed to manufacture the product. Additionally, while all this is going on, the business is incurring other costs which are not attributable to activities on the bold data path.

Expenditure on product research and management training are just two examples of such costs. The net effect of the delays along the bold path and the 'other costs' is a loss of correlation between the revenue and the total costs subtracted at Stage 6 to produce the profit. In an established business this is not a problem, since the stream of revenues from established products can 'fund' all these costs. It is, however, one of the difficulties which arise in launching a new business. In that case, there are no established products at the launch and funds must be obtained from elsewhere to sustain the business in its early life.

The marketing and sales functions are now examined by treating each as a 'black box', which transforms a set of inputs into a set of outputs. The inputs and outputs are those shown in Figure 9.2, and include the light data paths.

9.2.4 The role of marketing

The marketing function has three major responsibilities, which can be labelled:

(1) New profit opportunities.
(2) Product business plans.
(3) Promotional activities.

New profit opportunities

A major concern of marketing is the identification of promising new profit opportunities based on new or enhanced products. This requires two inputs: an appreciation of the strengths, weaknesses and ambitions of the business *and* market data.

The first input (labelled 'business data' in Figure 9.2) is vital. Ideally, there should be a good match between existing business resources (market knowledge, technologies, manufacturing capacity, work-force skills, management talent, finance, and so on) and those required to exploit the opportunity. Poor matching substantially increases the risk of failure. For example, many businesses operating in defence markets have failed to diversify profitably into civil markets, despite their advanced technical skills.

There are three strands to the market data input, relating to constraints, competitors and customers. A good understanding of the market constraints applying, or likely to apply, to its products is a necessity for all businesses. The growing concern about environmental damage, such as that arising from burning fossil fuels and chlorinated fluorocarbons (CFCs) in aerosols and refrigerators, illustrates the point. Knowledge of the competitors, and of their activities and products, is also critical. In some cases, useful data is public knowledge: the price, terms of offer and specification of consumer products, for instance. But it is difficult to obtain such information when trading is not in the public domain. Data relating to costs, future product plans and market share are always closely guarded, although much reasonably accurate data can be gleaned by 'detective' work. The pursuit of 'competitive intelligence' of this sort by ethical means is entirely proper and necessary. Industrial espionage also occurs but is generally frowned upon, particularly by those who suffer its consequences. The customer data that is sought has many facets, and the overall requirement goes beyond understanding the problems which might be addressed by a new or enhanced product. For example, the profitability of an opportunity will depend on the number of products sold, the price obtained for them and the cost of creating them. The timing and 'shape' of the **sales life cycle** (discussed in Section 3.3.1) is also critical.

The term **market research** is used to describe the work of obtaining and analysing market data. Its results are necessarily speculative, because forecasting is involved. The problem is not eased by the dynamic nature of the market. Competitors come and go, as do constraints. Customers' behaviour often seems to be capricious since, not unreasonably, they are more interested in solving their own problems than those of a market researcher.

To qualify as 'promising', a potential opportunity must be judged to meet criteria for profitability and, normally, for resource matching as well. Survivors of these tests usually involve one of more of the following situations:

- A current or anticipated 'gap' in the market, not currently satisfied by competitive action.
- Current products which can be technologically updated to yield more attractive features and/or better performance at the same or (better) reduced cost.
- A market expanding more quickly than the current rate of supply.

This list emphasizes the importance of competitor data, particularly with respect to product plans.

Product business plans

When a promising new profit opportunity has been identified, the next marketing task is to prepare a business plan. Generally, this relates to a **product range** (that is, to a family of similar products with increasing capabilities, costs and prices) rather than to a unique product. For simplicity, the term 'product' is retained in what follows. It can be interpreted as 'product range' where appropriate.

In the case of a new product, the plan treats the opportunity as a potential new 'mini-business'. The rationale of this approach is that each such product should become self-supporting and profitable in its own right. For enhancements to existing products, the plan is additive to an existing mini-business plan.

A plan describes the opportunity, specifies everything that has to be done to exploit it, and forecasts (in amounts and timing) its implementation costs and consequential revenues. A **risk analysis**, defining threats and vulnerabilities (such as those arising from competitive action), is also included. The planners liaise with the other business functions involved in the plan, principally in relation to technical feasibility and cost estimates. Note that plan costs predict cash-flows out of the business, and plan revenues predict cash-flows into it. So, from the financial perspective, the plan is regarded as a proposed investment/return project, where the costs are the investment and the revenues are the return. The evaluation of such plans is discussed in Chapter 11.

Generally, implementing a product business plan commits substantial resources, and the prior approval of top management is required. For this reason, a plan is usually prepared as an outline first, with the emphasis on its feasibility, financial aspects and risks. Subsequently, if the outline plan is approved, the details are filled in by the business functions concerned. In Figure 9.2, this detailed planning activity is initiated by the product brief.

Usually, marketing retains overall responsibility for plan implementation right through to the demise of the product, for one reason or another, at the end of its life cycle. This duty requires that it monitors progress against the plan and initiates corrective action as necessary. Responsibility for the individual sub-plans defining activity in the other business functions resides, of course, with the management of those functions.

Promotional activities

The third major responsibility of marketing is **product promotion**. Generally, this means all activities aimed at influencing potential customers to favour the products offered by the business over those offered by its competitors. As such, it includes selling. But, in this analysis, the term *selling* is reserved for sales function activities involving person-to-person customer contact. Here, therefore, promotion is regarded as the exclusive domain of the marketing function, and it does not include selling. The reasons for this unusual approach emerge shortly, in Section 9.2.6.

Promotion is concerned with established, enhanced and new products. Its most visible aspect (and that of marketing generally) is product advertising in the media. However, the total concept is broader than this, and is very market dependent. Promotion is covered in more detail in Sections 9.3.3 and 9.5.2.

9.2.5   The role of sales

The sales function has only two tasks, one of which is very straightforward. These are:

(1) Product dispatch.
(2) Selling.

Product dispatch

This task of the sales function has already been mentioned. It is at Stage 4 on the bold path of Figure 9.2. Here, an invoice is associated with the product, or product batch, and arrangements are made for its dispatch to the customer. But this is not a particularly demanding job and does not, in itself, justify the existence of the sales function.

Selling

In simple terms, the primary purpose of the sales function is to obtain confirmed orders for products from customers. The ordered products are then obtained either through an internal order placed on the production function or, more immediately, from the product store (if there is one).

Obtaining firm orders is the sole objective of selling. Selling is not a trivial task, although it is frequently regarded as such by engineers. Success or otherwise depends greatly on the personality of the salesperson. It is briefly discussed in Section 9.6.

9.2.6   Marketing and sales compared

Both the marketing and the sales function interface the business to its markets, and both are concerned with customers, competitors, products, prices and costs. Hence, they each bear a profit responsibility. But they have only the task of promotion, when broadly defined, in common. Promotion is more narrowly defined, in this book, to exclude selling – a decision which removes even this limited overlap between the roles of the two functions. Other, less arbitrary, distinctions are now examined.

Marketing and sales operate at different ends of the profit path through the business, as shown in Figure 9.2. The profit creation process starts with marketing and ends, apart from some simple arithmetic, with sales. Marketing is essentially a strategic function, being principally concerned with the longer-term issues of product planning and market influence. In contrast, the sales function is involved with the day-to-day implementation of product plans in their final 'pay-off' phase. It is essentially a tactical function.

In practice, the two functions are normally part of the same organization within a business. This organization is not always called 'marketing and sales', as it is in this book. The name 'marketing' is, perhaps, more common but numerous 'sales' and 'commercial' departments do exist. Whatever its name, it comprises both the marketing and the sales functions in a well-ordered modern business. Usually, sales is subordinate to marketing with, for example, the sales manager reporting to the marketing director. This real-life conjunction of the two quite distinct functions reflects their common interests in customers, competitors, products, prices and costs. There remains, however, some confusion in industry about their respective roles. Two reasons seem to underpin this situation.

Firstly, marketing has the higher status. It is perceived, oddly, as a more demanding and professional role than that of sales. It is certainly less dependent on the quirks of personality. Marketing can be analysed and taught as an academic discipline, as witnessed by the plethora of textbooks and university courses on the subject. This seems not to be the case with sales. Books and courses on selling tend to emphasize the persuasive element of the task. Neither are widely available in seats of academic learning, perhaps because the topic is too close to the harsh realities of industrial life. Also, it must be said, some of the methods propounded in such books and courses are less than ethical. Stories of dishonest selling pervade the media (for whom bad news is good news) and the public image of the salesperson is not good. Whether or not this is justified (generally it is not) is irrelevant, it is the fact that matters. So, naturally enough, sales people prefer to be known as marketeers, and will describe their jobs as such even when this is manifestly not the case.

The second reason is more important, because it reflects some facts of industrial life and qualifies the analysis of this section. This has focused on the roles of the marketing and sales functions. As a general rule, a description of the role of a business function can be equated with the role of the people working within that function. This rule is less true for marketing and sales than for any of the other business functions. For example, a marketeer will not hesitate to take an order should the opportunity arise, and sales personnel glean competitive intelligence as a matter of everyday routine. Thus, on occasions, salespeople are marketing and marketeers are selling. But the functions remain distinct.

9.2.7 Section end notes

This section serves two purposes. First, it collects together some further points which would have disturbed the flow of the argument if they had been included earlier.

Secondly, it introduces the more detailed discussion of marketing which absorbs the next three sections.

Further points

(1) The business depicted in this section could be described as **market-led** or, perhaps, **market-driven**. The guiding principle is the simple logic of trying to produce what customers want. This is the way with modern businesses, but it has not always been so. Traditionally, many businesses were **engineering-led** or **production-led**. Businesses which are dominated by engineers often try to sell technical excellence irrespective of cost. Nowadays, this only works in highly specialized **niche markets**. Production-led business, based on the flawed concept of 'we make it, they buy it' have mostly succumbed to more rational competitors.

(2) Not all businesses that survive are profitable. Some unprofitable businesses are sustained by government subsidies for political, social or economic reasons. National railway operations are a typical example. Very few of these are completely self-supporting.

(3) The assumption that the primary objective of a business is to maximize profit is too simplistic. A better assumption is that the first objective of most business managers is to survive and their second objective is to prosper. This might appear to be a cynical view, but it amounts to no more than observing that managers are also human. In a free market, achieving an adequate profit is the most obvious way of meeting these objectives. But not all managers are motivated entirely by self-interest. Some are genuinely more concerned with, for example, providing employment, equipment for the handicapped or food for the starving.

(4) Finally, the vision of marketing and sales provided in this section is idealistic. Real life is not as tidy as presented here. The principles are sound, but the way in which they are applied in practice varies widely in different businesses.

Marketing: Where from here?

Drucker (1989) cites marketing as a primary cause of American economic success. He identifies Cyrus McCormick, an American agricultural engineer and businessman, as its nineteenth century inventor. Today, marketing is conventionally introduced in terms of twin concepts labelled the **four Ps** and the **marketing mix**, respectively. This same approach is used, in the three following sections, to expand the analysis developed earlier in this section.

9.3 Marketing: The four Ps

The concept that marketing is about achieving:

- the **right product**
- at the **right price**
- with the **right promotion**
- in the **right place**

was originally formulated by McCarthy (1964), and has been elaborated by other writers since that time. 'Right' means right for the target customer *and* for the potential supplier.

9.3.1 Right product

This refers to a product, or product range, which both:

- adequately matches the identified needs or problems of the target customer, *and*
- is within the capabilities of the business to manufacture at a *competitive cost*.

The cost stipulation is important, because cost is a major factor in the profit equation. It also emphasizes the danger of over-specifying the product by providing optional features which are not cost-justified by their effect on sales. If product cost is not competitive it is difficult to set a competitive price and generate an adequate profit.

Products can be classified in market terms. The first major distinction is that between **tangible products** and **service products**. Tangible products have distinct physical characteristics, such as weight, size, shape and colour. Service products do not have a physical presence and are best described by example. Transport, insurance, education, consultancy and hairdressing are all service products. They are frequently based on specialist skills and facilities. This book is concerned mostly with tangible products. But the marketing of tangible products can involve a critical supporting service element. Typically, this applies when the customer requires a long-term solution to some need or problem. A product warranty, 'free' on-site maintenance for twelve months, and the ready availability of spares are examples of after-sales service. Such factors can be regarded as part of the product or as promotion elements. The provision of good documentation is also an important marketing tool for complex products. It is best regarded as an integral feature of the main product to which it refers.

Some of the principal marketing terms commonly used in classifying tangible products are now explained. The distinctions are useful when the marketing requirements of different sectors are considered in Section 9.4.

Industrial products

These are designed and manufactured for supply to corporate bodies, such as other businesses, public authorities and government departments. They are sometimes called **capital products**. However, the term 'capital' implies that customers purchase the products for long-term use. For example, office furniture, desktop computers and machine-tools are industrial products commonly purchased as capital items. However, items such as electrical relays and carburettors are industrial products but not usually capital products. This is because they are generally purchased as components destined for incorporation into the purchaser's own products.

Consumer products

The primary end users for consumer products are members of the general public, so they are sometimes called **domestic products**. Any home provides a wide range of examples: furniture, carpets, kitchen equipment, food, heating oil, paper towels, and so on.

Durable products

Products in this category are intended to have a long-term future in their own right. Some examples are machine-tools, computers, washing machines and software packages. A distinguishing feature is the need for maintenance, including inspection, servicing, preventive maintenance and repair. In an ideal world, software would be an exception to this rule.

Consumable products

These are products which are expended or changed in some way during use. Food is clearly a consumable. Paper and non-rechargeable batteries are further examples, as are the components a business purchases for incorporation into its own products. Consumable products have no long-term future in their own right. Maintenance is not usually applied to such products, because it is not needed, or not cost-effective or not possible. There are exceptions to this: wooden pencils need periodic sharpening, for instance.

9.3.2 Right price

The price obtained for a product is always important to the selling business, because it is a critical part of revenue. But there is a broad spectrum of customer response to product price, and this is another factor which distinguishes different types of market. At one end of the spectrum, price is the *only* feature which distinguishes competing products. It is then *the* critical competitive factor. At the other end, price is not important to the customer and other competitive weapons must be employed. Between these two extremes, price is just one of a number of product features which a customer considers in making a purchasing decision. But price occupies a special position in the list of features which describe a product. This is because it represents the purchasing capacity which the customer gives up in exchange for all the other product features. In other words, product purchasers have decided that they would rather have the product than the purchasing ability represented by its price. (A simplified analysis of the product purchasing decision can be found in Section 8.3.)

Petrol is an example in which price can be critical, because different brands are virtually indistinguishable in performance terms. So the smaller suppliers tend to compete with the giants of the industry solely on price, relying on sales volume to achieve enough revenue. The larger suppliers, whose prices are usually remarkably similar, largely ignore their smaller brethren and compete with each other in the number and positioning of outlets (a place factor) and 'freebies' offered (a promotion factor). Indifference to price is often associated with **necessity products**, such as food and clothing, when these are offered at prices well within the purchasing ability of the customers. Purchasing decisions then tend to be based on other factors, such as easy availability, convenience, appearance or functional performance.

In markets involving rational customers, such as the professional industrial buyers of machine-tools, the price of owning the product is often more critical than the initial price. **Price of ownership** includes the initial price of the product, together with its operating, maintenance and repair costs. In principle, this applies to all durable products, including those sold to the general public. However, the average member of the public probably only considers the initial product price. Irrational customers often equate high price with high quality and exclusiveness. This perception has a logical appeal, but it does not always apply in practice. Increasing the price of a luxury product may actually increase its rate of sales, so demonstrating a particularly bizarre facet of human nature.

9.3.3 Right promotion

Promotion is the customer persuasion aspect of marketing. As noted earlier, it is generally considered to include person-to-person selling. In this text, 'promotion' is used in a more restricted sense which excludes that activity. Selling is briefly discussed in Section 9.6.

Potential customers must be identified before they can be influenced. This trite statement raises a question that has been glossed over in the discussion so far: who is the customer? The answer to this question is market dependent, but two general points can be made. Firstly, the product purchaser is not always the product end user. Secondly, a product purchasing decision is often a complex matter involving more than one individual in a joint assessment of many factors. This situation is commonly the case with durable industrial products, but it can apply in any product category. Some examples will make this more clear.

The domestic end users for consumer products are many in number and widely dispersed. It is not usually economically feasible for a business which manufactures such products to sell directly to these end users. A typical arrangement in this case is illustrated in Figure 9.3.

Here, the product maker sells to **wholesalers**, wholesalers sell to **retailers**, and retailers sell to end users. There are three types of customer in this 'distribution channel', and all must be persuaded to buy the product.

At the opposite extreme, consider the case of a business bidding for a contract to supply an air-traffic control system to be installed at a major airport. Figure 9.4 illustrates the multiplicity of people and organizations that influence award of the contract.

The national aviation authority (the Civil Aviation Authority in Britain and the Federal Aviation Authority in the USA) is likely to be the system specifier and purchaser. But the end users are the airport operator, air-traffic controllers, and the many airline operators using the airport. Aircrew employed by the airline operators and their ground management are involved in the purchasing decision, as is the government department responsible for national transport. The government department responsible for national defence is also consulted, because airspace is a commodity shared by military and civil aircraft. All these parties are customers of a sort, and all must be persuaded that the proposed system is compatible with their interests. The situation is simplified, to some extent, by the fact that a evaluation team within the national aviation authority is responsible for bid adjudication.

The right promotion, therefore, must be directed at the right targets. Equally, the positive and negative factors which are likely to influence the different targets must be identified and emphasized or de-emphasized as appropriate.

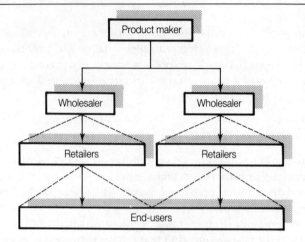

Figure 9.3 **A typical distribution channel: consumer product.**
The purpose of this figure (and of Figure 9.4) is to illustrate that 'the product customer' is rarely a single individual or organization. In the situation illustrated here, the maker of consumer products must recognize wholesalers, retailers and end users as different sorts of customers. Each has different needs that the products must satisfy. This multiple-customer environment must be considered in product design, pricing and promotion.

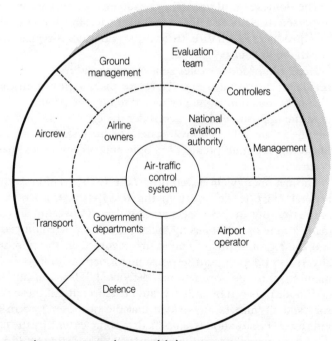

Figure 9.4 **A complex system product: multiple customers.**
The purpose of this figure (and of Figure 9.3) is to illustrate that 'the product customer' is rarely a single individual or organization. In the situation illustrated here, a business is bidding for a contract to supply an air-traffic control system for a major airport. The figure shows the many different people and organizations that influence award of the contract. All of these are customers of a sort, each with different needs that the (system) product must satisfy. This multiple-customer environment must be considered in product design, pricing and promotion.

9.3.4   Right place

The need for a product to be easily accessible by potential customers is self-evident but sometimes neglected. Inadequate attention to this factor can limit the growth of a small business, and has proved to be the fatal flaw in many otherwise excellent business plans. In McCarthy's original formulation of the four Ps, the alluring alliterative attraction of 'place' triumphed over descriptive accuracy. The phrase '. . . right place at the right time' is a better expression of the factor, since customer demand exhibits both geographical location and time parameters. Thus, ice-cream sells best at the seaside in summer, and textbooks in campus bookshops at the start of an academic session.

Nowadays, the right place factor is interpreted in three different ways, all concerned with right place and right time:

- The physical means of product distribution, which moves products from the original maker into the hands of end users.

- The structural organization of that physical distribution channel.

- Positioning at point of sale.

The physical transport issue is critical, because transport adds directly to the cost of the product. Factors for analysis include means of transport, routing, size of loads, transit time, product protection and transit insurance. Decisions also have to be made on the use and siting of intermediate storage depots. These depend on the extent to which the benefits of bulk loads and local accessibility are offset by the costs of storage and idle money tied up in stock. However, all these facets of the problem can be evaluated in reasonably precise numerical terms, in contrast to many aspects of marketing.

One form of distribution channel has already been mentioned: the maker–wholesaler–retailer arrangement commonly used in consumer markets and illustrated in Figure 9.3. But this is just one of a number of different arrangements between product makers and specialist distribution businesses. For example, the use of agents by industrial product businesses as an economical way of accessing overseas markets, and franchise arrangements in the consumer market place. Product distribution by mail-order direct to the end user is another mechanism which is usually associated with consumer markets. But it is increasingly employed for industrial products. One of the most successful desktop computer makers operates exclusively in this way.

9.3.5   The four Ps: Conclusion

The four Ps approach to marketing is a satisfactory way of illustrating the range and complexity of the task. But the four elements are not totally distinct. For example, discount pricing in the January sales is both a pricing and a promotional policy. Similarly, the easy availability of reasonably priced spare parts for a particular brand of motor car has product, price, promotion and place connotations. This classification fuzziness is a minor quibble of no real consequence. However, it does illustrate that only rarely does just one of the P factors totally dominate a marketing strategy. In most cases, it is the combination that matters. This combination of the four Ps is the so-called marketing mix.

9.4   Marketing: Mixing the four Ps

The marketing mix concept was originated (Borden, 1964) at about the same time as McCarthy's four Ps analysis. In terms of the four Ps, it is the notion that businesses must design and implement the right mixture of the product, price, promotion and place factors to survive and prosper in competitive markets. In a particular market, this right mixture varies with time, and it is different in different markets. For example, depending on the level of the local mouse population, kitten promotion should emphasize either hunting ability or cuddly charm. The fact that the four Ps are not independent variables is also implicit in the marketing mix concept. Low price, for instance, can compensate for low product quality and poor after-sales service, as observation of the desktop computer and hi-fi markets confirms.

9.4.1   Market segmentation

The concept emphasizes the need for a business to analyse the market in which it operates in order to determine the right mix. 'Divide and conquer' is the first rule for any analysis. In this case, the process is called **market segmentation**. Two major market segments are consumer and industrial. These have already been distinguished, to some extent, in the previous section.

Table 9.1 summarizes some of the differences in the marketing mix requirements of the consumer and industrial market segments. It shows that very different marketing (indeed, whole business) cultures are required in the two segments. This is one reason why individual businesses normally concentrate on just one segment, and find it difficult to switch from one to the other. A large company made up of many separate businesses can operate successfully in both segments, but the individual businesses within it generally follow the same rule. In practice, Table 9.1 is no more than a starting point for more detailed analytical work.

In the consumer market further segmentation is usually based on **socio-economic groups**. This approach classifies the target population primarily according to income, because this a good indicator of location, life style, type of employment, political leanings and purchasing habits. More detailed subdivisions based on age and sex are also made. The purpose is to create a descriptive profile of typical target consumers, and then shape a marketing mix that will capture them. A rather different approach to segmentation is used in marketing industrial products to corporate organizations. While relative affluence is obviously one factor that distinguishes such customers, other important distinctive features are geographical location and customer type.

9.4.2   Segmentation: A case study

As an illustration of segmentation techniques, the approach of a British business developing a marketing strategy to expand its total sales is now outlined. The procedure is loosely based on material prepared by Peter Greenwell of Weibmuller Klippon Electrics Ltd (Greenwell, 1989, private communication).

A hypothetical business designs and manufactures a range of electrical relays, typically used in various industrial control applications. Figure 9.5 summarizes its recent sales performance and current ambitions. It shows that annual sales have

	Consumer markets	Industrial markets
Situation	Product end users – widely dispersed members of the public – tend not to discriminate fine differences between the objective features of competing products. Demand is subject to seasonal variation. Product accessibility is important and promotion must cater for the multi-level nature of the distribution channels.	Product end users are corporate organizations who are discriminating purchasers, taking both product and maker features into account. Promotion must cater for multiple contributors to purchasing decisions. Distribution is normally direct from maker to customer, and relatively simple.
Product	Emphasis on *subjective* rather than objective performance features.	Emphasis on *objective* rather than subjective performance features.
Price	Initial price usually critical and more important than price of ownership for durable products.	Price always evaluated in relation to other product and maker features. Price of ownership critical for durable products.
Promotion	Promotion to distributors similar to that for industrial products. End user promotion a combination of image-based, low fact content advertising in the mass media, attractive packaging and a variety of 'special' product-related offers.	Factual advertising in specialist trade press, exhibitions and trade fairs employed to identify potential customers. Promotion then emphasizes product quality (fitness for purpose), commercial terms available and maker quality factors such as flexibility, punctuality and stability.
Place	'Instant' availability often critical. Multi-level distribution channels commonly employed, as are a variety of other more direct methods, such as mail-order, product parties and doorstep selling. Distribution costs are generally a significant part of end user price.	Distribution usually direct from maker to customer but wholesalers used in some cases. Agents are often employed in overseas markets, perhaps as a preliminary to establishing a foreign subsidiary.

Table 9.1 Illustrating the concept of marketing mix.

The 'marketing mix' is the mixture of the product, price, promotion and place factors which is 'right' (that is, most cost-effective) for a specific market. The table summarizes some of the differences in the marketing mix requirements of the consumer and industrial market segments. It illustrates that very different business cultures are needed to operate successfully in these two segments. This is one reason why individual businesses normally concentrate on just one such segment, and find it difficult to switch from one to the other.

increased (discounting inflation) by about fifty per cent over the last five years. A similar percentage increase is anticipated over the next five years if the current marketing strategy is retained. But the business wishes to more than double its revenue over the next five years. Thus, the figure defines a 'planning gap' to be filled as a result of the new strategy.

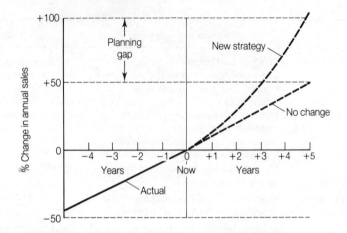

Figure 9.5   **Case study: the planning gap.**

The graphs describe a business situation used in the text to illuminate the marketing mix and market 'segmentation' notions. They summarize the recent sales performance and future ambitions of a business trading in a wide range of electrical relays. Annual sales have increased by about fifty per cent over the last five years. A similar increase is anticipated over the next five years if the current marketing strategy is retained. But the business wishes to more than double its revenue over the next five years. Thus, there is a planning gap to be filled as a result of a new marketing strategy.

The gap-filling options

The options for filling this gap are:

    (1) Better penetration of current markets with current products.
    (2) Better penetration of current markets with new products.
    (3) Penetration of new markets with current products.
    (4) Penetration of new markets with new products.
    (5) Acquisition of one or more competitors.

The first four options combine change/no change strategies in markets and products. Each calls for a different approach. Probably, Option 1 is the least risky, least expensive and least rewarding of the four; and, probably, Option 4 is the opposite extreme. But this is speculation at this stage. The fifth option does not employ **organic growth**. It achieves 'instant' growth by acquiring increased market share and, at the same time, reduces the intensity of competition. The options are not necessarily mutually exclusive, although they might become so when resource constraints are considered.

Market research

The first segmentation step merely partitions the whole market (all products and all customers) by location and customer type. This results in a matrix like that shown in Figure 9.6.

    Diagrams of this sort are often called 'market maps'. In this case, the 'cross-point' boxes represent areas for detailed market research. The following list describes the major objectives of the market research project.

Customer type → Location ↓	Electricity: power generation and distribution	Electricity: local distribution	Water and sewage processing	Gas distribution	Petro-chemicals	Food processing	Building services	Manufacturing industry	Transport industry	Mining industry	Defence industry	Media	
Britain													
Western Europe													
Eastern Europe													
North America													
Middle East													
Far East													
Australia and New Zealand													
South America													

Figure 9.6   Market map 1: location versus customer type.
This first market map in the segmentation case study merely partitions the whole market (all products and all customers) by location and customer type. Initially, the cross-point boxes only represent areas for detailed market research and they are shown empty for this reason. Ultimately, they could encapsulate figures describing (say) the size of the five-year accessible market for each product type in each geographical location.

(1) To identify actual and potential customers, and assess their product requirements over the next five years.
(2) To identify potential new products, together with outline product specifications and likely price levels.
(3) To derive a forecast, for each country, of the total market demand in each of the next five years, segmented by product and customer type.
(4) To identify actual and potential competitors, and their likely market status (strengths, weaknesses, products and market share).

All this is no small task. The work includes:

- Assessment of national statistics and forecasts to establish likely patterns of economic and industrial development in each country.
- Perusal of trade directories and journals to identify potential customers, competitors and products.
- Analysis of available financial and product information for both customers and competitors.
- Visits to trade fairs and exhibitions.
- Visits to typical actual and potential customers.

Product range \ Customer type	Electricity : power generation and distribution	Electricity: local distribution	Water and sewage processing	Gas distribution	Petro-chemicals	Food processing	Building services	Manufacturing industry	Transport industry	Mining industry	Defence industry	Media	Totals (units × 10000)
Reed relays	6		17		33			18					74
Printed circuit relays	5	6	8	12	17	2		7		3	13		73
Ligh current relays	7	11	16	17	21	17		7					96
Medium current relays	7	9	14	12	13	5	2	8	8	4	6		88
Power relays	16	22	10	5	16	5	6	7	3	4	5		99
Co-axial relays			3	4	16		30		15			28	96
Contactors: MK I	6	3	5	7	8	9	2	2	2	12		8	64
Contactors: MK II			20							52			72
Totals (units × 10000)	47	51	93	57	124	38	40	49	28	75	24	36	662

Figure 9.7   **Market map 2: product versus customer type.**
This market map typifies just one type of output from the market research project in the segmentation case study. It shows, for one country cited in Figure 9.6, the anticipated five-year aggregate total demand (in product units × 10,000), segmented by product range and customer type. This summary is supported by a number of more detailed *annual* demand maps (not shown), each identifying individual customers. Similar maps sets are produced for each country.

The market research project creates an enormous amount of data and segmentation is used to make this digestible. Figure 9.7 illustrates one of the data summaries.

This is a market map showing, for just one country, the anticipated five-year aggregate total demand (in product units × 10 000), segmented by product range and customer type. This summary is supported by a number of more detailed *annual* demand maps, each identifying individual customers. Similar maps sets are produced for each country.

Strategy formulation

The structured data created by the market research project is the launching pad for formulation of the new marketing strategy. Each country is considered, in turn, to determine the marketing mix with the (anticipated) best ratio of sales revenue to marketing cost. Forecasts of market share per product arising from this mix are also made. This share depends, among many other things, on competitor activity in the market. There are wide variations in the most cost-effective marketing mix between the different countries. Some of the major factors causing these variations are:

(1) *Product* Each country is likely to have marginally different product safety standards and, for some products, electrical interface requirements will also vary from country to country. Minor product variations are bad news from the

manufacturing point of view, but the problem can usually be accommodated by appropriate design modifications. However, the cost and time to accomplish such modifications must be taken into account.

(2) *Price*　Prevailing price levels are usually set by locally based competitors in each country, and country-to-country equivalence is rare. Additionally, currency exchange rate considerations enter into pricing, as do differences in local sales taxes and import tariffs. The customary commercial terms of supply (credit terms, say) also vary from country to country.

(3) *Promotion*　The appropriate methods and levels of promotional activity in any one country are largely conditioned by the extent of existing market penetration, and the strength of the local competition.

(4) *Place*　The optimum choice of physical and organizational distribution arrangements depends primarily on the distance between the market and the manufacturing base. In an extreme case, where a very attractive market exists in a remote location, it may be advantageous to establish (or purchase) a subsidiary manufacturing operation in that location.

The whole situation is reviewed when the most cost-effective marketing mix for each country has been determined. A dominant consideration is availability of the resources needed to implement the new marketing strategy. Resources are always limited, and this constraint influences the final choice of countries to include in the strategy. It may, of course, turn out that the initial ambition to more than double revenue over the five year period is too ambitious.

9.4.3　The defence systems market

The market for defence products, such as weapon systems, command and control systems, communication systems, and the like is a industrial market of a rather different sort to that cited in the case study. Currently, it is important to many technology-based businesses, although this may change if peace really does break out. This section concludes with a brief examination of the market in marketing mix terms.

Products

Defence system products invariably include many different technologies, ranging over the whole fields of mechanical, electrical, electronic and software engineering. Product specifications often stretch the limits of these technologies. So technology development projects are likely to be part of the whole programme. Great emphasis is placed on reliability and availability (in the system 'up-time' sense). Equally, the ability to function in extremes of temperature, humidity, dust, vibration and so on is a common requirement. Exhaustive testing and rigorous quality assurance are mandatory aspects of development, design and manufacture, as is the use of customer-approved hardware components and software languages. The system end-users, and their masters, invariably seek long and useful product life. This product requirement emphasizes the importance of such features as provisions for system enhancement and technological updating, long-term spares availability, user training, and good documentation.

Price

Product price is generally a less sensitive issue than in civil markets, but 'value for money' has received increased attention over the last few years. Procurement of systems of this sort is normally by way of a **turnkey contract** between the customer and a main contractor. The nature of such contracts, and their financial aspects, is discussed later (in Section 9.5.1, under the heading of 'Contract pricing'). For a variety of reasons, political as well as technological, the main contractor frequently employs other companies as subcontractors with specific responsibilities for parts of the total project. This always complicates the pricing problem, and increases the costs of project planning and control.

Promotion

In principle, the national government is the only customer in any one country. But this customer appears in many different guises: the armed forces as end users, different government departments, and the government defence establishments concerned (mostly) with defence technologies. Each such organization has a different perspective on forthcoming projects, and all these different interests must be understood and addressed in contract bids. All governments have a vested interest in preserving their national defence industries and this factor can influence the placing of contracts. Employment issues, too, can enter into the equation. Bidding for overseas contracts as a main contractor is rarely successful for these reasons. So international subcontracting and consortia 'teaming' arrangements are now commonplace when major new projects are in prospect. Promotion plays an essential role in setting up such arrangements, in which a partner might be a company treated as a competitor in other markets! So-called **offset provisions** are often a critical promotional factor in bids by international consortia. These seek to compensate a government for spending its taxpayers' money overseas with a reciprocal spending programme at home.

Place

There seems to be no distinctive aspect of this factor in the defence systems market except, perhaps, the secrecy requirement which is normally associated with military matters.

9.5 More on price and promotion

The concepts of right price and right promotion were introduced in Sections 9.3.2 and 9.3.3, respectively. This section develops these matters a little further, by examining a selection of pricing and promoting policies.

9.5.1 Pricing policies

Four types of pricing policy are considered:

(1) 'What the market will bear'.
(2) Pricing for growth or 'undercutting'.
(3) 'Cost-plus'.
(4) Contract pricing, including contract development pricing.

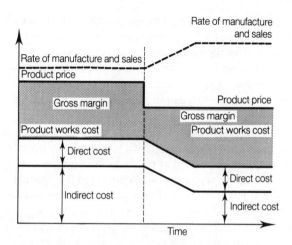

Figure 9.8 **Product price, works cost and gross margin.**
The figure shows how a business might increase profits as a result of reducing product price! Gross margin is the difference between the price of a product unit and its works cost (manufacturing cost). It is the gross profit per product unit sold. Part of works cost is the indirect cost. This is a share of the whole 'fixed' manufacturing cost, so-called because it does not vary with the rate of product manufacture. When product unit price is reduced, the rate of unit sales (and, hence, of unit manufacturing) gradually climbs to a new level. At first, the gross margin is also reduced. But, as the rate of manufacturing increases, the works cost reduces – as the fixed manufacturing cost is increasingly shared among more products units. Thus, the gross margin recovers to much the same value as before the price cut. The business is then selling more products than before at much the same gross profit per unit, so it has increased its market share and is making more profit.

Product suppliers can choose to operate one or other of the first three policies as they see fit. The 'ground rules' for contract pricing are usually set by the contract customer.

What the market will bear

This is a common product pricing policy in all types of market. The aim is to set product price as high as possible, subject only to selling enough units to achieve planned profit. It is most effective (from the supplier's point of view) when all the competitors have adopted the same strategy for equivalent products. However, formally agreed price-fixing arrangements between competing businesses are usually illegal. But there is no doubt that such situations do arise by simple price-matching mechanisms, without any formal agreement. The policy is always vulnerable to a competitor reducing price to gain an immediate, perhaps temporary, advantage. This is the pricing for growth, or undercutting, policy. It undercuts competitors' prices.

Pricing for growth

A business endeavouring to increase its market share can normally increase sales volume by reducing product price significantly below that of its competitors. This might reduce profitability. But this is not necessarily so, because economies of scale in manufacturing, if available, could also reduce costs. The situation is illustrated in Figure 9.8.

Here, **works cost** is the cost of making the product. It comprises a **direct cost** and an **indirect cost**. The first element depends only on the nature of the product. It is made up of the cost of the components that are assembled into the product plus the labour costs of assembling and testing it. The indirect cost element represents the fraction of the total manufacturing process cost which is assigned to the product. The manufacturing process cost comprises a facilities cost (due to machinery, equipment, buildings and so on) plus management costs. It is virtually fixed (constant) over a given period, irrespective of the number of product units made by the process in that period.

The difference between the product price and its works cost is the **gross margin** (sometimes called the **gross profit**). It measures profit at the product level. (This is more than profit measured at the business level, because it only takes costs attributable to making the product into account.) In the figure, product price and works cost are initially constant at a fixed rate of manufacture and sales. A constant gross margin, at about fifty per cent of product price, is shown. A decision is then made to reduce product price. This produces the desired effect and the rate of sales (and, hence, of manufacture) increases to a new level. At first, the price cut reduces the gross margin by the same amount. But, as the rate of manufacture increases the works cost reduces, such that the gross margin recovers to much the same value as before the price cut. The business is then selling more products than before the price cut at much the same gross margin, so it has increased its market share and retained its profitability.

The key to this pleasing situation is the reduction in works cost as the number of products made increases. This comes about because the fixed cost of the manufacturing process is now spread over more products, so the indirect part of the works cost is reduced. In other words, the manufacturing operation (represented by the fixed costs) is being used more efficiently. This is the economies of scale effect. It is discussed more fully in Chapter 7, particularly in Section 7.9.5.

Cost-plus

This old-fashioned pricing policy simply sets product price by adding some 'reasonable' percentage (as gross profit) to the product works cost. The technique has the merit of simplicity, but that is all that can be said in its favour. It is based on two notions that are fallacies in competitive markets. These are the concept of 'reasonable' profit and the belief that there is some mechanistic connection between cost and price. In reality, there is no such thing as a reasonable profit: all competitors need to make the best possible profit, and competitive pressure provides both the driving motivation and the limiting constraint. Equally, there is no trite formula connecting price and cost. The realistic price of a product is what a purchaser is willing to pay for it, and this is not related in any way to what the product cost its seller. However, some large businesses of national economic importance are in near-monopolistic supply situations. In such cases, government regulation is often employed as a substitute for competition in price control. Some of the larger telecommunication and 'utility' (such as water and electricity) companies are in this position.

Contract pricing

Many engineering businesses supply complex products to major corporate customers, such as government departments, national telecommunication companies, banks, and public or local authorities. Typical products are traffic (air, sea, road and rail) control systems, process control systems, military aircraft and other weapon systems, satellite communication systems and financial systems of various sorts. The procurement and supply of high-value products of this sort always involves a contract between the customer and the supplying business. This is because the products are costly custom-built items which cannot be designed and made on a speculative basis. The customers normally have immense purchasing power, which enables them to virtually dictate contract conditions. The contract, a legal instrument, usually covers the development, design, manufacture, installation, commissioning and subsequent support of the product. Contracts of this nature are sometimes called *turnkey contracts* because, in theory, all the customer has to do (some time after awarding the contract) is to turn the key which brings the product into service. (Occasionally, this theory is justified by events.) A contract is placed following issue of an **invitation to tender** (ITT), by the customer, to selected competitors deemed to have the requisite capabilities. A variety of marketing activities are involved in getting selected as a potential contractor and then achieving a fair share of contracts. But only the contract pricing aspects are of interest here. The ITT normally specifies the nature of the price 'bid' required, and there are three main types:

(1) Cost-plus.
(2) Fixed-price.
(3) Profit-incentive.

In all cases, a 'staged' price payment pattern is normally offered. This allows the contractor to claim partial payments at the satisfactory completion of 'milestone' stages on the path to contract completion. The facility is provided because projects costs can be very substantial and spread over many years. It is unreasonable to expect a business to totally fund the costs under these circumstances.

Cost-plus contracts are going out of fashion. In theory, the mechanism is straightforward. The customer and the supplier first agree the (estimated) cost that the supplier will incur in implementing the contract. A previously specified percentage of this cost, the profit element, is then added to the cost to yield the contract price. In practice, the price-setting negotiations can be a bureaucratic nightmare. The competitors have every incentive to demonstrate high cost levels to the customer, who is naturally reluctant to accept such bad news. Nor are the customer's price problems over when the contract has been placed. In major projects of this sort, the customer (beset by all the normal problems of limited budgets and demanding time-scales) is as solidly 'locked-in' to the project as the contractor, whatever the legal niceties of the contract. (The situation is not unlike that arising with a destitute borrower from a bank. If the borrower owes the bank £5,000 it is the borrower's problem. But, if the borrower owes the bank £50,000,000, it is the bank's problem.) Under these circumstances, the supplier may succumb to various temptations, such as:

- remembering some previously 'forgotten' costs, or
- arbitrarily increasing all costs, or
- charging excessively for (the inevitable) changes to product specification, or
- unduly extending contract duration, or
- doing all of these things.

(The term 'contract engineering' has been misused to describe activities of this nature.) Customers have become increasingly disinterested in offering cost-plus contracts. They are still sometimes used, however, when the contract work involves a substantial element of high technical risk, such that accurate cost estimating is genuinely impossible.

Fixed-price contracts avoid many of the problems corporate customers experience with cost-plus contracts, and the financial mechanism favours the more efficient suppliers. The principle is payment for results achieved. This seems more rational than payment merely for work done, which is the case with cost-plus arrangements. The financial mechanism is simple. A 'ceiling' price is included in the ITT and competitors are required to bid at, or below, that level. The way in which they arrange their price, cost and profit equations is entirely their own concern. The contract is then awarded (in theory) to the lowest price bid which is judged adequate in all other respects. The bid price is then the *fixed* contract price, without regard to *actual* contract cost. Generally, customers prefer fixed-price over cost-plus arrangements but suppliers are not as enthusiastic. There are problems, of course, for both parties. An early problem for the customer is choosing the ceiling price. ITTs may be declined if it is set too low. The selected contractor might make an 'excessive' profit if it is too high. This latter situation (if detected) is especially uncomfortable for government departments, who are supposed to spend taxpayers' money wisely. Customers sometimes solve their 'ceiling price' problem by placing a small study contract, aimed at assessing technical feasibility and realistic cost, before the main contract. Another difficulty relates to the financial risk inherent in all such major projects. In a fixed-price contract this risk is (legally) carried solely by the contractor, which is not the case with cost-plus contracts. If the successful contractor underestimates the cost, the planned profit will be correspondingly reduced. If the mistake is a big one, the contractor may be obliged to complete the work at a loss. Naturally, potential contractors prefer not be to exposed to this disaster, and they add substantial safety factors into their cost sums. The net effect of this is that a fixed-price contract is likely to be priced much higher than its cost-plus equivalent.

Profit-incentive contracts are a relatively recent development aimed at combining thé good features of cost-plus and fixed-price contracts but avoiding their bad features. Here, 'good' and 'bad' reflect the customer point of view. There are many detailed variations in the financial mechanisms of profit-incentive contracts, but the basic principle is reasonably consistent. This relates the profit earned by the contractor to contract performance on a proportional scale. Thus, 'poor' performance results in 'poor' profit, 'average' performance in 'average' profit, and so on. The concept has a clear logical appeal, but there are equally obvious difficulties. These centre around how performance is measured (cost, time and technical excellence are possible parameters), and on the definition of the scale.

Contract development

Some major businesses sell their expertise in technological innovation, commonly termed **research and development** (R&D), to corporate customers. The work is generally called 'contract development' by both customers and contractors. Contractual arrangements are much the same as those outlined for the complex industrial products. There has been a fairly recent move away from cost-plus towards fixed-price for such contracts. As a result, some research contracts with substantial inherent costing uncertainty are being placed at about twice the fixed price of the equivalent cost-plus contract. This situation is illustrated by a case study in Section 6.3.1.

9.5.2   Aspects of promotion

Three aspects of promotion are briefly reviewed here:

(1) Cost-effectiveness.
(2) Advertising.
(3) Supplier promotion in industrial markets.

Cost-effectiveness

Determining the cost-effectiveness of all forms of promotion is a long-standing problem. Advertising is a typical example. There seems to be no proven mathematical or empirical relationship between advertising expenditure and product sales volume. In consumer markets, experience suggests that the sales-generating effect of an increment of expenditure declines as memory of the advertisement fades in the consumer's mind. So, at the start of a sales campaign, a series of small increments is more effective than a single large increment. But a saturation effect can also occur and, beyond some threshold, further increments have no discernible impact on the rate of sales.

Advertising

Advertising is the most obvious means of promotion, and two levels can be distinguished. The first concerns business-level publicity, with only passing mention of products. It aims to present an attractive image of the business as a worthy contributor to local and/or national life. Thus, factors like the provision of employment and care for the environment are emphasized. Product-level advertising mostly employs national media for consumer products and the trade press for industrial products, but trade fairs and exhibitions are also used in both cases.

Generally, members of the public are relatively undiscriminating purchasers of consumer products. Advertising aimed at these end users tends to be 'glossy' with little factual content, often associating a desirable life style with the product as much as projecting the product itself. It is commonly associated with other promotional elements, such as:

- 'Free' offers of, say, gift vouchers and entries into prize-bearing competitions.
- Credit purchase on 'attractive' terms.
- Packaging designed to enhance the image of the product.
- Warranties extensible on 'attractive' terms beyond normal time limits.

Businesses offering consumer products must also deal with wholesale and retail distributors. These organizations employ professional buyers who are not as gullible as domestic end users, nor motivated by the same considerations. Their concern is solely that their organization should profit by distributing the product. Advertising aimed at these customers in the distribution channel promises them a profitable and trouble-free arrangement. This emphasizes volume-related discount price structures, the quality of the end-user promotional programme, anticipated end-user demand, security of supply, product reliability, shelf-life, invulnerability to transit damage, and a host of similar factors.

Industrial products are purchased by the professional buyers employed by corporate customers. So industrial product advertising is more factual than that for consumer products, and it is generally concentrated in specialist trade journals. Here, the emphasis is on the objective performance features of the product and the various product-related services that are available. Exhibitions and trade fairs are also widely used as a means of establishing initial contact with potential customers.

Supplier promotion in industrial markets

The prime purpose of promotional activity in industrial markets is to establish and maintain profitable supply relationships with the selected corporate customers. This goes beyond merely convincing potential customers that product performance (including quality) meets their requirements. Other critical factors in a promotion 'package' include:

- Commercial terms of supply, such as:
  - the levels of volume-related price discounts on 'one-off' prices
  - guarantees of continued supply for spares provisioning
  - credit arrangements
  - sale or return facilities
- Flexibility: the willingness and ability of the supplier to meet 'crisis' demands by the customer.
- Punctuality: the record of the supplier in meeting promised delivery dates.
- Accuracy: the willingness and ability of the supplier to deliver the required items to the agreed specification and in the quantities ordered.
- Stability: the financial strength of the supplier, which measures the probability that they will stay in business.

Professional buyers make independent enquiries to verify, so far as possible, the integrity of such offered packages. These include assessment of the financial position of the potential supplier and, probably, discussing their performance history with colleagues in the industry (even those employed by their own competitors). The promotional task is not finished when the supply contract is signed, since the purchaser then monitors supplier performance and does not hesitate to complain if it fails in any respect. Thus, the supply contract requires continuous marketing attention in order to retain the customer.

9.6 | More on sales

In this book, marketing and sales are regarded as distinct business functions where, using an agricultural analogy, marketing prepares the ground and sows the seed for sales to reap the harvest of orders. Thus, the primary purpose of the sales function is to obtain confirmed product orders from customers. Generally, this involves person-to-person contact between the salesperson and the customer and this is the essence of selling. Sales staff employed by industrial product makers must sell to the professional buyers, and others, who represent corporate organizations. Those employed by consumer product makers are generally in a similar position, because the immediate customer is likely to be a wholesaler, or one of the larger retail organizations.

This short section first explores the industrial selling environment, and then considers some of the characteristics of good sales people.

9.6.1 Industrial selling

In order to appreciate the complexity of this environment, consider first the case of **missionary selling**, where the salesperson is seeking the first-ever order from a new customer. Marketing will have prepared the ground with written material, glossy brochures and promotional packages. But all this does little more than get an appointment for the salesperson. The list of things which then have to be sold, eyeball-to-eyeball, to achieve that first order is formidable:

- The promised supplier performance of the selling business, in terms of punctuality, accuracy, and so on.
- The product, and any supporting services that go with it.
- The product price structure and terms of supply.
- The integrity and financial stability of the supplier business.

Thus, the salesperson probably has to deal with a range of people at different levels in the customer organization, each with a different interest. For example, part of the selling job is directed at the product end users, who might be design or production engineers. Another part of the task could be a presentation to top management. All of this absorbs substantial time: meetings have to be arranged, demonstrations mounted, visits to reference customers agreed and hosted, and prices and commercial terms negotiated.

Not all missionary selling projects succeed. When a supply contract is achieved, it becomes the salesperson's duty to monitor supplier performance and respond positively to any customer complaints. If this facet of the job is done properly, subsequent sales to the customer are more easily achieved and there is a good chance of retaining the customer as a source of future business. Selling is then in the **account development** phase.

Throughout the whole exercise, from first appointment to account development and beyond, the salesperson is aiming to establish a long-term relationship with the customer. This requires the identification, and cultivation, of those individuals in the customer organization who are:

- most influential in purchasing matters
- likely to know about future purchasing requirements
- directly affected by performance on existing supply contracts.

Thus, while the formal relationship is with the customer's purchasing department, many critical links need to be established and maintained in other parts of the organization. Good salespeople identify so closely with their customers that, over a period of time, the customers treat them almost as members of their own organization. What, then, are the qualities of a good salesperson?

9.6.2 Successful selling

Successful selling demands two sorts of ability. One of these is purely technical: product knowledge, numeracy, literacy, and familiarity with standard selling techniques. All of these things can be absorbed by any reasonably intelligent individual. The second, more distinctive ability, is largely inborn. It is a particular type of personality.

All good salespeople seem to have some personality characteristics in common. They are optimists who easily forget today's failure, secure in the belief that the sun will shine on them tomorrow. They genuinely believe in the merits of the product that they are selling, and can communicate this enthusiasm to their customers. They get on well with all sorts of people, appearing to be equally at ease in the board room and on the shop-floor. And they are trustworthy: keeping their customer's secrets and only making promises that they really do believe that they can keep.

9.7 Concluding summary

The material is an overview description of the marketing and sales functions in a typical large, technology-based, manufacturing business. The emphasis throughout is on industrial products and markets, but the consumer sector is not neglected. The inner workings of the two functions are exposed at a level of detail appropriate to those engineers outside the functions who must work with them.

The marketing and sales functions interface the business to its markets and so share a concern with customers, competitors, products, prices and costs. But their roles in the business are quite different. This is emphasized by analysing their duties in the business process which converts market data into profit. Marketing emerges as an essentially strategic activity, which contrasts with the more immediate tactical concerns of sales. The approach illuminates the critical roles of the technical and production functions in the same process, their relationship with each other, and with marketing and sales.

This introductory material is expanded in a more traditional description of marketing in terms of the four Ps (product, price, promotion and place) and their combination in the marketing mix. A case study, focused on an industrial market sector, and a brief analysis of the defence market are used to illustrate these concepts. Selected pricing and promotion topics of particular engineering significance are then reviewed. The chapter concludes with a brief examination of industrial selling and the demands that it places on sales personnel.

REFERENCES

Borden N. H. (1964). The concept of the marketing mix. *Journal of Advertising Research*, 2–7
Drucker P. F. (1989). *The Practice of Management*. London: Pan
McCarthy E. J. (1964). *Basic Marketing: A Managerial Approach*. Homewood, Ill: Irwin

SUGGESTED FURTHER READING

There is no shortage of specialist books on marketing, but only a relatively small number of these employ the analytical approach which most engineers prefer. Baker (1991) satisfies this criterion in a very readable manner. Kotler (1991) is a deservedly popular and comprehensive US-flavoured text, but too descriptive for some tastes. Selling is rarely covered in academic textbooks. However, the Lawrence and Lee (1984) management text does provide an entertaining introduction to the topic.

Baker M. J. (1991). *Marketing – An Introductory Text* 5th edn. Basingstoke: Macmillan
Kotler P. (1991). *Marketing Management* 7th edn. Englewood Cliffs, NJ: Prentice-Hall
Lawrence P. A. and Lee R. A. (1984). *Insight into Management*. Oxford: Oxford University
    Press (Chapter 7)

QUESTIONS

9.1 'The marketing and sales functions of a business are concerned with customers, competitors, products, prices and costs, so they bear substantial profit responsibility.' What is profit? Why is it important?

9.2 (a) Show how the product market-place in which a business operates can be represented as a structure containing:

- actual customers
- potential customers
- actual competitors
- potential competitors
- legislative, economic and social (market) constraints.

(b) Explain the meaning of the seven terms listed above. What is a substitute product? Give two examples of substitute product situations which are not cited in Chapter 9.

9.3 'A business is a system for turning market data into profit.'
(a) Justify this statement by describing the new product creation process within a typical manufacturing business.
(b) How does the business turn market data relating to established products into profit?

9.4 An analysis of the role of the marketing function can be started by partitioning the whole task into responsibilities for:

- new profit opportunities
- product business plans
- promotional activities.

Complete the analysis, and explain the relationships between the three parts of the whole marketing task.

9.5 Describe the role of the sales function.

9.6   Compare and contrast the roles of the marketing and sales functions.

9.7   (a) Section 9.3, which contains about 2000 words, explores the 'four Ps' concept of marketing. Summarize its principal messages in not more than 500 words. (Note-format and diagrams are allowed, even encouraged.)
(b) How does the four Ps concept relate to the 'marketing mix' concept?

9.8   In relation to the four Ps concept of marketing:
(a) Describe what is meant by 'right product'. Explain the meaning of the terms:
- tangible product
- service product
- industrial product
- capital product
- consumer product
- domestic product
- durable product
- consumable product.

(b) Is there such a thing as the 'right price' for a product? If so, why? If not, why not?
(c) A 'vector' is a quantity with both direction and magnitude. The 'right promotion' of a product is a vector. Discuss this notion.
(d) Describe what is meant by 'right place'.

9.9   (a) Describe the 'marketing mix' concept in terms of the 'four Ps' concept.
(b) Define, compare and contrast appropriate marketing strategies for the consumer and industrial product sectors.

9.10   A particular business wishes to increase the level of its sales significantly over the next few years. Identify five distinct marketing strategies which it might follow in pursuit of this objective. Are these strategies mutually exclusive?

9.11   Generally, there are wide variations in the most cost-effective marketing mix between different countries. Identify some of the major factors causing these variations.

9.12   Discuss the salient features of the market for defence systems.

9.13   (a) Describe the product pricing policies which are commonly termed:
- what the market will bear
- undercutting
- cost-plus.

(b) A business which adopts a 'pricing for growth' policy might achieve growth in market share and profit. Why?

9.14   (a) What is a 'turnkey contract'?
(b) Describe, in relation to such contracts, the pricing schemes known as:
- cost-plus
- fixed-price
- profit-incentive.

(c) Compare and contrast the relative advantages and disadvantages of these schemes from the customer perspective *and* the supplier perspective.

9.15   (a) What is the principal purpose of the promotional activities conducted by suppliers of industrial customers?
(b) Describe, in this context, the contents of a typical 'promotional package'.

9.16   Section 9.6, which contains about 700 words, is a brief examination of *selling*. Summarize its principal messages in not more than 200 words. (Note-format and diagrams are allowed, even encouraged.)

9.17   This book is a product. You are a potential or actual end user customer for the product. Describe your perception of its marketing mix on a five-point scale ranging from 'very good' through 'good' to 'very poor'. If we do it again, how can we improve it? (Answers, on a postcard please, to the acquisitions editor at the publishers. Please tell us who you are, where you work and/or study, which parts of the book you have read, and why you now have the book.)

The Production Function

Double, double, toil and trouble;
Fire burn and cauldron bubble.

William Shakespeare 1564–1616

10.1	Introduction	418
10.2	The manufacturing operation	421
10.3	Manufacturing support services	435
10.4	An arena of conflict	457
10.5	Current production technologies	460
10.6	Concluding summary	464

 Repetitions   The chapter contains no significant repetitions, but a number of topics introduced in other chapters are necessarily reviewed. These include budgets, the break-even concept and the profit equation, product works cost, quality-related product attributes, and product value. Cross-references are included in the text.

The overall objectives of this chapter are to describe the role of the production function in a large, technology-based, manufacturing business at a level of detail suited to engineers outside the function but who work with it. Objectives by section follow:

10.1 To review the purpose, configurations and relationships of the production function, and to describe the structure of the chapter.

10.2 To introduce the essentials of product manufacturing, and to describe the basic facility structures employed in different product environments.

10.3 To examine the role of the manufacturing support services in greater detail than provided by the summaries in Section 10.2.

10.4 To illustrate the variety of people-related problems which can arise in the production function.

10.5 To outline the current position in the developing areas of manufacturing process technologies and production management systems.

10.6 To identify its salient points and summarize its major messages.

10.1 Introduction

The **production function** is the wealth-creating 'engine' that powers the large, technology-based, manufacturing businesses at the focus of this book. This treatment of the topic owes much to Waters (1991) and Wild (1989). Here, the function includes the **manufacturing operation** and various **manufacturing support services**. The **technical function** has an important interface with production, which is the 'customer' for the product definition data created by its development and design teams. The **sales function** is the 'customer' for the finished products manufactured by production. These relationships are illustrated in Figure 9.2.

The manufacturing operation is the principal source of income in a manufacturing business. It is here that purchased raw materials and components are transformed into finished products for sale. The added value derived from this process is required to pay all the costs incurred by the business *and* provide a profit. For this reason, manufacturing performance is always closely monitored by top management, and sustained pressure to improve labour and capital productivity is a fact of manufacturing life. Most large manufacturing businesses have other sources of income, such as interest from investments and profit on **contract development** work in the technical function. But such income is usually trivial compared with that derived from manufacturing which, in terms of earnings capacity, is the heart of the business. Recognizing this, many businesses regard manufacturing as the single **direct** activity. All other tasks are perceived as **indirect** activities (also called **overhead** activities) needed to support manufacturing, which earns the funds to pay their costs.

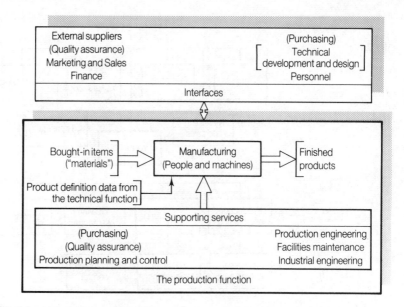

Figure 10.1 **An overview of the production function.**

The production function is the wealth-creating 'engine' that powers a manufacturing business. It is centred around the manufacturing operation, which transforms material inputs to finished product outputs in accordance with product definition data created by the technical function. This figure is an overview *system* diagram of the function, showing its major elements and the relationships between them. The most important interfaces between the function, other principal business functions, and external suppliers are also shown. Alternative positions for the purchasing and quality assurance support services are indicated by the parentheses.

Elements of the production function

The central role of manufacturing within the production function (and, hence, within the business) is illustrated in Figure 10.1. This is a system view rather than an organizational arrangement.

The figure sets the agenda for what follows. It shows the manufacturing operation as a transformation process which converts inputs to outputs. The process is supported by a set of local services activities, and the whole structure comprises the production function. This function has a number of critical interfaces with the other business functions, and these are also shown.

The position of the **purchasing** activity in the corresponding organizational structure varies from business to business, being a separate business-level function in some and a manufacturing support service in others. This same situation applies to **quality assurance**. Figure 10.2 shows a typical organization and some variations.

Alternative positions for quality assurance and purchasing are shown in this figure. The trend is to treat these activities as distinct functions in their own right, reporting directly to top management. For quality assurance, this arrangement may be a contractual requirement imposed by a major customer (such as a government department). The function manager then has more authority in negotiating with production and the other functions, so product quality is less likely to be compromised at times of commercial pressure. Also, quality assurance is commonly

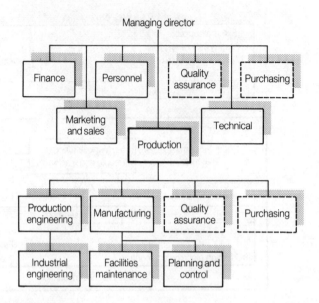

Figure 10.2 **A typical production function organization.**
This is a typical organizational structure corresponding to the system diagram of Figure 10.1.
Alternative positions are shown for the purchasing and quality assurance activities (dashed boxes).
These are increasingly recognized as critically important to the whole business, so the trend is to
treat them as 'top-line' business functions in their own right.

organized in this way by businesses which have adopted the **total quality** concept examined later, in Section 10.3.6.

Purchasing is increasingly recognized as a critical business activity, and it may be elevated to separate function status solely for this reason. But it does usually act as a buying agent for the other business functions, as well as for production. It is then sensible to centralize the activity, so that multiple orders for non-production items can be aggregated and improved volume discounts obtained. Additionally, a purchasing function which acts jointly for the technical and production functions can minimize the unjustified use of exotic and expensive components in product designs.

In Figure 10.2, the load on the managing director is, perhaps, too heavy when both purchasing and quality assurance report on the top line. A maximum of six is an accepted figure for the number of subordinates reporting to a manager. The load is reduced to five subordinates in an alternative structure, where purchasing and quality assurance report to the production director. Many variations are also found within production organizations and the arrangement shown in Figure 10.2 is just one possibility. Purchasing and quality assurance are covered in more detail in Sections 10.3.5 and 10.3.6, respectively, where they are treated as manufacturing support services.

Chapter structure

The production function is a meeting place for people and machines, and the trend is for less people and more machines. It is frequently an arena of human conflict. This topic is explored in Section 10.4, which follows discussion of the manufacturing operation and its supporting services in Sections 10.2 and 10.3, respectively. The treatment to this point takes little account of manufacturing process technologies and favours a more traditional production management perspective. This provides a useful background to the brief examination of current production technologies in Section 10.5.

10.2 The manufacturing operation

Following an introductory overview, this section examines what the manufacturing operation has to do and, to a lesser extent, how it does it. It concludes with an analysis of different types of manufacturing. Manufacturing support services receive only limited attention at this stage. Section 10.3 provides a more detailed treatment of those activities.

10.2.1 Manufacturing overview

Viewed from the narrow perspective of an **established product**, manufacturing can be regarded as a simple sequential (although usually re-entrant) process. It transforms product-related inputs into an output comprising a quantity of finished products. Matters become more complicated when several different established products are being manufactured at the same time, which is the normal situation in **batch manufacturing**. The real-life situation is also periodically disturbed by a number of planned interventions. Product-level interventions include those necessary to:

- enhance established products
- introduce new products
- phase out old products.

Process-level interventions also occur, such as:

- periodic maintenance and/or servicing of the machinery
- the introduction of new machines
- modifications to process procedures and techniques aimed at improving efficiency.

Virtually all planned interventions bring about changes in the work patterns of the people involved. Training in new skills may be required, and new working conditions may need to be negotiated and agreed. So, even when everything is proceeding as planned, manufacturing is likely to be in a state of change. But it is also subject to a variety of random disturbances, which further disturb the serenity of its management and staff. The causes of these major and minor crises are many and various. Just a few examples are cited here, as they might be presented to the manufacturing manager:

- The parent company, reacting to a forecast profit shortfall, requires an immediate reduction of ten per cent in all overhead costs.
- An external supplier has not delivered some urgently needed components.

- A critical machine has broken down, and the only other machine capable of the same work is stripped down for scheduled maintenance.

- A unexpected 'rush' order for a large quantity of an obsolete product has been received from the sales department.

- Urgently needed new product definition data has been delivered by the technical function, but it is incomplete in several important respects.

- A substantial stock of specialist components has been purchased against a 'firm' order from sales, but the order has now been cancelled.

- A deputation of irate assembly workers is waiting to discuss a grievance arising from a recent **time and motion** study.

This problem list illustrates how the performance of the manufacturing operation is critically dependent on the performance of a number of other organizations, both within and outside the business. John Donne (1571–1631) observed, some time ago, that 'no man is an Island, entire of itself'. The same is true of business functions and, indeed, whole businesses. The whole system works best when all its interconnected subsystems work properly together. The list also illustrates that life in the manufacturing operation is rarely dull, and that there are opportunities for conflict on several different fronts. This theme is developed in Section 10.4.

10.2.2   A specific established product

A typical (although simplified) manufacturing sequence for a batch quantity of a specific established product is now considered. An 'established product' is one that has been previously manufactured in substantial numbers, so a 'no surprises' exercise is anticipated. The sequence is started, in production, by acceptance of a **works order** received from the sales function. It terminates (in this illustration) when the ordered batch quantity of products is delivered to the finished-goods store. The works order specifies the product type, the quantity and the delivery date required. The anticipated maximum cost to sales is also stated.

The works order mechanism is part of an internal 'trading' relationship between the sales and production functions. An accepted works order becomes, in effect, a 'contract' between the two functions. It records an agreement for sales to purchase the product batch specified in the order from production. Both parties are bound by its time and cost provisions. The trading relationship is enshrined in the budget structure of the functions, which provides a means of financial planning and control. It is unlikely that real money will change hands. Normally, such transactions are simply recorded by equal and opposite entries in the 'actual' columns of the sales 'products purchase' budget and the production 'deliveries' budget.

(Budgets are relatively short-term financial *plans*, usually covering a twelve month period. Actual financial performance is measured by comparing progress with the corresponding budget. Budgets and budgeting are discussed in Sections 7.4 and 7.7. Trading between different units within a business is very common. A works order mechanism, or something like it, allows each unit to have its own set of budgets for financial planning and monitoring purposes. Works orders are sometimes called **inter-divisional orders**. Such documents are regarded as the only meaningful form of internal correspondence in some businesses!)

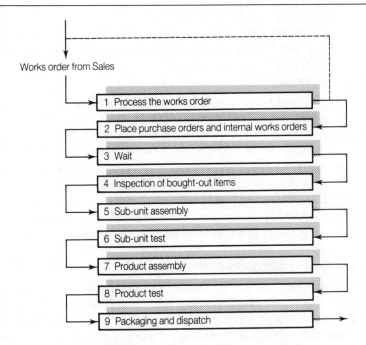

Works order from Sales

1 Process the works order

2 Place purchase orders and internal works orders

3 Wait

4 Inspection of bought-out items

5 Sub-unit assembly

6 Sub-unit test

7 Product assembly

8 Product test

9 Packaging and dispatch

Figure 10.3   **A manufacturing sequence for a product batch.**
An 'established' product has been previously manufactured in substantial numbers, so the
manufacture of another 'batch' should be straightforward. A typical manufacturing sequence for
such a batch is shown here. The diagram is simplified by not showing the effects of other product
batches which are being manufactured at the same time. It also illustrates an internal trading
relationship between the production and sales functions. The sales function, acting as a customer,
orders (and, subsequently, receives and pays for) the product batch from the production function,
acting as a supplier.

The activity sequence following receipt of the works order is outlined in Figure
10.3. It raises a number of topics which are developed in more detail later in the
chapter. The numbered notes that follow refer to the figure, and introduce the topics.

1   Process the works order

This activity has its own internal sequence:

- *Retrieve product data*   Product definition data is retrieved from archives,
  which are usually held as a computer database. The data defines the product in
  terms of everything that manufacturing needs to know in order to make and test
  it. It includes materials and parts lists, 'process sheets', drawings (possibly in
  machine-readable form), test specifications and details of any special machines,
  jigs, tools and test gear required. This data was originally provided by the
  product design and production engineering teams. It also includes the most
  recent product cost information, probably relating to when the product was last
  manufactured.

- *Establish deficiencies and lead-times*   The in-house availability of needed
  materials and parts is checked against existing stock levels, as is the existence
  and serviceability of any special processing facilities required. This usually

results in a deficiency list of items which must be obtained before manufacture can start. The time needed to rectify a deficiency is termed its **lead-time**. Those for time-critical items are assessed, since the longest may form part of the total in-sequence time.

- *Update product costs*   It is unlikely that all the historical product cost data still applies, so a new estimate must be made. This may involve negotiations with external suppliers for bought-out items on the deficiency list and, perhaps, internal discussions regarding shortcomings in special processing needs.

- *Accept works order*   Production management now review the works order in the light of all this information. It is accepted if they believe they can meet all its terms (quantity, delivery schedule and cost). Otherwise, they negotiate mutually agreeable new terms with sales. Occasionally, this may result in an agreement not to proceed further, but this possibility is not considered here.

2   Place purchase orders and internal works orders

The next step is to place purchase orders on selected external suppliers for bought-out items on the deficiency list. Similarly, if there are deficiencies in needed special processing facilities, internal works orders are placed on the appropriate local service organization (such as production engineering) to initiate rectification work.

3   Wait

A delay now occurs in the sequence, because of lead-times on the externally sourced items and/or the internal rectification work. If the whole deficiency list must be rectified before manufacturing can start then the delay is determined by the longest lead-time. But it may be possible to start before the longest lead-time has expired, if deficiency items are not required immediately.

4   Inspection of bought-out items

As lead-times expire (and assuming that the external suppliers meet their promises) the bought-out items are delivered to the goods-in store. Inspection of these items can then start. This is a very necessary precaution, aimed at ensuring that the ordered quantity of the ordered items has been delivered, and that the items perform to specification. Rectification costs increase dramatically as the degree of product assembly increases. A penny item can cost more than £100 (a 10,000:1 ratio) to replace when proved faulty in final product test.

Testing may be on a one hundred per cent basis, but a sampling technique is more usual. A whole batch might be rejected if the fault rate, assessed on a statistical basis, is more than a pre-defined (and very low) percentage. Rejection does present a problem, as a lead-time delay is reinstated. But it is generally the best choice, because it may be possible to accelerate the sequence to compensate for this early, unexpected, delay. On the other hand, an excessive number of faults emerging during the process could leave the delivery schedule agreed with sales in tattered ruins.

5   Sub-unit assembly

When all the low-level product parts are available, the various processing machines are loaded and the assembly of the product sub-units is started. The sequences and assembly techniques used are determined by the information previously extracted from the product data archives. Sub-unit assembly is typically a semi-automated operation, with the machines doing most of the repetitive work: for example, automatic component insertion into printed circuit boards. Assembly line operators supervise the machines and provide a first visual check on the quality of their output.

6   Sub-unit test

As a general rule, each completed sub-unit is tested as a stand-alone item before it is passed as 'finished'. The action taken when a faulty sub-unit is detected depends on the anticipated cost of correcting the fault. It is sometimes cheaper to scrap a faulty item, rather than repair it. **Fault-rate** and **scrap-rate** are important indicators of manufacturing process efficiency, and detailed records are always maintained. The raw figures only show overall trends and further analysis is required to isolate problem areas. Possibilities include faulty bought-in parts (which were not detected at goods-in inspection), machinery malfunction and operator problems. Occasionally, an assembly or testing procedure is faulty.

7   Product assembly

The finished sub-units are now assembled into completed products, again in accordance with the product archive data. Usually, this is largely a manual process. This is because the physical features of the sub-units to be assembled vary widely between different product types, and they cannot be manipulated by simple machines. However, 'smart' machines, such as the various types of industrial robot, are increasingly used in this stage of manufacture.

8   Product test

Each completed product is normally tested for overall functional performance before it is passed as 'finished'. Tests for immunity to extremes of various environmental factors (such as temperature, humidity and vibration) are also employed when required by product specification. A sampling approach is common practice in these cases. Product-level fault and scrap records are also maintained.

9   Packaging and dispatch

Finally, the finished products, together with any required documentation, are packaged in protective enclosures (as defined by sales) and passed to the finished-goods store. At this point, sales become the product 'owners', and the original works order is complete.

10.2.3   A broader view

Section 10.2.2 outlines a typical manufacturing sequence for a batch quantity of a specific product type. The treatment is somewhat unrealistic, as it assumes no interaction with other simultaneous activities within the operation. But it is useful introduction to the wider aspects of manufacturing (and of production), because each of the interfaces and the support services illustrated in Figure 10.1 is explicitly or implicitly cited. That initial narrow perspective is now expanded to reveal a broader view of manufacturing. The discussion takes some of the factors noted in the overview of Section 10.2.1 into account. It is still focused on batch manufacturing which, in practice, involves:

- many different products types being manufactured at the same time
- planned interventions at product and process levels
- random disturbances ranging in trauma level from mere irritations to major 'all hands to the pump' crises.

The way in which the last factor (random disturbances) is handled is a measure of management quality, and it is not considered further in this chapter. The significance of the two other factors is examined in summary descriptions of the manufacturing support services and the production interfaces. In this treatment, both purchasing and quality assurance are treated as manufacturing support services. But, as noted in Section 10.1, each of these activities might be business functions in its own right. Manufacturing support services are discussed in more detail in Section 10.3.

Summary: Manufacturing support services

The role of each of the manufacturing support services illustrated in Figure 10.1 is now briefly described.

(1) *Facilities maintenance*   Inspection, servicing, and repair of equipment and machinery used in manufacturing. The maintenance of complex items might be subcontracted to the original suppliers or to a specialist maintenance service business.

(2) *Industrial engineering*   Design and implementation of efficient systems of manual work, particularly at the operator–machine interface. This activity is often regarded as part of production engineering.

(3) *Production engineering*   Concerned with all aspects of manufacturing technology, including manufacturing system design, facilities layout, procedures and techniques, product cost and value engineering, new machinery evaluation, and so on. The activity might be restricted to the manufacturing operation, in which case the term **manufacturing engineering** is more appropriate.

(4) *Production planning and control*   Usually aimed at the most efficient use of the resources (people and facilities) which comprise the manufacturing operation. A central issue is **resource scheduling** in the multi-product situation, because (usually) the products must compete for the limited resources. 'Efficient' may be interpreted in a variety of ways which tend to be mutually exclusive. For example, minimum unit cost is likely to be incompatible with minimum throughput time, and achieving either one of these criteria is difficult when maximum quality is the dominant requirement.

(5) *Purchasing*   Traditionally concerned with the most efficient procurement of required goods and services from outside the business. Another major responsibility is efficient **inventory** planning and control. 'Inventory' is the buffer stock holding, in stores, of both externally purchased and own-build product parts. The meaning of the word 'efficient' is subject to similar qualifications as those expressed under the production planning and control heading.

(6) *Quality assurance* Conventionally defined to include all activities concerned with the achievement of product quality. In this context, the term **product quality** means the degree to which the product meets the requirements of the customer. Thus, 'quality' is used in the 'fitness for purpose' sense. Quality assurance includes the inspection and testing activities cited in Section 10.2.2, but the whole concept is much broader than this.

Summary: Production interfaces

Figure 10.1 indicates a number of important relations between the production function and other organizations. These interfaces are now briefly described.

(1) *External suppliers* interact principally with the purchasing activity. Most are businesses trading in the materials, components, piece-parts and sub-units specified for incorporation into the manufactured products. Others supply manufacturing equipment, machinery and test gear. This can range from simple tools up to complete production systems combining smart machines with the computers and software to control them. Purchasing may also deal with a number of different specialist service businesses providing, for example, machinery maintenance, contract cleaning and waste disposal.

(2) *The finance function* is involved in the preparation of production function budgets prior to the start of a financial year, and in its longer-term 'rolling' plans for subsequent years. During the course of a year, they monitor production performance against these budgets and provide helpful suggestions when adverse situations arise. This is part of the mechanism that subjects the production function to unrelenting pressure. It reflects its critical role in profit and cash generation.

(3) *The marketing function* works mostly with production planning and control to establish the production deliveries budget, at product-type level, for an approaching financial year. Their longer-term views on product requirements are also incorporated in the production 'rolling' plan.

(4) *The personnel function* has an extra link with production, as well as its routine involvement in remuneration, recruiting, training and so on. The special link concerns **industrial relations**. This term encapsulates the relationship between management and non-management employees, particularly those employed in manufacturing and often called the **shop-floor workers**. The emphasis is normally on the more formal relationship between employee representatives, who may be trade union officials, and management representatives. Thus, the focus is on overall working conditions and terms of employment rather than on individual cases.

(5) *The sales function* participates in an internal trading relationship with production (through its planning and control team). This is described in Section 10.2.2. A works order mechanism is used to initiate individual manufacturing projects which, in theory, are existing entries in both the sales purchase budget and the production deliveries budget.

(6) *The technical function* interface is principally between the product development and design teams and the production engineering teams. It concerns the introduction of new products into manufacturing and the enhancement of

established products. Some joint 'fire-fighting' activity also occurs when product definition data created by the technical function is (or is suspected to be) faulty in some way. The technical teams also get involved with purchasing on occasions, because they may specify that a particular bought-out item is obtained from a specific supplier.

10.2.4 The complexity of production

It is instructive to pause here to contemplate the awesome complexity of the task assigned to the production function. This often goes unrecognized by the denizens of the other business functions and, perhaps, by technical function personnel in particular. The major parameters contributing to this complexity are, in summary:

- It is subject to unremitting pressure to perform up to, and beyond, its budget commitments. Responding to it is not made easier by the poor appreciation of production problems frequently demonstrated by those who apply the pressure. 'Cost-saving' expenditure on facilities maintenance is a good example. A properly planned, funded and implemented maintenance programme more than pays for itself in the long run. But the required expenditure is *current*, whereas the savings are difficult to identify and occur in the *future*. So the programme is a prime target for immediate cost saving. When problems due to lack of maintenance arise later, as they always do, the primary cause is conveniently forgotten by those who instigated it; and they turn their wrath on the hapless manufacturing manager.

- The function has many critical interfaces with other business functions. Each presents an opportunity for communication difficulties and politics. So, production is also the central business function in this sense, as well as being the critical cash and profit earning centre.

- Production planning and control is a non-trivial scheduling problem at the best of times. But it is also subject to the vagaries of the product market-place and the sometimes erratic behaviour of external suppliers.

- The manufacturing operation usually contains the potentially least biddable section of the work-force, but it is totally dependent upon them. Commonly, many manufacturing shop-floor jobs are repetitive, and provide little intrinsic interest and intellectual stimulus. Not surprisingly, the people involved may look elsewhere for excitement and reward. Demands for shorter hours and better pay are an obvious example but the day-to-day problems are less dramatic and more subtle. Typical fascinations include safety-at-work issues, lack of overtime, demarcation disputes and the replacement of tea-ladies by soulless vending machines.

On balance the production function, and especially the manufacturing operation within it, is the most stressful arena in the business. Consequently, its management generally appears as a hard-bitten team of professional sceptics, whose brusque attitude to the rest of the business adequately conceals their hearts of gold.

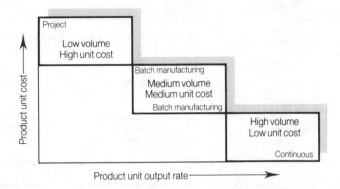

Figure 10.4   **Different types of manufacturing operation.**
The diagram shows manufacturing systems for a specific major technological product category classified according to product unit output rate and product unit cost. Products made (and sold) in small numbers tend to be specialized and expensive, because the cost of the system that makes them is spread over the small number of units. The extreme of this low-volume/high-unit-cost case is called **project manufacturing**, suggesting a **one-off** sequence which creates a unique product. Products made (and sold) in large numbers tend to be standard and cheap, because the cost of the system that makes them is spread over the large number of units. The extreme of this high-volume/low-unit-cost case is called **continuous manufacturing**, suggesting an uninterrupted process creating a stream of uniform products. The intermediate case is medium-volume/medium-unit-cost batch manufacturing. Economic considerations lead to each of these cases being associated with distinctive manufacturing facility layouts, as illustrated in Figures 10.5 to 10.8.

10.2.5   Manufacturing classifications

The discussion to this point has focused around batch manufacturing. However, this is only one of a number of different manufacturing situations. This section explores some basic distinctions. It classifies manufacturing systems for a major technological product category (civil, chemical, mechanical, electronic and so on) according to product unit output rate and product unit cost. The relationships and terminology are shown in Figure 10.4. The output rate (product units per unit time) reflects customer demand for the product, which depends on its degree of specialization.

Products produced (and sold) in low volumes tend to be highly specialized, with only a limited number of individual applications. Examples include motorways, selective antibiotics, oil-rigs and air-traffic control systems. Low volume products tend to have high unit costs, because the cost of the system that makes them is spread over a low number of units. Motorways and air-traffic control systems typify the extreme of the low-volume/high-unit-cost situation, because each such product is unique. No two motorways or air-traffic control systems are the same, because no two of the needs they satisfy are the same. This end of the manufacturing system spectrum is called **project manufacturing**, suggesting a **one-off** (not to be repeated) sequence of events and activities which creates a unique product.

Products produced (and sold) in high volumes tend to be highly standardized, repeatable items with a large number of individual applications. Examples include houses, petrol, most cars and calculators. High volume products tend to have low unit costs, because the cost of the system that makes them is spread over a large number of

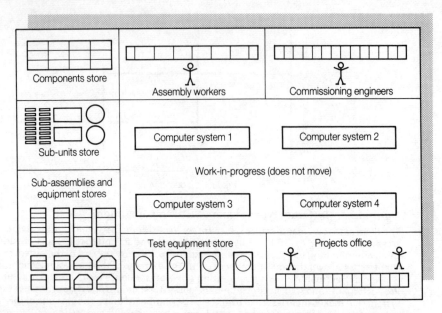

Figure 10.5 **Fixed position layout: low-volume/high-unit-cost manufacturing.**
In most manufacturing systems, mobile work-in-progress is moved to fixed manufacturing resources. But, as the figure shows, the reverse situation applies in this case – mobile resources are moved to fixed work-in-progress. This type of layout is inevitably applied to the manufacture of large and relatively immobile products such as bridges, aeroplanes and ships. Many small manufacturing businesses also start with this layout, because its start-up costs are relatively low. But its running costs per product unit are relatively high.

units. A brand of petrol typifies the extreme of the high-volume/low-unit-cost situation, because it is a uniform product which emerges from a **continuous manufacturing** process.

The intermediate situation between the extremes of project and continuous manufacturing is the medium-volume/medium-unit-cost batch manufacturing regime for a major technological product category. Examples include office blocks, fertilizers, some pleasure boats and answer-phones.

Low-volume/high-unit-cost manufacturing is often associated with a relatively low level of manufacturing technology and a correspondingly high level of intervention from a high skill work-force. This balance is typically reversed in the high-volume/low-unit-cost manufacturing systems, with a relatively high level of manufacturing technology needing only limited intervention from a low skill work-force. This perspective of manufacturing systems is developed a little further in Section 10.5.1.

Traditionally, a distinctive layout of facilities is associated with each manufacturing situation identified in Figure 10.4. The purpose in each case is to minimize costs. A fourth variant, known as **group technology** or **cell layout**, has emerged more recently. The three basic structures, and the hybrid variant, are now described, in association with the manufacturing class heading to which each is *normally* applied.

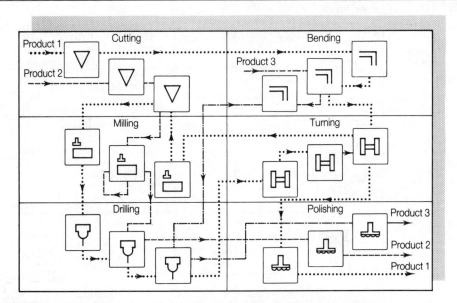

Figure 10.6   **Functional layout: medium-volume/medium-unit-cost batch manufacturing.**

The arrangement exemplified here is alternatively called sub-process layout, because operations of a like nature are co-located. It offers a wide variety of possible sequences and is thus suited for the batch manufacture of different products using different mixes of the same operations. Start-up costs are higher than for the previous case, but running costs per product unit are lower.

Fixed position layout: Low-volume/high-unit-cost

In this case, the resources are moved to the **work-in-progress** (the partially completed product), rather than the other way round. This is the reverse of the other cases. The arrangement is illustrated in Figure 10.5, where large computer-based systems are used as the example.

This form of facilities layout is inevitably applied to the manufacture of large and relatively immobile products such as bridges, aeroplanes and ships. It is less common (but no less important) than the other cases, because the sort of products to which it must be applied are less prevalent. But note that this system might be a rational choice for manufacturing any sort of product at low output rates. Many small manufacturing businesses start out with this approach because the start-up costs are relatively low.

Functional layout: Medium-volume/medium-unit-cost

Processing operations of a like nature are co-located in this arrangement. In other words, separate areas are assigned for each distinct sub-process: such as trimming, drilling, component insertion, soldering, wiring, inspection, test and so on. It is alternatively called **sub-process layout**, and is illustrated in Figure 10.6. This shows the sub-process sequences for batches of three simple mechanical products, called Products 1, 2 and 3 respectively.

The wide variety of possible processing sequences offered by this arrangement make it well suited to **batch manufacturing** of a range of different products using

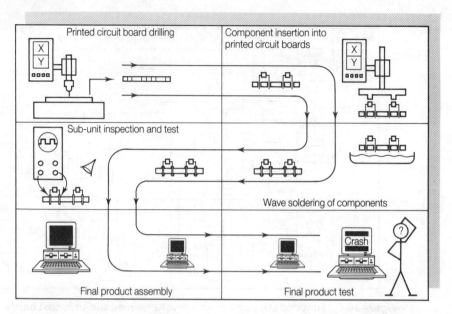

Figure 10.7 **Flow-line layout: high-volume/low-unit-cost manufacturing.**
In the scheme exemplified here, the layout matches the logical sub-process sequence(s) of the products, so it is very product-specific and inflexible. This type of layout is alternatively called product layout, and is best suited to the mass manufacture of a small range of nearly identical products in large quantities. Start-up costs are higher than for the previous case, but running costs per product unit are lower.

different mixes of the same sub-processes. Thus, simple products needing access to only a limited number of the sub-processes can be handled alongside more complex products needing all or most of the facilities. That sort of product mix presents real difficulties in the other two, more rigid, traditional layouts. The system also offers some operator and management advantages, because the grouping of operatives with similar skills encourages team spirit and eases supervision and training requirements. Also, the provision of local services, such as power, noise isolation and 'clean room' facilities is eased by the co-location of similar machines.

But the initial cost of the processing flexibility is comparatively high, and complex scheduling techniques are needed to obtain a satisfactory balance between machine usage and product throughput. Generally, product in-process time is longer than in the other layouts, because relatively high levels of work-in-progress are needed to keep the machines busy. The cost of internal transport for moving the work-in-progress around the system is also comparatively high.

Flow-line layout: High-volume/low-unit-cost

In this scheme, the facilities layout matches the logical sub-process sequence(s) of the products, making it very product-specific and non-flexible. It is alternatively called **product layout**, and is best suited to the **mass manufacturing** of a small range of nearly identical products in large quantities. Ideally, it is applied to just a single product with no variations, such as petrol. The structure is illustrated in Figure 10.7, which uses desktop computers as a product example.

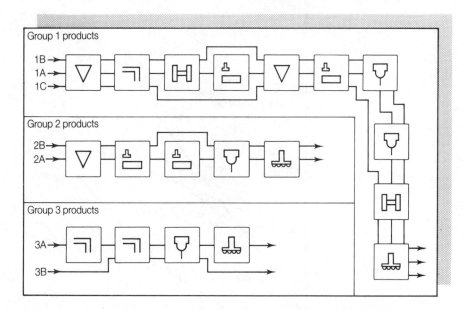

Figure 10.8   **Group technology (or cell) layout: batch manufacturing.**
The layout exemplified here is designed to yield the best features of the functional and product
layout schemes in batch manufacturing situations. It may be used when the products concerned can
be classified into a limited number of groups, with very similar sub-process sequences within a
group. A product-type layout is then installed for each group, based on the requirements of the
most complex product in the group.

All high volume electronic products follow a similar sequence. The technique was developed in the car industry, where it is still widely employed. Work-in-progress may be moved around by a conveyor belt system, but this is not always the case. Product throughput is comparatively high and, therefore, work-in-progress relatively low. Floor space requirements are low and it is used efficiently. The internal transport of work-in-progress is comparatively cheap with a high level of facilities utilization. Operator tasks are normally highly standardized (and de-skilled), so little specialized supervision is required and training needs are minimal.

These plus points are offset by some disadvantages and vulnerabilities. In the latter category, the breakdown of one machine in a sub-process brings the whole process to a halt, as does the lack of product parts at any stage. The provision of local services is less easy than in the previous case, since dissimilar machines are likely to be adjacent. Set-up costs are also comparatively high. Finally, the manual work is probably the most repetitive and boring in this layout, which may encourage operator aggravation.

Group technology (or cell) layout: Batch manufacturing

This facilities arrangement is a combination of the functional and product layout schemes, designed to realize the best features of each in batch manufacturing situations. The many different product types are first classified into a limited number of groups with very similar sub-process sequences. A product layout is then installed for each group, based on the requirements of the most complex product in the group. Figure 10.8 shows the basic principle.

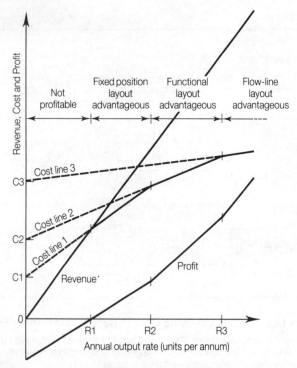

Figure 10.9 **Layout cost comparison for a specific product.**

The graphs illustrate the relative economics of the three basic manufacturing facility layout schemes (Figures 10.5. 10.6 and 10.7). Cost line 1 represents fixed position layout, Cost line 2 represents functional layout and Cost line 3 represents flow-line layout. The revenue line assumes that product units are sold, at a constant price per unit, as they are made. Note that the optimum (defined as 'most profitable') layout depends on the product unit output rate. This result is based on a break-even analysis, not unlike that introduced in Chapter 7.

Subject only to adequate group sizes and volumes, the group technology layout combines many of the advantages of product layout with much of the flexibility offered by the functional scheme. Of course, not all of the products within a group need all of the facilities provided for that group, and individual product-type flow patterns through group facilities also vary. But, provided the products within a group are sufficiently similar, machinery utilization is high. It is also probable, as Figure 10.8 suggests, that there is some commonality of requirements between groups, so that a built-in insurance exists against machinery failure.

The economics compared

Figure 10.9 illustrates the relative economics of the three basic layouts. It is another example of the **break-even concept** applied to the **profit equation**:

$$\text{Profit} = \text{Revenue} - \text{Cost} \tag{10.1}$$

Thus, annual (say) **profit** is the annual income from product sales (annual **revenue**) less the total cost of achieving those sales. The break-even concept was introduced in Section 7.6.2, and other examples of its application to the profit equation were explored in Section 7.9.

The figure plots annual revenue, cost and profit as *linear* (in this simplified analysis) functions of the number of units made, and sold, per annum. Each of the three basic layouts is associated with a particular cost line:

- Cost line 1 corresponds to the fixed position layout.
- Cost line 2 corresponds to the functional layout.
- Cost line 3 corresponds to the flow-line layout.

Each cost line is made up of a **fixed cost**, indicated by the intercept on the cost axis at zero output rate, and a **variable cost**. Fixed costs correspond to the initial facilities set-up costs (plus any other fixed costs), whereas variable costs represent process resources which are consumed in proportion to the number of products made.

Fixed cost is relatively low for fixed position layout (at C1 in the figure) and relatively high for flow-line layout (at C3). Functional layout lies between these two extremes (at C2). But the rate at which the total cost increases with output rate reverses this order, being relatively rapid for fixed position layout and relatively slow for flow-line layout. Functional layout is, again, the intermediate case.

Figure 10.9 demonstrates that fixed position layout is the most rewarding choice at output rates less than R2. But even this layout is not profitable until the output rate is greater than R1. This corresponds to the first break-even, at the point where Cost line 1 crosses the revenue line. The manufacturing process becomes profitable as the output rate increases beyond R1, but it is advantageous to switch to functional layout for rates greater than R2. This corresponds to the second break-even, at the point where the Cost line 2 crosses Cost line 1. It is advantageous to switch to flow-line layout for rates beyond R3. This is at the third break-even point, where Cost line 3 crosses Cost line 2.

Practical manufacturing operations

The preceding simplified analysis is no more than a starting point in the design of a real manufacturing layout. As always in design work, compromises are necessary. So the three basic layouts and the one hybrid are rarely found in exclusive pure form in real-life situations. Most practical manufacturing operations of significant size employ an appropriate mixture of these formats. In batch manufacturing there is, perhaps, a discernible trend favouring the group technology approach. Also, a particular layout might be retained even when the analysis suggests that it should be changed, because of the costs of changing over. But the analysis does demonstrate that organizations must develop as the business develops, a point discussed at some length in Section 4.3.2. Finally, it has been assumed that the optimum choice of manufacturing format should be determined on the basis of that which yields the best return on costs. There can be no quarrel with this. But a broader-based attack on this same target would pay more attention to the people parameters of the overall equation.

10.3 Manufacturing support services

Important manufacturing support services are briefly described in Section 10.2.3. This section expands the earlier material but its scope is still limited, because each cited services is a major topic in its own right. References to more detailed texts are included in the chapter bibliography.

10.3.1 Facilities maintenance

The performance of all physical facilities deteriorates as they are used and they are always vulnerable to total failure. Broadly, the purpose of facilities maintenance is to sustain (in a cost-effective way) the functional continuity of the manufacturing machinery at, or above, an acceptable quality level. It excludes the replacement of whole machines, but includes the replacement of components in faulty machines. 'Machine' includes both power driven equipment and simple hand tools. (The concept of 'maintenance' is actually wider than this, because all resources are subject to progressive degradation and failure. Thus, maintenance is also applied to the buildings, local services and, indeed, to the people involved. Here, however, the emphasis remains on the machinery.)

Facilities maintenance can be subdivided into five distinct activities:

- **inspection**
- **servicing**
- **preventive maintenance**
- **repair**
- **maintenance data collection and analysis**.

Each of these is now considered.

Inspection

This refers to the periodic check of every machine to assess its functional performance and whether unscheduled maintenance is required. Inspection may be merely visual, or it can include performance measurement on 'test pieces' or real work-in-progress. It may be informal, such as an operator might carry out visually, and/or be part of a formal programme of more extensive investigation. Policy in this respect depends on the complexity of the machine in question and its reliability characteristics.

Servicing

This term covers regular routine mechanical adjustments, resetting, lubrication, cleaning and so on. Servicing frequency normally depends on the usage rate of the machine. It is often regarded as an extension of the inspection work.

Preventive maintenance

This activity may include servicing, but its distinctive feature is the replacement of vulnerable machine parts before the (anticipated) end of their **working life**. This parameter is a statistical concept and the lifetimes of individual parts generally differ somewhat from the published figures. So preventive maintenance cannot entirely remove the possibility of machine failure, but it allows some of the inevitable 'downtime' to be scheduled at convenient times. It can be implemented on a regular basis or only when indicated by inspection. Both methods are often used together for complex and/or very critical machines. Preventive maintenance is a precautionary activity which, on balance, defers rather than prevents a breakdown. But it is not unusual for a well-maintained and inherently reliable machine to survive without failure until it is replaced by a more efficient successor.

Repair

Every physical machine ultimately fails, whether or not it has been subject to preventive maintenance. Repair work is then required to return the machine to service. Many different repair strategies are used. For example, preventive maintenance might be omitted prior to repair when records indicate that the cost of deferring breakdown is likely to exceed repair costs. Similarly, it is sometimes cheaper to replace a machine rather than repair it.

Data collection and analysis

This activity is an integral part of the planning and control of facilities maintenance which, in turn, is part of production planning and control. Records are kept of all maintenance work on every machine, including fault history and rectification cost. These assist in the development of a rational maintenance plan and, subsequently, allow its effectiveness to be monitored.

Planning facilities maintenance

The principal aim, when designing a facilities maintenance programme, must be to make best use of the costs involved. Maintenance incurs costs in two ways. Firstly, there is the cost of the maintenance activity itself (set-up and running) and, secondly, there is the cost of the disruption that maintenance causes to the manufacturing operation. Disruption can be minimized by providing 'spare' capacity but this, too, adds cost.

It is quite straightforward, in theory, to assess the optimum maintenance level measured (say) in team size. The aggregated running cost of inspection, servicing and preventive maintenance increase nearly linearly with team size. But the aggregated cost of repair and major disruption (caused by machinery breakdowns) decrease as team size increases. So there is a minimum in the total cost curve, which defines an optimum maintenance level. Figure 10.10 illustrates the argument.

Unfortunately, the real situation is more complicated than this figure suggests. The data needed to establish the nonlinear decreasing cost curve is statistical at best, and frequently only speculative. Even if this is not so, the analysis gives no guidance on choosing the relative levels of the various different activities comprising maintenance. A further objection is more subtle. In the figure, the increasing costs and the decreasing costs which are summed to obtain the total cost occur at different times. There are good reasons for questioning the validity of simply adding monetary sums which occur at widely separated times, as may be the case here. There are equally good ways of compensating for the time difference (which are discussed in Chapter 11). But the fact that relative timing enters into the analysis adds another uncertainty.

(Figure 10.10 illustrates a common business situation where two or more dependent variables, whose sum is of interest, exhibit converse behaviour with the independent variable. The data defining the curves is often somewhat dubious. Handling these situations calls for good judgement from the managers involved. Further examples arise later in the chapter.)

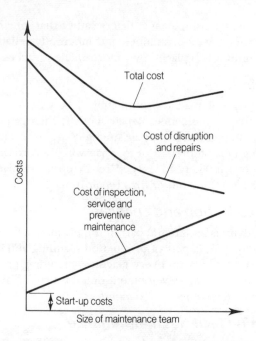

Figure 10.10   **Illustrating the behaviour of maintenance costs.**

A facilities maintenance programme must make best use of the costs involved. There are two sorts of maintenance cost: first, the cost of the maintenance activity itself (set-up and running), which increases nearly linearly, from its start-up cost, as team size increases; second, the cost of the disruption that maintenance causes to the manufacturing operation, together with the costs of repairs and stoppages. These costs decrease, from a high initial level, as team size increases. So there is a minimum in the total cost curve, shown in the figure, which defines an optimum maintenance level. The utility of this notion is limited by the difficulty of getting good data. The figure illustrates a common management situation involving the choice of an optimum operating point.

10.3.2   Industrial engineering

Industrial engineering relates to selected aspects of human work and behaviour in industry, a broad topic which is introduced in Chapter 4. There are some variations in the definition of 'industrial engineering', both between different businesses and between North American and European practice. Here, it is taken to include:

(1) The study and specification of working methods and procedures, sometimes termed **methods study**.

(2) The measurement of work and the determination of work standards, sometimes termed **work measurement**.

(3) Human factor considerations relating to the physical working environment.

Note that, taken together, the first two activities are sometimes termed **work study** or **time and motion study**.

This definition of industrial engineering is a fair consensus of current practice. In principle, it relates to all industrial work situations but it is most generally applied to the more repetitive aspects of manufacturing. The aim is to achieve high levels of

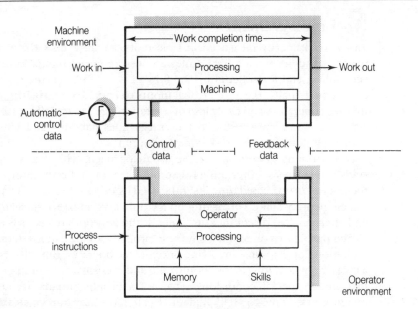

Figure 10.11 **The focus of industrial engineering.**

Industrial engineering relates to some aspects of human work and behaviour in industry, including methods study, work measurement and the people-related aspects of the working environment. It focuses on systems comprising human operators and machines, as illustrated symbolically in this figure, with the aim of maximizing labour and capital productivity. The system control loop is closed by the human operator. Feedback data from the machine (from a visual indicator, say) is processed by the operator to provide control inputs to the machine.

labour and capital productivity. In other words, it seeks the maximum possible output at the minimum rational cost. So industrial engineering is a sensitive area in the relationship between management and the work-force, because it impinges on working conditions and operator rewards. It focuses on systems comprising human operators and machines, as illustrated symbolically in Figure 10.11.

The system control loop is closed by the human operator. Feedback data from the machine (from a visual indicator, say) is processed by the operator to provide control inputs to the machine. The figure provides a context for the examination of the major facets of industrial engineering that now follows.

Methods study

This activity is applied to both new and existing tasks. Consider, for example, a new assembly operation. A number of feasible methods are explored and the most efficient selected for further development. This leads to a formal specification of the selected method in the form of a **method or process sheet**. The procedure for an existing task is similar, but normally starts with an analysis of the current method. The first consideration is the way in which the task is *actually* carried out by the operator(s), because this may not exactly conform with the method sheet. Methods study of existing tasks is **value engineering** (discussed in Section 10.3.3) applied to work. The term 'efficient' is interpreted in the economic sense, but the choice of methods is always constrained by operator and machine limitations.

Work measurement

Tasks are primarily measured in time units, because **task time**(-to-complete) is a major cost determinant. Task times are also required inputs for individual product scheduling, and for scheduling the flow of work through the whole manufacturing operation. Equally, they are critical inputs to **capacity planning**, which determines the size (operators and facilities) of operation needed to deliver the total throughput required. Work measurement necessarily goes hand-in-hand with methods study, because both emphasize task completion times.

Direct timing of tasks is still the usual approach, with data sampling followed by statistical analysis. Alternatively, some form of indirect timing is used. In this technique, an estimated time is synthesized by combining directly measured times for the elementary sub-tasks making up a whole task. Indirect 'measurement' is quicker and cheaper than direct measurement, if the appropriate records are available.

The raw figures obtained from these procedures measure task times under special conditions, perhaps just involving one specific operator. But what is really required is a measure of how long a task should take under normal conditions, not how long it did take under special conditions. Two sorts of adjustments are usually made to a measured task time to yield a quantity called the **standard task time**. The first is an averaging process to account for the 'standard rate of working'. This factor, despite the terminology used, is mostly a matter of local conditions. A second adjustment is then made to compensate for longer-term factors, such as operator fatigue, rest periods and any machine-related delays inherent to the task. Apart from their other uses, standard times commonly have a role in setting (or negotiating) basic and bonus payment levels for the operators. This factor can lead to difficulties in obtaining accurate raw figures at the start of the process.

The working environment

There is no doubt that physical working conditions, as well as monetary rewards, play a significant part in the efficiency of the work-force. Equally, a business has moral and legal obligations to ensure the health and safety of its employees. This aspect of industrial engineering is concerned, therefore, with such things as safety provisions and the levels of temperature, noise, vibration, lighting and hygiene. More specialized activities, involving human factors in job design for efficiency and enrichment, come under this same heading.

10.3.3   Production engineering

This activity is concerned with manufacturing and production technologies. It is conveniently divided into the overall system level and the product level. At the overall level, production engineers contribute to such matters as:

- Facilities layout design (reviewed in Section 10.2.5).
- Industrial engineering (reviewed in Section 10.3.2).
- Quality assurance (reviewed in Section 10.3.6).
- Production planning and control (reviewed in Section 10.3.4).
- Capacity planning.

- Evaluation of new machines.
- Introduction of new manufacturing technologies.

At the product level, the production engineers have a critical relationship with the product development and design teams in the technical function. This work concerns:

(1) Introduction of new products into manufacturing.
(2) Enhancement of established products.
(3) Modification of existing manufacturing methods.
(4) Resolution of any problems with established products.

The production engineering tasks involved include:

- Design of any special jigs, tools or fixtures or, perhaps, just their specification if they are to be purchased externally.
- Make-or-buy decisions regarding some product piece-parts and sub-units.
- Product level quality assurance (reviewed in Section 10.3.6).
- Review of product definition data created by the technical function.
- **Value engineering** and **value analysis**.
- Working with industrial engineers on the design of manufacturing sequences and procedures (reviewed in Section 10.3.2).

Most of the identified production engineering topics are either covered elsewhere or need no further comment. The three exceptions are now considered in more detail. Each involves working with the appropriate teams from the technical function.

The introduction of new manufacturing technologies

Introducing new (to the business) manufacturing technologies into the operation is an important production engineering task, which may include development work on the technology itself. This sort of technical innovation, which focuses on the product creation process rather than the products, is sometimes called **methods R&D**. The term covers (among other things) the initial creation, enhancement and/or customization of a manufacturing technology. Generally, the incentive to change is economic: that is, the new technology promises to be cheaper than the one it replaces. But other factors can be involved. For example, a new technology may offer previously unattainable product features, such as smaller size or greater reliability. An example from electronics manufacture is the replacement of conventional 'integrated circuit packages on printed circuit boards' technology with 'surface mount' technology, using naked chips on a special substrate.

The introduction of a new technology is normally treated as an 'off-line' project, so that it can be proved, learnt and assessed economically before being used on real products. The technical function can get involved in developments of this sort in two rather different ways. Firstly, it may be responsible for the methods R&D (instead of production engineering). Secondly, the technical teams must become familiar with new manufacturing technologies. This enables them to exploit any new product features made possible by the technology, and to recognize any new design constraints imposed on product innovation work.

Review of product data

Production engineers act as the first filter on product definition data created by the product development and design teams. Their review of this data has four major objectives:

(1) To assess ease of manufacturing and ease of testing. Each of these factors is a function of product design in relation to the nature of the manufacturing facilities available.

(2) To establish if any unusual manufacturing or testing operations are required, which might be expensive to provide. This, too, is a function of what is already available.

(3) To check that the product conforms with statutory and business-imposed health and safety standards. Most markets are subject to statutory health and safety regulations applying to all products sold in those markets. The business may also impose its own standards. This is often the case when a particular product is sold into markets with marginally different statutory regulations. In that situation, it may be more economic to adopt a comprehensive local standard rather than make product variants for the different markets.

(4) To examine the parts-list so as to identify any non-standard components and sub-units. Here, 'standard' is usually interpreted as 'preferred' or 'approved'. Most manufacturing businesses maintain lists of approved suppliers and acceptable bought-in items. The policy has a number of potent advantages, which are discussed in Section 10.3.5.

In theory, of course, the development and design teams are well aware of the manufacturing capabilities, and of policies on product safety and purchasing. Experience shows that this does not make the relevant checks any less necessary. When the production engineers detect a significant matter likely to spoil 'business as usual' manufacturing, they open negotiations with the technical team. The frequency and trauma of these meetings can be minimized by early involvement of production engineering in product development and design projects.

Value engineering and value analysis

Each of these terms is something of a misnomer, because the word 'value' is normally interpreted as 'cost' in both activities. Their purpose is to reduce the cost of manufacturing a product (commonly termed its **works cost**) without any detrimental effect on its performance, particularly its reliability performance. The terms are often used synonymously. Strictly, however, value engineering applies to new products, whereas value analysis refers to established products. The work is characterized by an orderly and structured approach, which distinguishes it from less formal cost-reduction actions. Major redesign is generally avoided. The costs of value engineering and/or analysis must always be considered. There is no merit in reducing the cost of a product if the cost of achieving the reduction cannot be more than recovered in product sales revenue. Both activities are usually joint efforts by production engineering and the technical function team responsible for the product.

The works cost of a product is discussed at length in Section 7.8. It has two major elements: a **direct cost** and an **indirect cost**. The first depends only on the nature of the product. It is made up of the cost of bought-in items incorporated in the product, together with the labour costs of assembling and testing it. The indirect element represents the fraction of the total manufacturing process cost which is assigned to the product. The manufacturing process cost comprises a facilities cost (due to machinery, equipment, buildings and so on) and management costs. Value engineering and analysis focus on individual factors (starting, usually, with the most significant) and seeks to reduce them, bearing in mind the need to retain (at least) product functions and reliability. Typically, the results that flow from this activity include the use of fewer and/or cheaper bought-in items, and less operator-hours consumed in assembling them into the product.

10.3.4 Planning and control

Planning and control are complementary tasks. **Control** is the management activity of assessing deviations from a plan and, if sensible and possible, taking action to minimize these deviations. A **plan** is a representation of intended progress from a specific start position to a specific end position, by means of a defined pattern of activities linking intermediate positions. In principle, production planning and control embraces strategic issues such as facilities layout and maintenance policy, and day-to-day activity scheduling in the manufacturing operation. In practice, the term is used almost exclusively in the later context, and this custom is continued here.

The relative importance of planning versus control is a function of the uncertainty level of the situation concerned. Of course, some degree of uncertainty exists in all planning situations, because the future is not precisely predictable. But in highly predictable cases, such as flow-line manufacturing, detailed planning is more critical than the more relaxed (give or take the occasional crisis) control function. On the other hand, in low-volume/high-value manufacturing, the reverse is the case. Here, the uncertainty level is generally high and tight control, which recognizes the possible need to rework aspects of the plan, is essential.

Production planning

Product scheduling in the manufacturing operation is a non-trivial problem. A schedule (which is a sequence, or sequences, of specific activities laid out in date order) is usually prepared for each next period in a series of such periods. Period duration depends on clarity of forward vision on manufacturing orders. Periods of one month (or less) are typical in flow-line and batch manufacturing, but they are normally much longer in the low-volume/high-value cases. An enduring major objective is to maximize the utilization of the available resources, thereby minimizing the cost impact of these resources on each unit of output. But achieving this aim is constrained by some human factors, and the need to provide acceptable service to the customer in terms of product delivery, price and quality. There are potential conflicts between these three basic measures of the (output) efficiency of a manufacturing operation. So a manufacturing schedule is always a compromise between a set of conflicting objectives. Wild (1989, Chapter 12) identifies four distinct types of scheduling problem. The treatment that follows is a simplified version of that analysis.

The essence of product scheduling is availability of the requisite time and resources (people, machinery, product piece-parts and so on). The available time is measured

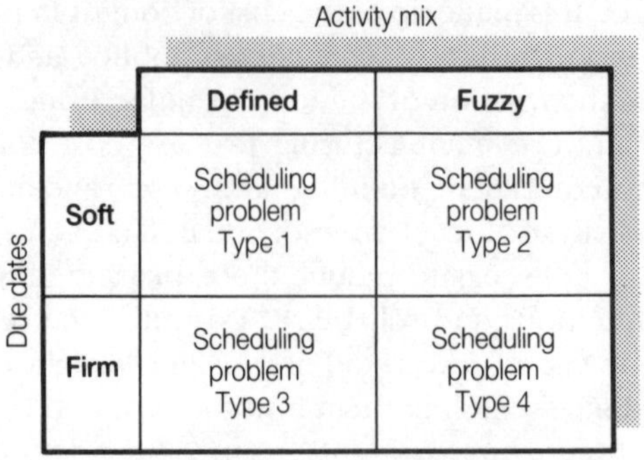

Activity mix

		Defined	Fuzzy
Due dates	**Soft**	Scheduling problem Type 1	Scheduling problem Type 2
	Firm	Scheduling problem Type 3	Scheduling problem Type 4

Figure 10.12   **Market factors and activity scheduling problems.**
A manufacturing schedule is a planned sequence, or sequences, of specific activities (manufacturing sub-processes) laid out in date order. The preparation of such a schedule, for a particular period, is conditioned by two main factors. These are the degree to which the requisite activity mix is known, and the degree to which the available manufacturing process time is limited by due dates for product delivery. A major planning target is to obtain maximum resource utilization, as this minimizes resource cost impact on each product unit. But the extent to which it can be achieved is limited by human factors and the need to meet product quality targets. This figure identifies four distinct types of scheduling problem by combining 'defined' or 'fuzzy' activity mix situations with 'soft' or 'firm' due date situations.

(backwards) from some critical date, termed the **due date**. Typically, this is the promised latest date of product delivery to an external customer. In multi-product multi-customer situations, a number of due dates may apply in a scheduling period. Assuming that adequate people and machinery resources are present within the manufacturing operation, their availability depends on their degree of utilization (how busy they are). In multi-product situations, competition between different products for resources is almost inevitable, and this often applies in the other situations as well. So scheduling usually implies the assignment of priorities. Due dates are one factor in determining relative priorities, and the product quantity required is another. These factors are not always precisely known.

The nature of an activities scheduling problem is largely determined by those features of the external market which define its *resource* and *time* parameters. There are four distinct boundary conditions:

(1) *Defined activity mix*   Here, there is certain knowledge of the types and quantities of established products to be delivered. Due dates may or may not be known. It is relatively easy to ascertain the total amounts of the different manufacturing activities required in the planning period. But scheduling them to meet resource utilization and due date constraints (if any) is another matter.

(2) *Fuzzy activity mix*   In this case, evaluation of the requisite activity mix is not possible. This can arise because the products concerned are not fully established and/or the quantities required are uncertain. Once again, due dates may or may not be known. The activity totals must then be predicted in some way, and this introduces unwelcome complexity and uncertainty into the scheduling process.

(3) *Soft due dates*   Here, the manufacturing operation aims to deliver products to

a stock 'buffer' (the finished-goods store) prior to due dates, if known, or in anticipation of forthcoming due dates if they are not known.

(4) *Firm due dates* This situation is the opposite of that above, because the manufacturing operation aims to deliver products on or before known due dates without the intervention of delivery to stock.

The first and second cases are mutually exclusive, as are the third and fourth. So there are four combinations to consider, each presenting a different scheduling problem. The matrix diagram of Figure 10.12 shows these four possibilities, labelling them Types 1 to 4.

(Type 4, which combines a fuzzy activity mix with firm due dates, exhibits basic conflict between its twin conditions. It is an exciting rather than attractive manufacturing problem. Wild (1989) suggests that this case is rare enough to be dismissed without further discussion. This author takes a contrary view based on sad experience. It is certainly not uncommon in low-volume/high-unit-cost and project manufacturing generally. When the latter situation applies to large, complex, one-off computer-based systems it is almost routine.)

The four types of scheduling problem identified in Figure 10.12 are summarized and compared in Table 10.1.

The market conditions which define the different types of scheduling problem are boundary conditions: that is, they represent the extremes of a variety of possible market situations. In practical cases, the scheduling team may have to cope with some mixture of these types. This does nothing to ease the problem.

The use of an output (stock) buffer simplifies any sort of scheduling problem, because it insulates the schedule from the external pressure of due dates. This enables business-determined scheduling criteria to be more nearly satisfied. In batch manufacturing, it can also enable economic batch sizes to be used. In some cases there is no choice but to deliver products to stock. For example, businesses manufacturing fireworks or toys operate in highly seasonal markets, and must deliver to stock for most of the year. The choice of delivering to stock or direct to the customers usually exists in situations where product demand is more constant. But products in stock represent idle money, and providing and administering the store also costs money. So the 'to stock or not to stock' decision turns on the relative economics:

- is it less costly to have near optimum manufacturing resource utilization offset by the costs of product stocking, or
- to accept some inefficiency in resource usage but avoid stock costs?

A variety of techniques are available to assist with solving scheduling problems, ranging from simple bar (or Gantt) charts through network methods, such as PERT, to a wide range of more complex systems. Bar charts and PERT are discussed in Chapter 6. Other, more specialized techniques, are beyond the scope of this book, but are covered in texts cited in the chapter bibliography.

Production control

The purpose of control is to ensure that, within reason, actual events conform to plan. (Engineering students will detect an analogy here with the concept of negative feedback.) In the present context, the plan is a schedule of manufacturing activities for

Type	Conditions and problems

Type 1   Defined activity mix + soft due dates

Conditions   Forward orders situation for the schedule period precisely defined in activity mix and product quantities required. Due dates may or may not be precisely known, but in either case are within the capacity of the manufacturing operation. Product delivery is to stock.

Problem   Relatively straightforward, because there are no external time constraints. Defined activities can be scheduled to satisfy internal criteria, such as optimum resource utilization.

Type 2   Fuzzy activity mix + soft due dates

Conditions   Forward orders situation for the schedule period not precisely defined in activity mix and/or product quantities required. Due dates may or may not be precisely known, but in either case are within the capacity of the manufacturing operation. Product delivery is to stock.

Problem   No external time constraints but more complex than for Type 1, because activity mix and/or activity volumes must be estimated in some way. When this has been completed, the estimated activities can be scheduled to satisfy internal criteria, as in Type 1.

Type 3   Defined activity mix + firm due dates

Conditions   Forward order situation for the schedule period is precisely defined in all respects: activity mix, product quantities and due dates. Product delivery is directly to the external customer with no intermediate stock holding.

Problem   The external time constraints imposed by the due dates add an extra dimension to the problem. These constraints probably have priority so the internal criteria, such as optimum resource utilization, may have to be compromised.

Type 4   Fuzzy activity mix + firm due dates

Conditions   Forward orders situation for the schedule period not precisely defined in activity mix and/or product quantities required. But due dates are firm! Product delivery is directly to the external customer with no intermediate stock holding.

Problem   Very unattractive – a potential disaster! Demands urgent management action to achieve a defined activity mix or to extend the due dates or (preferably) both of these reliefs.

Table 10.1   **Types of activity scheduling problem.**
This table complements Figure 10.12 by summarizing the conditions defining each type of scheduling problem and commenting on their nature. Note that the use of an output (stock) buffer simplifies scheduling problems, because it insulates the schedule from the external pressure of due dates. But it is not always feasible to make for stock and, when it is feasible, it is not always wise to do so (see text).

a specific period. It shows how a volume of work is intended to flow through the operation in a way which satisfies (more or less) various constraints. In most planning and control situations, the plan documentation (such as a bar chart, PERT diagram or financial budget) is also the control documentation. So, at detailed implementation levels, control techniques are as varied as planning techniques. Readers are again referred to the cited texts for details of specialized methods. But the principles of control are shared by all methods, and are now briefly examined in a manufacturing context.

Routine control is normally applied periodically: daily, weekly or monthly, say.

Assuming that a schedule exists which represents the desired progression of events and activities, the control function involves four steps:

(1) Measurement.
(2) Comparison.
(3) Assessment.
(4) Action.

Measurement

The actual values of a vast range of parameters can be measured in a manufacturing operation of significant size. This is particularly so when the progress of individual product batches must be tracked in a multi-product situation. So there are rich opportunities for setting up 'paralysis by analysis' situations. These must be avoided by judicious selection of those parameters which really matter. The aim is to obtain raw (uncooked!) accurate numbers. Typical of the product-level parameters that are measured are:

- the number of components type 'A' received and passed inspection
- the number of operator hours (classified by activity type) consumed on products type 'B'
- the number of operator hours (classified by product type) consumed on activity type 'C'
- the number of sub-units type 'D' actually completed.

Global parameters, such as:

- machine usage hours
- numbers and value (at cost) of faulty and scrapped items
- total normal and overtime operator hours

may also be measured. Increasingly, some degree of automation is employed in measuring parameters using, for example, bar codes on 'job cards' and data-logging facilities on the machines.

Comparison

The actual values of the selected parameters are now compared with their plan values. The results of these comparisons are termed **deviations** here. (The term **variance** is also used, but mostly in relation to financial parameters.) Usually, a deviation is simply the numerical difference between actual and plan values. The resulting figure may be either negative, zero or positive. By a convention (which is not always used), the subtraction is ordered such that negative signals worse than plan and positive signals better than plan. Clearly, a zero deviation indicates performance in accordance with plan. This is normally a fairly rare event. Deviations are commonly expressed both as absolute figures and as percentages of plan value.

Assessment

Assessment of the relative importance of the deviations is, perhaps, the most critical step. The individual problems flagged by the negative (worse than plan) deviations are rarely independent. They usually interact, because the activities draw on a common pool of resources. For example, removing one problem by switching resources may aggravate another problem, or even create a new one. Thus, a proper problem priority list is not simply produced by ranking the deviations from most negative through to zero. This ranking must be modulated by applying various other criteria to it. These are typically the internal and external pressures on the whole operation, such as resource utilization, profit and/or cash-flow targets, and due dates. Computer-based techniques can assist in this assessment exercise and, conceivably, the advent of expert, knowledge-based, systems will ultimately make it trivial. More probably, human judgement will remain heavily involved.

Action

The final step in a control sequence is executive action aimed at correcting the most important deviations. These usually stem from resource deficiencies and the usual corrective action is to switch resources from slack (positive deviation) areas to the problem areas. An expensive alternative is to use additional resources: by hiring, purchasing, subcontracting, overtime working and so on. There are economic limits on all options and some less important problems may have to remain unresolved.

Resource switching is not always a straightforward matter. Machines may have to be reset, and then reset again. The scheduled work-flow is always disturbed. Operators may need to be retrained. Other human factors can also intervene, because major changes present a variety of bargaining opportunities to the work-force.

Another source of negative deviations is failure by external suppliers to meet their delivery promises. Purchasing (discussed in Section 10.3.5) has special responsibilities in this area, but problems still arise. Resource switching may be possible when common standard items are involved. Emergency purchasing action is another option, but it is always expensive.

Random disturbances

This discussion of production control has focused on the normal routine activity. However, it is inevitable that this routine will be upset at random intervals by some unplanned event, such as a machine breakdown, an unscheduled rush order or a strike. These are testing times for production management, but they are not considered further here.

10.3.5 Purchasing

All manufacturing businesses purchase (rather than make) a substantial fraction of the materials, components and sub-assemblies that are incorporated into their products. These bought-in items may account for up to sixty per cent of product works cost, and even more in extreme cases. Moreover, their delivery in the right quantities, at the right time and to the right specification is critical if output schedules are to be met. For all of these reasons the purchasing activity is a critical element in the production function. Its objectives can be summarized as:

- To ensure continuity of external supply.

- To ensure timely delivery of externally purchased product parts to meet the requirements of the manufacturing schedules.
- To ensure that purchased items conform to quality requirements.
- To purchase other items and services as required.
- To manage the **input inventory**.
- To do all this things in a manner which ensures the best possible value for the money spent.

(In this context, an **inventory** is a store or stock of items. The input inventory is a stock of input items destined for incorporation into manufactured products. Such stocks are held to provide a degree of isolation between manufacturing schedules and the delivery delays which arise when dealing with outside suppliers. The finished-goods store, referred to earlier, serves a similar purpose with respect to customers. It is an **output inventory**).

Thus, purchasing is involved with two distinct but related problem areas: external purchasing and internal stocks. Each of these is now considered. Note that, in practice, inventory management is not always part of the purchasing organization. This structural variation is of no consequence here.

External purchasing

Ensuring continuity of supply (which is the continuing availability of the purchased items needed to keep manufacturing operating at the planned level) is, arguably, the most important purchasing task. Failures in this area are a guaranteed source of trouble for all concerned. The most common (but not infallible) provision against this risk is known as **multiple-sourcing**. In this strategy, at least two independent suppliers are contracted to supply a proportion of the total requirement for each item. But it clearly cannot apply to items available from just one source. Generally, this is only the case for very specialized items serving a small 'niche' market; and the purchasing team seeks to persuade their product development and design colleagues not to specify these. Multiple-sourcing may incur additional costs, because there is additional negotiation and administration, and volume discounts on list price can be reduced. Competition between the suppliers may mitigate the latter effect.

The key to availability, and to the other objectives of external purchasing, is held by the suppliers. So a primary aim of purchasing is to identify satisfactory suppliers. The process of assessing suppliers against various criteria is known as **vendor analysis**, and its results as **vendor ratings**. Purchasing applies the process to all potential suppliers and, periodically, to all actual suppliers. In the latter case, the exercise is eased by the maintenance of detailed records of supplier performance. Different businesses construe 'satisfactory' in different ways, but supplier assessment always includes:

(1) Commercial terms.
(2) Flexibility.
(3) Punctuality.
(4) Quality.
(5) Reliability.
(6) Stability.

Each of these factors is now examined.

(1) *Commercial terms* In industry, the 'one-off' list price of an item merely represents a starting point for negotiation. All external suppliers offer volume-related discounts on this maximum, which may rise to sixty or seventy per cent in extreme cases. (Of course, the one-off price may be adjusted to ease supplier pain.) The question of how the volume is assessed also arises. For example, does it apply to each batch supplied or to total annual volume? But negotiations go beyond the important question of price, to embrace such things as payment terms, guarantees of continued supply for spares provisioning and, perhaps, 'sale or return' arrangements. A supplier offering extended credit, by agreeing to payment up to (say) 60 days after the goods are supplied, makes a valuable contribution to the cash-flow of the purchasing business. Equally, those suppliers who are prepared to deal on a sale or return basis reduce the risk of the purchasing business being left with redundant input stock.

A manufacturing division in a large business usually purchases a proportion of its bought-out items from other divisions of the same business. Commercial relationships of this nature are rather different from those outside the 'family', and sometimes less satisfactory. It might be thought that security of supply is assured by internal trading. But the trading divisions of a **diversified** modern business are largely autonomous, with no obligation either to trade with each other or to look after each other. Supplies availability may then be particularly vulnerable, because it is difficult to enforce internal arrangements. In businesses where internal trading is obligatory, there may be little or no freedom to negotiate prices. In extreme cases, **transfer prices** are set at business headquarters and no negotiation is possible. This is typically the situation with large **vertically-integrated** businesses, such as in the car manufacturing industry. For example, the final assembly division purchases, at fixed transfer prices, engines from Division A, body-shells from Division B and so on. The mechanism presents multinational businesses with some control over where they make their profits.

(2) *Flexibility* This factor refers to the ability of suppliers to cope with unexpected demands made upon them by their customers. Their equanimity in such situations is also important: a manufacturer with supply problems has worries enough without having to deal with recalcitrant and awkward suppliers.

(3) *Punctuality* Suppliers who consistently meet promised delivery dates are valuable assets and, sadly, relatively rare. Equally important is their honesty in quoting delivery lead-times. Suppliers are inevitably tempted to make attractive, but unrealistic, delivery promises during the negotiation stage. Signing up with those who fall into this temptation only ensures future grief.

(4) *Quality* The quality of bought-in items, in the 'fitness for purpose' sense used here, is a self-evident requirement. But the cost of quality rises very rapidly as perfection is approached and an economic balance must be struck in determining the optimum level of supplies quality. The purchaser must specify the quality level, and the acceptable tolerance on that level, that is sought. Once again, suppliers who consistently meet the defined quality requirements are of great value to their customers.

(5) *Reliability*   In this context, the reliability factor covers a number of topics not specifically identified in the preceding list. This includes the apparently simple matter of actually delivering what was ordered in terms of the right quantity of the right items, complete with any loose accessories (nuts and bolts, say) and necessary documentation. But departures from this ideal are frequent enough to suggest that more than human error is involved. Oddly (at first sight) over-delivery is more common than under-delivery. Possibly unworthy suspicions are aroused in purchasing when the subsequent invoice matches the excessive delivery. All these problems take time and money to sort out, and are best avoided.

(6) *Stability*   The vulnerability of trading with a supplier which goes out of business is obvious. So the purchasing business normally investigates the financial strength of a potential supplier before trading starts, and periodically reviews the situation.

Input inventory management

The purpose of holding stocks of bought-in items (and any 'own-build' items used as inputs to manufacturing) is twofold. First, as noted earlier, the input stock insulates the manufacturing schedules from vagaries in supply. Second, it can reduce unit costs through volume discounts for bulk purchase. But, as with output stocks, items in the goods-in store represent unemployed money, and the store itself is also a cost factor. It is sometimes argued that, provided the credit period roughly equates with item storage time, much of the idle money is provided by the supplier and it is not a local problem. It is a specious argument, because credit costs incurred by suppliers are built into supply prices.

A relatively novel arrangement, known as **consignment stocking**, is increasingly used for standard items. Here, a substantial volume of such items is held in a 'bonded' store at the purchaser's premises, who pays for small batches as these are drawn from the store. Both parties benefit: the purchaser has instant availability and the supplier has a semi-captive customer. Financial details vary from case to case but the savings are normally shared between the cooperating parties. (This is an elementary version of the **just-in-time** notion reviewed in Section 10.5.2.)

Input **inventory management** is principally concerned with the choice of items to stock, batch order size, reorder levels, avoiding 'stock-out' crises and the economics of the whole system. The observed fact that actual inputs and outputs to and from the stock frequently relate only vaguely to planned quantities adds further spice to the practical situation. It is a problem of some complexity, and cannot be adequately treated here.

10.3.6 Quality assurance

Quality assurance embraces all activities directed at achieving and maintaining, at an economic cost, defined levels of product **quality**, **conformability** and **availability**. These three product attributes are defined very soon, and the market orientation of the definitions should be noted. Quality is defined from the product end user perspective, and both conformability and availability involve quality. Quality assurance also includes management activities such as quality planning and quality control.

In common parlance 'quality' usually means 'degree of excellence', and excellence, like beauty, is a fuzzy concept perceived differently by different people. More precision is needed for industrial purposes. The related product attributes of quality, conformability and availability are defined in Section 8.3.1, in the context of product purchasing decisions. Those definitions are repeated and expanded here.

Quality

The quality of a product is the degree to which its objective and subjective functional and performance features meet the customer requirements. This is the conventional 'degree of fitness for the user-defined purpose' definition. Observe that product quality is not measured on an absolute scale. It is measured by a customer as a fraction of perfection, where perfection is a complete match with the customer-defined product requirements. All products are imperfect, to some extent, because cost and price both rise sharply as perfection is approached. Customers have to accept some degree of initial and progressive imperfection.

Conformability

The conformability of a product is the degree to which it initially meets its **declared quality specification**, which is a statement by the product creators defining the intended objective and subjective performance features of the product. Actual products may or may not meet that specification, and conformability indicates the extent of any initial deviations. Note that the product (declared quality) *specification* may or may not match the user requirement. It is bad news if it does not, but it is nothing to do with product conformability. That deviation is a shortfall in specification quality, since the specification does not meet its intended purpose of defining a product that matches the user needs. The subject is part of the the **total quality** concept, which is examined later in this section.

Availability

The availability of a product is the degree to which it maintains its declared quality specification throughout its useful life. Availability measures the operational life of a product as a proportion of its useful life. It is related to **reliability** and **maintainability**. Most products deteriorate in use and with the passage of time. Availability measures the useful proportion of the intended in-service life of a product.

Reliability can be broadly defined as the ability of a product to perform a specific function, under specific conditions, for a particular time. Reliability calculations involve the probability of future failure and, because of variabilities within a group of notionally identical products, statistical techniques are generally employed. Typically, the **mean-time-to-failure** (MTTF) or **mean-time-between-failures** (MTBF) is quoted.

Maintainability can be defined as the time needed to repair a product when it fails. Again, there are variabilities between notionally identical products. This attribute depends on the design and manufacture of the product, *and* on the maintenance strategy in use. For example, transport delays are avoided, thereby improving maintainability, if spares are held at the product location. Maintainability is usually quoted as a **mean-time-to-repair** (MTTR).

The relationship between availability, reliability and maintainability is illustrated in the following simple example. Suppose a system of traffic-lights fails totally, on average, once a year. It then takes, on average, fifty hours to repair. The system is intended to be in operation twenty-four hours per day throughout the year. Then:

$$\text{System Availability} = \frac{\text{MTBF}}{\text{MTBF} + \text{MTTR}} = \frac{24 \times 365}{(24 \times 365) + 50} = 99.4\%$$

Note that the availability defined in this section should not be confused with the more general usage of the same word in Section 10.3.5, in the context of supplies availability.

Where things can go wrong

Assuming (boldly) that the **product brief** (which defines the targets for development and design work) *does* match the needs of the target users, then the focus falls on product conformability and availability. Each of these attributes depends on the design process and the manufacturing process. The emphasis here is on manufactured quality, but a brief diversion into design quality is appropriate.

Design quality

There are many reasons why conformability or availability can be compromised in the development and design phases. Apart from the possibility of human error or misunderstanding, the usual problem is that specified performance cannot be achieved within specified works cost. Situations where the development and design project budget (money or time) is in jeopardy can also arise. A decision may then be made to eliminate or reduce some performance features (spoiling conformability) or to specify cheaper, less reliable, components (spoiling availability). The initial (declared quality) specification is normally amended to reflect such changes, thereby accepting that product quality is reduced as fitness for purpose is marked down.

Manufactured quality

Specified conformability or availability can also be reduced within the manufacturing process. It is convenient to break the process into three distinct aspects. These are process inputs, transformation of inputs to outputs, and process outputs.

(1) *Inputs*   Process inputs include bought-in items and other 'consumables' such as management, supervision and operator effort. It is these resources which are transformed into finished product output in accordance with another (non-consumable) input: the 'how to make and test it' instructions. Clearly, undetected deficiencies in the bought-in items dilute output quality to some extent. This is equally so with the other inputs. The concepts of quality, conformability and availability can be usefully applied to all inputs to the manufacturing process, including the human effort inputs.

(2) *Transformation*   The transformation activities turn the inputs into the required outputs. Since input quality factors have been separated out, the primary concern here is with the machinery involved. So the purpose of facilities maintenance (discussed in Section 10.3.1) is not only to support the manufacturing schedules but also to sustain the quality and availability of these facilities.

(3) *Outputs*   There is always a delay between the emergence of finished products from the transformation activity and their employment by the user. Some of this delay may be deliberate, as with periods in the finished-goods store and/or storage at a retail outlet. Product distribution delays cannot be avoided. So some deterioration of quality is inevitable before the user receives the product, illustrating that the packing, storage and distribution activities also have a quality dimension.

National quality standards

There are a number of national and international quality assurance standards. British Standard BS-5750 (British Standards Institution, 1987) is a national example. It provides a reference framework on which a 'subscribing' business can build its own quality management system. This style contrasts with most other standard documents, which are generally more prescriptive. BS-5750 is now identical to ISO-9000 and EN-7000, the corresponding international and European standards, respectively. This is a fairly recent development which illustrates increasing harmony in some aspects of international trading.

Aggregate quality, cost and price

Aggregate quality is defined here as some combination of the three product attributes of quality, conformability and availability. Achieving and maintaining an 'acceptable' level of aggregate quality costs money, which is normally passed on to the customer in the product price. The cost, and hence the price, of providing it rises ever more steeply as perfection is approached. (Perfection corresponds to the unattainable one hundred per cent aggregate quality level. At this theoretical level, both cost and price are infinite!) But the *value* of aggregate quality perceived by the customer appears to diminish as perfection is approached. In theory, therefore, there is an aggregate quality level at which the customer perceives optimum value for money. Figure 10.13 illustrates this situation.

The concept of perceived **product value** is not well defined. But if a rational customer is presented with a choice of competing products to buy, then the customer buys the product which is perceived to have the best value in excess of product price. In other words, the customer would rather have that particular product (out of those on offer) than the money exchanged in acquiring it. Following this argument through leads to a definition of **customer benefit** as the difference of perceived product value and product price. This parameter is also plotted in Figure 10.13. Note that, as the aggregate quality level increases, customer benefit rises to a positive maximum and then declines through zero to become negative. The positive maximum indicates the target aggregate quality level to yield optimum value for money to the customer. The positive regime of the customer benefit curve defines the aggregate quality range over which the product is a viable sales proposition. (Readers should note that Figures 10.13 and 10.14 are drawn for clarity rather than to a realistic scale.)

The notions expressed here do demonstrate that there is an optimum target quality level. But their practical application is limited by the speculative nature of the two primary curves, particularly that for perceived product value. And any two economists will provide at least four unhelpful definitions of 'product value'. (A concept of product value, not unlike that considered here, is discussed in Section 8.3, where the

Customer benefit = perceived product value – product price

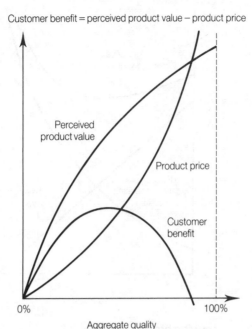

Figure 10.13 **Aggregate quality and customer benefit.**
Aggregate quality combines product quality, conformability and availability. Achieving and maintaining it at an acceptable level costs the supplier money, which is passed on to the customer in product price. The cost (and price) of providing it rises steeply as perfection is approached. But the value of aggregate quality perceived by the customer appears to diminish as perfection is approached. In theory, therefore, there is an aggregate quality level at which the customer perceives optimum value for money. The figure illustrates this notion by plotting customer benefit as the difference of perceived product value and product price.

purchasing decision in a competitive market is discussed).

A rational product customer considers both the initial price of a product and the subsequent costs of owning it, which comprise the **price of ownership**. For example, the purchase price of a car is but the first item on a long list of consequential expenses. Part of the operating cost of any product is due to its *out-of-service* time, so availability is also a customer consideration. Product availability is determined by the product itself and by the maintenance strategy applied to it, because it depends on reliability and maintainability. Again, the cost and price of providing availability rise steeply as the higher levels are approached. But out-of-service costs fall as availability increases. Other things being equal, these behaviours suggest a minimum in a plot of price of ownership against availability. This defines the optimum target availability in those situations where price of ownership is the primary customer interest. Figure 10.14 demonstrates the argument but, again, its practical utility is hampered by the difficulty of getting good data.

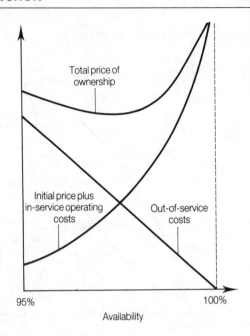

Figure 10.14   **Price of ownership versus availability.**

A rational product customer is concerned with initial product price and the costs of operating it, which together make up the price of ownership. Part of the operating cost is due to its out-of-service time, so availability is also a customer consideration. Availability is determined by the product itself and by the maintenance strategy applied to it. The cost (and price) of availability rise steeply as perfection is approached. But out-of-service costs fall from a high level as availability increases. So there is a minimum in a plot of price of ownership against availability, which defines the optimum target availability. This notion is illustrated in the figure.

The total quality concept

The dependence of product quality on both design quality and manufactured quality has already been noted. But, in fact, the dependence is much wider than this. For example, a product brief, prepared by marketing for the design and development team, must adequately reflect the needs of the target customers or the product will fail in the market-place. Every distinct function in a business contributes, directly or otherwise, to the product creation process. It is but a short step from this observation to propose that quality assurance should permeate every facet of business activity.

This is the total quality concept. The first steps in its implementation were taken in the USA in the early 1950s. It was subsequently adopted by some of the (now) large Japanese businesses, and is widely considered to have made a major contribution to the enviable reputation that they now enjoy for product quality. It is a life-cycle approach applied to products from their early birth pangs in a research laboratory to their ultimate demise on the scrap-heap of history. Experience has shown that, in the last analysis, a total quality programme is an exercise in human engineering. In other words, the mechanics may be perfect but the programme will fail unless the key people are dedicated to making it succeed. In this context, there are very few non-key people in a business.

10.4   An arena of conflict

It was observed earlier that the production function is, perhaps, the most stressful arena in a business. Its role as principal profit and cash creator, and its many interfaces with other business functions largely account for this unenviable position. This section introduces a note of human reality into the preceding, somewhat detached, discussion by outlining some of the conflicts which can arise.

10.4.1   External conflicts

The production function has critical relationships with:

- the product development and design teams in the technical function
- the finance function
- the sales function
- top management.

Development and design

Production depends on the development and design teams for product definition data relating to new products and to the enhancement of established products. They hope that the data will:

- Be delivered no later than its due date.
- Define products that can be made without recourse to exotic methods and/or machinery, or require the purchase of specialized 'single-source' components and/or components from 'non-approved' suppliers.
- Define products that can meet their specified works cost target.
- Define products that perform to specification and are testable as such.

But, too often, the product engineers cannot (or will not) see their role in this wider business context. They regard technology as the end rather than the means. Time and money take third place to technical excellence and/or the addition of technically challenging product features of dubious commercial merit. ('Marketing never got a spec right before, so why now?') The hopes of production are dashed again and some acrimony follows.

Finance

Conscious that their own prosperity is linked to business prosperity, the accountants analyse every facet of production activity. They rarely hesitate to bring their results to the attention of production management, nor to point out the disturbing nature of their conclusions. Messages of this sort do nothing to improve the temper of their recipients, and the more so when the problem is already receiving attention.

Some accountants equate profit only with manufactured output, irrespective of the content of that output. They may encourage the same damaging trait in like-minded manufacturing managers. A policy of 'deliver the budget, never mind the product mix' may follow. The sales function, rightly anxious to keep all their customers happy, can get very bitter about this.

Sales

Sales personnel are optimists. They expect production to produce the right products at the right time at the right cost (or less). The multiplication of three probabilities must produce unity if these expectations are to be realized. Even if each probability is as high as ninety-five per cent, sales will be disappointed in about fifteen per cent of the cases.

Sales, in their turn, visit some aggravation on production. Good sales staff know the limits of product performance, price flexibility and delivery time. They seek signed orders, with great enthusiasm, *within* these boundaries. Less good sales people find it easier to sell special price and/or delivery deals or (worse) novel product variants, leaving production to sort out the ensuing chaos.

Top management

Many senior managers, victims of their own history, do not understand the problems of production. But they do understand its paramount importance in meeting the demanding targets that they have been set. So they apply continuous pressure for more output at lower cost. Now, pressure accompanied by understanding is no bad thing. Any competent manager knows how to exploit that situation. But, too often, the pressure is accompanied by resource starvation. All 'indirect' production activities are prime targets, particularly those where very visible current costs promise future benefits. Maintenance, machinery updating programmes, new technology projects and quality assurance are typical casualties of this short-term policy. Managers in this sort of environment, where more and more is always expected from less and less, may lose their enthusiasm for the task.

10.4.2 Internal conflicts

Conflict inside the production organization usually involves:

- the purchasing team
- the quality assurance team
- the 'workers'.

Purchasing

A duty of purchasing is to procure the right items at the right time at the lowest cost. The manufacturing manager is responsible for meeting product output schedules. In a deliveries crisis, the manufacturing manager wants the the right items immediately, irrespective of cost. The cost problem can be worried about later. Emergency purchasing goes against all the instincts of purchasing managers, but they usually lose this battle. Victors and losers rarely enjoy a harmonious relationship.

Quality assurance

Those responsible for quality assurance take their job seriously. They believe, correctly, that product quality is important. The manufacturing manager understands that no quality programme can deliver perfection. What the manufacturing manager cannot understand (or chooses not to) is why it takes so long. A batch of urgently needed items gathering dust at goods-inwards inspection is one common source of (justified) irritation. Nor does the manufacturing manager find it easy to accept that some 'nit-picking little quality defect' is going to prevent achievement of the current month deliveries budget. A basic and enduring conflict between long-term and short-term objectives underlies such incidents. The danger that quality gets diluted at times of crisis is always present when the quality assurance organization belongs to the production function. (As noted in Section 10.1, this is one reason why quality assurance is often a 'stand-alone' organization reporting directly, say, to the managing director. This structure is also likely in businesses which have adopted the total quality approach discussed, briefly, in Section 10.3.6.)

The 'workers'

The production function employs the manufacturing operators, who are the potentially most awkward section of the total work-force. Sheer numbers and trade union membership contribute to the problem. But many shop-floor jobs are deadly dull, the working environment is rarely attractive, working hours per week are long, and pay and conditions are not always generous. A measure of discontent among the 'workers' is to be expected. They take the view, and it has merit, that they deserve a fair share of the cake that they help to cook. Sadly, the 'management' view of what is fair, or even possible, can differ sharply from theirs. This is not the place to debate the relative merits of these contrasting attitudes. But some of the effects are now illustrated.

Despite their media-exciting potential, all-out strikes are comparatively rare. Also, when they do occur, the grievance is usually reasonably clear and the parties involved generally share a common interest in its resolution. Solving 'working-to-rule' and absenteeism problems can be more difficult. But it is the steady day-to-day drip of less dramatic protest that is so wearying for both sides. Some typical flash points are:

- *Demarcation disputes*   These are situations when a member of one trade union is accused, correctly or not, of doing work regarded as the domain of another trade union. Disputes of this nature are now less fashionable than they were, but they still occur.

- *Rate-for-the-job*   There is a status hierarchy (skilled, semi-skilled, unskilled) on the shop-floor. The higher status groups are always concerned to maintain, or widen, pay 'differentials'. The lower status groups take a contrary view. Disputes under this same heading can also arise as a result of inter-business comparisons.

- *Safety issues*   These are always a good way of focusing management attention and, in many cases, rightly so.

- *Standard times*   Payment is frequently linked to labour productivity and this depends, among other things, on the standard times set for the various tasks. From the operator perspective, there is merit in longer rather than shorter times. Management do not share this view.

- *The 'right' to overtime*   Management take the view that overtime working is a flexible way of obtaining extra resources at times of peak load. But the workers may come to regard overtime, paid at greater than normal rates, as an entitlement which goes with the job.

- *Welfare provisions*   This covers a multitude of possibilities ranging from the entirely reasonable to the simply frivolous. Creches for the children of working mothers and paternity leave are popular at the time of writing.

10.5 Current production technologies

The technologies employed in modern production functions are currently changing quite rapidly. The driving motivation is the search for lower unit costs at consistently high quality delivered by systems able to cope with a broad range of product types and batch sizes. Computer technology contributes towards achievement of this demanding ambition, but other approaches depend more on organization, structure and attitudes. This section offers a brief review of the current situation. It is partitioned into manufacturing (process) technologies and production management technologies, although these areas are not entirely independent.

10.5.1 Manufacturing technologies

The discussion in Section 10.2.5 divides manufacturing processes into three broad classes. These range from the project manufacturing of a one-off product at one extreme, through batch manufacturing of similar products, to continuous manufacturing of a uniform product at the other extreme. This classification is summarized in Figure 10.4. A particular form of manufacturing system, characterized by its facilities layout, is traditionally associated with each class. The total cost characteristics of the three systems are compared by the 'cost lines' of Figure 10.9. In summary:

(1) Fixed position layout (Cost line 1 in Figure 10.9) is best used for low-volume/high-unit-cost products.
(2) Functional layout (Cost line 2 in Figure 10.9) is best used for medium-volume/medium-unit-cost products.
(3) Flow-line layout (Cost line 3 in Figure 10.9) is best used for high-volume/low-unit-cost products.

Low, intermediate and high technology

The fixed cost element in a total cost characteristic (the intercepts C1, C2 and C3 on the vertical axis in Figure 10.9) indicates the capital cost of the system facilities. This cost reflects the level of technology employed, which offers another way of classifying the three basic manufacturing systems:

(1) *Low technology 'manual' manufacturing*   Labour-intensive mostly manual operations best suited to low-volume manufacture of diverse products.
(2) *Intermediate technology 'mechanized' manufacturing*   'Balanced' combinations of labour and capital in mechanized operations best suited to batch manufacture of a variety of similar products.
(3) *High technology 'automated' manufacturing*   Capital-intensive automated operations best suited to high-volume manufacture of a limited range of virtually identical products.

The low-technology manual systems use relatively simple (and, perhaps, largely mobile) machinery with correspondingly high levels of operator intervention. Capital cost is low and product-type flexibility high. But operating cost increases rapidly as volume increases and unit costs are high. A highly skilled work-force is needed and output quality is likely to be variable.

The machinery used in the higher technology systems is largely immobile, so the work is brought to the machine, rather than the machine to the work. The positioning of the boundary between intermediate and high technology systems is debatable, and is shifting as manufacturing processing technology develops.

Manually controlled single-function machines, as suggested by Figure 10.6, are used in low-level intermediate systems. More sophisticated systems use some form of **numerically controlled** (NC) machine, which can be programmed to perform a sequence of operations without operator intervention. NC machines range from the early tape-controlled single-function units, to complex multi-function 'machine-tools' able to perform sequences of different operations on widely different product parts. Units with these features usually incorporate a control microcomputer, and are termed **computerized numerically controlled** (CNC) machines. Increasingly, **industrial robots** are also used in these systems. These are programmable machines which are able to manoeuvre tools and piece-parts with some precision. Typical current applications include spray painting, spot welding (as in vehicle assembly) and other simple assembly and inspection operations. They can operate in situations which are difficult and/or dangerous for human operators, such as tiny spaces and hazardous atmospheres. Installations of several individually programmed machines represent, perhaps, the upper boundary of the intermediate systems. The (vague) term 'intermediate' describes other important system parameters, such as capital cost, product-type flexibility, unit cost and requisite work-force skills. Output quality is generally higher and more consistent than that delivered by the more labour-intensive systems.

Combining the control mechanisms of two programmable machines to obtain coordinated processing is the next step, and it can be used to distinguish a low-level automated system from a high-level intermediate system. Increasing levels of automation are then obtained by integrating the computer-based control of several CNC machines and (possibly) industrial robots. The processing activities within this integrated 'cell' are then coordinated and optimized through a central computer.

FMS and CIM

From this point, it is but short step (in concept rather than practice) to the high level of automation which characterizes a **flexible manufacturing system** (FMS). These systems are also equipped with programmable internal transport and handling equipment. A central computer controls the processing machinery, the movement of work-in-progress between machines, its loading and unloading at the machines, and the whole coordinated manufacturing schedule. Capital cost is very high, but (subject to adequate volume) unit cost is low, as are the work-force skill requirements. Output quality can be high and consistent. Such systems are most commonly used at the high-volume/low-unit-cost end of the spectrum. But product-type flexibility is high, and the systems are increasingly used in the batch manufacture of similar products.

An FMS can be regarded as a low-level **computer integrated manufacturing**

(CIM) system, or as the machinery element in higher-level CIM systems. Opinions differ on what constitutes a CIM system, but the development thrust in manufacturing process technology is to bring all aspects of manufacturing under a single coordinated computer-based control. In some cases, this perspective is extended to include aspects of product design and product test.

10.5.2 Management technologies

Figure 10.1 shows the production function as a manufacturing operation supported by a set of local services activities. Production management technologies are directed at the efficiency of this whole system.

The manufacturing operation is a transformation process which uses some combination of machine facilities and human effort to convert bought-in supplies, commonly termed **materials**, into finished products. Manufacturing efficiency, however it is defined, is critically dependent on the ready availability of the right quantities of the right materials. Usually, a stock of materials (an inventory) is kept, to isolate the manufacturing process from short-term mismatches between supply to it and demand from it. Mismatches occur when there is a supply failure (due date, quantity, quality or content) or when an unexpected order is received. But, as indicated in Section 10.3.5, it is costly to provide the stocks and the space to store them. Administering the stock and the space is a further drain on resources. So minimizing stocks is a central issue in production management.

Traditional stocking policies are 'demand *independent*' systems. These set stock levels for individual items largely by analysis of historic demand patterns, with automatic reordering when the stock falls to some pre-ordained level. But extrapolating the past does not always provide an accurate vision of the future, and both stock shortage and stock redundancy problems occur. Over-ordering is commonly used as an insurance against 'stock-out', and it results in average stock levels (and stock costs) being higher than they need to be. A preferred approach is termed **materials requirement planning** (MRP).

Materials requirements planning

MRP is a 'demand *dependent*' system, based on the **master deliveries schedule** for a forthcoming production period. This defines the required manufactured output for the period in terms of product types, quantities and due dates. A parts list, or **bill of materials**, is associated with each product type, and the current stock holding of all individual items is also known. All this data is then combined with knowledge of delivery lead-times to create a **master materials ordering schedule** for the period. This is designed to keep average stock holdings to a minimum 'safety reserve' level. The system is still vulnerable to faulty demand forecasts and material supply problems. But it generally yields much lower stock costs than prevail in demand independent systems. It also offers:

- better customer service because fewer due dates are missed due to stock shortages
- better machinery utilization for the same reason
- less need for costly 'progress-chasing' and crisis management.

The MRP concept is not complicated, but its implementation involves a lot of simple arithmetic. So MRP operating economics depend heavily on the availability of cheap computing power, resulting in most developments and applications occurring since the mid 1970s. Many standard MRP software packages are available, but most MRP users have had to adapt both the software and their own procedures before obtaining the promised benefits.

Manufacturing resources planning

The generally satisfactory nature of MRP experience, coupled with its computer-based expression, has led to a variety of extensions. Initially, these were restricted to coping with the more variable demand and/or supply situations, supplier reliability and quality problems, and so on. The early development work led to a more ambitious concept, known as **manufacturing resources planning** (MRP II). The basic notion is that a master deliveries schedule for a period actually defines *all* the resources needed to generate the planned output, not just its materials requirement. So, MRP II systems offer integrated planning and control (through cost and cost variance reporting) of:

- ordering and purchasing of material requirements
- inventories
- processing facilities capacity
- facilities maintenance
- processing labour capacity
- finished product storage and distribution
- and so on.

Again, there are many standard software packages available which offer various MRP II recipes. Experience with MRP II has been generally less satisfactory than with the less complex MRP systems. However, those businesses which have invested substantial time, money and effort in MRP II generally reap very worthwhile rewards.

Both MRP and MRP II are sophisticated systems which stem from an attack on the economic problems posed by inventories. They are aimed, quite successfully, at improving the economic efficiency of traditional manufacturing systems with large doses of computer power. A more fundamental approach questions the need for inventories. This perspective has led to the **just-in-time** (JIT) concept of manufacturing which underpins the success of Japanese high volume manufacturing operations.

Just-in-time

In JIT terms, stocks are unnecessary evils. They exist only to cover short-term mismatches between input supply and output demand and impose an economic burden on the system in doing so. This is avoided if mismatches can be eliminated. So JIT aims to arrange that the right materials arrive where they are needed just as they are needed. In this sense, JIT is the logical extension of MRP. It (theoretically) eliminates stocks whereas MRP reduces them to a minimum safety level.

But the whole JIT concept is much broader than this introduction suggests. First, it demands a change in traditional attitudes. For example, the discussion on external purchasing in Section 10.3.5 suggests an adversarial relationship between the purchasing business and its material suppliers. The purchaser assumes that suppliers are unreliable and uses multiple sourcing both to encourage good supply perform-ance and to insure against it not being so. This approach works against the 'zero-stocks' JIT notion, which places total reliance on the timely delivery of 'zero-defects' material from suppliers working in close harmony with the purchaser. Similarly, successive machines in a manufacturing processing sequence are in a supplier–customer relationship, with work-in-progress being analogous to input stock. So excessive levels of work-in-progress, facilities under-utilization and wastage are problems to be solved rather than accepted as inevitable. JIT is most obviously applicable to stable, high volume, low product-diversity situations. But, as with the processing technologies, the thrust of production management development is towards applying some combination of JIT and MRP ideas in batch manufacturing.

10.6   Concluding summary

The chapter presents an introductory overview of the production function: the wealth-creating mechanism which dominates the present and determines the future of a technology-based manufacturing business. It has a critical relationship with the technical function, on which it depends for 'how to make and test it' data relating to new and enhanced products.

The production function is a system comprising a manufacturing operation and its supporting services. It has important interactive relationships with other business functions and external suppliers. A manufacturing operation employs some combina-tion of people and machinery in a process for converting bought-in items into complete tested products. Cost minimization dominates the design of (most) such operations and the degree of product diversity is a critical factor. Variations on three basic structures are used in practice, with people-intensive processes at one end of the diversity spectrum and machinery-intensive processes at the other. Whatever its structure, a manufacturing operation is supported by a production management system of supporting activities. The most important are concerned with:

- facilities maintenance
- industrial and production engineering
- production planning and control
- external purchasing and inventory management
- product quality assurance.

For the most part, the teams responsible for these activities also link the production function with:

- the marketing and sales functions
- the technical function
- the finance function
- the personnel function

- the external suppliers

in a set of critical business relationships.

People and machinery meet in the production function, which is normally under great pressure to deliver ever-better performance. It is probably the most stressful part of a manufacturing business and it can form an arena for human conflict.

There is an ongoing search for production systems able to deliver lower unit costs with consistently high quality over a broad range of product types and batch sizes. Both manufacturing process and production management technologies are involved. Flexible manufacturing systems (FMS), computer integrated manufacturing (CIM), sundry techniques for manufacturing resources planning (MRP and MRP II), and just-in-time (JIT) systems are all involved in a developing situation.

REFERENCES

British Standard Institution (1987). *Quality Systems* (BS 5750) London: BSI

Waters C. D. J. (1991). *An Introduction to Operations Management*. Wokingham: Addison-Wesley

Wild R. (1989). *Production and Operations Management* 4th edn. London: Cassell Educational

SUGGESTED FURTHER READING

The two principal references to this chapter (Waters and Wild) are wide-ranging texts which emphasize operations management, rather than focusing exclusively on production matters. Hill (1991) and Samson (1991) are in a similar vein and both are commended. At a more specialist level, Chapter 6 in Lawrence and Lee (1984) is a readable introduction to the human aspects of production; and Hill (1985) is an illuminating and comprehensive account of the strategic aspects of the whole subject. Browne *et al.* (1988) presents a fascinating perspective of the current situation and future outlook for computer-integrated manufacturing in its many forms. The other cited texts treat facets of production as topics in their own right. They are mostly directed at specialists in those areas.

Bailey P. and Farmer D. H. (1977). *Purchasing Principles and Techniques* 3rd edn. London: Pitman

Banks J. (1989). *Principles of Quality Control*. New York: John Wiley

Browne J., Harhen J. and Shivan J. (1988). *Production Management Systems*. Wokingham: Addison-Wesley

Corder A. (1976). *Maintenance Management Techniques*. New York: McGraw Hill

Hill T. (1985). *Manufacturing Strategy*. Basingstoke: Macmillan

Hill T. (1991). *Production/Operations Management* 2nd edn. Hemel Hempstead: Prentice-Hall

Kelly A. and Harris M. J. (1978). *Management of Industrial Maintenance*. London: Newnes Butterworth

Konz S. A. (1984). *Work Design: Industrial Ergonomics* 2nd edn. New York: John Wiley

Lawrence P. A. and Lee R. A. (1984). *Insight into Management*. London: Oxford University Press (Chapter 6)

Pall G. A. (1988). *Quality Process Management*. Englewood Cliffs, NJ: Prentice-Hall

Samson D. (1991). *Manufacturing and Operations Strategy*. Australia: Prentice-Hall

Van Hees R. N. and Monhemius W. (1973). *Production and Inventory Control – Theory and Practice*. London: Macmillan

Whitmore D. A. (1987). *Work Measurement* 2nd edn. London: Heinemann

QUESTIONS

10.1 'Manufacturing performance is always closely monitored by top management, and sustained pressure to improve labour and capital productivity is a fact of manufacturing life.' Why?

10.2 The production function of a typical manufacturing business may be regarded as an entity comprising:

- a manufacturing operation, and a number of
- manufacturing support services

which has a number of critical relationships with other entities both inside and outside the business.

(a) Illustrate this structure with a 'system' diagram, showing relevant relationships, which:

- describes the primary purpose of the manufacturing operation
- identifies the most important manufacturing support services
- identifies the most important other entities which cooperate with the production function.

(b) Illustrate this same structure in the form of a conventional organization chart of authority levels. Describe common variations in this structure which concern the scope of the production function.

10.3 A manufacturing company contains the five business functions of finance, marketing and sales, personnel, technical, and production. The production function contains the manufacturing operation and a set of supporting services comprising production engineering, industrial engineering, facilities maintenance, production planning and control, quality assurance and purchasing. Describe:

- the nature of the relationships between the production function and the other business functions cited above, and
- the role of each of the services, cited above, which support the manufacturing operation.

10.4 (a) List and describe the principal steps in a typical sequence for manufacturing a batch quantity of a specific established product.

(b) Such a sequence is subject to a number of possible interventions. These may be scheduled or unscheduled and at process level or product level, yielding four major classes. Give an example in each class.

10.5 Describe, briefly, the role of the manufacturing support services which are listed below:

- facilities maintenance
- industrial engineering
- production engineering
- production planning and control
- purchasing
- quality assurance.

10.6 Describe, briefly, the salient features of the relationships between the production function and the other organizations which are listed below:

- external suppliers

- the finance function
- the marketing function
- the personnel function
- the sales function
- the technical function.

10.7 (a) Show how manufacturing situations within a major technological product category can be partitioned into three broad classes reflecting the relationship between product unit output rate and product unit cost. What is meant, in this context, by the terms 'project manufacturing', 'batch manufacturing' and 'continuous manufacturing'?

(b) Choose any one major technological product category (civil, chemical, mechanical, electronic and so on) and identify products from this category which fall into each one of the three manufacturing situations.

(c) Describe, in comparative terms, how the levels of:

- operator skill
- operator intervention
- manufacturing technology

typically vary over the spectrum of manufacturing situations ranging from project manufacturing at one extreme to continuous manufacturing at the other.

10.8 (a) Describe the arrangement of manufacturing facilities which is traditionally associated with each of the three broad classes of manufacturing situation cited in Question 10.7(a), and justify its use in each case.

(b) Describe the 'group technology' (or 'cell') format of facilities layout. Under what circumstances is its use advantageous, and why?

10.9 (a) In the context of different arrangements of manufacturing facilities describe, in comparative terms, the manner in which the costs of:

- fixed position layout
- functional layout
- flow-line layout

vary with the rate of product output.

(b) Show that, for a specific type of product, the optimum economic choice of manufacturing facilities layout is a function of product output rate.

10.10 Figure 10.9 illustrates the relative economics of the three basic types of manufacturing layouts. Referring to that figure:

- the sales price of each product unit is £228
- C1 is £100,000 and the gradient of cost line 1 is £128 per unit
- C2 is £190,000 and the gradient of cost line 2 is £81 per unit
- C3 is £330,000 and the gradient of cost line 3 is £34 per unit

Assuming that the most economic manufacturing system is always used, calculate R1, R2 and R3 and the annual profit at each of these annual output rates.

10.11 Analyse the roles of the six manufacturing support services labelled (a) to (f) below under the headings of:

- Justification (answering the question '*why* is it needed?')
- Specification (answering the question '*what* does it have to do?')
- Implementation (answering the question '*how* does it do it?')

  (a) Facilities maintenance
  (b) Industrial engineering
  (c) Production engineering
  (d) Production planning and control
  (e) Purchasing
  (f) Quality assurance

10.12 The production function of a manufacturing business has been described as an 'arena for human conflict'. Discuss this view by examining relationships both inside the function and between it and other business functions. How can human conflict inside a business be minimized? ('By firing everybody' is *not* an acceptable answer.)

10.13 Section 10.5.1, which contains about 800 words, is an introductory overview of manufacturing technologies. Summarize its principal messages in not more than

200 words. (Note-format and diagrams are allowed, even encouraged.)

10.14 Section 10.5.2, which contains about 1000 words, is an introductory overview of production management technologies. Summarize its principal messages in not more than 250 words. (Note-format and diagrams are allowed, even encouraged.)

Technical Project Evaluation and Choice

Ah, take the Cash, and let the Credit go,
Nor heed the rumble of a distant Drum!

Edward Fitzgerald 1809–1883
(translating from Omar Khayyám)

11.1	Motivation and content	471
11.2	A review of project types	474
11.3	Project evaluation: Background	481
11.4	Evaluation of BR and AR projects	485
11.5	Evaluation of PD&D projects	489
11.6	Product creation projects	490
11.7	Project Evaluation Tool 1 (PET1)	493
11.8	The cash-flow model	497
11.9	Cash-flow shape techniques	501
11.10	The cost of negative cash-flow	506
11.11	A compounding technique	510
11.12	Discounting techniques 1: NPV	513
11.13	Discounting techniques 2: IRR	520
11.14	Project choice: NPV and IRR	524
11.15	Cash-flow models and inflation	533
11.16	Project Evaluation Tool 2 (PET2)	539
11.17	Concluding summary	543

Advanced material   Sections 11.10 to 11.16 contain material which is probably best appreciated by readers with some industrial experience. It covers project evaluation techniques which are based on 'time value of money' concepts. These are required because the cash-flow 'shape' techniques discussed in Section 11.9 do more to expose relevant questions than provide answers to them. (Other readers who feel frustrated by the sad conclusions of Section 11.9.3 are encouraged to read on. Elegant and useful solutions do emerge.)

 Repetitions Section 11.2.1 recalls visions of technology and products from Chapters 2 and 3; and Sections 11.2.2 and 11.2.3 review the four phase concept of technological innovation introduced in Sections 3.1 and 3.2. So Sections 11.2.1, 11.2.2 and 11.2.3 can be omitted if preferred. But they have 'stand-alone' merit as an integrated summary of the strategic and tactical aspects of technological innovation as presented in this book.

Section 11.8.1 develops the cash-flow model introduced in Section 3.3 to provide an investment perspective of a product creation project.

The overall objectives of this chapter are to examine a range of techniques for assessing the business merit of a proposed technological innovation project, both as a venture in its own right and as part of a larger programme. This is a long chapter, but it breaks into two largely self-contained parts. The first of these comprises Sections 11.1 to 11.9. It covers the evaluation and choice of technological innovation projects as stand-alone ventures, and introduces product creation projects and elementary cash-flow evaluation techniques. The second part, Sections 11.10 to 11.16, focuses on analytic techniques for evaluating cash-flow project models. Readers interested *only* in these techniques (which are applicable to many business situations) are recommended to start at Section 11.9. It provides a context for the subsequent discussion. Objectives by section follow:

11.1 To explain why technological innovation projects are important, why their investment prospects should be evaluated prior to launch, and how the chapter is structured.

11.2 To distinguish different types of technological innovation projects by identifying features which determine how they can be evaluated.

11.3 To establish the background of project evaluation in terms of project funding, the structure of project proposals and evaluation criteria.

11.4 To examine evaluation techniques suited to basic and applied research projects.

11.5 To examine evaluation techniques suited to product development and design projects treated as distinct ventures in their own right.

11.6 To describe the origin and structure of a product creation project as a multi-disciplinary 'mini-business' development programme encapsulating a product development and design sub-project and several other sub-projects.

11.7 To introduce the 'profile' method of evaluating the likely impact of a product creation project on the whole business.

11.8   To review the cash-flow model of a product creation project with special emphasis on its investment/return features.

11.9   To explore elementary cash-flow evaluation techniques which depend only on model 'shape'.

11.10   To explain why it costs money to get money to invest, and how a business can estimate the cost of investment money.

11.11   To introduce 'time value of money' cash-flow evaluation techniques by describing an unconventional method based on the well-known compound interest notion.

11.12   To examine the discounting concept, and to describe the conventional net present value (NPV) technique of cash-flow evaluation which is based upon it.

11.13   To describe the conventional internal rate of return (IRR)

technique of cash-flow evaluation with special attention to the meaning of IRR and the problems posed by this approach.

11.14   To illustrate the application of NPV and IRR, to examine project ranking methods, and to compare the relative merits of the two methods.

11.15   To establish the relationships between inflation rates and real interest rates, and to describe three ways of handling inflation in cash-flow evaluation work.

11.16   To illustrate the value of the NPV and IRR techniques by describing a near real-life application of a project planning tool for evaluating cash-flows.

11.17   To identify its salient points and summarize its major messages.

11.1   Motivation and content

This chapter is mostly about evaluating the business merits of proposed technological innovation projects, which are called 'technical' projects here.

The purpose of evaluating project proposals is to increase the probability of choosing the right projects to launch. Sadly, not all the projects that are launched then proceed as planned. So it is equally important to choose the right projects to stop. Mechanisms for evaluating proposed projects are equally applicable to projects in progress, and they can be based on better information.

The emphasis is on **private venture** (PV) projects. The term 'private venture' means that project costs are charged against profit by the project sponsor. That is, the profit earned by a business in an accounting period is reduced by the amount it spends on PV projects in that period. This is one factor which concentrates management attention on the proper choice of PV projects. Some technical projects may be wholly or partially funded by agencies outside the business. The principles involved in evaluating such projects are much the same as for PV projects, but the matter usually receives less attention. This is because business managers tend to focus on spending their 'own' money wisely.

(The abbreviation 'PV' is also commonly used to mean **present value**, which is a term explained later in the chapter. Normally, any potential confusion is removed by the context in which the abbreviation is used.)

11.1.1 Why invest in technology?

The primary aim of every business operating in a competitive environment is to survive and prosper. To do this, it must generate enough revenue (income) from product sales to pay all the costs incurred in achieving that revenue *and* leave an adequate profit. This basic fact of business life is encapsulated in the profit equation:

$$\text{Profit} = \text{Revenue} - \text{Cost} \tag{11.1}$$

which was introduced in Section 1.1.1. It is an underlying theme of the whole book. The purpose of every cost that a business incurs is to generate, directly or indirectly, an income. The costs of technical projects are no exception to this rule. Such costs are an investment in the future which, hopefully, will be returned together with substantial additional earnings.

Technological innovation offers three distinct ways of creating a more competitive product and thus improving the profitability of a business. These ways, which are not mutually exclusive, are:

- Providing attractive product features, which distinguish it in functional (*what* it does) terms from competing products.

- Improving the efficiency of delivering the product features, which distinguishes it in performance (*how well* it does it) terms from competing products.

- Reducing the cost of manufacturing the product, which distinguishes it in economic terms from competing products.

Technological innovation is important because it presents both opportunities and threats. It offers opportunities for survival and prosperity for those businesses which invest in it wisely. Equally, it poses the threat of oblivion to those businesses which do not.

11.1.2 Projects as investments

One corporate approach to building a technological strategy for the business is discussed in Chapter 2. This chapter assumes that such a strategy has already been formulated. In other words, it is assumed here that the longer-term aims of the technological innovation programme are already defined in terms aligned with the strategic ambitions of the business.

(In practice, this assumption is not always valid. In such cases, the senior scientists and engineers in the business must themselves assemble a technological strategy. This is likely to be a poor substitute for the real thing, which incorporates the combined wisdom of all the relevant business functions. But it is a great deal better than nothing.)

Individual technical projects are tactics aimed at implementing the technological strategy. A proposal to launch a technical project is also a proposal to spend resources in the immediate future in anticipation of earning an worthwhile reward in the longer-term future. So a technical project proposal is also an investment proposal. Evaluating the project proposal as a possible investment raises a problem which, in principle, is common to all investment proposals.

The basic investment evaluation problem

Given some resources to invest, the basic problem which faces all investors is how to choose the best single investment or portfolio of investments. There are three linked dimensions to this problem:

(1) The meaning of 'best' must be determined in relation to the context of the investment. In other words, a set of context-related investment criteria is required. For example, the appropriate investment criteria for a large and wealthy international business are unlikely to suit a small and struggling local enterprise, and would bring certain disaster to most widows and orphans.

(2) There are always more options for investment than there are resources to invest. So a central issue is the problem of choosing the best projects, from a wide range of possibilities, in which to invest limited resources.

(3) All investments are speculations. That is, the requisite resources must be committed (and, possibly, entirely consumed) before the rewards of using them become available and precisely known. So **risk** is an inherent feature of all investments: there is always the possibility that the reward will prove inadequate in relation to the investment. The need to forecast future events is an inherent feature of investment evaluation. Creating credible estimates of risk, and of the *reward to cost ratio*, is both demanding and critical. Inevitably, the cost estimate and the reward estimate each contain inaccuracies. But 'visibility' is better for cost than for reward, because cost is more immediate. This difference in quality must be recognized when the two estimates are compared.

Financial and non-financial evaluation

Proposals for technical projects range from vaguely defined research explorations into exotic new technologies to sharply specified product design exercises exploiting proven technologies in well-understood markets. There is no single evaluation technique which is applicable to this broad project spectrum. The issue is tackled in this chapter by distinguishing between financial and non-financial evaluation. An appropriate amalgam of each approach is then applied to the project in question.

In a sense, of course, this separation into financial and non-financial aspects is artificial, because the aim of all project evaluation work is to ensure the best possible return on the money invested. But the distinction is useful, because credible comparisons between forecast monetary investment and return are simply not possible for research projects.

11.1.3 Where from here?

The chapter continues with a review of distinctive features which determine how a project can be evaluated. This is followed, in Section 11.3, by the presentation of some background material about project funding, project proposals and evaluation criteria.

Non-financial evaluation

Sections 11.4 to 11.7 emphasize non-financial evaluation. The treatment of **basic and applied research projects** is necessarily limited to an evaluation of proposal quality in non-financial terms. Product **development and design projects** are discussed next. 'Stand-alone' proposal quality is again important, and is emphasized. Credible financial evaluation becomes tenable at this stage, because sharper product focus and improved market visibility distinguishes such projects. But a development and design project is just one critical part of a larger **product creation project** which also includes product marketing, manufacturing and selling activities. It is the financial investment/return prospects of this larger project which must be evaluated. Section 11.6 describes the origin and structure of product creation projects and Section 11.7 introduces a **profile** technique for evaluating their impact on the whole business.

Financial evaluation

The chapter then concentrates on the financial evaluation of the cash-flow models of product creation projects. Section 11.8 reviews the **cash-flow concept**, and some evaluation methods based simply on cash-flow 'shape' are considered in Section 11.9. These are not entirely satisfactory. The fact that it costs money to get money to invest is then developed, in Section 11.10, into the important concept of the **minimum attractive rate of return** for a project. This is used to explore a simple, but illuminating, approach to cash-flow evaluation based on the familiar **compound interest** notion. It forms a relatively unusual introduction to the examination of the more conventional **discounted cash-flow** evaluation techniques which follows in Sections 11.12 and 11.13. These cover the **net present value** (NPV) and **internal rate of return** (IRR) methods respectively. They are compared, as tools for choosing between mutually exclusive projects, in Section 11.14. **Inflation** has been mostly ignored in the preceeding discussions. The omission is corrected in Section 11.15, towards the end of the chapter. A near real-life example of cash-flow evaluation techniques is discussed in the penultimate section. This examines a project planning and performance tool which is a useful aid in the early formative stage of product creation projects.

The chapter concludes with a brief summary of its principle messages and a warning about the dangers of manipulating numbers into spurious conclusions. The wider application of cash-flow evaluation techniques is also mentioned.

11.2 A review of project types

In this book, technological innovation (commonly and confusingly called **research and development** or **R&D**) is treated as a sequence of four distinct phases. These are termed basic research, applied research, product development and product design. The concept is outlined in Figure 11.1. The figure identifies only three types of technical project:

- basic research (BR) projects,
- applied research (AR) projects, and
- product development and design (PD&D) projects

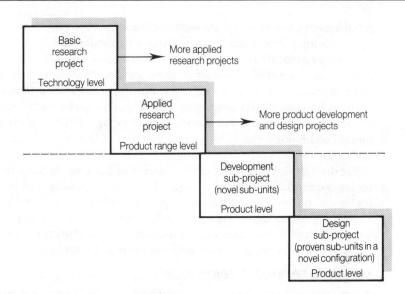

Figure 11.1   **Types of technical project.**
In this book, technological innovation is treated as a sequence of four distinct phases. The concept is outlined in the figure, which identifies only three types of technical project, because product development and design are normally taken together. The project types are basic research (BR), applied research (AR) and product development and design (PD&D). No single evaluation technique is applicable to this broad project spectrum. The issue is tackled by distinguishing between financial and non-financial evaluation. (It is shown later that all project types can be evaluated in non-financial terms. But financial evaluation is only sensibly applicable to PD&D projects, and then only in the context of a larger product creation project.)

because development and design activities are normally taken together.

The four phase concept of technological innovation is introduced in Sections 3.1 and 3.2 (where the terms are defined), and Figures 3.3, 3.4 and 3.5 extend the rudimentary vision of Figure 11.1. For convenience, a brief description of each technical innovation phase is included in this section. First, however, it is useful to recall some perspectives on technologies and products developed in Chapters 2 and 3. So Sections 11.2.1, 11.2.2 and 11.2.3 repeat earlier material and may be omitted if preferred. But they have 'stand-alone' merit as an integrated summary of the strategic and tactical aspects of technological innovation as presented in this book. The section concludes with an analysis of features which largely determine how different types of project proposal can be evaluated. This starts at Section 11.2.4.

11.2.1   Technologies and products

As it is used here, the term 'technology' means a science-based body of knowledge which is applied in industry and commerce. These are the **engineering or product technologies**. Each *major* product technology (such as electrical engineering, software engineering or mechanical engineering) can be regarded as a family hierarchy of progressively 'smaller' technologies, arranged in a series of levels. In this structure, technologies at the same level are distinguished by widely different skill requirements, whereas those at successive levels in the same family are distinguished by increasingly specialized application of a particular skill.

This hierarchical vision of product technologies leads directly to the concept of a product as a blend of a number of quite separate and distinct *minor* technologies. Here, the term 'minor' carries no suggestion of unimportance. It merely indicates that such technologies are constituent members of a major technology. For example, electric-arc welding is a part of welding technology which, in turn, is a part of metal-joining technology which, ultimately, is a part of the major mechanical engineering technology.

Product designing includes the process of defining the particular blend of minor technologies that comprise a product. In this same context, the lower-level technologies can be equated with specific product sub-units. This perspective makes the technological hierarchy concept entirely compatible with the **configuration view** of a product. It perceives a product as a unique configuration of distinct functional sub-units or components, and is reviewed in Section 11.2.3.

Example: A 'smart' telephone

An illustration of the blend of technologies notion is provided by a proposed (and hypothetical) 'smart' telephone product. This provides all the usual features of modern telephones, together with a combination of other facilities which distinguish it from most competing products. These include 'cordless' communication (by radio) with a local base-unit, call speech recording and play-back, and call cost monitoring and recording. The technological structure of this product is illustrated in the pie chart of Figure 11.2. The 'slices' of the pie represent the constituent minor technologies. System interface technology is concerned with the physical, speech signal and control signal relationships between the base-unit and the telephone network; and between the base-unit and the handset. Enclosures technology includes all the ergonomic and mechanical aspects of the 'boxes' which enclose and protect the other parts of the product. The terminology used to denote the other technologies is self-explanatory. Note that each technology carries a numerical rating. This corresponds to the fraction that the area of its slice bears to the area of the whole pie. This rating is explained shortly.

Competing with technologies

Each of the separate technologies which comprise a product can be assigned to one of three classes, depending on the contribution that it does, or might, make to the **competitive technological status** of the product. The three classes are:

(1) **Foundation** These are well-established technologies used in most of the products in a particular range, and in which most competitors are equally competent. Their limited potential for further development and wide availability means that they have virtually no effect on competitive status.

(2) **Critical** These technologies are usually still developing in their own right and/or in their application to the particular product range. They offer substantial opportunities for product differentiation and there are sharp differences in competence between competitors in the product market. So critical technologies are those with the greatest current impact on competitive status.

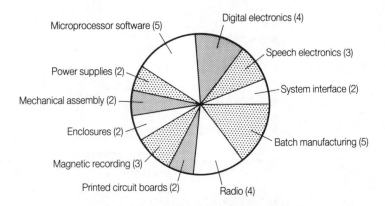

Figure 11.2   **A 'smart' telephone as a blend of technologies.**
The pie chart illustrates the notion that a product can be regarded as a blend, or recipe, of different product technologies. Here, each technology is assigned a numerical rating. These describe the relative perceived development potential of the technologies (in relation to the specific product) on a 5-point scale. A foundation technology with no development potential is rated at 1. A super-critical technology with maximum development potential is rated at 5. The higher rated technologies are the more important in creating competitive products.

(3) **Looming**   Technologies in this category are those which might develop into critical technologies. Generally, they are either embryonic technologies in their own right, and/or their application to the particular product range is still tentative and uncertain. They have no significant current impact on competitive status.

In practice, the divisions are not as sharply drawn as this list suggests. The critical category, for instance, covers a spectrum of technologies from near looming to near foundation.

In Figure 11.2, the numerical rating of a technology describes its perceived development potential in the context of that product application. A five point scale is used. A foundation technology with no development potential is rated at 1, whereas a super-critical technology is rated at 5. In this case, the business rates microprocessor software and batch manufacturing as the most important means of creating a competitive product. It is the potential of these technologies, and others which are highly rated, which may need to be nurtured and improved. But power supply technology, for example, is deemed to have little scope left for development and the business is unlikely to invest further in it.

Because of competitive activity, technologies have life cycles just as products do. This is illustrated in Figure 11.3, where the perceived development potential of a technology is plotted against time.

A technology first emerges as a looming technology with high perceived development potential. This diminishes as development occurs and the number of applications increases. As it becomes better established it is recognized as a critical technology, with a growing range of applications but still retaining substantial development potential. Eventually, this potential becomes exhausted and foundation status is achieved. Technologies can retain this position for many years, but may

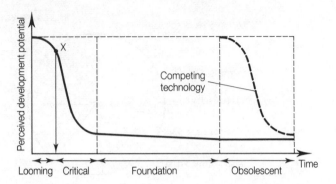

Figure 11.3 **The life cycle of a technology.**
Competitive activity causes technologies to have life cycles just as products do. This is illustrated in the figure (compare with the product life cycle in Figure 2.9), where the perceived development potential of a technology is plotted against time. It starts as a looming technology with high development potential, which diminishes as development occurs and applications increase. Survival beyond point X leads to critical status as applications further increase but substantial development potential remains. Eventually, this potential becomes exhausted and foundation status is achieved.

ultimately be displaced by a competing technology which allows the same product functions to be achieved more efficiently.

Not all technologies traverse all phases. Many looming technologies do not fulfil their early promise and 'die' at some point, such as X in the figure. Those that do progress into the critical phase often displace other critical technologies, which do not then mature into foundation technologies.

11.2.2 Research projects

Basic research: Technology level

A basic research (BR) project is normally concerned with the preliminary assessment, in terms of technical and economic feasibility, of a novel technological concept. Generally, the technology is a looming technology and the application concept relates to more than one specific product range. Just occasionally, it is the technology itself which is new. More usually, the aim is a significant extension to an existing technology. The advent of a major new technology – the jet engine, semiconducting materials and stored-program calculating machines are examples – is a rare event. Most BR projects, therefore, relate to extending the current boundaries of existing technologies.

Applied research: Product range level

Identification with a single specific product range is introduced in this phase. The aim of an applied research (AR) project is to resolve, in the context of a specific application, the principle uncertainties (technical and economic) carried over from the previous phase. The project should culminate in an outline specification (including preliminary costings) for the range of products, incorporating the now more precisely defined initial concept. A successful AR project can promote a looming technology into the critical category.

11.2.3 Development and design projects

Product development and design (PD&D) projects are focused on a single product within a product range. Their distinctive features are best explained with reference to the configuration view of a product. This perceives a complete product as a unique configuration of sub-units about which everything that needs to be known is known.

Many new products are designed and constructed solely in terms of **established** sub-units: those which are widely available, well-understood and proven. Product novelty then resides only in the relative numbers of the established sub-units incorporated into the product, and in the way in which they are interconnected. But other new products also incorporate a number of **novel** sub-units, which have not been used before in practical real-life situations.

Development: Product level

Development is concerned with novel sub-units, and its aim is elevate their status to that of established sub-units. It is the process of creating novel but well-understood and proven sub-units, destined for incorporation into the configuration of proven sub-units which is the complete product.

Design: Product level

Design is the complementary process. It is aimed at creating a novel configuration of well-understood and proven sub-units, some of which may be novel, which implements the pre-determined specification of the complete product.

Product development and design: Relative timing

Development is not always required because novel sub-units are not always required. When it *is* required it should, from a purist engineering perspective, be properly completed before the corresponding design activity is started. This arrangement minimizes opportunities to design with non-proven sub-units, which is a common cause of project overrun and, later, product failure. If development and design overlap is adopted, and it often is, the costs and time-scale of the combined development and design phases may be reduced. But the probability of product failure, sooner or later, is increased.

11.2.4 The project types compared

There are important differences, from the evaluation point of view, between BR, AR and PD&D projects. These are indicated in Figure 11.4, which shows a sequential relationship, with a degree of overlap, between the four phases of the product creation process.

A BR project is a highly speculative venture, launched when a coincidence of market and technological factors suggests a mechanism for advantageous product differentiation. It is an exploration of the unknown. The initial project objectives can be firmly defined but they might, quite properly, change as project activity uncovers

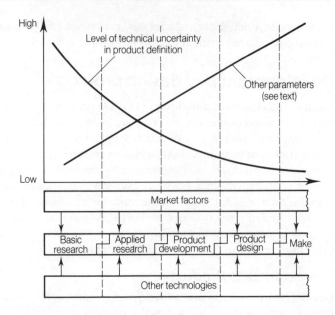

Figure 11.4   **Phases in the product creation process.**

The lower part of this figure shows a sequential relationship between the four technical phases of the product creation process. The graphs illustrate important differences between the BR, AR and PD&D projects within these phases. These differences determine how a project can be evaluated. The process is aimed at reducing technical uncertainties in the definition of the new product. These start at a high level in the BR phase but have diminished to a relatively risk-free low level in the 'how to make and test it' data emerging from the PD phase. Other parameters, such as definition of the commercial benefits, increase from a low level to a high level during the process.

more attractive targets. Similarly, the routes first planned to resolve the various uncertainties are subject to change as the project progresses. Predicting the time and cost needed to complete such a project is a challenging problem and only a broad-brush approach to project planning and control is feasible. A measure of the difficulty lies in the fact that the great majority of BR projects fail, in the sense that they do not spawn any AR projects.

At the other end of the uncertainty spectrum, PD&D projects are aimed at creating novel entities by combining other entities which are, for the most part, well-understood and proven. Project objectives can (and should) be sharply defined and immutable. Detailed project planning to establish credible project time and cost estimates is entirely feasible, as is tight project control. The great majority of these projects succeed, in the sense that they meet their technical objectives more or less according to plan.

An AR project is the intermediate case, with some characteristics of its predecessor and successor projects. However, AR projects can have relatively well-defined and firm objectives, and the probability of technical success is quite high (at about fifty per cent, say). So they are more akin to PD&D projects than to BR projects.

Thus, as Figure 11.4 shows, the product creation process is aimed at reducing technical uncertainties in the definition of the new product. These start at a high level in the BR phase but (in a successful progression) have diminished to a relatively risk-free low level in the 'how to make and test it' data emerging from the product design phase. Some other parameters increase from a low level to a high level during the process. These include:

- The clarity and stability of the technical and commercial objectives of the successive projects in the process sequence.
- The degree of focus on a single specific product.
- The detail, volume and integrity of the product definition data.
- The precision of the product costing data.
- The probability of technical and commercial success.
- The feasibility of detailed project planning and tight project control.
- The resource commitment and the cost of these projects (taking product development and design together).
- And finally, the importance of choosing the right projects, because of the progressively higher levels of resource commitment.

Note that, in connection with Figure 11.4, it not essential for all the four phases to be prosecuted within the same enterprise. It is essential, however, to obtain the technological information from a preceding phase before a successor phase can be sensibly started. This means that competitors who adopt a 'follow-the-leader' product strategy can largely dispense with research. But the benefits from this cost saving and risk avoidance can be dissipated as a result of late entry into maturing product markets.

11.3   Project evaluation: Background

The procedures employed for evaluating, choosing and funding private venture (PV) technical projects differ from business to business. The methods presented in this chapter are based on those used by many large businesses. This is appropriate, because small businesses practice is very variable. For example, they may not indulge in research to any real extent and their approach to development and design is often dangerously informal.

This section summarizes some background factors about project funding, project proposals and project evaluation. These are largely shared by PV technical projects of all types. Some special features of BR and AR project evaluation are considered in the following section. The remainder of the chapter is concerned, first explicitly and then implicitly, with the evaluation and choice of PD&D projects. Apart from the stand-alone quality of the project proposals, such projects must be considered in the broader context of a **product creation project** which encapsulates most of the product life cycle.

11.3.1   PV funding arrangements

Proposals for projects of any sort are directed, of course, at those who control the release of project funds. The identity of this individual or group of individuals is generally a function of the project type. Thus, for reasons that emerge later, most PV

BR projects are funded from the corporate centre of the business, and are launched (or relaunched) at the beginning of a financial year. In contrast, PV PD&D projects invariably depend on divisional support and can be launched at any time. Generally, AR projects are funded at divisional level but are launched (or relaunched) at the beginning of a financial year.

Agreements to spend PV funds very rarely carry over the end of a financial year. For this reason, PV projects are automatically terminated at a year end, unless (unusually) their continuation into the following financial year is specifically and individually authorized. A portfolio of project proposals contains, therefore, both proposals to continue current projects and proposals for new projects.

11.3.2 Proposal format

Technical project proposals are usually prepared in a prescribed format which differs somewhat between different businesses. The amount of detail required is another variable, which increases dramatically over the project spectrum from BR to PD&D. However, the information commonly required falls under the following headings:

        Part 1   Project history
        Part 2   Technical objectives, feasibility and deliverables
        Part 3   Commercial justification
        Part 4   Work breakdown structure
        Part 5   Estimated total cost and total time to complete
        Part 6   Estimated cost and time in the financial year
        Part 7   Project plan
        Part 8   Assumptions and vulnerabilities.

The content of these proposal sections depends, to some extent, on the type of project. Variations of this sort are identified in the summary descriptions that follow.

Part 1   Project history

This is an outline of any current or previous work on the project or on closely related projects. It describes the (sometimes anticipated) technical start position of the project (whether or not earlier related work is specifically identified).

Part 2   Technical objectives, feasibility and deliverables

This part mostly describes the technical goals that it is hoped to achieve. The plan may extend beyond the end of the financial year for which funding is sought. In this case, both the end-of-project objectives and end-of-year objectives are described. These distinct targets then correspond to the time and cost estimates provided in Parts 5 and 6, respectively.

A comparison of the technical objectives with the technical starting position, described in Part 1, defines the technical 'gap' which the project aims to close. Evidence which supports the feasibility of achieving this is presented here.

(Technical objectives should be formulated as events rather activities. It is, sadly, all too common for research project objectives to be stated as 'to investigate the ...' or words to that effect. This is an invitation to fund a journey with no destination. It is often refused, and rightly so. The situation rarely arises with PD&D project proposals.)

A statement of the proposed project **deliverables** is also included here. This term denotes the physical expression of the project results in the form in which they are to be delivered to the project customer. The project customer (sometimes called the project 'sponsor') is the source of the project funds or the nominee of that source. The results of BR, AR and PD&D projects are information which defines to what extent the project objectives have been achieved. This information can be packaged in a variety of ways. Examples include written reports, demonstration models or prototypes, and machine-readable design data on magnetic or other media. Each of these items is a deliverable.

Part 3   Commercial justification

This critical part describes the commercial benefits that should arise if the technical gap is adequately closed. They normally relate to product differentiation and competitiveness. The textual descriptions might be usefully assembled under the subheadings of:

- product functions
- product performance
- product cost

but this is not a universal practice.

The 'visibility' of these benefits and, hence, the integrity of their description depends on how far away they are in time. Thus, the commercial justification of a BR project is always tentative. But market and product visibility improve sharply through the AR and PD&D phases, which allows increasingly confident and detailed forecasts of the commercial benefits.

At the PD&D stage, the textual descriptions of the benefits might be supported by credible financial forecasts of the rewards flowing from product sales. However, such rewards really stem from the larger product creation project. That major project contains the PD&D project as a sub-project, and other sub-projects directed at the marketing, manufacturing and selling of the product. Thus the financial evaluation of a PD&D project is best absorbed into the evaluation of the product creation project which contains it. This topic is introduced in Section 11.8.

Part 4   Work breakdown structure

This is the anticipated project activity described as a configuration of distinct **work-packages**, which are linked together in a rational way to make up the whole project. Partitioning the project into logical work-packages aids project planning, cost and time estimating, and (later) project progress monitoring and control.

Part 5   Estimated total cost and total time to complete

These estimates include, but distinguish between, the actual cost and time (if any) spent on the project at the proposal date and the forecast cost and time to complete the project measured from that date.

Part 6   Estimated cost and time in the financial year

These are those parts of the total estimates entered in Part 5 which relate to the financial year for which funding is sought in the proposal.

Part 7   Project plan

The project plan can take a variety of forms, depending on the nature of the project and the particular requirements of the business concerned.

Plans for BR projects are generally presented, with descriptive text, in a bar chart format which aligns with the work-package structure in Part 4. The chart is usually supported with resource tables. A typical example is described in Section 6.2. The bar chart format is less commonly used (except in summaries) for AR projects, which always exhibit greater work-package interdependence. Some form of network planning technique (such as flow diagrams or PERT, either alone or in combination) is often more appropriate. Network planning techniques are discussed in Sections 6.3 and 6.4.

PD&D projects are usually sufficiently complex to require the use a network planning (and control) technique, and PERT, or one of its variants, is commonly employed. But plan summaries are often presented in bar chart form with resource tables.

Part 8   Assumptions and vulnerabilities

This part identifies the major assumptions which are incorporated in the proposal and considers the likely consequences of them proving faulty. Where possible, alternative courses of action aimed at circumventing such problems are also described.

11.3.3   Evaluation criteria

Consciously or not, project proposals are always evaluated with respect to a number of different criteria which are not equally important. This is illustrated here by ranking a few criteria in a three level hierarchy:

(1) *Decisive*   Criteria which must be judged to be adequately satisfied or the project proposal is rejected. Examples include:
  (a) Alignment with current technological strategy (for basic research).
  (b) Technical feasibility. (The 'pass' level increase from, say, thirty per cent probability for a BR project to more than ninety-five per cent probability for a PD&D project.)
  (c) Commercial prospects. (Rarely decisive at the BR stage but paramount for product creation projects.)
  (d) No infringement of adversely owned patents.
  (e) No operator exposure to hazardous substances during manufacture.
(2) *Critical*   Criteria which are not decisive on their own, but excite serious doubts about the proposal if they not judged to be adequately satisfied. Corrective action is possible in some cases. Examples include:
  (a) Quality of the proposal, especially with respect to the project plan.
  (b) Familiarity of the requisite manufacturing processes.
  (c) Work-force acceptability.

(3) *Supportive* Criteria which increase the attractiveness of the project if judged to be adequately satisfied. Examples include:
   (a) Licensing and/or patent potential.
   (b) Contribution to staff training and development.
   (c) Contribution to fixed expenses.

Different businesses take different views on what is important, and may rank the criteria cited in this illustration quite differently.

The fact that criteria come in hierarchies provides a useful insight into the evaluation process. In practice, the technique does not seem to be much used as a formal requirement, although its informal use is widespread. It appears, in a diluted form, in the well-known **profile** evaluation methods which are discussed in Section 11.7.

11.4 | Evaluation of BR and AR projects

Because of their high- to mid-range uncertainty levels, proposals for PV BR and AR projects can only be sensibly evaluated in subjective and largely non-financial terms. There are some differences in the methods adopted for the two types of project. These mostly reflect their sequential relationship, but both types of project share a strategic dimension. This aspect is examined first.

11.4.1 Strategy and research projects

As was noted earlier, this chapter assumes that a technological strategy for the business exists. Ideally, this has been formulated at corporate level as an integral part of the strategy for the whole business. Its principal author is likely to be the senior technologist within the business, who will have consulted senior marketing and production colleagues during its preparation.

Research themes

One facet of the technological strategy is (or should be) a document which classifies relevant product technologies into the looming, critical and foundation categories (discussed in Section 11.2.1). The rewards for further investment in the mature foundation technologies are likely to be small, so the document effectively defines a number of **research themes** in the looming and critical categories. Relative priorities may also be assigned within these two categories.

The research themes document, which is periodically updated, is made available to the research teams within the business. It is then their responsibility to prepare research project proposals within the areas defined in the document. This includes formulating a view on the commercial validity of the proposal, which is best done in association with marketing or production colleagues from the relevant trading division. Normally, the preparation of most research project proposals, and their subsequent adjudication, is part of the budgeting exercise for a forthcoming financial year.

11.4.2 Basic research projects

Figure 11.4 shows that BR activity:

- is at the high end of the uncertainty spectrum
- is a long way (in time) from the market-place
- has a low level of product focus.

BR project funding

The managers of the product trading divisions (which comprise the large business), being well aware of these features, are generally unwilling to fund BR. They argue, with some merit, that their task is to secure the present and immediate future of their part of the business. This, they claim, is demanding enough without being distracted by long-term speculations which (if history is a guide) will mostly prove irrelevant. Nor do they see any great virtue in paying for being so distracted out of the profit on which their job security (and bonuses) depends.

For these reasons and some others, such as continuity of funding, BR is normally funded at corporate level. To this end, a fund is created at the business headquarters which is called the **Corporate Research Fund**, the **Company Research Fund**, the **Central Research Fund** or some such title. In high technology businesses its annual value is typically about one per cent of the total annual sales revenue, and rather less in other businesses. BR project proposals are directed at the custodians of this fund. As a rule, this is a committee chaired by the senior technologist in the business. Committee members generally include corporate level marketing and production representation, and the senior technologists from the major trading divisions.

BR project selection

It is quite normal for the total financial support requested to exceed the value of the fund, sometimes by as much as two or three times. The question of how to distribute the fund then arises.

One 'solution' to this type of problem is to apply the **equal misery** principle. This is often employed by weak management in excessively democratic organizations. It removes the need for hard thinking and brave decisions by awarding all applicants the same proportion of their request, such that the whole fund is committed. For example, if the fund is initially over-subscribed by a factor of two, then all applicants are awarded just half of their requested funding. The only advantage of this approach is simplicity. It is an abrogation of management duty which makes a nonsense of what should be a merit-based allocation system. It is also an inefficient way of spending the limited funds available. This is because most projects have a **funding threshold**, below which the chances of success are very sharply reduced. If a project cannot be funded at, or above, its threshold it is better not funded at all. Finally, the approach has a built-in escalation mechanism, because applicants soon learn to ask for substantially more funds than they really require.

Happily, most businesses are not troubled by excessive democracy and the fund committee endeavours to operate a merit-based allocation mechanism which (usually) either totally accepts or totally rejects each project proposal. There is no magic formula, however, for identifying those projects which offer the best prospects of technical *and* commercial success. This observation applies to project proposals of whatever sort, but it applies to BR proposals more acutely than any others. Their unique blend of high technological uncertainty with the abysmal market and product visibility that was cited earlier ensures that this is the case. Thus, the fund committee must do its best with the unavoidably low quality data available to it. The evaluation process is, of necessity, relatively informal and dominated by subjective criteria reflecting the membership of the committee. There is no merit in any serious financial investment/return analysis, and it is rarely attempted.

The committee members bring great wisdom and wide experience, reinforced by their knowledge of the research teams, to the evaluation task. But the final selection can be no more than an educated guess. Historical evidence suggests that only about twenty per cent of the chosen BR projects will achieve results judged worthy of further investment. Fortunately, sad though it is, this situation does not matter very much. It is a well-known dilemma which applies in all fields of BR wherever, and by whoever, it is conducted. Everybody knows that eighty per cent of it will fail. But nobody knows, in advance, which eighty per cent!

BR programme strategy

It is for this reason that, by an unwritten convention, BR is an **open** activity. Researchers in a given field – from universities, research institutes and industrial laboratories world-wide – form a community of common interest: an informal 'research club'. They are encouraged to publish their results, to meet at seminars and conferences, and to exchange laboratory visits. Steady progress depends on this free exchange of information. It is largely unconstrained by considerations of commercial confidentiality (but is restricted when national security might be prejudiced).

A rational strategy for BR, therefore, assigns limited effort to all the more relevant and promising opportunities. The effort devoted to a particular topic need be no more than is required to make a contribution to the field (thereby qualifying for the club), and to monitor the world-wide activity. Thus, important advances can be followed-up, wherever they occur. Note that this policy implicitly assumes that the local BR team will not make a dramatic technological breakthrough of major commercial significance. Such events do occur, but so infrequently that the possibility is best ignored when planning a portfolio of BR projects.

11.4.3 Applied research projects

The transition from basic to applied research is accompanied, as Figure 11.4 shows, by a significant reduction in the level of technological uncertainty and much improved product and market visibility. The probability of technical success is now some fifty per cent. These factors justify the commitment of comparatively substantial resources to AR projects. In a high technology business, the average AR project typically costs about ten times more than the average BR project. However, because there are less of them, AR projects generally add only two or three per cent of the total annual sales revenue to the total annual cost of technical innovation.

AR project funding

AR is mostly funded at trading division level, rather than centrally. This policy is justified by the contrasts with BR which were noted earlier, and by the close coupling required with the subsequent PD&D phase. Each product trading division has its own budget for technical innovation, which must cater for both AR and PD&D. The major part of the budget is invariably assigned to PD&D. In high technology businesses, the total budget typically ranges from five to fifteen per cent of the annual sales revenue for the division. The divisional manager retains final authority over both the size and distribution of the budget, but usually delegates its day-to-day management to a small committee of senior colleagues. AR proposals generated within the division are directed at this committee, which is analogous to the central committee concerned with BR.

AR project selection

As with BR, it is quite normal for the total financial support requested to greatly exceed the resources available, so a project selection mechanism is again required. Choosing the 'right' AR projects is important because they absorb substantial resources and are the springboard for the creation of new products. Fortunately, the quality of the information on which to base project evaluation is much greater than in the case of BR.

As a rule, therefore, the project proposal evaluation process is more formal and searching than that employed for BR. All aspects of the proposal are considered, but the commercial justification, technical feasibility and the project plan are the most critical. If the commercial prospects do not appear sufficiently attractive then the proposal is likely to be rejected on these grounds alone. Severe doubts about technical feasibility can lead to the same result. Evaluation of the plan is likely to focus on structure, estimated cost and estimated time. Dissatisfaction with any one of these factors can lead to rejection of the plan and, probably, rejection of the proposal. But, if the proposal is otherwise satisfactory, it might be provisionally accepted subject to the plan being reworked into an acceptable form.

The selection procedures outlined so far concentrate on the project proposal as a self-contained entity. This is a critical but restricted perspective because, if the project is authorized, it will affect many aspects of the whole business. In some cases, therefore, the evaluation team takes the *wider* implications of the proposal into account by assessing its merit against a set of 'business level' criteria. These are typically assembled under the following headings:

- marketing and selling
- technical
- production
- financial.

In this respect the evaluation of AR proposals is very similar to the **profile** technique often employed for product creation projects. So discussion of the criteria and the ways in which they may be used is deferred to Section 11.7, which examines profile techniques.

Very occasionally, market visibility is sufficiently clear for a financial investment/ return analysis of an AR project proposal to be worthwhile. In such cases the procedure is again much the same as that employed for product creation projects. The topic is introduced in Section 11.8.

Evaluation of PD&D projects

A PD&D project is part of a product creation project which is normally funded by the product trading division concerned. The maximum acceptable time period between project launch and product availability is set by marketing considerations. And it is often uncomfortably short. For this reason, product creation projects and, hence, PD&D projects may be launched at any time (whereas most research projects are launched at the beginning of a financial year). This section briefly examines the evaluation of PD&D project proposals as *stand-alone items*, before attention is turned (in subsequent sections) to product creation projects.

All of the PD&D projects which are in progress during a year must be accommodated within the current technical projects budget and, as usual, there are generally more proposals than available resources. This is the normal mundane situation which sets one particular need for a project evaluation and choice mechanism. But, for PD&D projects, there is a more critical need. Figure 11.4 shows that PD&D activity:

- is at the low end of the technological uncertainty spectrum
- is comparatively close (in time) to the market-place
- has a high level of product focus.

These features mean that the project proposals can include relatively precise visions of the future. This is fortunate, because choosing the right PD&D projects is a survival issue. If a business does not offer competitive products it will, sooner or later, either die or be absorbed by a better managed business.

11.5.1 Evaluation of proposal quality

The fundamental purpose of a PD&D project is to transform a product specification into proven 'how to make and test it' data for the manufacturing operation. The specification defines product feature, performance and cost targets. It is derived from marketing data during the first part of the product creation project. The maximum acceptable project time is invariably similarly defined and, very often, so too is the maximum acceptable project cost.

Evaluation of a PD&D project proposal as a stand-alone item aims to measure its quality by assessing the extent to which it will:

- deliver proven manufacturing data which accurately reflects the product specification
- achieve this within the acceptable cost and time targets.

So attention is focused on the feasibility of the technical objectives and the credibility, in terms of structure, cost and time, of the project plan. The assumptions and vulnerabilities section of the proposal is also examined with some care.

Project time and cost estimates

Some of the problems and techniques of technical project time and cost estimating are examined in Chapter 6, principally in Section 6.5. It is an area of some complexity. The validity, or otherwise, of these estimates is often a sensitive issue in PD&D project evaluations. Their maximum acceptable levels are set by marketing and investment/ return considerations, and these factors do not recognize the nature of the technical challenge. But most projects seem to have a **natural time-scale**, which depends on the extent to which they can be partitioned into distinct tasks, and the logical sequence of these tasks. This natural time-scale is associated with a **natural cost** which reflects an efficient assignment of resources to the sub-tasks. There is no reason why the natural time and cost of a project *should* lie within the boundaries set by the non-technical considerations.

To some extent, project time can be reduced below its natural level by increasing the assigned resources (and, probably, the project cost). But the room for manoeuvre is quite limited, and disproportionate resource increases are needed to induce large time reductions. The temptation to compress the natural time and cost estimates too severely must be resisted by the project planners. Submitting honest estimates which fall outside the pre-set limits is certainly less dangerous, in the long run, than the easy alternative. It may be, of course, that estimates greatly beyond the limits so prejudice the investment viability that the project proposal is rejected. This is good news, because there is no merit in wasting resources in brewing a future disaster. On the other hand, realistic estimates lying marginally outside the limits might be accommodated in a number of ways. These include:

- Compensating for the excesses by reducing the time and cost allowances assigned to the other sub-projects making up the project creation project.
- Making the criteria for financial investment/return viability less severe (which amounts to extending the limits).
- Some combination of these two actions.

11.5.2 Investment/return evaluation

As noted earlier, a PD&D project is a part (albeit a critical part) of a larger product creation project. It is not possible, therefore, to evaluate it as a stand-alone investment/return proposition. It is the proposal for the product creation project, which embraces the PD&D project, that must be considered in that respect. This same situation applies, of course, to the other sub-projects (concerned with marketing, manufacturing and selling) which are also included within the product creation project. These subsidiary projects must also be evaluated with respect to their individual objectives, time-scales and costs, but their investment implications are those of the product creation project.

The discussion now switches to the broader issues of product creation projects and their evaluation as investment propositions.

11.6 | Product creation projects

This section examines the origin and structure of product creation projects.

11.6.1 The product brief

Usually, it is the divisional marketeers who initiate a product creation project by issuing a document describing a possible profit opportunity based on a new product. This document is called a **product brief** here. It comprises:

- An outline description of the new product, as currently perceived, in functional and performance terms.
- A description of the 'target' product customers (and, where appropriate, the target end-users), and an explanation of their need for the product.
- A description of the anticipated competitive situation including the identity of potential competitors and anything relevant that is known about their current products and future product intentions.
- Forecasts of the maximum acceptable product price, and of the size, timing and location of the accessible product market.

A product brief is normally approved by senior management prior to issue. A sample, which illustrates just one possible new product creation context, is included in Section A.2.2 of Appendix A.

11.6.2 Project structure

A product creation project consists of two major stages. The first is a planning activity. This defines the second stage of plan implementation, which will absorb significant resources. The arrangement provides a breakpoint at the end of the planning activity, so that the decision whether to enter the second stage can be made on the basis of good quality information. Figure 11.5 illustrates the structure of a product creation project. This shows its relationship with the product brief, the nature of the plan derived from the first stage, and the sub-projects making up the second stage.

Stage 1: Planning

The principal input to the initial planning stage of the product creation project is the product brief. Other relevant inputs are the constraints which are placed on the project by the business itself. These include such items as resource availability, any special requirements (safety procedures and quality assurance provisions, say) and the minimum acceptable level of financial performance. The output of this stage is a **product business plan** which models the second stage of the product creation project.

Preparing the business plan is a demanding task which requires a broad range of professional and management skills. This is because product creation involves, directly or indirectly, every facet of the business. But the business functions mostly concerned are marketing and sales, technical and production. The planning work includes the first (and most critical) phase of the product design process. This is the **requirements definition** phase, which is a major topic covered in Sections 8.5, 8.6 and 8.7. It leads to an *outline* design of the product, on which the PD&D sub-project plan and the initial product cost estimates are based.

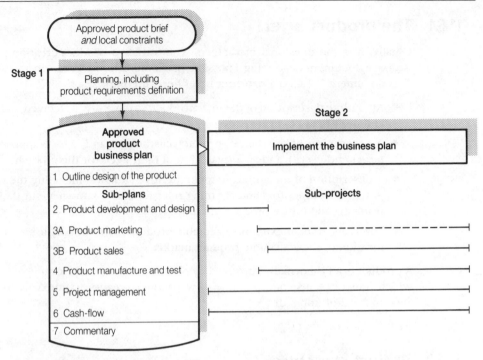

Figure 11.5   **The structure of a product creation project.**

A product creation project has two major stages. Stage 1 includes product requirements definition (as considered in Chapter 8, and culminating in the outline product design) and the preparation of an approved product business plan. Stage 2 is plan implementation. This figure shows the structure of each stage and the relationships between them.

The product business plan and Stage 2: Implementation

The product business plan is concerned with the prospective new 'mini-business' to be built around the new product. It serves two purposes:

(1) To define what has to be done to exploit the new opportunity.

(2) To provide data for the evaluation of that opportunity as an investment/return proposition.

The plan covers the venture from requirements definition through all the subsequent phases of the product life cycle until the ultimate demise of the product as sales decline towards zero. Stage 2 of the product creation project is implementing the plan. The aim is to manage the product life cycle to yield the best possible reward to the business.

The way in which that (major) part of the product life cycle which comprises Stage 2 is partitioned into activity phases varies to some extent between different businesses. In this formulation, the phases recognized are:

- product requirements definition
- product development and design
- production start-up
- marketing

- product manufacturing and sales:
  - sales rate growth
  - sales rate maturity
  - sales rate decline.

Stage 2 of the product creation project consists, therefore, of a number of linked sub-projects mounted by the business functions involved. Each of these sub-projects must be planned in Stage 1. So, in its completed form, the product business plan includes:

(1) The outline design of the product generated by the technical function.
(2) A sub-plan for detailed product development and design, which defines the PD&D sub-project to be mounted by the technical function.
(3) A sub-plan for marketing and sales. This defines the sub-projects concerned with product marketing before and during the anticipated sales life cycle and with sales activity and revenues during that life cycle. These sub-projects are to be mounted by the marketing and sales function.
(4) A sub-plan for product manufacture and test, which defines a sub-project to be mounted by the production function.
(5) A sub-plan for the management of Stage 2 of the product creation project (which comprises the linked sub-projects listed above).
(6) A sub-plan for the cash-flow of the whole product creation project. This includes all the cash-flows out of the business arising from planning and the sub-projects, and the cash-flow into the business arising from product sales. This sub-plan is the cash-flow model of the project.
(7) A commentary which summarizes the opportunity in terms of its apparent commercial and financial rewards, and the assumptions and risks attaching to them.

This list is numbered to align with the product business plan format shown in Figure 11.5, which shows the relative timing of the various sub-projects.

Now, to reiterate an earlier point, the sub-plan at item 2 in the list is the plan of the PD&D sub-project. This cannot be sensibly evaluated as a stand-alone investment proposition. The same observation applies equally to the other sub-plans. It is the whole product business plan which models the substance of the product creation project that must be evaluated. This topic largely accounts for the remainder of the chapter. Techniques relating to the impact of the project on the whole business are considered in the next section. Subsequent sections examines techniques for evaluating the financial performance of the project. These concern its cash-flow model.

11.7 Project Evaluation Tool 1 (PET1)

The substance of a product creation project is modelled by the corresponding product business plan. **Profile evaluation** is a generic term used here to denote a family of techniques which relate to the broader business issues raised by a product business plan. These techniques are characterized by some means of expressing the outcome of a multi-factored evaluation exercise in an easily absorbed format. **Project Evaluation Tool 1** (PET1) illustrates the approach and two variants are described here. PET1 is complemented by a tool called **Project Evaluation Tool 2** (PET2) which assists the planning and investment performance evaluation of projects. PET2 is described in Section 11.16.

11.7.1   PET1: Version A (PET1A)

A set of evaluation criteria is listed in Table 11.1 under the major headings of Marketing and Selling, Technical, Production, and Financial. The first three headings correspond to the business functions primarily involved in the proposed product creation project (which is modelled by the business plan). The criteria listed under 'Financial' are concerned with financial resources rather than with the investment/ return aspect of the project.

The business plan is evaluated by rating its status with respect to each criterion on a five-point scale, ranging from 'very good' to 'very poor'. These ratings are recorded in the table and subsequently joined up to reveal the business plan 'profile'. Clearly, the more this tends to the left the better the overall evaluation of the business plan in relation to the listed criteria.

11.7.2   PET1: Version B (PET1B)

A slightly more elaborate version of the same technique is shown in Table 11.2. Here, the 'very good' to 'very poor' ratings are assigned numerical values and each criterion is given a weighting factor in the range one to ten. Simple arithmetic then yields 'figures of merit' at the various levels from an individual criterion to the whole plan. This approach provides numeric evaluation measures and could be claimed (very arguably) to be more precise than the first version.

11.7.3   Profiles: For and against

It is not difficult to criticize this type of evaluation technique. For example, the terms 'very good', 'good', and so on used in PET1A are open to a variety of interpretations. The second version (PET1B) compounds this problem by assigning arbitrary numbers to these vague terms. Similarly, in the second version, choice of the weighting factors is a fruitful source of debate, often leading to an uneasy compromise which satisfies nobody. More seriously, as Twiss (1986) points out, a 'very poor' rating of critical importance might be lost in the overall evaluation, with tragic consequences at a later date. Direct conflict with adversely owned patents is just one possibility and untenable health and safety risk is another.

These very real problems must be weighed against some equally real virtues. Firstly, the technique provides a useful checklist of important questions which should be addressed in any event. They are essentially subjective questions permitting only equally subjective answers. And, if the questions are going to be asked, there is no merit in ignoring the answers. Secondly, the technique explicitly recognizes that the answers can only be judgemental answers, ranging from favourable to adverse. Offering such a range encourages better answers. The final plus point is more subtle. As presented, Tables 11.1 and 11.2 seek 'agreed by' ratifications by the heads of the four business functions. Probably, some of these individuals will be reluctant to

PET1A	17–Jan–91	VG	G	AV	P	VP

Marketing and selling   Agreed by: ....

- Compatibility with existing resources
- Availability of requisite resources
- Prospects for product and lifetime enhancement
- Effect on competitors
- Volume effects on current products
- Price effects on current products
- Lack of conflict with adversely owned patents
- Patent potential
- Licensing potential
- Government related advantages
- Effects of current and prospective legislation
- Work-force acceptability
- Public relations impact
- Effect of estimated additional resources:
  - Revenue per month £ –
  - Capital £ –

Technical   Agreed by: ....

- Compatibility with existing resources
- Availability of requisite resources
- Prospective project spin-offs
- Effect on other projects
- Work-force acceptability
- Effect of estimated additional resources:
  - Revenue per month £ 3,300
  - Capital £15,000

Production   Agreed by: ....

- Compatibility with existing resources
- Availability of requisite resources
- Availability of requisite materials and components
- Value added in manufacturing
- Vulnerability to supplier problems
- Cost effects on current products
- Freedom from health and safety hazards
- Work-force acceptability
- Effect of estimated additional resources:
  - Revenue per month £ –
  - Capital £ –

Financial   Agreed by: ....

- Availability of requisite additional resources
- Effect on other investment projects
- Effect of estimated additional resources:
  - Revenue per month £ 3,300
  - Capital £15,000

VG, Very Good; G, Good; AV, Average; P, Poor; VP, Very Poor.

Table 11.1   **PET1A: Product business plan profile (Version A).**

'Profile evaluation' is a generic term used here to denote a family of techniques which aid the assessment of 'whole business' issues raised by a product business plan. This table illustrates one such technique. The plan is evaluated by rating its status with respect to a set of criteria on a five-point scale, ranging from 'very good' to 'very poor'. A plan 'profile' is then obtained by joining the individual ratings. The more this tends to the left, the better the overall evaluation of the business plan.

PET1B	17–Jan–91	WF	VG 5	G 4	AV 3	P 2	VP 1	FoM
Marketing and selling	Agreed by:							
Compatibility with existing resources		8	1					40
Availability of requisite resources		5	1					25
Prospects for product and lifetime enhancement		8			1			24
Effect on competitors		5			1			15
Volume effects on current products		5			1			15
Price effects on current products		5			1			15
Lack of conflict with adversely owned patents		10	1					50
Patent potential		5				1		10
Licensing potential		8				1		16
Government related advantages		5					1	5
Effects of current and prospective legislation		10	1					50
Work-force acceptability		8		1				32
Public relations impact		5		1				20
Effect of estimated additional resources:		10	1					50
Revenue per month £ –								
Capital £ –								
	Marketing and selling %							76

Technical	Agreed by:	WF	VG 5	G 4	AV 3	P 2	VP 1	FoM
Compatibility with existing resources		8		1				32
Availability of requisite resources		5				1		10
Prospective project spin-offs		10	1					50
Effect on other projects		5	1					25
Work-force acceptability		8			1			24
Effect of estimated additional resources:		10				1		20
Revenue per month £ 3,300								
Capital £15,000								
	Technical %							70

Production	Agreed by:	WF	VG 5	G 4	AV 3	P 2	VP 1	FoM
Compatibility with existing resources		8	1					40
Availability of requisite resources		5	1					25
Availability of requisite materials and components		10		1				40
Value added in manufacturing		5			1			15
Vulnerability to supplier problems		10		1				40
Cost effects on current products		10	1					50
Freedom from health and safety hazards		10	1					50
Work-force acceptability		8	1					40
Effect of estimated additional resources:		10	1					50
Revenue per month £ –								
Capital £ –								
	Production %							92

Financial	Agreed by:	WF	VG 5	G 4	AV 3	P 2	VP 1	FoM
Availability of requisite additional resources		10				1		20
Effect on other investment projects		10		1				30
Effect of estimated additional resources:		10		1				30
Revenue per month £ 3,300								
Capital £15,000								
	Financial %							53
	Total %							77

WF, Weighting Factor; VG, Very Good; G, Good; AV, Average; P, Poor; VP, Very Poor; FoM, Figure of Merit.

record their views in case of future disaster. (A typical defence of this indefensible position cites 'paralysis by analysis' as an excuse for indecision.) Lack of commitment at any level, but especially at the top, only encourages disaster. The divisional manager can do something to minimize the problem by insisting on the appropriate signatures. This attitude can only improve the quality of thought which goes into the plan evaluation. So, provided that their limitations are recognized, profile techniques are useful tools for evaluating the broader business aspects of a product business plan.

The set of criteria listed in the tables should be regarded as illustrative rather than exhaustive. However, experience suggests that it covers most of the important factors. A number of standard software packages are available which extend the basic ideas discussed in this section.

11.8 The cash-flow model

A product business plan includes a sub-plan which is the cash-flow model of the product creation project. Evaluation of the project as a financial investment/return proposition is based on its cash-flow model. The form of the model is discussed in Section 11.8.1 following, which builds on some material from earlier chapters. The investment/return features are discussed in Section 11.8.2.

11.8.1 The form of the model

The product life cycle concept is introduced in Section 2.3.5. It is cited again in Section 3.3, where the cash-flow model of a product creation project is first discussed. Some of that earlier material is repeated in this section, where it provides the foundation of a more developed cash-flow model. In particular, Figure 11.6 is an expanded version of Figure 3.7.

The product creation project starts when an approved product brief (prepared by marketing) is available. Figure 11.6 illustrates important milestones on the route from this point (S in the figure) when the product is 'conceived', through its subsequent gestation, birth, life and death.

The cash-flow model of the product creation project is illustrated in the lower-half of the figure. This plots the variation with time of the **cumulative cash-flow** out of and into the business arising *solely* from the particular project under consideration. Conventionally, cash-flow out (expenditure or cost) is shown as negative, and cash-flow in (net revenue or income) is shown as positive. In the figure, straight line segments have been used to give greater emphasis to various break points. Real life cash-flow is rarely linear, but the form of the figure is real enough.

(Opposite page) *Table 11.2* **PET1B: Product business plan profile (Version B).**
This table demonstrates a more elaborate version of the same profile evaluation technique shown in Table 11.1. The 'very good' to 'very poor' ratings of the earlier version are replaced by numerical values and each criterion is given a weighting factor. Simple arithmetic then yields 'figures of merit' at the various levels, thus providing a numeric plan profile. Profile techniques can be criticized for a variety of reasons, including the possibility of losing a 'very poor' rating of critical importance in the overall evaluation. But, properly used, their virtues outweigh their disadvantages.

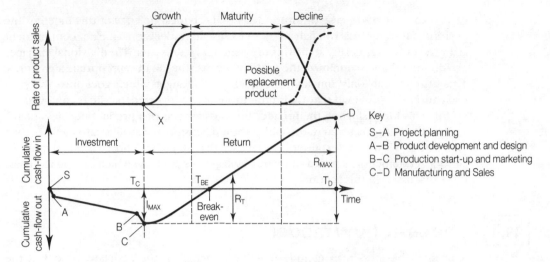

Figure 11.6 **The cash-flow model of a product creation project.**
A product business plan contains the cash-flow model of the product creation project. Financial
evaluation of the project as an investment/return proposition is based on this model. It is illustrated
in the lower half of the figure. The positive-going segment of the curve relates to the product sales
life cycle drawn above it. The figure illustrates important milestones on the route from when the
product was 'conceived' (at S) through its subsequent gestation, birth, life and death.

The cumulative cash-flow profile

Point S in the figure, where the cumulative cash-flow is zero, is the start of the planning
activity comprising Stage 1 of the project. Cash flows out of the business as the work of
the planning team proceeds, because of the costs of their employment (salaries and so
on) and because of costs of ownership and operating the facilities they need. The time
and money consumed in Stage 1 are comparatively small. It terminates, at point A in
the figure, when a product business plan has been produced and approved. This event
signals the start of Stage 2 of the product creation project, *and* the start of the PD&D
sub-project in the technical function. Other sub-projects (production engineering,
say) might also start at this point.

The PD&D sub-project also consumes money, not only because of its people-
related and facilities costs but also because various external purchases are made, such
as components for the prototypes. The sub-project terminates, at point B in the figure,
with the delivery of proven product definition data to the production function.

Cash continues to flow out of the business in the period between points B and C in
the figure. This stems from activity (assumed to start at point B) in the production,
marketing and sales functions. The product manufacturing sub-project is mounted by
the production function. The period B to C is the 'start-up' activity. It includes:

- planning
- the purchase and/or fabrication of any special equipment
- the purchase of sufficient components and other piece-parts for the initial
  manufacturing run.

Additionally, some **production prototypes** might be built, during this period, to confirm the integrity of the product definition data received from the technical function. While all this is going on, the marketing and sales functions launch their sub-projects, with an initial promotional phase aimed at conditioning the market to expect and accept the product.

At point C, which corresponds to time X on the sales life cycle diagram in the upper half of Figure 11.6, the first product units emerge from the manufacturing operation and selling starts.

The manufacturing, marketing and sales sub-projects all continue in the period bounded by points C and D, and each continues to incur costs. But, subject to certain assumptions (see later) and starting from point C, the cash-flow out is more than compensated by the cash-flow into the business stemming from product sales. Consequently, the gradient of the cumulative cash-flow curve becomes positive at point C. Net cash is now flowing into the business.

The sales life cycle

The (somewhat idealized) shape of the typical product sales life cycle shown in the upper half of Figure 11.6 is explained in Section 3.5.1. Briefly, this is a plot against time of the rate (units per month, say) of product sales. The initial period of rapid growth leads into a relatively stable period of market maturity. Ultimately, the rate of unit sales starts to decline towards zero, usually because of pending technological obsolescence. Of course, the business may choose to withdraw the product before it is totally rejected by the market. This option is commonly exercised when the business has created an enhanced version of the product to offer.

The basic assumptions

The shape and gradient of the cumulative cash-flow curve shown in the manufacturing and sales period (between points C and D in Figure 11.6) depends on some assumptions. These are:

- That the sale price of a product unit is greater than the sum of the cost of manufacturing it and its share of other relevant costs (marketing, selling, distribution and so on).
- That all sales are made on a cash basis (rather than on credit).
- That the products are sold as they are made: that is, products are not stored before sale.

Under these circumstances, each product unit generates a net incremental cash-flow into the business as it is sold. Provided that price and cost levels remain constant over the period, the shape of the positive-going segment of the cumulative cash-flow curve then tracks that of the *total* product unit sales curve (which can be derived by integrating the rate of product unit sales curve).

Only the first of the three assumptions noted earlier is critical. If that assumption is not satisfied the cumulative cash-flow becomes increasingly negative as manufacturing and selling the product proceeds. This is an unattractive business situation which invariably creates some excitement. It must be reversed, or at least stopped, very quickly.

The other two assumptions are, generally, only broadly true in practice. When they do not apply, the effect is to shift the positive-going segment of the cumulative cash-flow curve to the right by the appropriate time. This delay in positive cash-flow is wholly undesirable but it has to be tolerated in most businesses.

11.8.2   Investment/return features

The period from S to C in Figure 11.6 is the investment phase of the product creation project. In this period, the business is spending money in anticipation that it will earn an adequate future reward. The maximum investment is at point C, where the cumulative cash-flow is most negative.

The period from C and D in the figure is the return phase. The net incremental cash-flow is positive in this phase, and the cumulative cash-flow curve has a positive gradient. At the **break-even** point, where the cumulative cash-flow is (again) zero, the whole of the investment has been recovered. In other words, break-even occurs when the product has paid for its own gestation costs. Beyond this point, the cumulative cash-flow continues to increase until, at point D, the product dies.

The project starts to make a contribution to the financial health of the business as soon as the gradient of the cumulative cash-flow curve becomes positive (point C in the figure). The project, and the product, is commonly referred to as 'profitable' from that point forward. This is quite reasonable, because they are more than recovering the costs assigned to them from point C onwards. But the terminology is, strictly, inaccurate. 'Profit' is an accountancy concept and it is not the same as positive cash-flow (this point is discussed, very briefly, in Section 1.8.4 and it becomes very apparent in Chapter 12). However, in accord with common practice, the more relaxed interpretation of 'profit' and related terms are employed (sparingly) from now on.

The financial performance questions

The **cash-flow profile** of Figure 11.6 models the forecast financial performance of a product creation project. Assuming that this is a credible forecast, the question now arises as to whether or not the project promises to be a worthwhile investment. That is:

- Is it worth spending the money measured at point C in order to get back the money measured at point D?

- Or could the same investment have yielded a better return if spent in some other way?

- Or would the investment money be better employed earning a risk-free return in an interest-paying bank account?

These are important questions. Evaluating the cash-flow model of the project can make a substantial contribution to the answers.

Discounting and non-discounting evaluation methods

Most contemporary methods of evaluating cash-flow models are based on a concept called **discounting**, which is a relative of the familiar notion of compound interest.

Generically, these methods are termed **discounted cash-flow** (DCF) techniques, and they are introduced in Section 11.12. But first, some relatively crude *non-DCF* techniques are briefly examined. These provide useful guidance on the desirable features of a cash-flow model and expose the basic difficulties which discounting resolves.

11.9 Cash-flow shape techniques

In a typical cash-flow evaluation situation, a number of investment options (which, here, are product creation project proposals represented by their cash-flow models) are competing for limited resources. The aim, therefore, is to rank the options in merit order.

One choice that is always available is the **do-nothing** option. This is the decision to:

- either leave the available investment money on deposit to earn interest,

- or (if it is not available from current resources) not to seek it from outside the business and so avoid its acquisition cost (loan interest, say).

Of course, if this non-action is chosen, some other resources belonging to the business may become underemployed: part of the PD&D team, for example, or some of the manufacturing facilities. And underemployed resources cost money which does not earn a reward. But factors of this sort are part of the broader business situation which must be considered in every debate about investment options. Here, however, the focus is on cash-flow evaluation.

(Note that the do-nothing option is not the same as the **nil-investment** option. This latter option is a marginally useful theoretical concept which enters into the discussion further on in the chapter.)

11.9.1 Some shape parameters

A number of cash-flow evaluation techniques which do not involve discounting have been developed. These are all based, one way or another, on parameters which describe, rather crudely, the 'shape' of a cash-flow model. The more simple parameters, which are shown in Figure 11.6, are:

- The **maximum investment**, I_{MAX}, which occurs at the time, T_C, corresponding to the point where the incremental cash-flow becomes positive as profitable sales start.

- The **time to break-even**, T_{BE}, which is the point where the cumulative cash-flow curve crosses the zero cash-flow axis.

- The **return**, R_T, which is the net cumulative positive cash-flow measured at some time T, where $T > T_C$. (There is no return in the investment phase, and it is zero when $T = T_C$.)

- The **maximum return**, R_{MAX}, which occurs at time T_D, corresponding to the point where the incremental cash-flow becomes zero as the product dies or is withdrawn from the market.

Various criteria based on these parameters can be used to compare the relative merits of different cash-flow models. A few of these are now described.

The maximum investment and average rate of investment

When investment money is strictly limited, the maximum investment required by the competing options can, in itself, provide a definitive ranking criterion. Sometimes, it is the rate of investment which is critical. This rate clearly varies during the investment phase but the average rate, obtained by dividing I_{MAX} by T_C, is a useful indicator.

Time to break-even and average rate of recovery

At the break-even point, the cumulative cash-flow into the business (the return) has **recovered** (paid back) the maximum investment. The sooner this happens the better. So investment options with the smaller values of T_{BE} are preferred on this basis. The average rate of recovery, obtained by dividing I_{MAX} by $(T_{BE} - T_C)$, is another indicator. It is particularly useful when comparing options with very different values of I_{MAX}. The larger the better in this case.

The average rate of return

This criterion, obtained by dividing R_{MAX} by $(T_D - T_C)$, measures the average rate at which cash flows into the business over the sales life cycle of the product. The figure obtained may be much the same as that for the average rate of recovery. Options with the higher values are preferred.

The return to maximum investment ratio

This ratio, which is obtained by dividing R_T by I_{MAX}, can be derived for any value of $T > T_C$. It is unity at $T = T_{BE}$ and reaches its maximum value of (R_{MAX}/I_{MAX}) at $T = T_D$. At any given time, options with the higher values are preferred.

The maximum value, (R_{MAX}/I_{MAX}), measures how many times the maximum investment is recovered over the sales lifetime. It is an overall figure of merit for an investment option. But it needs to be handled with great care, because the options being compared may have substantially different lifetimes. This measure is sometimes called the **end ratio**.

Sales lifetime

The sales lifetime is $(T_D - T_C)$. Options with the longer (profitable) lifetimes are generally preferred. The longer the lifetime the less the need for further investment, either to extend the lifetime by enhancing the product or to create a replacement product.

New cash generated

The new cash generated at any time $T > T_{BE}$ is $(R_T - I_{MAX})$, which is the positive cumulative cash-flow into the business beyond the break-even point. It is a measure of the wealth created by the product. Options with the higher values at a given time are preferred.

	Project A		Project B		Project C	
	Incremental cash-flow In/(Out)	Cumulative cash-flow In/(Out)	Incremental cash-flow In/(Out)	Cumulative cash-flow In/(Out)	Incremental cash-flow In/(Out)	Cumulative cash-flow In/(Out)
EOY						
0	0	0	0	0	0	0
1	(40,000)	(40,000)	(65,000)	(65,000)	(30,000)	(30,000)
2	12,500	(27,500)	15,000	(50,000)	(30,000)	(60,000)
3	17,500	(10,000)	25,000	(25,000)	40,000	(20,000)
4	20,000	10,000	25,000	0	25,000	5,000
5	17,500	27,500	20,000	20,000	20,000	25,000
6	12,500	40,000	20,000	40,000	15,000	40,000

Table 11.3   **The cash-flow models of Projects A, B and C.**
The table shows the numerical cash-flow models of three projects. Only end of year (EOY) values are shown. Each project starts at the end of Year 0 (which is the beginning of Year 1) and continues until the end of Year 6. Negative cash-flow (out of the business) is shown in parentheses. The left-hand column in a project 'box' shows the net incremental cash-flow at the end of each year. The corresponding cumulative cash-flow at the end of each year is shown in the adjacent column to the right. This is the running total of the incremental cash-flows.

11.9.2   Example: Projects A, B and C

This example illustrates the use of criteria based on cash-flow shape parameters to evaluate the relative investment merits of three projects. The technique has a number of limitations which emerge during the discussion.

Table 11.3 shows the numerical cash-flow models of three projects, which are called A, B and C respectively. Only the **end of year** (EOY) figures are shown (in pounds sterling here, but the currency units do not matter).

In plan terms, each project starts at the end of Year 0 (which is the beginning of Year 1) and continues until the end of Year 6. In accord with a common convention, negative cash-flow (cash flow out of the business) is shown in parentheses: as (40,000), for example.

In each project 'box', the left-hand column shows the incremental cash-flow at the end of each year. This is the net change in the overall cash position which occurs between the beginning and the end of the year as a result of the project. It encapsulates all the finer detail of individual cash inflows and outflows which occur during the year. The corresponding cumulative cash-flow at the end of each year is shown in the adjacent column to the right. This is simply the running total of the incremental cash-flows.

In this example, the absolute maximum amount of money that can be invested during Year 1 is £65,000. So the projects are competing for limited resources and only one of them can be launched. But it can be any one of them. The problem now is to evaluate the cash-flow models, and so choose the best project to launch.

An easy way to solve this (particular) problem is to plot the cumulative cash-flow profiles of the three projects. These are shown in Figure 11.7. Note that these plots show the cumulative cash-flows changing linearly during the course of a year. This is an assumption which is unlikely to be satisfied in real life. Given the limited amount of

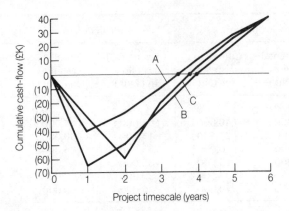

Figure 11.7   **Cumulative cash-flow profiles of Projects A, B and C.**

These graphs complement Table 11.3 by plotting the cumulative cash-flow models of the three projects. The associated example is arranged such that only one of the projects can be launched, so their relative merits as investments is of great interest. In this simple (and unrealistic) case, inspection of the graphs shows that the ranking, in merit order, is A–C–B.

detail in Table 11.3 it cannot be avoided here. It hardly matters, but it is re-examined later.

Now, all the projects generate the same amount of new cash (namely £40,000) at the end of Year 6, so that factor does not distinguish them. But it is clear that the order of merit ranking is A then C then B. Project A generates its new cash from the smallest investment, and also reaches break-even first. Project C is next best by the same measures, leaving Project B in third place.

The same conclusion can be reached by using the numerical data in Table 11.3 to calculate some merit factors selected from those identified earlier. The 'linear' assumption is implicit in the results, which are shown in Table 11.4.

The merit factors selected are:

(1) I_{MAX} is the maximum investment and the order of merit ranking adopted here is from low to high. This is justified on the basis that it puts the minimum amount of money at risk. (It is a somewhat dubious criterion, because it implicitly assumes that all the projects are equally risky, which is unlikely, and ignores the question of what to do with the residue of the available investment money.)

(2) T_{BE} is the time to break-even. The order of merit ranking adopted is from low to high. (Two of the break-even times in Table 11.4 are obtained by interpolation.)

(3) (R_{MAX}/I_{MAX}) is the maximum value of the return to maximum investment ratio, which is calculated at the end of Year 6. The order of merit ranking adopted is from high to low.

(4) $(R_{MAX} - I_{MAX})$ is the maximum value of the new cash generated, which is calculated at the end of Year 6. The order of merit ranking adopted is from high to low. (This criterion fails to distinguish the projects in this example.)

Shape parameter			A	B	C	Ranking 1 2 3
1.	I_{MAX}	£K	40.00	65.00	60.00	A C B
2.	T_{BE}	Years	3.50	4.00	3.80	A C B
3.	R_{MAX}/I_{MAX}	—	2.00	1.62	1.67	A C B
4.	$R_{MAX} - I_{MAX}$	£K	40.00	40.00	40.00	—

Table 11.4   Ranking the cash-flow models of Projects A, B and C.

The cash-flow profiles of Figure 11.7 are such that mere inspection reveals the investment ranking, in merit order, of A–C–B. This table illustrates a more formal way of reaching the same result. It compares some of the cash-flow 'shape' parameters discussed in Section 11.9.1. Note that cash-flow shape techniques are adequate in this case, but it is an unusual case.

11.9.3   Problems with shape techniques

Evaluation based on the shape of the cumulative cash-flow profile works well in the special case of Projects A, B and C. Those projects not only have the same lifetime, but they also generate the same amount of new cash at the end of this lifetime. Coincidences like this are unreal.

Suppose, for example, that Project B still breaks even at the end of Year 4 but generates £70,000 (rather than £40,000) of new cash at the end of Year 6. Under these circumstances, the merit factors in the Project B column of Table 11.4 change and the message of the ranking column is no longer decisive. The 'before' and 'after' rankings are:

	Before	After
(1)	A C B	A C B (same)
(2)	A C B	A C B (same)
(3)	A C B	B A C (different)
(4)	A=B=C	B A=C (different)

Another possibility, leading to similar consternation, is for Project B to perform exactly as advertised in Table 11.3. But it carries on beyond Year 6 to the end of Year 7, and generates another £20,000 of new cash in that last year. This circumstance poses the question:

- Which is better: £40,000 of new cash at the end of Year 6 or £60,000 of new cash at the end of Year 7?

This is a good question and the techniques considered so far cannot answer it.

So, one problem with shape techniques is that they can give conflicting messages and another is that there are some questions which they cannot answer. One of these unanswerable questions has just emerged. But there is another one, which is even more fundamental. This is:

- Is this project better than the do-nothing option?

('Do-nothing' either leaves the investment money on deposit to earn interest or does not acquire it from outside the business and so avoids the costs of acquisition.)

Sadly, it must be concluded that, while the shape techniques have an appealing simplicity and are useful in some circumstances, a better set of cash-flow evaluation tools is needed. This is where discounting comes in.

Discounting is covered in most books on business finance that include a discourse on 'capital budgeting' and/or investment-decision making. A small selection is cited in the chapter bibliography. An exhaustive treatment of discounted cash-flow evaluation techniques is given in a splendid text by White *et al.* (1989), which is devoted to engineering economics. But the approach to discounted cash-flow which is adopted in this book is a little unconventional. It first re-examines the familiar compound interest situation. Experience suggests that this introduction then allows discounting to be recognized as an elegant expression of economic reality, rather than as just another weapon used by accountants to confuse engineers (and many others).

However, a central feature of economics must be explored before the discussion of a compound interest approach to cash-flow evaluation. This is that money costs money!

11.10 The cost of negative cash-flow

The models of Projects A, B and C shown in Table 11.3 and Figure 11.7 are entirely orthodox cash-flow 'pictures' of such projects. But they do not, in fact, include all the financial factors which comprise the project environment. One missing factor is that it costs money to get money to invest. In other words, there is a cost associated with negative cash-flow. This insight allows a financial viability threshold to be set for investment projects. In broad terms, a project may be financially acceptable if it returns, as a minimum:

(1) the money invested in it, plus
(2) the cost of that investment, plus
(3) some additional amount as true earnings (discussed in Section 11.10.3).

Items 1, 2 and 3 constitute the threshold. Even if a project promises to pass the 'threshold test', it may still fail when compared with other projects competing with it for limited resources. So, surviving the threshold test is a necessary but not sufficient criterion for financial acceptability. Of course, if a project offers significant benefits which cannot be quantified in cash terms, it may still be approved even if it fails the threshold test.

It is clearly important to know the cost of the investment funds. This is usually expressed as an annual percentage rate, analogous to an interest rate. It depends, among other things, on how the capital that finances the resources and activities of the business is partitioned between its various sources. That is, it depends on the **capital structure** of the business.

11.10.1 Sources of investment funds

An established business has three major sources of investment funds:

(1) **Owners' (or equity) capital**   These funds belong to the owners of the business. They comprise the sum of their original and any subsequent investment in the business. This is the **share capital** of a limited liability business, which is obtained by selling shares in the ownership of the business.

(2) **Reserves (or retained profits) capital**   These funds also belong to the owners of the business, since they comprise profits earned which are then invested in the business, rather than paid to the owners (as dividends).

(3) **Loan (or debt) capital**   Funds of this type can be obtained from banks and other lending institutions, or by selling a variety of financial 'instruments' such as debentures and bonds. There is always an obligation to pay interest during the term of the loan, and to repay the amount borrowed at the end of that term.

Opportunity costs

At this stage it is useful to recall the concept of **opportunity cost**, which was introduced in Section 7.3, and discussed in some detail in Section 7.5.8. The opportunity cost of an amount of money which is used in a particular way is the amount sacrificed by *not* using it in its best other way. It is really a 'lost opportunity' cost! For example, the opportunity cost of keeping £1,000 under the bed rather than in a savings account with the local bank is the amount of interest lost: about £70 per annum, say.

11.10.2   Assessing the cost of capital

Now, so far as owners' capital is concerned, there is no legal obligation for the business to pay any reward to its owners in return for their investment in it. But they generally expect a reward in terms of periodic payments, called **dividends**, which are paid out of profit. (Additionally, the owners hope for growth in the value of their investment as a saleable asset.) If these expectations are not adequately realized, the owners will eventually withdraw their investment (sell their shares) and re-invest where the rewards are better. So the minimum cost of owners' capital is the opportunity cost borne by the owners as a result of their investment in the business, because the dividends must at least meet this cost. So the approximate minimum cost of owners' capital ($Cost_O$) is the dividend paid per share of ownership (D) expressed as a percentage of the share price (SP). That is:

$$Cost_O = \frac{100D}{SP}(\%) \tag{11.2}$$

Dividends are paid after the business has paid tax on the profit, so $Cost_O$ is an after-tax rate. The business must earn the dividend and the tax payable on it.

Tax must also be paid on that part of profit which is added to the reserves. The cost of the reserve capital ($Cost_R$) is the opportunity cost borne by the owners in sacrificing the dividends which they would have received had the transfer to the reserves not taken place. So, assuming that the tax rates for retained profits and dividends are the same, the cost of reserve capital is the same as for the owners' capital. That is:

$$Cost_R = \frac{100D}{SP}(\%) \tag{11.3}$$

Note (again) that the business must earn the profit which is transferred to the reserves and the tax payable on it, so $Cost_R$ is an after-tax rate.

The cost of the loan capital ($Cost_L$) is the interest rate (I) payable on the loan. Loan interest is regarded as a business expense (in contrast with dividends) and is deductible from profit for tax purposes. This reduces the effective after-tax interest rate below that charged by the lender. The reduction depends on the tax rate (TR). That is:

$$Cost_L = \frac{I(100 - TR)}{100} (\%) \qquad\qquad (11.4)$$

where both I and TR are expressed as percentages.

The approximate minimum cost of investment funds ($Cost_I$) is then:

$$Cost_I = O.Cost_O + R.Cost_R + L.Cost_L (per\ cent) \qquad\qquad (11.5)$$

where O, R and L are the respective proportions that the owners', reserve and loan capital make up of the total, such that:

$$O + R + L = 1 \qquad\qquad (11.6)$$

An example

A simple example will make this less obscure. Suppose that the capital structure of a large company is made up of:

- 15% owners' capital, so O = 0.15
- 25% reserve capital, so R = 0.25
- 60% loan capital, so L = 0.60.

The price per share (SP) has averaged £5 over the last 12 months, and the last annual dividend per share (D) was 45.5 pence. The company is paying 15.5% per annum interest (I) on its loan capital, and is subject to corporation tax at 35% (TR) on profits.

Using equations 11.2, 11.3 and 11.4 for $Cost_O$, $Cost_R$ and $Cost_L$ respectively, yields:

$$Cost_O = 9.1\% \ (tax\ paid)$$
$$Cost_R = 9.1\% \ (tax\ paid)$$
$$Cost_L = 10.1\% \ (tax\ paid)$$

Equation 11.5 then gives:

$$Cost_I = [(0.15 \times 9.1) + (0.25 \times 9.1) + (0.6 \times 10.1)] \% \ (tax\ paid)$$
$$= 9.7\% \ (tax\ paid)$$
$$= 14.9\% \ (before\ tax)$$

for the approximate minimum cost of investment funds.

11.10.3   The project rate of return

A financially viable investment project must return a *higher* rate than the equivalent interest rate cost ($Cost_I$) associated with obtaining investment funds. This is for two reasons:

(1) To compensate for investments that a business must make which do not earn a return quantifiable in cash terms. Examples include employee benefits (such as the provision of health insurance), safety features on manufacturing machinery and basic research projects.

(2) To provide some additional amount of real earnings (true profit).

Just how much higher than $Cost_I$ the minimum acceptable project rate of return should be is a controversial issue of some complexity. Different businesses resolve it in different ways, some of which are quite arbitrary. White *et al.* (1989) give the matter some attention and Kaplan (1986) identifies a dangerous tendency to use rates which are unrealistically high. An important factor is inflation, and this is mentioned in passing on several more occasions before it is examined in some detail in Section 11.15.

- For the present purposes, it is only necessary to appreciate that a minimum acceptable rate of return does exist, and why this is so.

In the literature, the minimum acceptable rate of return is variously called the **required rate of return**, the **return on investment**, the **discount rate**, the **hurdle rate**, the **marginal investment rate** and the **cut-off rate**. Here, the term used is that offered by White *et al.* (1989), which seems to capture the essence of the matter. This is the **minimum attractive rate of return** (MARR). It is a compound rate, in that unpaid interest is periodically added to the principal and the sum then attracts further interest. Following the usual convention, MARR is treated as an annual rate of interest which is compounded annually.

The MARR concept

The significance of MARR is as follows:

- If a project, as represented by its cash-flow model, promises to return at least:
  - the money invested in it, plus
  - the cost of that investment evaluated at MARR

  then it is a candidate for investment. Note that, in this expression of the financial viability threshold, item 3 of the earlier list ('some additional amount as true earnings') has been absorbed into the choice of MARR.

- In situations where projects are competing for limited resources, those projects promising the higher returns in excess of MARR are favoured. This particular statement must be interpreted with some care, because there are different ways of measuring the return. The topic is considered in Section 11.14.

- It is assumed that any available investment money which is not invested in a particular project is invested in some other project, or projects, where it earns not less than MARR.

- Finally, when a project is generating positive incremental cash-flows it is assumed that these are invested, and earn not less than MARR. (This might be achieved by using the positive cash-flows to reduce the overall business investment requirements.)

Thus the concept of MARR effectively establishes an interest rate regime for the business in which it can either borrow or lend money at MARR.

It is instructive to re-evaluate Projects A, B and C in the context of the interest rate regime which is established by the MARR concept. There are many different (but largely equivalent) discounting mechanisms for doing this. White *et al.* (1989) identify six related techniques. Only the most useful of these (author's choice) are covered in this chapter, starting at Section 11.12. Before that, an unconventional – but very illuminating – evaluation technique is examined. It is based on the notion of compound interest and is not a discounting technique.

11.11 A compounding technique

The particular cash-flow evaluation technique considered here is called **compounding forward**, to distinguish it from discounting techniques (which, as explained later, compound backwards). It is developed by means of an extended example focused on Project B discussed earlier. The MARR is assumed to be 18.00% per annum compound throughout this section.

11.11.1 Project B again

Now, consider Project B again, as it is modelled in Table 11.3 and Figure 11.7. There is an implicit 'linear' assumption (discussed later) about Project B as it is pictured in Figure 11.7. This simplifies the following analysis, but it is not essential to it. The analysis incorporates investment costs into the conventional cash-flow model of the project. All calculations are rounded to the nearest pound.

During Year 1, investment in the project increases linearly from zero to £65,000. The (interest) cost of this first year investment must be added to the principal (£65,000) at the beginning of Year 2. The average investment in Year 1 is half of £65,000, so the Year 1 investment cost is:

$$0.18 \times £32,500 \qquad = £5,850$$

and the net investment at the beginning of Year 2 is:

$$£65,000 + £5,850 \qquad = £70,850.$$

There is an incremental positive cash-flow of £15,000 during Year 2, so the net investment at the end of Year 2 is:

$$£70,850 - £15,000 \qquad = £55,850.$$

The average investment during Year 2 is the investment at the beginning of the year less half of the positive cash-flow during the year. So the Year 2 investment cost is:

$$0.18 \times (£70,850 - £7,500) = £11,403$$

and the net investment at the beginning of Year 3 is:

$$£55,850 + £11,403 \qquad = £67,253$$

and so on. Table 11.5 shows the figures for this algorithm.

	Project B: Interest Regime: 18% Incremental cash-flows			Cumulative cash-flow In/(Out) True
EOY	In/(Out) Project	In/(Out) Interest	In/(Out) True	
0	0	–	–	0
1	(65,000)	(5,850)	(70,850)	(70,850)
2	15,000	(11,403)	3,597	(67,253)
3	25,000	(9,856)	15,144	(52,109)
4	25,000	(7,130)	17,870	(34,238)
5	20,000	(4,363)	15,637	(18,601)
6	20,000	(1,548)	18,452	(149)

Table 11.5 **Cash-flow model of Project B incorporating costs of investment.**
The models of Projects A, B and C shown in Table 11.3 and Figure 11.7 are orthodox cash-flows. But they do not include all the financial factors which comprise the project environment! An important missing factor is an additional cost associated with negative cash-flow, which arises because it costs money to get money to invest. This insight (which is explored in Section 11.10) allows a financial viability threshold, called the minimum attractive rate of return (MARR) to be set for investment projects. This table builds a 'true' cash-flow model for Project B by adding in the annual cost of the money it invests as an interest charge borne by the project.

A more fascinating illustration of the same mechanism is shown in Figure 11.8, where the time-scale is 'zoomed' at the year boundaries to expose the detail. The vertical bars shown at the end of each year represent the *incremental* cash-flows arising from the project. The conventional cumulative cash-flow profile corresponding to these increments is also shown. This is identical to the Project B plot in Figure 11.7. The 'true' cumulative cash-flow takes into account the interest payments at the beginning of Years 2 to 7. After Year 1, the true profile is always more negative than the conventional uncorrected version shown above it. The interest payments are represented by the negative-going vertical steps in the true cash-flow profile.

Note that the true cumulative project cash-flow is (just) negative at the end of Year 6 (strictly, at the beginning of Year 7). This occurs because, while the positive cash-flow increments are more than enough to repay the initial (Year 1) investment, they cannot quite cope with the interest payments as well. The figures in Table 11.5 confirm this analysis. The end of Year 6 true cumulative cash-flow figure represents the net end value of the project: a cash deficit of about £150. So Project B fails the financial viability test at a MARR of 18.00%. That is, it does not promise to return, as a minimum:

(1) the money invested in it, plus
(2) the cost of that investment evaluated at the MARR

and so it is not a candidate for investment.

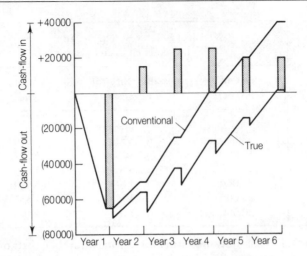

Figure 11.8 **Conventional and 'true' cash-flow models of Project B.**

This figure plots the values in Table 11.5 to provide a more striking comparison of the conventional and true cash-flow models of Project B. The vertical bars at each year-end (where the timescale is 'zoomed' to expose the detail) are incremental cash-flows. The conventional cumulative cash-flow profile is also shown. The 'true' cumulative cash-flow, which includes interest costs at the beginning of Years 2 to 7, falls just below it. Interest costs are represented by negative-going steps in the true cash-flow profile. This turns out to be (just) negative at the end of Year 6 because, while the positive cash-flow increments are more than enough to repay the the initial investment, they cannot quite cope with the interest payments as well. So Project B fails the financial viability test at the chosen MARR of 18.00%.

A borderline case

In practice, of course, a slightly more relaxed view might be taken in interpreting this close miss, especially if there is a shortage of candidates for investment or there are good non-financial reasons for launching the project.

> 'After all, the cash-flow model is no more than a view of the future and the actual investment required might be less. Or the actual returns might be more. Or both of these things could happen. And, even on the model figures, it would pass the test (just) if the MARR was 17.96% rather than 18.00%. Also, the 18.00% is just the guess today – who knows the right rate for six years from now?'

Arguments like this might carry the day, although some cynic (or realist) will point out that actual investment is always more than planned, actual returns are always less than planned, and the MARR rate used *is* chosen with a view to the future.

Comparing Project B with Projects A and C

However, in this example Projects A, B and C are competing for limited investment money and only one of the three can be launched. The reader may care to verify that the corresponding net end values of Projects A and C are £24,498 and £13,445, respectively. In each case, the positive amount represents new cash generated after the money invested in the project and the cost of that investment has been recovered.

So Projects A and C pass the financial viability test at a MARR of 18.00%. But Project A delivers substantially more new cash and, hence, is the one selected for launching.

11.11.2   For and against the technique

This result confirms the earlier analysis based on the cash-flow shape parameters. But the compounding forward technique (so called because the net investment is periodically increased by its MARR cost) is a much better tool. It offers the following advantages:

- The cash-flow model of a project is reduced to a single figure of merit at any specified future time (not only at the end of the project).

- The relative performance of projects with different lifetimes can be evaluated by comparing figures of merit at a specified future time.

- A figure of merit is related to the chosen MARR, and the degree of project financial viability with respect to this MARR is automatically obtained. In other words, a comparison with the do-nothing option is provided.

A weakness of the technique (as developed here) is that it assumes that the basic project cumulative cash-flow model is composed of a series of linear segments as in Figure 11.7. This is a handy (but not essential) simplification, because it eases the calculation of average cash-flow levels and, hence, of MARR costs (and incomes). But real cash-flow profiles are rarely linear and, perhaps for this reason, the technique seems not to be much used in practice. This is unfortunate, because it provides a vivid insight into the economic environment of project planning.

The economic rationale is a little less obvious in the more conventional cash-flow evaluation techniques which are now discussed. These are genuine discounted cash-flow techniques which assume that a project can be adequately represented as a stream of incremental cash-flows. In other words, the evaluation involves the incremental rather than the cumulative cash-flow model.

11.12   Discounting techniques 1: NPV

The first discounting mechanism examined is the **net present value** (NPV) technique. NPV is sometimes called **net present worth** (NPW). A related, but really quite different, approach involving a parameter called the **internal rate of return** (IRR) is considered in Section 11.13.

11.12.1   Introduction to discounting

Discounting is conveniently introduced in a personal context. Suppose that you are offered the choice of receiving £1 now *or* £1 one year from now. Which would you rather have? You may assume that the person making the offer is totally trustworthy, that the current inflation rate is zero and that you do not have to have £1 now, to make some absolutely critical purchase.

Here you should take the advice, quoted at the chapter head, of Omar Khayyám (an ancient Persian poet and an early economist). The correct answer is that you would rather have £1 now, because you could invest it in an interest paying situation and so have more than £1 one year from now.

So (in the absence of inflation) £1 today is worth more than £1 to be received at some future date, because today's pound can earn interest in the intervening period. The corollary of this observation is:

- £1 to be received at some future date is worth less than £1 now.

The whole basis of discounting lies within this statement.

For example, suppose that money can be invested at ten per cent compound annual rate. In this case, the value today of £1 promised one year from today is about 91 pence: because 91 pence could be invested today at ten per cent per annum interest to become £1 one year from today. The arithmetic is:

$$0.91 \times (1 + 0.1)^1 = 1.00 \text{ (nearly)}$$

Similarly, the value today of £1 promised two years from today is about 83 pence, because:

$$0.83 \times (1 + 0.1)^2 = 1.00 \text{ (nearly)}.$$

Assuming that the rate of inflation is zero is convenient, but not essential, in the development of the discounted cash-flow (DCF) notions that follow. Inflation is easily handled (mathematically, that is) by adjusting the interest rate used for discounting. That topic is explored in Section 11.15. Until that point is reached, it is implicitly assumed that the rate of inflation is either zero or (more realistically) that discount rates have been adjusted to cope with it.

11.12.2 Net present value (NPV)

Present values and future sums

The 91 pence and the 83 pence in the previous example are **present values** (PVs) and the promised £1s are **future sums** (FSs).

The present value (PV) of a future sum (FS) to be received n years from now is that amount which, when compounded for n years at a pre-determined rate r, becomes equal to the future sum. This formal definition is more clearly expressed as:

$$PV(1 + r)^n = FS \tag{11.7}$$

or, more usefully:

$$PV = FS(1 + r)^{-n} \tag{11.8}$$

So, a (positive) present value is compounded forward (increased in value) to yield a future sum (Equation 11.7). But a (positive) future sum is discounted backwards (reduced in value) to yield a present value (Equation 11.8).

The quantity $(1 + r)^{-n}$ is called the **discount factor**.

A note on calculations involving the discount factor

Calculations involving a discount factor are central to all DCF techniques. A spreadsheet program is undoubtedly the best general purpose tool for assisting these calculations, which can be very tedious if done 'by hand'. Modern spreadsheets are equipped with a range of financial functions which always include those most needed in DCF work. Some caution is needed in using these functions which, in some cases, make unjustified assumptions about the data presented to them.

Some calculators, particularly those of the 'business' variety, may serve in the absence of a spreadsheet. Access to a computer is more useful, because the DCF algorithms are not difficult to programme. As a last resort, published tables of the discount factor can be employed, using interpolation to determine intermediate values. For convenience, a limited table of discount factors is included in Appendix B. This is quite adequate for the chapter questions which concern DCF.

All the DCF-related tables and figures in this text have been created with the aid of a spreadsheet. In the tables, the discount factors appear as rounded to four decimal places but the spreadsheet program calculates with non-rounded discount factors of much greater precision. This enthusiasm can result in some apparent errors in the calculated figures. These are very minor illusions which can be safely ignored: the monetary amounts are correct to the nearest pound (unless stated otherwise). In practice, the precision employed in the tables is greater than justified by the nature of real-life cash-flow data. Outside a spreadsheet environment, it is quite usual to calculate with discount factors actually rounded to just two or three decimal places.

Present values and future sums (continued)

Figure 11.9 illustrates Equation 11.8. It shows the PVs of £1, promised for delivery at a range of future dates, in a ten per cent per annum compound interest rate regime. These conditions put FS = 1.00 and r = 0.1 into the equation. The 'present' in 'present value' is now(!). And 'now' is the end of Year 0 or the beginning of Year 1 (which amounts to the same thing). So the PV of a £1 promised at the end of Year 0 (now) is obtained by putting n = 0 in Equation 11.8. Not surprisingly, this PV is £1. The PV of £1 promised at the end of Year 1 is obtained by putting n = 1 in Equation 11.8, yielding 91 pence. And so on. The PVs in the figure are rounded to the nearest penny.

Cash-flow models and net present value

In Figure 11.9, the series of future sums (£1 at the end of Year 0, 91 pence at the end of Year 1 and so on) can be regarded as a sequence of positive cash-flow increments comprising a cash-flow model. The present value of the whole sequence, called its net present value (NPV), is obtained by summing the individual PVs. The figure shows that the NPV of this cash-flow model is £4.17. This is the current monetary equivalent of the whole sequence in the ten per cent interest rate regime. In other words, the NPV encapsulates the pattern of incremental cash-flows, magnitudes and timings, in just one sum of money deemed to be available now. It is an elegant notion.

The equivalence between a cash-flow model and its NPV can be visualized in either of two ways:

(1) The NPV is equivalent to the cash-flow model because the PVs comprising the NPV are obtained by *discounting* the FSs comprising the model *backwards* at the applicable interest rate. (This is the mechanism illustrated in Figure 11.9.)

(2) The cash-flow model is equivalent to the NPV because the sequence of FSs

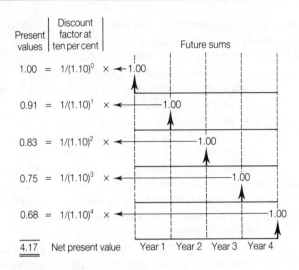

Figure 11.9 Illustrating the present value of future sum.
The present value (PV) of a future sum (FS) to be received n years from now in an annual compound interest rate regime of r is given by $PV = FS(1 + r)^{-n}$, where $(1 + r)^{-n}$ is the discount factor. So a future sum is discounted (reduced in magnitude) to yield a present value. The figure shows the FSs of some PVs (each of £1) arising at different future dates in a ten per cent per annum compound interest rate regime. The series of FSs can be regarded as a cash-flow model comprising a pattern of positive cash increments. The net present value (NPV) (£4.17 here) of this sequence is the sum of the individual PVs. It is the current monetary equivalent of the whole sequence in the ten per cent interest rate regime. Thus, NPV encapsulates the pattern of incremental cash-flows, magnitudes *and* timings, in just one sum of money deemed to be available now. It is a lovely idea.

comprising the model could be created by *compounding* the PVs comprising the NPV forward at the applicable interest rate.

Negative cash-flows

Only positive cash increments (positive FSs) flowing into into the reference system have been considered so far. But negative cash increments (negative FSs) flowing out of the reference system must also be handled. However, the discounting mechanism expressed in:

$$PV = FS(1 + r)^{-n} \qquad (11.8)$$

is indifferent to the sign of FS; and the discount factor, $(1 + r)^{-n}$, is less than 1 for all values of n > 0. So, when a FS is a negative incremental cash-flow the corresponding PV is a less negative incremental cash-flow. For example, if a cost of £1.00 is incurred 3 years 'downstream' in a ten per cent per annum compound regime (that is, FS = −£1.00, r = 0.10 and n = 3 years) then:

$$PV = -£1.00 \times 0.75 = -£0.75$$

This result can be interpreted by recalling that negative cash-flows attract an interest rate cost (whereas positive cash-flows attract an interest rate income). So PVs which are negative get more negative as they are compounded forward and, conversely, FSs which are negative get less negative as they are discounted backwards.

EOY n	Discount factor at r% = 18.00	Project A		Project B		Project C	
		Incremental cash-flow In/(Out)	PV at r% = 18.00	Incremental cash-flow In/(Out)	PV at r% = 18.00	Incremental cash-flow In/(Out)	PV at r% = 18.00
0	1.0000	0	0	0	0	0	0
1	0.8475	(40,000)	(33,898)	(65,000)	(55,085)	(30,000)	(25,424)
2	0.7182	12,500	8,977	15,000	10,773	(30,000)	(21,546)
3	0.6086	17,500	10,651	25,000	15,216	40,000	24,345
4	0.5158	20,000	10,316	25,000	12,895	25,000	12,895
5	0.4371	17,500	7,649	20,000	8,742	20,000	8,742
6	0.3704	12,500	4,630	20,000	7,409	15,000	5,556
		SUM	NPV	SUM	NPV	SUM	NPV
		40,000	8,326	40,000	(51)	40,000	4,569

Table 11.6   **Net present value and Projects A, B and C.**
The incremental cash-flow models of Projects A, B and C are reproduced in this table, and the project NPVs are calculated at MARR = 18.00% per annum compound. Comparison of the NPVs confirms the investment merit ranking of A–C–B. Note that NPV_B is negative. This confirms the diagnosis that, at this MARR, Project B loses, rather than makes, money.

11.12.3   NPV and Projects A, B and C

The incremental cash-flow models of Projects A, B and C were introduced in Table 11.3. They are reproduced in Table 11.6, which compares the three projects by evaluating the NPVs of their respective cash-flows.

The interest rate regime is that established by the MARR concept. MARR is set at 18.00% per annum compound (as previously) and this is the rate used to calculate the discount factors. In the table, the two left-hand columns indicate the end of successive years and the corresponding discount factors, respectively. The left-hand column within a project 'box' is the basic incremental cash-flow model of the project. The adjacent column to the right contains the PVs of those FSs. These are obtained by multiplying a FS by the corresponding discount factor, as required by Equation 11.8. The NPV for the project is then the sum of the individual PVs.

Comparison of the NPVs confirms the previous ranking of A then C then B. The fact that the NPV of Project B is negative also confirms the earlier diagnosis that, with MARR at 18.00%, it loses rather than makes money.

11.12.4   For and against the technique

The virtues of the NPV technique are very similar to those cited earlier in support of the compounding forward technique:

- The cash-flow model of a project is reduced to a single figure of merit (its NPV) which represents the 'now' value of the whole cash-flow sequence.

- The relative performance of projects can be evaluated by comparing their NPVs, even if they have different lifetimes.

- An NPV is a function of the chosen MARR, and the degree of project financial viability with respect to this MARR is automatically indicated. In other words, a comparison with the do-nothing option is provided.

One (commonly quoted) weakness is that the technique provides a comparative rather than an absolute measure of the value of a project, because it is basically a comparison against the MARR. The point is sound, but whether or not it should count against the NPV method is debatable. However, a simple extension of the technique does provide an absolute measure (which then has to be compared with the MARR). This extension is discussed very shortly, in Section 11.13.

A more fundamental problem lies in the basic assumption that a project can be adequately represented by a sequence of equally 'spaced' incremental cash-flows. In the development of the compounding forward method (Section 11.11) the simplifying (but not essential) assumption was made that cumulative cash changed linearly to create the increments. But the NPV method makes no assumptions at all about how the cumulative cash behaves in the periods between the increments. Except, perhaps, the implicit assumption that nothing alarming happens! But suppose, for example, that Project A needed to borrow £1,000,000 on Day 1 and planned to pay it back on Day 364, having also spent the advertised £40,000 over the year. This strange behaviour would create about £180,000 of additional investment cost early in the project, which is more than enough to sink it without trace. But it would not show up on the cash-flow model. The solution to this type of problem is to measure the increments more frequently: monthly or weekly, say. A project planning tool (PET2) which is considered later, in Section 11.16, uses this approach.

11.12.5   More interpretations of NPV

An NPV represents the today value, in a defined interest rate regime, of a sequence of future incremental cash-flows. Of course, one particular sequence that it represents is the sequence from which it was formed. As was pointed out earlier, this is so because that sequence could be re-created by compounding the individual PV elements of the NPV forward at the defined interest rate. But the NPV can also represent any number of other sequences. This is illustrated in the diagrams of Figure 11.10, which shows just some of the incremental cash-flow sequences which are equivalent to Project A.

The vertical 'T-bars' of Figure 11.10(a) are a 'to-scale' representation of the incremental cash-flows which comprise the basic cash-flow model of Project A.

Net end of year values

A **net end of year value** is the *single* value occurring at the end of a specified year which is equivalent to the original sequence. It is easily derived from the NPV of the sequence, by dividing it by the discount factor for the specified period. This is equivalent to compounding the NPV forward, at the MARR, for that period.

A set (as distinct from a sequence) of net end of year values is shown in Figure 11.10(b). These relate to the NPV of Project A evaluated at 18.00% per annum, as before. The scale of this diagram is normalized about the NPV.

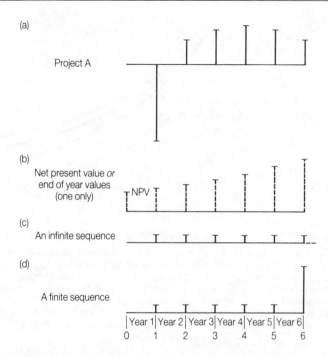

Figure 11.10   **Some cash-flow sequences equivalent to Project A.**

A net present value (NPV) represents the 'today-value', in a defined interest rate regime, of the particular sequence of future incremental cash-flows from which it was originally formed. But a NPV can also represent any number of other sequences. Diagrams (b), (c) and (d) exemplify this, by showing some incremental cash-flow sequences which are equivalent to Project A. The cash-flows are indicated with vertical T-bars. Diagram (a) is a 'to-scale' representation of Project A. Diagram (b) is a set (not a sequence) of net end-of-year values obtained by compounding the NPV forward, at the MARR, for the appropriate period. Diagram (c) is an infinite series of annual 'interest' payments obtained by investing the NPV at the MARR. Diagram (d) is a finite series of annual interest payments, as in (c), and terminated by repayment of the NPV.

An infinite series of interest payments

The NPV of (the cash-flow model of) Project A at a MARR of 18.00% is £8,326 (see Table 11.6). Suppose that this amount is invested, at the beginning of Year 1, in a situation returning interest at the MARR. This investment yields an infinite series of annual interest payments, each of which is equal to:

$$0.18 \times £8,326 = £1,499$$

This is illustrated in Figure 11.10(c). The NPV of the infinite series is £8,326. (This is intuitively fairly obvious, but it can be proved, if necessary, by recourse to the mathematics of infinite series.) This means that, contemplating the future from the beginning of Year 1, Project A is equivalent to an infinite series of annual cash-flow increments, each equal to the product of the MARR and the NPV of Project A evaluated at that MARR.

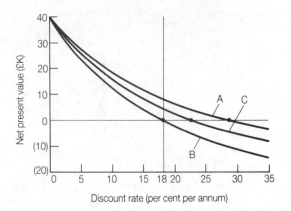

Figure 11.11 **Net present value (NPV) versus discount rate for Projects A, B and C.**
Project type cash-flow models start with investment (negative cash-flow out) and yield returns (positive cash-flow in). The NPV of such models may be positive, negative or zero. At low discount rates, positive increments occurring far downstream are not much reduced so the NPV is likely to be positive. But at high rates, the downstream increments are severely attenuated so the NPV is likely to be negative. So there is probably a discount rate at which the NPV is zero. This is illustrated in the figure, which shows how NPV varies with discount rate for Projects A, B and C. The discount rate at which the NPV of a cash-flow is zero is called its internal rate of return (IRR).

A finite series of interest and deferred repayment

This is an extension of the rationale underpinning the infinite series notion. It restricts the equivalent series of annual interest payments to a finite number, and compensates for the rest by repaying the original investment at the end of the series. For example, in the case of Project A, an equivalent finite series could comprise interest payments of £1,499 at the end of Years 1 to 6 inclusive plus repayment of the £8,326 at the end of Year 6. This possibility is shown in Figure 11.10(d). Readers may care to check that the NPV of this series does, indeed, evaluate to £8,326 at the MARR. This being the case, it is also equivalent to Project A. Note that this particular series is just one sample of its type, because such a series can be terminated at any time.

The 'finite series' equivalence concept is used later in the chapter when some differences in the NPV and IRR approaches are examined. (It is also the basic mechanism of the so-called 'interest only' mortgage loans used for property purchases, where the initial loan is ultimately repaid from the proceeds of an insurance policy.)

11.13 | Discounting techniques 2: IRR

With 'project' type cash-flows, such as those of Projects A, B and C, it is intuitively reasonable that NPVs can be either positive or negative, depending on the discount rate. At low rates, the positive cash increments occurring far downstream are not much reduced by the discounting process, so the NPV is likely to be positive. But at high rates, the far downstream contributions are severely attenuated, and the NPV becomes dominated by the early negative cash increments.

EOY n	Discount factor at r% = 28.17	Project A		Equivalent project	
		Incremental cash-flow In/(Out)	PV at r% = 28.17	Incremental cash-flow In/(Out)	PV at r% = 28.17
0	1.0000	0	0	0	0
1	0.7802	(40,000)	(31,208)	(40,000)	(31,208)
2	0.6087	12,500	7,609	11,269	6,860
3	0.4749	17,500	8,311	11,269	5,352
4	0.3705	20,000	7,410	11,269	4,175
5	0.2891	17,500	5,059	11,269	3,258
6	0.2255	12,500	2,819	51,269	11,563
		SUM	NPV	SUM	NPV
		40,000	0	56,347	0

Table 11.7 **An 'IRR equivalent' project to Project A.**
This table is designed to aid understanding of the IRR concept. Project A is on the left. Its IRR is 28.17%. The table builds another project on the right. This starts with the same investment as in Project A during Year 1, and its subsequent positive cash-flows are annual interest payments on this investment, calculated at a rate equal to the IRR of Project A. In the table, the cash-flow models of both projects are evaluated at a discount rate equal to the IRR of Project A. Note that the NPV of both projects is zero. So the cash-flow model of Project A is equivalent to an identical investment at an annual interest rate equal to its IRR. This is why the discount rate at which an NPV is zero is called the 'internal rate of return' of the cash-flow model which it represents. IRR is a measure of the true profitability of a project.

So, if the NPV of a cash-flow sequence can be either positive or negative at different rates, there is a rate at which it is zero. This is illustrated in Figure 11.11, which shows how NPV varies with discount rate for the Projects A, B and C.

The discount rate at which the NPV of a cash-flow is zero is called its **internal rate of return** (IRR) or (occasionally) its **yield**. It is the rate at which the sum of the discounted negative cash-flow increments (the discounted investment) is equal to the sum of the discounted positive cash-flow increments (the discounted return).

The problem of calculating an IRR (as distinct from obtaining it graphically) is considered shortly. However, as it turns out, the IRR of Project A is about 28.17%. The next section explores what this means.

11.13.1 Interpretation of the IRR

Project A is compared with an **IRR equivalent project** in Table 11.7. This equivalent project is of the 'finite series of interest and deferred repayment' type discussed in Section 11.12.5. But, in this case, the project starts with an investment (just like a real project). It invests the same amount (£40,000) as Project A during Year 1, and the subsequent incremental annual interest payments are calculated at a rate equal to the IRR of Project A. These payments of £11,269 occur at the end of Years 2 to 6 inclusive, and the investment is repaid at the end of Year 6 (so the repayment at the end of Year 6 is £11,269 + £40,000 = £51,269).

In the table, the cash-flow models of Project A and this particular IRR equivalent project are evaluated at a discount rate equal to the IRR of Project A. Note that the NPV of *both* projects is zero at this discount rate.

- This means that the cash-flow model of Project A is the equivalent of an identical investment at an annual rate equal to its IRR.

It is for this reason that the discount rate at which an NPV is zero is called the internal rate of return of the cash-flow model. IRR is a measure of the true profitability of a project.

Thus, the IRR of a cash-flow provides an absolute measure of its merit. This contrasts with the NPV technique, which invokes a MARR as a reference level when the NPV is calculated. So projects can be compared and ranked on the basis of their respective IRRs, without reference to a MARR. But an IRR can only be used to evaluate a project as a candidate for investment by comparing it with a reference level. The usual criterion is that:

- The IRR of the project shall be equal to or greater than the MARR for it to be accepted as a candidate for investment.

The IRR concept sounds like good news. But read on!

11.13.2   Calculating an IRR

To *calculate* an IRR it is necessary to solve for the rate, r, an equation of the form:

$$c_0 + c_1(1+r)^{-1} + c_2(1+r)^{-2} + .. + c_n(1+r)^{-n} = 0 \qquad (11.9)$$

where c_0, c_1 and so on are the cash-flow increments. An iterative trial-and-error method, using an initial guess, is needed. This can be very tedious if tackled 'manually'. Fortunately, some calculators and all modern spreadsheets provide a specific function for the task. In the absence of such tools, the calculation algorithm is not difficult to programme or, as a last resort, tables such as those in Appendix B can be used, with interpolation if necessary.

Here, a spreadsheet program reveals:

- IRR of Project A = 28.17%
- IRR of Project B = 17.96%
- IRR of Project C = 22.58%

The same program provides the curves of Figure 11.11, and solving for IRR graphically is normally sufficiently accurate (because the basic cash-flow data is only a best guess). So, once again, the project ranking of A then C then B is confirmed. Note, too, that the IRR for Project B is just less than the 18.00% used for the MARR in the earlier calculations. So, formally, Project B is not a candidate for investment at this value of MARR, as concluded before.

11.13.3   IRR: Multiple roots problem

Equation 11.9, which must be solved to calculate an IRR, is a polynomial of degree n in the variable $(1 + r)$. In general, therefore, it can have n different roots: suggesting that

EOY	Case 1	Case 2
	Incremental cash-flow In/(Out)	Incremental cash-flow In/(Out)
0	(1,000)	(50,000)
1	3,900	312,500
2	(5,008)	(776,875)
3	2,116	960,344
4	0	(590,363)
5	0	144,400
	SUM	SUM
	8	6

Table 11.8 **Cash-flows with multiple IRRs.**
Equation 11.9 (in the text) must be solved to calculate an IRR. It is a polynomial of degree n in the variable (1 + r). So it might have n different roots. That is, a cash-flow model might have more than one IRR. This is bad news, because it is not easy to interpret such results. The table shows two cash-flow models which exhibit this undesirable feature. Note that there is more than one sign change in these sequences.

a cash-flow profile might exhibit more than one IRR value. This is a bit sad, because it is not easy to interpret cash-flows which exhibit multiple IRR values.

Only positive real roots are of interest. For such roots, the 'rule of signs' indicates that:

- The maximum number of roots is equal to the number of sign changes in the cash-flow sequence.
- Sequences with an odd number of sign changes have an odd number of roots.
- Sequences with an even number of sign changes have either an even number of roots or no roots at all (zero is deemed to be an even number).

Happily, the incremental cash-flow models of most projects have only one sign change (a sequence of negative increments being followed by a sequence of positive increments) so, normally, there is just one value of IRR. But cash-flow models with more than one sign change should be handled with some care.

Table 11.8 shows two incremental cash-flow sequences, labelled Case 1 and Case 2, which are in this category. Case 1 has three sign changes in the sequence and has three values for the IRR. Case 2 has five sign changes in the sequence and also has three values for the IRR (because two of its five inherent real positive roots coincide with other roots). These features are illustrated in Figure 11.12, which plots NPVs against discount rate. The values of IRR are five, thirty and fifty-five per cent in each case, and the curves demonstrate conclusively that multiple values of IRR can exist.

The extent to which this is a real problem is less certain. The cash-flows of Table 11.8 were fabricated, after a fruitless search for some real-life examples, by working backwards from the answers. (This well-established engineering approach to problems of this nature will be familiar to all students.)

Note that, in each case, the sum of the incremental cash-flows is negligible in

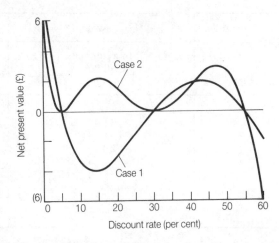

Figure 11.12 **Illustrating multiple values of IRR.**
These graphs are plots of NPV against discount rate for the cash-flow models in Table 11.8. They demonstrate that multiple values of IRR can exist. Whether or not this is a real practical problem is less certain. The matter is discussed in the text.

comparison with the magnitude of the individual incremental cash-flows. Note, too, that this same observation applies to the vertical scale ($+£6$ to $-£6$) in Figure 11.12. In fact, in comparison with the magnitude of the individual incremental cash-flows, the NPVs are sensibly zero over any reasonable range of discount rates (zero to sixty per cent, say). Another characteristic of these two cash-flow patterns is that their IRR performance is very sensitive to small variations in the figures. It would be unwise to conclude from all this that cash-flows of this nature do not arise in practice. But they are not hard to recognize if they do. It is recommended that graphs like those of Figures 11.11 and 11.12 are always constructed when cash-flows are investigated. It is very easy with a spreadsheet.

The multiple IRR problem can be avoided by modifying the calculation to deliver some other rate. Such modifications do not, of course, make any contribution towards avoiding those weird cash-flows sequences which are the more fundamental problem. The modifications are not considered here. White *et al.* (1989) do give the matter more detailed attention.

11.14 Project choice: NPV and IRR

The NPV and IRR approaches provide two ways of evaluating the cash-flow models of projects. General techniques for using these figures of merit to choose projects for launching are now examined. The problem is not quite as straightforward as suggested by the earlier study of Projects A, B and C.

11.14.1 Projects A, B and C again

When the business is able to invest in all of the projects that are being considered at a particular time, the NPV and IRR methods yield the same list of acceptable projects.

For example, suppose that the business has got (at least) £135,000 to invest, MARR is set at 18.00% and the available Projects are A, B and C (of Tables 11.3 and 11.6) as before. It will be recalled that the NPVs (at MARR = 18.00%) and the IRRs for these projects are:

	NPV (£)	IRR (%)
(1) Project A:	8,326	28.17
(2) Project C:	4,569	22.58
(3) Project B:	(51)	17.96

A sum of £135,000 is enough to launch A, B and C simultaneously if it makes economic sense to do so. Under these circumstances, the criteria for project acceptance are:

- NPV evaluated at the MARR is greater than or equal to zero, or
- IRR is greater than or equal to MARR.

The NPV criterion then accepts Projects A and C but rejects B, and the IRR criterion gives the identical message.

However, when the business is not able to invest in all of the projects that are being considered at a particular time, then simply ranking the individual NPV and IRR results from high to low may yield conflicting messages.

For example, suppose that the business has got only £65,000 to invest, MARR is set at 18.00% and the available projects are A, B and C as before. A sum of £65,000 is enough to launch any one of the projects, but is not enough to launch any two. In other words, because of the funding constraint, the projects are competing for limited resources and only one of them can be launched. Ranking the individual NPV results from high to low gives a merit list of A then C then B, so Project A is selected for launch. Ranking the individual IRR results from high to low gives an identical merit list, in this case, and there is no conflict between the two merit measures. Figure 11.11 shows why this is so for Projects A, B and C. Note that:

$$NPV_A > NPV_C > NPV_B \text{ for all discount rates} > 0$$

so the NPV curves intersect the zero axis, defining their IRR values, in the same high to low order (A then C then B).

11.14.2 Projects D, E, F and G

But, as noted before, Projects A, B and C represent a special case. The general case is illustrated by Projects D, E, F and G whose cash-flow models are shown, and evaluated, in Table 11.9. The MARR is set at 12.00% in this case. Note that NPV (at MARR = 12.00%) is greater than zero, and IRR is greater than MARR, for all four projects. So, if the business is able to fund all the projects (which together need £250,000 of investment funds in the first year) then all four can be launched simultaneously. That is, the NPV and IRR criteria for the 'no funding constraint' situation yield identical messages.

Conflict between NPV and IRR

But suppose that the business has only £85,000 available for investment. This

EOY n	Discount factor at r% = 12.00	Project D		Project E		Project F		Project G	
		Incremental cash-flow In/(Out)	PV at r% = 12.00	Incremental cash-flow In/(Out)	PV at r% = 12.00	Incremental cash-flow In/(Out)	PV at r% = 12.00	Incremental cash-flow In/(Out)	PV at r% = 12.00
0	1.0000	0	0	0	0	0	0	0	0
1	0.8929	(40,000)	(35,714)	(50,000)	(44,643)	(75,000)	(66,964)	(85,000)	(75,893)
2	0.7972	20,000	15,944	20,000	15,944	20,000	15,944	22,000	17,538
3	0.7118	17,500	12,456	25,000	17,795	25,000	17,795	28,000	19,930
4	0.6355	15,000	9,533	20,000	12,710	35,000	22,243	38,000	24,150
5	0.5674	15,000	8,511	20,000	11,349	32,500	18,441	35,500	20,144
6	0.5066	15,000	7,599	15,000	7,599	30,000	15,199	32,000	16,212
		SUM 42,500	NPV 18,329	SUM 50,000	NPV 20,754	SUM 67,500	NPV 22,658	SUM 70,500	NPV 22,081
		IRR % 32.57		IRR % 30.35		IRR % 23.84		IRR % 22.32	

Table 11.9 **The cash-flow models of Projects D, E, F and G.**

The NPV and IRR methods of preference ranking the investment merits of different projects can yield conflicting results! The table illustrates the problem by evaluating four specific projects by both methods. MARR is set at 12.00% per annum compound. Note that all the NPVs are positive, and all IRRs are greater than MARR. So it is economically sensible to launch all the projects simultaneously, if all can be resourced (funded, say) simultaneously. But suppose the business can only resource one of the four projects. The NPV ranking is F–G–E–D, but the IRR ranking is D–E–F–G. So the two tests for 'best' project do not agree at any level (in this case)!

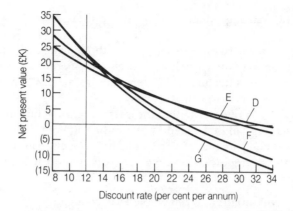

Figure 11.13   **Net present value (NPV) versus discount rate for Projects D, E, F and G.**
The graphs are plots of NPV versus discount rate for the four projects described and evaluated in
Table 11.9. They explain the NPV versus IRR preference ranking *conflict* exposed in that table. It
arises because the SUM (discount rate = 0) values of the cash-flow models are different (shown in
the table), and their cash-flow profiles are such that the NPV curves decline at different rates as the
discount rate increases. This situation is quite normal.

constraint means that only one of the four projects can be launched. Ranking the
individual NPV and IRR results from high to low gives the following merit lists:

	NPV rank	IRR rank
(1)	F	D
(2)	G	E
(3)	E	F
(4)	D	G

and the methods give conflicting messages. In fact, the two tests do not agree at any
level!

Figure 11.13, which plots the variations of NPV with discount rate, reveals the
reasons underlying this conflict. At low values of discount rate (less than ten per cent,
say) the NPVs are dominated by the positive incremental cash-flows and are ranked in
the order of their 'sum' (discount rate = 0) values (see Table 11.9). This initial
ranking, from high to low, is:

G–F–E–D.

However, as the discount rate increases, the NPVs decrease at different rates, with that
of Project G falling most rapidly and that of Project D least rapidly. Hence, the NPV
curves cross over and, in this case, do so before the NPV = 0 axis is reached. In fact,
the NPV curves for Projects G and F cross over before the discount rate reaches the
MARR at 12.00%. So, at the MARR, the NPV ranking is:

F–G–E–D.

The discount rate at which the NPV curve of a project intersects the NPV = 0 axis
equates with its IRR value. Ordering these points from high to low gives:

D–E–F–G

for the IRR ranking, which is the exact opposite of the NPV ranking at low discount rates.

This effect, where the NPV and IRR methods give conflicting results, arises because the sum values of the cash-flows models are different and their profiles are such that their NPV curves decline at different rates as the discount rate increases. This is, of course, an absolutely normal situation.

The problem of determining the correct *relative* ranking of projects under these circumstances can be tackled in two rather different ways. Both involve successive 'pair-wise' comparisons of the candidate projects. The first approach examined is termed the **aggregate** or **reserve account** method. It is the least popular of the two. However, it provides:

- a useful insight into the whole DCF concept,
- a simple rule for ranking projects in order of merit, and
- it points the way to the second, more elegant (but unnecessary), method of solving the same problem.

11.14.3 Ranking: Aggregate method

In the aggregate method, candidate projects are compared two at a time (pair-wise) as alternatives. The aim is to maximize the return on the *total* investment needed to launch the *larger* (in investment terms) of the two projects.

Since, in general, the investment needs of the two projects are different, the surplus funds not needed for the smaller project are invested (notionally) in a **reserve account** where they earn a return at the MARR. The comparison is then between the larger project and the aggregate of the smaller project with the reserve account. This concept is entirely in line with DCF and MARR notions, which assume that available investment funds which are not assigned to projects can earn a return (somewhere) at the MARR. The following example makes this more clear.

In Table 11.9, Projects D, E, F and G are assembled from left to right in size order. The first pair-wise comparison is between Projects D and E. The aggregate method of comparing these two projects is illustrated in Table 11.10. The first six columns of this table simply reproduce (for convenience) the same columns of Table 11.9.

The difference in the (initial) investment needs of Projects D and E at the end of Year 1 is £10,000. So this sum is invested in the reserve account at that time. There, it earns interest at 12.00% per annum (the MARR) up to and including the end of Year 6, when it is repaid. This sequence of incremental cash-flows is shown in the first column of the reserve account box. It has (of course) an IRR equal to the MARR at 12.00% and, not surprisingly, an NPV of zero because the cash-flow sequence is discounted at its IRR.

The first column in the aggregate box is a cash-flow sequence formed by adding corresponding cash-flows from Project D (the smaller project) and the reserve account. This comprises a 'dummy' aggregate project, which is now compared with Project E (the larger project of D and E).

Note that the NPV of Project E is greater than the NPV of the aggregate project. This indicates that Project E earns a better return on £50,000 than does the combination of

EOY n	Discount factor at r% = 12.00	Project D		Project E		Reserve account		Aggregate	
		Incremental cash-flow In/(Out)	PV at r% = 12.00	Incremental cash-flow In/(Out)	PV at r% = 12.00	Incremental cash-flow In/(Out)	PV at r% = 12.00	Incremental cash-flow In/(Out)	PV at r% = 12.00
0	1.0000	0	0	0	0	0	0	0	0
1	0.8929	(40,000)	(35,714)	(50,000)	(44,643)	(10,000)	(8,929)	(50,000)	(44,643)
2	0.7972	20,000	15,944	20,000	15,944	1,200	957	21,200	16,901
3	0.7118	17,500	12,456	25,000	17,795	1,200	854	18,700	13,310
4	0.6355	15,000	9,533	20,000	12,710	1,200	763	16,200	10,295
5	0.5674	15,000	8,511	20,000	11,349	1,200	681	16,200	9,192
6	0.5066	15,000	7,599	15,000	7,599	11,200	5,674	26,200	13,274
		SUM 42,500	NPV 18,329	SUM 50,000	NPV 20,754	SUM 6,000	NPV (0)	SUM 48,500	NPV 18,329
		IRR % 32.57		IRR % 30.35		IRR % 12.00		IRR % 27.35	

Table 11.10 **Comparing the cash-flow models of Projects D and E: aggregate method.**

The table illustrates one way of identifying the correct relative investment ranking of projects when NPV and IRR tests give conflicting results. Called the aggregate or reserve account method, it aims to maximize the return on the total investment needed to launch the larger of two projects treated as alternatives. Available surplus funds not needed for the smaller project are invested (notionally) in a reserve account to earn a return at the MARR. The larger project is then compared with the aggregate of the smaller project and the reserve account (in accordance with MARR notions). It is applied here to Projects D and E.

Note that NPV_E is greater than $NPV_{Aggregate}$. So Project E earns a better return on £50,000 than does the combination of £40,000 invested in Project D and £10,000 earning the MARR. Thus, Project E is preferred over Project D. Note, too, that $NPV_{Aggregate}$ is equal to the NPV_D (the smaller project). Hence, comparing NPV_E with $NPV_{Aggregate}$ is the same as comparing the NPVs of the alternative projects: the contortions with the aggregate project are comforting but unnecessary! So, as a general rule for alternative projects, the project with the largest NPV is preferred. (Figure 11.13 gives the same message, and shows that the 'best' project depends on the MARR used.) The IRR values are irrelevant.

£40,000 invested in Project D and £10,000 earning the MARR. So Project E is preferred over Project D.

This might seem to be an odd choice at first sight. That is, despite the fact that Project D has a higher profitability than Project E (because it has a bigger IRR), Project E is preferred. But profitability (return expressed as a fraction of the investment) is not the issue. It is the maximum actual cash return – *maximum 'profit'* – on the £50,000 that is sought, which clearly comes from Project E rather than from the aggregate project. This is because the higher profitability of Project D is not enough to compensate for the fact that Project E can earn substantially more than the MARR on the 'surplus' investment funds which become available if D is selected.

If this aggregate method of determining the relative ranking of Projects D, E, F and G were to be continued, the next step would be to compare Projects E and F. The 'winner' of these two projects would then be compared with Project G. Happily, it is not necessary to go to these lengths because a simple project ranking rule can be extracted from the analysis at this stage.

The NPV project ranking rule

Note that, in Table 11.10, both columns that represent the aggregate project are, or can be, formed by simple addition of corresponding figures from Project D and the reserve account (with the sole exception of the IRR figure). Since the NPV of the reserve account is zero (by definition), the NPV of the aggregate project is equal to the NPV of Project D. Hence, comparing the NPVs of Project E and the aggregate project is equally well performed by simply comparing the NPVs of Project E and Project D.

There is a general rule here, justified by its basis in the aggregate method, for determining the relative ranking of projects *solely* from their NPV measures. The rule is:

- Projects exhibiting positive NPVs when their cash-flow models are discounted at the MARR are candidates for investment.

- The project with the largest NPV is preferred if the circumstances are such that only one of a pair of projects can be launched at a given time. In the (unlikely) event that the two projects evaluate to the same NPV, the smaller project offers the higher profitability.

Applying this rule to Projects D, E F and G of Table 11.9 confirms that all of the projects are acceptable if all can be launched simultaneously. If this is not the case, the preference ranking is

F–G–E–D

in accordance with the NPVs. The IRR values of the projects play no part in formulating this decision. They are irrelevant.

11.14.4 Ranking: Differential method

The second method to be examined for determining the correct relative ranking of projects is sometimes called the **incremental** method. The term **differential** method is preferred here. It is a more satisfactory approach than the aggregate method, because it delivers the same message from NPV and IRR considerations. This can be important. It may be, for instance, that local management favour IRR rather

EOY n	Discount factor at r% = 12.00	Project (D – 0) Incremental cash-flow In/(Out)	PV at r% = 12.00	Project (E – D) Incremental cash-flow In/(Out)	PV at r% = 12.00	Project (F – E) Incremental cash-flow In/(Out)	PV at r% = 12.00	Project (G – F) Incremental cash-flow In/(Out)	PV at r% = 12.00
0	1.0000	0	0	0	0	0	0	0	0
1	0.8929	(40,000)	(35,714)	(10,000)	(8,929)	(25,000)	(22,321)	(10,000)	(8,929)
2	0.7972	20,000	15,944	0	0	0	0	2,000	1,594
3	0.7118	17,500	12,456	7,500	5,338	0	0	3,000	2,135
4	0.6355	15,000	9,533	5,000	3,178	15,000	9,533	3,000	1,907
5	0.5674	15,000	8,511	5,000	2,837	12,500	7,093	3,000	1,702
6	0.5066	15,000	7,599	0	0	15,000	7,599	2,000	1,013
		SUM 42,500	NPV 18,329	SUM 7,500	NPV 2,425	SUM 17,500	NPV 1,904	SUM 3,000	NPV (577)
		IRR % 32.57		IRR % 22.22		IRR % 14.37		IRR % 9.39	

Table 11.11   **The differential projects associated with Projects D, E, F and G.**

The table illustrates a different way (to that of Table 11.10) of identifying the correct *relative* investment ranking of projects when NPV and IRR tests give conflicting results. It is preferred by those who favour, for various odd reasons, IRR to NPV methods.

Suppose that the alternative projects to be compared are N_1 and N_2, where N_2 is larger than N_1. Now consider the identity: $N_2 = N_1 + (N_2 - N_1)$. This states that the performance of Project N_2 is identical to the performance of Project N_1, modified by the addition of the performance of a notional 'differential' project, called Project ($N_2 - N_1$). So, if the performance of differential Project ($N_2 - N_1$) is acceptable (that is, if its IRR is greater than the MARR) Project N_2 is preferred to Project N_1, but not otherwise.

This technique is used in the table to put Projects D, E, F and G in priority order, by forming a series of differential projects. It yields a preference ranking of F–G–E–D. Note that this is more easily obtained by simple comparison of the NPVs (evaluated at the MARR) of the original Projects D, E, F and G.

than NPV methods because rate of return is a familiar notion. Indeed, they may insist on basing their project choice decisions on IRR values. (This is a pity, because using IRR values to decide between two projects which are competing for the same resources is always more tedious than using an NPV approach. And it can be impossible.)

The differential method described here is based on a rationale similar to that which underpins the aggregate method examined earlier.

Suppose that the two projects to be compared are called N_1 and N_2, where N_2 is larger than N_1 in the sense that it requires a larger initial investment. A third *notional* project, called the **differential project**, can be formed by applying the identity

$$N_2 = N_1 + (N_2 - N_1) \qquad \qquad \textbf{(11.10)}$$

to the corresponding cash-flow increments which model Projects N_1 and N_2. In effect, the identity states that the performance of Project N_2 is identical to the performance of Project N_1 modified by the addition of the performance of Project $(N_2 - N_1)$. So:

- if the performance of differential Project $(N_2 - N_1)$ is acceptable, Project N_2 is preferred to Project N_1, but not otherwise.

An example is needed to make this more clear. The performance of the four differential projects associated with Projects D, E, F and G (from Table 11.9) is shown in Table 11.11. MARR remains at 12.00% as before.

There are four differential projects because Project D is first compared with a 'nil-investment' project. This is not an entirely pointless piece of symmetric pedantry, because it does demonstrate that investing in Project D is better than not investing at all. The other three projects are formed by taking Projects D, E, F and G two at a time and subtracting the cash-flows in corresponding periods. The direction of the subtraction is always such that differential projects start with a negative increment, indicating investment.

IRR considerations

Consider first the IRR performance measures of the differential projects in relation to the MARR of 12.00%. The IRR for Project $(D - 0)$ is greater than the MARR so Project D, which is the larger of the two projects, is selected to go forward for comparison with Project E. Similarly, Project E is selected to go forward for comparison with Project F and, subsequently, Project F goes forward for comparison with Project G. But the IRR of Project $(G - F)$, at 9.39%, is less than the MARR. This means that Project $(G - F)$ is not acceptable: that is, that Project F is preferred over Project G. This being the case the overall preference ranking is

F–G–E–D

as was determined earlier by a simple comparison of the NPVs (evaluated at the MARR) of the original Projects D, E, F and G.

NPV considerations

Note that the same conclusion can be reached by selecting the project to carry forward to the next comparison (if any) in accordance with the *sign* of the NPV of the differential project. If this is positive the larger original project is selected whereas, if it is negative, the smaller is selected.

NPV and IRR compared

Note, too, that the IRR and NPV tests for the differential projects now yield the same message, which is an advantage of the differential method. But formulating the differential projects and calculating their IRR values is not really necessary. Project ranking by a simple comparison of their NPVs yields the right answers more quickly and easily.

There is a potential hazard in formulating the differential projects which can limit the utility of the differential method. This is that the cash-flow model of a differential project may exhibit more than one sign change, which can result in more than one value of IRR for the model. The problem was examined in Section 11.13.3. It is quite general to IRR project evaluation methods, and is another good reason for avoiding them when it is possible to do so.

11.15 Cash-flow models and inflation

The problems that inflation imposes on the construction and evaluation of cash-flow models have been largely ignored up to this point. The omission was covered by assuming that rate of inflation is either zero or that discount rates have been adjusted to cope with it. This section examines some problems arising from inflation.

11.15.1 General remarks

Inflation is the term used to describe persistent increases in commodity prices which are *not* justified by a corresponding increase in the benefits provided by the commodities to their purchasers. Here the term **commodity** is used to mean any and every sort of purchased item. In principle, the phenomena of inflation applies to every sort of commodity: tangible products, service products and human effort. Inflation erodes the purchasing power of money.

Economists continue to debate the reasons for inflation and no attempt is made here to rehearse the various arguments. Begg *et al.* (1984) provide, in Chapter 27 of their text, a very readable overview of the whole topic, including an illuminating section on the costs of inflation.

There is almost universal agreement that inflation is a bad thing and government fiscal policies are generally focused at its removal. However, despite this attention, prices in Britain have increased every year since 1945 and other 'developed' economies show a similar pattern. The evaluation of cash-flow project models is based on numbers which purport to represent the future. Inflation is a current and future event. No discussion of discounted cash-flow techniques can sensibly ignore inflation.

There are no substantial conceptual difficulties in modifying DCF techniques to deal with inflation. The real problems are of a practical nature. In general, different commodities inflate at different rates and the problem of which rate (or which **basket** of weighted rates called an **index**) to use is ever present. A number of such indices are regularly updated and published in the business press. The best known are the Retail Prices Index (RPI) in Britain and the Consumer Price Index (CPI) in the USA. Historical records of all of these indices are widely available. But, even when an appropriate index for a particular situation has been selected, the problem is not over.

Future rates are of most interest when evaluating cash-flow project models. But history is not always a reliable guide to the future. Economists generally have a consistent record of inaccurate predictions. Forecasts made by politicians are no better, usually reflecting pious hope rather than analytic conviction.

Two facets of inflation are considered in this section. First, its impact on investment is reviewed so as to establish the **inflation rate** as a link between **nominal interest rates** and **real interest rates**. This is followed by a examination of DCF techniques in an inflationary environment. Three ways of handling inflation in that context are explored.

11.15.2   Inflation and interest rates

In an inflationary situation, the price of a quantity of a needed commodity increases with time. But, in some circumstances, an immediate purchase can be postponed until a later time. In this case, as an alternative to immediate purchase, the money available for the purchase could be lent (invested) to grow by earning interest in the interim period.

The question of whether it is better to purchase the commodity now or later then arises. It only makes (economic) sense to postpone the purchase if it will be possible to purchase a larger quantity of the commodity later with the purchase money which is available now. In other words, when it is possible to postpone purchasing, it makes sense to do so if the interest rate on money invested is still positive when corrected for inflation.

Correcting interest rates for the effects of inflation is now considered. First, however, some terms and variables are defined.

Some definitions

(1) The **annual inflation rate** (denoted by f) for a commodity is the proportionate increase in the unit price of the identical commodity in one year. Suppose the annual inflation rate for commodity X is five per cent. Then, if the price of a quantity of the commodity is £1 at the beginning of the year, the price of the same quantity at the end of the year is £1.05 [= £1(1 + f)]. Note that the purchasing power of £1 at the beginning of the year has eroded to £(1/1.05) at the end of the year. The erosion is slightly less than five per cent.

(2) The **nominal annual interest rate** (denoted by m) is the proportionate increase in the number of pounds obtained by investing £1 for one year in an interest earning situation. Thus, £1 invested for one year at a nominal annual interest rate of ten per cent becomes £1.10 [= £1(1 + m)].

(3) The **real annual interest rate** (denoted by a) is the proportionate increase in the amount of the commodity that can be purchased at the end of a year with the £1 that was invested at the beginning of the year.

The real interest rate

Now, suppose that f = five per cent for commodity X and m = ten per cent. The corresponding value of the real annual interest rate, a, is obtained by comparing the amount of commodity X which can be bought, with the £1, at the beginning of a year with the amount of the same commodity which can be bought at the end of the year, with the £1.10.

Let Q_0 be the number of units which can be bought at the beginning of the year (denoted by $t = 0$). Let Q_1 be the number of units which can be bought at the end of the year (denoted by $t = 1$). Then:

$$\text{At } t = 0, \text{ unit price} = \frac{\pounds 1}{Q_0}$$

$$\text{At } t = 1, \text{ unit price} = \frac{\pounds 1.05}{Q_0}$$

But, at $t = 1$, there is £1.10 available to purchase units. Therefore:

$$Q_1 = \frac{1.10}{1.05} Q_0 = 1.048 \, Q_0 \text{ (very nearly)}$$

So,

$$a = \frac{Q_1 - Q_0}{Q_0} = 4.8\% \text{ (very nearly)}$$

This sample result is easily generalized to yield an expression for the real annual interest rate, denoted by a. This is:

$$a = \frac{(1 + m)}{(1 + f)} - 1$$

or:

$$a = \frac{(m - f)}{(1 + f)} \tag{11.11}$$

Note that the magnitude of the real annual interest rate is less (but usually only slightly) than the simple difference of the annual nominal interest rate and the annual inflation rate. This is because the extra money available at the end of the year to purchase more of the commodity, has to purchase it at the inflated price. However, the $(1 + f)$ factor in Equation 11.11 is commonly (but sometimes unwisely) taken as unity. With this simplification, the real annual interest rate becomes the difference of the annual nominal interest rate and the annual inflation rate, which is, perhaps, its intuitive value.

Note, too, that the real annual interest rate is negative when the inflation rate, f, is greater than the nominal rate, m. Thus, if $f = 10\%$ and $m = 7\%$ then $a \simeq -3\%$ (-2.72% more exactly). Situations like this are not attractive to lenders: there is no future in paying, in real terms, for the privilege of lending money. The message of Equation 11.11 under these circumstances is 'buy now, not later'. This is one mechanism by which inflation encourages inflation.

11.15.3   Cash-flow models and inflation

There are two conventional analytic approaches to handling inflation when discounting techniques are used to evaluate cash-flow models. They are termed here the

1	Constant-value method					Composite-rate method		
	2	3	4	5	6	7	8	9
EOY n	Then-current incremental cash	Inflation factor at f% = 6.00	Constant-values incremental cash	Discount factor at d% = 12.00	PVs of constant-values incremental cash	Then-current incremental cash	Composite discount factor at (f+d+df)% 18.72	PVs of then-current incremental cash
0	0	1.0000	0	1.0000	0	0	1.0000	0
1	(40,000)	0.9434	(37,736)	0.8929	(33,693)	(40,000)	0.8423	(33,693)
2	12,500	0.8900	11,125	0.7972	8,869	12,500	0.7095	8,869
3	17,500	0.8396	14,693	0.7118	10,458	17,500	0.5976	10,458
4	20,000	0.7921	15,842	0.6355	10,068	20,000	0.5034	10,068
5	17,500	0.7473	13,077	0.5674	7,420	17,500	0.4240	7,420
6	12,500	0.7050	8,812	0.5066	4,464	12,500	0.3572	4,464
	SUM 40,000		Net CV 25,813		Net PV 7,587	SUM 40,000		Net PV 7,587
	IRR % 28.17		IRR % 20.92			IRR % 28.17		

Table 11.12 **Cash-flow models: two ways of handling inflation.**

Two conventional ways of handling inflation in DCF calculations are illustrated here. Column 2 is Project A from Table 11.3. It is (now) labelled 'then-current incremental cash' to emphasize that it defines the actual numbers of cash-flow pounds anticipated at the EOYs. These amounts are *not corrected* for inflation. Column 3 is the 'inflation factor', which is the eroded purchasing power of £1 at each EOY. Column 4, labelled 'constant-values incremental cash', is the 'corrected for inflation' cash-flow model equivalent of column 2, obtained by multiplying by the inflation factor. Note that Net CV is less than Sum, showing inflation erosion of the cash generated.

The cash-flow model of column 4 can now be evaluated by any or all of the techniques examined earlier. The MARR rate must be a 'zero-inflation' rate if it to be discounted. Columns 7 to 9 in the table illustrate the composite-rate method of inflation correction. This is essentially the same as the constant-value method of columns 2 to 6, but it corrects for inflation and does the discounting in one step rather than in two. The expression for the composite discount factor is derived in the text.

constant-value method and the **composite-rate method**. They amount to much the same thing, but the constant-value method is more illuminating. Both are demonstrated in Table 11.12.

The constant-value method

Column 1 of the table indicates the end of successive years and columns 2 to 6 inclusive illustrate the constant-value method. Column 2 is the incremental cash-flow model of Project A (from Table 11.3). This column is now labelled **then-current incremental cash**. This terminology emphasizes that the figures represent the actual numbers of pounds that it is anticipated will be spent or received at the end of the various years. These amounts of money have not yet been corrected to reflect the erosion of their purchasing power due to inflation. Note that this cash-flow profile sums to £40,000 at the end of Year 6, and its IRR is 28.17%.

The rate of inflation, f, is assumed (probably unwisely) to be constant over the whole six-year period. Now, the purchasing power of £1 available at the beginning of Year 1 (EOY = 0) erodes to £1/(1 + f) at the end of Year 1. Similarly, at the end of Year 2 its purchasing power is £1/(1 + f)^2 and so on, losing purchasing power in each successive year. Column 3 in the table is labelled **inflation factor**. It represents the purchasing power of £1 at the end of the successive years. Here, the rate of inflation is taken as 6.00% per annum: and £1 loses some 30% of its purchasing power over the six-year time horizon of the model cash-flow, because 1/(1.06)^6 is about 0.7.

Column 4 in the table, labelled **constant-values incremental cash**, is the then-current cash-flow profile of column 2 corrected for loss of purchasing power. It is obtained by multiplying corresponding figures in columns 2 and 3. Column 4 is the 'corrected for inflation' cash-flow model equivalent of the then-current cash-flow model of column 2. Note that the net sum of the constant-values (Net CV), at £25,813, is substantially less than the corresponding then-current figure of £40,000. The difference shows how the new cash generated by the project is eroded by inflation. The cash-flow model of column 4 can now be evaluated by any or all of the techniques examined earlier. The rate used must be a **zero-inflation** rate if it is discounted, because the inflation correction has already been done.

Here it is discounted at 12.00% (in columns 5 and 6) to yield a NPV of £7,587: indicating that the project is profitable at that discount rate even after inflation at 6.00% per annum. This is confirmed by its IRR figure of 20.92%. Note that this latter result could have been obtained more directly from Equation 11.11, by recognizing the IRR of column 2 as the nominal annual interest rate. Then,

$$\text{IRR of column 4} = \frac{28.17 - 6.00}{1 + 0.06} = 20.92\%$$

The composite-rate method

Columns 7 to 9 in the table illustrates the composite-rate method of inflation correction. This is essentially the same as the constant-value method, but it corrects for inflation and does the discounting in one step rather than in two.

Column 7 is merely a copy of column 2, but it is again labelled 'then-current' to emphasize that the figures it contains are numbers of pounds with different purchasing powers. Column 8 contains the **composite discount factor** derived (in the usual way) from a **composite (discount) rate**. This rate is a function of the inflation rate, f, and the zero-inflation discount rate, d.

An expression for the composite-rate, denoted by c here, is obtained by considering how column 2 in Table 11.12 is transformed into column 6. At the end of any year, n, the figure in column 2 is multiplied first by $1/(1 + f)^n$ and then by $1/(1 + d)^n$ to yield the figure in column 6. Expressing this in terms of the composite-rate gives:

$$\frac{1}{(1 + c)^n} = \frac{1}{(1 + f)^n} \times \frac{1}{(1 + d)^n}$$

or:

$$(1 + c) = (1 + f)(1 + d)$$

or:

$$c = f + d + df \tag{11.12}$$

So, if f = 6.00% and d = 12.00% then c = 18.72%, as in the table. Note that column 9 is identical to column 6, thereby demonstrating the sameness of the two methods.

In developing the twin approaches for the analytical treatment of inflation the rate of inflation, f, has been assumed constant over the whole period. This assumption is not likely to apply in practice. But it is quite straightforward to use different inflation rates in different years so this is only a minor inconvenience (from the calculation point of view).

11.15.4 Inflation: A summary

In summary, the two *analytic* options for dealing with inflation are:

(1) Express the cash-flow model in constant-value amounts and then use a zero-inflation discount rate and/or compare the IRR with a zero-inflation MARR. This is the constant-value method demonstrated in columns 2 to 6 of Table 11.12. The constant-value amounts of column 4 are obtained from the then-current amounts of column 2 by applying the inflation factor of column 3.

(2) Express all cash-flows in then-current amounts and then use a composite discount rate and/or compare the IRR with a composite MARR. This is the composite-rate method demonstrated in columns 7 to 9 of Table 11.12. The composite discount rate accounts incorporates both the inflation rate and a zero-inflation discount rate.

There is a third, quite popular, approach to inflation in this cash-flow evaluation context. This is to ignore it. It is an attractive solution to an uncomfortable practical problem, because correctly predicting inflation rates is not easy. Perhaps the best justification for adopting this approach can be illustrated by inspecting Table 11.12 again, but from a different perspective.

When a cash-flow model is first constructed it is generally in constant-value terms. That is, the future incremental cash-flows are expressed in terms of the purchasing power of current pounds: inflation is assumed to be zero. In Table 11.12 this means that, in practice, column 4 comes first rather than column 2, as the structure of the table suggests. This being the case, and provided that the appropriate MARR is employed, there seems little virtue in creating cash-flow models which incorporate inflation. In other words, column 2 is redundant in the constant-value method, and the composite-rate method is merely an intellectual curiosity.

There is merit in this argument. But it still puts a figure on inflation because it cites an 'appropriate' MARR. And it becomes more dubious when the reality of time-varying inflation rates is recognized. There are also occasions when inflation must be specifically forecast and included in estimates. Bidding for a contract offered by an external agency is one example.

On balance, it is recommended that inflation is explicitly accounted for in evaluating cash-flow models. The constant-value approach, while a little more long-winded than the composite-rate equivalent, is probably better structured to deal with time-varying inflation rates.

11.16   Project Evaluation Tool 2 (PET2)

The discussion of cash-flow evaluation now concludes with a description of a way of using DCF techniques in the planning of product creation projects. It is focused on a spreadsheet program called **Project Evaluation Tool 2** (PET2). PET2 is a financial performance assessment and planning aid which complements the PET1A and PET1B tools described earlier (in Section 11.7). Those tools assist the construction of evaluation profiles for examining projects in the context of the whole business.

Table 11.13 is a sample output from PET2, obtained at an early stage in preparing a business plan which will (ultimately) describe a particular product creation project. The table is divided horizontally into four parts, concerned with project timing, investment (costs), return (net income) and financial performance. Each part is now considered.

11.16.1   Part 1: Phase durations

The project is partitioned into three sequential phases relating to:

> Phase 1   Preparing the business plan
> Phase 2   Preparing the manufacturing data
> Phase 3   Manufacturing and selling the product

Phases 1 and 2 together comprise the initial investment period of the project, which includes the product development and design project. Phase 3 is the return period of the project. Referring back to Figure 11.6, which graphs the project cash-flow model, phases 1 and 2 of Table 11.13 correspond to the period S to C and phase 3 corresponds to the period C to D in that earlier figure.

Three-times estimating

The expected duration of each phase is derived using a technique called **three-times estimating**, which is described more fully in Section 6.4.5. In summary, the expected duration of a phase is derived from three other estimates called the **optimistic time** (t_O), the **most likely time** (t_M) and the **pessimistic time** (t_P). The **expected time** (t_E) is then given by:

Phase durations (months)		Optimistic	Most likely	Pessimistic	Expected	Expected cumulative (months)
Phase 1	Prepare business plan	3.0	3.0	3.0	3.0	3.0
Phase 2	Prepare manufacturing data	5.0	6.0	7.0	6.0	9.0
Phase 3	Manufacturing and sales	46.0	42.0	38.0	42.0	51.0

Investment (£K)		Optimistic	Most likely	Pessimistic	Expected	Expected average (£K/mth)
1.1	Prepare business plan	3.5	3.5	3.5	3.5	1.2
2.1	Project management	16.7	20.0	23.3	20.0	
2.2	Marketing and sales	4.6	5.5	7.0	5.6	
2.3	Development and design	160.0	230.0	250.0	221.7	
2.4	Production engineering	47.0	52.4	57.0	52.3	
2.5	Factory costs	9.0	10.2	11.0	10.1	
	Total Phase 2	237.3	318.1	348.3	309.7	51.6
Phase 1+2	Total investment	240.8	321.6	351.8	313.2	34.8

Return (£K)		Optimistic	Most likely	Pessimistic	Expected	Expected average (£K/mth)
3.1	Sales revenue	3,900.0	3,700.0	3,400.0	3,683.3	
Less 3.2	Factory costs	(2,535.0)	(2,590.0)	(2,550.0)	(2,574.2)	
Less 3.3	Project management	(117.0)	(140.0)	(163.0)	(140.0)	
Less 3.4	Distribution	(156.0)	(185.0)	(204.0)	(183.3)	
Less 3.5	Units returned	(39.0)	(55.5)	(68.0)	(54.8)	
Less 3.6	Marketing and sales	(234.0)	(296.0)	(340.0)	(293.0)	
Less 3.7	Development and design					
Less 3.8	Production engineering					
	Total return	819.0	433.5	75.0	438.0	10.4

Performance of the expected cash-flow
@ MARR % = 15.0 compound annual rate

	Maximum invest.	Break-even	Maximum return	End ratio	NPV	
Undiscounted (£K)	313.2	*	438.0	1.4	124.8	0%
Discounted at MARR (£K)	290.6		310.1	1.1	19.5	MARR %
At month number	9	40	51	51	0	

IRR % = 19.1 Compound annual rate

Table 11.13   **Project Evaluation Tool 2: an example.**
This is a sample print-out from a project plan evaluation tool used as a financial performance
assessment and planning aid. It comprises four parts, concerned with project timing, investment
(costs), return (net income) and financial performance. A 'statistical' estimating technique
(described in Section 6.4.5) is used to obtain the 'expected' values of the various plan parameters.
Plan evaluation is based on the expected phase durations and average monthly rates for
investment and return. These figures are in the right-hand column. They are used to construct an
incremental cash-flow model for the project which is then evaluated using DCF techniques. The
results are summarized in the performance section at the bottom of the table.

$$t_E = \frac{t_O + 4t_M + t_P}{6} \tag{11.13}$$

The statistical argument behind this relationship is fragile, and the definitions of 'optimistic', 'most likely' and 'pessimistic' included in Chapter 6 are not very precise. But the formula is generally found to provide better results than a single estimate, perhaps because it encourages realism in the estimators.

The last column in this first part of the table shows the expected whole project time-scale. This is the sum of the expected phase durations, and it amounts to 51 months in this example.

11.16.2 Part 2: Investment

The project investment costs are incurred on a number of sub-projects of which the first (1.1 in the table) is 'Prepare the business plan' and the largest (2.3 in the table) is 'Development and design'. Other sub-projects are concerned with project management, pre-launch marketing and sales activity, some production engineering work, and the fabrication of a few product samples in the factory to prove the manufacturing data.

The expected total cost of each of these sub-projects is also estimated on an optimistic, most likely, pessimistic basis in a manner analogous to that used for time estimating.

The last column in this second part of the table indicates the *average* expected cost per month during phases 1 and 2: obtained by dividing a total expected phase cost by the expected phase duration. The purpose of these average expenditure figures is explained later.

11.16.3 Part 3: Return

The total project return, or net total income, is obtained by subtracting a number of different phase 3 cost totals from the total revenue arising from product sales. The costs are items 3.2 to 3.8 in the table. The largest, by far, are the factory costs (item 3.2). These are the (anticipated) costs of manufacturing products for sale. Once again, the optimistic, most likely, and pessimistic method is used to obtain the expected totals.

The last column in this third part of the table indicates the average expected return per month during phase 3: about £10.4K per month for 42 months in this example.

11.16.4 Part 4: Financial performance

The last part of Table 11.13 is an approximate evaluation of the financial performance of the project.

The evaluation is largely based on the expected phase durations and the expected average monthly rates for investment and return. These figures are in the last column of the table. They are used to construct an incremental cash-flow model for the project which comprises:

(1) Negative increments of £1.2K at the end of Months 1, 2 and 3.

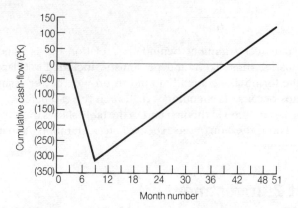

Figure 11.14   **PET 2 example: assumed cumulative cash-flow.**

This figure complements the PET 2 sample print-out of Table 11.13. It is a plot of the cumulative cash-flow version of incremental cash-flow project model developed in that table. It emphasizes the linear nature of the approximation, which stems from using the average incremental cash-flows. It is quite adequate, however, for its purpose as a project planning aid.

(2) Negative increments of £51.6K at the end of Months 4 to 9 inclusive.

(3) Positive increments of £10.4K at the end of Months 10 to 51 inclusive.

The cumulative cash-flow version of this model is shown in Figure 11.14. It emphasizes the linear nature of the approximation, which stems from using the average incremental cash-flows. It is quite adequate, however, for its purpose as a project planning aid.

In this example, the business has set a MARR of fifteen per cent compound annual rate and the NPV is calculated by discounting the incremental cash-flow model at this rate. The IRR for the cash-flow is obtained by using a built-in function provided in the spreadsheet software. The **end ratio** is another measure of the performance of the cash-flow. It is obtained by dividing the maximum return by the maximum investment. This is a rather crude measure, because it has no inherent time sensitivity.

Annual and monthly compound interest rates

Note that the MARR is set as compound annual rate. But a compound monthly rate is required for discounting, because the incremental periods are months. For the same reason the IRR is first calculated as a compound monthly rate but it is required as a compound annual rate.

The equivalence relationship between an interest rate, a, which is compounded annually and an annual interest rate, m, which is compounded monthly is:

$$(1 + a) = (1 + m/12)^{12} \tag{11.14}$$

Translations between the two forms of rate are built into the spreadsheet program in accordance with this equation.

11.16.5   PET2 summary

The sample cash-flow models employed during the earlier exploration of discounting were expressed in convenient yearly increments. These are rarely encountered in real-life situations. The PET2 example, which is expressed in periods of one month, demonstrates how such situations can be handled. The principles employed can be easily extended to provide more or less detail, as required by project circumstances.

PET2 does not have to be implemented as a spreadsheet program. However, this expression of the tool is particularly useful, because it enables rapid exploration of *'what-if'* type questions. For example, suppose that the MARR has been set and that good estimates for all costs other than those for the product design and development (PD&D) project exist. The maximum acceptable cost of the PD&D project can then be rapidly determined by observing the behaviour of the performance parameters as this cost is varied.

When tools of this nature are used in practice, staff costs are normally calculated in conventional 'labour and overhead' terms, as discussed in Section 7.7.1. Purists may point out that the inclusion of an overhead element in these costs compromises their treatment as cash-flows. This is a valid point, but it is best ignored. As a rule, correcting for the approximation is too complicated to contemplate seriously and it is not justified by a commensurate improvement in the results.

11.17   Concluding summary

Technology offers opportunities to those businesses which use it wisely, and poses threats to those businesses which do not. Part of using it wisely lies in choosing the right technological innovation projects. This requires that the proposals for such projects – the project plans – are evaluated in the light of some pre-determined criteria.

Proposals for research projects can be checked for alignment with the techno-logical strategy of the business, and their quality as stand-alone project plans can be assessed. But it is not possible to evaluate them as prospective financial investments. This is most disturbing in the case of applied research, because those projects can absorb substantial resources.

Proposals for product development and design projects are the most critical. These projects usually absorb the greater part of the available technical innovation resources and have a relatively immediate impact on the future of the business. Proposals should be assessed both for stand-alone quality and for their financial investment merits. This latter requirement can only be met by recognizing that a product development and design project is part of a larger product creation project.

The financial investment and return features of a product creation project are encapsulated in its cash-flow model. Possible evaluation techniques for such models range from inspecting simple shape parameters through forward compounding to discounting. The NPV method of discounting is the most satisfactory. But it is some-times necessary to use the less useful IRR approach. The realities of inflation should be incorporated into cash-flow models and this presents no analytic problems. In practice, coping with inflation in cash-flow models is fraught with difficulty. This is because accurate forecasts of inflation rates are rarely achieved.

The preparation and subsequent evaluation of project proposals requires an insight into the future. The probability that such predictions will be totally accurate is vanishingly small and diminishes as the time-scale of the prediction increases. Numerical values are attached to some predictions for investment/return evaluation purposes. Most of the investment evaluation techniques explored in this chapter involve massaging such numbers. There is a human tendency to assume that manipulating numerical forecasts somehow improves their quality. This is sometimes valid when statistical data is processed. Otherwise, the assumption is a snare and delusion to be guarded against.

The cash-flow evaluation techniques described in this chapter are applicable to a wide range of business situations which can be described in cash-flow terms. Examples are lease or buy alternatives for equipment provisioning, assessing the relative merits of different items of production machinery and questions relating to different machinery maintenance schedules.

REFERENCES

Begg D. K. H., Fischer S. and Dornbusch R. (1984). *Economics*. Maidenhead: McGraw-Hill. (A US edition is also available)

Kaplan R. S. (1986). Must CIM be justified by faith alone? *Harvard Business Review*, **64**(2), 87–95

Twiss B. C. (1986). *Managing Technological Innovation* 3rd edn. London: Longman

White J. A., Agee M. H. and Case K. E. (1989). *Principles of Engineering Economic Analysis* 3rd edn. New York: John Wiley

SUGGESTED FURTHER READING

Twiss (1986) (cited above as a reference), Oakley (1984) and Parker (1985) are specialist texts which give detailed attention to the problems of evaluating and selecting basic and applied research projects. Waters (1989) gives a straightforward introductory account of discounted cash-flow techniques. These methods are developed in more detail in the various specialist accounting texts cited, of which Sizer (1989) is particularly good value. Parkin (1990) is another splendid economics text offering, among many other things, a highly readable account of inflation.

Arnold J. and Hope T. (1990). *Accounting for Management Decisions* 2nd edn. Hemel Hempstead: Prentice-Hall

Canada J. R. and White J. A. (1980). *Capital Investment Decision Analysis for Management and Engineering*. Englewood Clifs, NJ: Prentice-Hall

Horngren C. T. and Sundem G. L. (1990). *Introduction to Management Accounting* 8th edn. Englewood Cliffs, NJ: Prentice-Hall

Oakley M. (1984). *Managing Product Design*. London: Weidenfeld & Nicolson

Parker R. C. (1985). *Going for Growth*. Chichester: John Wiley

Parkin M. (1990). *Economics*. Reading, MA: Addison-Wesley (Chapter 22). A British edition is also available: Parkin M. and King D. (1992). *Economics*. Wokingham: Addison-Wesley

Sizer J. (1989). *An Insight into Management Accounting*. Harmondsworth: Penguin

Waters C. D. J. (1989). *A Practical Introduction to Management Science*. Wokingham: Addison-Wesley

QUESTIONS

Note: EOY = end of year, NPV = net present value, IRR = internal rate of return and MARR = minimum attractive rate of return.

11.1 (a) Why should a business invest in technology?
(b) Why is a proposal to launch a technical project also an investment proposal?
(c) What problems are shared by all investors? What additional problems are faced by investors in technology?
(d) How, in broad terms, can these additional problems be tackled?

11.2 Explain the following concepts:
- major and minor product technologies
- a family hierarchy of technologies
- a product as technological recipe
- the configuration view of a product
- the competitive technological status of a product
- foundation, critical and looming technologies
- technological life cycles.

11.3 The 'smart' telephone example in Section 11.2.1 illustrates how a product can be described as a blend of technologies. Using this as a guide, create such a description for any other product and rank the competitive importance of its constituent technologies on a five-point scale.

11.4 Summarize the purposes of basic research and applied research, with special emphasis on features which distinguish projects in these two types of research.

11.5 Summarize the purposes of product development and design, with special emphasis on features which distinguish development and design projects, including their time relationship.

11.6 Sections 11.2.1, 11.2.2 and 11.2.3, which contain about 1600 words, comprise an integrated summary of the strategic and tactical aspects of technological innovation as presented in this book. Summarize their principal messages in not more than 400 words. (Note-format and diagrams are allowed, even encouraged.)

11.7 The level of technical uncertainty in new product definition diminishes as product creation progresses through basic research, applied research, product development, product design and manufacturing.
(a) Illustrate this process with a diagram and identify seven project parameters and one management, or business, parameter which increase during the process.
(b) Which single parameter from this multitude of parameters provides an objective indicator of technical project type during the process?

11.8 Describe the format of a typical technical project proposal.

11.9 (a) Show how criteria for evaluating project proposals can be structured into an 'importance' hierarchy.
(b) Why is this a useful concept?

11.10 Section 11.4, which contains about 1800 words, outlines the background and procedures concerned with the evaluation and choice of private venture research projects in a large technology-based manufacturing business. The presentation has a serial structure. Summarize the principal messages in this section into not more than 450 words and arrange the summary in a parallel structure, as illustrated below:

- technological strategy and private venture research projects
- funding mechanisms for private venture research projects
- selection mechanisms for private venture research projects
- a staffing policy for basic research.

(Note-format and diagrams are allowed, even encouraged).

11.11   (a) In the context of evaluating and choosing private venture PD&D project proposals as stand-alone items:

- *Why* is choosing the right projects a business survival issue?
- *What* features of a proposed project must be evaluated?
- *How* are these features evaluated?

(b) Why are requests sometimes made to reduce the estimated time and/or cost needed to complete a proposed PD&D project? What problem does this present to the project planners? How can they best resolve it?

(c) Why is it not (sensibly) possible to evaluate a proposed PD&D project as a stand-alone financial investment/return proposition?

11.12   (a) What (briefly) is a 'product creation project'?

(b) Describe the origin, purpose and content of a 'product brief'?

(c) Describe, with the aid of a diagram, the nature of a product creation project in terms of a two-stage structure comprising a planning phase and an implementation phase. The description should list the major elements of the plan, explain their purposes, and show how they relate to the implementation phase.

(d) What are the overall purposes of the project plan? Show how the project

structure serves these purposes.

11.13   (a) Describe the use of 'profile techniques' for evaluating aspects of a product business plan other than its financial investment/return prospects.

(b) Do the advantages of such schemes outweigh their disadvantages? Would a profile evaluation help to answer that last question?

11.14   (a) Explain the meaning of the terms:

- profit
- cash-flow
- positive cash-flow
- negative cash-flow
- incremental cash-flow
- cumulative cash-flow.

(b) Show how the predicted financial consequences of a product creation project can be expressed as a cash-flow model by devising, and explaining, a diagram which:

- combines the structure of Figure 11.5 with
- the concepts of the sales life cycle and cumulative cash-flow.

State the principal assumptions incorporated in the model, and the consequences if they are not met in practice.

(c) Why is the ratio:

$$\frac{\text{Cumulative cash-flow at the end of the project } (R_{MAX})}{\text{Most negative cumulative cash-flow during the project } (I_{MAX})}$$

of special interest? Why is the amount of elapsed time between I_{MAX} and R_{MAX} of special interest?

11.15   (a) Sketch a typical cumulative cash-flow diagram for an investment/return project which shows the position and magnitude of:

- the maximum investment (I_{MAX})
- the time (T_C) when the incremental cash-flow becomes positive
- the time to break-even (T_{BE})
- the return (R_T) defined as net cumulative positive cash-flow

- the maximum return (R_{MAX})
- the time (T_D) when the incremental cash-flow becomes zero.

(b) Describe eight criteria, based on these project parameters, which can be used to compare the relative investment merits of different cash-flow models. Why is comparing such merits often important?

(c) This technique fails under certain circumstances. Describe some of these circumstances.

11.16 (a) Why does it cost money to get money to invest? Why does this mean that negative cash-flow costs money? (Hint: These questions ask 'why?', not 'how much?') If negative cash-flow costs money, does positive cash-flow earn money?

(b) Show how these notions contribute to the concept of the 'minimum attractive rate of return (MARR)' financial viability criterion for investment projects.

(c) 'The concept of the MARR effectively establishes an interest rate regime for the business in which it can either borrow or lend money at the MARR.' What are the features of the MARR concept, and how does it meet this claim?

11.17 (a) Describe a compounding forward technique, which explicitly recognizes investment costs, for evaluating investment project cash-flows. Why is this a better evaluation technique than those techniques which consider only the 'shape' of cash-flow profiles?

(b) Project A is modelled in Table 11.3. Evaluate this project as an investment/return situation, using the compounding forward technique described in (a) above, at an MARR of 18% per annum compound. (Hint: Table 11.5 provides an appropriate format for the calculations.)

11.18 (a) Assuming that the true (that is, after allowing for inflation) zero-risk compound interest rate is 3% per annum, how long will it take to (really) double your money in a zero-risk investment situation?

(b) A future sum (FS) is to be received in n years time, during which period the interest rate regime is r per annum compounded annually. Derive an expression for the present value (PV) of this future sum.

(c) In Figure 11.9, the series of future sums (£1 at the end of Year 0, £1 at the end of Year 1 and so on) can be regarded as a sequence of positive cash-flow increments comprising a cash-flow model. Calculate the NPV of this model in an interest rate regime, r, of 20%. (Hint: Now might be a good time to look at Appendix B.)

(d) Repeat the calculation requested in (c) above, but assume that the first three cash-flow increments are negative (that is, costs) rather than positive (that is, incomes).

(e) The cash-flow sequence established in (d) above could represent an investment project, because it starts with (investment) costs and then returns incomes. Is it an attractive investment project? Explain your answer.

11.19 (a) A company is considering the relative merits of two product creation projects, called Project P and Project Q, which are mutually exclusive. It has been agreed that the most likely incremental cash-flow profiles are as in the table below.

The company has set a financial acceptability threshold of 10% per annum compound for such projects. What investment options are open to the company? Which of these options should

		Cash in/(out) (£M)				
	EOY 0	EOY 1	EOY 2	EOY 3	EOY 4	EOY 5
Project P	(1.50)	0.25	0.50	0.75	0.50	0.50
Project Q	(1.25)	0.50	0.75	0.50	0.25	0.25

it choose *on the basis of the given data*? Is this the best choice?

(b) Calculate the NPVs of projects P and Q at an MARR of 28%. Comment on the results.

(c) List the good and bad features of the NPV cash-flow evaluation technique.

11.20 (a) When evaluated at an MARR of 10%, the NPV of a particular project is £0.53M. Calculate the single values, in the same MARR regime, occurring at the end of Years 1, 2, 3, 4 and 5 which are equivalents of this project.

(b) Show that, in the same MARR regime, this project is also equivalent to a project comprising a series of payments of (MARR × NPV) at the end of Years 1 to 5 inclusive plus a payment of NPV at the end of Year 5.

11.21 'The IRR of Project Q, described in Question 11.19 (a), is about 28.13%.' What does this statement mean?

11.22 Two variations of Project B (see Table 11.3) were postulated in Section 11.9.3, to illustrate the limitations of evaluation techniques based on the 'shape' of cash-flow models. The original project is labelled B1 in the table below, and the variations are called B2 and B3.

(a) Compare the NPVs of projects B1, B2 and B3, computed at a MARR of 18%, and the IRR of each project.

(b) Rank Projects B1, B2 and B3 in order of financial merit.

(Hint: Save yourself some work – the projects are very similar.)

11.23 In December 1990 a company was considering the launch, in January 1991, of a product creation project. It was assumed that manufacturing and sales would start in January 1993 and that the product sales lifetime would be four years. The following incremental cash-flow estimates were agreed:

In 1991: PD&D costs = £675K
In 1992: PD&D, marketing and production start-up costs = £1,050K
In 1993: Net income from sales = £675K
In 1994: Net income from sales = £900K
In 1995: Net income from sales = £675K
In 1996: Net income from sales = £450K

(a) Calculate, using the tables in Appendix B or otherwise, the approximate (to 1 decimal place) maximum cost of borrowing at which the project can still break even.

(b) In January 1991, the company borrowed £675K at 15% per annum compounded annually and launched the project. In December 1991, a review of the project revealed that:

- the cost of further borrowing would be 20% per annum compounded annually
- the £675K PD&D cost planned for 1991 had been spent
- the initial PD&D estimate was faulty, and a further £250K would have to be spent in 1992 to complete the work
- the competitive situation had changed such that the estimates for net income from sales were reduced by £200K in each of the years 1993, 1994, 1995 and 1996
- other estimates remained valid.

| | Cash in/(out) (£K) | | | | | | |
	EOY 1	EOY 2	EOY 3	EOY 4	EOY 5	EOY 6	EOY 7
Project B1	(65)	15	25	25	20	20	–
Project B2	(65)	15	25	25	30	40	–
Project B3	(65)	15	25	25	20	20	20

Analyse the financial implications of this new situation and, hence, suggest what course of action the company should consider.

(c) How could the problem posed by the the increase in borrowing rate with effect from January 1992 have been minimized?

11.24   A company is evaluating the investment merits of two possible projects, called Project X and Project Y. Their incremental cash-flow models are as outlined in the table below and the company is not able to invest more than £75,000.

(a) Calculate:

- the NPV of both projects at an MARR of 14%
- the NPV of both projects at an MARR of 22%
- the IRR of both projects.

(b) Explain the results of these calculations and, assuming that there are no other factors to take into account, advise how the company should invest the available funds.

11.25   (a) Explain, in the context of commodity price inflation, the meaning of the following terms:

- annual inflation rate (denoted by f)
- nominal annual interest rate (denoted by m)
- real annual interest rate (denoted by a)

(b) Show that the real interest rate is related to the inflation and nominal rates by the expression:

$$a = (m - f)/(1 + f)$$

(c) Under what circumstances does this relationship suggest 'buy now, not later', and why is this so?

11.26   Describe the 'constant-value method' of incorporating the effects of inflation into cash-flow models.

| | | | Cash in/(out) £K | | | |
	EOY 1	EOY 2	EOY 3	EOY 4	EOY 5	EOY 6
Project X	(52)	25	20	20	20	15
Project Y	(75)	25	30	30	30	25

Basic Financial Accounting

*Annual income £20, annual expenditure
£19.975, result happiness.
Annual income £20, annual expenditure
£20.025, result misery.*

*Charles Dickens 1812–1870
(slightly modified to incorporate decimal
currency)*

12.1	Introduction	552
12.2	Basic accounting principles	555
12.3	The birth of Adastra	571
12.4	Adastra: The end of Year 1	585
12.5	Adastra: Year 1 accounts analysis	596
12.6	Concluding summary	613

Advanced material The derivation and interpretation of funds flow statements commonly causes engineers more consternation than do the source accounts on which they are based. The method used here is chosen to appeal to engineers, but it remains a little more challenging than the rest of the material. So Sections 12.3.6 and 12.5.2 may be omitted at first reading.

Repetitions The financial aspects of business operations were introduced in Chapter 1 (*Business basics*) and some of that material is necessarily repeated in this chapter. In particular, Sections 1.6, 1.7 and 1.8 built and exercised a 'physical financial' model of an established manufacturing business. That material was classified as 'somewhat demanding' for readers with no prior knowledge of business notions. It complements rather than competes with this chapter, which builds and develops a broader perception of the same model. A concept introduced in Chapter 7 (*About cost and costing*) is used later in the chapter as an analytic tool to extract some less obvious information from a P&L account. All these repetitions are detailed below.

Some material in Section 12.2.1, about accounting entities, was first covered in Section 1.2.3.

Section 1.6 was a selective summary of Sections 12.2.2 to 12.2.6 inclusive, which describes some primary accounting principles.

Sections 1.7 and 1.8 covered much the same material as Section 12.3 (the birth and first active month of a new company), but from a rather different perspective. The approach in Chapter 1 developed a *physical* model of an *established* manufacturing business and exercised it over a *complete trading cycle*. It complements, rather than repeats, the accounting story starting at Section 12.3.

Section 12.5.3 illustrates the use of break-even notions to analyse a profit and loss account. The break-even concept was introduced in Section 7.6.2 and was explored in some depth in Section 7.9.

The overall objectives of this chapter are to introduce the basic principles of financial accounting and illustrate their use and language in an extended example. Engineers often find it difficult to grasp accounting concepts which, when first experienced, seem to describe an abstract and unreal world. But engineers are accustomed to manipulating equations. So the approach adopted here focuses on the accounting model of a business expressed in the 'balance sheet' equation and its variants. It differs in this respect from more conventional introductions to accounting. Discussion is limited to traditional 'historical cost' accounting which ignores inflation. The book-keeping aspect of accounting is not covered. Objectives by section follow:

12.1 To explain the general nature and major purposes of business accounting, why engineers should be competent users of accounting data and the structure of the chapter.

12.2 To describe the most important principles, techniques, conventions and terminologies of accounting.

12.3 To introduce the basic accounting model of a business by tracking the creation of a small company from inception to the end of its first trading month.

12.4 To extend the overview of Section 12.3 by describing the preparation of the profit and loss account and balance sheet which report the financial results of the company's first trading year.

12.5 To illustrate how the primary accounts developed in Section 12.4 are analysed to reveal illuminating insights into the business by determining its flow of funds, the minimum activity level for profitable operation, and the ratios between selected parameters.

12.6 To identify its salient points and summarize its major messages.

12.1 | Introduction

A business must make adequate profits to ensure its long-term survival, and it must consistently make profits greater than the survival threshold to prosper. The overriding requirement for profit underpins every aspect of business management. It is the central theme of this book.

Management skill is the most critical factor determining profit performance and, hence, the prospects of a business. But even the most expert managers can only succeed if they have up-to-date information about that profit performance. This information is provided in **management accounts**. A new set of these accounts is prepared and issued periodically (monthly, say). Within this set, there are three major accounts which are concerned with the *whole* business. Each reports on one distinct aspect of the financial affairs of the business. The major accounts are:

(1) A **balance sheet**, which states the financial condition of the business as it stands at the end of a specific period. This statement is concerned with resources. It puts a value on those resources which belong to the business and shows how it acquired them.

(2) A **profit and loss account**, which reports the income earned and the cost incurred by the business during the specific period. This enables the profit earned (or loss incurred) for the period to be calculated. The way in which this profit is used (or loss is absorbed) may also be shown.

(3) A **funds flow statement**, which illustrates how funds have moved into, out of, and around the business during the specific period. The availability of **liquid funds** (cash or 'near-cash') is also shown.

A funds flow statement is derived from the associated balance sheet and profit and loss account. So it contains no new information, but it does present some existing information in a more useful way. The three major accounts are normally accompanied by an analysis which reveals how the overall position was achieved and suggests how it might be improved in the future.

In addition to the three major accounts, a set of management accounts generally includes a multitude of other financial reports. These relate to individual facets of the business. For example, the production control manager needs periodic reports on stock holdings for scheduling purposes. Similarly, technical project managers need to compare cost with progress on a regular basis. This chapter is not about that very broad range of diverse and detailed financial reports. It is about the three major accounting statements.

Businesses which are also companies are required to *publish* statements of financial status and performance at least once a year. These **final company accounts** are based on the major reports circulated more frequently inside the business.

Accounts and accounting are about money. Their purposes, language and techniques form a common thread which links all the distinct functions which comprise a business. There are a number of reasons why engineers need to understand something of these matters:

- The engineering role in technological innovation (basic and applied research, product development and design, and production engineering) is part of the profit-making process. Engineers must communicate with, negotiate with, and sell their ideas to accountants and other financially literate managers.

- The costing and costs of technical projects and of products are fundamental engineering topics (which are discussed in Sections 7.7 and 7.8). They are also fundamental accounting topics.

- Some engineers develop into technical and generalist managers within the business or within the industry of which it is a part. Financial competence is a prerequisite for career progression of this sort.

- Many engineers are potential business entrepreneurs in their own right, with an inclination to launch their own business enterprise. To do so without some knowledge of accounting is an invitation to disaster, which is too often accepted.

12.1.1   About accounting in general

The financial concerns of a business cover a spectrum from longer-term strategic issues to the day-to-day tactics of current operations. **Accounting** (as distinct from **finance**) is generally considered to be at the tactical end of this spectrum, linking into business strategy through the budgeting process. Budgeting is reviewed in Section 7.4. It translates immediate business objectives into financial plans (budgets) for a forthcoming financial year. Accounting is then the process of:

- identifying
- measuring
- recording
- classifying
- monitoring (comparing with plan)
- analysing
- communicating

the financial information arising from the operations of the business. The first four activities on this list make up the **bookkeeping** aspect of accounting. It is the essential, but not very interesting, prerequisite to the latter part of the process. This latter part summarizes the bookkeeping data into specific reports and statements designed to meet the needs of a range of different users. The users fall into two broad categories: those outside the business and those inside the business. Their needs are so different that, after the bookkeeping stage, two types of accounting are recognized. They are termed **financial accounting** and **management accounting**. Both employ the same accounting principles and both stem from a common bookkeeping activity, so they are distinguished by purpose rather than method.

Financial accounting

The primary purpose of financial accounting is to provide financial information about the business to interested parties outside the business. These include owners (shareholders), stock market analysts, investors, lenders (such as banks), customers, suppliers, trade unions, trade associations, taxation authorities, other government departments and economists. The information is published in the form of the three major accounts previously described (balance sheet, profit and loss account and funds flow statement), together with some explanatory notes. When these are issued as company accounts, they must comply with certain statutory requirements. These define (in terms of type and detail) the minimum amount of information that must be included. (This legal minimum is rarely exceeded, because the information is available to competitors and there is nothing gained by telling them more than the law allows them to know.) Final company accounts, which report on a complete trading year, must also be **audited** (verified as a 'true and fair view') by an independent qualified authority. The content and format of published accounts is also greatly influenced by the various professional accountancy institutions. Their requirements impose a degree of standardization on published accounts which is not dependent on the nature of the company concerned.

Management accounting

The purpose of management accounting is to provide financial information about the business to interested parties inside the business. These are mostly the managers at various levels. They need the information to help them plan, monitor, control and improve financial performance within their area of responsibility. Much of this information is provided in the form of internal reports which are customized for particular purposes. Examples include the 'resource tables' of Table 6.1 and the cash-flow comparisons of Table 11.6. Standard formats for the presentation of specific management accounting information may be used inside a particular business. But there are no universal standards, because the range of applications is too diverse.

12.1.2   Where from here?

Some important engineering aspects of management accounting are examined in Chapter 7 (*About Costs and Costing*), Chapter 11 (*Technical Project Evaluation and Choice*) and, to a lesser extent, in Chapter 6 (*Technical Project Planning and Control*). This chapter concentrates on financial accounting. The basic principles of accounting are discussed first. These are then explored by means of an extended example, which is presented in a somewhat different style from the rest of the book. This takes the form of an accounting story about the birth and early life of a new company. It describes and debates, in accounting terms:

- the creation of this enterprise
- the preparation of its accounts at the end of the first **trading** (buying, making and selling) year
- an analysis of those accounts aimed at learning more about the business.

The final section of the chapter briefly reiterates its salient points.

Any one of the texts by Arnold *et al.* (1985), Barrow (1988), Berry and Jarvis (1991), Glautier and Underdown (1986), Harrison (1989), Meigs and Meigs (1987) and Wilson (1990) is recommended as a follow-up reference. All of these books develop and expand the material in this chapter in a digestible form. Some suggestions for further reading are also noted in the bibliography.

12.2 | Basic accounting principles

Accounting principles impose substantial uniformity of treatment on most areas of accounting. They have been developed over many years for three major reasons:

(1) To allow the financial results of a specific business to be properly compared from period to period.
(2) To allow the financial results of different businesses to be properly compared, whether or not the businesses operate within the same industry.
(3) To aid the detection of carelessness or fraud in business transactions.

Conformity with some of the principles is a legal requirement. In Britain, most of the accounting principles are enshrined in 'Statements of Standard Accounting Practice' (SSAP), which provide a framework of rules, conventions and standards. These largely correspond to the 'Generally Accepted Accounting Principles' (GAAP) which apply in the USA. These documents continue to evolve as principles are modified, deleted or introduced in response to changes in the business environment.

Eight primary accounting principles are identified here. These are:

(1) Accounting entities.
(2) Double-entry accounting.
(3) The basic accounting, or 'balance sheet', equation.
(4) The distinction between capital and revenue.
(5) Matching.
(6) Going concern.
(7) Prudence.
(8) Consistency.

There is also a number of secondary (but important) accounting principles. The primary principles are discussed first.

12.2.1 Accounting entities

The material in this section is first covered in Section 1.2.3.

Business accounting treats trading organizations as things which are totally distinct from their owners. An 'accounting entity' may be an individual, a (deliberately) non-profit making organization such as a charity, or a business. This book is only concerned with businesses. There are three sorts of accounting entity which are classified as businesses.

Sole-traders

A sole-trader business is wholly owned by a single individual who, usually, also manages it. In accounting terms, the financial affairs of the business are separate from the financial affairs of its sole-trader owner. But there is no legal distinction between the business and its owner. That is, a sole-trader business is not a distinct legal entity. This means that the owner is legally responsible for all the debts incurred by the business. As a rule, sole-trader businesses are relatively small retail or service operations: a village shop, say, or a freelance programmer.

Partnerships

A partnership business is owned by two or more individuals who are the **partners**. In every other way, partnerships are the same as sole-trader businesses. So, while the accounts of the business and the personal accounts of the individual partners are separate, the business is not a separate legal entity. The partners, therefore, are fully liable for the debts of the business. They can deal with the its profits (or losses) in any legal way that they choose. Partnerships are commonly small to medium-sized retail or service businesses, but the category also includes some large businesses which are typically accountancy, legal or consultancy firms.

Companies

A company is a legal entity which is created (**incorporated**) in accordance with the laws of the countries in which it 'resides'. It is distinct from its owners in both accountancy and legal terms, and its separate legal status distinguishes it from sole-trader and partnership businesses. Companies are usually the larger businesses. The ownership of a company is divided into a number of **shares**, and **shareholders** participate in the rewards of ownership in proportion to their holding of issued shares. Shareholders may be either individuals or other entities.

Shares in a **private limited company** are not publicly traded (bought and sold) on a stock exchange. In Britain, this type of company is identified by the descriptor **Limited** (Ltd) following the company name. Private limited companies usually have a relatively small number of shareholders who are often personally involved in managing it. Shares in a **public limited company** (PLC) are listed on a stock exchange where they are publicly traded. Public limited companies usually have a large number of shareholders, most of whom are not directly involved in managing it.

The term **limited** has special significance. It indicates that the shareholders of a limited company are only liable up to the amount of their investment in the company. This means that they cannot lose more than this amount, whatever difficulties the company gets into. The safeguard of limited liability and the wide marketability of their shares has resulted in most industries being dominated by public limited companies.

12.2.2 Double-entry accounting

Section 1.6 is a selective summary of Sections 12.2.2 to 12.2.6 inclusive, which describe the remaining primary accounting principles.

The technique of **double-entry accounting** was invented in Italy during the fourteenth century. It stems directly from the accounting entity principle and is neither as complicated nor as wicked as it sounds. Business transactions are described in terms of **assets** and **liabilities**. Assets are things that the business *owns* and liabilities are debts that the business *owes*. The mechanics of double-entry result in every transaction being entered twice into the accounts, because:

- the acquisition of an asset implies either
- the acquisition of an equivalent liability, or

(a)	Before	Liabilities (owes) £		Assets (owns) £
	Sundry debts	4,000	Sundry things	10,000
	Owner's capital	8,000	Money at bank	2,000
	Total:	12,000	Total:	12,000

(b)	After	Liabilities (owes) £		Assets (owns) £
	Sundry debts	4,000	Sundry things	10,000
	Bank loan	1,000	Van	1,500
	Owner's capital	8,000	Money at bank	1,500
	Total:	13,000	Total:	13,000

Table 12.1 **Victorian Values: balance sheets at the end of Day 1 (a) and Day 2 (b).**
Proper application of the double-entry accounting principle ensures that the (accountancy) value of things a business owns (its assets) is always equal to what it owes (its liabilities). Table 12.1(a) shows this balance of assets and liabilities in a small business at the end of a particular day. On the next day, the business pays £1,000 borrowed from the bank into its bank account and buys a van for £1,500 with a cheque. Table 12.1(b) shows that assets and liabilities still balance after these transactions. But note that each has increased by £1,000 and only £500 in cash has left the business.

- an equivalent reduction in another asset, or
- an equivalent mixture of those two events.

One important consequence of double-entry accounting is that the total asset value of a company is (or should be) always equal to its total liabilities. An example will make all this more clear.

Example 1: Acquiring an asset

Victorian Values is an antiques shop, operating as a sole-trader, which has been in business for some time. This example evaluates its financial position at the end of two successive days. On Day 1, the owner of Victorian Values decides to purchase a van for use in the business. The local garage has a suitable second-hand vehicle and the owner agrees to pay £1,500 for it. She does not want to spend more than £500 of the cash in the business bank account on this purchase. So, on the morning of Day 2, she negotiates (on behalf of the business) a £1,000 loan from the bank to make up the remainder of the purchase price. The purchase of the van is completed on the afternoon of Day 2.

Table 12.1 illustrates the assets and liabilities situation of the business before and after purchasing the van. Assets are listed on the right and liabilities on the left.

Before the purchase of the van, the business owned sundry things valued at £10,000 and had £2,000 in its bank account. So its total assets were £12,000. At the same time, the business had sundry debts of £4,000, owed to some other businesses. There is also a debt of £8,000, called **owner's capital**, which the business owes to its owner. So its total liabilities were £12,000. Note that, before the purchase transaction, total assets are equal to total liabilities.

After the purchase of the van, the business owns the same sundry things as before (valued at £10,000) and it has acquired another asset, the van, valued at £1,500. But the money-at-bank asset is reduced from £2,000 to £1,500 since £500 has gone towards the cost of the van. So its total assets are now £13,000. At this time, the sundry debts (£4,000) and the owner's capital debt (£8,000) are unchanged. But the business has acquired another debt, because it now owes £1,000 to the bank. So its total liabilities become £13,000. Note that, after the purchase transaction, total assets are still equal to total liabilities.

Now, this example shows that the total business assets are exactly equal to the total business liabilities both before and after the purchase transaction. Under these circumstances, total assets and total liabilities are said to be 'balanced', and Tables 12.1(a) and (b) are *balance sheets*. The purchase transaction does not disturb the balance of total assets and total liabilities because both change, in the same direction, by the same amount. This change is an increase of £1,000. On the asset side of the balance sheet, it arises because the increase of £1,500 due to the van is offset by the £500 paid from the business bank account. On the liability side of the balance sheet, the increase is the £1,000 now owed to the bank.

Further insight into the balance sheet mechanism (which flows from the double-entry principle) is obtained by breaking the purchase transaction down into its basic steps. Total assets and total liabilities are in balance before the transaction, so only those balance sheet items which change during the transaction need be considered. The steps are:

(1) Borrow £1,000 from the bank and pay it into the business bank account.
   The liabilities increase by the £1,000 now owed to the bank and the assets increase by the same £1,000 paid into the bank account, which then stands at £3,000. Total assets and total liabilities remain in balance and each has increased by £1,000.
(2) Pay for the van with a cheque for £1,500, drawn on the business bank account.
   The assets now increase by £1,500 due to acquisition of the van, but this is exactly offset by the reduction in the bank account from £3,000 to £1,500. Total assets and total liabilities remain in balance at £1,000 more than before the transaction.

Assets

Assets are the economic resources owned by the business, which it uses in some way to aid the flow of money into the business. They can be tangible or intangible. Tangible assets include such things as buildings, equipment and items held in stock. In contrast, **debtors** are intangible assets. Debtors are entities that owe the business money, because they have already received something of value from it. In other words, the debtors asset represents promises of future income. Typically, it arise from sales made on credit. A patent is another, less commonplace, example of an intangible asset.

A business resource is only recognized as an asset if a reasonably accurate monetary value can be assigned to it. This is normally the price paid to acquire the asset. Thus, in the earlier example, the van asset appears in the balance sheet of Table 12.1(b) at £1,500. However, the value of some resources cannot be precisely measured in money terms and these do not appear in the accounts. Resources in this category include valuable skills, such as exceptional selling abilities and management expertise.

Liabilities

Liabilities are debts that the business owes. They represent claims by **creditors** on the assets of the business. A creditor is an entity that has provided an asset to the business in exchange for a promise of something of value, which is usually money. Thus, in the earlier example, the bank loan appears in the balance sheet of Table 12.1(b) as a liability of £1,000. The bank has become a creditor of the business. It has provided a cash asset to the business in exchange for a promise of periodic interest payments on the loan. The effect of these interest payments on the balance sheet is not shown in Table 12.1(b), because none had been made when it was prepared. Most liabilities arise, as in the example, from the acquisition of assets.

In practice, the term 'liabilities' is always understood to mean **external liabilities**. These are the debts that the business owes other than that which it owes to its owner(s). Henceforth, this chapter follows that convention and 'liabilities' should be understood as 'external liabilities'. The other part of the total debt is most generally termed the **owner's capital**. It is distinguished from (external) liabilities for reasons that shortly emerge.

Owner's capital

Table 12.2 shows the balance sheet of Table 12.1(b) recast into a more conventional **vertical or report format**. This balance sheet first lists assets and liabilities, and then subtracts total liabilities from total assets to yield **net assets**, which is £8,000 in this case. The net assets have been funded by (that is, provided by) the owner's capital of £8,000, and they belong to the owner. This arrangement of a balance sheet demonstrates the equality of net assets and owner's capital, rather than the equality of total assets and total liabilities.

The table also shows that the owner's capital is made up of two elements. (This detail is omitted in Table 12.1.) The first of these is the owner's initial investment of £2,000 made when she established the business. The second element, of £6,000, is **retained profits**. This is that fraction of the total (after tax) profit earned, up to the date of the balance sheet, which has been re-invested in the business. (The fraction not so re-invested has been paid to the owner.)

The business owes the owner's capital to the owner. It represents her financial stake in the business. (Note that it is *not* immediately available as a lump sum of money, because it is 'locked up' in the net assets.) The concept is equally applicable to all types of business entity. The owner's capital is sometimes called **capital of the business** or, less commonly, the **capital employed** (in the business). (But note that a wider, and better, definition of 'capital employed' is more commonly used than that just stated. That wider definition is examined in Section 12.5.4.)

The notion of 'capital employed' illuminates another way of regarding a balance

Assets:		£
	Sundry things	10,000
	Van	1,500
	Money at bank	1,500
	Total:	13,000
Liabilities:		
	Sundry debts	4,000
	Bank loan	1,000
	Total:	5,000
Net assets:		8,000
Financed by:		
	Owner's investment	2,000
	Retained profits	6,000
	Owner's capital	8,000

Table 12.2 **Victorian Values: balance sheet at the end of Day 2 (vertical format).**

In balance sheets, 'liabilities' means 'external liabilities'. These are amounts owed by the business excluding what it owes to its owner(s). This latter debt is most generally termed 'owners' capital'. This table is the balance sheet of Table 12.1(b) recast into the more usual vertical or report format. It shows that:

Assets − Liabilities = Net assets = Owner's capital

That is, the net assets have been purchased with the owner's capital and they belong to the owner. Here, the owner's capital is an initial investment of £2,000 plus £6,000 of retained profits, which have been invested in the business rather than paid to its owner.

sheet, which the vertical format of Table 12.2 is designed to expose. The table shows that the owner's capital employed in the business has been employed to purchase the net assets. In other words, the **employment of owner's capital** has been to purchase the total assets at a value offset by the total liabilities. Because of this perspective, alternative terms for 'capital employed' and 'employment of capital' are **source of funds** and **application of funds**, respectively.

Unfortunately, the term 'capital' is used somewhat loosely in business circles. For example, the funds which a company gets from selling its shares are often called 'the capital of the company'. Probably, however, those funds are only part of the real capital belonging to the owner(s), which is made up of:

(1) The amount invested in the company by the owner(s) when it was first established, together with any subsequent investments made by the owner(s).
(2) The addition of that fraction of profits earned by the company which has been retained in the company.
(3) The subtraction of any losses that the company has incurred which have been absorbed by the company.

The capital that a business owes to its owner(s) can also be called **equity or funds**, as in:

- the owner's or proprietor's capital or equity or funds, or
- the partners' capital or equity or funds, or
- the owners' capital or equity or funds, or
- the shareholders' capital or equity or funds

depending on the type of accounting entity in question. For example, a company owes the shareholders' funds to its shareholders, who are its owners. The shareholders participate in the benefits of ownership that the company earns for them. But if the company is **liquidated** for any reason (that is, if all its assets are sold and converted into cash) then the **external creditors** (that is, people or entities owed money by the business) have a prior legal claim on this cash. So the company debt represented by the shareholders' funds is the **residual claim** of the owners on the assets of the company. They only get back what is left (the residue) after the other creditors have been paid. The residue may be zero, because assets liquidated in a forced sale may not realize their balance sheet values.

Note that, as shown in Table 12.2, profit accrues to (that is, adds to) the owner's capital. It belongs to the owner(s). A major aim of a business is to increase the capital belonging to its owner(s) by making profits.

Example 2: Making a profit

In the morning of Day 3, the owner of Victorian Values buys (on behalf of the business) an attractive old desk for £450. She pays cash for it, in the form of a cheque drawn on the business bank account. In the afternoon, she sells the desk to a another dealer for £800. This is a credit sale, with the money being due within 30 days.

Table 12.3 is the balance sheet for Victorian Values at the end of Day 3. It shows the effects of the cash purchase of the desk and its subsequent credit sale. The liabilities do not change on Day 3.

Money-at-bank is reduced to £1,050 because the desk cost £450. But a new asset, a debtor, at £800 is introduced. This is the customer who has purchased the desk on credit. So total assets increase by £800 − £450 = £350, (as do net assets in this case). This amount represent the profit made on the whole 'purchase then sale' transaction. The profit accrues to the owner's capital, which increases from £8,000 to £8,350 and thereby maintains the balance between owner's capital and net assets.

Note that, strictly, the £350 should be termed the **gross profit** because it is the 'margin' (difference) between the sale price of the desk and the directly attributable costs of acquiring it prior to sale. The business also incurs many other costs on Day 3, such as petrol for the van and rent for the shop. These other costs are only partially attributable to acquiring the desk. To simplify matters, they are not taken into account at this stage in the discussion.

For and against double-entry accounting

There are two major merits of double-entry accounting. Firstly, it allows the capital employed (however defined) in the business to be separated into its constituent parts. Secondly, it provides a degree of automatic cross-checking against carelessness or

Assets:		£
	Sundry things	10,000
	Van	1,500
	Debtor (re desk)	800
	Money at bank	1,050
	Total:	13,350
Liabilities:		
	Sundry debts	4,000
	Bank loan	1,000
	Total:	5,000
Net assets:		8,350
Financed by:		
	Owner's investment	2,000
	Retained profits	6,000
	Profit (re desk)	350
	Owner's capital	8,350

Table 12.3   Victorian Values: balance sheet at the end of Day 3.
This balance sheet is that of Table 12.2, but modified to incorporate a trading transaction. This is the purchase, for £450 cash, of an item of stock and its subsequent sale for £800 on credit. Note that, comparing Tables 12.2 and 12.3, cash at bank diminishes by £450 (cash purchase) but a debtor asset of £800 is acquired (credit sale). So (because liabilities are unchanged in this case), net assets increase by £800 − £450 = £350. And this profit accrues (adds) to owner's capital. A major aim of a business is to increase owners' capital by making profits.

dishonesty by those people who perform the business transactions. But, largely because of the double-entry principle, accounts are traditionally kept in terms of *original* cost. This means that, unless complex corrections are applied, the effects of inflation are ignored. The system also has a built-in anomaly, which is illustrated in Table 12.1(b). The purchase of the van has the same effect on both sides of the balance sheet, but the value of the van to the business must be greater than the £1,500 paid for it. Because, if this is not so, there is no reason to buy it! However, despite these objections, double-entry accounting has worked reasonably well for some 500 years and remains the basis of almost all business accounts.

12.2.3   The basic accounting equation

The **basic accounting equation** (which is alternatively called the **balance sheet equation**) is introduced in Section 1.6, where it is labelled Equation 1.10. It is the mathematical expression of the double-entry principle. The equation is:

Total Assets = Total Liabilities   (12.1) which is more commonly written as:

$$\text{Assets} = \text{Liabilities} + \text{Owners' Capital} \tag{12.2}$$

In this generalization of the basic accounting equation:

(1) Assets should be understood to mean total assets.
(2) Liabilities are the external liabilities, which relate to the external creditors of the business.
(3) Owners' capital is either owner's capital, partners' capital or share-holders' capital, depending on whether the business is a sole-trader, a partnership or a company. The terms equity or funds might be used instead of capital.

The basic accounting equation underpins everything that follows in this chapter. In passing, and using a company example, note that:

(1) If assets are greater than liabilities plus shareholders' funds then either carelessness has intervened or some sort of fraud is being perpetrated.
(2) If assets are less than liabilities plus shareholders' funds then either careless-ness has intervened or the business is unable to meet its financial obligations. In other words, it is **bankrupt**.

12.2.4 Capital and revenue

Accounts are produced periodically and, in terms of the statutory requirements for formal external reporting, the normal **accounting period** is one year. Management accounts are usually produced at the end of each month, but weekly reporting is not unknown.

A balance sheet shows the financial position of the business at the end of a defined period. It is a 'snapshot', which measures the business at a specific time. But businesses are dynamic and the financial position measured at one instant changes as soon as the next transaction occurs. It would be possible to produce balance sheets at, say, daily intervals but a more efficient process is always adopted to keep track of day-to-day activity. This process records the revenue (income) earned and the corresponding cost (expenditure) incurred during the period in a profit and loss account (**P&L account**) for that period. The difference between the revenue and the corresponding cost is the profit (or loss) for the period, in accordance with the **profit equation** (introduced in equivalent form as Equation 1.3 in Chapter 1):

$$\text{Profit} = \text{Revenue} - \text{Cost} \tag{12.3}$$

Now, assuming that the profit is retained in the business, there is an equivalent change in the owners' capital during the period. A P&L account is thus the trading link between the balance sheets produced at the end of two successive periods. It shows how the *trading* activities have modified the owners' capital from one balance sheet to the next by recording changes to some of the assets and liabilities. This linking role of the P&L account is illustrated in Figure 12.1, which also shows the position of the funds flow statement in the overall scheme.

Accounting procedures recognize two broad categories of cost. These are **capital costs**, which are shown (strictly) only on balance sheets, and **revenue costs** which are shown only on P&L accounts. This cost classifying convention is now examined.

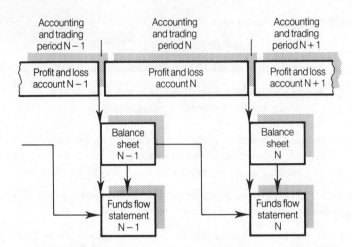

Figure 12. 1 **The relationships between the three major financial statements.**

Generally, the major statements describing the financial condition of a business are produced at fixed intervals and the normal accounting period is one year. The figure shows the relationships between the major statements. A balance sheet details the pivotal Net assets = Owners' capital equality at the end of a specific period. A profit and loss account shows how profit/loss arises from increases/decreases in net assets as a result of trading transactions during the specific period. So it forms a 'trading' link between balance sheets reporting the end of successive periods. A funds flow statement shows how funds have moved into, out of, and around the business during the specific period. It is built from the opening and closing balance sheets of the period and its profit and loss account.

Capital costs and fixed assets

Capital costs relate to the acquisition of assets which, at the time of purchase, are expected to aid the earning process for more than one accounting period. In other words, it is anticipated that the useful life of such assets will be more than one year. Examples include land, buildings, manufacturing machinery and vehicles. It is not equitable to assign the whole cost of such items to the P&L account of the year in which they are acquired. To do so would unfairly depress the profit in that period and unfairly increase it in some subsequent periods. For this reason, **capital assets** are recorded in the balance sheet, where they are called **fixed assets** and are listed under that heading.

However, fixed assets do have a finite useful life. For example, it might be assumed that a computer printer will operate usefully for three years before increasing 'downtime' and maintenance charges require its replacement. In this case, it is reasonable to assign one-third of its initial cost to the three corresponding annual P&L accounts. This is an illustration of the **depreciation** mechanism, which is used to measure the 'consumption' of fixed assets. It forms another link between balance sheets and P&L accounts.

Revenue costs

Revenue costs relate to the purchase of items which, it is anticipated, will be completely consumed (used up) within one year. In other words, it is anticipated that the benefits purchased with revenue costs will be consumed within one year of their purchase. These are the day-to-day operating costs of the business. Examples include salaries and wages, rent and business rates, insurance premiums, and the costs of electricity, heating, machinery maintenance and repairs, and so on. It is entirely reasonable to assign the cost of such items to the P&L accounts of the year in which their benefits are 'delivered'. It is in those accounts that the revenue costs are related to the revenue, and hence the profit, that they have helped to earn. Note that revenue costs are often termed **expenses**, in this text and elsewhere.

12.2.5 Matching and accruals accounting

The assignment of revenue costs to the P&L account of the period in which their benefits are fulfilled is an illustration of the **matching** principle. This requires that the costs incurred to generate a particular revenue are 'matched' (compared) with that same revenue, so that it can be seen if the costs are worthwhile. This is achieved by recording the costs in the same period as that in which revenue arises. For example, the costs of making a product are recorded alongside the revenue arising from its sale. The depreciation mechanism mentioned earlier is also motivated by the matching principle. It creates revenue costs which spread the consumption of fixed assets over their useful lives.

Current assets

Application of the matching principle also results in **current assets** being assigned to the balance sheet. In a manufacturing business, this group of assets includes:

- **stocks** of raw materials and components destined for incorporation into products
- **work-in-progress**, which is raw materials and components in the process of being converted into products
- **finished products** held in store, prior to dispatch to customers.

Stocks are purchased in anticipation of future needs and held in a local store for immediate availability when required by the manufacturing operation. When an item of stock leaves this store, it first becomes a part of work-in-progress, and then it becomes a part of a finished product. But the matching principle requires that the cost of the item is only recognized as a revenue cost (as a part of product cost, in this case) when that product is sold. The product making and selling operations are essentially continuous activities. (Assuming all is well with the business!) So it is virtually certain that quantities of stock, work-in-progress and finished products will exist at the end of an accounting period. The costs that these quantities represent must be recorded on the balance sheet for that period, because they cannot yet be matched with a corresponding revenue.

Items like stock, work-in-progress and finished products are termed 'current assets', because they are not (unlike fixed assets) deliberately held for use during a number of successive accounting periods. Their existence in a particular form is (hopefully) only temporary. Current assets are sometimes called **circulating assets** because of their transient nature within a continuous trading cycle. This illuminating notion is illustrated in Figure 12.2.

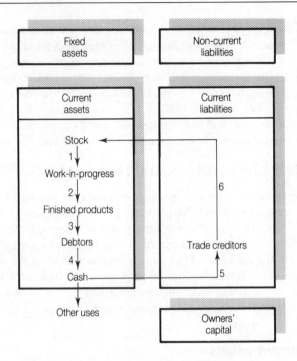

Figure 12.2 **Circulating assets in a manufacturing business.**

Current assets, unlike fixed assets, are not held for use during successive accounting periods. They stay in a particular form (such as stock, work-in-progress and finished products) only briefly, and are sometimes called 'circulating assets' because of their part in the trading cycle. This is illustrated in the figure, which mimics a balance sheet. Fixed and current assets are separated on the left, and non-current and current liabilities on the right. Non-current liabilities are borrowed funds held for use during a number of successive accounting periods. Current liabilities are short-term debts which are usually paid off in the same period as they are incurred.

The figure is constructed in balance sheet format and, on the left, shows fixed and current assets separately. An analogous distinction is made on the right, where **non-current liabilities** and **current liabilities** are separated. Non-current liabilities are borrowed funds held for use during a number of successive accounting periods. A long-term bank loan is a typical example. Current liabilities are short-term debts which, for the most part, are paid-off in the period that they are incurred.

The 'circulation loop' within Figure 12.2 assumes that normal trading conditions apply. That is, products are being sold on credit to create debtors and stock is being purchased on credit to create creditors. Starting with stock, and moving anti-clockwise round the loop, current assets are transformed in the following sequence:

(1) *Stock* moves out of the 'input' store into the manufacturing operation, where it is termed 'work-in-progress'.
(2) *Work-in-progress* is converted, in the manufacturing process, to finished products, which are then held in an 'output' store.
(3) *Finished products* are sold to customers on credit and so become debtors.
(4) *Debtors* pay the amounts that they owe and so become cash (usually at the bank).

(5) *Cash* is used to pay **trade creditors** and to purchase new stock on credit, thereby creating more trade creditors.

(6) When the new stock is delivered it is placed in the input store and the cycle is repeated.

Trade creditors are other businesses that supply stock on credit. The credit period is normally relatively short, such as 30 or 60 days. Creditors of this nature are listed under the current liabilities heading in a balance sheet.

Note that the cash current asset is not only used to buy stock to sustain trading. It has a range of other uses, such as paying the day-to-day operating costs and purchasing more fixed assets to increase the earning capacity of the business. Alternatively, it may be paid as dividends to the owner(s) of the business.

Limitations of matching

The maxim 'the purpose of every cost that a business incurs is to create an income' is well founded. But there are some inescapable costs which cannot be (easily) matched with a corresponding income. Examples include top management salaries, and the costs of heating and cleaning the offices and factory. Costs of this nature are sometimes called **period costs**. They are **recognized** (entered into the P&L account) either in the period in which they occur or in the period in which the benefits they provide are consumed. Thus, the chairman's salary for fiscal year 1990/91 occurs and is charged against income in that year. Equally, the (estimated) cost of electricity used in the last quarter of 1990/91 is charged against income in that year. This is despite the fact that the relevant electricity bill is not available, and is not paid, until the first quarter of 1991/92.

A different sort of matching problem is presented by 'investment-type' costs which occur in a particular period. The purpose of such costs is certainly to produce an income, but the income can be scheduled for later periods and, indeed, may not happen at all. Marketing costs are often of this nature, as are product research, development and design costs. It is usual in most, but not all, businesses to **write-off** such costs as they occur. That is, they are normally charged against income (entered into the P&L account) in the period in which they occur. This is not legally required for other than research costs. Alternatively, investment-type costs may be **capitalized**. That is, they are recorded in the balance sheet as assets. This practice assumes that the investment will be successful, and it can lead to severe problems (like business failure) when this proves not to be the case.

In summary, therefore, matching is not always possible and/or is not always prudent. This means that some costs which are shown on a particular P&L account may not relate to the revenue (income) shown on that same account. The matching principle is compromised in such cases by the (usually justified) intervention of expediency and caution.

The accrual concept

The (sales) revenue figure shown in a P&L account is the sum total of the cash and credit product sales made during the relevant accounting period. It does not include any other income from, say, interest received on deposit accounts or the sale of fixed assets. Importantly, the revenue is likely to be greater than the actual cash received during the period. This is because some of the cash due from credit sales will still be pending at the end of the period. (The outstanding amounts are included as debtors on the balance sheet.) So revenue is recognized (entered into the P&L account) when everything that has to be done to earn the revenue has been done. This occurs before the receipt of the corresponding cash. Similarly, as has been discussed earlier, costs are recognized in the period when they are incurred rather when the corresponding payment is actually made.

This process which recognizes revenue and cost only during the periods in which they occur is called **accrual accounting**. Its purpose is to aid the matching of associated revenue and cost items. The alternative is **cash or cash-based accounting**, which is based on actual cash receipts and actual payments made. That approach, while it deals with facts rather than expectations, can only match associated items when they occur in the same (one year) period. It is unsatisfactory in this respect. There is a legal requirement for limited liability companies to use accrual accounting for all external financial reporting. Cash-based accounting is rarely used in practice, even when such use is permitted.

12.2.6 Other primary principles

The last three accounting principles from the list of those awarded 'primary' status can be explained quite briefly.

Going concern

Under normal circumstances, business accounts are prepared on the basis that the business will stay in business. In other words, the accounts assume that the business is a **going concern**. This means that the asset values used are based on this rather than on assessed liquidation values, which are likely to be smaller.

Prudence

Accountants believe (rightly) that it is less dangerous to understate a profit than to overstate it. This cautious outlook is embodied in the **prudence** principle. It requires that:

- if two estimates of an income are equally likely then the smaller one should be selected, and
- if two estimates of a cost are equally likely then the larger one should be selected.

The use of judgement-based estimates is unavoidable in accrual accounting. Accountancy prudence biases these estimates towards pessimism rather than optimism.

Consistency

The **consistency** principle requires that, in relation to a particular business, the accounting treatment of similar items does not change either within a period or from period to period. Adherence to this principle allows the performance of the business in different periods to be properly compared.

12.2.7 Secondary principles

Secondary, but important, accounting principles include:

(1) Clarity
(2) Comparability
(3) Cost-effectiveness
(4) Materiality
(5) Monetary basis
(6) Periodicity
(7) Relevance
(8) Reliability.

Each of these is now briefly discussed.

Clarity

A central purpose of accounting and accounts is to provide intelligible information to decision makers. This requirement is encapsulated in the **clarity** principle. Accountants must make an assumption about the financial competence of accounts users. They regard competent users to be those with a reasonable understanding of business and financial matters, who are willing to study the accounts with some care. Note that this definition aims to covers all managers. It is not confined to financial professionals.

Comparability

One of the main purposes of accounting standards is to allow the financial performance of different businesses to be reasonably compared. **Comparability** measures the extent to which a set of accounts meets this requirement.

Cost-effectiveness

This principle does no more than state a criterion that should be applied to all service activities within the business. It requires that the benefits of the service provided should be greater than the cost of providing it. It is a constraint which limits the amount of detail and the degree of accuracy in the accounting information.

Materiality

Materiality is, perhaps, a concession rather than a principle. It allows minor details to be omitted and other principles to be breached if the consequences make no material (significant) difference to the meaning of the accounts. For example, a sum of £1,000,100 may be entered into the accounts as £1,000,000, because £100 is immaterial in the context of £1,000,000. Similarly, small items of capital equipment (office clocks, say) may be written-off in the P&L account rather than being assigned to fixed assets, where they strictly belong.

Monetary basis

This principle is noted earlier. It requires that the accounts only report factors which can be measured in money. This (inevitable) restriction excludes, for example, the quality of the work-force and the value of excellent management.

Periodicity

The periodicity principle requires that accounts are produced at discrete intervals, preferably of equal duration. Legal obligations are placed on companies with respect to their published financial statements. Public limited companies must report at least twice a year and all limited companies must report at least once per year. Annual reports must be audited by an independent authority.

Relevance

Clarity and relevance are related requirements. The relevance principle requires that accounts contain all the information pertaining to the user's purpose. This is usually a straightforward matter in customized management accounts, but less so in financial accounts which are aimed at a diverse set of users.

Reliability

The reliability principle requires that accounts do not contain errors, do contain all the significant data and, importantly, are verifiable.

12.2.8 Section summary

Accounting technology is a vast topic. It has been introduced in this section by partitioning it into primary and secondary principles, which are then briefly explored. The remainder of the chapter is aimed at developing and reinforcing an appreciation of the primary principles, and of the language in which they are conventionally expressed. The definitions of the accountancy terms introduced in this section are reiterated and, sometimes, expanded in the Glossary.

Everything that follows has its roots in the basic accounting equation:

$$\text{Total Assets} = \text{Total Liabilities} \tag{12.1}$$

The claim that to understand this equation is to understand business accounting is an exaggeration. But not a big one. However, the equation is rather more subtle than it appears at first sight. It is the top level accountancy model of a business. At the next (and lower) levels the model employs:

- fixed assets
- current assets
- current liabilities
- non-current liabilities
- owners' capital

as its major elements. A common conceptual difficulty, implicit in the model, relates to the accountancy notion of 'funds'. Engineers, and other non-accountants, tend to regard funds as cash. Accountants have a broader vision of reality. A sale made on credit adds to the fund of debtors within current assets. A purchase made on credit adds to the fund of creditors within current liabilities. A fund is a store of value. To accountants, these funds are as real as cash, even though they represent promises rather than facts. Similarly, a depreciation charge is a real part of 'funds', but it is not cash. So the reader is asked to think about funds rather than cash while Equation 12.1 is unravelled in the rest of the chapter. Cash is just a special type of fund.

12.3 The birth of Adastra

Sections 1.7 and 1.8 cover much the same material as this section, but from a rather different perspective. The approach in Chapter 1 develops a physical model of an established manufacturing business and exercises it over a complete trading cycle. It complements rather than repeats the following accounting story.

Once upon a time, Arthur Starr had an idea for a novel product. At the time, he was an electronics engineer employed by a large company as a senior product designer. The novel product was directed at a gap in an industrial market sector already exploited by his employers. They decided, after a short investigation, that its commercial potential was too small to justify any further investment on their part. Arthur found this view difficult to accept. He believed that visible trends in the market promised rosy prospects for the product, and its derivatives, over the next few years.

Now, Arthur had always wanted to run his own business. He decided (after some sleepless nights) that the product idea represented, perhaps, the opportunity to do so. Accordingly, over a period of about two months, he spent most of his free time and some of his own money in developing and designing the product at his home. This activity culminated in a working prototype, which performed more or less exactly to specification. Arthur demonstrated this prototype to several potential customers, some of whom said that they would buy the product in significant numbers if it were available at the right price. Arthur had a shrewd idea of what this right price was. The potential customers were not apparently deterred when he increased that figure by twenty per cent and tested it on them. He was much encouraged by this response.

At about this time, early November 1990, Arthur talked over the whole situation with one of his neighbours. This lady, an accountant with her own practice in the town, was impressed with the progress that Arthur had made. They discussed the sales prospects for the product family, the potential competition, and probable product costs and prices. They agreed that Arthur would need about £10,000 to launch the business. The accountant advised him that (if he decided to go ahead) the business should be a private limited company rather than a sole-trader or partnership operation. She pointed out that, of the three options, a limited company would be the most costly to set up and operate. This is because of the initial cost of forming the company, and the subsequent costs of preparing and auditing its accounts to meet statutory requirements. On the other hand, the limited liability provisions would give Arthur valuable protection should the business fail 'under normal circumstances'. Arthur was a bit disturbed by the concept of business failure being a normal circumstance. The accountant explained that the law does not penalize company directors whose business fails because they are unlucky or stupid. Under those circumstances, they are only liable up to their investment (if any) in the business. But the protection of limited liability does not apply to directors convicted of fraud. Marketing considerations also favoured the company option. The product family is aimed at company customers. Companies usually prefer their suppliers to be companies rather than individuals, because they are less ephemeral, and because of the ready availability of independently audited financial information. This argument would become increasingly persuasive when Arthur started to exhaust his list of influential friends working for prospective customers. She offered to form the company, and to prepare and audit its first year accounts, for the all inclusive price of £600. Arthur, who had made enquires elsewhere, thought that this was a bargain offer, and said as much to the lady. She explained that she, too, was anxious to grow her business and was quite prepared to invest some of her time in helping prospective long-term clients. But payment in advance was part of the deal. Having obtained her assurance that 'occasional' advice would be available during the first year, Arthur accepted the offer and gave her a *personal* cheque for £600. They agreed that the company name would be 'Adastra' (if that name was available) and the initial owners' capital would be in the form of 7,500 £1 shares issued at par (face) value. These would be subscribed for (purchased) by Arthur and his wife in equal amounts. Arthur would be the sole director (and the secretary) of the company.

At the end of November 1990 Arthur bravely (or stupidly, because the distinction is not always clear at the time of the action) gave his employers the required one month notice of his pending resignation. Adastra Limited came formally into being as a legal entity on the 31st December 1990 and, in January 1991, Arthur began the task of building the company.

12.3.1   Actions in the first month

Arthur had a hectic and, sometimes, confusing first month as a business man rather than an engineer. At the end of the month, in an attempt to measure the progress made, he listed all the significant actions that he had taken. The list is shown below:

On 31st December 1990
(1) Set up a business bank account for Adastra Ltd, and paid into it £7,500 from a building society account held jointly with his wife. He and his wife each received a share certificate for 3,750 £1 Adastra shares in exchange for their investment.

   Paid £2,500 borrowed from his bank into the Adastra bank account. The bank required him to assign an insurance policy to them as security for the loan. The interest on the loan was set, initially, at 17% per annum payable monthly in arrears.

   Paid, by cheque, £600 from the Adastra bank account into his personal bank account to recover his earlier advance payment of that amount for company formation and other costs.

In January 1991
(2) Bought for cash a small workshop on an industrial estate at £5,000.
(3) Bought for cash some tools, second-hand electronic test gear and fittings for the workshop amounting to £2,500.
(4) Bought all the components to make five product units for £750 on credit.
(5) Assembled and tested three product units.
(6) Sold one of them for £1,000 on credit.
(7) Paid himself £500 as salary from the business bank account. (This was about a sixth of his previous monthly salary, but he consoled himself with the thought that his sacrifice was being shared by the taxman.)

Having made the list, Arthur still could not be sure if Adastra and its owners were winning or losing. So he called his accountant. She agreed to give Arthur an accounting tutorial, and then to analyse Adastra's end-of-January situation. A meeting was arranged.

12.3.2 An accounting tutorial

Arthur opened the meeting by presenting the accountant with his list of significant actions, and asked 'Where am I?' The accountant, who is a bit pedantic, replied 'You are here with me. And we want to know where your business is, which is a quite separate matter.' She then gave Arthur a brief lecture on:

- A business as an accounting entity (quite separate from its owners) which can own things called assets and owe money called liabilities.

- Double-entry accounting with assets, liabilities and owners' capital as its main elements.

- And, finally, the basic 'balance sheet equation' written first as:

      Assets = Liabilities + Owners' Capital

and then as:

      Net Assets = Assets − Liabilities = Owners' Capital

where it is understood that 'liabilities' means 'external liabilities' and that owners' capital is also a liability, because the business owes it to its owners.

12.3.3 Month 1 actions analysis

The accountant then analysed Arthur's list of actions on a double-entry accounting basis. The results of this analysis are displayed in Table 12.4. This table is constructed on the same basis as Table 12.3. Its major elements are assets, liabilities, net assets and owners' capital. Before the build-up of Table 12.4 is examined in detail, note that net assets (which is the difference between assets and liabilities) is equal to owners' capital after each action. Note, too, that owners' capital has decreased between the formation of the company (action 1) and the end of the first active month (action 7). At first sight, this is not good news. A major objective of a business is to increase its owners' capital. So, at this stage, Arthur and his wife appear to be losing.

The accountant 'walked' Arthur through the table by correlating the figures in each action column with the action list. Her explanations were as follows:

On 31st December 1990
(1) The owners' start-up investment of £7,500 and the bank loan of £2,500 are paid into Adastra's bank account. So Adastra *initially* acquires an asset of £10,000 in the form of cash-at-bank. Net assets become £7,500 because a creditor liability (the bank) has also been acquired at £2,500, which is the bank loan. The net assets are financed by (provided by) the owners' capital of £7,500.
      The cheque for £600 paid out of the bank account then reduces the cash-at-

	1990	←		JANUARY	1991		→
Action number:	1	2	3	4	5	6	7
	£	£	£	£	£	£	£
Assets:							
Premises		5,000	5,000	5,000	5,000	5,000	5,000
Equipment			2,500	2,500	2,500	2,500	2,500
Prepayment	600	0	0	0	0	0	0
Components				750	300	300	300
Finished goods					450	300	300
Debtors						1,000	1,000
Cash at bank	9,400	4,400	1,900	1,900	1,900	1,900	1,400
Total:	10,000	9,400	9,400	10,150	10,150	11,000	10,500
Liabilities:							
Creditors:							
Trade				750	750	750	750
Bank	2,500	2,500	2,500	2,500	2,500	2,500	2,500
Total:	2,500	2,500	2,500	3,250	3,250	3,250	3,250
Net assets:	7,500	6,900	6,900	6,900	6,900	7,750	7,250
Financed by:							
Start up	7,500	7,500	7,500	7,500	7,500	7,500	7,500
Profit/(Loss)		(600)	(600)	(600)	(600)	250	(250)
Owners' capital:	7,500	6,900	6,900	6,900	6,900	7,750	7,250

Memo:
1. Components consumed per product (£): 150
2. Salary for month (Mr A. Starr)   (£): 500

Table 12.4 **Adastra: the initial transactions.**
This table illustrates the use of double-entry accounting and the balance sheet equation to express the action list in Section 12.3.1 as a sequence of seven balance sheets. Note that Net assets = Owners' capital after each action. Note, too, that owners' capital has decreased between the formation of the company (balance sheet 1) and the end of the first active month (balance sheet 7), because a trading loss has been incurred during the month.

bank asset to £9,400. But total assets do not change, because a **prepayment asset** of the same value is acquired at the same time. This asset is the future benefit of company formation, and the preparation and auditing of its first year accounts. This benefit will arise in 1991, which is the first full year of Adastra's operation, whereas it was purchased in 1990.

In January 1991
(2) As soon as 1991 starts, the matching principle requires that the prepayment asset is 'written-off' (reduced to zero). This is because the cost of the benefit must be set against the income of the period where the benefit arises. This action reduces total assets (and net assets) by £600. There is a corresponding

reduction in the profit. In other words, the business makes a loss of £600 as a result of the asset write-off. Note that, in Table 12.4, negative amounts are enclosed in parentheses, which is a common accountancy convention.

The other transaction in column 2 is less complicated. The purchase of the small workshop reduces the cash-at-bank asset by £5,000, but the premises asset increases by the same amount. There is no net effect on total assets.

(3) The transaction to purchase tools, test gear and fittings (collectively called 'equipment') for the workshop follows the same pattern as the premises transaction described above.

(4) The purchase of components on credit is not quite as simple. A components asset valued at £750 is acquired, as is a 'trade' creditor liability of the same amount. Total liabilities become £3,250 but net assets are unchanged, because total assets have similarly increased.

(5) Each product unit uses £150 worth of components at cost, so the three completed units become an asset called 'finished goods' valued at £450. There is a corresponding reduction in the components asset. (The accountant prefers the term 'finished goods' to 'finished products'.) Note that the finished goods are valued at (component) cost. This is an example of the accountancy prudence principle.

(6) Here, one of the completed units is sold on credit for £1,000. So the finished goods asset is reduced by the cost of this unit (£150) to £300, and a debtor asset (the customer) of £1,000 is acquired. So total assets increase by £850 (= £1,000 − £150) which is the profit on the sale. Net assets increase by the same amount (because no liabilities change in this transaction). A corresponding increase in profit (which brings it to £850 − £600 = £250) maintains the balance between net assets and owners' capital. (Adastra owes the profit to Arthur and his wife, because profit accrues to owners' capital.)

(7) The salary payment reduces the cash-at-bank asset by £500. The corresponding reduction in net assets is accompanied by a matching reduction in the profit, which becomes negative, to leave a net loss of £250 at the end of the month.

Arthur was somewhat concerned that Adastra's first month of trading had ended in a loss rather than a profit, even though he had taken such a small salary from the business. The accountant, on the other hand, was not at all worried. It emerged that her serenity was not only because she was not holding the loss. She pointed out that it was still early days in the life of Adastra, and early losses were entirely normal with business start-up situations. Also, she could have chosen to phase the write-off of the £600 prepayment asset over the whole year, at £50 per month. If this procedure had been adopted than Adastra would have shown a profit at the month end. She had chosen not to do this on the basis of accountancy prudence, taking the view that it is better to understate rather than overstate a profit where a choice exists.

The accountant then warned Arthur that her analysis was, in any case, somewhat unrealistic, because Adastra had incurred a number of other costs during the month that were not on his list. She promised to return to the problem later on, after discussing balance sheets.

Adastra Ltd (Mr A. Starr)
Balance sheet at 31st January 1991

		£	£
Fixed assets:			
	Premises	5,000	
	Equipment	2,500	
			7,500
Current assets:			
	Prepayment	0	
	Stocks	300	
	Finished goods	300	
	Trade debtors	1,000	
	Cash at bank	1,400	
			3,000
Current liabilities:			
	Trade creditors		750
Net current assets:			2,250
Total assets *less* current liabilities:			9,750
Non-current liabilities:			
	Bank loan		2,500
Net assets:			7,250
Financed by owners' capital:			
	Paid up capital	7,500	
	Profit and loss A/c	(250)	
			7,250

Table 12.5   Adastra: Month 1 balance sheet (Version 1).
The balance sheet shown here is a more formal version of balance sheet 7 in Table 12.4. 'Stocks' now encapsulates the components (current) asset of that table, and the owners' start-up investment has become 'paid up capital'. The profit entry apparently comes from a P&L account (shown later). The structure of this balance sheet follows that used by many companies. It shows net current assets ('working capital'), which is a measure of 'liquidity'. Note that the long-term total capital employed (defined as owners' capital plus non-current liabilities) has been employed to provide the total assets less current liabilities.

12.3.4   Some balance sheets

She pointed out that her analysis of the initial transactions (Table 12.4) was structured as a sequence of seven balance sheets, each describing the financial position of Adastra at the end of an action. She then went on to draw up a more formal Month 1 balance sheet, based on the data at the end of action 7.

Month 1 balance sheet (Version 1)

This is shown in Table 12.5. It is cast in a format used by many companies. Note that the components asset of Table 12.4 is now within the broader category of 'stocks'. Note, too, that the start-up (investment) is now termed the **paid up capital**, and that the profit entry is derived from a P&L account (which has not yet been formulated).

It will be recalled that a balance sheet is a financial 'snapshot' of the status of a business at a specific time. It shows, in tabular form, the balance expressed by the basic accounting equation:

$$\text{Assets} = \text{Liabilities} + \text{Owners' Capital} \qquad (12.2)$$

or, in this case:

$$\text{Net Assets} = \text{Owners' Capital} \qquad (12.4)$$

where

$$\text{Net Assets} = \text{Assets} - \text{Liabilities} \qquad (12.5)$$

A company balance sheet must show fixed assets separately from current assets, and current assets and liabilities separately from non-current assets and liabilities. Conventionally, the boundary between 'current' and 'non-current' is set at one year.

So current assets are either already cash (or near-cash), or expected to become cash within the year. Assets are normally listed in **liquidity** order with cash (the most liquid asset) listed last. 'Liquidity' measures the amount of time required to convert an asset into cash. Similarly, current liabilities includes all those debts which are to be paid within the year. The non-current liability category includes the long-term (longer than the year) debts, such as the bank loan in this case.

The balance sheet of Table 12.5 shows **net current assets**, as well as net assets, where:

$$\text{Net Current Assets} = \text{Current Assets} - \text{Current Liabilities} \qquad (12.6)$$

This parameter is commonly called **working capital**, and it is a critical element in a balance sheet. Indeed, the format of Table 12.5 is specifically designed to expose it. It is a measure of the extent to which the current assets, when translated into cash, are able to pay off the current liabilities (Figure 12.2 illustrates this translation process). So working capital is a useful indicator of the short-term financial stability of the business. (But the ratio of current assets to current liabilities is a better one.)

The next line in this balance sheet, which is labelled 'total assets less current liabilities', is obtained by adding the fixed assets to the working capital. This is another important parameter which is exposed by the arrangement of Table 12.5. It is equal, by way of the basic accounting equation which governs balance sheets, to the sum of the non-current liabilities and the owners' capital. That is:

$$\begin{matrix} \text{Fixed Assets} \\ + \\ \text{Working Capital} \end{matrix} \quad = \quad \begin{matrix} \text{Non-Current Liabilities} \\ + \\ \text{Owners' Capital} \end{matrix} \qquad (12.7)$$

The two items on the right-hand side of this equation comprise the long-term debt which, as the equation shows, is financing the company. This long-term debt is commonly termed the **capital employed**. That is:

$$\text{Capital Employed} = \text{Non-Current Liabilities} + \text{Owners' Capital} \qquad (12.8)$$

It was noted earlier that the owner's capital is sometimes called the capital employed. However, the definition encapsulated in Equation 12.8 is preferred. It is the *whole* of the long-term capital available to the company, rather than just part of it.

Adastra Ltd (Mr A. Starr)
Balance sheet at 31st January 1991

Source of funds (or capital employed)

	£	£
Paid up capital	7,500	
Profit and loss A/c	(250)	
		7,250

Application of funds (or employment of capital)

Fixed assets:

	£	£	£
Premises		5,000	
Equipment		2,500	
			7,500

Current assets:

	£	£	£
Prepayment	0		
Stocks	300		
Finished goods	300		
Debtors	1,000		
Cash at bank	1,400		
		3,000	

Current liabilities:

Trade creditors	(750)	

Net current assets:	2,250
Non-current liabilities:	
Bank loan	(2,500)
	7,250

Table 12.6   Adastra: Month 1 balance sheet (Version 2).

This is different (and not much used) arrangement of the balance sheet of Table 12.5. It defines capital employed as owners' capital (which is an unsatisfactory definition), and details how funds from that source are applied (employed) to provide the net assets.

Month 1 balance sheet (Version 2)

At this point, the accountant reminded Arthur that the structure of the balance sheet of Table 12.5 reflects the basic accounting equation written in the form:

$$\text{Assets} - \text{Liabilities} = \text{Owners' Capital} \tag{12.9}$$

She then showed him a rather different way of presenting this same basic structure. It is known as the **source and application of funds** format, and is illustrated in Table 12.6.

This form of balance sheet *does* treat the source of funds used in the business as the owners' capital. (That is, it adopts the non-preferred definition that the capital employed is the owners' capital.) These funds are applied (used) to acquire the net assets, which are shown on the other 'side' of the balance sheet as applications of funds (that is, as the **employment of capital**).

Adastra Ltd (Mr A. Starr)
Balance sheet at 31st January 1991

	£	£			£	£
Owners' capital:			Fixed assets:			
Paid up capital	7,500			Premises	5,000	
Profit and loss A/c	(250)			Equipment	2,500	
		7,250				7,500
Current liabilities:			Current assets:			
Trade creditors		750		Prepayment	0	
				Stocks	300	
Non-current liabilities:				Finished goods	300	
Bank loan		2,500		Debtors	1,000	
				Cash at bank	1,400	
						3,000
Liabilities + Owners'						
capital:		10,500	Assets:			10,500

Table 12.7   **Adastra: Month 1 balance sheet (Version 3).**
This second rearrangement of the balance sheet of Table 12.5 reflects the basic accounting equation in the form: Assets = Liabilities + Owners' Capital. It has the merit of simplicity, but balance sheets in the format of Table 12.5 are more common in practice.

In this case, as is commonly the case, the source funds have been mostly applied to the acquisition of fixed assets. Note that liabilities are shown as negative entries under applications of funds. The liabilities are, in effect, funds held in trust by the business, because they are owed to creditors (the bank and the component supplier in this case). Such funds do not belong to the owners and, therefore, (with this interpretation of capital employed) do not belong under the source of funds heading. Note, too, that the creditors are making a valuable contribution to the health of the business. This is shown in the table by the offsetting effect of the negative entries. Thus, the owners' capital (valued at £7,250) has provided only part (about 69%) of the funds used to acquire the assets (valued at £10,500).

Month 1 balance sheet (Version 3)

Finally, the accountant drew up a third version of Adastra's month 1 balance sheet. This is shown in Table 12.7.

The structure of this balance sheet reflects the basic accounting equation written in its original form as:

$$\text{Assets} = \text{Liabilities} + \text{Owners' Capital} \tag{12.2}$$

Arthur found this format rather more clear than the equivalent earlier versions. The accountant, however, commended that shown in Table 12.5 to him, because it is more commonly used in practice.

Adastra Ltd (Mr A. Starr)
Profit and Loss account for the month ending 31st January 1991

		£	£	Notes
Sales revenue:			1,000	1. Sale of 1 unit
less Cost of sales:				2. No data
	Direct labour	???		2. No data
	Direct materials	150		3. Made 1 unit
	Fixed production costs	???		4. No data
			150	5. Understated
Gross profit			850	6. Overstated
less Operating expense:				
	Salary	500		7. Mr A. Starr
	Legal and professional	600		8. Prepayment 1990
	Other fixed costs	???		9. No data
			1,100	10. Understated
Operating profit/(loss):			(250)	11. Loss understated

Table 12.8   Adastra: Month 1 profit and loss account.
A complete P&L account shows the revenues (income), expenses, profit retained or loss funded, dividends paid to the owners, accumulated net profits or losses from previous periods, and tax liabilities for the defined period covered by the account. This simplified example omits many such items and is inaccurate because some data is missing, but it is otherwise satisfactory. It determines a gross profit by subtracting the cost of sales from the sales revenue. The operating profit/(loss) is then derived by subtracting the operating expense from the gross profit.

12.3.5   The P&L account

The accountant reminded Arthur that a balance sheet is one of three major financial statements used to report the financial position of a business. The next one to be considered is the P&L account. This covers a defined period of time whereas a balance sheet reports the situation at a defined point in time.

Normally, a P&L account shows the:

(1) revenues (income) and expenses
(2) amount of profit retained or loss funded
(3) dividends paid to the owners
(4) accumulated net profits or losses from previous periods
(5) tax liabilities

for the defined period covered by the account.

The P&L account for Adastra's first month is not complicated by many of these factors, as the accountant illustrated in Table 12.8. The table shows how a **operating loss** of £250 (note 11) arises from the sale of a single product unit (note 1). Note that the £600 write-off of the 1990 prepayment appears (note 8) as a **legal and professional** cost. This is conventional terminology for such items.

In broad terms, the account determines a **gross profit** (note 6) by subtracting the **cost of sales** (note 5) from the **sales revenue** (note 1). The **operating profit/(loss)** is then derived (note 11) by subtracting the **operating expense** (note 10) from the gross profit.

(Readers may find it illuminating to compare Figure 1.1 with the structure of the P&L account in Table 12.8. The arithmetic of the table corresponds to Equations 1.1 and 1.3 in Section 1.1.1.)

This account is an illusion

The accountant was careful to point out that this P&L account, while the best she could do with the information supplied, is really an illusion. The account, as presented, understates the operating loss because it understates both the cost of sales and the operating expense.

The primary problem is that various costs that Adastra has incurred (but not paid) during the month have not been taken into account. These omissions contravene the critical matching principle, which demands that profit is determined by comparing the income with all the costs incurred in obtaining it. The unrecorded expenses relate to items like:

- a proportion of the annual business and water rates
- heat, light and power consumed
- post and telephone charges
- marketing, selling and product distribution costs
- interest on the bank loan.

Depreciation has also been ignored. (The depreciation mechanism creates cost items which recognize the consumption of the fixed assets during the month.) Costs such as those identified are referred to as **fixed costs**, because they are largely incurred whether or not any products are made. A proportion of the total fixed costs for the month can be assigned to the production operation (note 4), where they add to the cost of sales. The remainder of the fixed costs combine (note 9) with those that have been identified (notes 7 and 8) to make up the operating cost (note 10). Fixed costs are also commonly called **overhead costs** or **indirect costs**.

In contrast, **direct costs** are incurred in direct proportion to the number of products made. One direct cost relates to the **direct materials**, meaning the components in this case, which are incorporated into the manufactured product which has been sold. This contributes (note 3) towards cost of sales.

The secondary problem with the P&L account is that there is no way to determine the remaining element of cost of sales, which is the **direct labour** (note 2). This refers to some unrecorded fraction of Arthur's time (costing the business about £25 per working day) which is directly attributable to assembling and testing the product that has been sold. This omission only contributes towards the understatement of the cost of sales. It has no overall effect, because the whole cost of Arthur's time is recorded elsewhere (note 7).

At this point, Arthur was tempted to ask how these problems of overstatement and understatement could be corrected. But the accountant had already moved on to the third, and final, major financial statement which illustrates funds flow.

12.3.6 The funds flow statement

She pointed out that balance sheets and P&L accounts, while communicating a great deal of information about the business and its operations, do have some limitations. A balance sheet only shows:

- *where* the total funds available to a business at a specific date have come from, and
- *how* they are being used on that date.

The corresponding P&L account only shows:

- whether *trading* has increased or decreased those funds in the period up to the date of the balance sheet.

These 'primary' statements do not provide a clear insight into the liquidity of the business, nor of its flow of funds or cash during the period. A third type of financial statement is needed to correct these deficiencies. This is the funds flow statement. It is concerned with the movement of funds which change values in the system of assets, liabilities and owners' capital which comprises the accounting model of the business. The funds flow statement complements the primary statements, by explaining how the financial status of the business has changed over the period as a result of trading *and* non-trading transactions. Its particular value lies in its emphasis on changes in working capital and/or cash, which determine the liquidity of the business.

The accountant went on to explain that a number of different interpretations of the term 'funds' are used in practice, and that there are no prescribed formats for fund flow statements. However, all such statements are compiled from information in the primary statements. To illustrate the principles involved she then returned to Table 12.4, and reminded Arthur that it consists of a sequence of balance sheets. Simple funds flow statements can be extracted from this table, by comparing Adastra's position immediately following action 7 with that immediately following action 1. This period defines the active life of the business, from its creation (measured from having funds available) to the end of Month 1. For convenience, it is called 'Period 1–7' from now on.

Funds flow as cash flow

One common interpretation of 'funds' is 'cash', where 'cash' means the cash-at-bank asset. So, with this interpretation, the funds flow statement presents an analysis of the flow of cash into and out of the bank account during the period covered by the statement. Cash is an asset so, by separating assets into non-cash assets and cash, the basic accounting equation:

$$\text{Assets} = \text{Liabilities} + \text{Owners' Capital} \tag{12.2}$$

can be rewritten as:

$$\text{Cash} = -\text{Non-Cash Assets} + \text{Liabilities} + \text{Owners' Capital} \tag{12.10}$$

Now, funds flow statements are about *changes*, and Equation 12.10 indicates how cash flows are caused by unbalanced changes in non-cash assets, liabilities and owners' capital. (The meaning of 'unbalanced' in this context emerges very shortly.) Note that non-cash assets (which is a fundamentally positive fund) is preceded by a negative sign on the right-hand side of this equation. This means that if non-cash assets decrease then cash may increase and, conversely, if non-cash assets increase then cash may decrease.

From Equation 12.10, cash must increase (flow into the bank account) to balance either:

(1) a decrease in non-cash assets, or
(2) an increase in liabilities, or
(3) an increase in owners' capital.

Similarly, cash must decrease (flow out of the bank account) to balance either:

(1) an increase in non-cash assets, or
(2) a decrease in liabilities, or
(3) a decrease in owners' capital.

Note, however, that Equation 12.10 also indicates that cash will not change if changes on the right-hand side of the equation are equal and opposite (that is, balanced). For example, a decrease in non-cash assets which is accompanied by a decrease of equal magnitude in owners' capital has no effect on cash. (This particular case is illustrated in Table 12.4, by the write-off of the prepayment asset in the period between the end of action 1 and the end of action 2.)

Cash flow sources and applications

At this point, the terminology of cash flow **sources** and cash flow **applications**, or **uses**, must be introduced. Cash flows *in* to the bank account *out* of sources. For example, when payment is received for products sold on credit, cash flows into the bank account out of the debtor asset source, which is thereby decreased. Conversely, cash flows *out* of the bank account *in* to applications or uses. For example, when payment is made for stock purchased on credit, cash flows out of the bank account into the creditor liability, which is thereby decreased. This is an application, or a use, of cash.

The implications of Equation 12.10 can now be encapsulated in a rule for identifying sources of cash flow in to the bank account and uses of cash flow out of the bank account. This rule is:

Sources of cash-flow in	*Examples*
A decrease in a non-cash asset	Receive payment for goods sold on credit
An increase in a liability	Borrow more cash from the bank
An increase in owners' capital	Make and retain a profit

Uses of cash-flow out	*Examples*
An increase in a non-cash asset	Buy some equipment for cash
A decrease in a liability	Pay a creditor
A decrease in owners' capital	Pay a dividend

Note, in passing, that the rule for owners' capital follows that for (external) liabilities, since it is also a liability.

	1	7	In	Out	In/(Out)
	£	£	£	£	£
			Sources	Uses	
Non-cash assets:			Decrease	Increase	
Premises	0	5,000	–	5,000	(5,000)
Equipment	0	2,500	–	2,500	(2,500)
Prepayment	600	0	600	–	600
Components	0	300	–	300	(300)
Finished goods	0	300	–	300	(300)
Debtors	0	1,000	–	1,000	(1,000)
Total:	600	9,100	600	9,100	(8,500)
Liabilities:			Increase	Decrease	
Creditors:					
Trade	0	750	750	–	750
Bank	2,500	2,500	–	–	0
Total:	2,500	3,250	750	–	750
Owners' capital:			Increase	Decrease	
Paid up capital	7,500	7,500	–	–	0
Profit	0	(250)	–	250	(250)
Total:	7,500	7,250	–	250	(250)
Net cash-flow at bank account:					(8,000)
Provided by:			Decrease	Increase	
Cash at bank	9,400	1,400	8,000	–	(8,000)

The top of the table is headed: Cash-flow at bank account

Table 12.9   Adastra: Period 1–7 funds flow statement.
This is a funds = cash-flow statement created from the basic accounting equation written as:
Cash = – Non-Cash Assets + Liabilities + Owners' Capital. Columns 1 and 7 are the opening and
closing balance sheets for the period (from Table 12.4) rearranged to isolate the cash asset. The
differences between corresponding items in these columns are fund flows which combine to
produce the net effect on cash (at bank). The statement shows (right-hand column) £8,500 of
cash is used to acquire various non-cash assets during the period. A further £250 cash is used to
fund the trading loss, making £8,750 in all flowing out. This is offset by a £750 inflow (due to
trade creditors), so net cash flow out is £8,000.

A funds = cash flow statement

Table 12.9 is a 'cash-oriented' funds flow statement for Adastra during Period 1–7. The
columns labelled '1' and '7' are balance sheets extracted from Table 12.4 which have
been rearranged to isolate the cash-at-bank asset (at the bottom of the columns). The
differences between corresponding items in the two balance sheets are the discrete
fund flows (the changes) which combine to produce the net effect on the bank
account. These discrete flows are separated, in the next two columns, into flows in
(sources) and flows out (uses) using the rule derived earlier. The final column merely
collects the discrete flows together. Negative flows (leading to cash flows out of the

bank account) are enclosed in parentheses in this column. Note that the analysis yields a net cash flow out at bank account of £8,000. The validity of this result is confirmed by inspection of the two balance sheets. (The accountant referred to this useful cross-check as 'proving the cash'.)

The funds flow statement of Table 12.9 illustrates that Adastra used cash of £8,500 to acquire various non-cash assets during Period 1–7. A further £250 of cash is used to fund the trading loss, making £8,750 in all flowing out to applications. Only £750 of this flow is sourced externally, by the trade creditors, thereby demanding a net flow of £8,000 cash out of the bank account.

12.3.7 Meeting conclusion

Arthur was still concerned about overstating profit and understating product cost. But, at this stage, he felt that he had absorbed about as much accounting as he could handle at one time and said as much to his accountant friend. Over lunch (paid for by Arthur), she expressed some concern about the gross profit shown in the P&L account. This might be too low, she suspected, to provide a reasonable operating profit when the unrecorded expenses are brought into account. She wondered if the product price could be increased to ease this problem, or its cost greatly reduced. Arthur agreed to think about these problems, reflecting that it must be easier to bring a price down than to put it up! As they parted company, the accountant wished him good luck for the future and suggested one or two books (referenced in the bibliography) that he might read to improve his still very basic accounting knowledge.

Arthur resolved to invest some of his future efforts in learning more of accountancy, recognizing that such knowledge is part of the essential skills of any business manager.

12.4 Adastra: The end of Year 1

Adastra prospered reasonably well during the rest of the year and Arthur kept meticulous note of all the financial transactions. His bookkeeping technique was based on double-entry principles, with separate 'ledgers' (accounts) for each major class of items. The early promise of his (Adastra's, strictly) first product was confirmed by further sales, and he developed and designed an enhanced version during the year. Several of these were also sold. He found it necessary to employ a technician to do most of the product assembly and testing work. He also bought some office furniture. Bills for various services arrived and had to be paid. Interest on the bank loan was paid in monthly instalments. A variety of other expenses were incurred for postage, product distribution, and for sundry stationery items.

At the end of the year, Arthur prepared the Adastra accounts using his double-entry bookkeeping records and Chapters 1 and 2 of a 'do-it-yourself' book on accounting as a guide. These accounts are now considered. The P&L account is examined first because, in its detailed form, it explains quite a lot about Adastra's first trading year.

Some whole year expenses, which are not separately identified elsewhere, are listed here for reference:

Adastra Ltd: Profit and loss account
For the year ended 31st December 1991

	£	£	Note
Sales revenue:		67,500	1
less Cost of products sold:			2
Direct labour	13,357		3
Direct materials	8,550		4
Production overhead	11,430		5
		33,337	
Gross profit:		34,163	6
less Operating expense:			7
Salary (A. Starr 50%)	10,000		8
Rates (25%)	700		9
Electricity (25%)	900		10
Insurance (25%)	255		11
Marketing and selling	3,038		12
Product distribution	876		13
Post and telephone	667		14
Office supplies	97		15
Development and design	12,123		16
Depreciation (part)	123		17
Legal and professional	600		18
		29,379	
Operating profit:		4,784	19
less Interest paid:		425	20
Profit before tax:		4,359	21
less Tax payable:		1,444	22
Profit after tax:		2,915	23

Table 12.10 **Adastra: Year 1 profit and loss account (detail).**

The 'management accounting' version of Adastra's Year 1 P&L account shown here is more detailed than the corresponding published 'financial accounting' version (Table 12.13). It determines gross profit by subtracting cost of products sold from sales revenue, and then operating profit by subtracting operating expense from gross profit. Interest paid is a 'financing' cost (one which is allowable against tax) rather than 'operating' cost. It is subtracted from operating profit to yield profit before tax. Tax (due) is then subtracted from this to obtain profit after tax.

(1) Salary   £20,000 (A. Starr)
(2) Salary   £ 9,025 (technician: amount paid to end of Year 1)
(3) Rates   £ 2,800 (business and water)
(4) Electricity   £ 3,600 (heat, light and power)
(5) Insurance   £ 1,020 ('buildings and contents')

Note that some cost factors (such as value-added and payroll taxes) are ignored in everything that follows. The aim is to avoid obscuring the main issues with too much detail. Note, too, that all calculated monetary amounts are rounded to the nearest pound before they are entered into the accounts.

12.4.1 Year 1 P&L account (detail)

Arthur's 'management accounting' version of the Year 1 P&L account is shown in Table 12.10. This includes more detail than would be provided in a published 'financial accounting' version. In broad terms, the account identifies the sales income achieved by Adastra during the year, and the various costs which must be set against it before a profit (or a loss) is declared. The costs items are grouped in a conventional way which aids analysis of the account. Most of the figures in the table are associated with a note number in the right-hand column. These numbers are used in the following commentary to link the table to the text.

Sales revenue (1)

Sales revenue is the total cash and credit sum arising from products sold during the year. It does not include any other sort of income, such as interest earned on a deposit account. Part of the sales revenue is usually still in credit form at the year end and this part is listed as debtors on the balance sheet.

Note that a variety of terms are used to describe business income. **Sales** and **turn-over** both mean income or revenue from product sales. The terms 'income' and 'revenue' used on their own can include any or every sort of income.

Adastra sold 60 product units at an average price of £1,125 each in Year 1:

$$\text{Sales revenue (1):} \qquad\qquad 60 \times \pounds1{,}125 = \pounds67{,}500$$

Cost of products sold (2)

This cost relates only to the 60 product units sold during the year, so it matches the sales revenue. The cost of products sold is sometimes called the **total works (or factory) cost**. It is made up of three parts which are termed **direct labour**, **direct materials** and **production overhead**.

Now, while 60 product units were sold during the year, the number of product units actually made and tested (that is, produced) was 63. So the cost of products produced is calculated first, by evaluating the total direct labour, direct materials and production overhead consumed.

Direct labour is the cost of the human effort which is directly attributable to making and testing the products. Arthur estimated that, over the year, all of the technician's time and twenty-five per cent of his time was spent in this way:

$$
\begin{aligned}
&100\% \text{ of technician:} && = \pounds\ 9{,}025 \\
&25\% \text{ of Arthur Starr:} && 0.25 \times \pounds20{,}000 = \pounds\ 5{,}000 \\
&\text{Total direct labour (63 units):} && = \pounds14{,}025
\end{aligned}
$$

Direct materials is the cost of those externally purchased items which are directly attributable to making the products. In other words, it is the cost of all the 'materials' incorporated into the products (or otherwise consumed) during manufacture. Arthur obtained a five per cent 'volume purchase' discount on the original list price of the components (which was £150 per product):

Total direct materials (63 units): $0.95 \times £150 \times 63 = £8{,}978$

The production overhead (or production indirect) cost is made up of a number of cost elements which are attributable to the product making and testing activity, but are 'fixed' in the sense that they do not vary with the number of products made and tested. Arthur decided that only the depreciation of Adastra's tools, test gear and fittings (the 'equipment') was wholly chargeable to the production activity. He then used relative floor area as a basis for partitioning costs associated with the whole workshop such as rates, electricity, insurance and depreciation of the premises. The production activity used seventy-five per cent of the workshop floor area. Arthur also estimated that twenty-five per cent of his time was spent on supervising the production activity and calculated the production overhead as:

Equipment depreciation: $= £ \ 1{,}250$
75% of (rates, electricity, insurance): $0.75 \times £7{,}420 = £ \ 5{,}565$
75% of premises depreciation: $0.75 \times £250 = £ \quad 187$
25% of Arthur Starr: $0.25 \times £20{,}000 = £ \ 5{,}000$

Total production overhead (63 units): $= £12{,}002$

(The depreciation charges used here are calculated in Section 12.4.2, which examines the Year 1 balance sheet.)

Then, for the 63 units:

Cost of products produced: $£14{,}025 + £8{,}978 + £12{,}002 = £35{,}005$

The cost of products sold is then obtained by apportionment, as follows:

Direct labour (3): $(60/63) \times £14{,}025 = £13{,}357$
Direct materials (4): $(60/63) \times £ \ 8{,}978 = £ \ 8{,}550$
Production overhead (5): $(60/63) \times £12{,}002 = £11{,}430$

Cost of products sold (2): $= £33{,}337$

Gross profit (6)

Gross profit is the excess of sales revenue over the cost of products sold. In other words, it is the net income earned by the production activity. It has to pay for all the other costs that a business incurs and provide a residue as operating profit. Because of its critical role, the production activity it often referred to as the 'direct' activity, whereas all the other activities, which it supports with its earnings, are 'indirect' (or 'overhead') activities. In this case:

Gross profit (6): $£67{,}500 - £33{,}337 = £34{,}163$

Operating expense (7)

Operating expense, or cost, is made up of day-to-day running costs of the business which are not directly incurred in making and testing products. Such items are often termed 'indirect' or 'overhead' costs and are relatively independent of the number of product units made or sold. Most of the items included under operating cost in the (detailed) Adastra P&L account require very little explanation.

Half of Arthur's salary is included in the cost of products produced. This is the other half.

Salary (A. Starr 50%) (8): $0.5 \times £20,000 = £10,000$

Most of the following costs are included in the cost of products produced. These are the residues.

Rates (25%) (9): $= £700$
Electricity (25%) (10): $= £900$
Insurance (25%) (11): $= £255$

At note 12, marketing covers the design and printing of business and product brochures for dispatch to actual and prospective customers. Selling costs refer to Arthur's expenses incurred in follow-up visits and presentations. Arthur realized that some fraction of the whole cost is of an investment nature, because it would (hopefully) lead to product sales in 1992. He could have **capitalized** this fraction by treating it as an asset to be carried forward in the balance sheet. This would have the effect of increasing the 1991 profit but reducing the 1992 profit when the asset is written-off. He chose not to do this, and entered the whole sum into the accounts as an expense to be set against the 1991 sales. This is an example of the accountancy prudence principle triumphing over the matching principle. Arthur regarded it as an example of normal engineering caution. He was surprised that these 'commercial' costs were so high, at about 4.5% of sales revenue.

Marketing and selling (12): $= £3,038$

Product distribution refers to the packing, transit insurance and transport (by a specialist distribution company) of the products sold. Arthur considered this cost to be higher than necessary at about £15 (average) per product.

Product distribution (13): $= £876$

The costs here refer to postal and telephone charges, and items of stationery.

Post and telephone (14): $= £667$
Office supplies (15): $= £\ 97$

Development and design is a major cost item (about eighteen per cent of sales revenue) which reflects Arthur's plan to reduce product cost. Development and design cost is generally of an investment nature, because the benefits that it purchases are likely to be received after (perhaps long after) the money has been spent. Arthur wisely chose not to capitalize this cost, although he could have done so. (Note that research costs, as distinct from development and design costs, must not be capitalized. This is to avoid the dangers of holding assets of very uncertain real value in a balance sheet.) Arthur found that he was not able to devote much of his own time to product innovation. He concentrated, therefore, on defining two 'custom' silicon integrated circuit 'chips' aimed at replacing most of the individual chips in the current products. Together, these will probably cost rather more than the components that they replace. But they should allow very substantial reductions in product assembly and test costs. The entry in the P&L account covers the cost to date of a development and design contract, placed on a specialist supplier, for the custom chips.

Development and design (16): $= £12,123$

Most of the total depreciation charge is assigned to cost of products produced. This is the residue, made up of twenty-five per cent of premises depreciation and all of the furniture depreciation. (The depreciation charges used here are calculated in Section 12.4.2, which examines the Year 1 balance sheet.)

Depreciation (part) (17): $(0.25 \times £250) + £60 = £123$

The cost at note 18 is the write-off, as an expense in the 1991 accounts, of the 1990 prepayment of formation and auditing costs.

Legal and professional (18): $= £600$

This completes the individual costs contributing to operating expense, so:

Operating expense (7): $= £29,379$

Operating profit (19)

This measures the efficiency of the trading activity before interest costs and taxation are taken into account. It is obtained by subtracting operating expense from the gross profit:

Operating profit (19): $£34,163 - £29,379 = £4,784$

Interest paid (20)

Loan interest is a **financing cost** which *is* allowable against tax, but is not considered to be part of operating expense. It arises here because of the 17% per annum interest charge on the bank loan:

Interest paid (20): $0.17 \times £2,500 = £425$

(Dividends paid or payable to shareholders are a financing cost which is *not* allowable against tax. It does not arise here, because Arthur has chosen not to pay a dividend.)

Profit before tax (21)

This is simply the operating profit less the interest paid:

Profit before tax (21): $£4,784 - £425 = £4,359$

Tax payable (22)

Business tax is government-imposed charge against profits, rather than an expense incurred in earning them. It is normally payable some months after the end of the business financial year. Companies are subject to **corporation tax** on **taxable profit** at 'company' rates which depend on the profit level. (The rates applicable to a sole-trader business are the same as the personal income tax rates of its owner.) **Taxable profit** and **accounting profit** are rarely identical. Typically, a substantial difference arises because the tax authorities set their own rules for calculating the depreciation of fixed assets which do not coincide with those used by the business. Other factors include the disallowance of some business expenses for tax purposes, and timing differences between when some expenses are set against profit and allowed against tax. In general, the assessment of business tax is a complex matter which is not eased by periodic changes in the rules and the rates. It is best left to professional accountants. Arthur did not follow this advice. His calculation is shown in Table 12.11.

Adastra Ltd: tax payable for the year ended 31st December 1991

	£	£	Note
'Accounting' profit before tax:		4,359	from P&L account
Add back:			
Depreciation	1,560		Disallowed
Formation costs	400		Disallowed
Entertainment costs	355		Disallowed
Total disallowed:		2,315	
Subtract:			
4% of premises	200		Depreciate over 25 years
25% of equipment	625		Depreciate over 4 years
25% of furniture	75		Depreciate over 4 years
Total capital allowance:		(900)	
Taxable profit:		5,774	
Tax payable @ 25%:		1,444	Small business tax rate

Table 12.11   **Adastra: Year 1 tax payable.**
Corporation tax is a government levy on profits, not a cost contributing to earning them. Taxable profit and accounting profit are rarely identical, because some business expenses are not tax deductible and the tax authorities use their own depreciation algorithms. The table shows how Adastra's accounting profit (at note 21 of Table 12.10) is adjusted to taxable profit, so that the tax due can be calculated.

The accounting profit before tax comes from the P&L account at note 21 of Table 12.10. This is first adjusted by 'adding back' three disallowed costs. These are depreciation, formation costs (part of legal and professional at note 18) and entertainment costs (part of marketing and selling at note 12). (Arthur cannot understand why taking potential customers out to lunch is not regarded as an acceptable marketing expense by the tax authorities. But he is glad that he has kept the receipts that support all of his personally incurred marketing and selling costs.) The depreciation adjustment is then partially compensated by subtracting a **capital allowance** to yield the **taxable profit**. The capital allowance is calculated on the first cost of the fixed assets at 'write-off' rates which are determined by the tax authorities and noted in Table 12.11. The tax payable is then calculated as twenty-five per cent of the taxable profit, this being the tax rate that is applicable to 'small' businesses:

Tax payable (22): $0.25 \times £5,774 = £1,444$

Profit after tax (23)

This is simply the profit before tax less the tax payable:

Profit after tax (23): $£4,359 - £1,444 = £2,915$

This calculation completes the detailed management accounting version of the P&L

account for Adastra's first year of operations. Attention is now turned to the corresponding balance sheet, which Arthur constructed from his detailed records of transactions during the year.

12.4.2 Year 1 balance sheet

The Year 1 balance sheet associated with the P&L account of Table 12.10 is shown in Table 12.12. In fact, balance sheets for 1991 (Year 1) and 1990 (Year 0) are displayed in the 1991 balance sheet statement. This is a standard practice which allows easy comparison of the status of the business at the end of two successive years. As a rule, the same practice is used in P&L accounts but Adastra did no trading in 1990. The 1990 balance sheet in Table 12.12 is a simple affair illustrating the start-up position of Adastra. It is derived from the 1990 column (action 1) of Table 12.4, which is examined in Section 12.3.3.

Overview

In broad terms, the account of Table 12.12 expresses the basic accounting equation formulated as:

$$\text{Net Assets} = \text{Owners' Capital} \tag{12.4}$$

by describing the balance of assets less liabilities with owners' capital as it appears at the end of the year. Values are first obtained for:

- fixed assets (FA)
- current assets (CA)
- current liabilities (CL)
- non-current liabilities (NCL).

Net current assets (NCA), also called working capital, is then:

$$\text{NCA} = \text{CA} - \text{CL} \tag{12.11}$$

and net assets (NA) is:

$$\text{NA} = \text{FA} + \text{NCA} - \text{NCL} \tag{12.12}$$

The net assets are balanced against the owners' capital on the other 'side' of the balance sheet. The owners' capital comprises paid up capital (which is the owners' initial investment in this case) and the **retained profit** (profit after tax and dividends) derived in the P&L account.

Most of the figures in Table 12.12 are associated with a note number in the right-hand column. The following commentary concerns the 1991 entries, and the numbers are used to link the table to the text.

Fixed assets (1)

In this presentation, the individual fixed assets (premises, equipment and furniture) are listed at their first cost. An aggregated depreciation adjustment is then applied to obtain total fixed assets. Alternatively, the individual fixed assets may be listed at their **book values**. The book value of a fixed asset is its first cost less total depreciation at

Adastra Ltd: Balance sheet at 31st December 1991

	1991 £	1991 £	1990 £	Note
Fixed assets:				1
Premises at cost	5,000		–	2
Equipment at cost	2,500		–	3
Furniture at cost	300		–	4
less Depreciation	1,560		–	5
		6,240	–	
Current assets:				6
Stocks	713		–	7
Finished goods	1,668		–	8
Trade debtors	4,500		–	9
Prepayments	735		600	10
Cash at bank	2,324		9,400	11
		9,940	10,000	
Current liabilities:				12
Trade creditors	1,425		–	13
Tax	1,444		–	14
Accruals (salary due)	396		–	15
		3,265	–	
Net current assets:		6,675	10,000	16
Total assets *less* Current liabilities:		12,915	10,000	17
Non-current liabilities:				18
Bank loan	2,500		2,500	19
		2,500	2,500	
Net assets:		10,415	7,500	20
Financed by capital and reserves:				21
Paid up capital	7,500		7,500	22
Retained profit (P&L account)	2,915		–	23
Owners' capital:		10,415	7,500	24

***Table 12.12*   Adastra: Year 1 balance sheet.**
The balance sheet for the previous year is shown, for comparison purposes, alongside this 1991 balance sheet. It expresses the balance of net assets (in terms of fixed assets, current assets, current liabilities and non-current liabilities) with owners' capital. This comprises paid up capital (which is their initial investment here) and the retained profit (profit after tax and dividends) from the P&L account (Table 12.10).

the time it is measured. A depreciation adjustment measures the 'consumption' of a fixed asset over the year and it appears as a cost in the P&L account. Note that the principles of prudence and matching dominate these techniques. Assets are accounted for at the lower of cost or market value (the prudence principle). Depreciation is even applied to the premises which, generally, could be expected to increase in value over the years. The book values of the equipment and furniture do represent approximate market value. The depreciation mechanism aims to spread the purchase cost of a fixed asset over its useful life, thereby matching its consumption with the benefits it provides.

Many different algorithms are used for assessing depreciation charges. That employed here assumes that book values decline linearly to zero over defined asset lifetimes. These are taken as:

- premises: 20 years
- equipment: 2 years
- furniture: 5 years.

The assumed lifetime for the equipment is short because the asset was well-used when purchased, and it is ageing rapidly. The depreciation calculations are shown below.

Premises (2):
Depreciation $0.05 \times £5{,}000 = £\ \ 250$
Book value at the end of Year 1 $£5{,}000 - £250 = £4{,}750$

Equipment (3):
Depreciation $0.5 \times £2{,}500 = £1{,}250$
Book value at the end of Year 1 $£2{,}500 - £1{,}250 = £1{,}250$

Furniture (4):
Depreciation $0.2 \times £300 = £\ \ 60$
Book value at the end of Year 1 $£300 - £60 = £\ \ 240$

Aggregate Depreciation (5) $£250 + £1{,}250 + £60 = £1{,}560$

Fixed assets (1) $£7{,}800 - £1{,}560 = £6{,}240$

Current assets (6)

Current assets are tangible and intangible resources held by the business which should be converted into cash within one year.

Stocks are valued at the lower of purchase cost or market value (prudence concept). In this case, five 'product kits' of components are held in store and they are valued at cost.

Stocks (7): $5 \times 0.95 \times £150 = £713$

Completed products which are held in store prior to sale are valued at the lower of cost or market value (prudence concept). In this case, three completed products are held in store, and they are valued at cost of products produced less cost of products sold.

Finished goods (8): $£35{,}005 - £33{,}337 = £1{,}668$

Trade debtors represents cash due from customers who have purchased products on credit but not paid at the end of the accounts period. It is valued at the amount due less any allowance for anticipated bad debts (prudence concept). No bad debts are anticipated in this case, and cash is due on four product units sold on credit.

Trade debtors (9): $4 \times £1,125 = £4,500$

Prepayments are (usually unavoidable) payments of expenses made in advance of the purchased benefits being received. Rent, for example, is normally paid in advance. Such items count as assets because they represent future benefits. Adastra paid rates in two equal instalments of £1,470 on 1st April and 1st October 1991. The October payment created a prepayment relating to the first quarter of 1992.

Prepayments (10): $0.5 \times £1,470 = £735$

(Note that the rates payment for the first quarter of 1991 was £595, so rates for the whole year is $£595 + (3 \times £735) = £2,800$.)

Cash-at-bank is a portmanteau term, which covers cash held and near-cash items, such as cheques held, as well as the contents of the bank account:

Cash at bank (11): $= £2,324$

Current assets (6): $= £9,940$

Current liabilities (12)

Current assets are debts which are to be repaid within one year.

Trade creditors is the amount owed to external suppliers for goods and services purchased on credit but not paid for at the year end. Adastra owes its component supplier for ten 'product kits' of components.

Trade creditors (13): $10 \times 0.95 \times £150 = £1,425$

Adastra has not yet paid any tax, so it is liable for the whole amount shown in the P&L account.

Tax (14): $= £1,444$

As illustrated here, **accruals** are liabilities which increase progressively until paid, and which must be recorded to maintain matching between revenue and expense. The P&L account records the whole year cost of the technician, but Adastra pays his salary on the 15th of each month. So, at the end of December 1991, there is an accrued liability equivalent to 16 days pay.

Accruals (15): $(16/365) \times £9,025 = £396$

(Accruals can also be income items. For example, a property company might be due rental income which has not yet been billed to a tenant. The amount due adds to income in the P&L account and is shown as a debtor in the balance sheet.)

Current liabilities (12): $= £3,265$

Net current assets (16) = working capital

This is the working capital: the excess of current assets over current liabilities. It is an indicator of the short-term financial stability of a business:

Net current assets (16):   £9,940 − £3,625 = £6,675

Total assets less current liabilities (17) = capital employed

This parameter is equal to the capital employed (when conventionally defined as non-current liabilities plus owners' capital). It is a long-term indicator of financial stability, because fixed assets cannot (usually) be quickly converted to cash (unless offered at substantially below normal market value). It is obtained by adding the fixed assets to the working capital:

Total assets less current liabilities (17):   £6,240 + £6,675 = £12,915

Non-current liabilities (18)

These are debts which are not due to be paid within one year.
The only item, in this case, is the loan from the bank.

Bank loan (19):   = £2,500

Non-current liabilities (18):   = £2,500

Net assets (20)

This is the excess of total assets over total liabilities. It is sometimes called the **net worth** of the business. This is a potentially misleading term, because it suggests that the business could be sold for its net worth. The net assets value, or net worth value, is a factor in the market value of a business but the circumstances of the sale determines the price obtained. Net assets is obtained by subtracting non-current liabilities from total assets less current liabilities:

Net assets (20):   £12,915 − £2,500 = £10,415

Capital & reserves (21) = owners' capital (24)

The owners' capital equates to net assets. It is made up of the capital and reserve elements: the initial investment by the owners:

Paid up capital (22):   = £7,500

and the the retained profit as assessed in the P&L account:

Retained profit (23):   = £2,915

Owners' capital (24):   £7,500 + £2,915 = £10,415

This calculation completes the Year 1 balance sheet. Arthur was both pleased and surprised that it did show a balance between net assets and owners' capital. He regarded this as a convincing demonstration of the logic of double-entry accounting and of the accuracy of his bookkeeping.

12.5 Adastra: Year 1 accounts analysis

Arthur had already arranged another meeting with his accountant to launch her promised 'preparation and audit' of Adastra's first year accounts. They reviewed the

Adastra Ltd: profit and loss account
for the year ended 31st December 1991

	£	Note
Product sales:	67,500	1
Cost of products sold:	33,337	2
Gross profit:	34,163	3
Distribution costs:	876	4
Administration costs:	16,380	5
Development and design costs:	12,123	6
Operating expense:	29,379	7
Operating profit:	4,784	8
Interest payable:	425	9
Profit before tax:	4,359	10
Tax payable:	1,444	11
Profit after tax:	2,915	12
Dividend payable:	0	13
Retained profit this year:	2,915	14
Retained profit from prior years:	0	15
Retained profit at end of this year:	2,915	16

Table 12.13   **Adastra: Year 1 profit and loss account (summary).**
This is the 'management' P&L account of Table 12.10 condensed into a 'financial' format suitable for publication. It is, perhaps, slightly unusual in displaying development and design costs as a distinct item. Many such accounts absorbs such costs under the 'administration' heading. Note that dividends (another 'financing' cost), if paid, are paid out of profit after tax.

results of his excursions into accountancy at the start of the meeting. She congratulated him on the progress of Adastra during the year and on his accounting efforts. Arthur was eager to decipher the less obvious messages that he felt that the accounts contained. The accountant agreed to lead him through the initial stages of analysis before starting her own work. She began with the P&L account.

12.5.1   Year 1 P&L account (summary)

The Year 1 P&L account shown in Table 12.10 is in a management accounting format, which reveals more detail than would appear in a P&L account prepared for publication. The accountant thought that Arthur should witness how the management data is condensed into a financial accounting format suitable for publication. The process is quite straightforward and the result is displayed in Table 12.13.

As before, the table contains a series of note numbers in the right-hand column for reference purposes. However, in this case, most of the data in the account is extracted unchanged from the detailed P&L account (of Table 12.10) and needs no further comment. Some points of special interest are now examined.

Cost of products sold (2)

Note that only the total is revealed. No information is provided about the structure of this major cost item. There is no sense in giving more information to competitors than must be published to meet legal requirements.

Operating expense (7)

Most published P&L accounts collect the costs making up operating expense under just two subheadings: distribution costs and **administration costs**. Arthur pointed out that development and design are nothing to do with 'administration'. He also felt that there is some merit in advertising Adastra's commitment to technological innovation in the accounts. The accountant agreed. So distribution costs (4) and development and design costs (6) are extracted directly from the detailed account. Administration costs (5) is then a balancing figure which covers all the other items listed under operating expense in Table 12.10.

Retained profit this year (14)

As shown, this item is the same as profit after tax (12), which is extracted from the detailed P&L account. But suppose that Arthur had chosen to reward Adastra's owners (his wife and himself) with a dividend for their investment in the company. In this case, the dividend paid (or proposed for payment) would be subtracted, at note 13 in this account, before declaration of the retained profit this year.

Dividends are a financing cost rather than a business expense, and they are paid out of profit *after* tax. Thus, in effect, the shareholders (the owners) pay the company's tax liability.

Retained profit at end of this year (16)

This is a *cumulative* figure recording the whole history of retained profits and absorbed losses from the foundation of the business up the end of 'this year'. The retained profit at end of this year is alternatively called the **reserves**.

In this case, retained profit from prior years (15) is nil, because Adastra has no prior trading years.

12.5.2   Year 1 funds flow statement

The accountant then turned her attention to the balance sheet of Table 12.12. She pointed out that cash at bank (11) has decreased from £9,400 to £2,324 during the 1991 year. In other words, there has been a net cash flow of:

$$£9,400 - £2,324 = £7,076$$

out of Adastra's bank account during 1991. Similarly, net current assets (16), which is the working capital, has decreased from £10,000 to £6,675 during 1991. In other words, there has been a net fund flow of:

$$£10,000 - £6,675 = £3,325$$

out of Adastra's (notional) store of working capital during 1991. Part of this outflow is due to tax (14) which, once a profit has been declared, is not controllable by Adastra's management. But the remaining outflow of working capital:

$$£3,325 - £1,444 = £1,881$$

arises from the managed operations of the business as, indeed, does the cash outflow (noted earlier) which it includes.

The accountant thought that it would be illuminating to find out why these flows had happened before discussing their significance. She reminded Arthur that this type of analysis is the purpose of a funds flow statement. Arthur produced the funds flow statement for Adastra's first trading month from his files. (This is Table 12.9, which is developed in Section 12.3.6. It emphasizes cash flow.) The accountant explained that the statement she was about to prepare would be formulated on the same basis as that earlier document. However, the format would be arranged to:

- illustrate changes in working capital
- illustrate cash flow at the bank account
- conform with the mandatory requirements of the British professional accountancy institutions relating to funds flow statements.

The conventional funds flow format

This conventional form of funds flow statement is commonly called a **statement of source and application of funds**. Its structure is most easily explained in terms of the basic accounting equation:

$$\text{Net Assets} = \text{Owners' Capital} \tag{12.4}$$

which underpins the balance sheet of Table 12.12 (and, indeed, every other balance sheet).

Now, Equation 12.4 can be expanded in terms of its basic elements, which are:

- fixed assets (FA)
- current assets (CA)
- current liabilities (CL)
- non-current liabilities (NCL)
- owners' capital (OC)

to read:

$$FA + CA - CL - NCL = OC$$

which is then rearranged as:

$$(OC + NCL - FA) \quad\ = (CA - CL) \tag{12.13}$$

The quantity $(CA - CL)$ is the working capital (WC), which is conventionally termed net current assets in balance sheets. So Equation 12.13 becomes the 'twin' equation:

$$(OC + NCL - FA) \quad\ = WC = (CA - CL) \tag{12.14}$$

This is an interesting expression of the basic accounting equation. Its left-hand side is a store of funds provided by the excess of the long-term liabilities (owners' capital plus non-current liabilities) over the long-term assets (fixed assets). Its right-hand side is a store of funds provided by the excess of the short-term assets (current assets) over the short-term liabilities (current liabilities). The difference in liquidity between the opposite sides of the equation is largely accommodated by the 'circulation' of day-to-day trading transactions on the right-hand side of the equation, and the accrual of profit to owners' capital. (This circulation concept is discussed in Section 12.2.5 and it is illustrated in Figure 12.2.)

A source and application of funds (flow) statement is conventionally based on Equation 12.14, which effectively defines 'funds' as working capital. The flows of these funds during a period are the changes, between the end and beginning of the period, in the left-hand side and the right-hand side of the equation. Clearly, an increase in the quantity $(OC + NCL - FA)$ increases working capital. Equally, a decrease in the quantity $(OC + NCL - FA)$ decreases working capital. In the language of a source and application of funds (flow) statement:

- an increase in the quantity $(OC + NCL - FA)$ is a **source** of (working capital) funds, and
- a decrease in the quantity $(OC + NCL - FA)$ is an **application** of (working capital) funds.

Thus, a rule can be formulated for identifying sources and applications of working capital funds. The rule is:

Sources of working capital funds	*Examples*
An increase in owners' capital	Make and retain a profit
An increase in non-current liabilities	Increase long-term debt
A decrease in fixed assets	Sell a building
Applications of working capital funds	*Examples*
A decrease in owners' capital	Pay a dividend
A decrease in non-current liabilities	Decrease long-term debt
An increase in fixed assets	Buy some equipment

Note that 'source' and 'application' are defined in a way which means long-term (that is, relatively stable during the year) source and application. Equation 12.14 shows that increases and decreases in the quantity $(CA - CL)$ are also sources and applications of working capital. But these short-term changes are not described in that way in a source and application of funds (flow) statement!

Now (recognizing that the following statement is a blinding glimpse of the obvious) a transaction that changes any one side of Equation 12.14 must generate an equal change on the other side of the equation. (Because this is what equations are about!) So, over a period of time embracing many transactions:

$$\text{Aggregate Sources} - \text{Aggregate Applications} = \text{Net Increase or Decrease in Working Capital} \qquad (12.15)$$

This is the relationship expressed in a (conventional) statement of source and application of funds, which has three parts:

(1) A record of sources, which is where new funds have come from.
(2) A record of applications, which is what the new funds have been used for.
(3) An analysis of how the net inflow or outflow of the funds is reflected in the elements comprising the working capital of the business including, importantly, the movement (flow) in **net liquid funds**.

Net liquid funds has been previously called cash-at-bank or cash and near-cash. It is the aggregate of all cash, cheques to hand, the net cash balance at the bank (credit less any overdraft) and any other 'immediately' available money.

Statement overview

The statement of source and application of funds which the accountant constructed for Adastra is shown in Table 12.14. It is based on Equation 12.15, but excludes the effects of tax and dividend liabilities on profit and on working capital. This approach focuses attention on fund flows that relate to business transactions. (As it happens, Adastra has no dividend liability at the end of 1991.)

The flows identified and classified in this statement are either extracted from the 1991 P&L account (Table 12.10) or are calculated by comparing the 1991 balance sheet with that for the previous year (both in Table 12.12).

As before, the numbers in the note column are used in the following commentary to link the table to the text. Broadly, the upper part of the statement (notes 1 to 7) concerns the left-hand side of Equation 12.15 and the lower part (notes 8 to 17) concerns its right-hand side.

Note that applications, which are fund flows out of the business, are taken as negative. The same convention applies, for the same reason, to decreases in current assets (of which there are none) and increases in current liabilities.

Source of funds (3)

Generally, source items are any increases in owners' capital and non-current liabilities, and decreases in fixed assets (see Equation 12.14).

There is one entry in this case, which is the profit before tax (1). The profit for the period increases owners' capital. It is derived, in the P&L account, by subtracting all relevant costs from the revenue. However, not all costs involve an actual *movement* of funds. Depreciation, which is an accounting adjustment to profit made for matching purposes, is the most common cost of this type. Such costs must be 'added back' to yield a proper measure of funds flow from the profit source. Here depreciation (2) from the balance sheet is added back to yield the aggregate sources, which are:

Funds generated from operations (3): £4,359 + £1,560 = £ 5,919

Applications of funds (6)

Generally, application items are any decreases in owners' capital and non-current liabilities, and increases in fixed assets (see Equation 12.14).

There are two entries in this case. The first, tax and dividend paid (4), is included only as an illustration because it is a zero flow here. In principle, it decreases owners' capital but no tax has yet been paid and no dividend has been (or will be) paid. The second item is the purchase of fixed assets (5) extracted, at cost, from the balance sheet. So:

Adastra Ltd: Statement of source and application of funds
for the year ended 31st December 1991

	£	£	Note
Source of funds:			
Profit before tax	4,359		1
Adjustments:			
Add depreciation	1,560		2
Funds generated from operations:		5,919	3
Application of funds:			
Tax and dividends paid	0		4
Purchase of fixed assets	(7,800)		5
		(7,800)	6
Inc/(dec) in funds:		(1,881)	7
Comprising			
Inc/(dec) in current assets:			
Stocks	713		8
Finished goods	1,668		9
Trade debtors	4,500		10
Prepayments	135		11
		7,016	12
(Inc)/dec in current liabilities (excluding tax and dividend):			
Trade creditors	(1,425)		13
Accruals	(396)		14
		(1,821)	15
Flow of net liquid funds:			
Cash at bank		(7,076)	16
Inc/(dec) in working capital:		(1,881)	17

Table 12.14   Adastra: Year 1 funds flow statement.

This conventional form of funds flow statement is commonly called a statement of source and application of funds. It is arranged to emphasize changes in working capital (and cash) during the year. The basic accounting equation can be manipulated to show that increases in owners' capital and non-current liabilities, and decreases in fixed assets are sources of working capital. Conversely, decreases in owners' capital and non-current liabilities, and increases in fixed assets are applications of working capital. The statement is based on these notions, but excludes the effects of tax and dividend liabilities on profit and on working capital. This focuses attention on fund flows that relate to managed business transactions. Note that the funds generated from operations account for about 76% of the increase in fixed assets. In the other half of the statement, the increase in (non-cash) current assets is nearly matched by the decrease in cash; and most of the decrease in working capital relates to the increase in current liabilities.

Application of funds (6):   = (£7,800)

Increase/(decrease) in funds (7)

This is the excess of sources over applications. It summarizes the first half of the flows balance, and is a net outflow in this case:

Increase/(decrease) in funds (7):   £5,919 + (£7,800) = (£1,881)

Increases/(decreases) in working capital (17)

This summarizes the second half of the flows balance. An increase in working capital flows from an increase in current assets or a decrease in current liabilities. Conversely, a decrease in working capital flows from a decrease in current assets or an increase in current liabilities (see Equation 12.14).

This part of the statement first shows the changes in all the current assets *except* net liquid funds (cash-at-bank in this case). The purpose of this structural feature is explained shortly. The items at notes 8, 9, 10 and 11 in the statement are extracted from the balance sheet. In this case, they are all increases, and are summed at note 12 where:

Inc/(dec) in current assets (12): £713 + £1,668 + £4,500 + £135 = £7,016

The items at notes 13 and 14 are increases in current liabilities, which are also extracted from the balance sheet. They are summed at note 15 where:

(Inc)/dec in current liabilities (15):   (£1,425) + (£396) = (£1,821)

The change in net liquid funds, which is simply the change in cash at bank here, is entered next (note 16) as an isolated item:

Flow of net liquid funds (16):   = (£7,076)

This structural feature focuses attention on the critical net cash flow parameter, which is the flow of net liquid funds. It is this flow (of the most liquid asset) which, in effect, achieves the overall balance demonstrated by the equality:

Increase/(decrease) in funds = Increase/(decrease) in working capital
            at note 7   at note 17

Funds flow statement: Discussion

The accountant opened the discussion of the funds flow statement. She pointed out that, generally, a reduction in working capital (even before the tax liability is included) is not good news. And such situations are worsened when, as here, it is accompanied by comparatively substantial net cash outflow. But, she consoled Arthur, this gloomy view is not justified in this case. In fact, recognizing its start-up status, Adastra has performed well in its first year, when heavy spending is almost inevitable. She noted that the funds generated from operations, at note 3 in Table 12.14, had made a very substantial (some 76%) contribution towards the purchase of fixed assets (note 5). Similarly, in the other half of the statement, virtually the whole of the current assets (note 12) has been purchased with cash (flow) at bank (note 16). Similarly, most (about 97%) of the decrease in working capital (note 17) relates to the increase in current liabilities (note 15). She cautioned Arthur that this perspective is just one particular interpretation of the statement. Other interpretations are possible. The one that she had presented clearly did not align with the day-to-day flow of funds that had occurred during the year. The fixed assets, for example, had actually been purchased with cash out of the bank. During the year, however, this cash outflow had been largely compensated by inflow of funds from operations.

Other forms of funds flow statement

The accountant reminded Arthur that other forms of funds flow statement could be constructed, because there is no universally accepted definition of the term 'funds'. In Table 12.14, 'funds' means 'working capital'. Another common definition of 'funds' is 'cash'. A cash-oriented funds flow statement can be constructed by expressing the basic accounting equation in the appropriate form (as in Equation 12.10). The cash format is preferred by some managers to the working capital version. She suggested that they should postpone examining that approach to funds flow until some other time. She wanted to consider some implications of the P&L account.

12.5.3 Break-even analysis

The break-even concept is introduced in Section 7.6.2 and is explored in some depth in Section 7.9. Its application to Adastra's first trading year exposes some interesting information. For the purpose of the analysis, it is assumed that *all* of the 63 product units produced in the year are sold (at the average price of £1,125 each) during the year. This assumption enables the *whole* cost of production to be dealt with in a notional P&L account, and the fact that Adastra sold only 60 units during the year becomes irrelevant to the argument.

The basic theory

In a P&L account, both the sales revenue and the cost of products sold relate to the product units which are sold during the year. The gross profit (GP) is the excess of sales revenue (SR) over cost of products sold, and this relationship may be written as:

$$GP = (SR - TPC) - POH \tag{12.16}$$

where TPC is the **total prime cost** defined by:

$$TPC = \text{Direct Labour} + \text{Direct Materials} \tag{12.17}$$

and POH is the production overhead.

Now, subject to certain assumptions which are examined later under the 'Assumptions and conclusions' heading in this section, SR and TPC both vary in direct proportion to the number of product units sold during the year. On the other hand, POH is a fixed cost, in the sense that it does not vary with the number of product units sold. (It comprises assigned fractions of annual depreciation, rates, electricity and insurance costs together with a fraction of Arthur's salary representing his production manager role. The details are in Section 12.4.1.) So Equation 12.16 can be rewritten as:

$$GP = C.US - POH \tag{12.18}$$

where C is a constant given by:

$$C = \frac{(SR - TPC)}{US} \tag{12.19}$$

and US is the corresponding number of product units sold. The constant, C, is the average sales revenue per product unit sold *minus* the average prime cost per product unit sold. This is an important parameter called the **product contribution**. The terminology recognizes that C is the (average) contribution that the sale of a single product unit makes towards the fixed costs. Alternatively, it may be regarded as the (average) net incremental income earned from the sale of one additional product unit.

The operating profit (OP) is obtained by subtracting the operating expense (OE) from the gross profit. The operating expense is also a fixed cost in the sense that it does not vary with the number of product units sold, so:

$$OP = C.US - TFC \tag{12.20}$$

where TFC is the **total fixed cost** given by:

$$TFC = POH + OE \tag{12.21}$$

Adastra: The relationships between profit and unit sales

Using the figures derived in Section 12.4.1, the product contribution, C, is very nearly £760 (from Equation 12.19), and the production overhead and total fixed costs are £12,002 and £41,381 respectively. Equations 12.18 and 12.20 then become:

$$GP = £(760.US - 12,002) \tag{12.22}$$
$$OP = £(760.US - 41,381) \tag{12.23}$$

Clearly, if no products are sold during the year (US = 0) the gross profit is a negative value (that is, it is a loss rather than a profit) equal to the production overhead. It increases linearly from this negative value as the number of product units sold increases, and it becomes zero when the number of product units sold is about 16. This is the break-even point for the gross profit. It occurs when the aggregated contributions of the products sold have paid for the fixed production overhead. Beyond this point the gross profit is positive.

The behaviour of the operating profit is similar, except that it shows an initial loss equal to the total fixed costs, and breaks even when the number of product units sold is about 54. This occurs when the aggregated contributions of the products sold have paid for the total fixed costs. Beyond this point the operating profit is positive.

The **profit equations** 12.22 and 12.23 are plotted over a limited range of units sold in Figure 12.3. This figure (while still subject to the assumptions referred to earlier) describes the Year 1 profit performance of Adastra as a function of the number of product unit sold during the year. Note that at an output level of 60 units per annum, some 90% of the net variable income (aggregate contributions) is needed to pay fixed costs. This observation illustrates the vulnerability of profit performance to the factors in Equations 12.19 and 12.20. It emphasizes the need to:

- Maximize product contribution by obtaining the best possible price per product and minimizing prime cost per product.
- Maximize the number of products sold.

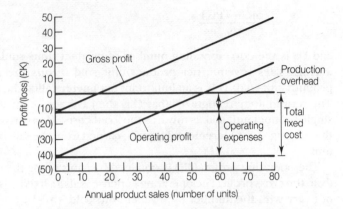

Figure 12.3 **Adastra: Year 1 variation of profit with unit sales.**

Profit is revenue minus cost. Subject to some simplifying assumptions and considering a whole year, the direct product cost incurred and the revenue earned both increase linearly with the number of product units made and sold. But the production overhead and operating costs incurred are essentially fixed amounts, irrespective of the number of units made and sold. Using values from Section 12.4.1, these observations lead to relationships between annual gross profit (GP), operating profit (OP) and unit sales (US) of the form: GP = £(760US − 12,002) and OP = £(760US − 41,381). These are plotted in the figure, which shows there is a threshold activity level (rate of production and sales) for profitable operation. Note that the slope of the graphs is £760 per product unit, which is the *contribution* each unit sale makes to the fixed costs.

- Minimize the fixed costs of product production.
- Minimize the other fixed costs of operating the business.

The internal conflicts among this list of objectives are self-evident. Designing and operating an adequately profitable compromise of the objectives is the principal task of business management.

Assumptions and conclusions

Three major assumptions underpin the break-even analysis presented here. These are:

(1) That sales revenue increases linearly with the number of product units sold. This assumption can break down in practice, when product price is reduced in order to increase the rate of unit sales.

(2) That total prime cost (that is, the total variable cost) increases linearly with the number of product units produced. In practice, the gradient of the variable cost curve is rarely completely constant over any significant range.

(3) That the fixed costs really do not vary with the number of product units produced and sold. But there are a few subtle relationships between the rate of production and/or sales and some so-called 'fixed' costs. Generally, these are (quite reasonably) ignored in practice.

Despite these objections (which can be accommodated in a more detailed treatment) the concepts of 'break-even' and 'product contribution' provide a valuable insight into business operations. They are related to **marginal analysis**, which is a nice idea that accountants and engineers have borrowed from the economists. All of these matters are explored in more detail in Section 7.9.

At this point, the accountant abandoned the discussion of profit performance as a function of activity level in favour of **business ratios**. She explained that this topic concerned another way of extracting interesting messages from a set of accounts.

12.5.4   Ratios and ratio analysis

The accountant returned to the P&L account and balance sheet of Tables 12.10 and 12.12, respectively. She pointed out that, while the absolute levels of the reported figures is always of interest, more significant information is often revealed by *comparing* selected figures. For example, the Adastra P&L account for Year 1 reports a profit after tax of £2,915 (note 23). This is interesting but, without further analysis, there is no way of deciding whether it is a good or bad result. The balance sheet shows, however, that Adastra's owners (Arthur and his wife) originally invested £7,500 in launching the business. The return on this investment is, therefore, the ratio of 2,915 to 7,500, which is about thirty-nine per cent. This is good going by any standards. (The fact that this return is locked up in the net assets of the company is another matter.)

Ratio analysis expresses the relationship between key elements of a P&L account and balance sheet in ratio form. Ratios can be used as management tools inside the business to assess progress over a period of time, and as an aid to problem analysis. They can also be used (cautiously) to compare the relative performance of different companies, and to assess their credit worthiness and financial stability.

The main areas of application

The accountant went on to explain that 'ratios and ratio analysis' is a vast topic which can be subdivided into five main areas:

(1) **Activity**
(2) **Coverage**
(3) **Financial**
(4) **Liquidity**
(5) **Operational**.

Activity ratios yield some indication of how efficiently various resources are being used. For example, the ratio:

Sales Revenue/Total Assets

measures the 'sales productivity' of the business assets.

Coverage ratios generally relate the degree to which a financing cost is covered by earnings. An example is the ratio:

Profit After Tax/Dividends.

The level of this ratio tends to reflect the growth rate (or growth ambition) of the company, because high growth companies usually re-invest most of their profits, rather than disburse them as dividends.

Financial ratios are designed to indicate aspects of financial strength and stability. For example, the ratio:

Non-Current Liabilities/(Non-Current Liabilities + Owners' Capital) measures the proportion of long-term *external* debt in the total capital employed by the business. This ratio is called the **gearing**. High gearing may represent a vulnerability, because it implies a high level of fixed (with respect to output) interest costs, and the possibility of early loan recall.

Liquidity ratios measure the ability of the business to meet its short-term financial obligations. One example is the so-called **acid test**:

(Current Assets − Stocks)/Current Liabilities.

Stocks (broadly interpreted) are taken out of current assets in this ratio, because they can be difficult to convert into immediate cash at balance sheet values, especially if the business is in difficulties.

Operational ratios, of which there are a large number, are aimed at assessing management effectiveness in achieving returns on product sales and capital invested. An example is the ratio:

Profit After Tax/Owner's Capital at Year Start

which is calculated earlier for Adastra.

Arthur and the accountant agreed that they would limit further discussion to some of the more important ratios. Perhaps *the* most important operational ratio is the **return on capital employed** (ROCE).

Return on capital employed and related ratios

It is noted earlier that the term 'capital' is used rather loosely in the business community. In particular, it is sometimes used to describe the owners' or shareholders' stake in the business. This is the owners' capital: the debt that the business owes to its owners. Owners' capital is not usually what is meant by 'capital' when the term **capital employed** is used. Normally, and logically, this means the sum of non-current liabilities and owners' capital (that is, the total long-term debt). This sum funds the quantity 'total assets less current liabilities' in a balance sheet (for example, at note 17 in Table 12.12). Apart from the current liabilities, capital employed defined in this way represents the whole capital available to management. Current liabilities are excluded because of their short-term nature and, typically, close association with the current assets.

It is this definition of capital employed that is used in Figure 12.4. This illustrates how the ROCE ratio forms a link between a P&L account and its associated balance sheet. The figure also introduces a number of other important ratios.

The upper half of the figure describes relationships between major P&L account items, culminating in the operating profit. It has the same structure as the P&L account of Table 12.10. The lower half of the figure describes relationships between major balance sheet items, culminating in the capital employed. In this case, the structure follows that arrangement of the basic accounting equation which defines capital employed. This arrangement first equates fixed assets (FA) plus working capital (WC) to capital employed (CE), which it then equates to non-current liabilities (NCL) plus owners' capital (OC):

$$FA + WC = CE = NCL + OC \tag{12.24}$$

Figure 12.4 then traces the derivation of two important intermediate ratios, **return on sales** and **capital turnover**. These subsequently combine to form ROCE. The

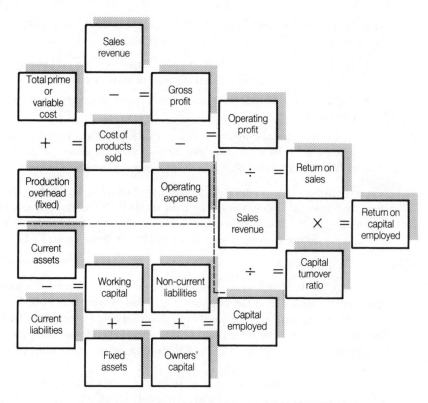

Figure 12.4   **Return on capital employed (ROCE) as the linking ratio.**
ROCE is an important ratio which measures the merit of a business as an investment/return
situation, where the investment is its capital employed and the return is the profit earned by
employing it. The figure shows how ROCE forms a link between profit and loss account items (top
half) and balance sheet items (bottom half). The derivation of the return on sales and capital
turnover ratios is shown. The three ratios are different indicators of management skill in using
company resources to generate profit, and powerful diagnostic tools for locating problem areas
when performance is poor.

definitions of these three ratios are encapsulated in the following equations:

$$\text{Return on Sales} = \frac{\text{Operating Profit}}{\text{Sales Revenue}} \tag{12.25}$$

$$\text{Capital Turnover} = \frac{\text{Sales Revenue}}{\text{Capital Employed}} \tag{12.26}$$

$$\text{ROCE} = \frac{\text{Operating Profit}}{\text{Capital Employed}} \tag{12.27}$$

or

$$\text{ROCE} = \frac{\text{Operating Profit}}{\text{Sales Revenue}} \times \frac{\text{Sales Revenue}}{\text{Capital Employed}} \tag{12.28}$$

or

$$\text{ROCE} = = \text{Return on Sales} \times \text{Capital Turnover} \tag{12.29}$$

The three ratios are indicators of management skill in using company resources to generate profit:

- Return on sales (also called the **profit ratio** or the **net margin**) measures the profit generated from a given volume of sales revenue.
- Capital turnover measures the sales revenue generated from a given volume of capital.
- Return on capital employed measures the profit generated from a given volume of capital. It is probably the best overall measure of **profitability**, which determines (ultimately) whether a business prospers, merely survives or dies.

Capital employed is adequately defined by Equation 12.24, but the balance sheet items involved are likely to change over the year. Because of this, average values are commonly used (as here) but this is not invariably the case. For Adastra's first year, and calculating on the liabilities side of the balance sheet (Table 12.12):

$$\text{Capital employed:} \qquad £(2,500 + 7,500 + 2,915/2) = £11,458$$

Note that, on the other side of the balance sheet, this figure is obtained by averaging the capital employed at the beginning and end of the year (note 17).

A P&L account provides a number of different profit levels. The best level to use for assessing overall performance is profit before any deductions for interest, tax or dividends. This coincides with the definition of the operating profit of £4,784 in Adastra's P&L account (Table 12.10) at note 19.

So, for Adastra's first trading year, the three ratios are (approximately):

Return on sales:	4,784/67,500 = 7.1%
Capital turnover:	67,500/11,458 = 5.9
Return on capital employed:	4,784/11,458 = 41.7%

The return on sales is, perhaps, rather too low for comfort. It can be investigated further by calculating the **gross margin**. This ratio measures the earning power of the production operation. It is a critical parameter because, in a manufacturing business, the production function is the only significant source of income. The ratio is defined by:

$$\text{Gross Margin} = \frac{\text{Gross Profit}}{\text{Sales Revenue}} \qquad \qquad \textbf{(12.30)}$$

So, here:

$$\text{Gross Margin} = 34,163/67,500 \qquad \qquad = 50.6\%$$

This is a very acceptable level. It implies that product cost is less (just) than fifty per cent of product price, which is better than typical for such companies. It is now clear that the return on sales is comparatively low, mostly because the operating expense is comparatively high. This is running at about forty-four per cent of sales revenue. With one exception, the individual cost items comprising the operating expense are at, or below, typical levels. The exception is the development and design cost at £12,123, which represents some forty-one per cent of the total. An expense of this nature is commonly termed a **research and development** cost, or perhaps just an R&D cost. (This potentially misleading terminology is examined in Chapter 3.) The **R&D ratio** is a useful indicator of the level of investment in technological innovation. The ratio is defined by:

$$\text{R\&D Ratio} = \frac{\text{R\&D Cost}}{\text{Sales Revenue}} \tag{12.31}$$

So, here:

R&D ratio = 12,123/67,500   = 18.0%

This unusually high level reflects Arthur's ambitions to grow the business. Typical levels for established 'high-tech' businesses range from about five per cent to fifteen per cent. If Adastra's R&D ratio had been fifteen per cent the return on sales would have been about ten per cent, which is reasonably typical of a prosperous high-tech business.

Adastra's return on sales may be a bit low at some seven per cent. But its capital turnover and ROCE ratios are unusually high, at about six and forty-two per cent respectively. A factor of the order of 2 is involved. Since the operating profit is not excessive, Equation 12.28 suggests that this is because the capital employed is unusually low. Equation 12.29 confirms this diagnosis. The build up of the capital employed is illustrated in Figure 12.4. It is clear from the balance sheet (Table 12.12) that the working capital (note 16) is not unusually low at about ten per cent of sales revenue and more than fifty per cent of capital employed (note 17). This all suggests that the level of fixed assets is unusually low. At this point, Arthur confessed that his 'small workshop' is, in fact, both tiny and tatty (being a decaying structure of about 100 square feet), which accounts for its low initial cost. This factor, together with the purchase of second-hand equipment and furniture, had minimized the risk implicit in launching Adastra. But that (wise) policy now poses problems for Adastra. Firstly, the workshop is too small to accommodate further growth. Secondly, the image of Adastra presented by the workshop and facilities is not consistent with its planned future as a valued supplier in a sector of the professional equipment market. Solving those problems is outside the scope of this chapter. But it is reasonably certain that the solutions will result in more capital being employed.

Some other ratios

There are many other ratios, of varying significance, which can be extracted from a balance sheet and its associated P&L account. To illustrate the point, a limited selection of other ratios is presented here.

The **current ratio** is a liquidity test which compares current assets with current liabilities:

$$\text{Current Ratio} = \frac{\text{Current Assets}}{\text{Current Liabilities}} \tag{12.32}$$

So, here:

Current ratio = 9,940/3,265 = 3.0 (say)

This indicates that short-term liabilities are reasonably well covered by the 'buffer' of short-term assets, even if these were to decline substantially in value for some reason.

The **quick ratio** (also known as the acid test) is a more severe liquidity test than the current ratio, because it excludes stock items from the current assets. In this context 'stock' certainly includes work-in-progress and, usually, **output stock** (finished goods) as well as input stock:

$$\text{Quick Ratio} = \frac{\text{Current Assets} - \text{Stock (see text)}}{\text{Current Liabilities}} \qquad (12.33)$$

So, here:

$$\text{Quick ratio} = (9,940 - 2,381)/3,265 = 2.3 \text{ (say)}$$

This is still quite reasonable. The rationale for the exclusions is that all forms of stock are not, in an emergency, readily transformed into cash at balance sheet values.

The **interest cover** ratio relates profit to interest payments on loans:

$$\text{Interest Cover} = \frac{\text{Operating Profit}}{\text{Interest Paid}} \qquad (12.34)$$

So, here:

$$\text{Interest cover} = 4,784/425 = 11.3 \text{ (say)}$$

High ratios are attractive to actual and prospective lenders, because they suggest that the business meets its interest payments without difficulty. But this can be an illusion. Profit is not the same as positive cash flow and, ultimately, it is positive cash flow that pays business expenses.

The **gearing** ratio is the proportion of long-term (as distinct from 'permanent') debt in the capital employed:

$$\text{Gearing} = \frac{\text{Non-Current Liabilities}}{\text{Non-Current Liabilities} + \text{Owners' Capital}} \qquad (12.35)$$

So, here:

$$\text{Gearing} = 2,500/(2,500 + 7,500 + 1,458) = 21.8\% \text{ (say)}$$

This low ratio is quite satisfactory. High ratios tend to make lenders and investors (actual and prospective) nervous about the ability of the business to meet high interest charges and, perhaps, repayments of principal. Such costs do not depend on activity level and can cripple highly-geared business in times of economic recession. Profit and, hence, dividend levels are also vulnerable in highly-geared businesses for the same reasons.

12.5.5 Section summary

Arthur was slightly bemused, by this time, with the wealth of additional information that had emerged from Adastra's first year accounts. To conclude the meeting, the accountant condensed some of the more fundamental points that she had made into a brief summary.

A P&L account and its associated balance sheet are the two basic financial statements. They summarize the performance of a business during an accounting period and its status at the end of that period. This section has shown that these basic accounts can be analysed, alone and in combination, to reveal more information about the business than is immediately obvious from the source documents. Three aspects of analysis have been introduced, summarized as funds flow, break-even and ratios.

Funds flow statements merely rearrange data extracted from the two basic accounts, and they come in a variety of forms. The format which emphasizes changes in working capital is, perhaps, the most usual. But an interpretation, not considered in detail here, which emphasizes cash flow is often more useful.

Break-even analysis focuses on the P&L account. The notion depends on distinguishing costs which do vary (more or less directly in practice) with the level of production and sales from costs which do not. This leads to the derivation of a break-even activity level, where the net income contribution from the products sold pays-off the fixed costs. Sales beyond this point make the business profitable. The analysis demonstrates with great clarity what has to be done to achieve and maintain that happy position.

Ratio analysis can yield illuminating insights into several distinct areas of business performance, strengths, weaknesses, and prospects. It is a well-established technique which offers its messages by forming selected ratios between various figures extracted from the accounts. Only a few of the more useful ratios have been considered here, but this has served to introduce the topic. Some experience of, or access to, comparative data is required to interpret ratios, and there are traps for the unwary. In particular, when comparing different businesses, analysts must take care to compare like with like. Different businesses may well treat depreciation, stock valuation, development and design costs, bad debts, and other judgemental factors in quite different ways.

12.6   Concluding summary

The need to make at least adequate profits dominates the conduct of all businesses operating in competitive environments. Engineers perform a number of critical tasks in the profit-making process of manufacturing businesses. An appreciation of business finance is essential for proper discharge of these duties. Engineers must learn to communicate with, negotiate with, and sell their ideas to accountants and other financially literate managers. Understanding business finance is also an essential first step for those engineers who wish to develop their careers into the broader fields of technical and business management.

Accounting technology is a vast topic. It is introduced in this chapter by partitioning it into primary and secondary principles. The primary principles are then explored in some detail, mostly in the context of an extended example. Budding engineers often have difficulties with this material, however it is presented. There are, perhaps, two main reasons for this.

First, the language of accounting is quite new to most engineering students. This is unfortunate, but the deficiency must be overcome. The language of accounting is also, to a large extent, the language of business. Accountants can (and do) survive and prosper in industry without any real understanding of engineering and its language(s). Ambitious engineers must understand the language of accounting as a prerequisite to career development.

The second problem is of a clash of cultures. Engineers tend to think in terms of cash. For them, a sale has occurred when the cash is received. Similarly, a purchase is made when the cash is paid out. Accountants extend reality beyond this narrow view. For them, cash is just one form of 'funds'. This is a word much used but rarely defined in the world of accountancy. But a sale made on credit adds to the fund of debtors, and a purchase made on credit adds to the fund of creditors. To accountants, these funds are as real as cash, even though they represent promises rather than facts. This perception is valid because the prudence principle requires them to discount the value of dubious promises. Similar difficulties can arise with the depreciation concept. A depreciation charge in a P&L account is totally unreal in cash terms. The fixed asset to which it relates has already been purchased. No further movement of cash is involved. But accounting is not, primarily, about cash. It is about funds, which include cash. The matching principle and natural justice each require that the cost of the fixed asset is set against the earnings it helps to create. So a depreciation charge measuring the annual consumption of the fixed asset is created. It is a real part of 'funds', but it is not cash.

Unhappily for cash-oriented engineers, it has long been recognized that cash-based accounting cannot meet the needs of interested parties inside or outside the business. The problem is essentially one of time. If a business could be measured over a time long enough for all credit transactions to come to fruition and all the fixed assets to be consumed then cash flow and profit would coincide. But businesses must be measured, monitored and controlled very much more frequently than this. Accrual accounting is here to stay!

The accountants have created a beautiful model of a business (any business). Its major elements are:

- fixed assets
- current assets
- current liabilities
- non-current liabilities
- owners' capital.

This model is the business balance sheet. Business transactions causes changes in the elements comprising the model. It is too tedious to update the balance sheet model after each transaction, so this is only done periodically. In the intervals between these periodic updates, the changes in the balance sheet elements are recorded in another model. This is the P&L account. A third model is also employed which is, in effect, another form of balance sheet. This is a funds flow statement. It is built on the premise that the changes in corresponding elements occurring between successive balance sheets must also be in balance. These changes reflect the way in which funds have been exchanged (moved or flowed) among the elements in the period between the balance sheets. A funds flow model is derived from the balance sheet and P&L account models. It adds no new information to the overall picture but it does show quite clearly where new funds have come from and how they have been used.

Engineering is largely about building and understanding models of the real world. So is accounting. Hopefully, this chapter has demonstrated that engineering and accounting have more in common than is frequently supposed.

REFERENCES

Arnold J., Hope T. and Southworth A. (1985). *Financial Accounting*. Hemel Hempstead: Prentice-Hall

Barrow C. (1988). *Financial Management for the Small Business* 2nd edn. (A *Daily Telegraph Guide*) London: Kogan Page

Berry A. and Jarvis P. (1991). *Accounting in a Business Context*. London: Chapman & Hall

Glautier M. W. E. and Underdown B. (1986). *Accounting Theory and Practice* 3rd edn. London: Pitman

Harrison J. (1989). *Finance for the Non-Financial Manager*. Wellingborough: Thorsens

Meigs W. B. and Meigs R. F. (1987). *Accounting: The Basis for Business Decisions* 7th edn. New York: McGraw-Hill

Wilson P. (1990). *Financial Management for the Small Business*. (A Barclays Guide) Oxford: Blackwell

SUGGESTED FURTHER READING

Bird & Rutherford (1990), Droms (1990), Foster (1986) and Warren (1990) are written for account users rather than embryonic accountants. The Droms text has a US flavour which only marginally limits its value outside that country. It is particularly commended, as is the Warren book. Lewis and Gillespie (1986) is an introductory specialist text which employs an equation-based approach, making it very acceptable to engineers. Marriott and Simon (1990) is an unconventional specialist text which takes this idea somewhat further by expressing the concepts in spreadsheet programs.

Bird P. A. and Rutherford B. A. (1990). *Understanding Company Accounts* 3rd edn. London: Pitman

Droms W. G. (1990). *Finance and Accounting for Nonfinancial Managers* 3rd edn. Reading, MA: Addison-Wesley

Foster G. (1986). *Financial Statement Analysis* 2nd edn. Englewood Cliffs, NJ: Prentice-Hall

Lewis R. and Gillespie I. (1986). *Foundations of Accounting 1* 2nd edn. Hemel Hempstead: Prentice-Hall

Marriott N. and Simon J. (1990). *Financial Accounting – A Spreadsheet Approach*. Hemel Hempstead: Prentice-Hall

Warren R. (1990). *How to Understand and Use Company Accounts* 3rd edn. London: Business Books

QUESTIONS

12.1 Describe the major purposes and procedures of business accounting and, in that context, explain the meaning of the following terms:

- book-keeping
- management accounting
- financial accounting
- balance sheet

- profit and loss account
- funds flow statement
- final company accounts
- accounts audit.

12.2 (a) What is an 'accounting entity'? Describe the legal and accounting factors which distinguish the following types of business:

- sole-traders
- partnerships
- companies.

(b) How do private limited companies differ from public limited companies, and what is the significance of the term 'limited'?

12.3 (a) What are business 'assets' and business 'liabilities'? Describe the basic principle of double-entry accounting in terms of assets and liabilities.

(b) Explain the meaning of the following terms:

- tangible asset
- intangible asset
- debtor
- external liability
- external creditor
- net assets
- owners' capital.

(c) If the business described in Table 12.3 is liquidated at the end of Day 3, how much money would its owner receive?

12.4 Table 12.3 shows the balance sheet of a small sole-trader business at the end of Day 3 in a particular week. Its owner conducts only two transactions on Day 4:

(1) Pays £400 to a trade creditor by means of a cheque drawn on the business bank account.

(2) Transfers £500 out of the business bank account into her personal bank account as the weekly instalment of the annual salary she charges the business for her services.

Calculate, and explain, the balance sheet values of:

- money-at-bank
- total assets
- sundry debts

- total liabilities
- net assets
- profit
- owner's capital

at the end of Day 4. Comment on the performance of the business during the week to date, by comparing its position at the end of Day 4 with its position at the end of Day 1 (which is is shown in Table 12.1).

12.5 (a) Describe the accounting concepts known as:

- the basic accounting (or balance sheet) equation
- a balance sheet
- an accounting period
- the profit equation
- a P&L account

and show, with the aid of a diagram, how they are related. What is a 'funds flow statement', and how is it related to the other items in the diagram?

(b) Distinguish between 'capital' costs and 'revenue' costs.

(c) 'Depreciation is a mechanism for converting capital costs into revenue costs.' Explain this statement.

12.6 (a) Section 12.2.5, which contains about 1400 words, discusses the 'matching' principle and the related technique of 'accrual' accounting. Summarize its major messages in not more than 350 words. (Note-format and diagrams are allowed, even encouraged.)

(b) The profit position of a business calculated, at a given time, on an accrual accounting basis is likely to be quite different from its cash-flow position determined at that same time. Describe three situations which can cause this discrepancy.

(c) Is profit or positive cash-flow the more important factor in determining the survival of a business?

12.7 Explain the accountancy principles commonly called:

- 'going concern'
- prudence
- consistency.

12.8   Explain, briefly, the accountancy principles commonly called:

- clarity
- comparability
- cost-effectiveness
- materiality
- monetary basis
- periodicity
- relevance
- reliability.

Note: Questions 12.9 to 12.13 form a sequence which explores many of the basic accounting principles, and they are most usefully answered in the order offered. Question 12.11 is about cash and funds flow, and it may be omitted by those readers who are not yet concerned with the 'advanced material'. But an easy way of answering it is shown in the answer section.

12.9   Small Business Ltd is a manufacturing enterprise which was incorporated, on 31st December 1990, as a private limited company with a paid-up share capital of £15,000. The following list records the significant actions taken by its owner-managers on incorporation and, subsequently, during its first trading month of January 1991.

On 31st December 1990
(1)   Paid £20,000 into the business bank account, comprising £15,000 from their own resources and £5,000 borrowed from the bank. Interest on the bank loan was set at seventeen per cent per annum payable monthly in arrears.
      Paid, by cheque, £1,200 from the business bank account into their personal bank account to recover their advance payment of that amount for company formation and other costs.
In January 1991
(2)   Bought for cash a small workshop on an industrial estate at £8,000.
(3)   Bought for cash tools, second-hand test gear and fittings for the workshop amounting to £6,000.
(4)   Bought all the components to make ten product units for £5,000 on credit.

(5)   Assembled and tested seven product units.
(6)   Sold two product units for £1,500 each on credit.
(7)   Wrote-off one-twelfth of the prepayment asset as 'legal and professional' expenses.
      Paid salaries for the month of £3,000 by cheques drawn on the business bank account.

(a) Analyse these actions on a double-entry accounting basis to determine the financial status of the business at the end of January 1991. (Hint: Table 12.4 provides an appropriate format for this analysis.)
(b) An alternative treatment of the prepayment asset would be to write-off the whole amount in January 1991. How would the reported end-of-January profit be affected if this approach had been adopted? Which of the two treatments is to be preferred?

12.10   The information in column 7 of Table 12.15 (p. 664) relates to the financial status of Small Business Ltd at the end of January 1991.
(a) Rearrange this information into the conventional balance sheet format exemplified by Table 12.5.
(b) In terms of this balance sheet, what are the values of working capital and capital employed for Small Business Ltd at the end of January 1991? Explain the significance of these two parameters.

12.11   Table 12.15 (p. 664) illustrates transactions conducted by Small Business Ltd in January 1991. It shows that £17,000 in cash flows out of the business bank account during that period. By arranging the basic accounting equation in a form which equates cash with the remaining balance sheet elements, or otherwise, show that the cash flow out of the business bank account is made up of:

- £20,900 spent on acquiring non-cash assets, together with
- £1,100 spent on funding the end-of-January loss, but offset by
- £5,000 of creditor funds.

12.12 Tables 12.15 (p. 664) and 12.16 (p. 665) relate to the financial status of Small Business Ltd at the end of January 1991.
(a) Use the information in these two tables to construct, in the format exemplified by Table 12.8, a profit and loss account for the period ending January 1991.
(b) The validity and usefulness of this particular profit and loss account is compromised by various omissions and simplifications in its source documents. Explain what these are.

12.13 The owners of Small Business Ltd are unhappy with the balance sheet of Table 12.16 (p. 665) and the P&L account of Table 12.17 (p. 666) because:

- No adjustment has been made for the depreciation ('consumption') of fixed assets over the period of the account, causing the profit to be overstated.
- Various other costs (such as those due to rates, electricity used, telephone and loan interest) have been incurred, but not paid, during the month. These other costs do not appear in either account, also causing the profit to be overstated.
- The balance sheet understates the asset value of the finished goods retained in store. These have been valued at component cost, but this is only part of their works cost.
- The P&L account does not show the true cost of sales (cost of products sold).

In order to correct this situation, the owners estimate that:

- The total value of the fixed assets has depreciated by £200 over the month, and this sum should be partitioned on a 140:60 basis between the production operation and the rest of the business.
- The other (committed but unpaid) costs amount to £1,000, and should be partitioned on a 705:295 basis between the production operation and the rest of the business.
- Of the £3,000 spent on labour during the month, £700 is attributable to making and testing product units, £1,500 is attributable to supervising that work, and

the residue is attributable to the rest of the business.

It will be recalled (from Question 12.9) that components to make ten product units were purchased for £5,000 (on credit), seven product units were made and tested, and two of these were sold for £1,500 each.
(a) Modify, by incorporating the new information contained in the owners' estimates, the balance sheet of Table 12.16 (p. 665) and the P&L account of Table 12.17 (p. 666) to correct the identified deficiencies.
(b) What is the principal factor contributing to the substantial difference between the two sets of accounts?

12.14 Describe, in the context of a typical annual P&L account for a manufacturing company, the nature and content of the following account items:

- sales revenue
- cost of products sold
- gross profit
- operating expenses
- operating profit
- interest paid or payable
- profit before tax
- tax payable
- profit after tax
- dividend paid or payable
- retained profit this year
- retained profit at the end of this year.

12.15 (a) Describe, in the context of a typical end-of-year balance sheet for a manufacturing company, the nature and content of the following account items:

- fixed assets (FA)
- current assets (CA)
- current liabilities (CL)
- non-current liabilities (NCL)
- owners' capital (OC).

(b) A company balance sheet is an expression of the basic accounting equation which, in its most simple form, is:

Total Assets = Total Liabilities

Hence, show (using the notation defined

in (a) above) how a balance sheet illustrates:

- that the owners' capital has been used to acquire the net assets of the company, and
- that capital employed by the company (defined as the whole of the long-term debt) has been employed to acquire the fixed assets and working capital of the company.

(c) The *fundamental* definition of profit earned during an accounting period is the increase in owners' capital (or 'wealth') between the opening and closing balance sheets for the period. Show that the period profit is also the increase in net assets between the opening and closing balance sheets.

(d) The P&L account associated with a balance sheet derives a trading profit arising from the normal buying and selling activities of the company. Is this profit necessarily the same as that shown on the corresponding balance sheet? If so, why? If not, why not?

12.16 Table 12.12 shows the 1991 and 1990 balance sheets for Adastra Ltd.

(a) Calculate the cash flow during 1991.

(b) Calculate the funds flow arising from the acquisition of liabilities of *all* sorts during 1991.

(c) Calculate the funds flow arising from the acquisition of non-cash assets during 1991.

(d) Show that the cash flow calculated in (a) is equal to the sum of the funds flows calculated at (b) and (c), and explain this result.

12.17 A particular manufacturing company is able to sell as many products as it can produce. Show that the rate of product manufacture must attain a certain threshold level before profitable operation is achieved.

12.18 (a) Explain, in the context of assessing business performance, the meaning of the term 'ratio analysis'.

(b) Define the ratios:

- return on sales
- capital turnover ratio
- return on capital employed.

What is the significance of each of these ratios, and how are they related?

A requirements definition example

*Member of the flock: 'Rabbi, why do rabbis
always answer a question with another
question?'
Rabbi: (Pause for thought) 'Tell me, my son, is
there a better way?'*

Traditional

A.1 Introduction 621
A.2 Case study context 622
A.3 TCM requirements definition 630
A.4 Concluding summary 642

 Repetition The opening discussion in Section A.3 is a very concise summary of the requirements definition methodology designed in Section 8.5. It includes two figures extracted from Chapter 8.

This appendix is an adjunct of Chapter 8. It can be read as a stand-alone module, but it is better perused after a study of that chapter up to, and including, Section 8.5.3. The overall objectives of this appendix are to provide a realistic illustration, by means of a case study, of the structured product design methodology developed in Chapter 8. Objectives by section follow:

A.1 To explain the background of the case study and describe its content and structure.

A.2 To provide the case study context by describing company organization, the new product to be designed, the associated commercial factors, and the product design environment.

A.3 To derive a requirements definition for the new product by structured analysis of the case study context.

A.4 To identify its salient points and summarize its major messages.

A.1   Introduction

The first and most critical problem of product design is to obtain a description of the right product to design. Here, 'right' means the most rewarding compromise between what the customer wants and what the designer is able to provide. The difficulty arises because the initial description of the new product provided, directly or indirectly, by its prospective customer is usually flawed in several important respects. Typically, it lacks precision rather than ambition in defining the functional and performance features of the product, but sets firm limits on delivery time and price. Additionally, technical restrictions on design freedom are commonly imposed when the customer wishes to retain compatibility with an earlier product.

Requirements definition (RD) is the first phase of the product design process. Its purpose is to create a statement (also called a 'requirements definition') of the *whole* problem that the design of the new product presents to its designer. So an RD is a problem statement not a problem solution; and the requirements it defines are those of the prospective customer *and* those of the prospective product producer. The RD is the platform for building a proper description of the right new product. This description, which is created in the second phase, is termed the **product architecture** (PA). The PA is the platform for the subsequent, more detailed, design work. Figure A.1 illustrates this vision of the product design process. It uses the terminology introduced in Chapter 8.

This appendix illustrates the methodology for creating an RD which is developed in that chapter. It is intended to be a realistic case study. This ambition leads to a lengthy exercise, because the design context must be established before the problem that it presents is considered. This context is provided in the next section. An RD of the new product is contained in the following section. It includes a brief excursion into the design of the PA, which illustrates the relationship between the PA and the RD.

To aid realism, a specific product must be chosen as a vehicle for the case study. The product selected is a relatively simple high (sales) volume item using mostly electronic and computing technologies. The **product sponsor** is the marketing department of the product producer business, because the product is to be sold (hopefully) to many widely dispersed

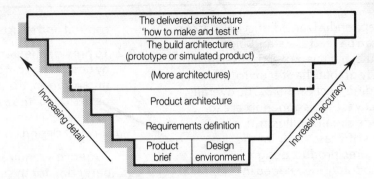

Figure A.1 **The design process as a hierarchy of platforms.**

This is a vision of the product design process which expresses the structure established in Figure 8.8 in a rather different way. It emphasizes the model-to-model transformation nature of the process by showing the phases of the earlier figure as a developing series of 'platforms'. Thus, the requirements definition is built on a combination of the product brief and the design environment. It supports the product architecture, and so on.

end user customers. A duty of the sponsor is to ascertain, evaluate and represent the views of the product customers during the design process.

- The need to focus the case study on a specific product and its technologies does not compromise the generality of the design methodology, which is fundamentally technology independent.

A.2   Case study context

The context of the product RD exercise comprises:

- A short description of the business concerned with the design and supply of the new product (that is, the producer company).
- A description of the new product as it is first perceived by its sponsor. This description is called the **product brief**.
- A description of the product design environment in the producer company.

The RD analysis is concerned, principally, with the second and third items in this list.

A.2.1   The producer company

The basic organization of the company concerned with the design, manufacture and supply of the new product is shown in Figure A.2. It includes only those business functions directly involved in the product design process.

The company has a new business development department, whose task it is to plan and manage projects directed at product-related new business opportunities. Usually, the full-time team members assigned to such a project are engineers seconded from the technical department. They can call on the services of any of the other departments (on a paid-for basis) to assist in project planning and implementation. Both the new business development department and the technical department report to the technical director. The technical department is primarily concerned with the technological aspects of product innovation.

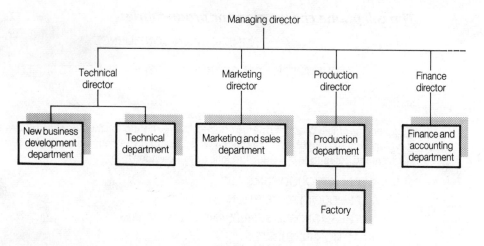

Figure A.2 **Basic organization of the producer company.**

The outline organization illustrated here includes only those departments (functions) directly involved in the new product creation process. Note that this company has a new business development department (not all companies organize this way), whose task is to plan and manage projects directed at product-related new business opportunities. Usually, the full-time team members assigned to such a project are engineers seconded from the technical department. They can call on the services of any of the other departments (on a paid-for basis) to assist in project planning and implementation.

A.2.2   The product brief

The first significant event in the product design process is the creation of the product brief. In this case study, the marketing director sent the product brief to the technical director in September 1991, together with a covering memorandum. Both documents are reproduced here.

Covering memorandum

MEMORANDUM

From: Donna O. Daring, Marketing Director   *Date*: 21st Sept 1991
   To: Trevor E. K. Merlin, Technical Director
Subject: **Telephone Charge Monitor – Product Brief**
Following the board meeting last week, I now forward the TCM product brief and an IDO to launch the project.
I think that this is an exciting opportunity for the company which will, I hope, result in the development of a new business area.

(Signed)
Donna O. Daring

(Note: An IDO is an inter-departmental order. This is a document in which one department agrees to pay some other department to do some defined work on its behalf.)

The telephone charge monitor product brief

COMMERCIAL-IN-CONFIDENCE

THE TELEPHONE CHARGE MONITOR – PRODUCT BRIEF

1. INTRODUCTION

This document is a product brief produced by marketing for the attention of new business development. It describes a potential new product for the company, and the commercial background relating to it, under the following headings.

2. BACKGROUND SUMMARY
3. PRODUCT DESCRIPTION
4. THE PROPOSED SUPPLY AND SUPPORT CONTRACT
5. ACTION REQUESTED
6. PLANNING COSTS AND PROGRESS MONITORING

This product brief was approved (subject to minor amendments now incorporated) by the main board on 16th September 1991.

2. BACKGROUND SUMMARY

2.1 The Customer
We have had a good relationship for many years with W H Jones PLC (WHJ), who have marketed several of our products (under their own label) via their high-street outlets. *Their* customers are principally in the domestic and small business sectors. We believe they are currently forecasting declining sales of 'high-tech' products in both areas, because many of the products they now offer are becoming obsolescent. They also face increasing pressure from a number of other high-street retailers. The opportunity described here arises from their response to that situation.

Following discussions with their marketing people, we have conditionally agreed to design, manufacture and supply a new product for sale by them. It is called the telephone charge monitor (TCM).

2.2 The Competition
WHJ intend to invite at least one other company to supply the same, or similar, product. This is their normal practice in such cases. It might be wise to assume that WHJ have approached our usual two competitors.

2.3 The Risk
It has not been possible, because of the competitive situation, to negotiate a customer-funded product design, supply and support contract. Hence, if we are to develop a new mini-business around the TCM, the whole of the costs must be company funded as a private venture project. This is why our current agreement with WHJ is conditional: we have reserved the right to withdraw should the venture appear (to us) commercially non-viable at any stage. (In this event, we would retain all rights to the product and would be free to market it, if this was desirable, in any other way.) More details of the proposed contract with WHJ are given at 4, which also includes some speculative market numbers and timings.

2.4 Main Board Approval
It is emphasized that, for the present, main board approval for the venture extends only to preparation of a business plan in our standard format. Progress beyond that point is subject to main board approval of that plan.

3. PRODUCT DESCRIPTION

3.1 Primary Feature
The primary functional requirement of the TCM product is that it allows the end user to monitor the cost of a telephone call *while the call is in progress*. You will recall that the 'connect cost' of an ordinary dialled telephone call depends on:

- The call unit charge
- The time of the day.
- The day of the week.
- The day in the year (Christmas Day etc.)
- The type of the call (local, national, international etc.)
- The duration of the call
- The rate of value added tax (VAT).

British Telecommunications (BT) produce a helpful leaflet called 'Your Guide to Telephone Charges' which explains all this in some detail.

It is believed that, given an 'on-line' charge monitoring facility, (responsible) users would modify their telephone habits to significantly reduce the cost of their telephone usage. For example, they might reduce the duration of calls, and/or arrange to make calls at cheap-rate times, and/or limit the number of long-distance calls.

3.2 Marketing Considerations
Thus, the principle selling point for a basic product is economic. The product represents an investment by the end user which should repay its initial cost many times. The product also has a high-tech novelty appeal which should not be overlooked.

WHJ are to target two classes of end user – the domestic customer and the small business customer – believing (we think correctly) that both are increasingly concerned by escalating telephone charges. They have estimated that the average telephone bill for the domestic user is about £400 per annum. Some of this is due to fixed rental charges, but the variable element due to call charges usually dominates and is estimated to be some £350 annually. Proper use of the TCM could reduce these charges by, in WHJ's opinion, some thirty per cent. On this (admittedly not well-researched) basis they believe that an acceptable price to the domestic end user would be about £50 (including VAT) for a basic model. An end user price at about this level would enable product promotion based on suggestions of 'your money back in six months' to be a tenable proposition.

WHJ are continuing to refine the basic pricing argument outlined above, and to extend it to the small business case. They have promised to keep us informed of developments. But it would be unwise to assume that we shall have definitive information much before product launch. So it is suggested that we assume, for planning purposes, an end user price (including VAT) in the range £45 to £55 for a basic model.

We believe that WHJ seeks a minimum gross margin of about thirty per cent (on selling price) on products of this nature (where promotion and support costs are to be shared, to some extent, between the producer and WHJ). This suggests that our price to WHJ should be in the range £27 to £33 (excluding VAT). Assuming that we take a similar mark-up, it seems that the works cost target range is about £19 to £23.

3.3 Secondary Features

All of the above applies to a basic model offering only the mandatory on-line charge monitoring function. But an attractive part of the whole concept is that there could be a range of models providing additional functions at, presumably, increased prices. (On the other hand, the provision of additional functions at a price not too different from that of the basic model might be a potent means of overcoming the opposition.) WHJ are enthusiastic about possibilities here and they have made the following suggestions:

Group 1

- A time display   (image)
- A calendar display   (image)
- A pre-set alarm(s) feature   (useful)

Group 2

- Auto totalling of charges   (for bill audit)
- Print out of the above   (a convenience)
- Built-in telephone directory   (a convenience)
- A loud-speaking (conference) facility   ('look, no hands')
- A call recording facility   (some business users)
- Some provision for call inconvenience after a pre-set
  time, to discourage persistent long-duration users, e.g.
  a tone of increasing volume and/or frequency   (a teenager fix)

Group 3

- Last number re-dial   (but see later)
- 'Short-code' dialling for popular numbers   (but see later)
- Monitoring of transfer-charge calls   (but see later)

The first three items on the above list should be fairly easy (and cheap) to provide since a built-in clock/calendar and display will be required for the charge monitoring.

The middle group would be useful additions: extending the basic product from a mere TCM into a 'telephone-users friend'. But we imagine that significant extra costs (both development/design and manufacturing) would be involved. However, it is certain that an enhanced product would command a significantly higher price. The additional features are listed in no particular order of merit. There may be other useful add-on facilities not listed above.

The last three possibilities are long-shots. We suspect, to provide these, there would have to be a physical connection between the TCM and the telephone instrument. This would need the TCM to be approved by BT prior to connection to their network. Getting it approved would be both time-consuming and costly. (And BT may not bubble with enthusiasm about the TCM idea.) We recommend that such features are avoided, at least until the product business is well established. However, some non-invasive way of allowing the TCM to know what the telephone instrument is doing would be very useful: for automatic call-distance detection, say, by detecting the dialled area code.

3.4 Other Features

Clearly, the TCM will need to be visually attractive and weight/size compatible with a telephone environment. It must cope with both the modern tone-dialling and the old-fashioned step-by-step instruments (if it matters). Its reliability must equate to that of the telephone. We discuss product support at 4.

The TCM must be 'programmable'. That is, it must be possible for the user to:

- Set up the clock/calendar.
- Enter new charge parameters when these are changed by BT or by government (value added tax).
- Control the the TCM during call monitoring. For example, in the basic case, the user will probably have to signal the start and end of a call to the TCM.

We envisage programming to be done by 'buttons' in the most simple case. This approach might be made more user-friendly (possibly to the extent of eliminating user intervention during a call) if a non-invasive data channel can be established between the TCM and its telephone. This might be a difficult technical problem. WHJ have no firm views on power supply provision. The choice between battery and mains-driven is left to us. Power consumption should be minimal.

4. THE PROPOSED SUPPLY AND SUPPORT CONTRACT

If our current understanding with WHJ becomes a contract, then that contract will cover the matters outlined in 4.1, 4.2, 4.3 and 4.4 below. We provide some notes on these in 4.5. While such a contract is in force, we will not be permitted to market the TCM, in any of its forms, to any other customer. If the product is a success, there is the possibility of follow-up contracts after the first.

4.1 The TCM Product Range

The basic TCM must provide, as a minimum, facilities which allow the user to monitor the cost of a telephone call while that call is in progress. WHJ are interested in enhancements to this 'core' requirement, where enhancement refers to either additional functions or user-friendliness or both.

Products must be warranted with a free replacement guarantee for 12 months from date of sale to end user. The costs implicit in this warranty are to be borne by the producer.

WHJ are responsible for point-of-sale product promotion to end user customers. This activity may be based on material supplied by ourselves.

4.2 Market Timing and Numbers

WHJ has provided the following data on a 'best-guess' basis:

- Supplies to WHJ to commence in July 1992.
- Initial sale price per unit to end users in the range £45 to £55 (including VAT) for the basic model.
- Sales lifetime 40 to 45 months.
- A total sales volume over this period of 250,000 to 350,000 units.

4.3 Sales Periods

In order to minimize their promotion costs and potential stock losses, WHJ are only prepared to consider changes in product specification and/or price to them at quarterly intervals during the sales life. Thus, the sales life is divided into a number of quarterly sales periods. WHJ has agreed to provide a forecast of their total sales demand (measured in product units) for each such period. The forecast will be available 'just before' the period starts.

4.4 WHJ Purchasing Policy

WHJ are not prepared to guarantee any particular level of product purchases to any one of their suppliers, either during any one sales period or over the whole sales life. Their purchasing policy will be as follows:

- During a sales period, WHJ will place purchase orders on their suppliers summing to a number of units approximately equal to their forecast total demand for that period. They will place these orders in descending priority order, giving first priority to the supplier, or suppliers, who in their judgement are offering them the best 'value for money' and product support.

- This process will continue until either their demand for that period has been met or their suppliers are unable to supply any more units during the period.

4.5 Notes

We expect the shape of the product market outlined in 4.2 to conform to the normal pattern for novel products, but we have no firm views on the timing of the build-up and decline curves.

The WHJ purchasing policy emphasizes the importance of their perception of the 'value' of the product in relation to its price. This underlines the need for an adequate marketing effort during the sales periods, both for product support (promotion and after-sales service) and to influence WHJ's judgement of 'product value for money' to them.

5. ACTION REQUESTED

That the new business development department prepare a business plan for the TCM venture as outlined above. This should be ready for evaluation by the main board not later than 16th December 1991.

6. PLANNING COSTS AND PROGRESS MONITORING

The costs of preparing the business plan will be taken as a charge against the marketing projects budget. We accept your estimate of 160 engineer-hours and £3,500 for this assignment. An IDO in this amount, on a 'not to exceed' basis, is attached herewith.

We assume that you will, as usual, monitor project progress and keep us informed of any problems. We will continue our discussions with WHJ and let you know of any substantive changes in the situation if these arise.

The managing director has requested that a brief progress report be presented, under Agenda Item 6 (Current Projects), at subsequent board meetings. I assume that you will handle these.

Donna O. Daring   18th September 1991

(Signed)

Marketing Director

It will be appreciated that this product brief is not a model of precision. It is better, however, in this respect than many documents of its kind.

A.2.3 The product design environment

In practice, this part of the context is rarely contained within a single document. The unified description that follows is culled from the typical mixture of formal directives, common knowledge and 'custom and practice' which comprise a real product design environment. It contains only that part of the total data which is relevant to the initial RD phase. Substantially more data, relating to costing and planning assumptions, is required for the subsequent phases.

Company facilties

The technical department is provided with a range of modern electronic development and test equipment, including computer-aided facilities for the design of printed circuit boards and 'custom' integrated circuits. It includes a small drawing-office and a mechanical engineering 'model shop'. Facilities for relatively small-scale software projects are also available.

The factory is a self-contained unit equipped for modern electronic product 'batch' manufacture, with a range of automatic and semi-automatic machinery. It includes facilities for:

- 'bare' printed circuit board manufacture and test
- automatic component insertion, soldering and test
- cable-forming and test
- plastic-injection moulding for product enclosures and similar items
- product assembly and test.

There are no in-house facilities for the *manufacture* of custom or semi-custom integrated circuits. If such circuits are required, they are contracted for with specialist suppliers on the basis of design data created by the technical department. It is not possible to give any general guidance on the bought-in costs of such circuits: each case must be treated individually.

Financial criteria

The company defines two financial targets for private venture product creation projects of this nature. These are:

- A minimum **gross margin** (unit sale price − unit works cost) of thirty per cent of sale price.
- A minimum **internal rate of return** (IRR) of (currently) twenty per cent.

The minimum gross margin target relates to immediate trading profit, and is regarded as highly desirable rather than mandatory. The minimum IRR target is more critical. The IRR of a project measures its profitability in a way which takes into account its pattern of negative and positive **cash-flows** over the whole project life. These concepts are discussed in Chapter 11, starting at Section 11.8. Section 11.13 focuses on the IRR concept.

A.2.4   Section end note

Note that the product brief calls for the preparation of a **business plan**. This refers to the prospective new 'mini-business' based on the TCM product. Conceptually, the plan covers the whole venture: from its first definition in the product brief through planning, marketing, design, manufacture and sales. The plan has two purposes. Firstly, it defines what has to be done to exploit the new opportunity. Secondly, it evaluates that opportunity as an investment/return proposition. When completed, the business plan includes:

(1) The outline design of the product.
(2) A sub-plan for its detailed development and design.
(3) A sub-plan for its marketing and sales over its anticipated sales life.
(4) A sub-plan for its manufacture and test.
(5) A sub-plan for the management of the whole mini-business project.
(6) A sub-plan for the cash-flow of the whole mini-business project.
(7) A commentary which evaluates the opportunity in terms of its apparent commercial and financial rewards, and the assumptions and risks attaching to them.

It is this document that must be submitted for board approval in mid-December. Its preparation is considerably eased by the use of a number of 'planning assumptions' which the company has developed over several years of experience. These assumptions are not presented here.

This RD case study is concerned with only the first part of the first item in the business plan. In the plan, the outline design is the PA, which is then the basis for the sub-plan describing the detailed product development and design activity (at item (2) above).

In the structured product design methodology developed in Chapter 8, the design of the PA immediately follows the initial RD phase. PA is derived by applying the **design constraints** identified in the RD phase to the **functional architecture** established in that phase. The functional architecture is a structured description of the product as it is first conceived by its sponsor (with no attempt to remove any blemishes in that description). It is obtained by **context analysis** of the product brief and makes no reference to implementation technologies. On the other hand, the PA is expressed in terms of real elements: components, modules, sub-assemblies and so on. *Its* derivation *does* require an excursion into the technologies. This is not the purpose of the case study, which therefore terminates with the first speculative version of the PA.

A.3   TCM requirements definition

The opening discussion in this section is a very concise summary of the requirements definition methodology designed in Section 8.5 of Chapter 8. It includes two figures extracted from that chapter.

Most of this section is the derivation of the RD for the TCM product. It uses the methodology developed in Chapter 8. The fundamentals of that technique are encapsulated in two figures in that chapter, which are reproduced here for convenience. The first of these, Figure A.3, partitions the work into three connected analyses using a **why–what–how** construct.

These analyses, labelled context analysis, functional architecture and design constraints, constitute a hierarchy of three levels in the RD. They are termed **vantage points** to emphasize the notion of relative height.

Figure A.4 illustrates further decomposition of the RD derivation task. Here, each vantage point level is separated into three elements by recognizing that each primary design

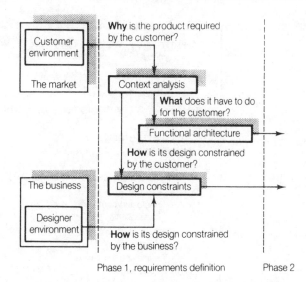

Figure A.3   **The basic structure of the requirements definition methodology.**

This is Figure 8.4. Examination of the customer environment yields the context analysis, which provides a statement for further analysis. This leads to the functional architecture, and to the customer facets of design constraints. These are completed by adding supplier constraints from the designer environment.

Requirements definition	Viewpoints					
	Technical		Economic		Operational	
Why is it required Context analysis	?		?		?	
What has it to do Functional architecture	?		?		?	
How is it constrained Design constraints	c	s	c	s	c	s
	?	?	?	?	?	?

(Vantage points — left axis label)

Key: c – customer
        s – supplier

Figure A.4   **Further partitioning of the requirements definition phase.**

This is Figure 8.5. It extends Figure A.3 by partitioning the vantage point levels with three critical viewpoints. The net effect is to decompose the big question of how to create a proper RD into twelve smaller (and hence, easier) questions.

question must be considered from technical, economic and operational **viewpoints**. Note that, at the third level, design constraints arise from both customer and company sources. The net effect of all the partitioning is decomposition of the RD derivation task into 12 relatively distinct areas. In practice, further logical subdivisions are often possible and this is the case with the TCM.

Context analysis 1: **Why** is the TCM required by WHJ?
- technical
- time and/or money
- operational

Context analysis 2: **Why** is the TCM required by the end users?
- technical
- time and/or money
- operational

    Functional architecture 1: **What** *must* it do?
    - technical
    - time and/or money
    - operational
    Functional architecture 2: **What** *might* it do?
    - technical
    - time and/or money
    - operational

Design constraints 1: **How** does WHJ constrain the design?
- technical
- time and/or money
- operational

Design constraints 2: **How** does the end user constrain the design?
- technical
- time and/or money
- operational

Design constraints 3: **How** does the company constrain the design?
- technical
- time and/or money
- operational

Figure A.5 **Structure of the requirements definition: a word picture.**

The structure of this word picture is based on Figure A.4, but advantage has been taken of features within the product brief to introduce additional partitioning. Thus, the context analysis is in two parts, as is the functional architecture, and the design constraints is in three parts. Note how textual indentation has been used to impose the block structure of Figure A.3 on the equivalent of Figure A.4 in this figure.

A.3.1 TCM RD: Basic structure

The TCM RD is based on analysis of the product brief of Section A.2.2, and the description of the product design environment in Section A.2.3. Happily, the product brief contains two factors which allow the RD to be partitioned to a greater extent than shown in the general case of Figure A.4. The factors are:

(1) WHJ is the product customer because it is the prospective purchaser of TCM units from the producer company. But it is the needs and limitations of the product end users which must dominate the product design. So the context analysis and design constraints must recognize both the intermediate (WHJ) and the final (end user) customers.

(2) The product brief distinguishes two sorts of product feature. These are the mandatory primary feature (for on-line connect cost monitoring) and a number of secondary features (for making the product more attractive to end users). This allows the functional architecture (which is an abstract entity) to be further partitioned by separating primary and secondary features. (It is a luxury which is not available at the PA stage. That construct must define the primary feature and the selected secondary features within a single non-abstract entity.)

These initial considerations lead to the RD structure shown in Figure A.5. Note that the RD derivation task is now partitioned into 21 relatively distinct areas, rather than the 12 areas of Figure A.4. Note, too, that 'economic' has been expanded to 'time and/or money'.

Figure A.5 is a **word picture**, which uses textual indentation to indicate relationships and groupings. The technique is used by users of structured programming languages, such as Pascal, C and Ada. Indentation is more generally employed as a 'shorthand' for presenting outlines and summaries. It is used in that way, reinforced by a numbering scheme, in the textual presentation of the TCM RD in Sections A.3.2, A.3.3, and A.3.4 which now follow. This follows the structure of Figure A.5, and employs two simple conventions to aid further analysis:

- References to implementation details (if any) are flagged with 'square' brackets to emphasize their [*aide-mémoire*] status.

- Outstanding questions needing early resolution are flagged with two question marks, as in ??.

These flags allow the marked items to be rapidly isolated, by automatic text searching techniques, for subsequent attention. This is not critical in the relatively small exercise considered here, but it becomes increasingly useful as product complexity increases. In this exercise, the outstanding questions are collected in Section A.3.5.

A.3.2 Context analysis (CA)

CA 1: Why is the TCM required by WHJ?

(A) *Technical*
    (1) To sustain image of supplying useful high-tech products

(B) *Time and/or money*
    (1) Forecast decline in sales to domestic and small business sectors
        (a) lack of distinction between two customer types ??
    (2) TCM sales to start July 1992
    (3) Forecast sales life 40 to 45 months ??
    (4) Forecast total sales 300K +/− 50K units ??
        (a) at £38 to £47 per unit (pre-VAT) ??
        (b) say 300K @ £43 ⇒ about £12.5M total revenue
        (c) margin @ 30% ⇒ about £3.8M gross margin

(C) *Operational*
    (1) Retain or increase market share of high-tech products

CA 2: Why is the TCM required by end users?

(A) *Technical*
    (1) Easy alternative to manual calculation of connect costs
        (a) manual calculation of connect costs while on-line not tenable

(2) Some useful and (nearly) free secondary features

(B) *Time and/or money*
    (1) Minimize connect cost of calls
        (a) an investment purchase: money back, then profit
    (2) Some secondary feature may save user time hence user money

(C) *Operational*
    (1) Easy to use alleviation of escalating telephone charges
    (2) Other useful secondary features
    (3) High-tech image and fascination

A.3.3   Functional architecture (FA)

This part of the analysis is divided into two parts, as in Figure A.5. The first part, FA 1, describes the *mandatory* features of the TCM and the second, FA 2, describes some possible non-mandatory features. But FA 1 is also divided into two parts, which are not shown in Figure A.5. It is presented first, textually, in overall terms and then, graphically, in more detail. This approach seeks confirmation that elements which must be present for the mandatory primary feature also enable many non-mandatory features to be provided relatively easily.

FA 1: What must the TCM do? (overall)

(A) *Technical*
    (1) Display connect cost of dialled outgoing calls while in progress
        (a) national and international calls
        (b) ?? accuracy not specified
        (c) see FA 1 detail (next) for a connect cost algorithm
    (2) Visually attractive: ?? shape, size, colour(s), image
    (3) Weight and size compatible with telephone environment: ?? numbers
    (4) At least as reliable as a telephone instrument: ?? numbers
    (5) Minimal (why, assumes battery PSU ??) power consumption: ?? numbers

(B) *Time and/or money*
    (1) Encourage user to adopt economical telephone habits

(C) *Operational*
    (1) Easy to understand, program and use: user manual needed
    (2) Present high-tech image

FA 1: What must the TCM do? (detail)

BT charges for normal 'dialled' telephone calls in *whole* connect-time units at a fixed fee (to which VAT is added) per unit. A unit fee buys an amount of connect time which depends on the date, time and type of the call. Call type depends mostly on distance. But there are other categories, such as free calls and calls to mobile telephones. Taken together, the national and international services result in some twenty **charge bands**, one for each call type. The time allowed per unit fee for a particular call is then determined by the intersection of its charge band with the **charge period**. The principle is shown in the illustrative **allowed time tables** of Figure A.6. The connect cost algorithm needs access to tables of this nature.

A unit fee is recorded at **call start**, which occurs when the called number answers. If the call is still in progress when the time allowed for that first unit fee expires a second unit is recorded, and so on until **call finish** is signalled by either party **hanging up**. An algorithm

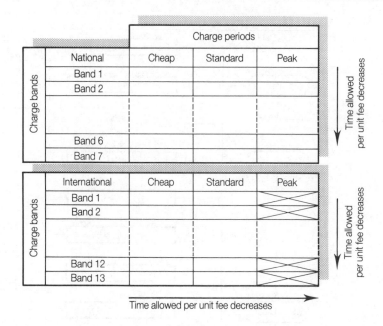

Figure A.6 **Telephone charge monitor: illustrative time allowed tables.**
BT charges for 'dialled' telephone calls in *whole* connect-time units at a fixed fee (to which VAT is added) per unit. A unit fee buys an amount of connect time which depends on the date, time and type of the call. Call type depends mostly on distance. This figure illustrates the basic principle. The connect cost algorithm (Figure A.7) needs access to tables of this nature.

which calculates the connect cost of a call while it is in progress is illustrated in Figure A.7. This flow-chart uses the notation introduced in Figure 6.6.

The various 'registers' (CBR, UCR and so on) store variables (CB, UC and so on) used by the algorithm for calculation and control purposes. The symbol '⇒' should be read as 'becomes'. For example, the notation:

CBR ⇒ Charge Band, or
CBR ⇒ CB

means that the value in the charge band register becomes the charge band.

A call monitoring sequence is initiated by the call-type input becoming available. A little time later, a call-start input sets the call status register (CSR) to 'on'. The algorithm is self-explanatory from that point and it is not considered further here.

FA 2: What might *the TCM do?*

FA 2 describes the possible non-mandatory secondary features. These features are grouped into four categories which do *not* coincide with those used in the product brief.

    (A) *Technical*
        (1) Group 1 = ?? cheap and easy extras
            (a) display time when not monitoring calls
            (b) display date on request
            (c) provide a number of pre-set alarms

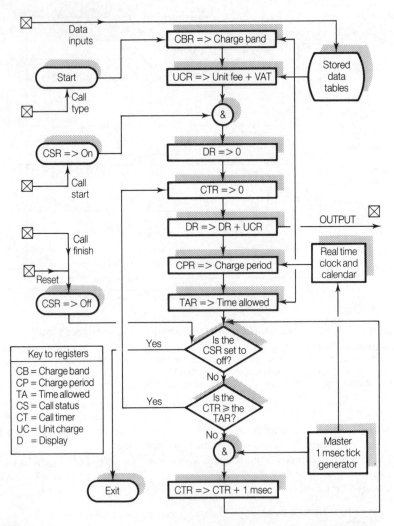

Figure A.7   **Telephone charge monitor: FA1 as the connect cost algorithm.**
This flow chart describes an algorithm which calculates the connect cost of a call while it is in progress. It uses the 'RPD' notation introduced in Figure 6.6.

[needs additional hardware for the alarm]
  (d) warning of pending charge increment (not in product brief)
  (e) recall last call charge (not in product brief)
  (f) auto totalling of charges for last quarter
  (g) built-in directory of popular numbers
  (h) optional auto call disruption for irresponsible users
     [can use alarm hardware]

(2) Group 2 = obvious omissions from product brief
  (a) handle calls via the operator
  (b) handle calls on the Mercury network

(3) Group 3 = the big one [but how ??]
    (a) totally automatic operation (after initial programming)
      (see detail later in PA 1)

(4) Group 4 = ?? too expensive and really fancy telephone features
    (a) short code dialling facility for popular numbers
    (b) loud speaking facility
    (c) call recording facility
    (d) optional auto redial for engaged numbers
    (e) print out charges for last quarter

(B) *Time and/or money*
    (1) Group 1 features offer time and money saving, convenience and image
    (2) Group 2 extend primary economic benefit
    (3) Group 4 as Group 1, but probably too expensive to provide

(C) *Operational*
    (1) Group 3 feature offers greatly improved ease of use
    (2) But other features make more difficult to understand, program and use
      (a) need bigger and better user manual
    (3) Enhanced high-tech image

A.3.4 Design constraints (DC)

DC 1: How does WHJ constrain the TCM design?

(A) *Technical*
    (1) 'Required' secondary features not well defined ??
      (a) (see what might the TCM do)
    (2) WHJ would like to offer a product range
      (a) extensible design required
      (b) marketing strategy required asap!
    (3) User-friendly: fully automatic best but how ??
      (a) handle both line interrupt and tone dialling
    (4) Needs to be rugged and reliable

(B) *Time and/or money*
    (1) Whole project to be company funded: funds might be tight
    (2) Probably two competitors, so will restrict market share ??
    (3) WHJ purchasing policy high risk to producers ??
    (4) Assume get one-third market share $\Rightarrow$ about 100K units ??
      (a) assume unit price to WHJ $\Rightarrow$ about £30 (midrange)
      (b) so total revenue $\Rightarrow$ about £3M
      (c) so gross margin (@ 30%) $\Rightarrow$ about £0.9M
    (5) Assume want five times investment back over about 4 years
      (a) so maximum project cost $\Rightarrow$ about £180K (first crude guess)
    (6) First deliveries to WHJ July 1992
      (a) need 3 months to plan (part-time effort)
      (b) so just 6 months from start of plan to first sales
    (7) Unit price to WHJ about £27 to £33 ??
      (a) probably too low to provide the more fancy (Group 4) features ??
    (8) Mandatory free replacement warranty at our expense
      (a) puts a premium on ruggedness and reliability

(C) *Operational*
    (1) Planning problems:
        (a) ?? fuzzy technical spec and works cost limits
        (b) ?? number of competitors uncertain so ?? credible market share
        (c) ?? shape of market growth–maturity–decline curve
        (d) can only change product features and price every 3 months
    (2) Competitive purchasing policy priority based
        (a) on product value for money to WHJ
          ?? WHJ technique for assessing product value
        (b) on quality of product promotion support from producers so plan for more than average product marketing support

DC 2: How does the end user constrain the TCM design?

(A) *Technical*
    (1) Non-technical users, so must
        (a) be easy to understand, set up, operate
        (b) guard against invalid data entry
        (c) have rugged user-proof mechanical design

(B) *Time and/or money*
    (1) End user pricing based on dubious data ??
    (2) Whole concept based on economic problems of prospective end user
        (a) ?? risk these not severe enough to ensure adequate sales

(C) *Operational*
    (1) User-friendliness a must
    (2) Must be user-proof – input and handling
    (3) First class user manual required [adds to works cost]

DC 3: How does the company constrain the TCM design?

(A) *Technical*
    (1) Lack own facilities to make custom/semi-custom integrated circuits
        (a) no real problem

(B) *Time and/or money*
    (1) Need 3 months to plan because only part-time effort available
        (a) puts rest of project under time pressure
        (b) 9 months from now to first sales!
    (2) Business plan needed by mid-December
    (3) Private venture project may limit funds (£180K max first guess)
    (4) Minimum gross margin $\Rightarrow$ 30%
    (5) Minimum IRR whole project $\Rightarrow$ 20%
    (6) Works cost target range about £19 to £23 ??
        (a) ?? probably too small to provide more fancy (Group 4) features

(C) *Operational*
    (1) Planning problems:
        (a) only part-time planning effort available
        (b) need a basic marketing strategy fast
          ?? sell large number of cheap basic units or
          ?? sell smaller number of expensive multi-featured units or
          ?? a middle of the road approach or

?? some combination of these
(2) Defined format for business plan
(3) Defined design methodology
(4) Weekly meetings with technical director
(5) Get direct access to planners in WHJ ??

A.3.5   TCM RD: Outstanding questions

This section is a commentary on the outstanding questions identified in the (mostly) textual RD of Sections A.3.2, A.3.3, and A.3.4. The comments are assembled under the viewpoint headings: technical, time and/or money, and operational. As before, commentary relating to implementation details is enclosed in square brackets.

Technical

(1) Output accuracy is not specified. Display to nearest penny should be acceptable. It is probably more important to ensure that the TCM measures call durations identical to those measured by BT (and Mercury).
(2) 'Visually attractive' needs to be better defined.
(3) Maximum weight and size must be defined by comparison with telephone instruments, as must the minimum reliability.
(4) Maximum power consumption needs to be defined. [The answer will be depend on type of power supply: mains, battery or some combination. The use of mains power will allow a brighter display but the stored data is then vulnerable to loss of power. Mains with battery back-up is probably the best choice. A need for access to mains power compromises TCM location.]
(5) Group 1 features must be confirmed as 'cheap and easy'. (Group 2 features are to be included.)
(6) Group 3 feature of totally automatic operation is highly desirable. It requires auto-detection of call type, start and finish. [Maybe use a non-invasive transducer (probably electromagnetic) monitoring the telephone cable. Then implement detection of call type by using a learning mechanism to avoid need for massive customized stored table.]
(7) Group 4 features need to be confirmed as too expensive.
(8) Domestic and business customers are not currently distinguished by WHJ. But their needs might be sufficiently distinctive to justify separate 'domestic' and 'business' models.

Time and/or money

All of the available time and money numbers, which affect commercial viability, are forecasts of unknown precision. This applies to the product sales life (duration and 'shape'), total sales over that life, unit price to WHJ, works cost and the number of competitors.

Operational

(1) All the normal planning problems due to fuzzy technical specification, speculative works cost limit and uncertain other 'commercial' numbers.
(2) The competitive purchasing policy is vicious. There is an urgent need to understand how WHJ assess product value. [Maybe do our own survey of end user reaction to sundry features and then 'help' WHJ to implement a rational way of assessing product value: discuss this with marketing.]

(3) A marketing strategy is urgently required. Basic options are:
    (a) aim to sell large number of cheap basic units or
    (b) aim to sell smaller number of expensive multi-featured units or
    (c) adopt a 'middle of the road' approach or
    (d) adopt some combination of these.
(4) Direct access to WHJ planners would be very helpful.

An alternative design concept

Each subscriber line provided by BT is monitored by a meter (at the telephone exchange end) which counts call units. The algorithm which 'drives' this meter must be similar to that illustrated in Figure A.7. BT are willing, on receipt of an initial fee and subsequent quarterly rental payments, to connect the pulses that drive this meter to the subscriber line. Then, provided the TCM is able to detect these pulses, its mandatory cost monitoring function is reduced to merely forming a running pulse count and displaying it in money terms.

This is an attractive concept which may offer a cheaper solution to the mandatory TCM function than the algorithm in Figure A.7. Evaluating the relative economics of the two approaches is complicated by the ongoing rental payments in the pulse counting method. However, if pulse counting is adopted for the mandatory on-line connect cost monitoring, then additional hardware and software will be needed to provide any of the non-mandatory secondary features. But, if additional modules are to be provided for the non-mandatory features, they can equally provide the mandatory feature!

This dilemma has both cost and marketing dimensions. It is resolved remarkably promptly by WHJ insisting (when consulted) that the TCM should have 'at least a minimum set of secondary features'.

A.3.6   Where from here?

The earlier parts of this section have taken the RD work about as far as it can go with available information. Purists, however, would round off the analysis with formal statements on output specification and input characterization. Creating these statements is not difficult, but they are omitted here for the sake of brevity.

The RD analysis has identified several further questions which need to be resolved. Two of these are critically important. Firstly, it appears that there is a conflict between implementing the whole list of features suggested by WHJ and the limits set on works cost. Secondly, the company urgently needs to select a specific marketing strategy. The two problems are not unrelated, and solutions should emerge during the next phase in the design process.

This next (and second) phase in the design process is 'design of the PA'. As noted earlier, the PA is a constrained version of the FA expressed in terms of real elements: components, modules, sub-assemblies and so on. It is formed by 'filtering' the FA through the design constraints. A likely consequence of the works cost constraint is that the Group 4 secondary features will be sacrificed. Defining this situation in numerical terms is a priority task. It needs realistic estimates of works cost, for a number of different product configurations, before any significant detailed design is done. Given experience of similar products, this estimating can normally be completed without much difficulty. The works cost part of the resulting relationship between works cost and feature list is then easily translated into price terms. Armed with this data, it should be possible to agree a much tighter functional specification with WHJ. When that has been achieved, the right marketing strategy should be more obvious, and work can then proceed on the detailed design. Reasonable first steps in design of the PA are now outlined.

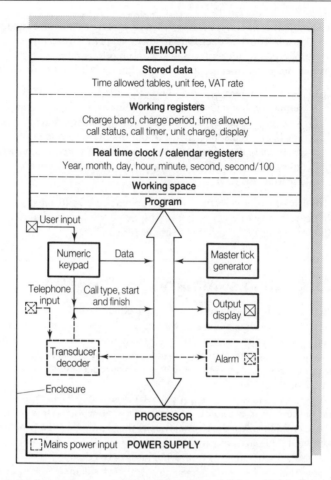

Figure A.8 **Telephone charge monitor: the major modules of PA1.**

Product architecture (PA) is a constrained version of the functional architecture (FA) expressed in terms of real elements: components, modules, sub-assemblies, and so on. It is formed by 'filtering' the FA through the design constraints. This figure illustrates the first PA to be costed.

Architecture 1: An example

The first TCM product configuration to be costed is shown in Figure A.8. This envisages the TCM as a microprocessor-based electronic product. It is equipped with only the minimum hardware and software required to provide:

(1) The mandatory on-line call charge monitoring feature, extended to include operator-controlled calls and (switchable) compatibility with the Mercury network (the Group 2 features).

(2) Those Group 1 features which, given the hardware needed to provide the mandatory feature, require only additional software. The additional software may have an adverse effect on works cost if more memory is required to accommodate it. But the effect is likely to be small. Providing more software will, of course, increase the product design cost, and it will have to created within the already tight time-scale.

This product configuration is regarded as comprising the irreducible minimum feature specification. The final decision on power supply provisioning is deferred, pending the advent of credible figures for power consumption.

A number of enhancements to this minimum feature list are also to be costed. These are:

(3) As in (1) above, but including the alarm and auto call disruption features. These require additional software and additional hardware to implement the alarm.

(4) A version of the TCM which includes automatic detection of call type, start and finish. The transducer which monitors the telephone cable is the only technical problem of any consequence in this concept. Permission will be sought for the immediate launch of a small applied research/development project directed at creating this device.

Note that all Group 4 features have been excluded at this first stage. This is because it may not be necessary to cost them if, as suspected, the works cost limit is already vulnerable following inclusion of the less costly features.

A.4 | Concluding summary

This case study has demonstrated that product design is not only about manipulating technologies in a cost-effective way, particularly in its early stages. The telephone charge monitor used as an example in the discussion is, technically, a relatively simple product. But the range of marketing, profit and cost issues which must be considered substantially complicates the task of achieving a proper product specification. This is an entirely normal situation.

The basic structure of the product RD is provided by the why–what–how vantage points and the technical, economic and operational viewpoints. It provides a useful framework on which to build an exhaustive analysis of the product design problem as that is initially presented. This analysis provides a more secure foundation for the subsequent design work than the basic documents from which it is derived.

Note that the FA derived in Section A.3.3 is fundamentally implementation independent, although a certain amount of technical jargon has crept into the description. (Rules, it will be recalled, are for the guidance of wise men and the adherence of fools.) But the on-line connect cost algorithm (Figure A.7) is genuinely independent of technology. Subject only to considerable dexterity with a stop-watch, and a split personality, the end user could use it to 'manually' monitor on-line call costs.

Designers using this RD methodology for the first time can waste time debating the best 'slot' for some particular data item. This debate should be strictly limited, because some items can quite reasonably fit into a number of different slots. It only matters that they are recorded somewhere. Another trap to avoid is spending too much time answering intermediate questions. If the answer to such questions is not immediately obvious, then they should be deferred for later consideration. Answering questions too soon tends to remove design options too soon. And many deferred questions actually disappear, without trace, as a consequence of answering other questions.

Tables of discount factors

This appendix is an adjunct of Chapter 11 (Technical Project Evaluation and Choice). It contains tabulated values of the discount factor:

$$(1 + r)^{-n}$$

for values of the discount rate, r, ranging from 1% to 60% and values of the years hence, n, ranging from 1 to 10. The discount rate is incremented in steps of 1%. Values of the discount factor at intermediate values of the discount rate can be estimated by interpolation.

The discount factor is the present value of one currency unit scheduled for delivery n years from now in an discount (interest) regime of r compound annual rate.

The tables may be used in connection with those questions relating to discounted cash-flow which are associated with Chapter 11.

Table B.1 covers values of r from 1% to 30% and values of n from 1 to 10; and Table B.2 covers values of r from 31% to 60% and values of n from 1 to 10.

Years hence	1%	2%	3%	4%	5%	6%	7%	8%	9%	10%
1	0.9901	0.9804	0.9709	0.9615	0.9524	0.9434	0.9346	0.9259	0.9174	0.9091
2	0.9803	0.9612	0.9426	0.9246	0.9070	0.8900	0.8734	0.8573	0.8417	0.8264
3	0.9706	0.9423	0.9151	0.8890	0.8638	0.8396	0.8163	0.7938	0.7722	0.7513
4	0.9610	0.9238	0.8885	0.8548	0.8227	0.7921	0.7629	0.7350	0.7084	0.6830
5	0.9515	0.9057	0.8626	0.8219	0.7835	0.7473	0.7130	0.6806	0.6499	0.6209
6	0.9420	0.8880	0.8375	0.7903	0.7462	0.7050	0.6663	0.6302	0.5963	0.5645
7	0.9327	0.8706	0.8131	0.7599	0.7107	0.6651	0.6227	0.5835	0.5470	0.5132
8	0.9235	0.8535	0.7894	0.7307	0.6768	0.6274	0.5820	0.5403	0.5019	0.4665
9	0.9143	0.8368	0.7664	0.7026	0.6446	0.5919	0.5439	0.5002	0.4604	0.4241
10	0.9053	0.8203	0.7441	0.6756	0.6139	0.5584	0.5083	0.4632	0.4224	0.3855

Years hence	11%	12%	13%	14%	15%	16%	17%	18%	19%	20%
1	0.9009	0.8929	0.8850	0.8772	0.8696	0.8621	0.8547	0.8475	0.8403	0.8333
2	0.8116	0.7972	0.7831	0.7695	0.7561	0.7432	0.7305	0.7182	0.7062	0.6944
3	0.7312	0.7118	0.6931	0.6750	0.6575	0.6407	0.6244	0.6086	0.5934	0.5787
4	0.6587	0.6355	0.6133	0.5921	0.5718	0.5523	0.5337	0.5158	0.4987	0.4823
5	0.5935	0.5674	0.5428	0.5194	0.4972	0.4761	0.4561	0.4371	0.4190	0.4019
6	0.5346	0.5066	0.4803	0.4556	0.4323	0.4104	0.3898	0.3704	0.3521	0.3349
7	0.4817	0.4523	0.4251	0.3996	0.3759	0.3538	0.3332	0.3139	0.2959	0.2791
8	0.4339	0.4039	0.3762	0.3506	0.3269	0.3050	0.2848	0.2660	0.2487	0.2326
9	0.3909	0.3606	0.3329	0.3075	0.2843	0.2630	0.2434	0.2255	0.2090	0.1938
10	0.3522	0.3220	0.2946	0.2697	0.2472	0.2267	0.2080	0.1911	0.1756	0.1615

Years hence	21%	22%	23%	24%	25%	26%	27%	28%	29%	30%
1	0.8264	0.8197	0.8130	0.8065	0.8000	0.7937	0.7874	0.7813	0.7752	0.7692
2	0.6830	0.6719	0.6610	0.6504	0.6400	0.6299	0.6200	0.6104	0.6009	0.5917
3	0.5645	0.5507	0.5374	0.5245	0.5120	0.4999	0.4882	0.4768	0.4658	0.4552
4	0.4665	0.4514	0.4369	0.4230	0.4096	0.3968	0.3844	0.3725	0.3611	0.3501
5	0.3855	0.3700	0.3552	0.3411	0.3277	0.3149	0.3027	0.2910	0.2799	0.2693
6	0.3186	0.3033	0.2888	0.2751	0.2621	0.2499	0.2383	0.2274	0.2170	0.2072
7	0.2633	0.2486	0.2348	0.2218	0.2097	0.1983	0.1877	0.1776	0.1682	0.1594
8	0.2176	0.2038	0.1909	0.1789	0.1678	0.1574	0.1478	0.1388	0.1304	0.1226
9	0.1799	0.1670	0.1552	0.1443	0.1342	0.1249	0.1164	0.1084	0.1011	0.0943
10	0.1486	0.1369	0.1262	0.1164	0.1074	0.0992	0.0916	0.0847	0.0784	0.0725

Table B.1   Discount factors for rate, r, in [1% . . . 30%] and years hence, n, in [1 . . . 10].

Years hence	31%	32%	33%	34%	35%	36%	37%	38%	39%	40%
1	0.7634	0.7576	0.7519	0.7463	0.7407	0.7353	0.7299	0.7246	0.7194	0.7143
2	0.5827	0.5739	0.5653	0.5569	0.5487	0.5407	0.5328	0.5251	0.5176	0.5102
3	0.4448	0.4348	0.4251	0.4156	0.4064	0.3975	0.3889	0.3805	0.3724	0.3644
4	0.3396	0.3294	0.3196	0.3102	0.3011	0.2923	0.2839	0.2757	0.2679	0.2603
5	0.2592	0.2495	0.2403	0.2315	0.2230	0.2149	0.2072	0.1998	0.1927	0.1859
6	0.1979	0.1890	0.1807	0.1727	0.1652	0.1580	0.1512	0.1448	0.1386	0.1328
7	0.1510	0.1432	0.1358	0.1289	0.1224	0.1162	0.1104	0.1049	0.0997	0.0949
8	0.1153	0.1085	0.1021	0.0962	0.0906	0.0854	0.0806	0.0760	0.0718	0.0678
9	0.0880	0.0822	0.0768	0.0718	0.0671	0.0628	0.0588	0.0551	0.0516	0.0484
10	0.0672	0.0623	0.0577	0.0536	0.0497	0.0462	0.0429	0.0399	0.0371	0.0346

Years hence	41%	42%	43%	44%	45%	46%	47%	48%	49%	50%
1	0.7092	0.7042	0.6993	0.6944	0.6897	0.6849	0.6803	0.6757	0.6711	0.6667
2	0.5030	0.4959	0.4890	0.4823	0.4756	0.4691	0.4628	0.4565	0.4504	0.4444
3	0.3567	0.3492	0.3420	0.3349	0.3280	0.3213	0.3148	0.3085	0.3023	0.2963
4	0.2530	0.2459	0.2391	0.2326	0.2262	0.2201	0.2142	0.2084	0.2029	0.1975
5	0.1794	0.1732	0.1672	0.1615	0.1560	0.1507	0.1457	0.1408	0.1362	0.1317
6	0.1273	0.1220	0.1169	0.1122	0.1076	0.1032	0.0991	0.0952	0.0914	0.0878
7	0.0903	0.0859	0.0818	0.0779	0.0742	0.0707	0.0674	0.0643	0.0613	0.0585
8	0.0640	0.0605	0.0572	0.0541	0.0512	0.0484	0.0459	0.0434	0.0412	0.0390
9	0.0454	0.0426	0.0400	0.0376	0.0353	0.0332	0.0312	0.0294	0.0276	0.0260
10	0.0322	0.0300	0.0280	0.0261	0.0243	0.0227	0.0212	0.0198	0.0185	0.0173

Years hence	51%	52%	53%	54%	55%	56%	57%	58%	59%	60%
1	0.6623	0.6579	0.6536	0.6494	0.6452	0.6410	0.6369	0.6329	0.6289	0.6250
2	0.4386	0.4328	0.4272	0.4217	0.4162	0.4109	0.4057	0.4006	0.3956	0.3906
3	0.2904	0.2848	0.2792	0.2738	0.2685	0.2634	0.2584	0.2535	0.2488	0.2441
4	0.1924	0.1873	0.1825	0.1778	0.1732	0.1689	0.1646	0.1605	0.1565	0.1526
5	0.1274	0.1232	0.1193	0.1155	0.1118	0.1082	0.1048	0.1016	0.0984	0.0954
6	0.0844	0.0811	0.0780	0.0750	0.0721	0.0694	0.0668	0.0643	0.0619	0.0596
7	0.0559	0.0533	0.0510	0.0487	0.0465	0.0445	0.0425	0.0407	0.0389	0.0373
8	0.0370	0.0351	0.0333	0.0316	0.0300	0.0285	0.0271	0.0257	0.0245	0.0233
9	0.0245	0.0231	0.0218	0.0205	0.0194	0.0183	0.0173	0.0163	0.0154	0.0146
10	0.0162	0.0152	0.0142	0.0133	0.0125	0.0117	0.0110	0.0103	0.0097	0.0091

Table B.2 Discount factors for rate, r, in [31% . . . 60%] and years hence, n, in [1 . . . 10].

Answers to Selected Questions

Chapter 1

1.2 All in Section 1.1.1. This is an exercise in manipulating Equations 1.1 to 1.5. The numerical answers are:

Added value = 75%
Gross profit = 40%
Operating Profit = 10%

1.9 First part is all in Section 1.4.1. The numerical answers are:

Labour productivity per employee = £10,000
Return on capital employed = 5%

1.13 First part in Section 1.7.2. Under the planned circumstances, the effect of the purchase is to decrease annual operating profit by £1,000 in each of the four years. Under the actual circumstances, operating profit in Years 1 and 2 is decreased by £1,000 as before. In Year 3, the decrease is £2,000. There is no effect in Year 4.

1.15 This tests understanding of the balance sheet equation:

$$(FA + CA) - (CL + NCL) = OC$$

which is introduced in Section 1.6. The material in Sections 1.7 and 1.8 is also helpful.
(a) FA and CL increase by the same amount, so no change in OC.
(b) No change in FA but CA increases by £500, so OC increases by £500.
(c) CA and CL increase by the same amount, so no change in OC.
(d) CA decreases by £3,000, so OC decreases by £3,000.
(e) A debtor current asset of £12,000 becomes a cash current asset of £12,000, so no change in OC. The information about product cost is irrelevant, because the profit on this transaction was taken when the products were sold on credit.
(f) A finished products current asset valued at £12,000 becomes a debtor current asset valued at £20,000, so OC increases by £8,000.
(g) NCL and CA increase by the same amount, so no change in OC.
Net change in OC = +£500 − £3,000 + £8,000 = +£5,500.

Chapter 2

2.2 A complete answer should first explain the usual meaning of 'technology' (at Section 2.1.3), and then examine the concept of strategic factors (at Sections 2.1.1 and 2.3.2). This answers the 'is it?' part of the question. The material in Section 2.1.4 answers the 'why?' part.

2.5 The first two parts are bookwork only, from Section 2.3.2. The purpose of the last part is to illustrate how difficult it is to answer this question. There is no indisputably correct general-purpose answer, although there might be in specific cases. In general, there are powerful arguments for choosing 'people' and 'markets' as, respectively, the most important internal and external types of factor.

2.11 This question is more challenging than it appears at first sight. The answer to the first part is certainly 'no'. Answering the 'if not, why not?' part is more demanding. There are clues in the earlier sections of the chapter, in particular in the 'General investment criteria' of Section 2.3.3 and in the 'Traditional investment criteria' of Section 2.3.4. The unhappy position of a business investing heavily in a technology which is suddenly superseded by a technological 'switch' should also be mentioned. (Of course, no directors would consciously strive to be in that position. But many arrive there due to a combination of ignorance and bad luck.)

Chapter 3

3.6 This is a challenging question based on the whole of Section 3.2. It tests both the understanding of that material and the ability to extend it a little. An answer is sketched out below.

Projects at the start of the technical innovation process are speculative attempts to extend distinct technologies. Projects at the end of the process aim to arrange well-understood data in new ways to define distinct products. Many project features change dramatically over this spectrum. Examples are:

- clarity and rigidity of technical and financial objectives
- optimum staffing strategies (from dispersion to concentration)
- typical staff temperament (from scientists to engineers)
- probability of success
- typical project cost
- susceptibility to detailed planning and tight control
- business consequences of failure.

The differences are such that very different project management regimes are appropriate at different ends of the process. The relaxed approach suited to the start of the process is best matched to the tight regime demanded at its end by an intermediate stage. This requirement conveniently coincides with the switch from technology emphasis to product emphasis which must occur within the process. Thus, basic research is distinguished from applied research. It is then rational, so as to minimize the risk of technical failure, to design and prove novel sub-units before designing them into the complete product. Thus, product development is distinguished from product design and the whole process becomes separated into four stages.

A two-stage approach is vulnerable to three dangers:

- Use of inappropriate project management techniques, which upsets project staff and yields poor planning and control.
- Poor control of the switch from technology to product emphasis, resulting in inadequate product range definition and, perhaps, failure to identify critical sub-units.
- Project time and/or cost overrun, project failure and/or product failure in service due to designing with unproven sub-units.

3.8   The first part is an invitation to reproduce and explain Figure 3.7, but starting with the cash-flow rather than the sales life cycle (as in the text). The material is in Sections 3.3.1 and 3.3.2. The second part can only be answered in subjective terms at this stage in the book. There are clues in Section 3.3.2, but the features are reasonably self-evident:

- Maximum investment – should be as small as possible.
- Time to break even – should be as soon as possible.
- Rate of positive cash-flow – should be as high as possible.
- Positive cash-flow – should last as long as possible.
- Ratio of total positive cash-flow to maximum investment – should be as high as possible.

Chapter 4

4.2   The first part is in Section 4.2.1. The second part is more challenging; it is not specifically answered in the text. The material on motivation in Section 4.2.2 gives adequate clues.

4.7   This seeks a summary of Sections 4.4.1, 4.4.2 and the first part of 4.4.3. This is a demanding but rewarding exercise. It also provides a foretaste of the design technique developed in Chapter 8.

Chapter 5

5.5   The enormous scope of this question is limited by the time available to answer it (30 minutes, say). This, in itself, is one answer to the second part of the question, which might appear to be unrelated to the first part. Thus (as always), the design of the answer is constrained by the time available to produce it. Within this constraint, the first part of the question is adequately answered in Section 5.3.2. The second part can be answered by showing that conflicts arise between the organizational design objectives. (Which are *what* the organization has to do.) So some objectives must be compromised, to some extent, in the final design. This, too, is covered in Section 5.3.2.

5.7   All in Section 5.4.2, under the 'Bonds and barriers concept' heading. Figure 5.2 aids the explanation sought in the first part of the question, and Figure 5.4 illustrates one acceptable answer to the second part.

5.10   First two parts in Section 5.5.5. The third part is a small design exercise not specifically covered in the text.

Chapter 6

6.4   Mostly in Section 6.2.2, but Equation 6.1 in Section 6.2.1 defines the total cost variance. The figures required to complete the (end of) Month 04 control report are:

- the actual cumulative headcount
    = 10.5 people-months
- the effort variance
    = -20.75% *under*
- the actual cumulative effort cost
    = £43.313 K
- the actual cumulative total cost
    = £48.513 K
- the total cost variance
    = 17.29% *under*

This report, of itself, reveals nothing definitive about the technical status of the project. It shows that it is underspending with respect to cost plan, and that it is underresourced with respect to effort plan. So project progress is likely to be lagging behind schedule. But this is an assumption which may or may not be valid.

6.6   This exercises some of the notions in Section 6.3 under the 'Estimating a single activity loop' heading. Let T_1 be the elapsed time between the wake-up alarm and finishing breakfast, and T_2 be the elapsed time between finishing breakfast and going fishing (at the exit of the 'and' gate). Then, working throughout in minutes:

(a) minimum T_1 is $t_1 + t_2$ = 105
    minimum T_2 is t_4 = 30
    so minimum $(T_1 + T_2)$ = 135

The probability of achieving this time on *any* day is:

$$P_1 \times (1 - P_2) \times (1 - P_3) = 0.137$$

(b) See Figure 6.7 and the accompanying explanation.
(c) The first three possible values for T_1, with corresponding probabilities, are obtained in (b). T_2 can only be either 30 or 60 minutes, at 0.600 and 0.400 probability, respectively. So the first six possible times for going fishing and their associated probabilities are:

135 minutes at 0.480 probability ($T_1 = 105$ at 0.800 probability)
165 minutes at 0.320 probability ($T_1 = 105$ at 0.800 probability)
195 minutes at 0.576 probability ($T_1 = 165$ at 0.960 probability)
225 minutes at 0.384 probability ($T_1 = 165$ at 0.960 probability)
255 minutes at 0.595 probability ($T_1 = 225$ at 0.992 probability)
285 minutes at 0.397 probability ($T_1 = 225$ at 0.992 probability)

6.10   In Section 6.4.5, under the 'The three times combined' heading. The calculated expected activity times are shown in Table 6.11, which also shows the standard deviation (s) and variance (s^2) for each activity.

Activity	T_O	T_M	T_P	T_E	s	s^2
01.02	3.0	4.2	4.8	4.1	0.30	0.09
03.18	14.5	16.0	18.1	16.1	0.60	0.36
04.08	1.8	2.5	3.2	2.5	0.23	0.05
04.15	6.8	7.8	10.0	8.0	0.53	0.28
05.10	1.5	1.8	2.1	1.8	0.10	0.01
05.16	7.9	9.2	10.5	9.2	0.43	0.19
08.15	9.8	11.0	11.6	10.9	0.30	0.09
10.16	1.2	1.5	1.8	1.5	0.10	0.01
15.17	1.6	3.4	4.0	3.2	0.40	0.16
16.17	0.8	1.0	1.2	1.0	0.07	0.00
17.18	0.6	0.8	1.0	0.8	0.07	0.00
18.20	4.4	6.0	6.4	5.8	0.33	0.11

Table 6.11 **Activity times (weeks).**

(a) Path 01.02.03.18.20	26.0
(b) Path 01.02.04.15.17.18.20	21.9
(c) Path 01.02.04.08.15.17.18.20	27.3
(d) Path 01.02.05.16.17.18.20	20.9
(e) Path 01.02.05.10.16.17.18.20	15.0

Table 6.12 **Expected path times (weeks).**

	E01	E02	E03	E04	E05	E08	E10	E15	E16	E17	E18	E20
Earliest time	0.00	4.10	4.10	4.10	4.10	6.60	5.90	17.50	13.30	20.70	21.50	27.30
Latest time	0.00	4.10	5.40	4.10	10.50	6.60	18.20	17.50	19.70	20.70	21.50	27.30
Slack	0.00	0.00	1.30	0.00	6.40	0.00	12.30	0.00	6.40	0.00	0.00	0.00
Critical path	*	*		*		*		*		*	*	*
	E01	E02	E03	E04	E05	E08	E10	E15	E16	E17	E18	E20

Table 6.13 **Event time parameters (weeks).**

6.12 In Section 6.4.3, under the 'The critical path' and 'Event times and slack' headings. The numerical answers are in Tables 6.12 and 6.13. The critical path is 01.02.04.08.15.17.18.20 = 27.3 weeks.

6.14 In Section 6.4.3, under the 'Activity starts, finishes and floats' heading. The numerical answers are in Table 6.14.

Activity	CPath	T_E	TF	FFE	FFL	IF
01.02	*	4.10	–	–	–	–
02.03		–	1.30	–	1.30	–
02.04	*	–	–	–	–	–
02.05		–	6.40	–	6.40	–
03.18		16.10	1.30	1.30	–	–
04.08	*	2.50	–	–	–	–
04.15		8.00	5.40	5.40	5.40	5.40
05.10		1.80	12.30	–	5.90	–
05.16		9.20	6.40	–	–	–
08.15	*	10.90	–	–	–	–
10.16		1.50	12.30	5.90	–	–
15.17	*	3.20	–	–	–	–
16.17		1.00	6.40	6.40	–	–
17.18	*	0.80	–	–	–	–
18.20	*	5.80	–	–	–	–

Table 6.14 **Activity float times (weeks).**

6.15 All in Section 6.4.5, under the 'An example of three-times estimating' heading. The question follows the example in the text quite closely, but requires calculations for two paths. Numerical answers are:

Critical path: 01.02.04.08.15.17.18.20
Expected time = 27.3 weeks, standard deviation = 0.71 weeks

Next most critical path: 01.02.03.18.20
Expected time = 26.0 weeks, standard deviation = 0.75 weeks

Estimates: (i) about four per cent
(ii) about ninety-five per cent

The path times and probability calculations are plotted in Figure 6.35, which is similar to Figure 6.28.

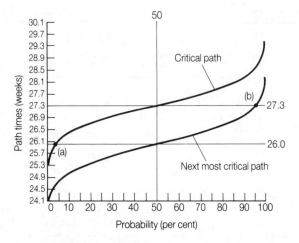

Figure 6.35 **Path times and probability.**

This approach to a solution differs slightly from that in the text, because it is *wholly* spreadsheet based. The alternative approach, using published tables, is equally valid but less illuminating and more tedious. Note that the two path length curves are virtually 'parallel', because their standard deviations are much the same.

The 'usual' assumptions look a bit dubious, especially with respect to path 01.02.03.18.20. In fact, the question really turns on the probability performance of path 04.08.15.17.18 in comparison with that of the single activity 03.18. This is not examined here.

6.17 Equation 6.23 is derived in Section 6.5.2 under the 'Estimating divisible tasks: The f factor method' heading. The answer to the second part of the question (obtaining an appropriate value for f) is contained within that derivation. But it can also be obtained as follows.

Let T_2 be a credible estimate, made without reference to Equation 6.23, for the value of T when P = 2Ps. Then, from Equation 6.23:

$$T_2/Ts = 1/2 + f/2$$

or

$$f = \frac{T_2 - (Ts/2)}{(Ts/2)}$$

So, f is the proportion by which T exceeds Ts/2 when P = 2Ps.

6.18 This an exercise in understanding Equation 6.23, which is derived in Section 6.5.2 under the 'Estimating divisible tasks: The f factor method' heading. The first part of the question is answered in Table 6.15. Columns (1) to (5) summarize the question and column (10) gives the answers.

The difference between the T values for task C at P = 4 and P = 8 is nil: they are equal at 6 months. This indicates that no reduction in completion time is achieved by doubling the team size over its sparse estimate value! The effect occurs because the contribution to T from column (7) decreases as P increases, whereas that from

(1)	(2)	(3)	(4)	(5)	(6)	(7)	(8)	(9)	(10)
						$\dfrac{1}{(P/Ps)}$	$\dfrac{f(P/Ps - 1)}{2}$		
Task	Ts	Ps	f	P	P/Ps	(P/Ps)	2	T/Ts	T
A	6	4	0.0	2	0.5	2.0	0.000	2.000	12.00
A	6	4	0.0	4	1.0	1.0	0.000	1.000	6.00
A	6	4	0.0	8	2.0	0.5	0.000	0.500	3.00
B	6	4	0.5	2	0.5	2.0	(0.125)	1.875	11.25
B	6	4	0.5	4	1.0	1.0	0.000	1.000	6.00
B	6	4	0.5	8	2.0	0.5	0.250	0.750	4.50
C	6	4	1.0	2	0.5	2.0	(0.250)	1.750	10.50
C	6	4	1.0	4	1.0	1.0	0.000	1.000	6.00
C	6	4	1.0	8	2.0	0.5	0.500	1.000	6.00

Table 6.15 **The f method for task times.**

column (8) increases as P increases. So, as P increase from a low value, T decreases to a minimum and then increases. This is shown rather nicely by the $f = 1.0$ curve in Figure 6.30.

The final part of the question asks for the derivation of:

$$(P/Ps)_{opt} = + (2/f)^{1/2} \tag{6.24}$$
$$(T/Ts)_{min} = + 2(f/2)^{1/2} - f/2 \tag{6.25}$$

which are obtained by differentiating Equation 6.23. For Task C, $f = 1.0$, $Ps = 4$ and $Ts = 6$ (months). So, rounding to 1 decimal place:

$(P/Ps)_{opt} = 1.4$ and $(T/Ts)_{min} = 0.9$
$P_{opt} = 5.6$ and $T_{min} = 5.4$ months.

Fractional people are inefficient, so $P = 5$ is a reasonable practical choice. This gives a completion time estimate of about 5.5 weeks.

6.20 All in Section 6.6.1. The numerical answers are:

Project	DT (months)	DC £K	DT %	DC %
A1	0.5	9	8	15
B2	0.0	0	0	0
C3	−3.0	−180	−17	−40

Project A1 is a small project (PC = £60K), which appears to be running ahead of time schedule and spending less than planned. This is an unusual progress situation, which might be explored in more detail at some time. But not now, because there are more urgent enquiries to make. Project B2 is a large project (PC = £1,100K). It has completed 20 months of its 22 month time plan, and appears to be exactly on plan for both time and cost. At first sight, these are very suspicious circumstances which must be urgently explored. Hopefully, the project has been re-planned recently and the report merely confirms that the new plan is a good one. (More cynically, perhaps the new technical manager is about to find out why the previous technical manager has moved to fresh pastures.) The Project C3 report is also disturbing. This project appears to have slipped 3 months in 3 months and is promising a forty per cent overspend of £180K. These are the early signs of a future disaster. The technical manager calls for more details (by the end of the day), before asking the leader of Project B2 to come for a chat.

Chapter 7

7.1 Figure 7.1 is explained in Section 7.2.2. The numbers for constructing the required diagram are:

	£s	%
Sales revenue	67,500	100.00
Cost of products sold	33,337	49.39
Gross profit	34,163	50.61
Marketing, selling and distribution	3,914	5.80
Research and development	12,123	17.96
Administration cost	13,342	19.77
Interest paid	425	0.63
Profit before tax	4,359	6.46

7.3 Mostly in Section 7.3.2; bonus points for bringing the purchase of fixed assets and depreciation into the discussion, as noted in Section 7.5.1. (Note: Struggling with this question brings special rewards. The difficulty that many engineers have with accounting concepts stems from misunderstanding the distinction between profit and cash-flow. The topic – which is on the boundary between financial and management accounting – is introduced, almost imperceptibly, in Chapter 1. Section 7.3.2 develops it a little further, and it is an important issue in Chapter 12.)

7.5 The first two parts are answered in Section 7.5.1, although careful reading is required. The completed table is:

	Start Year 1	End Year 1	End Year 2	End Year 3
Incremental profit £	0	−300	−300	−300
Cumulative profit £	0	−300	−600	−900
Incremental cash-flow £	−1,000	0	0	+100
Cumulative cash-flow £	−1,000	−1,000	−1,000	−900

The final 'comment' should note that, at the end of the useful life, the cumulative *loss* is the same as the *net cash-flow out* of the business, and explain why this is so. This is what depreciation aims to do. Two further points on this question: (1) examination of the table columns provides a nice answer to Question 7.3; (2) readers may care to compare the answer table with Table 1.1 in Chapter 1, which yields another insight into the same question.

7.8 This is a more conventional example of break-even analysis than that discussed in Section 7.6.2. Working to the nearest £, a step-by-step approach to the first part is:

Sales price per product unit	= 70,875/63	= 1,125
Direct cost of 63 units (35 005 − 12 002)		= 23,003
Direct cost per unit	= 23,003/63	= 365
Contribution per unit to fixed costs	= 1,125 − 365	= 760
Number of units to recover fixed costs	= 12,002/760	= 15.8

(This part of the question is solved graphically in Figure 12.3.) The second part of the question is a bit ambiguous! In accountancy terms, the answer is 'by the end of March 1991'. But there is not enough information to answer the question in cash terms. Because: (1) if units are sold on credit, cash income lags sales revenue, and (2) the production overhead cost increases with time, in some unspecified way, even though it does not vary with the number of units made.

7.9 Because of the 'economies of scale' effect noted in Section 7.6.2 (and discussed in more detail in Section 7.9.5). The direct cost per unit is unchanged, but the fixed cost per unit decreases because there are more units to share the fixed cost. Thus:

- at 63 units made, works cost = 365 + 12,002/63 = £556 (per unit)
- at 100 units made, works cost = 365 + 12.002/100 = £485 (per unit)

7.11 This exercises understanding of all of Section 7.7. Part (a) is simple, part (b) is less straightforward but more entertaining. Readers should note that, while budgeting technique (b) is *not* formally recommended, it is quite commonly used in practice.

(a) Labour rate = £19,600/1,702   = £11.52 per hour
   Overhead rate = £1,048,875/53,190   = £19.72 per hour
   Number of direct engineers needed   = 53,190/1,702
                         = 31.25 (rounded average)

(b) Labour rate = £19,600/1,702   = £11.52 per hour (as before)
   Adjusted overhead rate   = £20.71 per hour (rounded up)
   L+O/H before = £11.52 + £19.72   = £31.24 per hour
   Price increase of safety factor   = (£20.71 − £19.72) per hour
            = £ 0.99 per hour   = 3.2% (about)
   Increase in overhead cost   = 53,190 × £0.99
                         = £52,658

   Safety factor = 52,658/11.52 direct hours
               = 4,571 direct hours
               = 8.6% of budget direct hours

The additional £52,658 is dispersed among the existing overhead items in a series of small upward adjustments to the estimates. In effect, this increases the waiting time provision in the budget (see Section 7.7.1, under the 'Total overhead cost' heading) without increasing the waiting time entry!

7.12 Mostly in Section 7.8.1, but some relevant material is in Section 7.5.3. A good answer notes wider use of multiple labour rates and greater diversity of mechanisms for overhead allocation in the product case. Bonus points for recalling variation of works cost with volume, and why it happens (see Questions 7.8 and 7.9).

7.14 This exercises the whole of Section 7.8.2. A completed version of the variance report is shown in Table 7.12.

The most serious issue revealed by the report is the adverse variance of some £7 (about fifty-five per cent of the total adverse variance). It arises from the consumption of excessive (compared with standard) quantities of too expensive (compared with standard) printed circuit board material. The unit cost variance makes up about sixty-seven per cent of this problem.

Note: Questions 7.15 and 7.16 are essentially the same; 7.16 is longer than 7.15, but less brutal.

7.16 In Sections 7.9.1, 7.9.2 and most of 7.9.3. Some pointers are now outlined.

(b) UP_0 is the lowest unit price at which there is no demand ($r = 0$) for products. $1/D$ is the demand in the unlikely event of products being given away ($UP = 0$)! The marginal demand is $-1/(D \times UP_0)$, but D is really the price-volume discount factor in the recast version of Equation 7.13a:

$$UP = UP_0(1 - rD) \qquad (7.13)$$

which helps with the sketch.

(c) This starts the build-up of a diagram like Figure 7.15. Revenue = unit demand × unit price, so

$$R = UP_0(1 - rD)r \qquad (7.14)$$

which shows that R = 0 when r = 0 and when r = 1/D (at UP = 0)! The slope of the R curve is the marginal revenue:

Product X Period: FY 1992/93 Weeks: 01–48	Units	Actual costs AQOU Aq	£ ACPU Ac	£ Item	1 off £ Total Aq × Ac	Standard costs SQOU Sq	£ SCPU Sc	£ Item	1 off £ Total Sq × Sc	Variances (£s) Unit Cost	Unit Quantity	Total	1 off
1. Direct labour:	hours	9.67	5.34		51.64	9.30	5.15		47.90	1.84 A	1.91 A	3.74 A	
2. Direct materials:													
Chips type A	–	122.00	0.94	114.68		120.00	0.95	114.00		(1.22) F	1.90 F	0.68 A	
Chips type B	–	15.00	4.45	66.75		15.00	4.50	67.50		(0.75) F	0.00 F	(0.75) F	
PC board	sq cm	27.50	0.62	17.05		22.30	0.45	10.04		4.67 A	2.34 A	7.01 A	
					198.48				191.53	2.71 A	4.24 A	6.95 A	
3. Overheads:													
Variable	hours	9.67	1.41	13.66		9.30	1.26	11.70		1.49 A	0.47 A	1.96 A	
Fixed	hours	9.67	2.70	26.15		9.30	2.81	26.16		(1.05) F	1.04 F	(0.01) F	
					39.81				37.86	0.45 A	1.51 A	1.95 A	
		1.00 product units			289.93	1.00 product units			277.29	Total variance:		12.64 A	
Note: Total weeks 01–48		Var £ 35,637	Fx £ 68,200	Hours 25,222		Var £ 30,200	Fx £ 67,500	Hours 24,000		Var £ 5,437 A	Fx £ 700 A	Hours (1,222) A	

Table 7.12 Works cost of Product X during 1992/93.

$$MR = UP_0(1 - 2Dr), \text{ so } R \text{ is a maximum when } MR = 0 \text{ and } r = 1/2D$$

(d) Equation 7.18 is the traditional simplifying assumption that total cost is a linear 'semi-variable', as in Figure 7.4(c). The marginal (total) cost is the slope of the TC curve, so K is the marginal (total) cost.

(e) P = R − TC, so the sketch can be constructed by subtracting the TC sketch from the R sketch. P is a maximum when the slope of the P curve, which is the marginal profit, is zero. That is, when:

$$\frac{d(P)}{d(r)} = \frac{d(R)}{d(r)} - \frac{d(TC)}{d(r)} = MR - MC = MP = 0$$

7.17 This example closely follows 'Example 1: Revenue, cost and profit' in Section 7.9.4 and illustrated in Figure 7.15. But, in this case, the revenue curve just fails to cross the cost line and the maximum profit is actually the minimum loss. Answers are:

(a) No break-even value(s), so no corresponding values of revenue and total cost.

(b) Output rate for maximum revenue = 66,667 units per annum, and
       maximum revenue = £3,333,333 per annum.

(c) Output rate for maximum profit   = 41,574 units per annum, and
       minimum loss   = maximum profit = −£3,697 per annum.

Chapter 8

8.2 All in Section 8.3. Some specific points are:

(d) No: product value has still to be compared with product price.

(g) Relative, in two senses: (1) as between the different products, and (2) as between different customers, because assessment of value involves subjective evaluations.

(h) No: benefit ratio (= competitiveness) may be less than 1 for the most competitive product.

8.3 In the introduction to Section 8.4 and the first part of Section 8.4.1. Note that it is necessary but not sufficient for product price to be adequately greater than product cost. The product must also be sufficiently competitive (in the benefit ratio sense) at this price.

8.10 This is a challenge to summarize the whole of Section 8.5 in support of the requirements definition procedure illustrated in Figures 8.4 and 8.5. It a demanding but rewarding exercise.

8.14 (a) 'Design constraints' are defined in Section 8.4.3 under the 'Constraints' heading. Their critical nature emerges in Section 8.5.4 (and is summarized under the 'Constraints' heading) and is illuminated from another perspective in Section 8.6.1. The 'six types' classification is first described in Section 8.5.5 under the 'Further partitioning of the RDM' heading and is illustrated in Figure 8.5. It is summarized at the start of Section 8.7.

(b) All in Section 8.7.1.

(c) All in Section 8.7.2.

8.17 Some clues in Section 8.9.

Chapter 9

9.1 A 'scene-setting' question answered in Section 9.2.1. Bonus points for recalling that PV-funded technological innovation (also needed for business survival) is paid for, in effect, out of profit; and that positive cash-flow is needed to pay business costs, so liquidity can be more important than profit.

9.3 There are others ways of doing it, but this question is best recognized as an invitation to reproduce and explain Figure 9.2. The material is all in Section 9.2.3.

9.8 (a) All in Section 9.3.1.
(b) The first answer is 'yes'. Explaining why is more challenging. Product suppliers want high price and product purchasers want low price. 'Right' means 'right for both parties'. So there is a right price somewhere between 'high' and 'low'. This is all a bit simplistic, but it represents a start. Further clues are in Sections 9.3.2, 9.5.1 and Section 8.3. And 'Example 1: Revenue, cost and profit' in Section 7.9.4 is also relevant.
(c) All in Section 9.3.3.
(d) All in Section 9.3.4.

Chapter 10

10.2 All in Section 10.1, under the 'Elements of the production function' heading. Reproduction and limited explanation of Figures 10.1 and 10.2 is required.

10.7 In the introduction to Section 10.2.5. Figure 10.4 is required. The notions underlying part (c) are developed a little further in Section 10.5.1 under the 'Low, intermediate and high technology' heading.

10.10 For R1: $228R1 = 100{,}000 + 128R1$, so $R1 = 1{,}000$ units per annum, and
profit at $R1 = 0$

For R2: $100{,}000 + 128R2 = 190{,}000 + 81R2$, so $R2 = 1915$ units per annum (to the nearest unit), and
profit at $R2 = 1{,}915(228 - 128) - 100{,}000 = £91{,}500$ per annum.

For R3: $190{,}000 + 81R3 = 330{,}000 + 34R3$, so $R3 = 2{,}979$ units per annum (to the nearest unit), and
profit at $R3 = 2{,}979(228 - 81) - 190{,}000 = £247{,}900$ per annum.

10.11 All in Section 10.3, under the appropriate headings. Note that the requested format for the analyses employs the powerful partitioning rationale introduced (overtly, at least) in Section 8.5. Its effective use for precis of the sort requested here takes a little practice, but it repays the effort.

10.12 Material for the requested discussion is in Section 10.4. The 'how can human conflict ... be minimized?' question is one of the very big ones. The only clue in this chapter is in some rather trite observations towards the end of Section 10.2.1. Other prescriptions are scattered throughout the book: Chapters 4 (especially) and 5 are particularly relevant. Industry is still searching for the right answer(s). A good answer here 'would cite leadership, motivation, a common sense of purpose, involvement. and awareness of colleague's duties, jargon and problems.

Chapter 11

11.7 (a) Mostly in Section 11.2.4, but reference to earlier material may be required. Figure 11.4 is sought. The *importance of choosing the right projects* is the management (or business parameter) in the list of those which increase during product creation.

(b) This is a tough question which is avoided in the main text! There are two reasons for this: (i) in practice, project boundaries are drawn by management influenced by local conditions as well as theoretical considerations and, (ii) most of the cited project parameters are subjective and/or comparative indicators. Probably the most reliable and objective indicator is the degree of focus on a single specific product. Because BR is at technology level, AR is at product range level and PD&D is at single product level.

11.12 (a) 'Product creation project' is first defined (in this chapter) in Section 11.1.3 and it is explained again in Section 11.5, before becoming the focus of Section 11.6. Answers to (b), (c) and (d) are all in Section 11.6. Figure 11.5 is required.

11.14 This is (mostly) quite a demanding challenge to condense Section 11.8.1 and 11.8.2 into a slightly different format, including a more explicit version of Figure 11.6. Bonus points for explaining why profit is not the same as cash-flow (see, for example, the answer to Question 7.3, which indicates a trail to follow). In (b): the most critical assumption equates a net incremental positive cash-flow with every product unit sold. This turns on, among other things, product works cost ('the cost of manufacturing it') which, generally, decreases from a high level as the rate of manufacture increases. This is the economies of scale effect examined in Section 7.9.5. It is ignored in Section 11.8 as a potential confusion, but recalled here for completeness. In (c): the time aspect is not covered in Section 11.8.1 and 11.8.2 (although it becomes central later) but it is in Section 3.3.2, under the 'Evaluating the cash-flow performance' heading.

11.16 All in Section 11.10, although the answer to the last question in (a), which is 'yes', is only covered by implication: consider positive cash-flow from one project being used to reduce negative cash-flow on another project, so reducing cost, hence earning income.

11.17 (a) All in Section 11.11.
(b) The algorithm is in Section 11.11.1, answer in Table 11.14.

For interest(!): read the last question in Question 11.16 (a) again, and then inspect the interest column in this table.

11.18 (a) This asks for $1 \times (1 + 0.03)^n = 2$ to be solved for n. The answer is about 23.5 years!
(b) In Section 11.12.2, under the 'Present values and future sums' heading. Derivation of Equation 11.8 is required.
(c) In Section 11.12.2 under the 'Cash-flow models and net present value' heading. Answer is £3.59.
(d) −£1.47.
(e) No, it is truly awful. The NPV of the investments is about −£2.53 and the NPV of the returns is about £1.06 (treating them separately) yielding a total NPV of

| | Project A: interest regime: 18% Incremental cash-flows | | | Cumulative cash-flow |
EOY	In/(Out) Project	In/(Out) Interest	In/(Out) True	In/(Out) True
0	0	–	–	0
1	(40,000)	(3,600)	(43,600)	(43,600)
2	12,500	(6,723)	5,777	(37,823)
3	17,500	(5,233)	12,267	(25,556)
4	20,000	(2,800)	17,200	(8,356)
5	17,500	71	17,571	9,215
6	12,500	2,784	15,284	24,498

Table 11.14 **Cash-flow model of Project A incorporating cost of investment.**

−£1.47. So only about half the investment cost has come back after four years. Just keeping the investment money under the mattress is more rewarding than this.

11.19 (a) For the most part, this follows the NPV example in Section 11.12.3. At MARR = 10%, NPV_P = £0.36M and NPV_Q = £0.53M, so the company should choose project Q rather than project P rather than 'do-nothing'. The purpose of the 'is this the best choice' question is to remind you that financial viability is a necessary but not decisive test. So the answer to this question is 'don't know'. The company should also evaluate the proposed projects against all the 'PET1 factors' (see, for example, Table 11.1 in Section 11.7) and ensure that the project estimates are of similar (high) quality.
(b) NPV_P = −£0.31M and NPV_Q = £0.00M (= £2,699 more nearly). So project P is not viable at this MARR (because its NPV is negative), and project Q is just viable. If you know about IRRs at this stage, you might guess that the IRR for project P is about 19% (by assuming that its NPV declines linearly between 10% and 28%). This is quite a good guess. Guessing that the IRR of project Q is about 28% is even better, but is it more or is it less?.
(c) is answered in Section 11.12.4.

11.20 (a) In Section 11.12.5, under the 'Net end of year values' heading. The set (not series) of equivalent 'lump sum' values is:

	EOY 0	EOY 1	EOY 2	EOY 3	EOY 4	EOY 5
Net EOY £M	0.53	0.58	0.64	0.70	0.77	0.85

because, for example, $0.53 \times (1.1)^3 = 0.70$ (nearly).
(b) Also in Section 11.12.5, under the 'A finite series of interest and deferred repayment' heading. The two projects are equivalent because their NPVs are the same. The arithmetic is:

$$0.053 \times (1.1^{-1} + 1.1^{-2} + 1.1^{-3} + 1.1^{-4} + 1.1^{-5}) + (0.53 \times 1.1^{-5}) = 0.53$$

11.21 This is an invitation, which leaves some scope for initiative, to explain the IRR concept. The material is in the introduction to Section 11.13 and in Section 11.13.1. For enthusiasts, the 'IRR equivalent project' of project Q (project R) is:

Cash In/(Out) (£M)

	EOY 0	EOY 1	EOY 2	EOY 3	EOY 4	EOY 5
Project R	(1.25)	0.35	0.35	0.35	0.35	1.60

11.22 This ties up some loose ends, and tests understanding of Sections 11.12 (NPV) and 11.13 (IRR). Answers:

$$NPV_{B1} = -51 \qquad NPV_{B2} = 11\,729 \qquad NPV_{B3} = 6228 \text{ (in £s)}$$
$$IRR_{B1} = 17.96 \qquad IRR_{B2} = 25.77 \qquad IRR_{B3} = 22.22 \text{ (in \%)}$$

So ranking is B2 then B3 then B1 by both criteria.

11.23 (a) The only way to answer this question is to 'calculate' the IRR. The approach here illustrates using the tables of Appendix B, but rounds the discount factors to 2 decimal places to minimize the tedium. Columns (a) to (e) of Table 11.15 are the sums in the guessing game. The first two guesses, in columns (a) and (b), show that the IRR lies between 10% and 20%, but closer to 20%. The next two guesses, in columns (c) and (d), show that the IRR lies between 18% and 19%, but closer to 18%. Linear interpolation then suggests that the IRR is: $(23 \times 18\% + 14 \times 19\%)/(14 + 23) = 18.4\%$, say. Checking this out, in column (e), shows that the NPV at this rate is near enough zero, in relation to the cash-flows, to claim that the answer required is 18.4%.

(b) First note that, if the 'new situation' had been known in 1990, the project would (should) not have been launched. Because, even before discounting, it is just a way of taking six years to lose £75,000. But this is hindsight. The £675K spent in 1991 is a 'sunk' cost which has gone forever (see Section 7.5.2), and it should play no part in the (financial) analysis of the new situation. So the new situation is as shown in the in the four right-hand columns of the table. The NPV of the modified project is just negative at the twenty per cent borrowing rate, indicating that the project is no longer financially viable. This suggests that the company should terminate the project. Under the circumstances, it is suggested that the suggestion is made from a safe distance. It might be made more convincing by pointing out that the project ought to earn *more* than the borrowing rate, to compensate for 'non-earning' costs (basic research, say). But companies do find it hard to make this sort of decision. And they might be right to carry on with the project if its non-financial merits are very attractive.

(c) By borrowing the whole of the (first) estimated investment cost (£1,725K) at fifteen per cent at project start. The £1,050 not needed in 1991 could have been re-invested at about the same rate, so making keeping it for a year nearly free. Of course, it is the twenty-twenty vision of hindsight that makes this the right answer. If interest rates had fallen rather than risen the original gamble would have paid off.

11.24 Results are (in £s and percentages):
- at MARR = 14% $NPV_X = 16,185$ and $NPV_Y = 18,429$, so Y > X
- at MARR = 22% $NPV_X = 6,165$ and $NPV_Y = 4,066$, so X > Y
  $IRR_X = 29.15\%$ and $IRR_Y = 25.03\%$, so X > Y

This is one of those situations where the NPV and IRR criterion can give conflicting messages. The explanation is in Section 11.14.2 under the 'Conflict between NPV and IRR' heading. Resolving the conflict is covered in Sections 11.14.3 and 11.14.4. It matters in this case, because there are only enough funds to launch one project. Some more sums are needed before the company can be (best) advised. Note that

	In/(Out) £K	DF @ % 10.0	(a) PVs	DF @ % 20.0	(b) PVs	DF @ % 18.0	(c) PVs	DF @ % 19.0	(d) PVs	DF @ % 18.4	(e) PVs	New situation EOY	In/(Out) £K	DF @ % 20.0	(f) PVs
EOY															
In 1991	1	(675)	0.91	(614)	0.83	(560)	0.85	(574)	0.84	(567)	0.84	(567)	1	(1,300)	0.83	(1,083)
In 1992	2	(1,050)	0.83	(872)	0.69	(725)	0.72	(756)	0.71	(746)	0.71	(746)	2	475	0.69	330
In 1993	3	675	0.75	506	0.58	392	0.61	412	0.59	398	0.60	405	3	700	0.58	405
In 1994	4	900	0.68	612	0.48	432	0.52	468	0.50	450	0.51	459	4	475	0.48	229
In 1995	5	675	0.62	419	0.40	270	0.44	297	0.42	284	0.43	290	5	250	0.40	100
In 1996	6	450	0.56	252	0.33	149	0.37	167	0.35	158	0.36	162				
Sum=		975	NPV=	303	NPV=	(43)	NPV=	14	NPV=	(23)	NPV=	4	Sum=	600	NPV=	(19)

Table 11.15 Project analysis.

NP_X declines from £16,185 at fourteen per cent with a 'slope' of about £1,252 per per cent, and NPV_Y declines from £18,429 at fourteen per cent with a slope of about £1,795 per per cent. So the curves cross (as in, for example, Figure 11.13) at about:

$$14\% + [(18{,}429 - 16{,}185)/(1{,}795 - 1{,}252)]\% = 18\%, \text{ assuming linearity}$$

So, rounding to integers, the advice is:

- in 0% < MARR < 18% choose project Y
- in 18% < MARR < 29% choose project X
- in 29% < MARR do not invest in either project.

Chapter 12

12.3 All in Section 12.2.2. Part (c) can only be answered accurately after the liquidation is complete! The most obvious answer (which is £8,350) is almost certainly wrong, because it assumes that the assets can be turned into cash at their balance sheet values. This is unlikely. For example, the local garage will not repurchase the van for £1,500 and a private sale, without the benefit of warranty, is unlikely at that price.

12.4 All in Section 12.2.2. Working in £s, after transaction 1:

- money-at-bank = 1,050 − 400 = 650
- total assets = 13,350 − 400 = 12,950
- sundry debts = 4,000 − 400 = 3,600
- total liabilities = 5,000 − 400 = 4,600
- net assets = 12,950 − 4,600 = 8,350 (*unchanged*)
- profit = 350 (unchanged)
- owner's capital = 8,350 (*unchanged*)

Note that transaction 1 involves equal changes in assets and (external) liabilities, so there is no compensating change in profit and, hence, no change in owner's capital.
   Working in £s, after transaction 2 (= end of Day 4):

- money-at-bank = 650 − 500 = 150
- total assets = 12,950 − 500 = 12,450
- sundry debts = 3,600 (unchanged)
- total liabilities = 4,600 (unchanged)
- net assets = 12,450 − 4,600 = 7,850 (*changed*)
- profit = 350 − 500 = −150 (changed to a loss)
- owner's capital = 8,000 − 150 = 7,850 (*changed*)

Note that transaction 2 involves unequal changes in assets and (external) liabilities, so there is a compensating change in profit and, hence, also in owner's capital.
   Comment on performance: Owner's capital has reduced from £8,000 at the end of Day 1 to £7,850 at the end of Day 4, because the profit earned (£350) is not enough to cover the salary increment (£500) paid to the owner. So the business has made a loss of £150 over these few days.

12.6 Parts (a) and (b) are covered in Section 12.2.5. Three circumstances which can cause (accounting) profit and cash-flow to differ are (1) credit selling and purchasing, (2) the retention of purchased current assets on the balance sheet pending receipt of a matching revenue, and (3) the depreciation charges associated with fixed assets are 'matching' adjustments rather than cash costs. Part (c) is not specifically covered in the main text. In fact, most businesses that fail do so because they are unable to pay their creditors due to a lack of cash (a 'liquidity' problem). A business which is trading unprofitably, in accountancy terms, may survive for a long time by selling assets to provide the necessary cash, although this clearly cannot go on for ever. So positive cash-flow is more critical than trading profit in ensuring the survival of a business.

12.9   (a) The required analysis closely follows that discussed in Section 12.3.3, differing only in its treatment of the prepayment asset. It is shown in Table 12.15.

	1990	January 1991					
Action number:	1	2	3	4	5	6	7
	£	£	£	£	£	£	£
Assets:							
Premises		8,000	8,000	8,000	8,000	8,000	8,000
Equipment			6,000	6,000	6,000	6,000	6,000
Prepayment	1,200	1,200	1,200	1,200	1,200	1,200	1,100
Components				5,000	1,500	1,500	1,500
Finished goods					3,500	2,500	2,500
Debtors						3,000	3,000
Cash at bank	18,800	10,800	4,800	4,800	4,800	4,800	1,800
Total:	20,000	20,000	20,000	25,000	25,000	27,000	23,900
Liabilities:							
Creditors:							
Trade				5,000	5,000	5,000	5,000
Bank	5,000	5,000	5,000	5,000	5,000	5,000	5,000
Total:	5,000	5,000	5,000	10,000	10,000	10,000	10,000
Net assets:	15,000	15,000	15,000	15,000	15,000	17,000	13,900
Financed by:							
Start up	15,000	15,000	15,000	15,000	15,000	15,000	15,000
Profit/(Loss)						2,000	(1,100)
Owners' capital:	15,000	15,000	15,000	15,000	15,000	17,000	13,900

Memo:			
1.	Components consumed per product £:		500
2.	Salaries for month £:		3,000

Table 12.15   **Small Business Ltd: double-entry accounting transaction analysis.**

(b) The end-of-January profit is $-£1,100$ (that is, it is a loss of £1,100) when write-off of the prepayment asset is phased over the year, as shown in Table 12.15. The loss is increased to £2,200 if the whole amount is written-off in the month. From the accountancy perspective this is the preferred treatment because it is more prudent (see Section 12.2.6). The owner-managers seem to prefer the phased write-off, probably because it reduces the perceived end-of-January loss.

12.10   (a) Table 12.5 in Section 12.3.4 under the 'Month 1 balance sheet (version 1)' heading provides the model for the requested balance sheet, shown in Table 12.16.
(b) All in Section 12.3.4 under the 'Month 1 balance sheet (version 1)' heading. Numerical answers are:

Working capital   = net current assets = £4,900.
Capital employed = non-current liabilities + owners' capital
$$= £5,000 + £13,900 = £18,900,$$ which funds the
total assets − current liabilities.

Small Business Ltd
Balance sheet at 31st January 1991

		£	£
Fixed assets:			
	Premises	8,000	
	Equipment	6,000	
			14,000
Current assets:			
	Prepayment	1,100	
	Stocks	1,500	
	Finished goods	2,500	
	Trade debtors	3,000	
	Cash at bank	1,800	
			9,900
Current liabilities:			
	Trade creditors		5,000
Net current assets:			4,900
Total assets *less* current liabilities:			18,900
Non-current liabilities:			
	Bank loan		5,000
Net assets:			13,900
Financed by owners' capital:			
	Paid up capital	15,000	
	Profit and loss A/c	(1,100)	
			13,900

Table 12.16   **Small Business Ltd: Month 1 balance sheet.**

12.11 By suggesting this particular arrangement of the basic accounting equation (see Equation 12.10), the question invites the construction of a 'funds = cash' flow statement along the lines discussed in Section 12.3.6. This is a rewarding but tedious exercise. An 'otherwise' approach merely searches columns 7 and 1 of Table 12.15 for differences in corresponding items, because such differences must be caused by fund flows. Other than noting that it is −£17,000 (= £1,800 − £18,800), the cash at bank difference (flow) is ignored in the search. The rationale behind this neglect is that the whole of Table 12.15 is 'balanced', so the sum of the other differences must equate to the cash difference. Working in £s and in Table 12.15 sequence, the search proceeds as follows:

Acquiring asset items =
− 8,000 − 6,000 + 100 − 1,500 − 2,500 − 3,000 = −20,900
Offset from trade creditor funds = + 5,000
Funding the end-of-January loss = − 1,100

So net cash flow at the bank account = −17,000 (out).

12.12 (a) Table 12.8 in Section 12.3.5 provides the model for the requested P&L account, shown in Table 12.17.
(b) All in Section 12.3.5, under the 'This account is an illusion' heading.

12.13 This is a challenging question at this stage in the chapter. It exercises many of the basic ideas in Section 12.3 and, in particular, probes understanding of the basic accounting equation (as in Equation 12.2, say). Table 12.18 is the modified P&L account.

Small Business Ltd
Profit and Loss account for the month ending 31st January 1991

	£	£	Notes
Sales revenue:		3,000	1. Sale of two units
less Cost of sales:			
Direct labour	???		2. No data
Direct materials	1,000		3. Re two units sold
Fixed production costs	???		4. No data
		1,000	5. Wrong
Gross profit:		2,000	6. Wrong
Less operating expense:			
Salaries	3,000		7. All staff
Legal and professional	100		8. (Prepayment)/12
Other fixed costs	???		9. No data
		3,100	10. Wrong
Operating profit/(loss):		(1,100)	11. Wrong

Table 12.17 **Small Business Ltd: Month 1 P&L account.**

The modified total cost of sales (at Note 5) is two-sevenths of the total production cost, because only two of the seven units made were sold. Total production cost is £700 of direct labour plus £3,500 of direct materials plus total fixed production costs at £140 depreciation, £705 other costs and £1,500 supervisory labour (= £2,345), making £6,545 in all. So the modified total cost of sales is £1,870, made up as shown at notes 2, 3 and 4. Total labour costs attributable to production are £2,200, so the residual labour cost attributable to the rest of the business is £800, at Note 7. Other (fixed) costs assigned to the rest of the business are £60 depreciation plus £295, making £355 at Note 9. The modified 'profit', therefore is a loss of £125 at Note 11.

Table 12.19 is the modified balance sheet. At Note 1, the depreciation of £200 reduces the total fixed assets by the same amount. Finished goods, at Note 2, become five-sevenths of total production cost (= £4,675) and total current assets are also increased. The 'other (committed but unpaid) costs' of £1,000 are a current liability entered at Note 3, and the subsequent arithmetic at Notes 4 and 5 completes the calculations. The profit increase between the balance sheets of Tables 12.16 and 12.19 is £975. This is made up of £4,675 − £2,500 = £2,175 due to capitalizing the whole value (at cost) of the the finished (unsold) goods, less £200 due to depreciation less £1,000 due to the 'other costs'. Alternatively, the 'Table 12.19' profit (−£125) is obtained from the 'Table 12.16' profit (−£1,100) in the following way:

$$-£1,100 - £200 + £2,175 - £1,000 = -£125$$

So the principal factor in the difference between the two sets of accounts is the additional capitalization of the finished goods.

Small Business Ltd
Modified P&L account for the month ending 31st January 1991

	£	£	Notes
Sales revenue:		3,000	1. Sale of two units
less Cost of sales:			
Direct labour	200		2. See text
Direct materials	1,000		3. Re two units sold
Fixed production costs	670		4. See text
		1,870	5. Re two units sold
Gross profit:		1,130	6. Modified total
Less operating expense:			
Salaries	800		7. See text
Legal and professional	100		8. (Prepayment)/12
Other fixed costs	355		9. See text
		1,255	10. Modified total
Operating profit/(loss):		(125)	11. Modified result

Table 12.18 Small Business Ltd: modified Month 1 P&L account.

Small Business Ltd
Modified balance sheet @ 31st January 1991

	£	£	Note
Fixed assets:			
Premises	8,000		
Equipment	6,000		
Less depreciation	(200)		1
		13,800	1
Current assets:			
Prepayment	1,100		
Stocks	1,500		
Finished goods	4,675		2
Trade debtors	3,000		
Cash at bank	1,800		
		12,075	2
Current liabilities:			
Trade creditors	5,000		
Other creditors	1,000		3
		6,000	3
Net current assets:		6,075	4
Total assets *less* Current liabilities:		19,875	4
Non-current liabilities:			
Bank loan		5,000	
Net assets:		14,875	5
Financed by owners' capital:			
Paid up capital	15,000		
Profit and loss A/c	(125)		5
		14,875	5

Table 12.19　**Small Business Ltd: modified Month 1 balance sheet.**

12.15　(a) All in Section 12.4.2. Table 12.12 is particularly useful.

(b) Again, all in Section 12.4.2. The balance sheet equation can be rewritten as:

$$(FA + CA) = (CL + NCL) + OC.$$

Now, net assets = total assets − total (external) liabilities, so:

$$net assets = (FA + CA) - (CL + NCL) = OC,$$

which answers the first part. Then, capital employed (defined as long-term debt) is $(NCL + OC)$ and working capital is net current assets, which is $(CA - CL)$. So, rearranging the balance sheet equation:

$$FA + (CA - CL) = (NCL + OC),$$

which answers the second part.

(c) Note, first, that this *fundamental* definition of profit is introduced (without special emphasis) in the opening of Section 12.2.4, where the relationship between a balance sheet and the corresponding P&L account is discussed. Note, too, that the figures at Notes 23 and 24 in Table 12.12 illustrate the definition. The question is answered by observing that net assets are equal to owners' capital (as shown in (b) above), so the two definitions of profit are equivalent. The figures at Note 20 of Table 12.12 illustrate the 'net assets' definition.

(d) The trading profit in the P&L account is *not* necessarily the same as the profit shown on the corresponding balance sheet. Expressed in terms of net assets, the balance sheet equation is:

$$(FA + CA) - (CL + NCL) = OC$$

so any 'unbalanced' transaction occurring on the left-hand side of the equation cause a change in OC (which is a profit or a loss) on the right-hand side of the equation. Product sale transactions normally create a profit, because of the net increase in CA. But suppose a fixed asset is sold for less than its book value. The reduction in FA is then more than the increase in CA, so a loss is created which is not shown on the P&L account.

12.16   It is important to remember, throughout this question, that the term 'flow' means 'change'. Referring to Table 12.12, and working in £s:

(a) At Note 11, cash flow $= (2,324 - 9,400) = -7,076$ (out)

(b) At Notes 24, 12 and 18, funds flow $= (10,415 - 7,500) + (3,265 - 0) + (2,500 - 2,500) = 6,180$ (in, because these funds come from the acquisition of liabilities, including profit which is owed to the owners).

(c) At Notes 1 and 6, but excluding cash at Note 11, funds flow $= -(6,240 - 0) - (7,616 - 600) = -13,256$ (out, because these funds go on the acquisition of assets).

(d) $-7,076 = 6,180 - 13,256$, so cash flow calculated in (a) is equal to the sum of the funds flows calculated at (b) and (c). The result can be explained by rewriting the basic accounting equation as: cash $= (OC + CL + NCL) - (FA + \text{non-cash } CA)$ and recognizing that changes (flows) between two balance sheets must also balance. Note that the technique used in answering this question is a quick way of analysing the cash flow without constructing a formal 'funds = cash' flow statement.

Glossary

*'When I use a word,' Humpty Dumpty said in a
rather scornful tone, 'it means just what I
choose it to mean – neither more nor less.'*

Lewis Carroll 1832–1898

This glossary explains a *selection* of words and phrases as they are used in the text. Glossary entries which appear in other entries are emphasized with **bold** type.

Accounting entities Bodies which are financially distinct from their owner(s).

Accounting period The time lapse between the issue of successive sets of accounts. It should be not more than one year for published **financial accounts** and is usually one month for **management accounts**.

Accounting profit The excess of **revenue** over corresponding **cost**, where some cost items (notably **depreciation**) may not be wholly acceptable for tax purposes. See **Taxable profit**.

Accrual accounting Entry of **revenue** and corresponding **cost** into the **profit and loss account** when they are earned and incurred respectively (rather than when received or paid) to aid **matching**. See also **Cash-based accounting**.

Activities In the **project** sense, these are elements which consume time and (usually) also effort and money. See also **Dummy activities**.

Annual inflation rate For a **commodity**, the proportionate increase in the unit price of the commodity in one year. See also **Nominal annual interest rate** and **Real annual interest rate**.

Applied research (AR) At *product-range* level. It aims to resolve uncertainties (technical and economic) carried over from the earlier **basic research** stage, and to specify a **product range** (in functional and cost terms) based on the technological concept explored in the preceding basic research.

Assets **Resources** owned by the **business** to aid its **revenue** earning process, and to which a reasonably accurate monetary value can be assigned.

Audits Examinations, by independent qualified authorities, of things (such as accounts) which need to be checked for compliance with pre-set standards.

Balance sheet States the financial position of the business (in terms of **assets**, **liabilities** and **owners' capital**) as it stands at the *end* of a specific **accounting period**.

Balance sheet equation   See **Basic accounting equation**.

Bar charts   Simple **project plan** and control documents where **activities** are represented as horizontal bars scaled in proportion to estimated duration. Activity dependencies are not (usually) explicitly shown. The charts are commonly supported by tables showing the phased consumption of planned and actual project **resources**.

Basic accounting equation   **Assets = Liabilities + Owners' capital**, where 'liabilities' means **external liabilities**. It is the mathematical expression of the **double-entry accounting** principle. Also called the **balance sheet equation**.

Basic research (BR)   At *technology* level. It aims to assess the technical and economic feasibility (in relation to a possible profit opportunity) of a new technological concept.

Batch manufacturing   Characterized by the simultaneous manufacture, in relatively small numbers (batches), of many similar products.

Benefit ratio   (**product value**)/(**price of ownership**) of a product. It is a measure of product competitiveness.

Bonds and barriers concept   Relates to communication channels between a technical **projects** team and a **customer** organization within the same **business**. The position of the team relative to the customer defines four possible communication situations involving combinations of location and organization.

Book value of a fixed asset   Its purchase cost less accumulated **depreciation** at the time it is measured.

Break-even   A general term denoting the equality of two parameters whose difference is of interest.

Brooks's Law   (Modified to broaden its application) states that adding people to a late project makes it later.

Budget reconciliation   The process of 'netting out' (to avoid double counting) transactions between the **trading** divisions of a **business** when their budgets are combined to form the whole business budget.

Budgets   **Plans** expressed in financial terms, usually covering just one **financial year**.

Business   An entity which aims to transform inputs to outputs in a way which increases their *value*. The value added to the inputs is **wealth**.

Business creation project   See **Product creation project**.

Business function   See **Professional function** and **Stage function**.

Business ratios   See **Ratio analysis**.

Capital allowance   The annual **depreciation** (as a fraction of fixed asset purchase cost) which *is* accepted as a charge against pre-tax profit by the tax authorities.

Capital and reserves   A **profit and loss account** entry (equating to **owners' capital**) comprising direct investment by the owners (**paid up capital**) and **retained profits**.

Capital assets   See **Fixed assets**.

Capital costs   These purchase **fixed assets**.

Capital employed   Capital used by the business is sometimes regarded as the **owners' capital**. It is better defined as the whole **long-term** debt of the business, which comprises **non-current liabilities** plus **owners' capital**. This sum funds its **fixed assets** and **working capital**.

Capital item   See **Fixed assets**.

Capital of the business   Another (poor) name for **owners' capital**.

Capital products   **Industrial products** which are purchased for **long-term** use.

Capital structure   Shows how the **capital employed** is partitioned between its various sources (**owners' capital**, **retained profits** and borrowings).

Capitalized costs   Those of an investment nature which, because they promise **long-term** benefits, are recorded as **assets** in the **balance sheet**. Alternatively, such costs may be **written-off** as they occur.

Cash accounting   See **Cash-based accounting**.

Cash-at-bank   A term embracing cash and 'near-cash' items (such as cheques) held in the **business**, as well as the contents of its bank account. Also called **net liquid funds**.

Cash-based accounting   Based on actual cash receipts and actual payments made. **Businesses** normally use **accrual accounting**.

Cash-flow   The actual physical movement of cash *out* of (negative cash flow) or *into* (positive cash flow) the **business**.

Cash-flow model   A financial **plan** of a **project**, usually expressed as a time sequence of estimated **incremental cash-flows** out of and into the **business**.

Cash-flow profile   A **cash-flow model** of a **project** expressed graphically, usually in terms of **cumulative cash-flow** out of and into the **business**.

Cell layout   The same as **group technology** facilities layout.

Chief programmer team (CPT)   An organizational concept increasingly used in **software engineering**.

Circulating assets   A term used to describe **current assets**, because of their transient nature in a continuous **trading cycle**: where **input stock** becomes **work-in-progress** which becomes **finished products** which become **debtors** which become cash, which is then used to buy more input stock.

Clarity   An accounting principle requiring that accounts provide intelligible information to **competent users**.

Commodity   Any sort of purchased item, including **tangible products**, **service products** and human effort.

Company (business)   An **accounting entity** which is also a legal entity. It is formed (**incorporated**) in accordance with the laws of the country where it 'resides', and is distinct from its owners in both financial and legal terms.

Comparability   An accounting principle requiring that accounts be constructed such that the financial performance of different **businesses** can be reasonably compared.

Competent users (of accounts)   Those who have a reasonable understanding of **business** and financial matters, and who are willing to study accounts carefully. See also **Clarity**.

Competitive status   The extent to which the business (or product) favourably compares with its competitors in critical areas.

Competitive technological status   That part of the **competitive status** of a product which derives from its technological 'mix'. See also **Foundation technologies**, **Critical technologies** and **Looming technologies**.

Competitors   Other **businesses** which offer solutions to the same needs and problems of the same **customers** as those addressed by the business.

Compound interest   Compound interest situations are characterized by the periodic addition of interest (at the compound rate) to the investment. The sum then becomes the investment and it attracts further interest, so 'interest on interest' is obtained.

Configuration view of a product (type) This perceives it as a unique configuration of distinct functional sub-units. See also **Established sub-units** and **Novel sub-units**.

Consistency A principle requiring that accounting policy does not change either within a period or from period to period, so that the performance of the **business** in different periods can be properly compared.

Constraints Boundary conditions which restrict freedom to manoeuvre during a design exercise. In the case of **product design**, they are imposed by product **customers** and product suppliers; and as classified as technical, economic or operational.

Consumable products Products which are expended or changed in some way during use.

Consumables Purchased items (tangible or otherwise) which are expected to be wholly used up within a year of purchase. See also **Current assets**.

Consumer products Those aimed at members of the general public, the so-called 'consumers'.

Context analysis (CA) This answers the question 'why is the **product** required by the **customer**?'

Contingency concept This concept of task **management** suggests that the ideal approach depends on the interplay of subordinate and task characteristics. It recognizes four basic management styles: telling, selling, participating and delegating.

Continuous manufacturing A form of manufacturing characterized by the uninterrupted manufacture of totally uniform products.

Contract development (CD) **Technological innovation** work carried out, under contract, for a **customer** outside the **business**. The term is also commonly used to describe the customer-provided **funds** which support the work.

Contract funding Financial support under a contract with an agency outside the **business**. See also **Contract development**.

Contract pricing The rules are usually set by the contract **customer**. The mechanisms include **cost-plus contract**, **fixed-price contract** and **profit-incentive contract**. **Contract development** pricing is similarly constrained.

Contribution At the **business** level, this is the difference between the **revenue** earned and the corresponding **variable costs** incurred in a period. This 'contributes' towards (offsets) the **fixed costs** incurred during the period to yield a **profit**. See also **Product contribution**.

Corporation tax A government charge on **taxable profit**. It is levied at rates depending on **profit** level.

Cost Ultimately, cash which flows out of the **business** in exchange for purchased goods, services and benefits. An exchange and the corresponding cash outflow rarely coincide, as most items are purchased on credit and some benefits are paid for before consumption.

Cost card This shows the standard cost build-up of a **product**.

Cost-effectiveness An accounting principle requiring that the benefits obtained from the accounts must be greater than the cost of providing them. It restricts their detail and accuracy.

Cost of employment (COE) The sum of an employee's salary, **social costs**, and any benefits or 'perks' provided as part of remuneration.

Cost of products sold A **profit and loss account** entry **matching** the period **sales revenue** by referring only to **product** units sold, as distinct from produced, during the period. See also **Product cost**.

Cost of sales See **Cost of products sold**.

Cost-plus A **product** pricing method which simply adds a **profit** to **product cost** to determine **product price**.

Cost-plus contract **Customer** and supplier **business** agree the (estimated) contract cost. An agreed percentage of this cost is then added, as profit, to yield contract price.

Creditors People or organizations who have supplied **assets** to the **business** in exchange for a promise of future payment. See also **Liabilities**.

Critical criteria These are not decisive on their own, but excite serious doubts about the proposal being evaluated if they are not judged to be adequately satisfied. See also **Decisive criteria** and **Supportive criteria**.

Critical path The longest duration forward path through a PERT network.

Critical path method (CPM) A **project** planning and control technique of the network variety which is similar to PERT.

Critical technologies Technologies that are still developing in their own right and/or in their application to the particular **product range**, thus offering important opportunities for **product differentiation**. They have the greatest *current* impact on **competitive status**. See also **Foundation technologies** and **Looming technologies**.

Cumulative cash-flow Obtained by summing a time sequence of incremental cash flows.

Current assets (CA) Either cash (or near-cash), or expected to become cash within the year. That is, **short-term** items *not* (unlike **fixed assets**) acquired for use during successive accounting periods. They exist only transiently in a particular form because they participate in the **trading cycle**. Also called **circulating assets**.

Current cost The cost of purchasing an item now. See also **Past cost**.

Current liabilities (CL) **Short-term** debts which are to be paid-off within a year of being incurred. See also **Trade creditors**.

Customer Actual or potential customers of a business have three attributes. They have a requirement which matches a (current or potential) **product**; they are able to pay a price for it which allows the **business** to make an adequate **profit**; they are willing to pay that price.

Customer benefit Derived from **product** ownership, this is the difference between the **product value** perceived by the **customer** and product **price of ownership**. See also **Benefit ratio**.

Cut-off rate See **Minimum attractive rate of return**.

Dangle PERT jargon for an event which is not followed by an activity. This feature is disallowed except for end events.

Debt capital See **Loan capital**.

Debtors Debtors owe the **business** money, because they have received something of value from it on credit. They are intangible **assets** representing promises of future income.

Decisive criteria These must be judged to be adequately satisfied or the proposal being evaluated is rejected. See also **Critical criteria** and **Supportive criteria**.

Deliverables   The physical expression of **project** results in the form which they are to be delivered to the project **customer**.

Delivered product model   The set of proven 'how to make and test it' instructions delivered to the **production function** at the end of the design process. It describes (models) the product in a form intelligible to, and compatible with, the manufacturing operation.

Delta analysis   A simple and widely applicable technique for describing **project** progress in terms of *total* planned time and cost, *actual* time and cost at assessment time, and *forecast* time and cost to complete measured from assessment time.

Demand curve   This expresses a relationship between the unit price of a **product** and its rate of sales, where 'demand' is rate of sales.

Depreciation   This measures the 'consumption' of a **fixed asset** by creating notional **revenue costs** (depreciation charges or costs) which spread net asset purchase cost over its useful life. It is motivated by the **matching** principle.

Design(ing)   See **Product design(ing)**.

Design constraints (DC)   These answer the question 'how is the design of the **product** to be constrained by the **customer** and by the supplier?'

Design options   Different ways of solving design problems which are evaluated with regard to relevant **design constraints**.

Differential resources   Those which distinguish between competing **businesses**. They are mostly the people resource, because **competitors** have much the same access to identical non-people resources but people quality is very variable.

Direct   A term used to describe things which are attributable to some other particular thing or activity, such that they do not arise unless the other thing or activity arises. See also **Indirect**.

Discount factor = $(1 + r)^{-n}$ This relates a **present value** (PV) to its **future sum** (FS). That is, the PV of a FS due in n years time in a **compound interest** rate regime of r, is given by $PV = FS(1 + r)^{-n}$.

Discount rate   Most generally, any (interest) rate used for **discounting**. In some circumstances it means **minimum attractive rate of return**.

Discounted cash-flow (DCF)   Techniques which adjust **cash-flow models** to recognize that promised future cash is less valuable than cash now. This allows widely different cash-flow models to be sensibly compared. The principle techniques are **net present value** (NPV) and **internal rate of return** (IRR). See also **Discounting**.

Discounting   £1 now is worth more than £1 later, because the £1 now can earn interest in the intervening period. So *£1 due later is worth less than £1 now* (assuming the **compound interest** rate exceeds the rate of **inflation**). This is the basis of discounting. See also **Discounted cash-flow**.

Diseconomies of scale   See **Economies of scale**.

Distinction between capital and revenue   An accounting principle classifying costs according to whether the benefits they purchase are **long-term** or **short-term**. See also **Capital costs** and **Revenue costs**.

Dividends   Monetary rewards to **shareholders** for their investment (by way of **shares**) in the **business**.

Divisible task   A task which can be partitioned into a number of smaller, relatively independent, sub-tasks which may be assigned to different people. So, within limits, task completion time decreases as the number of people assigned to it increases.

Divisionalization An organizational technique which divides a large **business** into a set of semi-autonomous smaller **businesses**, called 'divisions'.

Do-nothing The (always available) investment option to either leave available **funds** on deposit earning interest, or not to borrow them and so avoid acquisition costs.

Domestic products See **Consumer products**.

Dominant constraints theory This claims that all complex planning and design situations contain a limited number of critical constraints which, when identified and applied, eliminate a great number of apparent options for progress.

Double-entry accounting This involves every **business** transaction being recorded twice in the accounts: because acquiring an **asset** implies either acquiring an equivalent **liability**, or an equivalent reduction in another **asset**, or an equivalent mixture of those two events. The **basic accounting equation** expresses this mathematically.

Dummy activities PERT elements used to indicate dependencies between events. Unlike 'real' activities, 'dummies' consume neither time nor any other resource.

Durable products Products intended to have a **long-term** future in their own right.

Economies of scale The economies of scale effect is the decline in **product** unit cost as the rate of product output (scale of production) increases from a low level. The subsequent increase in product unit cost as the rate of product output is further increased is the **diseconomies of scale** effect.

End ratio A measure of **cash-flow model** performance, obtained by dividing maximum return by maximum investment. It is a crude parameter which ignores the 'time value of money'.

Engineering The application of technology to **wealth** creation by providing cost-effective solutions to human needs and problems.

Engineering technologies See **Product technologies**.

Equal misery principle A way of sharing out limited resources where all bidders receive the same fraction of their bids, such that the sum of the fractions equates to the available resources.

Equity (capital) See **Owners' capital**.

Established products Those which have been previously manufactured in substantial quantities.

Established sub-units Those which are widely available, well-understood and proven. See also the **Configuration view of a product** and **Novel sub-units**.

Evaluation criteria (for project proposals) These come in a hierarchy: see **Decisive criteria**, **Critical criteria** and **Supportive criteria**.

Event slack A PERT parameter measuring the 'freedom' of an **event** to move inside the boundaries set by its latest acceptable time and its earliest possible time.

Events Specific auditable happenings in the PERT representation of a **project**. They occur at an instant of time and consume neither time nor other resources.

Expense See **Operating expense** and **Revenue costs**.

External creditors People or organizations outside the **business** who are owed money by the business. The owners of the business are internal creditors.

External liabilities The debts that the **business** owes other than that which it owes to its owner(s), which is the **owners' capital**. See **Liabilities**.

f factor method   A technique for determining the approximate relationship between the completion time of a divisible task and the number of people assigned to it.

Facilities maintenance   The inspection, servicing and repair of equipment and machinery used in manufacturing.

Factory cost   See **Works cost** and **Product cost**.

Federal decentralization   A North American term for 'divisionalization'.

Final company accounts   These are published annually as a statutory requirement, and must be **audited** (verified as a 'true and fair view') by an independent qualified authority.

Finance function   Finance function activities permeate every facet of the **business**, because all have financial consequences. Its major tasks include cash control, accounting, investment planning and evaluation, tax collecting and payroll matters.

Financial accounting   The process of producing, analysing and communicating **financial accounts**.

Financial accounts   These are produced (mainly) for users outside the **business**. They include the **balance sheet**, **profit and loss account** and **funds flow statement** relating to a whole business.

Financial viability threshold   This concept applies to investment **project** proposals. To reach the threshold, a project must return the money invested in it plus the cost of that investment plus some 'true earnings'. See also **Minimum attractive rate of return**.

Financial year   The actual period between successive publications of the formal annual financial accounts of a business. It rarely coincides with the calendar year.

Financing (or finance) costs   These are incurred in obtaining **funds** from external agencies to invest in the **business**.

Finished products   Complete and tested **product** units. Also called finished 'goods'.

Fiscal year   See **Financial year**.

Fixed assets (FA)   Long-term items acquired to aid earning over more than one **accounting period**, so their useful life is (expected to be) more than one year. Also called **capital assets**. See also **Depreciation**.

Fixed costs   These do not (unlike the **direct** or **variable costs** with which they are associated) vary with the activity level of interest. Also commonly called overhead or **indirect** costs. See also **Semi-variable costs**.

Fixed position layout   In manufacturing facilities this layout is used for low-sales-volume/high-unit-cost products which are usually large, heavy and relatively immobile. Manufacturing resources are moved to the **work-in-progress**, rather than the other way round.

Fixed-price contract   Customer and supplier **business** agree a price for the contract work which then remains constant irrespective of actual contract cost incurred by the supplier.

Flow-line layout   In manufacturing facilities this layout is used for high-sales-volume/low-unit-cost products. The layout matches the logical sub-process sequence(s) of the products, so it is product-specific and non-flexible.

Foundation technologies   Well established technologies used across the **product range** by most **competitors** with about equal competence. They have little effect on **competitive status** because of limited development potential and wide availability. See also **Critical technologies** and **Looming technologies**.

Four Ps   This concept summarizes the aim of **marketing** as the achievement of the right product at the right price with the right promotion in the right place, where 'right' is right for **customer** and supplier.

Full cost analysis This takes both the variable and fixed elements of total cost into account. See also **Marginal (cost) analysis**.

Function See **Professional function** and **Stage function**.

Functional architecture (FA) This answers the question 'what is the **product** to do for the **customer**?' It is the product **functional specification** (derived from the **context analysis**) before the **design constraints** are applied. So it is what the **customer** *wants*, rather than what the customer *can have*. See also **Product architecture**.

Functional decentralization A North American term for '**functional partitioning**'.

Functional layout In manufacturing facilities this layout is used for medium-sales-volume/medium-unit-cost products. Similar manufacturing sub-processes are co-located, such that the arrangement provides the variety of possible processing sequences needed for **batch manufacturing** of similar products.

Functional partitioning An organizational technique which divides a **business** into a set of business functions (people groups). Partitioning can be by common professional skills (**professional function**) or by common activity (**stage function** or sub-process function). The two arrangements may co-exist.

Functional specification See **Functional architecture**.

Funding threshold A project-dependent support level, below which the probability of success is very sharply reduced. See also **Equal misery principle**.

Funds Stores of value and may be as tangible as cash, or as intangible as promises to pay made by **debtors**.

Funds flow statement This shows how **funds** have moved into, out of, and around the **business** during an **accounting period**. It is derived from the associated **balance sheet** and **profit and loss account**.

Future sum (FS) An **incremental cash-flow** (into or out of the **business**) which is expected to occur in the future. See also **Discount factor**.

Gantt chart See **Bar charts**.

General investment criteria A set of features sought (but rarely wholly obtained) in all **business** investment proposals. They include low risk with high return, minimum cost, compatibility with internal and external business environments, minimum 'lock-in' and synergy.

Going concern An accounting principle which, unless there is reason not to, values **assets** on the basis that the **business** is to continue trading. This usually values assets higher than their **liquidation** level.

Gross margin A ratio (**gross profit/sales revenue**) measuring the earning power of the production activity. Also used to describe the difference between the unit price and unit **works cost** of a **product**.

Gross profit (GP) **Sales revenue** − **Cost of products sold**. The net income earned by the production activity, which pays (one way or another) all other **business** costs and provides **operating profit**. See also **Gross margin**.

Group technology (or cell) layout In manufacturing facilities this layout is commonly used for **batch manufacturing** as an alternative to facilities layout. Products are grouped according to the manufacturing sub-process they require, and a **flow-line layout** is then used for each group.

Hardware   Commonly means the tangible sub-units of a computer, as distinct from 'software'. The term is used in this book to distinguish *all* tangible products from service products. Both hardware and software products are created by **manufacturing businesses**.

Headcount   The number of people.

Hierarchy of human needs   A concept in motivation theory which ranks human needs into distinct priority levels. It then proposes that lower level needs must be satisfied (to an extent determined by the individual) before energy is spent on seeking satisfaction of the next higher level needs.

High-technology automated manufacturing   These processes are capital-intensive automated operations best suited to high-volume manufacture of virtually identical products. See also **Flow-line layout**.

High-volume products   See **Repeatable products**.

Historical cost   See **Past cost**.

Hurdle rate   See **Minimum attractive rate of return**.

Hygiene factors   Features of the working environment which (it is proposed) cause reduced job performance and satisfaction when perceived as negative, but do not necessarily cause the converse effects when perceived as positive. See also **Motivators**.

Income   Usually means **sales revenue**. But it sometimes means **profit**, although this is more commonly termed net income. It can also mean any or every sort of **revenue**.

Incorporate   The process of forming a **company** (a corporation) as a distinct legal entity.

Incremental cash-flow   This occurs (sometimes notionally) as a lump sum at a specific time. See also **Cumulative cash-flow**.

Index   A summation of weighted inflation rates for different commodities, selected to represent aggregate inflation in specific purchasing areas.

Indirect   A term used to describe things which are to be distinguished from associated **direct** things. The magnitude of indirect things is not attributable to the particular thing or activity on which the magnitude of the associated direct things depends. See also **Direct**.

Indivisible tasks   These tasks have completion times which are independent of the number of people assigned to them beyond a certain minimum, which might be zero.

Industrial engineering   The design and implementation of efficient systems of manual work, particularly at the operator–machine interface.

Industrial products   Products that are designed and manufactured for supply to corporate bodies, such as other **businesses**, public authorities and government departments.

Inflation   Persistent increases in commodity prices which are not justified by a corresponding increase in the benefits provided by the commodities to their purchasers.

Inflation factor $1/(1 + f)$, where f is the appropriate **annual inflation rate**. It measures the annual erosion in monetary purchasing power due to **inflation**.

Inflation rate   Commonly means **annual inflation rate**.

Initial product model   The **product brief** (document). Its issue marks the first formal event in the product design process.

Input stock or inventory   Bought-in items (mostly **current assets**) stored in the **business** prior to use.

Interest paid or payable A **financing cost** allowable against tax. It is not classed as an **operating cost**.

Intermediate-technology mechanized manufacturing This technique employs 'balanced' combinations of labour and capital in mechanized operations best suited to **batch manufacturing** of a variety of similar products. See also **Functional layout**.

Internal rate of return (IRR) The **discount rate** at which the sum of the discounted *outflow* (investment) increments of a **cash-flow model** equates to the sum of its discounted *inflows* (return) increments, such that the **net present value** of the model is zero. This rate measures **project profitability** and it is an absolute indicator of financial merit. It is sometimes called **yield**.

Intrinsic work content The intrinsic work content of a divisible task excludes all but the inescapable minimum effort dispersed in learning time and in person-to-person communication. See also **Sparse estimate**.

Inventory Items held in **stock**.

Lead-time The delay between placing a purchase order on a supplier and receiving the item concerned.

Liabilities The debts (promises to pay) that the **business** owes, representing claims by **creditors** on the **assets** of the business. **Owners' capital** is strictly classed under 'liabilities', but the term usually means **external liabilities**.

Life cycle This analogy applies principally to products. It partitions **product** existence into conception, gestation, and birth; followed by sales rate growth, maturity and decline to death. The latter period is the 'sales life cycle'.

Life cycle cost The sum of all the costs of an item (product or otherwise) attributable to that item, measured from when it is first identified as a separate entity to when it becomes of no further economic interest.

Limited A descriptor used in Britain to denote a **private limited company**. See also **Limited (liability)**.

Limited (liability) When used as a company descriptor 'limited' means that the company owners (**shareholders**) are only liable for their investment in the company. This is the most they can lose, whatever difficulties the company gets into.

Line functions **Business** functions of the **stage function** (sub-process) type within the vertical 'line-reporting' chain of business command, rather than being 'set off' to the side, as with **staff functions** which have advisory and consultative roles.

Liquid funds Cash and near-cash items (such as cheques in hand).

Liquidate To sell non-cash **assets** and so convert them to cash.

Liquidity A relative term indicating the time needed to convert an **asset** into cash, the most liquid asset.

Loan capital Obtained from banks and other lenders, or by selling financial 'instruments' such as debentures and bonds. There is an obligation to pay interest during the term of the loan, and to repay the amount borrowed at the end of that term. Usually a **non-current liability**, that is, a **long-term** debt.

Long-term Means more than one year, which is the normal maximum duration of an **accounting period**. See also **Short-term**.

Looming technologies These are possible future **critical technologies** with no significant *current* impact on **competitive status**. They are either new technologies in their own right, and/or their application to the particular **product range** is still tentative.

See also **Critical technologies** and **Foundation technologies**.

Low-technology manual manufacturing This comprises labour-intensive, mostly manual, operations best suited to low-volume manufacture of diverse products. See also **Fixed position layout**.

Magic questions Why, what and how. They form a recursive **partitioning rationale** which divides **design** and **management** problems into justification, specification and implementation stages.

Management What managers do. It always involves some mixture of planning, organizing, controlling and leading. Relative leadership ability is the attribute which most sharply distinguishes one manager from another.

Management accounting The process of producing, monitoring, analysing and communicating **management accounts**.

Management accounts Produced for use inside the **business** and may relate to only part of it. They are usually more detailed and 'customized' than **financial accounts**.

Managerial grid This concept classifies different management leadership styles by plotting their location on a matrix, or grid, with axes scaled in degrees of 'concern for people' and 'concern for task'.

Manufacturing business Those which create tangible products, rather than intangible 'service-type' products.

Marginal (cost) analysis This is concerned with *changes*, taking only the variable elements of the situation into account. See also **Full cost analysis**.

Marginal cost (MC) The change in total cost, at a particular output level, arising from producing one more (or one less) **product** unit. It is the gradient of the total cost versus output level curve at that output level.

Marginal investment rate See **Minimum attractive rate of return**.

Marginal profit (MP) The difference between **marginal revenue** and **marginal cost**.

Marginal revenue (MR) The change in revenue, at a particular output level, arising from selling one more (or one less) **product** unit. It is the gradient of the revenue versus output level curve at that output level (assuming that product units are sold as produced).

Market-place The commercial environment in which the **business** operates. It contains **customers**, **competitors** and **constraints**.

Market rejuvenators Technological changes which are substantial natural extensions of the critical technology currently employed in the **market-place**. So, while dealing a mortal blow to the current **product generation**, they allow the creation of a new generation based on the extended technology, thereby breathing new life into the original market. See also **Market terminator**.

Market research The process of obtaining and analysing data about the product market-place.

Market segmentation The process of dividing (on some basis) a total **market-place** into smaller pieces as an aid to analysis.

Market share The proportion of the market which is claimed by a **business**. It is an indicator of its **competitive status** in that market.

Market terminators Technological changes which switch from one form of **product technology** to another which is completely different (from mechanical to electronic, say), such that the market based on the outdated technology is virtually destroyed. See also **Market rejuvenators**.

Marketing The task of capturing and keeping **customers** by ensuring that the right **product** is available at the right price with the right promotion at the right place and time.

Marketing mix The concept that the **business** must choose the right mixture of the **four Ps** to survive and prosper in competitive markets. This right mixture varies with time, and it is different in different market segments.

Mass manufacturing Characterized by the simultaneous manufacture, in relatively large numbers, of virtually identical **products**.

Matching The central principle underlying **accrual accounting**. It requires that costs incurred to generate a particular revenue appear in the **profit and loss account** which recognizes that revenue, so that they can be compared. Because of matching, **sales revenue** and **revenue costs** usually contain both cash and credit elements.

Materiality An accounting principle (or concession) allowing details to be omitted and other principles ignored if doing so makes no significant difference to the accounts.

Matrix organization This combines project **management** and professional discipline management in a grid-like structure. Project teams are formed by assignment of the requisite staff at the appropriate matrix cross-points. The scheme can be used for any sort of multi-discipline project.

Method-oriented technical innovation Directed at using technology to improve some facet of the **product** creation process, rather than at creating a product with the process. It is sometimes called 'methods R&D'.

Minimum attractive rate of return (MARR) An annual interest rate which is compounded annually. It is the **discount rate** which defines a *financially* viable investment **project**. See also **Internal rate of return**, **Net present value** and **Financial viability threshold**.

Monetary basis A principle which confines accounting to items that can measured reasonably accurately in money terms.

Motivators Features of the working environment which (it is proposed) cause increased job performance and satisfaction when perceived as positive, but do not necessarily cause the converse effects when perceived as negative. See also **Hygiene factors**.

Natural justice equation Effort + Achievement = Reward. The equity theory of motivation suggests that people react to a perceived mismatch in this equation by adjusting their behaviour to restore the balance.

Necessity products Those which customers must obtain.

Net assets (NA) Assets − Liabilities. The excess of assets over (external) liabilities. It belongs to the owners of the **business**: see **Basic accounting equation**.

Net current assets (NCA) See **Working capital**.

Net liquid funds This is the same as **cash-at-bank**, comprising cash, cheques in hand, net cash balance at the bank and any other 'immediately' available money.

Net present value (NPV) The NPV of a sequence of **future sums** is the sum of the **present values** obtained by **discounting** the future sums at a specific **discount rate**. It is the current monetary equivalent of the sequence at that rate. See also **Discount factor**.

Net worth This is the same as **net assets**, but is a misleading term because it suggests that the value of a **business** is its net asset value.

Nominal annual interest rate The proportionate increase in the number of pounds obtained by investing £1 for one year in an interest earning situation. See also **Annual inflation rate** and **Real annual interest rate**.

Non-current liabilities (NCL) **Long-term** debts relating to borrowings held for use over more than one accounting period.

Novel sub-units Those which have not yet been used in practical real-life situations. See also the **Configuration view of a product** and **Established sub-units**.

One-off products See **Unique products**.

Operating cost See **Operating expense**.

Operating expense (OE) The day-to-day running costs of the **business** which are not **directly** incurred in making and testing products. It is a **fixed cost** in that it does not vary with the number of **product** units made. Also called **operating cost** and **revenue cost**.

Operating loss Negative **operating profit**.

Operating profit (OP) **Gross profit** – **Operating expense**. The reward earned by managing the business resources. It measures the efficiency of the business before interest costs and taxation are taken into account.

Opportunity cost The opportunity cost of a resource which is used in a particular way is the benefit sacrificed by not using it in its best other (economic) way. It is really a 'lost opportunity' cost.

Organizing Dividing people into groups with assigned sub-tasks, and providing **management** within and between the groups so as to achieve the whole task. An organization is such a group or a system of such groups.

Output inventory See **Output stock**.

Output stock **Finished products** (finished goods) stored by the **business** prior to dispatch to **customers**.

Owners' capital (OC) The debt (a **liability**) that the **business** owes to its owners. In this context, 'capital' can also be called **equity** or **funds**, as in owner's or proprietor's equity or funds; or partners' equity or funds; or owners' equity or funds; or shareholders' equity or funds depending on the **accounting entity** in question.

Paid up capital The part of **owners' capital** which the owners have invested directly in the **business** (by buying **shares**, say). The other part is **retained profits** (or losses).

Partially divisible tasks Separable into **indivisible** and **divisible** sub-tasks; they are the general case.

Partitioning rationale A logical tool for cleaving a big problem into a relatively self-contained set of smaller problems.

Partnership business An **accounting entity** owned by two or more individuals (partners) where there is no legal distinction between the business and its owners.

Past cost The previous cost of an item. See also **Current cost**.

Period costs Day-to-day running costs not easily matched (see **matching**) with a corresponding revenue. So they are recorded as **revenue costs** (in the **profit and loss account**) in the period when they occur or when the benefits they buy are consumed.

Periodicity An accounting principle requiring that accounts are produced at discrete intervals, preferably of equal duration.

Personnel function Responsible (usually also with line managers) for the people

resource of the **business**. It ensures that the resource matches what is required in skills, numbers and location, and that the employment environment is such that the people within it can give of their best.

Plan   An (intended) orderly progression from a defined start position to a defined end position, which is the plan objective(s). It is an instrument for implementing change while maintaining stability and a sense of purpose. The difference between the start and end positions is termed the 'planning gap'.

Prepayment assets   These relate to costs, called prepayments, which purchase benefits arising in a future **accounting period**. They are 'carried forward' in the **balance sheet** until recorded as **revenue costs** in the appropriate period.

Present value (PV)   The present value of a **future sum (FS)** to be received n years from now is the amount which, when compounded for n years at a predetermined rate r, becomes equal to the future sum. That is, $PV(1 + r)^n = FS$. See also **Discount factor**.

Price of ownership   A **product** attribute which includes its purchase price, together with any subsequent operating, maintenance and repair and disposal costs.

Prime cost   Direct Labour + Direct Materials. The part of **product cost** which is directly attributable to making and testing the product. Total prime cost is the **variable cost** part of the cost of products produced.

Private company   One owned privately rather than publicly. That is, its **shares** are not publicly **traded** on a stock exchange. See also **Public company**.

Private limited company   See **Private company** and **Limited (liability)**.

Private venture (PV)   A **project** which is paid for by the **business** (rather than by some agency outside the business), such that profit earned by the business is reduced by the amount it spends on the project. Funds spent or to be spent on PV projects are termed 'PV funds'.

Product architecture (PA)   This describes the **product** as a configuration of *real* tangible elements or sub-units. It results from 'filtering' the **functional architecture** through the **design constraints**. It is what the **customer** can have, rather than what the customer wants.

Product attributes   Primarily, **quality**, conformability, availability, delivery time, confidence and **price of ownership**. **Product value** and **benefit ratio** are further attributes derived from the primary list.

Product brief   A new **product** description as it is first perceived by its **customer** (actual or proxy). Also called 'product concept', 'product requirement specification' or 'user requirement specification' in the literature. It marks the first formal event in the product design process and is the **initial product model**.

Product business plan   This relates to the possible 'mini-business' focused on a new **product**. It defines what has to be done to exploit the new **profit** opportunity represented by the product and provides data allowing that opportunity to be evaluated as an investment/return proposition.

Product contribution   Product price − **Prime cost**. The net income obtained by selling the product which contributes (towards paying) the **fixed costs** of the **business**.

Product cost   See **Works cost**.

Product creation project   This relates to the whole **life cycle** of a new product from conception in the **product brief** to its ultimate demise as **sales** decline to zero. The initial planning stage is followed by sub-projects for **product development and design**, production start-up, **marketing**, manufacturing and **selling**. It is a (mini-)business creation project.

Product design(ing)   The process of seeking a match between a set of customer-derived product requirements and a way of meeting those requirements, or of finding an acceptable compromise. It includes **product development and (technical) product design**.

Product design environment   This reflects the product supplier business. It comprises internal constraints applying to the performance of the **product creation project** and the resources available for implementing it.

Product development and design (PD&D)   This comprises the distinct **technical function** activities of product development and *technical* product design. Both are part of the comprehensive **product design(ing)** process defined earlier. Product development is the process of creating well-understood, proven, **novel sub-units** which are destined for incorporation into the pre-determined configuration of proven sub-units comprising the complete product. (Technical) product design is the process of creating the novel configuration of well-understood and proven sub-units to implement the pre-determined specification of the complete product. See also **Configuration view of a product**.

Product differentiation   An attribute which distinguishes similar products offered by competing supplier **businesses**. **Technological innovation** activity can be directed at functional and/or performance and/or economic differentiation.

Product generation   An aggregate of a class of competing products which have broadly similar features and performance at corresponding points in the price range. It generally represents a well-defined stage in **product** and manufacturing technologies.

Product layout   See **Flow-line layout**.

Product price   Notionally, the price at which a product is offered for sale. But it is really the price a purchaser is prepared to pay for it. See also **Price of ownership**.

Product range   A family of similar products offered by the **business**. Product capability, cost and price usually increase across the range.

Product range focus   A **technical function** organization in which each second-level unit is concerned with a distinct **product range**. See also **Professional-discipline focus** and **Project focus**.

Product requirements definition (PRD)   See **Requirements definition**.

Product sponsor   A 'proxy' **customer** which is able to describe the requirements of the real prospective customer for the product.

Product technologies   Science-based bodies of knowledge applied in industry and commerce. Each major product technology (such as electronic engineering or mechanical engineering) comprises a 'family' hierarchy of progressively 'smaller' technologies. The concept allows a product to be viewed as a technological blend, recipe or mix.

Product value   Perceived by a **customer** as an aggregate of product **quality**, conformability, availability, delivery time and confidence. See also **Benefit ratio**.

Production engineering   This relates to all aspects of manufacturing technology, including process design, facilities layout, procedures and techniques, **product cost**, **value analysis**, **value engineering** and new machinery evaluation.

Production function   The wealth-creating 'engine' that powers a **manufacturing business**. It includes the manufacturing operation and various manufacturing support services.

Production overhead (POH)   The part of total **fixed costs** (**indirect** or overhead costs) assigned to the **production function**. Some fraction of this cost is assigned to each **product** produced: see **Product cost**.

Production planning and control   Usually aimed at the most cost-effective use of manufacturing resources (people and facilities). But other criteria, such as throughput time and quality targets, can compromise this aim.

Productivity   This is some measure of how efficiently a **business** uses its resources.

Products   Things created by the human mind and human labour as tangible items *or* services offered for sale by **businesses**. All products are **systems**.

Professional-discipline focus   A **technical function** organization in which each second-level unit is concerned with a distinct professional technical discipline. See also **Product range focus** and **Project focus**.

Professional function   A group of **business** employees who share a specific professional skill. See also **Stage function**.

Profit   The excess of **revenue** over **cost**: see **Profit equation**.

Profit after tax (PAT)   **Taxable profit** less the **tax paid or payable**.

Profit and loss (P&L) account   This reports the **revenue** earned and the corresponding **cost** incurred by the **business** *during* a specific **accounting period** and, hence, the **profit** for that period.

Profit before tax (PBT)   **Operating profit** less **interest paid or payable**.

Profit equation   Profit = Revenue − Cost. To make sense, both **revenue** and **cost** must refer to the same period and, ideally, they should be totally **matching** quantities. But **prudence** usually compromises matching. A **profit and loss account** expresses the detail of this equation.

Profit-incentive contract   **Customer** and supplier **business** agree the (estimated) contract cost. **Profit** earned by the contractor in excess of this cost then depends on performance in implementing the contract.

Program evaluation and review technique (PERT)   A **project** planning and control technique which represents a project as a network of dependent **events** and **activities**.

Project   A set of **activities** with a (or some) pre-defined objective(s). It consumes time and other resources, such as effort and money. Usually the activities and the target objective(s) have some degree of novelty.

Project budget   A **cost** (and other **resources**) **plan** of the project which covers its estimated duration.

Project control   A **management** activity aimed at ensuring that the conduct of a project conforms (so far as is possible and sensible) to its current **plan**.

Project focus   A **technical function** organization in which each second-level unit is concerned with a distinct technical project. See also **Product range focus** and **Professional-discipline focus**.

Project manufacturing   A 'one-off' sequence of manufacturing sub-processes which creates a unique **product**.

Project parameters   (Basically) progress, time and cost. See also **Project plan**.

Project plan   A model of the project created before the real project is launched. It defines an intended relationship between the project parameters of progress, time and cost, and links these parameters such that specifying any one of them defines unique values of the other two.

Project profitability   Return expressed as a fraction of the investment. See also **Internal rate of return**.

Project work capacity   The total **direct** hours of project effort available.

Prudence   An accounting principle which requires that **profit** should be understated rather than overstated when uncertainty exists. It takes precedence over the **matching** principle in **accrual accounting**.

Public company   One owned publicly rather than privately. That is, its **shares** are traded on a stock exchange. See also **Private company**.

Public limited company (PLC)   See **Public company** and **Limited (liability)**.

Purchasing   This is concerned with the most efficient procurement of required goods and services from outside the **business**, and with **inventory** planning and control.

Pure research   Carried out in universities, polytechnics and (sometimes) in government research establishments but seldom, if ever, in industry. It is motivated by curiosity, hopes of fame, career ambitions or prospective benefits for humanity. Potential commercial gain is rarely a factor. It is the basis of modern industry, but it is not examined in this book.

Quality   The degree to which the objective and subjective performance features of an entity meets the requirements of its user. It is fitness for purpose measured by the user as a fraction of perfection.

R&D cost   See **Research and development** and **Research and development (R&D) cost**.

Ratio analysis   This expresses relationships between some key elements of a **profit and loss account** and **balance sheet** in ratio form. These **business ratios** are used internally to aid to problem analysis and externally to assess credit worthiness and financial stability.

Real annual interest rate   The proportionate increase in the amount of a **commodity** that can be purchased at the end of a year with the £1 that was invested at the beginning of the year. At low values, it is nearly equal to **Nominal annual interest rate − Annual inflation rate**.

Realizable value   The net return from selling an **asset** after its disposal costs have been paid. The term is usually applied to the sale of redundant **fixed assets**.

Recognize   An accounting term meaning 'enter into the **profit and loss account**' or, equivalently, 'treat as a **revenue cost**'.

Recover   A financial term meaning 'get (money) back'.

Relevance   An accounting principle related to **clarity**. It requires that accounts contain all the information relevant to accounts users.

Reliability   An accounting principle requiring that accounts contain no errors, include all the significant data and are verifiable by **audit**. It is also a **product** attribute related to product availability.

Repeatable products   Products manufactured in substantial quantities (high volumes) as exact replicas of each other, and sold in the same substantial quantities to many different customers.

Replacement cost   See **Current cost**.

Required rate of return   See **Minimum attractive rate of return**.

Requirements definition (RD)   A concise and accurate statement of the *whole* problem that the design of a new **product** presents to its designer. It includes the requirements of the prospective product **customer** and those of the prospective product supplier.

Research and development (R&D) Traditional jargon denoting **technological innovation** (which is the technical aspect of the **product** creation process). In this book, the activity is treated as the distinct tasks of **basic research**, **applied research**, **product development** and **(technical) product design**.

Research and development (R&D) cost This refers to **technological innovation**. It is an investment cost aimed at creating **revenue** in future periods. **Product development and design** cost may be **capitalized** whereas **research** cost must not. See also **Research and development**.

Research planning diagram (RPD) A particular form of flow chart used in technical **project** planning and **plan** analysis. It is particularly useful in **activity** looping situations (which PERT cannot handle).

Reserves or reserve capital The accumulated retained profit part of **owners' capital**. See also **Paid-up capital**.

Residual claim The lowest priority debt owed by a **company**, which is the debt it owes to its owners (= **owners' capital**).

Resources The people and things (such as buildings, machinery, tools, furniture and computers) which **businesses** need to operate. All resources incur **cost**, both to acquire and to employ or use.

Retailers Part of a **product** distribution channel. They purchase products from **wholesalers** and sell them (at increased prices) to end-user **customers**.

Retained profits See **Reserves or reserve capital**.

Return on capital employed (ROCE) ratio Operating profit/Capital employed. It measures **management** skill in using **funds** invested in the **business** to generate **profit**, and is probably the best overall measure of **profitability**.

Revenue Usually means **sales revenue** but, used on its own, it can mean any or every sort of **business** income.

Revenue costs These buy **short-term** items and benefits expected to be completely 'consumed' (used up) within one year of purchase. These day-to-day **operating costs** of the **business** (also called 'expenses') are recorded in the **profit and loss account**.

Sales See **Sales revenue**.

Sales function Primarily concerned with **selling**.

Sales revenue The total cash and credit **income** arising from selling **products**. It excludes every other sort of income. Also called **sales** or **turnover**.

Salvage value See **Realizable value**.

Selling The non-trivial task of obtaining confirmed (and profitable) orders for **products** from **customers**.

Semi-variable cost The sum of a **variable cost** and an associated **fixed cost**.

Service businesses Those which create non-tangible 'service' **products** based on specialist skills and facilities, or a particular location, or a combination of these features.

Share capital That part of **owners' capital** obtained by selling shares in the ownership of the **business**.

Shareholders Part owners of a **company** who enjoy the rewards of that ownership in proportion to their holding of issued **shares** of ownership. They may be individuals or organizations.

Shares Fractions of **company** ownership, denoting part ownership of its **net assets**.

Short-term This means less than one year, which is the normal maximum duration of an **accounting period**. See also **Long-term**.

Slack See **Event slack**.

Social costs Part of **cost of employment**, including, for example, contributions to national insurance and pension funds made by an employer on behalf of an employee.

Software engineering **Technological innovation** directed at the creation of software products.

Sole-trader business An **accounting entity** owned by one individual where there is no legal distinction between the business and its owner.

Sparse estimate A sparse estimate of the *effort* required to complete a **divisible task** is obtained by assigning to it the absolute minimum number of full-time people demanded by the different skills its completion entails. It is the best possible measure of the **intrinsic work content** of the task.

Staff functions See **Line functions**.

Stage function A group of **business** employees who share a specific business purpose, stage or sub-process in the whole business mission.

Stakeholders Groups, institutions or organizations who have a vested interest in the performance and behaviour of the **business**, and who are able to apply pressure in pursuit of that interest.

Standard costing A technique for planning and controlling costs, usually **product costs**. It separates cost planning from cost control in an orderly way by using **variances**. See also **Cost card**.

Stock(s) Comprises **input stock** and **output stock**.

Strategic A term used to describe issues, objectives, plans and activities which concern the long-term survival and prosperity of the **business**, and which can have tragic consequences if badly managed. See also **Tactical**.

Structured product design Orderly decomposition of big questions into successive layers of smaller questions, until the questions become small enough to answer; followed by construction of big answers by amalgamating successive layers of smaller answers.

Sub-process layout See **Functional layout**.

Substitute products These address the same needs or problems as the 'original' products but use very different **product technologies**.

Sunk costs Those parts of a **past cost** which are not recoverable.

Supplier rating See **Vendor ratings**.

Supportive criteria These increase the attractiveness of the proposal being evaluated if judged to be adequately satisfied. See also **Decisive criteria** and **Critical criteria**.

Systems Configurations of interacting entities. System **products** are also 'tools' for aiding the achievement of specific human purposes. Not all systems are products.

Tactical A term used to describe issues, objectives, plans and activities which relate to the immediate short-term survival and prosperity of the **business** within a **strategic** framework.

Tangible products Manufactured items with the physical properties of size, shape and weight. Unlike service products, they can be stored (rather than sold) when demand is low. See also **Service businesses**.

Tax paid or payable A government-imposed charge on business **taxable profit**, rather than a cost incurred in earning it. See also **Corporation tax**.

Taxable profit Obtained by adjusting **accounting profit** to comply with tax rules on **depreciation** and the disallowance of certain other costs for tax purposes.

Technical function A stage, or sub-process, in the primary business process of creating and selling **products** to customers. It includes all **technological innovation** activities within the **business**, and normally employs most of its technically qualified staff.

Technical innovation See **Technological innovation**.

Technical product design See **Product design(ing)** and **Product development and design**.

Technological innovation This activity is the technical aspect of the **product** creation process. It normally relates to new and enhanced products to be offered for sale by the **business**. In this treatment, the activity is partitioned the distinct tasks of **basic research**, **applied research**, **product development** and **(technical) product design**. See also **Research and development**.

Technological profile A set of technology-related factors which are characteristic of an industry at a particular stage in its development and, to some extent, of the individual **businesses** within that industry.

Technology This is really any organized body of knowledge which is applied in a field of human endeavour, such as industry. But, as used in the book, the term means one of the science-based **engineering technologies** or **product technologies**.

Technology vector The combined 'force' acting to change the **strategic** position of a business due to technology-induced **market-place** and **competitive status** changes.

Theory X and Theory Y Sets of conflicting assumptions (and, perhaps, self-fulfilling prophesies) about how people behave at work.

Three-times estimating A probability-based technique aimed at improving on single time estimates of activity duration. Optimistic, most likely and pessimistic time estimates are combined in a simple expression to yield an expected time for the activity duration.

Time-sheets Records of **direct** effort (usually measured in hours/week) spent on **projects**.

Total quality A policy aimed at applying **quality** concepts to *every* facet of business activity.

Trade creditors Other **businesses** that supply **stock** on credit. They are listed as **current liabilities** in the **balance sheet**.

Trading Buying, making (perhaps), and selling activity. It is what **businesses** do.

Trading cycle See **Circulating assets**.

Turnkey contract This covers the development, design, manufacture, installation, commissioning and subsequent support of a large 'system' **product**. The **customer** has then only to 'turn the key' which brings the product into service.

Turnover See **Sales revenue**.

Unique products Those tailored, to some degree, to match the unique requirements of a specific customer.

Value analysis This aims to reduce the cost of **established products** without damaging their functions, performance and reliability.

Value engineering This aims to reduce the cost of new products without damaging their functions, performance and reliability.

Vantage points Successive levels, called **context analysis**, **functional architecture** and **design constraints**, which form the 'horizontal' structure of the requirements definition methodology developed in Chapter 8. See also **Viewpoints**.

Variable costs Those which vary with an associated activity level. See also **Fixed costs** and **Semi-variable costs**.

Variance In business, this denotes the difference between the planned (or budgeted) and actual values of a parameter. The term also has a statistical meaning.

Vendor analysis The process of assessing actual and potential suppliers to the **business** against various criteria.

Vendor ratings The results of **vendor analysis**.

Viewpoints These form the 'vertical' structure of the requirements definition methodology developed in Chapter 8. They comprise technical, economic and operational viewpoints. See also **Vantage points**.

Volume discounts Reductions in **product** unit price offered as the number of units purchased increases.

Wealth The added value generated in a business when it transforms purchased inputs to **product** outputs which have a sale value greater than the cost of the inputs consumed in making them.

Wholesalers Part of a **product** distribution channel. They purchase products from **manufacturing businesses** and sell them (at increased prices) to **retailers**.

Why–what–how A 'divide and conquer' **partitioning rationale** which seems universally applicable to **design** and **management** problems. See also **Magic questions**.

Work-in-progress A **current asset** comprising raw materials, components and sub-units (and any other purchased items) which are being converted into **products**.

Working capital (WC) **Current assets − Current liabilities**. It is the same as **net current assets**. It is an indicator of the **short-term** financial stability of the **business**.

Works cost The works cost of a **product** includes a **direct** cost and an **indirect** cost. The direct element is the cost of bought-in items incorporated in the product (direct materials) plus the 'people' cost of assembling and testing it (direct labour). The indirect element is a fraction of the total **fixed cost** of the **production function** which is assigned to the product.

Written-off Written-off costs are those of an investment nature which (even though they promise **long-term** benefits) are charged, as they arise, against *current* income (in the **profit and loss account**). Alternatively, such costs may be **capitalized**.

Yield See **Internal rate of return**.

Index

This index is topic-oriented rather than word-oriented.

AC (actual cost) (in delta analysis)   260
account analysis
    summary of   612–13
accounting
    cash-based   568
    overview of   553–4
    primary principles of   555–68
    principles of   570, 555–71
    secondary principles of   569–70
    summary of   570–1
    why & what of   552–4
accounting entity   555–6
accounting period   563
accrual   595
accrual accounting   278, 567, 614
    aims of   568
    & matching   565–8
    & prudence   568
ACPU (actual cost per unit)   314
activity   219
    elapsed time of   224
    finish time of   See earliest finish & latest finish
    float of   See float
    mutually exclusive   207
    start time of   See earliest start & latest start
activity (cost behaviour context)   296
activity loop   207, 210–17
    estimating of   210
actual cost   See AC
actual cost per unit   See ACPU
actual quantity of units   See AQOU
actual time   See AT
Adastra: end of Month 1   571–85
Adastra: Month 1
    accounting review for   573
    action analysis of   573–5
    actions in   572–3
    balance sheet of   576–9
    funds flow statement of   582–5
    P&L account of   580–1
        flawed   581
Adastra: Year 1
    accounts analysis of   596–613
    accounts preparation of   585–96
    balance sheet of   592–6
    & break-even analysis   604–7
    funds flow statement of   598–604

P&L account of
    detailed   587–92
    summarized   597–8
    & ratio analysis   See ratio analysis
added value   5, 418
administration costs   598
advertising   392
Agee M. H.   506, 509, 510, 524
aggregate quality   454
    value of   454
Ansoff H. I.   47, 161
applied research   See AR
AQOU (actual quantity of units)   314
AR (applied research)   86, 92–3, 157, 474
    evaluation of   474, 487–8
    funding of   482, 487
    product range level of   478
    & project selection   488
    as treasure-hunting   88
asset   28, 558
    accrued   See accrual
    prepayment   574
AT (actual time) (in delta analysis)   260
availability   344, 369, 452
average (unit) cost   300

balance sheet   552
    asset & liabilities format of   579
    as business model   614
    conventional format of   559, 576
    overview of   592
    & P&L account   563
    source & application format of   578
    structure of   577
balance sheet equation   562–3
    & compensating transactions   29
    incremental   33, 32–3
    & non-compensating transactions   29
bar chart   202–3, 264
    for & against   206–8
    & precedence information   233
bar chart & resource table   201–8
basic accounting equation   See balance sheet equation
basic research   See BR
batch manufacturing   421, 425, 430, 431
    & group technology layout   433
Battersby A.   219

BCG (Boston Consulting Group)   61
BCG matrix   61
    criticisms of   64
    extension of   64–8
    & investment criteria   62
Begg D. K. H.   318
benefit ratio   345–6, 356
Blake R. R.   130
Blanchard K. H.   130
board function   18
bonds & barriers concept   170
    See also DC on technical organization,
        location
book-keeping   553
Borden N. H.   400
Boston Consulting Group   See BCG
bought-in item   424
BR (basic research)   86, 92, 157, 474
    evaluation of   474, 486–7
    funding of   482, 486
    openness of   487
    & project selection   486
    strategy for   487
    technology level of   478
    as treasure-hunting   88
break-even concept   298–301, 321, 434
    & activity level   604
British Standards Institution   See BSI
Brooks F. P.   190, 251
BSI (British Standards Institution)   219, 454
BT (British Telecommunications plc)   625
budget   281–7
    & company model   281
    costs   307
    departmental   305–10
    elements of   302–5
    linking sales & costs   308
    preparation of   284, 281–6
        imperfections in   310
    real   309
    reconciliation of   285
    sales   305
    structure of   283
    & trading concept   302, 422
budgeting   See budget, preparation of
business
    balance model of   29–30
    basic mechanism of   5–7
    basic model of   5
    basic terminology of   5–7
    capital structure of   506
    engineering-led   394
    financial model of   27–30
    liquidity of   582
    manufacturing   See manufacturing business
    manufacturing & service compared   9
    market-driven   394
    market-led   394
    ownership classification of   10–11
    product classification of   8–9
    production-led   394
    service   See service business
    size classification of   9–10
    summary of   7–8
    trading equations of   6
    types of   8–11

business creation project   See product creation
        process/project
business function   See function
business income
    terminology of   587
business model
    as balance sheet   614
business objective   22–5
    critical   22–5
    hierarchy of   46
    innovation as   23
    manager performance as   25
    market standing as   23
    productivity as   23
    profitability as   24
    public responsibility as   25
    resources as   24
    worker performance as   25
business organization   118–19
    basic structures of   18–21
    & birth-rate   146
    classic principles of   131
    compared with university   166
    & death-rate   146
    decisions in   136
    design of
        company level   135–42
    design overview of   131–5
    divisionalization of   See divisionalization
    forecast changes in   144–8
    by function   18
    functional partitioning of   See functional partitioning
    future
        in summary   148–9
    future of   142–9
    by geography   20
    growth of   133–5
    implementation of   138–42
    & industrial trends   148
    & job content   146
    & job swapping   147
    & job trends   149
    justification of   136
    large   20
    & leisure   147
    life cycle of   133
    & matrix structures   149
    owner of   See business, ownership classification of
    pressures for change in   143
    by product   19
    relationships in   138
    signs of change in   143–4
    specification of   136–8
    technical   See technical organization
    & technological prospects   144
    tiny, small, medium & large   9
    traditional hierarchy of   131–3
    traditional structure of   131
    & trend to part-time work   144
    & working hours   147
business plan
    product   See product business plan
business planning   52–68
    major objective of   52–4
    problem of   54–6
    SBU level   60

Buxton J. 190, 259, 339, 343

CA (context analysis) 357
  Phase 2 373
  as reference document 362
CA (current asset) 29
  accounting for 594
  & FA 565
  & matching 565
capital
  terminology of 560, 608
capital asset *See* FA
capital cost
  & FA 564
capital employed 577
  long-term debt as 596
capital structure 506
Case K. E. 506, 509, 510, 524
case studies
  Acquiring an Asset 557–8
  Adastra Ltd: The First Year 571–613
  Break-Even Analysis Applied to Alternative Vehicles
    298–301
  Break-Even Analysis Applied to a P&L Account
    604–7
  Building a Departmental Budget 301–10
  Building a Technological Strategy 73–81
  Estimating Activity Loops: Example 1 212–17
  Estimating Activity Loops: Example 2 217
  Evaluating Project B by Compounding 510–13
  Evaluating Projects A, B & C with NPV 517
  Evaluating Projects A, B & C with Shape Parameters
    503–5
  Exercising the Manufacturing Business Model 34–9
  How to Ruin a Good Project 249–52
  Inflation & Project A 535–8
  Make or Buy Decision 326–8
  Making a Profit 561
  Market Segmentation & Marketing Strategy 400–5
  PERT & Probability 244–7
  Pipework Project 233–4
  Portfolio of Mini-Businesses 328–30
  Pricing for Growth 407–8
  Project Choice: NPV v. IRR – General Case 525–8
  Project Choice: NPV v. IRR – Special Case 524–5
  Requirements (RD) Definition Example 621–42
  Revenue, Cost & Profit 324–6
  Standard Costing & Product X 314–17
  Technological Recipe of a Smart Telephone 476–7
cash-flow
  application of 583
  cost of negative 506–10
  cumulative 104–6, 498, 499
    with investment costs 511
  incremental 499
  & profit 39
  sign conventions of 503
  source of 583
  source & application rule 583
  & TCM 629
cash-flow model 497–501
  basic assumptions in 499
  break-even in 500
  & compounding 510
  & discounting (IRR) 520–4
  & discounting (NPV) 513–20

form of 497–500
  & inflation 533–9
  investment/return features of 500–1
  performance of 105
  & PET2 539
  shape evaluation of 501–6
  shape parameters of 501–2
Cather H. vi, 217, 233
CD (contract development) 110
  See also source of project fund 305
central/corporate/company research fund *See* CRF
CF (contract funding) 110
Channon D. F. 9, 133
Chapman C. B. 287
chief programmer team *See* CPT
CIM (computer integrated manufacturing) 461
circulating assets *See* CA
CL (current liability) 29
  accounting for 595
clarity principle 569
Clark C. E. 219
CNC (computerized numerically controlled) 461
CNC machines 461
Coate M. B. 64
COE (cost of employment) 303
company 556
  limited liability 11, 556
  private 556
  public 556
company organization *See* business organization
comparability principle 569
competitive status
  & technological innovation 48
competitiveness 345
competitor 387
compound interest 474
  & cash-flow model 506
compounding forward technique 510–13
  for & against 513
computer integrated manufacturing *See* CIM
confidence 344
conformability 344, 452
consistency principle 568
constraint
  market *See* market, constraint in
context analysis *See* CA
contract
  bids for 215
contract development *See* CD
contract funding *See* CF
contribution 330
  & fixed cost 605
  product *See* product contribution
conventional funds flow statement 599
  discussion of 603
  overview 602
corporate planning 47
  model of 61, 56–61
  sequence 58
cost
  & activity level problem 280
  & allocation problem 280
  business level structure of 273–6
    as average product 276
    as P&L account 276
  capital & revenue 563–5

cost (*cont.*)
 & choice problem   277–8
 depreciation   *See* depreciation
 direct   *See* direct cost
 disposal   *See* disposal cost
 of employment   *See* COE
 & engineers   276–7
 fixed   *See* fixed cost
 future   *See* future cost
 historical   *See* historical cost
 indirect   *See* indirect cost
 investment nature of   278
 L+O/H   *See* L+O/H cost
 life cycle   *See* life cycle cost
 opportunity   *See* opportunity cost
 other direct   *See* ODC
 prime   *See* prime cost
 & profit   272–7
 purpose of every   472, 567
 sunk   *See* sunk cost
 & time problem   278–9
 types of   287–96
 variable   *See* variable costs
 variation of   296–301
 works   *See* works cost
 written-off   567
cost & costing
 approach to   272
 problems of   277–81
cost card   314
cost deviation   *See* DC
cost-effectiveness principle   569
cost efficiency   320
cost of employment   *See* COE
cost of products sold   587, 598
cost source   286–7
 facilities   287
 financing   287
 labour   286
 materials & services   286
CPM (critical path method)   219
CPT (chief programmer team)   190
creativity   168
 & the technical function   127
CRF (central/corporate/company research fund)   306
critical path   226
critical path method   *See* CPM
critical technology   77, 476, 478, 485
 opportunities of   79
 threats of   79
current asset   *See* CA
current cost   *See* replacement cost
current liability   *See* CL
customer   386
 identity of   397
 project   483
customer benefit   454

Davies D. G. S.   208
DC (cost deviation) (in delta analysis)   262
DC (design constraint)   139, 166, 349, 357, 366–70
 on business organization
  general   139
 customer-imposed   356, 368–70
 as good news   166
 as next phase input   362

supplier-imposed   356, 366–8
 financial   366
 miscellaneous   368
 resources   367
DC on technical organization   166–77
 location   170–4
 people-related   166–9
 performance measurement as   174–5
 project planning & control as   174
 source of funds as   175–7
DCF (discounted cash-flow)   474
 basic assumption of   513
 basics of   513–14
 & cash-flow model   500
 & inflation   534
 negative   516
defence market   405–6
 place in   406
 prices in   406
 products in   405
 promotion in   406
definitive product specification
 & Phase 2 CA   373
delivery time   344
delta analysis   260–2, 264
 deviation matrix in   262
 for & against   262
 time & cost deviations in   260
demand curve   318–20
depreciation   32, 287–9
 & book value   32, 288
 & FA   564
 & funds flow   601
 & matching   565
deviation   199, 447
direct cost   280, 292–3, 303
direct hours
 total   304
direct labour cost   310
 total   303
direct labour rate   305
direct materials cost   310
direct staff   302
director function   18
discount factor   514
 calculations using   515
discount rate
 composite   538
 zero-inflation   537
discounted cash-flow   *See* DCF
diseconomies of scale   300, 331
disposal cost   291
distribution costs   598
divisionalization   140
 compared with functional partitioning   141
double-entry accounting   556–62
 for & against   561
 mechanics of   556
Drucker P. F.   22, 135, 394
DT (time deviation) (in delta analysis)   262
due date   444
dummy activity   220

earliest (possible) time   *See* ET
earliest finish   230
earliest start   230

economies of scale   290, 300, 331, 387, 407
effort   248
effort variance   205
engineering
   industrial   *See* industrial engineering
   production   *See* production engineering
engineers
   & accounting   552, 613–14
   & cash   613
   & cost   276–7
   & funds   570
   production   276, 423, 427, 441
EOY (end of year)   503
equal misery principle   486
equity   *See* OC
estimating tasks   *See* task estimating
   See also f Factor Method
ET (earliest) (possible) time (for event)   228
event   219
event time   228
expenses   *See* revenue cost

f Factor Method   253–8
FA (fixed asset)   29
   accounting for   592
   & CA   565
   depreciation of   36
FA (functional architecture)   223, 357, 362–6
   creation of   363–6
   inputs to   365
   as next phase input   362
   outputs of   364
   & PA   362–3
   as universal concept   362
   as what customer wants   362, 630
facilities maintenance   425, 436–8
   cost of   437
   data collection & analysis in   437
   & inspection   436
   planning of   437
   preventive   436
   & repair   437
   & servicing   436
facility layout
   fixed position   431, 435
   flow-line   432, 435
   functional   431, 435
   group technology   433
   & relative economics   434
   types of   430–35, 460
Fazar W.   219
FC (forecast cost) (in delta analysis)   261
FFE (free float early)   232
FFL (free float late)   232
final year project   376
finance function   14–15, 427
financial accounting   553, 554
financial viability threshold   506
   true earnings element of   509
financing cost   590
finished good   *See* finished product
fixed asset   *See* FA
fixed cost   280, 296–8
   & contribution   605
flexible manufacturing system   *See* FMS
float   231

flow diagram   *See* RPD
FMS (flexible manufacturing system)   461
forecast cost   *See* FC
forecast time   *See* FT
foundation technology   77, 78, 476, 478, 485
four Ps   394–9
   & marketing mix   399
   & right place   399
   & right price   396–7
   & right product   395–6
   & right promotion   397–8
free float early   *See* FFE
free float late   *See* FFL
Freedman A. L.   vi, 339
FS (future sum)   514, 515
FT (forecast time) (in delta analysis)   261
full cost analysis
   compared with marginal costing   322
function
   as activities   136
   personnel   427
   types of   12–18
functional architecture   *See* FA
functional partitioning   139
   compared with divisionalization   141
functional specification   *See* FA
funding threshold   486
funds
   & credit purchase   570
   & credit sale   570
   & depreciation   570
   increase/(decrease) in   603
funds as cash   582
funds flow statement   552, 563
   & balance sheet   582
   & cash-flow   584
   conventional   *See* conventional funds flow statement
   forms of   604
   & P&L account   582
   & working capital   598
funds generated from operations   601
future cost   278, 292

GAAP (Generally Accepted Accounting Principles)   555
Gantt chart   *See* bar chart
Glautier M. W. E.   554
going concern   568
Greenwell P. E.   vi, 400
gross profit   588
   & activity level   605

Handy C. B.   142, 144, 145
Harrison J.   554
Hedley B.   61
Hellriegal D.   49
Henderson B. D.   61
Hersey P.   130
Herzberg F.   122
high-volume/low-unit-cost manufacturing   430, 432
historical cost   278, 289–90
hours per direct (staff member)   304

IDO (inter-divisional order)   422
IF (independent float)   232
incremental cost   *See* marginal cost
independent float   *See* IF

indirect cost 280, 292–3
  allocation of 311
  See also overhead
indirect staff 303
industrial engineering 13, 426, 438–40
  & methods study 439
  & work measurement 440
  & working environment 440
inflation 290, 509, 513
  basics of 533–4
  & cash-flow model *See* cash-flow model, & inflation
  & composite-rate method 537
  & constant-value method 537
  & DCF 534
  ignoring 538
  & interest rates 534–5
  summary of 538–9
  terms relating to 534
information services function 17
integrity 369
inter-divisional order *See* IDO
interest paid/payable 590
interest rates
  annual & monthly 542
internal rate of return *See* IRR
inventory
  management of 462
investment
  basic problems of 473
  cost of funds for 507–8, 510
  general criteria 60
  source of funds for 506–7
investment strategy 53
invitation to tender *See* ITT
IRR (internal rate of return) 474, 520–4
  calculating 522
  compared with NPV 533
  conflicting with NPV 525
  interpretation of 521–2
  & multiple roots problem 522–4
  project choice using 532
  & project profitability 522
  & TCM 629
ITT (invitation to tender) 216

JIT (just-in-time) 291, 451, 463
Judd R. 52
just-in-time *See* JIT
Justis R. 52

Kaplan R. S. 509
Knott G. 272

L+O/H (labour+overhead) 302
L+O/H cost 302
L+O/H rate 305
labour+overhead *See* L+O/H
latest (acceptable) time *See* LT
latest finish 230
latest start 230
Lawler E. E. 121
leadership 129
lead-time 424
legal function 17
Levy F. K. 219
liability 28–9, 559

accrued *See* accrual
life cycle cost 293–4
liquidity 577
looming technology 77, 477, 478, 485
  threat of 81
Lorange P. 49
low-volume/high-unit-cost manufacturing 429, 431
LT (latest) (acceptable) time (for event) 228

McCarthy E. J. 395, 400
McDonnell E. J. 47
McGregor D. 119
Macro A. 190, 259, 339, 343
maintainability 344, 452
make or buy
  example of 326
Malcolm D. G. 219
management 25–7
  hierarchy of 26–7
  production *See* production management
  quality of 552
  tasks of 26
  technical *See* technical management
  & why–what–how 376
management account 552
management accounting 554
manager
  personal qualities of *See* manager attributes
manager attributes 26, 125
management style 128–31
  democratic 128
  dictatorial 128
  ideal? 129
manufacturing business 8
  model of *See* manufacturing business model
manufacturing business model 30–4
  exercising 34–9
  overview of 30–2
  sequence in 34–6
manufacturing operation 418, 421–35
  & established product 422–5
  high-technology 'automated' 460
  intermediate-technology 'mechanized' 460
  low-technology 'manual' 460
  operator skills & technology levels in 430
  overview of 421–2
  practical 435
  support services & interfaces of 425–8
  types of 429–35
manufacturing resources planning *See* MRP II
manufacturing support services 418, 43–56
  outline of 13
  summary of 426
manufacturing technology 460–62
marginal analysis 272, 321–4, 606
  compared with full costing 322
  concept of 318
marginal cost *See* MC
  & standard cost 328
marginal profit *See* MP
marginal revenue *See* MR
market 386–8
  age status of 69–71
  constraint in 387
  consumer 400
  defence *See* defence market

market (*cont.*)
  industrial 400
  maps of 402
  segmentation of 400
market research 402
marketing function 384, 390–2
  & four Ps *See* four Ps
  & marketing mix *See* marketing mix
  & new profit opportunities 390
  & product business plans 391
  & product price *See* pricing policy
  & product promotion 392, *See* promotion
  See also marketing & sales function
marketing mix 399, 400–6
marketing & sales function 12–13, 427
  comparison of 392–3
  & mousetrap making 384–5
  overview of 385–94
  & profit creation process 388–90
  & profit equation 385–6
  role summary 414
MARR (minimum attractive rate of return) 474
  interest rate regime of 509, 510
  significance of 509
Maslow A. H. 121
mass manufacturing 430, 432
matching principle
  & accrual accounting 565–8
  limitations of 567
  prudence principle versus 589
  & writing off 574
material requirement planning *See* MRP
materiality principle 569
MC (marginal cost) 300, 321
  effect of shifts in 323
medium-volume/medium-unit-cost manufacturing 430, 431
Meigs R. F. 554
Meigs W. B. 554
Mills H. 190
minimum attractive rate of return *See* MARR
Mitchell T. R. 120
monetary basis principle 569
motivation theory 120–4
  equity & natural justice 124
  hierarchy of human needs 121
  hygiene factors 122
  & individuals 124
  motivators 122
mousetrap 384
Mouton J. S. 130
MP (marginal profit) 321
MR (marginal revenue) 321
  effect of shifts in 323
MRP (materials requirement planning) 462
MRP II (manufacturing resources planning) 463
MTBF (mean-time-between-failures) 370, 452
  See also reliability
MTTF (mean-time-to-failure) 452
  See also reliability
MTTR (mean-time-to-repair) 370, 452
Myers F. A. vi, 212

NC (numerically controlled) 461
NC machines 461
NCL (non-current liability) 29

accounting for 596
NDV (new diesel van) 299
net assets 596
  & OC 592
net present value *See* NPV
net present worth *See* NPV
network analysis 225–38
  reduction in 226
network dictionary
  activity table 225
  event table 225
network synthesis 221–5
  & detail design 223
  & outline design 222
new diesel van *See* NDV
NIH (not invented here) 159
non-current liability *See* NCL
NPV (net present value) 474, 514–16, 513–20
  basic interpretation of 515
  compared with IRR 533
  conflicting with IRR 525
  & finite series 520
  for & against 517–18
  & infinite series 519
  interpretations of 518–20
  & net end of year value 518
  project choice using 530, 532
  variation with discount rate of 520
NPW (net present worth) 513

OC (owners' capital) 29, 558, 559
  elements of 507, 596
  & net assets 592
  & profit 561
  terminology of 28, 561
ODC (other direct cost) 205, 292, 303
operating expense 588, 598
operating profit 590
  & activity level 605
opportunity cost 278, 294–6, 507
other direct cost *See* ODC
overhead 280
  total 304
  See also indirect cost
overhead cost *See* indirect cost
overhead rate 305
owners' capital *See* OC

PA (product architecture) 223, 362
  design of 373–4
  as design platform 621
  & FA 362–3
  partitioning of 375
  as what customer can have 362, 630
Parker R. C. 47, 167
Parkin M. 318
partitioning rationale 349, 375
  & why–what–how 360
partnership 11, 556
PAT (profit after tax) 275, 591
path 221
PBT (profit before tax) 274, 590
PC (plan cost) (in delta analysis) 260
PD&D (product development & design) 93–4, 158, 442, 474
  accounting for 589

PD&D (product development & design) (*cont.*)
  distinctions between   94
  evaluation of   474, 489–90
    as investment   490
    investment/return   490
    & proposal quality   489–90
  funding of   482
  & PET2   539
  & product creation process/project   489
  product level of   479
  relative project timing in   479
  time & cost of   489
PD&D cost   279
PD&D projects
  review of   479
people at work   119–31
  conservative & revolutionary traits in   128
  future of   142–9
  & industrial engineering   438
  job performance of   120
  personality aspects of   125–8
periodicity principle   570
personnel function   15
PERT (Program Evaluation & Review Technique)   94,
    219–48, 264
  basic concepts of   219–21
  calendar network   *See* PERT, squared network
  conventions of   221
  dependent & independent activities in   239
  for & against   248
  free float & dummies in   241
  loops & dangles in   240
  matrix calculator for   235
  network analysis in   *See* network analysis
  network synthesis in   *See* network synthesis
  network tuning in   235
  parallel activities in   240
  precedence in   238
    See also precedence rule
  predecessors & successors in   238
  & probability   242–7
    for & against   247
  rules of   238–42
  shorthand for   222
  & squared network   232
  & three-times estimating   *See* three-times estimating
PET1 (Project Evaluation Tool) 1   493–7
PET2 (Project Evaluation Tool) 2   494, 539–43
  & cash-flow model   539, 541
  financial performance phase in   541–2
  investment phase in   541
  phases in   539–41
  return phase in   541
  summary of   543
  & three-times estimating   539
PET1A (Project Evaluation Tool) 1A   494
PET1B (Project Evaluation Tool) 1B   494
P&L (profit & loss)   276
P&L account   38–9, 552
  & balance sheet   563
  contribution format of   330
  financial accounting version of   597
  management accounting version of   587
  marginal cost format of   330
  structure of   580
P&L centre   283

plan cost   *See* PC
plan time   *See* PT
planning
  basic sequence of   50
  basics of   49–52
  conventions of   49
  overview of   48–52
planning environment   49
planning gap   198
  options for filling   402
Porter L. W.   121
PRD (product requirements definition)   223
precedence rule   206, 221, 238
present value   *See* PV
price of ownership   345
pricing policy   406–11
  & contract pricing   408
  cost plus   408
  pricing for growth   407
  what the market will bear   407
prime cost   292
  & activity level   604
private venture   *See* PV
product   339–40
  assembly of   425
  capital   395
  consumable   396
  consumer   395
  defence   405
  durable   396
  industrial   395
  packaging & dispatch of   425
  as problem solution   384
  serial innovation of   91–2
  software   *See* technological innovation, software
  standard cost of   *See* standard cost, product
  sub-unit of   *See* sub-unit
  substitute   387
  & system   342
  as technologies blend   76, 74–7, 476
  test of   425
  uniform   430
  unique   429
product architecture   *See* PA
product attribute   344–5
product brief   348, 354, 361, 391, 491
  initial product model as   370
  quality of   453
product business plan   391
  cash-flow model of   *See* cash-flow model
  elements of   493
  evaluation of   493
  & profile techniques   493
  purposes of   492
  TCM   *See* TCM business plan
product concept   *See* product brief
product configuration   89–91, 476, 479
  building analogy of   89
  new   90
product contribution   605
product cost   272
  & benefit ratio   346
  & costing   310–18
  elements of   310–12
  responsibility for   310
  variation of   330–1

product creation process/project   187, 293, 490–3, 497
  cash-flow model of   *See* cash-flow model
  evaluation of   474, 493
  implementation stage of   492
  major stages in   86
  & PD&D   489
  planning stage of   491
  structure of   492–3
  variation of product parameters in   481
  See also product business plan
product definition data   157
  proven   92
  See also production engineering
product design   346–52
  basic techniques of   349–52
  communication problem in   355
  critical problem in   349–52
  definition of   342
  & 'divide & conquer'   349
  & engineering products   342–3
  environment of   353, 361
  first error in   354
  fundamental aim of   351
  fundamental problem of   351
  model phases of   372
  objective & subjective options in   350
  phases after Phase 2 in   374–5
  & profit   347–8
  quality of   367, 453
  responsibility for   347
  reusable   189
  as sequence of models   370–3
    Phase 2 in   374
  supplier margin conflict in   356
  terminology of   339–43
  whole process of   370–5
product design (technical)   93, 342
  as blending technologies   476
  & standard sub-unit   479
  as treasure-hunting   88
  See also PD&D
product designers   346–52
  skills of   348–9
product development   93
  & novel sub-unit   479
  as treasure-hunting   88
product development & design   *See* PD&D
product differentiation   472, 483
product feature   *See* product function
product price
  & benefit ratio   346
product purchasing decision   343–6, 396
product range   91
product requirement specification   *See* product brief
product requirements definition   *See* RD
product sponsor   352
product technology   75, 475–8
  classifying   77
  relative importance of   77
product value   345–6, 367, 454
product value, price & cost   7
production control
  actions of   448
  deviation assessment in   447
  deviation comparison in   447
  measurement in   447

  principles of   445
production engineering   13, 426, 440–43
  & new manufacturing technology   441
  & product definition data   442
  & value analysis   442
  & value engineering   442
production function   13–14
  complexity of   428
  elements of   419
  & external conflict   457–8
  interfaces of   428
  interfaces summary of   427
  & internal conflict   458–9
  overview of   418–21
  people & machines in   420
  role & situation summary of   464
production management   448, 462–4
production overhead
  & activity level   604
production planning
  as product scheduling   443
production planning & control   426, 443–8
  & resource scheduling   428
  relative importance of   443
production technology
  manufacturing & management   460–64
productivity   23
  See also business objective
profile techniques   488
  for & against   494–7
profit
  accounting   590
  & cash-flow   279
  & cost   272–7
  & OC   561
  as primary business objective   385, 394
  role of   273, 385
  taxable   590
profit after tax   *See* PAT
profit before tax   *See* PBT
profit creation process   385, 388
  practical aspects of   389
profit distribution policy   53
profit equation   272, 318–31, 434, 472
  activity level example of   324
  examples of   324–30
  variable elements in   320–1
profit & loss   *See* P&L
Program Evaluation & Review Technique   *See* PERT
project   197
  administration of   206
  business creation   *See* product creation
    process/project
  competing   503
  evaluation of   *See* project evaluation
  IRR equivalent   521
  as investment   472–3
  natural time & cost of   490
  rate of return on   508–10
  review of   96
  technological innovation   197
project choice
  aggregate method of   528–30
  differential method of   530–3
  NPV & IRR in   524–33
  summary of   544

project control   199, 259–64, 264
  action in   262–4
    types of   263
  action or not in   263
  delta analysis technique of   *See* delta analysis
project cost   272
  & costing   301–10
project cost variance   202
project evaluation
  & AR   *See* AR, evaluation of
  background of   481–5
  & BR   *See* BR, evaluation of
  BR & AR   485–8
  & cash-flow shape   501–6
  by compounding   *See* compounding forward
    technique
  criteria of   484–5
  financial   473, 474
    See also financial viability threshold
  financial, key questions of   500
  non-financial   473, 474
  & PD&D   *See* PD&D, evaluation of
  profile   *See* profile techniques
  & product creation process/project
    See product creation process/project
  summary of   543
  why & what of   471–4
project manufacturing   429, 445
project plan   197
  precedence rule in   *See* precedence rule
project planning   94, 197
  & activity loop   *See* activity loop
  as low risk high return investment   264
project planning & control
  background to   196–201
  & bar chart   *See* bar chart
  basic concepts of   197–200
  basic problems of   200–1
  level of   201
  & network technique   *See* PERT
  & resource table   *See* resource table
  & RPD *See* summary   264
project proposal   482–4
  assumptions & vulnerabilities of   484
  commercial justification of   483
  cost in year of   484
  deliverables in   483
  feasibility of   482
  history in   482
  as investment proposal   472
  objectives of   482
  plan in   484
  time in year of   484
  total cost of   483
  total elapsed time of   483
  work breakdown structure in   483
project ranking rules   *See* project choice, NPV & IRR in
  See also NPV, project choice using
project types
  comparison of   479–81
  review of   474–81
project work capacity   302
promotion   411–12
  advertising aspect of   411
  cost-effectiveness of   411
  in industrial market   412

prudence principle   568
PT (plan time) (in delta analysis)   260
purchase order   424
purchasing function   16, 426, 427, 448–51
  & external suppliers   449, 463
  & inventory management   451
  & multiple-sourcing   449
PV (present value) (in DCF)   472
PV (private venture) (fund/project)   110, 514, 515
PV fund   305, 481–2

quality   344, 427, 452
  cost of   450
  manufacturing   453
  product design   453
  specification of   452
  standards of   454
quality assurance function   16, 427, 451–6

ratio
  activity   607
  coverage   607
  financial   607
  liquidity   608
  operational   608
  selected   611
ratio analysis   607–12
  uses of   607
R&D (research & development)   86, 474
  & external customers   410
R&D cost   274
RD (requirements definition)   223
  data for   352–3
  design of   352–62
  as design platform   621
  why & what of   621–2
RD example
  context of   622–30
RDM (requirements definition methodology)   353
  basis structure of   358
  design approach to   353
  example of   *See* Appendix A
  implementation of   358–61
  justification of   353–5
  outputs of   361–2
  principal features of   356
  secondary features of   357
  specification of   355–8
  summary of   630
  using   642
  & vantage points   360
  & viewpoints   360
real interest rate
  expression for   534
realizable value   278, 291–2
recursion   *See* recursion
relevance principle   570
reliability   344, 370
reliability principle   570
replacement cost   278, 291, 290–1
requirements definition   *See* RD
requirements definition methodology   *See* RDM
research
  accounting for   589
  & strategy   *See* technological strategy, & research
research cost   279

research & development   *See* R&D
research planning diagram   *See* RPD
research project
    review of   478–9
research themes   485
reserves   598
resource scheduling
    defined activity mix   444
    firm due dates   445
    fuzzy activity mix   444
    soft due dates   444
resource table   204–5
    cost   205
    headcount   204
resource table & bar chart   201–8
retained profit   598
revenue cost   36, 564
RFS (ready for service)   112
robot   461
ROCE (return on capital employed)   608
    & P&L account   608
    & related ratios   608
Roseboom J. H.   219
Ross D. T.   169, 339
RPD (research planning diagram)   208–18, 264
    for & against   217–18
    See also TCM, algorithm of

sales function   384, 392, 412–14
    & industrial selling   413–14
    & product dispatch   392
    & product orders   392
    & successful selling   414
    See also marketing & sales function
sales life cycle   64, 103–4, 499
    age indicators in   66
    decline phase of   104
    growth phase of   103
    maturity phase of   103
    total unit sales in   499
sales revenue   587
    & activity level   604
    & credit   567
Salter M. S.   133
salvage value   *See* realizable value
SBU (strategic business unit)   57
    example   73–4
    investment in   61–4
SBU competitive status   67, 71
SBU movement
    & drift to oblivion   68–9
    horizontal   70
    vertical   71
Schoman K. E.   339
SCPU (standard cost per unit)   313
second-hand gas guzzler   *See* SHGG
semi-variable cost   296–8
service business   8
shape parameter
    average rate of investment   502
    average rate of recovery   502
    average rate of return   502
    maximum investment   502
    new cash generated   502
    problems with   505–6
    return to maximum investment ratio   502

sales lifetime   502
    time to break even   502
shareholder   556
SHGG (second-hand gas guzzler)   299
shop-floor workers   428
slack   230
Slocum J. W.   49
small company   134
    & budgeting   286
software engineering   114, 190, 343
software innovation   *See* technological innovation, software
software organization   *See* technical organization, software
sole-trader   10, 555
source of project fund   110
SQOU (standard quantity of units)   313
SSAP (Statements of Standard Accounting Practice)   555
stakeholders   56
standard cost
    & costing   272, 291, 312–17
    & marginal cost   328
    product   312
    & variance   314
standard cost per unit   *See* SCPU
standard quantity of units   *See* SQOU
standard target path time   *See* STPT
Stanley A. V.   177
Stephens D.   52
Stewart J. M.   47, 161
Stewart R.   56
stock
    consignment   451
STPT (standard target path time)   245
strategic business unit   *See* SBU
strategic factor
    external   56
    internal   54
strategy
    & tactics   45–6, 80
    marketing   401
        & four Ps   404
        & resource availability   405
Structured Analysis & Design Technique (SADT)   339
structured product design   343, 351, 621
    basic notion of   360
    key mechanism of   376
    summary of   376, 630
    why & what of   338–9
sub-unit   89
    assembly of   424
    proving novel   98
    standard & novel   479
    test of   425
sunk cost   289–90
    & fallacy   289
suppliers
    external   427, 428
system   340–2
    'how' definitions of   340
    'what' definition of   341
    See also product, & system
system design   *See* product design

tactics
    & strategy   45–6

TAM (technical assistance to manufacturing)   108
target path time   *See* TPT
TAS (technical assistance to sales)   108
task estimating   248–59
  constant effort fallacy in   251
  curvaceous   252–9
  divisible   253
    See also f Factor Method
  indivisible   253
  & large software project   258
  linear   249–52
  & task type   252
task time & task effort   *See* task estimating
tax
  corporation   590
TCM (telephone charge monitor)   622
  algorithm of   635
    See also RPD
  alternative design of   640
  design environment of   629
  primary functions of   625
  secondary functions of   626
  supplier of   622
TCM business plan   628
  elements of   630
TCM CA
  & end-users   633
  & WHJ   633
TCM DC
  & end-users   638
  & supplier   638
  & WHJ   637
TCM design environment   632
  financial criteria   629
  supplier facilities   629
TCM FA
  mandatory functions of   634
  optional functions of   635
TCM PA
  design of   640
  example of   641
  as outline design   630
TCM product brief   623–9, 632
  elements of   624
TCM RD   630
  CA in   633–4
  DC in   637–9
  derivation of   630–42
  FA in   634–7
  steps following   640–1
  structure of   632–3
  unresolved questions in   639–40
  word picture of   633
TCM requirements definition   *See* TCM RD
technical assistance to manufacturing   *See* TAM
technical assistance to sales   *See* TAS
technical function   13, 283, 418
  commercial objectives of   111
  & creativity   127
  justification of   161
  & licences and patents   107
  & non-company products   107
  organization of   *See* technical organization
  & other functions   108–9
  primary tasks of   89–102
  & production engineers   427, 441

  & project evaluation and choice   111
  & project proposals   109–10
  & research 'clubs'   111–12
  role summary of   157–61
  secondary tasks of   106–12, 159–60
    problem of   160
    specification of   161
    why & what of   161
technical innovation   *See* technological innovation
technical organization   156
  by phase   182–3
    advantages   183
    disadvantages   183
  by product range   179–80
    advantages   180
    disadvantages   180
  by professional discipline   177–9
    advantages   178
    disadvantages   178
  by project   180–2
    advantages   180
    disadvantages   181
  DC on   *See* DC on technical organization
  design objectives of   165
  extended matrix type of   187–9
  software   189–91
  matrix type of   184–6
    advantages   185
    disadvantages   185
  objectives of   161–5
  profiles of   161–5
  types of   177–91
technological innovation   85–9, 157–9
  & clarity of objectives   99
  & competitive status   48, 476
  & external customer   410
  investment as   102–6
  investment/return situation as   472
  overview of   86–7
  practical aspects of   94–9
  software   112–14
    & complexity   112–13
    definition of   114
    & flexibility   113
    & people   113
    problem summary   189
  treasure-hunting as   88–9
technological innovation phase
  comparison of   159, 479–81
  features of   99–102
  & probability of success   100
  recognition of   97
  & relative costs   100
  review of   474–81
  sequence of   98
  & staffing   100
technological profile   161–5
  & coupling   163
  factors of   162
  & primary activities   162
  & product life-cycle   164
  & R&D investment ratio   164
  & secondary activities   163
  & technological 'state-of-the-art   165
technological strategy   73–81
  product aspects of   78–80

technological strategy (*cont.*)
  & research 485
  research aspects of 80–1
technology 47
  competing with 77–8, 476
  engineering 475
  hierarchy of 475
  importance of 47–8, 472
  life cycle of 477
  & market demand 70
  & market outlook 80
  market rejuvenator as 70
  market terminator as 70
  opportunities & threats of 48, 472
  product *See* product technology
  sharper definition of 74
  & strategic position 68–73
  strategic role of 45–8
technology vector 71–3
  & market regime 71
  segment of 72
  & status regime 71
TF (total float) 231
Theories X & Y 119–20
three-times estimating
  definitions in 243
  example of 244
  formula of 243
  & PET2 539
time deviation *See* DT
time value of money 294
total cost (as in profit equation) 274, 320
total float *See* TF
total quality 452, 456
TPT (target path time) 245
trading cycle 33–4, 554
  & balance sheet 566
  manufacturing 36–7
  tracing 566
  whole business 38
trading division 281
  & AR 487
  & BR 486
  as set of mini-businesses
    See also SBU
turnkey contract 406, 409

turnover *See* sales revenue
Twiss B. C. 47, 494

Underdown B. 554
university organization
  compared with business 166
user requirement specification *See* product brief

value analysis 442
value engineering 442
vantage point of product design
  & TCM 630
variable cost 280, 296–8
variance 312, 447
  adverse 317
  favourable 317
vendor analysis
  elements of 449
viewpoint of product design 360
  & TCM 631
volume *See* activity (cost behaviour context)

Wassell H. J. A. vi, 339
wealth 502
Weist J. D. 219
White J. A. 287, 506, 509, 510, 524
White U. K. 177
WHJ (W H Jones plc) 624
why–what–how
  as partitioning rationale 360, 376
  as three magic questions 357
Wild R. 443, 445
Woodgate H. S. 219
working capital
  application of 601
  increase/(decrease) in 603
  & net CA 577, 595
  source of 601
  source & application rule 600
works cost 274, 292
  & bought-in item 448
works order 422
  processing of 423

yield, project *See* IRR